Hitler's
Jewish Soldiers

Hitler's Jewish Soldiers

The Untold Story of Nazi Racial Laws and
Men of Jewish Descent in the German Military

Bryan Mark Rigg

UNIVERSITY PRESS OF KANSAS

© 2002 by the University Press of Kansas

Published by the University Press of Kansas (Lawrence, Kansas 66049), which
was organized by the Kansas Board of Regents and is operated and funded by
Emporia State University, Fort Hays State University, Kansas State University,
Pittsburg State University, the University of Kansas, and Wichita State University

Library of Congress Cataloging-in-Publication Data
Rigg, Bryan Mark, 1971–
   Hitler's Jewish Soldiers: the untold story of Nazi racial laws and men of Jewish
descent in the German military / Bryan Mark Rigg.
      p.cm.—(Modern war studies)
   Includes bibliographical references and index.
   ISBN 0-7006-1178-9 (alk. paper)
      1. Jewish soldiers—Germany—History—20th century.   2. World War, 1939–
   1945—Participation, Jewish.   3. Children of interfaith marriage—Germany—
   History—20th century.   4. National socialism.   5. Germany—History,
   Military—20th century.   I. Title.   II. Series.
   DS135.G3 R54 2002   2001007626

British Library Cataloguing in Publication Data is available.

Printed in the United States of America

10 9 8 7 6 5 4 3 2 1

The paper used in this publication meets the minimum requirements of the
American National Standard for Permanence of Paper for Printed Library
Materials z39.48-1984.

To my pillars of strength

Grandmother, Edna Davidson
Aunt, Mary Rigg-Dalbey
Mother, Marilee Rigg
Daughter, Sophia Rigg
Wife, Stephanie Rigg

Knowledge is better than ignorance; history better than myth.

—Ian Kershaw, *The Nazi Dictatorship*

CONTENTS

Writing the history of Jews and men of Jewish descent who served in the Wehrmacht has a history of its own. The story opens in a Berlin movie theater and follows the trajectory of an idea that became a nine-year obsession leading me from an undergraduate thesis at Yale University to a doctoral dissertation at Cambridge University to this book that you, the reader, now hold in your hand. It started in 1992 when I was at the Goethe Institute in Berlin to learn the language and research my family's background. One of my teachers recommended viewing *Europa Europa (Ich war Hitlerjunge Salomon)* as a way to improve my German. This film is about the Jew Shlomo Perel, who falsified his identity and served in the Wehrmacht from 1941 to 1942 and studied at a Hitler Youth boarding school from 1942 to 1945. At the movie theater, I sat next to an elderly gentleman who helped translate the dialogue for me. Afterward, I asked him what he thought. He told me that the film was close to his own story and asked if I wanted to talk over a drink.

Over a few glasses of beer, Peter Millies told me of his experiences during World War II. He was a quarter-Jew who was drafted into the Wehrmacht in 1941 and spent three years on the Russian front. After the war, he was taken prisoner by the Russians and did not return to Germany until 1950. Our conversation led me to wonder if there were others like Perel and Millies who served in the German armed forces during World War II.

When I returned to Yale University to begin my sophomore year, I started to look into the subject, despite being discouraged by professors about its feasibility. I believed that if I could find twenty men like Perel and Millies, I would have enough material to write an interesting senior essay.

By my junior year, I had identified only seven living persons of Jewish descent who had served in the Wehrmacht. However, I knew more existed and that locating them meant a fight against time because these elderly veterans were dying by the thousands every day. Therefore, with funding from Yale, I took a year off between my junior and senior years and lived in Germany. I bought a laptop computer, a small printer, a video camera, and a large backpack. I videotaped every interviewee, and sometimes my backpack weighed over one hundred pounds. My goals for the year were to find thirty German veterans of Jewish descent, to look for supporting documents in German archives, and to become fluent in German.

In the first month alone, I documented the experiences of over thirty men. My research benefited from the snowball effect: most of those I met entrusted me with the names of friends and family members who had also served in the Wehrmacht under similar circumstances. I traveled throughout Western Europe, primarily Germany and Austria, interviewing men and collecting documents from their personal collections.

During the fall and winter of 1994, I lived in Berlin and studied at a language institute there. Because many interviewees lived in Berlin, I scheduled meetings there on weekdays and also frequented the Deutsche Dienststelle archive in Berlin, which houses most of the files of German navy personnel. On weekends, I would travel to other cities to interview the veterans I had contacted during the week. To make the interviewing process more efficient, I frequently biked to meetings. Sometimes biking was the only way to get to a person's home. I biked over one hundred miles round-trip to reach Alexander Stahlberg, Field Marshal von Manstein's adjutant, who lived in a castle in the small town of Gartow. One month after my visit, Stahlberg died. During the winter, spring, and summer of 1995, I lived in Freiburg to be near the military archive there. I continued to take German classes during the week at the Goethe Institute and traveled every weekend to interview veterans and collect documents. These men also gave me important information about what to look for in the archives. By September 1995, when I returned to Yale, I had documented hundreds. Many of these veterans had been high-ranking officers (colonel or higher) in the Wehrmacht.

After graduating from Yale, I did my graduate work at Cambridge University. During 1996 and 1997, I spent many weeks in Germany interviewing veterans and collecting more documents. I also returned to several of the German archives.

Besides a few hundred documents in the Bundesarchiv in Berlin and the Institut für Zeitgeschichte in Munich, the archives do not have much that is classified as pertaining to Jews or *Mischlinge* in the Wehrmacht. But by interviewing eyewitnesses, I uncovered thousands of pages of invaluable primary source material. The bulk of this study's documents came from interviewees.

Many still have their letters, diaries, and even official government documents bearing the signatures of Göring, Keitel, and Hitler.

Most interviewees signed consent forms that allowed me to research their personnel files in the archives. Between 1994 and 1998, I conducted 430 interviews. An average interview lasted around ninety minutes. The questions were divided into three parts: I would first ask them about their backgrounds, then discuss their time in the Wehrmacht, and then ask them about their motivation for serving in the Wehrmacht and their knowledge of the Holocaust. Most of these interviews gave me keys to archives that opened doors to thousands of documents about *Mischlinge*. To the best of my knowledge, no one had examined these documents before. Interviews with these people filled in many of the gaps that the documents left. Fortunately, most veterans were now ready to talk, and many of them said things that had never been expressed before.

During the interviews, they returned to a forgotten and repressed landscape, intermixing anecdotes of the past with knowledge gained after the fact. They would get very excited about their past and talk endlessly about their youth. Often an eighty-year-old man would appear to revert to his twenty-year-old self and recount his thoughts and feelings about the Third Reich as if he were still there. Many times, his wife or children (or both) were surprised by what they heard from their husband or father.

Many have chosen to forget their pasts, because soldiers of countries that lost a war rarely have as many listeners, or at least sympathetic ones, as soldiers of victorious countries. This is especially true in the case of Nazi Germany. But when presented with a young and interested student, most opened their homes and their hearts.

I believe the majority of my interviewees were honest. Most did not feel threatened by a person about the same age as their grandchildren, who wanted to understand what a *Mischling*'s life was like. They struggled to explain, sometimes for the first time, their humiliating and painful past, knowing well that today's society would not fully understand their situation. Their testimonies seem to undermine stereotypes about the Wehrmacht, Nazi persecution, and moral conduct, and their stories bear witness to a horrific and obscure history.

In this work I necessarily refer to and analyze a number of terms ("Mischling," "Mischlinge," "half-Jew," and "quarter-Jew") that are Nazi in origin and originally designed to denigrate and discriminate against all individuals who Hitler so classified. Let me emphatically state here what I hope is eminently apparent throughout the rest of my book: these terms and the intent that lay behind them (but not the individuals who were so labeled) were part of a mindset and genocidal plan that the civilized world must never forget and forever condemn.

ACKNOWLEDGMENTS

I am indebted to so many people and organizations that listing and thanking them all for the different ways they helped me would fill hundreds of pages. My heartfelt thanks go to all of the people who helped me these past nine years, particularly the 430 interviewees. I thank especially Professors Paula Hyman, General William Odom, Jeffrey Sammons, and Henry Turner of Yale University for their guidance throughout my undergraduate years.

Thanks to all those who read the prepublication manuscript and gave me invaluable feedback: Andy Baggs, American Military University; Michael Berenbaum, Jewish University; Mark Bernheim, Miami (Ohio) University; Michael Briggs, University Press of Kansas (his professionalism and advice have been greatly appreciated); Leslie Brisman, Yale University; Lawrence Burian, J.D.; Peter Cahn (Hochschule für Musik in Frankfurt); Chris Clark, Cambridge University; James S. Corum, School of Advanced Airpower Studies at Maxwell Air Force Base; Leo Daugherty; Hans-Joachim Fliedner, director of Kulturamt Stadt Offenburg; John Fout, Bard University; Vigor Froehmke, J.D.; Joachim Gaehde, Brandeis University; William Godsey, Institute for Economic and Social History, University of Vienna; retired USMC major Bruce Gudmundsson, Marine Corps Command and Staff College; Paula Hyman, Yale University; Eberhard Jäckel, Stuttgart University; Dr. Stan Leavy, Yale Medical School; Geoffrey Megargee, Holocaust Museum; Manfred Messerschmidt, Freiburg University; Georg Meyer (German Military Research Center, Freiburg); Archive Director Günther Montfort, Bundesarchiv/Militärarchiv (he knows how much I have appreciated his help); Kevin Murphy, J.D.; Norman Naimark, Stanford University; retired captain Horst von Oppenfeld (Stauffenberg's adjutant); Patricia von Papen-Bodek (Ph.D. from Columbia University); Heinz Puppe, Texas A&M University; Dr. Fritz Redlich, Yale Medical School; Alex Romain, J.D.; Jeffrey Sammons, Yale University; former chancellor Helmut Schmidt *(Die Zeit);* Hans Schmitt, University of Virginia; Baron Niklas Schrenck von Notzing, Schrenck von Notzing Archive; Freiderich Schuler, Portland State University; Dennis Showalter, Colorado College; Frank Snowden, Yale University; Jonathan Steinberg, Penn University; Laura Sudhaus;

Nathan Stoltzfus, Florida State University; Steven Welch, Melbourne University; Charles White, American Military University; and Lothar Zeidler, Rutgers University.

Thanks to the mathematicians and statisticians who gave me helpful advice for the chapter on assimilation: (USMC) Lt. Edmund Clayton, Ph.D. in physics from Louisiana State University; instructor Sybille Clayton, Louisiana State University; Monnie McGee, Hunter College; and Stan Stephenson, Southwest Texas State University.

Special thanks to the *Mischlinge* who read this work for their invaluable comments and criticism: Fredrich Baruch, Gerhard Bier, Dr. Robert Braun, Klaus Florey, Werner Goldberg, Michael Günther, Dr. Rudolf Hardy, Michael Hauck, Helmut Krüger, Otto Lüderitz, Ernst Ludwig, Emil Lux, Hanns Rehfeld, Richard Riess, Udo Rühl, Peter Schliesser, J.D., Captain Helmut Schmoeckel (commander of *U-Boat 802*), and Dr. Hans Weil (Yale University).

Several others throughout the years helped me tremendously in various ways: Paul Barby, Martin Bloch, Piers Brendon (Churchill Archives, Cambridge University), Dr. Kelly D. Brownell (Yale University), Marlies Flesch-Thebesius, Dean Hugh Flick Jr. (Yale University), John Francken, Dr. Jürgen Gronau, Dean Susan Hauser (Yale University), Barbara Jacoby, Toni Klein, Ramsay MacMullen (Yale University), Beate Meyer, Dan Nyhus, Marilee Rigg, Mary Rigg-Dalbey (Yale Nursing School), Colonel Martin Senekowitsch (Bundesministerium für Landesverteidigung: Abteilung Ausblidung), Barry Smith, Henry Soussan, Dr. Howard Spiro (Yale Medical School), Georg Sudhaus, John Weitz, and Dr. Kwan-sa You. Thanks to all of you.

Thanks to the theologians and rabbis who provided helpful insight and advice concerning the chapter titled "Who Is a Jew?": Guy Carter, the Jesuit College of New Jersey; Rabbi Zalman Corlin, Ohr Somayach Yeshiva; Rabbi Baruch Frydman-Kohl, Beth Tzedec Congregation; Rabbi Dovid Gottlieb, Ohr Somayach Yeshiva; Rabbi Avraham Laber, Congregation Beth Tephilah; Sheila Rabin, the Jesuit College of New Jersey; Regina Schneider, Walter Bader Realschule; and Wolfgang Schneider, Städtisches Stiftsgymnasium.

I was deeply impressed with the staffs at the archives and libraries throughout the world where I worked. Those who helped me the most these past nine years are David Lowe at the Cambridge University Library, the entire staff at the Marine Corps University Library, the entire staff at the Yale University Library, Director Peter Tamm of the Institut für Schiffahrts-und Marinegeschichte, Dr. Milton Gustafson at the U.S. National Archives in Washington, D.C., Torsten Zarwel in the Bundesarchiv in Berlin, Bernd Gericke and Peter Gerhardt in the Deutsche Dienststelle in Berlin, Ronald Meentz in the Bundesarchiv in Aachen, and Oberarchivrat Günther Montfort and Director Manfred Kehrig in the Bundesarchiv/Militärarchiv in Freiburg.

I wish I could mention by name the countless others who assisted and supported me. Hundreds of people fed me and gave me money to support this research. Scholarships enabled me to conduct this research: Richter scholarships from Silliman College at Yale University, the Horowitz Scholarship from Yale's Hillel Foundation, the Dean's Discretionary Scholarship for Senior Projects awarded by Dean Judith Hackman and Dean Richard Brodhead of Yale University, the Marshall-Allison Scholarship awarded twice by the Margaret Laughlin Marshall–John M. S. Allison Fellowship Committee of the Department of the History of Art at Yale University, the several scholarships awarded by the German Academic Exchange Service (DAAD), the Henry Fellowship for study at Cambridge University, the Darwin College travel grant, the Claussen *Stiftung,* and the Zeit *Stiftung.*

For their guidance I also thank my examiners, Richard Evans (Cambridge University) and Mac Knox (London School of Economics).

Finally, I thank my patient wife, Stephanie, for five years of valuable counsel and editing.

Because of the extreme sensitivity of this material, I consulted many people from diverse backgrounds. I realized early on that the more constructive criticism I could gather, the better this work would be. I hope that I have produced a well-documented work that reveals a dark chapter of the Third Reich and a facet of Hitler's activities that has not been fully documented until now. I hope that this work honors the experiences that so many shared with me. Any mistakes in this manuscript are mine alone. The majority of the people mentioned in this work had a chance to read what I wrote about them before I published this book. Any mistakes in representing their histories are mine alone. I have done all the translations except where I note that I used a translation from another author. Any mistakes in translations are mine alone.

ABBREVIATIONS

AWOL	Absent Without Leave
DAK	(Deutsches Afrika-Korps) German African Corps
EKII	(Eisernes Kreuz Zweiter Klasse) Iron Cross Second Class
EKI	(Eisernes Kreuz Erster Klasse) Iron Cross First Class
Gestapo	(Geheime Staatspolizei) Secret State Police
KdF	(Kanzlei des Führers) The Führer's chancellery (not to be confused with the same abbreviation used for Kraft durch Freude of the German Labor Front)
NCO	Noncommissioned officer
NSDAP	(Nationalsozialistische Deutsche Arbeiter-Partei) the Nazi Party
OKH	(Oberkommando des Heeres) army high command
OKL	(Oberkommando der Luftwaffe) air force high command
OKM	(Oberkommando der Marine) navy high command
OKW	(Oberkommando der Wehrmacht) armed forces high command
OT	(Organization Todt) forced labor camps
POWs	prisoners of war
RMI	(Reichsministerium des Innern) Reich Ministry of the Interior
SA	Sturmabteilung storm detachment, a Nazi Party paramilitary formation
SD	(Sicherheitsdienst) security and intelligence service of the SS
SPD	Social Democratic Party of Germany
SS	(Schutzstaffel) the most feared organization of the Third Reich: the Gestapo, SD, and the Waffen-SS were all part of the SS
Waffen-SS	Armed forces of the SS

SS and Waffen-SS	*Wehrmacht*	*U.S. Army Equivalent*
SS-Mann	Soldat/Funker/Kanonier/ Flieger/ Schütze/Matrose	Ordinary
Sturmmann	Obersoldat/Oberschütze/ Oberfüsilier	Private (Senior)
Rottenführer	Gefreiter	Private First Class
N/A	Obergefreiter	Acting Corporal
N/A	Stabsgefreiter/Hauptgefreiter	Administrative Corporal
Unterscharführer	Unteroffizier[a]/Maat	Corporal
Scharführer	Unterfeldwebel/Obermaat	Sergeant
N/A	Offiziersanwärter	Officer Candidate
N/A	Fähnrich/Fähnrich z. S.	Officer Candidate
Oberscharführer	Feldwebel/Wachtmeister/ Bootsmann	Staff Sergeant
Hauptscharführer	Oberfeldwebel	Technical Sergeant
N/A	Oberfähnrich/ Oberfähnrich z. S.	Senior Officer Candidate
Sturmscharführer	Stabsfeldwebel	Master Sergeant
Untersturmführer	Leutnant/Leutnant z. S.	Second Lieutenant
Obersturmführer	Oberleutnant/ Oberleutnant z. S.	First Lieutenant
Hauptsturmführer	Hauptmann/Kapitänleutnant	Captain
Sturmbannführer	Major/Korvettenkapitän	Major
Obersturmbannführer	Oberstleutnant/ Fregattenkapitän	Lieutenant Colonel
Standartenführer	Oberst/Kapitän. z. S.	Colonel
Oberführer	N/A	N/A
Brigadeführer	Generalmajor/Konteradmiral	Brigadier General
Gruppenführer	Generalleutnant/Vizeadmiral	Major General
Obergruppenführer	General der Inf. usw./Admiral	Lieutenant General
Oberst-Gruppenführer	Generaloberst/Generaladmiral	General
Reichsführer	Generalfeldmarschall (field marshal)/Grossadmiral	Five Star General (general of the army)

Source: These ranks have been tabulated according to the *Handbook on German Military Forces,* ed. United States War Department Technical Manual (Washington, D.C., 1945), pp. 16–17; Hilde Kammer and Elisabet Bartsch, eds., *Nationalsozialismus. Begriffe aus der Zeit der Gewaltherrschaft 1933–1945* (Hamburg, 1992), pp. 204–5.

[a]Unteroffizier, although translated as corporal, was in reality more like a U.S. Army staff sergeant or a U.S. Marine Corps sergeant. This rank marked the beginning of a professional soldier for an enlisted man.

Hitler's
Jewish Soldiers

Nur für den Dienstgebrauch

im Heerespersonalamt

Liste von a k t i v e n Offizieren,
die selbst oder deren Ehefrauen jüdische Mischlinge sind
und vom Führer für deutschblütig erklärt wurden

Name u. Vorname	Dienstgrad u. R.D.A.	Dienststelle	Geburts-datum	Bluts-anteile
Adlhoch Franz	Gen.Major 1.11.42 (11)	Kdt. St.O.Kdtr. Rudnja	17. 6.93	Ehefrau 50%
Altmann Helmut	Oberst 1.2.42 (101)	Kdr. A.R.347	4. 1.97	selbst 25%
Andresen Hans	Major 1.1.42 (424)	b. Kw.Trsp.Abt.356 als/Kdr. Abt.	6. 8.07	selbst 25%
Arnold Reinhard	Major 1.6.43 (6)	St. Gen.d.Pi. H.Gru.Nord	21. 5.12	selbst 25%
Aschenbrandt Heinrich	Gen.Major 1.12.41 (10)	Kdt. F.Kdtr.238	–	Sohn aus 1.Ehe, 25%
Behrens Wilhelm	Gen.Major 1.1.42 (5)	Kdr. Div. Nr.193	23. 8.88	selbst ?
Belli von Pino Anton	Oberst 1.4.58 (33)	F.Res.OKH, Dienst regelt Chef Kriegs-gesch.Abt.	13.12.81	selbst 25%
Bieringer Ludwig	Gen.Major 1.7.43 (1)	F.Res.OKH, kdt.zum Mil.Befh.i.Frkr.zur Einweis.i.d.G.eines Feldkdt.	12. 8.92	Ehefrau 50%
Bloch Dr. Ernst	Obstlt. 1.7.41 (45)	F.Res.OKH, kdt.zur 213.I.D. z.Verw.als Btls.Kdr.	1. 5.98	selbst 50%
Bonin Swantus	Oberst 1.4.42 (544)	Vorstand Bekl.Amt Erfurt	–	Ehefrau 50%
Borchardt Robert	Major 1.6.43 (32d)	Pz.Aufkl.Abt.7 Wiedereinberufung als akt.Offz.genehmigt, aber noch nicht arisiert	9. 1.12	?
Borowietz Willibald	Gen.Lt. 1.7.43 (7)	Pz.Jäg.Tr.Schule, hat Ritterkreuz, ist in engl.Gefangenschaft	17. 9.93	3 Kinder (50%) arisiert, Ehe-frau(Jüd)verstb.
Braune Günther	Oberst z.V.	z.Zt. Gehilfe beim Mil.Attaché Madrid	18.10.88	selbst 50%
Bruhnke Dr. Johannes	Oberst-Vet. 1.8.41 (1)	Wehrkr.Vet.IX	–	Ehefrau 25%
Colli Robert	Oberst 1.7.43 (36a)	Kdr. Gren.Rgt.547	27. 6.98	selbst 50%
Emmenthal Karl	Oberst 1.10.42 (50)	Bev.Trsp.Offz.beim AOK 1	26. 6.01	Ehefrau 25%

"List of active officers, who are either *Mischlinge* or married to *Mischlinge*, whom the Führer has declared of German blood." Page 1 of 5 is shown here. Note the far right *Blutsanteile* (blood percentage).

One approaches the study of the Holocaust with a profound sense of humility, respect, and responsibility. The subject itself encompasses a tragedy so enormous that we have yet to fully grasp its terrible meaning, although the contributions of countless books and articles that have preceded the present work have brought us ever closer to that goal. However, numerous areas relating to the Holocaust and the Nazi era in general remain largely unexamined or poorly understood. This book represents a close study of one such area, and while it does not presume to offer the final word, the hope is that it will provide readers with a new way of looking at one of the central issues in the history of the Third Reich and Holocaust, namely, Jewish identity.

More specifically, this book explores the historical phenomenon of Jews and men of partial Jewish descent, called "Jewish *Mischlinge*"[1] (singular of *Mischlinge* is *Mischling*), who fought in the German armed forces during World War II. It discusses how it was possible for Jews and *Mischlinge*, also called "half-" and "quarter-Jews," to have served in the Wehrmacht.[2] Many historians assume the Wehrmacht automatically excluded anyone of Jewish ancestry from serving between 1933 and 1945. Others believe that a small number may have fought in the Wehrmacht, but reject the ideas that this happened on a large scale and that any of them played a significant military role. All three of these assumptions are wrong. Many professors and historians initially doubted that this study would uncover anything historically significant. This assumption is also wrong. This book demonstrates that tens of thousands of men of Jewish descent served in the Wehrmacht during Hitler's rule. Although the exact number of *Mischlinge* who fought for Germany during World War II cannot be determined, they probably numbered more than 150,000.[3] That is both startling and important for what it tells us about how Jewish identity was viewed, constructed, and contested by German citizens, Nazi leaders, military commanders, and the Jewish community within German borders, and for what it tells us about how these perceptions saved some while condemning others to the death camps.

Even more startling, this study demonstrates that Hitler played a direct role in permitting *Mischlinge* to serve in the Wehrmacht. He even allowed some to become high-ranking officers. Generals, admirals, navy ship captains, fighter pilots, and many ordinary soldiers served with Hitler's personal approval. Possible reasons why Hitler allowed their service are also explored. Furthermore, this book examines what Hitler might have done with them had Germany won the war. To show the development of *Mischling* policy, most chapters are organized chronologically.

First, because the question "Who is a Jew?" is central to this study, several possible answers to it are discussed. Some call a person with any Jewish ancestry a Jew. Others, primarily Orthodox Jews, claim that anyone of Jewish descent who served in the Wehrmacht could not have been Jewish at all. Both extreme views are wrong. This section also discusses the Nazi definition of a Jew.

Second, the Nazi term *Mischlinge* is explored. It is impossible to understand how and why *Mischlinge* served in the Wehrmacht without understanding the several categories and particularities of this group. The term meant something very different before the Nazis used it to describe people of partial Jewish descent. After the war, the term was largely left out of works of scholarship because of its derogatory connotations. Moreover, there seemed to be little interest in researching the plight of the *Mischlinge* until recently. To understand the history of *Mischlinge* in the Wehrmacht, one must look at how the Nazis defined this term and how the *Mischlinge* themselves reacted to it.

Third, an overview of Jewish assimilation in Germany and Austria is presented to establish the probable number of *Mischlinge* during the Third Reich.[4] Students of this history often forget that the majority of German Jews had fully integrated into society and did not live as a separate ethnic group. The existence of hundreds of thousands of Christian Germans with Jewish ancestry, resulting from generations of intermarriage, is also often overlooked. These *Mischlinge* especially did not perceive themselves as a minority until Hitler classified them as such.

Fourth, the history of German and Austrian Jews who served in their countries' armed forces for over a century is discussed briefly. Since military service provided an effective path to social acceptance, many Jewish families had strong military traditions. Jews often shed their Jewishness as quickly as the surrounding society allowed. These people felt fully assimilated into German and Austrian society and had served their countries honorably.

Fifth, the regulations for Jews and *Mischlinge* in the Wehrmacht from 1933 until 1945 are explained in detail. The Wehrmacht's policies dealing with *Mischlinge* were complicated and perplexing. *Mischling* policy developed in spurts with tangential exploration and backtracking. Yet, it resulted in tens of thousands of *Mischlinge* wearing the Wehrmacht's uniform. This section provides a fine case study of a polycratic regime in action. In *Mischling* matters, there were competing views, personal power rivalries, and different agendas on the part of the civil service, Wehrmacht, SS, the Party, and the Führer. This section also deals with what the Nazis planned to do with *Mischlinge* had Germany won the war. Some have claimed *Mischlinge* never had to fear extermination because the Nazis did not concern themselves with them as they did the Jews. Yet, the Nazis had planned to ostracize, sterilize, and ultimately exterminate half-Jews. After the Nazis finished annihilating the Jews, half-Jews would have been next.

Sixth, official exemptions from racial discrimination which Hitler personally granted to *Mischlinge* are investigated. Some historians have noted that Hitler gave a limited number of such exemptions to important people of Jewish descent. Most failed to acknowledge that Hitler granted as many as several thousand such exemptions to members of the armed forces ranging from generals to privates and that he paid far more than cursory attention to them. Hitler's role in personally deciding on their cases showed how obsessed he was with racial policy.

Finally, the question "Who knew about the Holocaust?" is examined because some *Mischlinge* in the Wehrmacht found themselves in a unique position from which to observe Hitler's racial persecution. Many knew about isolated atrocities such as shootings and deportations, and most had experienced Nazi persecution, but the majority did not know about the systematic extermination of millions of Jews.[5] One would think that they should have known what was happening to their Jewish relatives and what ultimately would have happened to them had Hitler won or prolonged the war, but the evidence in this study proves that most were unaware of the scope of the Holocaust.

Until now, Nazi policies toward *Mischling* Wehrmacht personnel have not yet been fully explored. Jeremy Noakes's essay about *Mischlinge* in the 1989 *Leo Baeck Yearbook*, while only briefly mentioning Wehrmacht policy, provides the foundation for this book. Ursula Büttner wrote a social history of *Mischlinge* in her 1988 book, *Die Not der Juden teilen,* based on the experiences of several families. Werner Cohn wrote an essay about the Paulus Bund, a self-help organization formed by *Mischlinge,* in the 1988 *Leo Baeck Yearbook.* Aleksandar-Saša Vuletić also wrote about the Paulus Bund in his book *Christen Jüdischer Herkunft im Dritten Reich. Verfolgung und Organisierte Selbsthilfe, 1933–1939,* published in 1999. Nathan Stoltzfus dedicated a chapter to *Mischlinge* titled "Hitler's Army" in his 1996 book, *Resistance of the Heart: Intermarriage and the Rosenstrasse Protest in Nazi Germany.* Steven Welch wrote a short essay about eight half-Jewish Wehrmacht deserters in the 1999 *Leo Baeck Yearbook.* Beate Meyer's book *Jüdische Mischlinge: Rassenpolitik und Verfolgungserfahrung, 1933–1945,* published in 1999, does a good job of exploring the different aspects of *Mischling* life, but devotes only a short subchapter to *Mischlinge* in the armed forces. H. G. Adler's book on the deportation of German Jews, Raul Hilberg's work on the Holocaust, Manfred Messerschmidt's book on the Wehrmacht, Rolf Vogel's book *Ein Stück von uns,* and Saul Friedländer's history titled *Nazi Germany and the Jews* mention *Mischlinge* in passing. None of these works thoroughly documents the history of *Mischlinge* or Jews in the Wehrmacht. Noakes's essay and Meyer's book focus more on *Mischlinge* in the Wehrmacht than the other works; however, both dedicate only a few pages to this subject.

This book provides an in-depth look at Jews and *Mischlinge* in the Wehrmacht, especially high-ranking *Mischling* officers whom Hitler granted, after reviewing applications from them, some form of clemency. Moreover, the significance of Hitler's personal involvement with *Mischlinge* and policy affecting them supports his personal involvement in the Holocaust—an aspect of *Mischling* history not closely analyzed. This book provides new insight into the minority group of the *Mischlinge* torn between their Christian German culture and the Jewish heritage some of whom did not even know they shared. Although this group was large, it has been overlooked, primarily because the extremely polarized discussion of Hitler's anti-Semitism left little room for *Mischlinge* in the middle. Through this discussion of *Mischlinge* and their experiences in the Wehrmacht, some of the conflicting loyalties that many Germans felt during the Third Reich are brought to light. Also, by studying the history of *Mischlinge* in the Wehrmacht, one comes to learn about Nazi racial policy as a whole.

Understanding the racial state at the margins clarifies the central problems of Nazi Jewish policy. This study is about the nature and presence of Jewish identity in the armed forces of the Nazi state and, by implication, about the nature and presence of Jewish identity within the entire state itself. In the end, this study shows just how flawed, dishonest, corrupt, bankrupt, and tragic were the racial theories and policies of Hitler and the Nazis.[6]

Who Is a Jew?

The question "Who is a Jew?" has sparked heated debate throughout the ages. Even today in Israel, the intensity of the preoccupation with this question is, according to law professor Asher Maoz of Tel-Aviv University, "second only to Israel's preoccupation with problems of security and peace. This is unsurprising as many regard both subjects as matters of national survival."[1]

The Term "Jew"

The word "Jew" derives from the name of the tribe of Judah, named after one of the twelve sons of Israel (Jacob). The Jews descend from Aramean nomads who crossed the Euphrates into the land of Canaan under Abraham's leadership around 1850 B.C.E.[2] They were called the *Ivrim* (Hebrews).[3] Many today call Abraham the "first Jew"[4] and the first monotheist.[5] Some focus on the collective experiences of Jews during their bondage as slaves in Egypt and their eventual exodus out of Egypt that led to their becoming a nation. Others emphasize that God's chosen people officially became a nation of Jews when Moses received God's laws (the Torah[6]) on Mount Sinai around 1200 B.C.E. soon after they left Egypt.[7] This is when the people of Israel entered into a covenant *(B'rit)* with God, and the Torah was the "sacred writ of that covenant."[8]

In biblical times, a child "inherited" his Jewishness from his father. According to one common interpretation, in the Book of Leviticus, a "half-caste Danite"[9] man who had a Jewish mother but an Egyptian father was rejected as not "belonging."[10] This example illustrates that at the time,

Jewishness depended on descent through the father, contrary to today's practice. For example, Joseph's children are considered Jews, though their mother Asenath was the daughter of an Egyptian priest of On,[11] and Moses' children, though their mother Zipporah was a Cushite from present-day Ethiopia.[12] Before the giving of the Torah, Jewishness was a function of one's lineage, beliefs, and customs. For example, circumcision was an identifying factor for Abraham and his descendants. To join the Hebrews, one just had to adopt their culture; no formal procedure of conversion was required. In this sense, all of the Israelites prior to Sinai were Jewish. Only after Sinai was a formal procedure of conversion necessary.[13]

Present-day Definitions of a Jew

Today, observant Jews look to the Tanach (Jewish bible)[14] and Talmud (the oral Torah)[15] to define Jewishness. According to rabbinical law (Halakah)[16] today, a Jew is a person born of a Jewish mother or one who properly converts to Judaism.[17] Orthodox rabbi and professor Jacob Schochet of Humber College commented, "The father's status is altogether irrelevant."[18] The father does, however, play an important role in deciding whether a male child is of the priestly cast or not (i.e., a Cohen or a Levi).[19]

Why do observant Jews follow the law of maternal descent? Most observant Jews simply say that is how God set it up. When asked why God did it this way, some suggest that this law probably was adopted because a child's mother could almost always be identified in biblical times. This humane law also may have served to protect children fathered by foreign soldiers in wartime by accepting them into Jewish society. Moreover, most Jews consider a child born of a Jewish mother Jewish regardless of the parents' future actions. For example, most Jews would consider a child Jewish even if the parents baptized the child at birth. The child's Jewishness is its birthright, which its parents cannot take away.[20]

According to Halakah, once a person is born Jewish or properly converts to Judaism, that status remains forever.[21] One might think that a Jew would no longer be Jewish if he professed another religion, but this is not the case.[22] Orthodox rabbi Dovid Gottlieb remarked, "Once a Jew, always a Jew."[23] For example, most consider that political philosopher Karl Marx, poet and writer Heinrich Heine, and composer and conductor Felix Mendelssohn-

Bartholdy were all Jews, although they all converted to Christianity.[24] Shlomo Perel, a Jew who served in the Wehrmacht (under the assumed name of Josef Perjell), wrote, "It's hard to be a Jew, but it's even harder to try not to be one [if you were born one]."[25] The satirist Kurt Tucholsky, in Swedish exile in 1935, echoed Perel when he wrote, "I left Judaism in 1911," but then added, "I know that this is in fact impossible."[26]

For many Jews, however, religion plays little or no role in defining their Jewishness. They believe Jewishness means first and foremost an ethnic allegiance (i.e., belonging to the Jewish people). They also hold certain ideals very dear to their hearts, such as education, family values, and charity. Religious beliefs are secondary. Many in the world who consider themselves Jews in every respect would deny that they have any religion at all.[27]

Most Jews consider themselves part of a unique family. Every day, observant Jews say the Shema, the holiest Jewish prayer which comes from Deuteronomy 6:4. It reads, "Hear, O Israel! *Adonai* is our God. *Adonai,* the one and only."[28] This prayer is a declaration to a nation, the people of Israel. Nicholas De Lange writes, "To be a Jew is thus to acknowledge an attachment to an historic experience. To become a Jew is essentially to join a people."[29] Moses Hess, an early advocate of Zionism, said in 1862, "Jewry is above all a nationality; its history goes back several thousand years and marches hand-in-hand with the history of mankind."[30]

The Jews are not a "race";[31] there are no genetic features that all Jews, and only Jews, share. Furthermore, because non-Jews have always been able to convert to Judaism, common physical traits could hardly be expected. Because Jews have spread throughout the world, they have taken on different ethnicities, cultures, and traditions. Nevertheless, they all have some attachment to Israel, and those who have remained observant share a spiritual allegiance to the Torah. In modern times, tensions sometimes arise when groups from the Diaspora immigrate to Israel. Israeli officials who have to define whether the people entering Israel are Jews sometimes have trouble addressing this delicate issue. Recently the arrival of destitute Ethiopian Jews *(Falashas)*[32] in Israel sparked debate about who is a "kosher Jew."[33] The government airlifted these persecuted people to Israel and gave them Israeli citizenship, homes, food, and education, but that did not automatically confirm their status as Jews. After discussing Ethiopians' cultural and religious differences, Israel's supreme court concurred with the chief Rabbinate's judgment that Ethiopian Jews "were *doubtful Jews* requiring a restrictive conversion *(giyur lechumra)*[34] in order to qualify for [Jewish] marriage [author's italics]."[35] Many religious leaders questioned these Ethiopians' Jewishness, maintaining that these African Jews only observed a form of "crypto-Judaism."[36] Many Russian Jews are also looked upon as "doubtful Jews." Since the fall of the Iron Curtain, tens of thousands of Russian Jews have immigrated to Israel. Most have fled persecution and poverty in Russia. They view Israel as a land of hope where they can live a free and self-determined existence. However, the Rabbinate views some of these Russians' Jewishness skeptically, maintaining that many of these people have either falsely claimed to be Jewish to escape the poverty in Russia, have an imperfect understanding of what it means to be Jewish, or only have Jewish fathers.[37]

The variations in cultural values and historic legacy among certain Jews can create confusion regarding how Jewish or Israeli they are perceived as being. Although the Israeli government uses a definition similar to the Halakic one to recognize a Jew — that is, one must be born of a Jewish mother or convert to Judaism and not belong to another religion (called the "Law of Return") — the nation of Israel is strongly split over the issue.[38] For example, in 1998, two Russian-Israeli soldiers died in combat while stationed in Lebanon. The Rabbinate refused them a Jewish burial in a military graveyard because they had only Jewish fathers. They were not considered Jews.[39] One would think that dying while serving in the Israeli army would prove that one felt Jewish and believed in the state of Israel, but the Rabbinate does not hold such actions and convictions sufficient to declare someone Halakically Jewish. The Rabbinate views Jewishness as a formal definition of status as opposed to one of self-perception or commitment to Israel or the Jewish people. A person could consider himself Jewish, be a dedicated Israeli citizen, and even an Israeli war hero, but not formally be considered Jewish. So for many, differences in religious belief, cultural background, ethnic makeup, and self-perception make the answers to the question "Who is a Jew?" complex and unresolved.

Strong differences also exist between the Orthodox, Conservative, and Reform movements within Judaism.[40] For example, the Orthodox and Conservative movements adhere to the Halakic law of maternal descent or conversion for one to be a Jew.[41] Most Reform Jews believe paternal descent is also enough to be a Jew. While Conservative Judaism "affirms the divinity of Halacha but questions its immutability," Reform Judaism "denies the authority of both principles."[42] Orthodox Judaism believes these two movements are not Halakically sound. The ideological differences between these three movements have caused heated debate. In Israel, the Orthodox passionately fight to keep Reform and Conservative organizations from establishing themselves. For example, for many Orthodox Jews, Jews in the Reform and Conservative movements, especially gentiles by birth who have converted into those movements, are not really Jews.[43] The "Ministry of Religions" in Israel does not recognize people as Jewish who convert under non-Orthodox auspices. In fact, the ministry had been keeping lists provided by informers overseas or in Israel that registered some ten thousand immigrants whose Judaism was called into question. Although these people were not denied entrance into Israel under the Law of Return, many rabbis would not perform marriage ceremonies or Jewish burials for them.[44] In other words, for Orthodox Jews, if a Reform or Conservative Jew does not have a Jewish mother or an Orthodox conversion, then he or she is "not Jewish, period."[45] One of the Orthodox Jewish movement's objectives is to "de-legitimize the non-orthodox streams."[46] These schisms cause many to worry about Israel's future. The conflict jeopardizes the entire social fabric of Israel and the unity of the nation. Different groups threaten one another and Israel with "boycotts, financial blackmail and sanctions."[47] Orthodox Rabbi Schochet wrote, "Self-interest, arrogance and narcissism (on the individual and organizational levels) within our own people threaten to achieve what our worst enemies could not."[48] With all the controversy surrounding the questions "Who is a Jew?" and "What is Jewish?" one can see the difficulties this study encountered when discussing issues of people's Jewishness. Quite often, to discuss *Mischlinge* and their Wehrmacht service, readers must first acknowledge their own prejudices and beliefs. The definition of Jewishness and "Who is a Jew" strongly influences how one reads this history. Ironically, the current problems in Israel often came up during this research, and that is why they are addressed in such detail.

Jewish Law (Halakah) and Mischlinge

Mischlinge were confused by these religious definitions. Some did not know what Halakah meant before it was explained to them during the interviews conducted for this study. Helmut Krüger complained that he is tired of some Jews trying to make him into a Jew. He struggled for twelve years to convince the Nazis he was not Jewish but rather a loyal German patriot. He survived the Nazi onslaught but never convinced them that he was fully "Aryan."[49] Even now, observant Jews asked about his case unwaveringly state that Krüger is Halakically Jewish because he had a Jewish mother. Krüger insists that he had nothing to do with his mother's Jewishness. He was born German and raised as a Christian. Krüger dislikes being called a Jew, not because he is anti-Semitic but because he does not feel Jewish. Halakah means nothing to him. He added, "Should I be called a Nazi because my uncle, Hermann Krüger, was an Ortsgruppenleiter[50] of the NSDAP?[51] The answer is no just as much as it's no that I'm a Jew."[52] Some rabbis claim that people like Krüger demonstrate Jewish self-hatred; they renounce their Jewishness because they are afraid to admit who they are. Krüger believes that he is just Helmut Krüger, born a German not by choice but by chance to a German-Jewish mother who, like many Jews, assimilated and shed her Jewishness to integrate fully into the dominant society. Krüger's opinion is common among *Mischlinge*. The vast majority do not know how to describe their own Jewish heritage and are confused when observant Jews tell them they are Jewish. Some feel Jewish in their own way, not because they have Jewish mothers but because the Nazis persecuted them for being partially Jewish. Their Jewish identity was born of persecution rather than religious or cultural heritage.

Eastern Jews versus German Jews

Examining the tragic conflict between German Jews and Eastern Jews (*Ostjuden*) before Hitler came to power helps explain the *Mischlinge*'s confusion over what it meant to be Jewish. Prior to the rise of Nazism, many German Jews had unfortunately discriminated against *Ostjuden*. Many felt that the poor, culturally backward, and "dirty" *Ostjuden* gave the typically well-educated and cultured German *Jeckes*[53] a bad name.[54] Although many German Jews had contempt for the *Ostjuden*, some did help the *Ostjuden* philanthropically. They felt compassion for these Jews who left the East because of Communism, pogroms, and economic strife. Unfortunately, such German Jews who did help *Ostjuden* were a minority. Many German

Jews felt that the *Ostjuden* lived in anachronistic ghettos and only learned "Polish Talmudic barbarism" in comparison to refined German *Bildung* (education).[55] For German Jews, these "ghetto-Jews" from the East followed an irrational and superstitious religion of the Jewish mystics that no longer could function properly in a world based on a religion of reason and knowledge. Most *Ostjuden* felt that their heretical *daitsch* (German) brothers had left *Yiddischkeit* (Judaism) by shaving off their beards, adapting modern ways, and not keeping the Sabbath holy.[56] Many of them denounced the Reform movement which had been started in Germany.[57] In Austria, the situation was no different than in Germany. For example, many Viennese Jews also did not welcome *Ostjuden* and showed contempt for the "bearded, caftan-clad people."[58]

Thus, many German Jews and *Mischlinge* thought Hitler based his anti-Semitic tirades on *Ostjuden* who had emigrated from the "land of Bolshevism." The Nazis reinforced this preconception when they issued decrees against *Ostjuden* in 1933[59] and later when they forced eighteen thousand of them to leave the Reich in 1938.[60] Wolf Zuelzer, a 75 percent Jew, explained that German Jews maintained their prejudice against *Ostjuden* because of their cultural isolation and "primitive" lifestyle. Zuelzer wrote that "for the majority of German Jews, the Orthodox *Ostjuden* dressed in his caftan, fur hat and ritual side-locks was a frightening apparition from the Dark Ages."[61] At the beginning of the twentieth century, "[m]any of the local Jewish communities in Germany refused to allow Eastern Jews to vote in community elections on the grounds that they were not German nationals."[62] Dr. Max Naumann, a Jew and a retired World War I army major and founder of the militant right-wing organization of National German Jews, wrote Hitler on 20 March 1935 that he and his followers had fought to keep *Ostjuden* out of Germany. Naumann felt that these "hordes of half-Asian Jews" were "dangerous guests" in Germany and must be "ruthlessly expelled."[63]

Naumann wanted Hitler forcibly to remove the *Ostjuden* from Germany.[64] He strove for Nazi acceptance by displaying his organization's adherence to what he thought was Hitler's *Weltanschauung*.[65] Naumann hoped to gain Hitler's approval of his organization. He failed to recognize how impossible that was. Naumann's organization was not alone. The

Deutsche Vortrupp (German Vanguard), a group of university students led by Hans Joachim Schoeps, believed that what lay at the center of Nazism was the regeneration of German society, "not racialism and race hatred." Schoeps and his group wanted to take part in supporting the Nazis in rebuilding Germany. They wanted the Nazis to see that they, as nationalistic German Jews, were a part of the German nation. They admitted that problems did exist between Jews and Aryans, but not surprisingly, they "blamed the *Ostjuden* for it."[66] The Nazis would dissolve Naumann's and Schoeps's organizations in 1935.[67] Many German Jews saw the *Ostjuden* as a grave danger to their social standing who, if allowed to stay in Germany, would only intensify anti-Semitic feelings. In several public statements during the 1920s and 1930s, liberal German Jews labeled *Ostjuden* "inferior" and asked for state assistance to combat their immigration.[68] Many Germans, including Jews, thought Hitler would stop the immigration of *Ostjuden,* which dramatically increased after World War I, and approved of such a policy.[69] By the 1920s, some estimates claim that well over one-hundred thousand foreign Jews, mostly Polish, lived in Germany.[70] Many German Jews probably felt that the large number of *Ostjuden,* who would work for cheaper wages, threatened their jobs. Perhaps some German Jews also reacted as they did because *Ostjuden* represented a part of themselves they wanted to deny. All German Jews knew that at one time in history they or their ancestors looked like the *Ostjuden* they were condemning.[71] That fact embarrassed most, and many responded to *Ostjuden* with disdain and arrogance. *Ostjuden* simply represented all that many German Jews had fought to distance themselves from.

Robert Braun recalled that his Jewish father, Dr. R. Leopold Braun, was an anti-Semite who did not like *Ostjuden.*[72] Many German Jews and *Mischlinge* felt that since their families had lived in Germany for several generations, they should be treated differently from *Ostjuden.* For example, retired Lieutenant Colonel Albert Benary, a half-Jew and a well-known military writer,[73] wrote to the Nazi government on 25 September 1933 in response to the *Arierparagraph*[74] (racial laws that persecuted "non-Aryans *[Nichtarier]*" in the civil service).[75] He felt outraged that a battle-tested officer, whose family had lived in Germany for more than a century, should be excluded from "building the new Germany at the very moment of its fulfilment." Benary requested that he and his family be recognized as German citizens who through their contact with German *Blut und Boden*[76] had become German.[77] He repeated his plea on 16 October 1933:

> My family doesn't come out of the Eastern ghettos. They came from the West through North Africa and Spain to Germany and certainly picked up non-Jewish blood along the way. However, my family's not ashamed of its Jewish blood. We can trace our Jewish origins back to the priestly cast of the Jewish people, and our family's motto, battle-cry if you will, comes from the book of Maccabees:[78] "If our hour comes, then let us die chivalrously for our brothers' sake, to preserve our honor." I believe this motto resonates in the National-Socialist heart as well. . . . I believe I have the right to ask not to be treated as a second-class German.[79]

Benary failed to understand Nazi intentions. The Nazis did not care how honorably his ancestors or he had behaved or what class or region his Jewish family had come from. For them, he was a non-Aryan. Although the fact that the Nazis treated him like a "second-class German" should have made him more aware of the drastic changes happening in Germany, he did not yet understand that while Hitler maintained power, his ancestry excluded him from Aryan society. Perhaps out of a sense of loyalty to a fellow officer, the chief of the Reichswehr's[80] ministerial office, Colonel Walter von Reichenau, wrote on Benary's behalf saying that his noteworthy service to the fatherland should allow him to remain at his post. Apparently, despite Reichenau's help, Benary continued to experience difficulties.[81] The majority of Nazis did not sympathize with Benary and paid little attention to what Western and Eastern Jews thought of each other or what a German half-Jew thought he was entitled to.

How Hitler and the Nazis Identified Jews

Hitler's anti-Semitism matured into a "murderous East European anti-Semitism"[82] while he lived in Vienna before World War I[83] and from his experiences after the Great War when revolution swept through Germany.[84] When Hitler started writing and talking about the Jews in the early

1920s, he directed much of his hatred toward Eastern Jews and Jewish Communists.[85] He believed the Jews killed Christ and were the vermin of the world. He also hated Communists and felt that Communism was a Jewish movement. He was present in Munich when Kurt Eisner, whom Hitler called "the international Jew,"[86] led his Socialist revolution from 1918 to 1919.[87] Hitler felt that "Judeo-Bolsheviks" like Eisner were responsible for and had profited from Germany's defeat in World War I.[88] After half-Jew Count Anton Arco-Valley assassinated Eisner in February 1919, the Red Terror only intensified in Munich as the Reds tried to gain more power, under the leadership of people such as the Russian Jew Eugen Leviné, whom Rosa Luxemburg had sent to Munich from Berlin.[89] As a witness to this chaos in Bavaria, Hitler described it as being a "rule by the Jews."[90] So, since Hitler felt that Communism was a Jewish movement and inherently dangerous, he directed his hatred toward the Jews.

Later, Hitler hated all Jews regardless of origin or political orientation. Hitler's government officially designated a Jew in 1935 as anyone who was more than "50 percent Jewish."[91] However, how did Hitler describe Jews or Judaism? Even Hitler acknowledged some positive traits about Jews:

> In hardly any people in the world is the instinct of self-preservation developed more strongly than in the so called "chosen." . . . What people, finally, has gone through greater upheavals than this one— and nevertheless issued from the mightiest catastrophes of mankind unchanged? What an infinitely tough will to live and preserve the species speaks from these facts.[92]

The praise Hitler gives the Jews is astonishing. Hitler acknowledged the Jews' ability to persevere against heavy odds. Recognizing this fact, one can understand what monumental task Hitler knew he had undertaken to get rid of Jews. Hitler's quote implies that he wanted to create a transhistorical, unbeatable race by destroying the one that already existed. Hitler had once said, "There cannot be two chosen people. We are the people of God. Does that not explain it all?"[93] Hitler thought the "Aryan race" should replace the "Jewish race." He overestimated the power of the Jews. Hitler's statement here displayed a strange admiration he had for the Jews and what he thought they represented.

Yet Hitler's attitude toward Jews changed throughout his life. During his youth, his attitude toward Jews seemed ambiguous. For instance, Hitler said during his Vienna days that the Jews made up the first civilized nation because they discovered monotheism.[94] Hitler often praised the respected Jew Gustav Mahler, whose productions of Wagner's *Tristan and Isolde* and *The Flying Dutchman* were performed in the Imperial Opera House of Vienna.[95] Yet, during this same time, Hitler was prone to sudden anti-Semitic rages.[96]

After World War I, Hitler's anti-Semitism seemed to blossom. He frequently spoke out against Jews in his speeches and placed them at the center of his Party platform. For example, on 6 April 1920, Hitler claimed that in getting rid of the Jew, Germans were justified in allying themselves even with Satan.[97] Hitler alleged that Jews were evil, the counter-ideal of Aryans, of which the Germans were the nucleus. As a result, a Jew by definition behaved differently from an Aryan. Hitler also believed Jews were obsessed with sex. "With satanic joy in his face," wrote Hitler, "the black-haired youth lurks in wait for the unsuspecting girl whom he defiles with his blood, thus stealing her from her people. . . . Just as he himself systematically ruins women and girls, he does not shrink from" destroying the "blood" of others.[98] Hitler's morbid sexual ravings illustrate how strongly he believed that Jews destroyed society through racial defilement. After the loss of World War I and the humiliating Versailles treaty, Hitler used the "Jew-enemy" as political bait for the disgruntled German masses. The Jews remained the focal point of his drive to power and ultimately of the enactment of most of his racial policy. He said that if the Nazis did not have them as an enemy, they would have to invent one: "It is essential to have a tangible enemy, not merely an abstract one."[99] Defining that Jew enemy would be one of Hitler's most difficult tasks. Until the 1930s, German society generally understood Jewishness as being a religion, although there had been several movements in certain universities to define Jewishness as a race. Before Hitler, German social and political conventions allowed and encouraged Jews to shed their Jewishness by converting to Christianity. When Hitler came into power, Jewishness officially became a "race."

Similar to Halakah, Nazi doctrine said Jewishness was inherited. However, Hitler argued that a Jewish father passed as much Jewishness to a child as a Jewish mother.[100] Nazi scientists tried to classify Jews according to their phenotypical traits by projecting onto them big ears, large noses, short bodies, flat feet, hairiness, and dirtiness.[101] Julius Streicher, the editor of the notoriously anti-Semitic and vulgar newspaper *Der Stürmer*, claimed that the shape of Jewish blood cells and Aryan blood cells differed, but that experts were unable to describe that difference because the "wicked Jew had prevented scientific research in this field."[102] Streicher did not specify how "the Jews" had prevented this research. Dr. Bruno Kurt Schultz, chief of Prague's Nazi Racial Office, argued that half-Jews inherited twenty-four Jewish chromosomes and twenty-four Aryan chromosomes. However, he did not explain how to tell Jewish and Aryan chromosomes apart.[103]

These prejudices inherent in phrenology and other pseudo-scientific research had their detrimental effects on Jews and *Mischlinge*. On 24 November 1936, a certain Herr Volkmann of Munich's Nazi Party Court recommended that the Main Office for Racial Research not certify Aryan descent for Nazi Party member Dr. Heinrich Neumann because he looked Jewish. His family tree did not reveal any Jewish descent, but Neumann's appearance was enough to declare him Jewish.[104] Half-Jew Rudolf Sachs remembered that SA[105] Brownshirts beat up a high school classmate because he had a large nose. His classmate protested and claimed that "he wasn't Jewish." As they brutally punched him, they answered that "a person with such a big nose can only be a Jew."[106] Other SA men mistook a Gestapo[107] agent for a Jew in a Kassel public swimming pool and brutally beat him.[108] Reich's minister of the interior, Dr. Wilhelm Frick, claimed that officials could have ancestry investigated when a person's name sounded Jewish.[109] Normally, however, the Nazis had to rely on church or local court records rather than appearance or the sound of a name to define Jewishness.[110]

As hard as he tried, Hitler could not disconnect Jewishness from the Jewish religion.[111] For the Nazis, Jews who had converted to Christianity remained Jewish,[112] but most Christians who had converted to Judaism were considered racially 100 percent Jewish.[113] Nazis called these converts *Geltungsjuden*,[114] meaning they were full Jews by legal fiction. For instance, on 3 July 1942, the minister of justice said of a Christian who in 1920 had married a Jew, converted to Judaism, been circumcised, and later raised his son as a Jew: "Anyone who so attaches himself to Judaism has removed himself from the German *Volk*[115] and will be treated as a Jew."[116]

Interestingly, Reichsleiter[117] Martin Bormann, head of the Parteikanzlei and Hitler's personal secretary, issued a circular that stated that Hitler did not require all Aryans to be Christians. In 1943, Hitler declared that "Germans who were Muslims could remain Nazi Party members. Faith is a matter of private conscience."[118] However, the Nazis saw the Jewish religion as irredeemably evil and a constant source of danger.

Thus, Nazi policy treated converts to Judaism the same way Halakah treats them: as full Jews capable of passing this Jewishness on to their children. However, Jewish converts to Christianity still remained Jewish for the Nazis. For instance, the Nazis sent the philosopher Edith Stein to Auschwitz although she had converted to Christianity. She was sent to the gas chambers.[119] As Martin Gilbert wrote, "[T]ens of thousands of German-Jews were not Jews at all in their own eyes."[120]

In conclusion, one must not ignore the importance of Halakah, especially when looking at the history of Jews and *Mischlinge* who served in the German armed forces during World War II. Such definitions strongly affect the way some view this history today. According to the Halakic definition, the statement that "thousands of Jews served in the Wehrmacht" is correct. This is especially the case, since 60 percent of the half-Jews and 30 percent of the quarter-Jews documented in this study were Halakically Jewish.[121] However, a discussion of this history must use Nazi definitions concerning Jewishness because ultimately only what the Nazis believed counted. Most of the people in this study would not describe themselves as Jews or partial Jews, but Hitler's racial theories and policies did. Thus, when Jewishness is discussed in this study, it is according to the Nazi racial laws, not Halakic definitions.

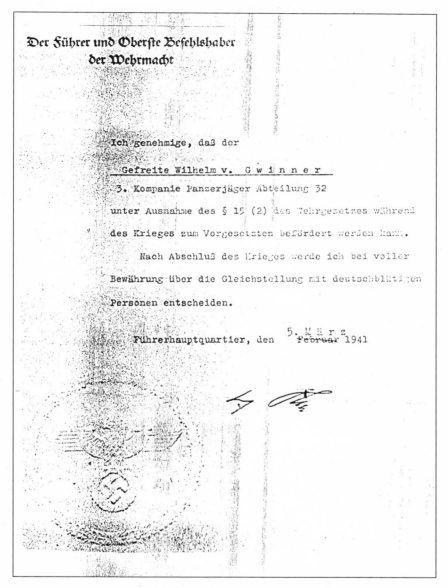

Der Führer und Oberste Befehlshaber
der Wehrmacht

Ich genehmige, daß der

Gefreite Wilhelm v. G w i n n e r

3. Kompanie Panzerjäger Abteilung 32

unter Ausnahme des § 15 (2) des Wehrgesetzes während

des Krieges zum Vorgesetzten befördert werden kann.

Nach Abschluß des Krieges werde ich bei voller

Bewährung über die Gleichstellung mit deutschblütigen

Personen entscheiden.

Führerhauptquartier, den 5. März 1941

Hitler's *Genehmigung* (exemption) for the Gefreiter Wilhelm von Gwinner, a quarter-Jew (last rank lieutenant). It reads: "I approve Private First Class Wilhelm v. Gwinner in 3rd Panzerjäger Company, Section 32, to be allowed to be promoted to ranks of authority during the war according to the exemption clause of §15 (2) of the military law. After the war, I will decide whether to declare Wilhelm von Gwinner of German blood according to his performance as a soldier. Führerhauptquartier, 5 March 1941. Signed: Adolf Hitler."

Der Leiter
der Reichsstelle für Sippenforschung

Berlin NW 7, den 15. Dezember 1939
Schiffbauerdamm 26   Fernsprecher: 42 33 83
Drahtanschrift: Reichssippenforschung

Nr. I 1150 G. (68)
Es wird gebeten, dieses Geschäftszeichen bei
weiteren Schreiben anzugeben.

Bescheinigung

über die Einordnung des

Hauptmanns Walter Hollaender,

Infanterie-Regiment 46,

geboren zu Verden am 15.10.1905,

im Sinne der ersten Verordnung zum Reichsbürgergesetz vom 14. November 1935
(R G Bl. I S. 1333):

deutschblütig

An official German blood certificate for half-Jew Walter H. Hollaender (last rank Colonel). It reads: "Certificate of classification of Captain Walter H. Hollaender, Infantry Regiment 46, born on 15 October 1905 in Verden in accordance with the first supplementary decree to the Reich citizenship law from 14 November 1935 (RG B1. I S. 1333): German blooded. Signed: Kurt Meyer."

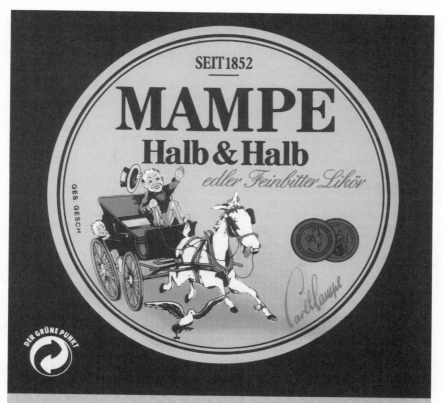

SEIT 1852

MAMPE

Halb & Halb

edler Feinbitter Likör

GES. GESCH

DER GRÜNE PUNKT

Feine Kräuter und ausgewählte Bitter-Orangen bilden die Grundlage für seine Geschmacksfülle und wohltuende Bekömmlichkeit.

In der Lizenz der Carl Mampe GmbH Berlin, Vertrieb in Berlin: Mampe Vertrieb 12099 Berlin

31 % vol   1,0 ℓ

Many half-Jews, especially those living in Berlin, called themselves *Mampe,* a term derived from the name of a popular cocktail in Berlin at the time; it is a well-known brand of brandy *(Kräuterlikör),* which is half sweet and half bitter.

Top: Quarter-Jew Fritz Binder in 1994 (last rank second lieutenant); *right:* ca. 1941. According to Binder, Hitler declared him an *Ehrenarier* (Honorary Aryan) in 1945. (Military awards: EKII, Assault Badge, Wound Badge, and Eastern Campaign Medal 1941–1942.)

Ich erkläre durch meine Unterschrift ausdrücklich, daß ich deutschen bzw. artverwandten Blutes bin.

Unterschrift des Bewerbers

Das Lichtbild und die eigenhändige Unterschrift des Bewerbers sowie die nebenstehenden Personalangaben werden hiermit beglaubigt.

Der Bewerber hat sich durch Vorlage des (Name, Nr. und Datum) amtlichen Ausweises *Bud. Kirdu* genügend ausgewiesen.

(Nichtzutreffendes ist zu streichen)

Stempel und Unterschrift einer amtlichen Stelle (Militär- bzw. Polizeibehörde, Hochschule oder Schule) einer zuständigen NS-Gliederung oder Ortsgruppe des Nationalsozialistischen Reichsbundes für Leibesübungen.

Reichs-Sport-Medal Document, 1941. Age 21 as soldier.
Signature missing below:
"I declare to be of German or racially equivalent blood

Institut für Leibesübungen
Universität Leipzig

2   104

Half-Jew Dieter Bergmann (last rank Unteroffizier).

Half-Jew Wilhelm Dröscher in the early 1970s (*top*) and ca. 1942 (*bottom*); he became a first lieutenant and received Hitler's *Genehmigung*. After the war, he became a very influential politician in the SPD. (Military awards: German-Cross in Gold, EKI, EKII, Close Combat Badge First Class, Silver Wound Badge, and Eastern Campaign Medal 1941–1942.)

Half-Jew and Unterarzt Robert Braun.

Half-Jew Colonel Walter H. Hollaender, decorated with the Ritterkreuz and German-Cross in Gold; he received Hitler's *Deutschblütigkeits-erklärung.* (Military awards: Ritterkreuz, German-Cross in Gold, EKI, EKII, Wound Badge, Assault Badge, and Close Combat Badge.)

Quarter-Jew Jürgen Krackow
(last rank second lieutenant); he
received Hitler's *Genehmigung*.
(Military awards: EKI, EKII,
Golden Wound Badge, and
Panzer Assault Badge in Silver.)

Half-Jew Helmut Krüger (last
rank Gefreiter). (Military awards:
EKII and Wound Badge.)

Quarter-Jew Admiral Bernhard Rogge wearing the Ritterkreuz and oak leaves; he received Hitler's *Deutschblütigkeitserklärung.* (Military awards: oak leaves to Ritterkreuz, Ritterkreuz, samurai sword from the emperor of Japan, EKI, and EKII.)

Half-Jew Karl-Arnd Techel (last rank Unteroffizier). (Military awards: EKI, EKII, Paratroop Assault Badge, and Wound Badge.)

Half-Jew and field-marshal Erhard Milch (*left*) with General Wolfram von Richthofen. Hitler declared Milch Aryan. He was awarded the Ritterkreuz for his performance during the campaign in Norway in 1940.

Half-Jew Herbert Lefévre (last rank Hauptgefreiter); he received Hitler's *Genehmigung* and was a Nazi Party member.

Quarter-Jew and Nazi Party member Franz Mendelssohn (last rank Marine-Oberbaurat). A direct descendant of the famous German-Jewish philosopher Moses Mendelssohn, Franz Mendelssohn helped build torpedo boats and U-boats. *Top*: At his daughter's wedding: Marine-Baurat Müller-Thode, Eva-Irene Mendelssohn, Werner Müller-Thode, Marine-Oberbaurat Franz Mendelssohn. *Bottom*: At his desk in 1940. (Military awards: War Service Cross Second Class.)

Half-Jew Helmuth Kopp (last rank Gefreiter) (*second from right, front column*). (Military awards: He should have received the Wound Badge, but was afraid to report his wounds because he thought the authorities might discover that he was a half-Jew when they reviewed his army file.)

Half-Jew Helmuth Kopp next to the grave of his Jewish mother, Helene.

Quarter-Jew Rolf von Sydow (last rank Obergefreiter). Sydow was eventually promoted to lieutenant, but he was demoted soon thereafter because the authorities found out he had lied about his ancestry—a grave offense in the Wehrmacht. The photograph in which he is smiling was taken after he had become a Fahnenjunker and was on his way to becoming an officer. The second photograph was taken after his demotion and subsequent time in jail. (Military awards: EKII and Panzer Assault Badge in Silver.)

Who Is a *Mischling*?

Many have spent the years since 1945 trying to forget about the days when they were labeled as *Mischlinge* by Hitler. However, being labeled *Mischlinge* and treated like second-class citizens by the Nazis made an indelible impression on them that has greatly influenced the way they view this history, their society, and themselves. Although most *Mischlinge* would prefer not to use this term to define themselves, they have to use it to describe their personal histories and the development of their identities. In many ways, this term gives meaning to their experience, pain, behavior, and personalities. The following anecdote is telling:

> In 1937, five-year-old Erwin Fuchs, a half-Jew, boarded a streetcar with his older brother. Both boys had been informed that Jews were no longer allowed to sit in public transportation, so they remained standing. A woman sitting near the boys made a little room for Erwin on her seat and said, "Here's half a seat for you, little one." Doubtful, little Erwin looked up at his brother and asked, "Which side of me is Jewish, the right or left?"[1]

The Term Mischling

The word *Mischling* means "half-caste, mongrel or hybrid."[2] Everyone originates from mixed backgrounds. Ironically, Hitler conceded that "we all suffer from the illness of mixed, spoiled blood."[3] The term *Mischling*, however, is primarily used to describe animals of mixed breeds. In keeping with the idea of a *Mischling* as a mixture of different "races," this term apparently was first applied to people with one black and one white parent in Germany's African colonies. Some Germans at the time called these children the "Rehoboth bastards."[4] In the 1920s, when French colonial soldiers had affairs with women in German territories they occupied,[5] the children who resulted were called *Mischlinge.* Hitler believed that the Jews brought these French blacks to Germany to destroy the "White Race."[6] The offspring of these unions, the so-called Rhineland Bastards, would be sterilized during Hitler's rule. There were at least two hundred who the Nazis subjected to this horrible treatment.[7]

In 1933, General Helmut Wilberg defined a *Mischling* as the offspring of a black person and a Spaniard.[8] To Wilberg's great surprise, the 1935 Nuremberg Laws labeled Wilberg a *Mischling* because he had a Jewish mother. Wilberg felt horrified that this label now applied to him. Most Germans agreed that blacks and whites were different enough to declare their offspring *Mischlinge,* but not everyone saw the difference between German Christians and Jews, much less than that between German Christians of non-Jewish descent and those with one or two Jewish grandparents. The German author Carl Zuckmayer, a half-Jew, wrote, "The term *Mischling* is total nonsense when applied to people with the same culture, language and skin color. A raving lunatic must have thought of this."[9] The Nazi term *Mischling* conveyed a strong negative image and encouraged Aryans to shun those classified as such.

Two years after seizing power, the Nazis implemented laws to separate *Mischlinge* from Aryans. In 1935, the Nuremberg Laws created two new "racial" categories: the half-Jew (Jewish *Mischling* first degree), and the quarter-Jew (Jewish *Mischling* second degree). A half-Jew had two Jewish grandparents; a quarter-Jew had one. Since Nazi racial policy declared anyone of the Jewish religion a full Jew regardless of ancestry, most *Mischlinge* were by definition Christians.[10] These laws implied that anyone with less than 25 percent Jewish "blood" would be considered German.[11] Those in the SS and the Party had to prove pure Aryan ancestry back to 1800 to remain in their positions.[12] SS officers had to take their ancestry back to 1750.[13] Officially though, only those with 25 percent or more of so-called Jewish blood would be handled as second-class citizens. Most affected by the Nuremberg Laws did not argue against these new stipulations. They did not foresee what they would mean for their lives, nor did they see any chance of opposing them in this authoritarian state. As half-Jew Hans-Geert Falkenberg said, "These laws were nonsense and weren't discussed by anybody in Germany. Don't forget that!"[14]

Mischlinge, according to Hitler, were the products of "unholy unions." Hitler claimed that *Mischlinge* "are the sad products of the irresistibly spreading contamination of our sexual life; the vices of the parents are revealed in the sickness of the children. . . . Blood sin and desecration of the race are the original sin in this world and the end of humanity which surrenders to it."[15] Hitler also said that *Mischlinge* were "bastards . . . monstrosities halfway between man and ape."[16]

The 1935 Nuremberg Laws defined the categories of *Mischlinge* according to the religion of a person's grandparents. Left without a reliable "scientific" method for physically identifying *Mischlinge,* Nazi officials had to turn to church archives[17] or local court records for evidence of a person's "race." Birth certificates kept in churches and synagogues identified every baby born in Germany as either Christian or Jewish. To prove the purity of one's Aryan ancestry, one had to produce birth, baptismal, or marriage certificates (or a combination of these documents) for all of one's grandparents. Conversion to Christianity at any stage more recent than a great-grandparent did not remove the stain of Jewish blood. The Nazis detested assimilation. Hitler cynically described this process: "If worst came to worst, a splash of baptismal water could always save the business and the Jew at the same time."[18] Frick declared on 4 October 1936 that "the ability to camouflage ancestry by changing religions will completely disappear."[19] After the advent of Nazi rule in 1933, the process of assimilation came to a halt, but the results of that assimilation, namely *Mischlinge,* confounded many Nazis.

Nazis were confused about *Mischlinge,* since they were both Jewish and German. Adolf Eichmann, SS-Obersturmbannführer[20] and chief of the Jewish Evacuation Office of the Gestapo, acknowledged that the unclear racial position of *Mischlinge* temporarily protected them.[21] For the Nazis, *Mischlinge* were also half or three-quarters German, and thus 50 percent or 75 percent valuable. Probably frustrated by all the confusion surrounding Jews and *Mischlinge,* Hermann Göring,[22] head of the Luftwaffe and second in command after Hitler, was rumored to have said, "I'll decide who's a Jew! *(Wer Jude ist, bestimme ich)."*[23] Göring allowed several

Mischlinge to serve in his Luftwaffe, three of whom eventually became generals.[24] However, Göring could only protect so many *Mischlinge,* usually those whom he knew personally or who had come to his attention through a contact. Once he decided that the person in question was "not Jewish," he still had to get Hitler's approval for most of them. If they wanted their racial status officially changed, only Hitler could truly decide "who was a Jew" or not.[25]

Most *Mischlinge* soon discovered that the Nazis took away their rights. For example, the Nazis denied *Mischlinge* citizenship in practice.[26] *Mischlinge* could not hold positions of authority. *Mischlinge* and Jews could be severely punished for sleeping with an Aryan, a crime called *Rassenschande* (race defilement),[27] which was loosely interpreted by the Nazis and affected people in many ways. Werner Eisner, a half-Jew and severely wounded Wehrmacht veteran, was deported to Auschwitz because he had slept with an Aryan.[28] But a person did not have to have sexual intercourse with an Aryan to commit *Rassenschande.* Dr. Hans Serelman, a German Jew, was sent to a concentration camp in October 1935 because he gave blood to a non-Jew to save that person's life. His crime was *Rassenschande.*[29] Dieter Bergmann's Aryan father, Ernst, a convinced Nazi, experienced difficulties with the authorities because he lived in the same house with his *Mischling* son. One night, after discussing their situation, Dieter sardonically told his father that just as long as they did not sleep together, the Nazis had no grounds to separate them.[30]

The fear of committing *Rassenschande* did not prevent most *Mischlinge* from having relations with Aryans. In a joint interview in 1996, Robert Braun, a half-Jew, and his wife, Margot, were asked whether they had been scared about the consequences if caught sleeping together. Margot, whom Robert had married after the war, looked confused. Suddenly, Robert looked up with a smirk. He had kept information about *Rassenschande* secret from his wife for five decades. She had had no idea of the punishments they could have incurred as a result of this most natural of behaviors for lovers. When asked why he did not tell her, Robert said, "Well, I think it's quite obvious why I didn't." We all laughed; however, the punishment back then could often be deadly.[31] At other times, the punishment for *Rassenschande* was mild. For example, Rudolf Sachs and his Aryan girlfriend, Traute Siedler, when caught having a relationship, were just forced to sign declarations that they would stop seeing each other. They were told that there would be no second chances.[32] Sachs thought that the SS implied that they would be deported if again found guilty of *Rassenschande.* They made sure they were not caught again.

The Nazis banned most *Mischlinge* from many popular activities, including certain university studies, specific civilian and military occupations, and places of Christian worship. Most could not enter Nazi organizations such as the Party and SA. At universities, several could not study medicine or law unless they had had distinguished military careers. The Wehrmacht drafted many, but they often could not become NCOs[33] or officers without an exemption. Gerhard Fecht wrote, "I was a quarter-Jew and was allowed to finish high school. Yet, I couldn't study in the University. I had to serve in the army, but I could never become an Unteroffizier;[34] I was generally inferior to everyone else."[35]

Fecht struggled with the limitations enforced on *Mischlinge*. Opportunities open to most Aryans were closed to many of them, and they felt excluded and disgraced. Not only were *Mischlinge* sometimes excluded from certain billets and ranks in the armed forces and from studying certain subjects in the universities, but they were excluded from some churches. For instance, the Evangelische Landeskirche officially announced that "racially Jewish Christians have no place and no rights" as members in the Protestant Church.[36]

Various officials predicted a bleak future for *Mischlinge* if the government enforced "racial" restrictions on them. The desk officer for racial law in the Reich Ministry of the Interior (RMI), Dr. Bernhard Lösener, stated on 30 October 1933 that *Mischlinge* suffered a double psychological blow, first by being associated with the Jews and second by being driven out of the German society to which they felt completely bonded.[37] Erwin Goldmann, the leader of the Stuttgart organization for non-Aryan Christians, went further, arguing in November 1934 that "*Mischlinge* suffer emotionally more than the 100 percent Jews who had voluntarily separated themselves from the German *Volk*."[38] Lösener warned on 10 November 1935 that persecuting them would make them dangerous because their "German blood" would make them formidable enemies.[39] Lösener argued that "half-Jews as enemies should be taken more seriously than Jews" because they had intelligence, the benefits of a good upbringing, and both Jewish and German attributes.[40] Lösener further warned that "a dangerous situation will develop in that half-Jews will no longer feel united with Jews and be pushed in between the races [of Jews and Aryans]." If this happened, Lösener argued, they would become "pariahs" and "desperados."[41] He felt that this estrangement could force some to feel so desperate that they would turn against the government with a vengeance.

All these predictions, however, underestimated the loyalty of most *Mischlinge* to Germany. Few were willing to risk their lives to resist the regime, although many thought about doing it at some point. Some took part in the White Rose and 20 July 1944 resistance groups.[42] However, most did not have the opportunity to resist, and most did not participate in the few groups that existed. They tried to avoid calling attention to themselves, aware that any transgression would be judged most severely. For example, after being denounced to the Gestapo for anti-Hitler activities, half-Jew and ex-soldier Erik Blumenfeld was sent to Auschwitz.[43]

Lösener believed that most half-Jews felt German and had rejected Judaism. He also warned that separating *Mischlinge* from the *Volk* not only could turn them into enemies, but also might drive many to suicide. If the government labeled them as Jews, Lösener warned, the suicide rate would rise significantly.[44] Lösener accurately observed that many *Mischlinge* did not want to be associated with Jews. After the Nuremberg Laws, most felt shocked to think that anyone might identify them with Jews, particularly *Ostjuden*. *Mischling* families had lived in Germany for generations, and most had lost all contact with their Jewish heritage. They had helped develop German society, fought in her wars, and furthered her culture. Some had not known of their Jewish heritage until Hitler came to power. Suddenly, they had to accept that they were categorized with so-called enemies of society. Half-Jew Hans Pollak learned of his Jewish ancestry in 1935. He had read about Jews in school and the press and felt upset to be associated with them.[45] This distaste at being identified with Jews sometimes resurfaces in the present. Hans Herder said that finding out he had a Jewish grandfather was his worst experience during the Third Reich. "I tell you honestly, I don't like Jews," he said in 1996. "I just don't like Jews. That's correct. I would never do anything to a Jew, I must also tell you that, because the Jew is also a human being. . . . When I get to know a Jew, then he's no longer a Jew, but a mensch like you and me."[46] As Robert Braun, a half-Jew and Unterarzt[47] in the medical corps put it, "Generally, *Mischlinge* are very anti-Semitic."[48] Half-Jew Joachim Gaehde described this more graphically: "I had a feeling that most of the *Mischlinge* felt more German than Jewish and venture to say some, not me, would have gladly joined the SS had they not been tainted by Jewish blood."[49] Most felt Aryan and did everything they could to disassociate themselves from Jews and to be viewed as faithful Germans.

Moreover, when the Nazis stereotyped how Jews looked and behaved, the Nazis affected not only society's perception of Jews, but also the way Jews and *Mischlinge* perceived themselves. Consequently, many agonized over aspects of their appearance and behavior that seemed to fit the Jewish stereotype. Half-Jew Dieter Bergmann hoped his blond hair and blue eyes would counterbalance his big nose. He remembers constantly—whether in the bathroom, lying in bed, or studying—pushing his nose back and up to make it look less "Jewish."[50] The "nose problem" became so serious for half-Jew Hartmut Ostendorff (birth name Link) that he had plastic surgery in the 1930s so his nose would look less Jewish.[51]

The following anecdote illustrates a typical episode of how the Nazi view of physical Jewishness could affect society's perception of people. When Marine-Oberbaurat[52] Franz Mendelssohn, a quarter-Jew, attended a party, he entered the foyer with a nobleman who was short, fat, and unkempt but nonetheless Aryan. Without asking, the maître d'hôtel introduced the fat man as Mendelssohn, and Mendelssohn, who was six feet, three inches tall, slender, and handsome, as the nobleman. When the men clarified who they were, it not only embarrassed those around, but it also deeply troubled Mendelssohn.[53]

The Nazis' description of Jews being sexual perverts also affected *Mischlinge* and how they viewed their own sexual development. As a teenager, quarter-Jew Rolf von Sydow felt greatly troubled by the fact that descriptions of Jews and *Mischlinge* in biology textbooks as being sexual perverts seemed to describe him, too. He felt that masturbation and the sexual fantasies of a typical teenage male were a sign of his Jewish depravity. He wrote, "I'm inferior. No one can ever know."[54] Nazi propaganda had convinced this perfectly normal teenager that sexual acts and thoughts were peculiar to Jews and therefore vile.

Mischlinge who were homosexuals suffered even more because they were persecuted for being both Jewish and "sexual degenerates." Most *Mischling* homosexuals documented in this study were successful in hiding their sexual orientation, but not their ancestry. Since homosexuality was illegal in the Third Reich, when a *Mischling* was found guilty of this crime, he often was judged quite harshly. For example, half-Jew Hauptgefreiter[55] Herbert Lefévre had received Hitler's *Genehmigung*[56] and served in the Kriegsmarine[57] as a cook. He was also a member of the SA and Party. In 1944, the court found him guilty of homosexuality and sentenced him to death. He had misused his position as a cook by giving extra food to fellow sailors in return for sexual favors. Amazingly, Oberbereichsleiter Werner Blankenburg in the Kanzlei des Führers (KdF)[58] wrote the court on 24 March 1944 on Lefévre's behalf. He had known Lefévre since 1928 and wrote that Lefévre was an outstanding individual who had learned of his ancestry after 1933. Hitler had awarded him a "special exemption *(Sondergenehmigung)*" to remain in the Wehrmacht. During his acquaintance with Lefévre, Blankenburg never noticed that Lefévre was a homosexual. To support the assumption that he was heterosexual, Blankenburg wrote that Lefévre had applied for permission to marry a woman in Hamburg. It is impressive that such a high-ranking official in the KdF was willing to write a letter of support for a person who was not only gay but also a *Mischling.* However, even with such support, the evidence was unquestionable concerning Lefévre's sexual persuasion. Marinestabsrichter (naval judge) Dr. August Berges ruled that as a half-Jew, Lefévre should have taken advantage of the opportunity he had to prove himself as a worthy member of the Wehrmacht. Instead of seizing this opportunity, his true "Jewish heritage of criminal instincts *(jüdischen Erbteils verbrecherische Instinkte)*" had revealed itself. His Party membership and Hitler's *Genehmigung* did not excuse his dastardly behavior as a sailor. The court reasoned Lefévre should have been more conscious of his duties and obligations to the German government because of his privileged status. The court showed no mercy. He was hanged on 6 July 1944. The authorities noted that it took him seven minutes to die.[59]

Mischlinge's *Views of Themselves and the Racial Laws*

When *Mischlinge* were forced to deal with their Jewish background after 1933, some went through a stage of denial; they could not believe they were associated with such an unpopular minority. Further, many had difficulties defining Jewishness. After 1935, despite all the racial laws and anti-Jewish propaganda, *Mischlinge* were extremely unsure how to view themselves. For instance, on 5 November 1941, Heinz Gerlach wrote Minister of Education Bernhard Rust[60] about his Jewish mother's Aryan attributes to mitigate her situation and thereby help his own case: "I don't believe that my mother is 100 percent racially Jewish, because none of our relatives or acquaintances can believe it! There is nothing even the slightest bit Jewish about my mother. She consciously avoided Jews because she found them distasteful."[61] Twenty-two-year-old Gerlach lived in a world where the rules of social interaction had radically changed; he could no longer be sure of things he had taken for granted all his life. By Halakah, Gerlach was a Jew, but he felt completely Aryan and German. The Nazis considered him a half-Jew. His case typified the confusion of most *Mischlinge* about what it meant to be called Jewish. Rolf von Sydow wrote after watching the Nazi film *Jud Süß*:[62] "[T]his film doesn't characterize me at all. I'm not a Jew. I don't go to the synagogue. . . . I don't betray other people. . . . I don't look Jewish. I'm a German. I'm from the aristocracy. . . . I'm better than the others. . . . I hate my grandparents because they're guilty. I hate my friends because they're Aryans. I hate the world. I hate myself."[63]

Most *Mischlinge,* like Sydow, agonized over what the Nazis described as Jewish. Feelings of shame, inferiority, and self-hatred were all manifestations of being labeled "Jewish" by the Nazis. Most did not feel an emotional attachment to Judaism, and the Judaism the Nazis described horrified them. They quickly learned to behave in a manner that would prove to their fellow Germans that they were not Jewish but Aryan. Some started to hate that side of themselves that was Jewish and became somewhat anti-Semitic to prove it. For example, half-Jew Unteroffizier Hans Mühlbacher was described by one of his superiors as being a "product of Nazi education" and that he fully identified with Nazi philosophy especially concerning the "Jewish enemy." However, his superior added that while Mühlbacher tenaciously adhered to his Germanness, he still had "racial problems."[64]

Although German Jews and *Mischlinge* were not regarded as 100 percent German according to Nazi laws, most still thought of themselves as Germans. They could not fully redefine themselves according to Nazi ideology. Jewish professor of Romance literature Viktor Klemperer of the Technical

University in Dresden wrote on 10 January 1939 that the differences and friction between Jews and Aryans were "not even half as big as that between Protestants and Catholics . . . or between Eastprussians and Southern Bavarians. . . . The German Jews were always a part of the German *Volk*. . . . They feel at home within German life. . . . They are and will remain German."[65] For the *Mischlinge,* the concept of being half-German was just as foreign as "being half-Jewish or trying to explain to someone why you're half-circumcised."[66] Another claimed, "There was no such thing as being half-Catholic or half-Protestant, and the Nazi laws made just as little sense as these categories did."[67]

Many *Mischlinge* simply were passionate Germans. In 1940, Unteroffizier Dieter Bergmann wrote to his Jewish grandmother, Elly Landsberg née Mockrauer:

> Don't you realize how much I'm with my whole being rooted in Germany. My life would be very sad without my homeland, without the wonderful German art, without the belief in Germany's powerful past and the powerful future that awaits Germany. Do you think that I can tear that all out of my heart? . . . Don't I also have an obligation to my parents, to my brother who showed his love to our Fatherland by dying a hero's death on the [battlefield]?[68]

Bergmann wrote this letter in defense of his grandmother attacking him for being a "Nazi." He had passionately performed his military duty and felt loyal to Germany. His grandmother felt scared for his future and believed Bergmann was not living in reality. However, Bergmann hoped that his army service and behavior would prove his Germanness: "Someday, I want to be a German amongst Germans and no longer a second-class citizen only because my wonderful mother is Jewish."[69] The *Mischlinge*'s tragedy was that they could not accept that they were no longer 100 percent German. For Hitler, they were separate from the *Volk*. However, they believed that they were and would remain German regardless of what Hitler said or did. This conviction explains why most remained in Germany during the increasing severity of Nazi laws beginning in 1933, and then subsequent to the end of the war, in 1945. As Klemperer wrote on 30 May 1942, "I'm German and I'm waiting for the Germans to return once again; they have disappeared somewhere."[70]

Regardless of how illogical the racial laws seemed, the majority of *Mischlinge* felt obligated to honor the very laws that infringed upon their natural rights. They, like most Germans of this time period, had been raised to be law-abiding citizens. The great German-Jewish philosopher Moses Mendelssohn wrote in his work *Jerusalem,* "The man who does not believe in laws must obey them, once they have received official sanction."[71] Mendelssohn might have changed his mind had he witnessed what would happen to his descendants during Nazi rule.[72] But his conviction about law typified how most viewed Nazi laws. Anything official had to be obeyed.

Some tried to change their racial status by denying their Jewish relatives. As early as 1935, Dr. Achim Gercke, appointed in 1933 to the RMI as an expert for racial research,[73] wrote that families with Jewish ancestry had done everything within their power to prove that a parent or grandparent was not a Jew but an Aryan. They denied the existence of Jewish relatives to free their children from the laws and, thus, to allow them to become "full-blooded Germans."[74] The Nazis knew that many would deny their Jewish past or claim an Aryan lover as the parent of their children instead of their Jewish spouse to protect themselves and loved ones. For example, on 26 July 1944, Himmler's office sent SS-Hauptsturmführer[75] Volk material the Parteikanzlei had compiled on *Mischlinge.* Among other things, this report discussed the problem of women inventing Aryan lovers to change their children's racial status. The protocol stated that "it has been established through experience that every mother is willing to commit perjury when it's a question of the German ancestry of her child."[76] Field Marshal and State Secretary of Aviation Erhard Alfred Richard Oskar[77] Milch's "Aryanization" was the most famous case of a *Mischling* falsifying a father. In 1933, Frau Clara Milch went to her son-in-law, Fritz Heinrich Hermann, police president of Hagen and later SS general, and gave him an affidavit stating that her deceased uncle, Carl Bräuer, rather than her Jewish husband, Anton Milch, had fathered her six children. After SA Colonel Theo Croneiss denounced Milch to Göring, Göring took Milch's mother's affidavit to Hitler.[78] In 1935, Hitler accepted the mother's testimony and instructed Göring to have Dr. Kurt Meyer, head of the Reich Office for Genealogy Research,[79] complete the paperwork. On 7 August 1935, Göring wrote Meyer to change Milch's father in his documents and issue him papers certifying his pure Aryan descent.[80] After the war, according to one of Göring's interrogators, John E. Dolibois, Göring was proud that he had helped "the half-Jew Milch" remain in "his Luftwaffe."[81] Ironically, many have suspected that Milch's mother was Jewish, since her maiden name was Rosenau.[82] Robert Wistrich claims that she was indeed a Jew; however, he does not give his evidence for this.[83] No documents have been presented that prove Milch's mother was Jewish. If Wistrich is correct, then Milch was 100 percent Jewish and not a half-Jew, making his position back then more precarious. In Milch's case, the Nazis did not object to incest, but Jewish ancestry was indeed a problem. Milch became a powerful field marshal, who according to historian James Corum, "ran the Luftwaffe and was its most powerful figure per personnel and planning issues, production and even strategy."[84] In addition, Milch had close contact with many of the Nazi elite, entertaining the likes of Himmler, Goebbels, Heß, and Blomberg at his home.[85] Milch's mother sacrificed her reputation as well as her husband's to protect her children. Without her lie, Milch might have lost his career and, along with it, his ability to protect his youngest daughter, Helga, who had Down syndrome, from Hitler's euthanasia program.[86] Moreover, Milch's mother's affidavit allowed her daughter to remain married to her husband, an SS general. Milch's mother's actions typified how thousands of Aryan mothers attempted, some successfully, most unsuccessfully, to erase their children's racial stigma.

However, once a mother successfully changed the racial status of her children through perjury, this act could have deadly consequences for her sons. After his military discharge on 30 October 1940, Klaus Menge had his mother swear that an Aryan lover was his father instead of her Jewish husband. The courts accepted her claims and Klaus happily returned to the army on 26 April 1941. A few months later, on 24 September 1941, he died in battle.[87]

Wise to the trick, the courts did not always believe women's claims about their children's fathers. When Wolfgang Spier's mother claimed that he and his sister Ruth came from her Aryan lover, the Nazis sent the children to a racial institute in Hamburg (Racial Biological Institute of the Hanseatic University)[88] for testing. After the scientists measured and photographed their heads, noses, ears, and bodies, the institute concluded that Ruth definitely descended from an Aryan, but that Wolfgang descended from the Jew (Julius).[89] Spier thus had to remain a half-Jew.

Often, to prove that they had been fathered by an Aryan, most had to attack their mothers' and grandmothers' characters by claiming they had had several affairs.[90] Joachim Löwen[91] said, "My own brother [Heinz] went to the Gestapo and claimed that our mother was a slut and had been a prostitute. The Gestapo reviewed our case and declared us *deutschblütig* (of German blood)." This ordeal destroyed Löwen's mother. Heinz died on the Russian front in the ranks of the Waffen-SS as an Oberscharführer,[92] and Joachim served the entire war in a Panzer company as an Unteroffizier. Although the brothers both knew they had a Jewish father, they felt it necessary to deny him to live a better life.[93] One half-Jewish soldier claimed his parents were not really his parents because, after his birth, they had mistaken him for their child in the hospital — they had taken the wrong child. Later, he changed his story and claimed that his mother had just been promiscuous.[94] Beate Meyer researched forty-two cases in Hamburg where half-Jews changed their status by proving the Jewish father was not really the father.[95] Most often, as Meyer notes, those who made such claims also were careful to claim that the Aryan father was a distant relative, a tenant, a coworker, or boss who also happened to be dead. Such people could not be brought to court to testify. Often, the authorities used racial tests to verify a *Mischling*'s Aryan father.[96] Jürgen Grün,[97] whose mother died before 1933 and who was raised by his half-Jewish father, claimed to a Nazi court that he had not been fathered by the half-Jew, but by a childhood friend of his mother's, an Aryan who had died in World War I. After the court investigated the matter and an institute racially tested him, the authorities declared him Aryan. Two years later, while fighting at the outskirts of Moscow in 1941, his commander called him into his tent and informed him that his father, the fallen soldier, had turned out to be a full-Jew. Grün, now registered as a half-Jew, was discharged.[98]

Officials often warned each other that such lying about a Jewish father was common for *Mischlinge*. On 30 July 1942, Oberbereichsleiter Werner Blankenburg in the KdF wrote Commander Richard Frey, who worked in the General Wehrmacht Domestic Office,[99] that Joachim Leftin had tried to enter the Wehrmacht by denying his Jewish father. Blankenburg explained that this was not true. Leftin did know his father. He further expressed his disbelief with Leftin's German mother, who had converted to Judaism on 28 March 1934 after Hitler had already been in power for over a year. Consequently, Blankenburg wrote that Leftin's letter "is typical Jewish insolence *(typisch jüdische Frechheit)*."[100] Blankenburg warned Frey that *Mischlinge* typically denied their Jewish fathers and instead claimed that their true fathers were "German blooded" men. He wrote that such statements from *Mischlinge* must be handled "with the utmost caution."[101]

Although some denied their ancestors, they still could not escape the fact that they descended from Jews, whether it became public knowledge or not. Quarter-Jew Admiral Bernhard Rogge said that "one could curse one's birth and ancestry; however, one cannot make it not to have happened. One can never step out of his family tree, no matter how much one wants to. . . . He may keep it a secret, may hate it, may feel ashamed because of it; however in his secrecy, his shame, his hate, he will in his disgust have to recognize it."[102] Rogge knew that no matter how much one lied about or doctored his ancestry, he would always remain who he was. Any *Deutschblütigkeitserklärung* (German blood certificates)[103] from Hitler or official Aryan certificates from courts would not alter the truth no matter how much one wished it to. Many successfully hid their ancestry, but sometimes living as an Aryan required them to do and say things that caused them emotional and psychological distress.

Those *Mischlinge* who had Aryan-sounding names had an easier time hiding their ancestry than those with Jewish-sounding names. The family name affected the way a *Mischling* viewed himself as well as how others viewed him. Those named Cohn, Mendelssohn, or Levy had a much more difficult time escaping the stigma of being Jewish than those named Bergmann, von Sydow, or Gerlach.

Mischlinge who had contact with Jewish relatives or observed some Jewish practices in their own homes understood Nazi persecution better, or at least knew where it was coming from, because they felt somewhat Jewish. From this study, half-Jews with Jewish fathers were more likely to feel a connection with Judaism than those with Jewish mothers, who by Halakah were Jews. This fact shows that Halakah in many respects was out of step with social reality — namely, that a father's religious convictions influenced a child's upbringing more than the mother's did. Perhaps this was because of the generally patriarchal nature of most German households. This is corroborated by the fact that most in this study who were circumcised had Jewish fathers.[104] Wolfgang Behrendt claimed that "my father loved his

Judaism. . . . I learned my Hebrew prayers from my father. . . . My heart is Jewish — that's for sure. It'll never leave me. . . . Wonderful — Jews, that's my world."[105] The only contact some had with Judaism was through their parents. As a result, many of those who learned about Judaism from a parent feel attached to Judaism. They describe this attachment as private — something they have a hard time sharing with others. But this attachment is real and lives strongly with them today.

Social Rejection of Mischlinge

Often friends, lovers, and even both the Jewish and Aryan sides of their families rejected *Mischlinge*.[106] Half-Jew Wilhelm Dröscher wrote in his diary in 1938 that he did not want anyone to know about his ancestry except his girlfriend (Ruth). "I wonder if anybody can tell how this weighs on my poor, tortured heart. Only she can know, later, but when? When? When?"[107] When Dröscher finally got up the courage to tell Ruth, she left him.[108] Such experiences made many hesitate to date or engage in intimate contact with Aryan women.[109] The racial laws forced *Mischlinge* to change their lifestyles dramatically, causing many to live without confidence.

Divorces often ensued because of so-called racial reasons. Some Aryans lacked the courage to stand by their Jewish spouses during hard times. Some Jews, mostly women, selflessly asked their Aryan spouses for a divorce, knowing that such action would benefit their spouse and children tremendously. Nazi officials had no trouble convincing many Aryans to file for divorce from their Jewish or *Mischling* spouses. While the Nazis told those Aryans that divorcing their Jewish spouses would help them, the opposite proved true. The Jewish partner lost the protection of the "privileged mixed marriage"[110] and in most cases was subsequently deported, especially after 1941.[111] For example, Robert Braun's mother divorced his father, who was immediately sent to a concentration camp at Drancy, France. She had left her husband because she was scared, and the Gestapo convinced her that she and her husband would be better off if she did.[112] Also, some Aryan men "*pro forma* divorced their Jewish wives" so they could keep their jobs and support themselves and families.[113]

Some Jewish spouses decided to commit suicide. They reasoned that their existence only caused their Aryan partners to lose their jobs and distressed

their children. Many felt guilty for bringing this "burden" upon their families. They reasoned that their deaths would simply be "best for the family."[114]

Several Aryan parents forsook their half-Jewish children. Ex-Oberschütze
Peter Scholz visited his father Julius after the Wehrmacht had discharged him
for racial reasons. His parents had been divorced for several years. Scholz
hoped that his wealthy father, although a miser and anti-Semite,[115] could
find him a job, an increasingly difficult task for *Mischlinge*. During their
conversation, they started arguing. Scholz called his father a coward for not
having fought in World War I. Enraged, his father stood up and yelled,
"Get out, you Jew! Out, you dirty Jew."[116]

Max Scheffler worried that he would lose his business if he remained
married to a Jew. He said that his greatest mistake in his life was marrying
a Jew, which left him three Jewish sons to support. In 1937, he divorced his
Jewish wife, Helena Weiss. The sons (Günther, Hubertus, and Karl-Heinz)
did everything they could to protect their mother. They felt army service
would be the best method.[117] Although two were later discharged, Unteroffizier Günther Scheffler remained with his unit during the whole war and
earned the Iron Crosses Second (EKII) and First Class (EKI).[118] He hoped
that as long as one of them served in the Wehrmacht, the Gestapo would
leave their mother alone. Helena survived the war. Max became a Nazi and
ignored his sons throughout the Third Reich.[119] Some Aryan parents even
refused to protect their *Mischling* children, "leading to the children's deportations from the Jewish Hospital in Berlin."[120]

Even more amazing, some Jewish grandparents rejected their half-Jewish
grandchildren. Helmuth Kopp remembered how, on the few occasions he
saw him during the 1920s and early 1930s, his Jewish grandfather, Louis
Kaulbars, hit him with a whip and called him goy.[121] Although he had a
Jewish mother, his grandfather did not consider him Jewish. One day his
grandmother protested this treatment, telling her husband, "That's our
daughter Helene's child!" The grandfather replied, "No, that's Wilhelm's
goy!" "My soul was damaged," Kopp said in 1995. He later added, "The
situation was pure *meshuga* (madness)." When his mother died on 18 November 1925, Kopp moved in with his Jewish aunt and uncle, who forced
him to go to an Orthodox school. He often got into trouble when he
brought sausage and butter to school for his lunch. His aunt, Sarah Moses
née Kaulbars, also forced him to have a traditional, although belated *bris*[122]

at the age of twelve. After the operation, he had to walk with a cane for six weeks. Years later, Kopp escaped this environment and entered the Wehrmacht in 1941.[123]

Sometimes *Mischlinge* were raised Jewish, but when they decided to take on other beliefs, their Jewish relatives rejected them. Alfred Bütow, who was raised Jewish by his Jewish mother and grandfather, later converted to Christianity. After he did this, his grandfather told him that from then on, Alfred was dead for him.[124] With convictions such as Kopp's and Bütow's grandfathers displayed, it was not surprising that some Orthodox Jews welcomed the Nuremberg Laws because they prevented intermarriage.[125] When *Mischlinge* were forced to deal with the racial laws, they soon found that they had few people to rely on for support. Whichever side of the family they turned to, whether Aryan or Jewish, many encountered painful episodes of rejection. For example, Hanns Rehfeld wrote:

> I have been discriminated against in my life for three things I could do nothing about. First, my Jewish relatives discriminated against me because I had a Christian mother *(Schickse)*.[126] Secondly, the Germans discriminated against me because I had a Jewish father. And [after the war], when I worked in the foreign service for many years, people discriminated against me because I was a German (i.e., I must be a Nazi).[127]

Rehfeld remembers that when his father, Martin, died in 1940 in a Breslau[128] prison run by the Gestapo,[129] he and his siblings did not have any means to support themselves. Their Jewish relatives refused to help them and told them to go to the Germans, but when they went to the Germans, they were told to go to the Jews. Rehfeld's Jewish grandmother, Nathalie née Schey, had a gravestone made for his father. On the stone was written, "Here rests my dear son." There was no mention of husband or father. Rehfeld concluded, "My Jewish relatives never recognized the marriage of my parents."[130] Rehfeld's experience typified the experiences of many *Mischlinge*. They felt alone in a world that progressively became more hostile to them from all sides.

Tragically, as some *Mischlinge* were pushed further into the "Jewish camp" by being rejected by German organizations, they discovered that most Jewish organizations did not want anything to do with them either. Many *Mischlinge* may have been rejected because of their hostility to Jews. In periods of persecution, Jewish communal institutions felt that their resources should be used to help Jews, not those who resented their Jewish ancestry and were trying to escape the stigma of Jewishness. Others were probably rejected not because they were embarrassed of their Jewish past, but because they were not viewed as Jewish enough to warrant assistance. Lösener in RMI wrote on 10 November 1935 that, almost without exception, the Jewish community denied "half-Jews any help."[131] For example, when Rehfeld and his siblings asked Jewish organizations to help them emigrate, they rejected them because they were *Mischlinge*.[132] Lösener wrote that many "half-Jews have already decided to avoid dealing with the Jewish communities."[133] This was probably because they either did not feel Jewish or had already had negative experiences with Jewish organizations (or both). *Mischlinge* felt caught in the middle in more ways than one. For the Nazis, they were products of sexual sins, and for religious Jews, one of their parents had broken a sacred covenant not to marry outside the Jewish community. Either way, they were shunned by both ends of the social spectrum in Nazi Germany. Frau Olga Mühlbacher, an Austrian Jew, wrote in her diary in 1943, "It's a proven fact that Jews always thought it to be the biggest disgrace to marry a 'Christian,' although this totally baffles the Gestapo agent."[134] Because many religious Jews abhorred intermarriage and ostracized those who practiced it, many young *Mischlinge* did not know about their Jewish heritage. Since many Jewish grandparents had rejected their father or mother when they married a non-Jew, many *Mischlinge* grew up outside the Jewish communities.[135] So *Mischlinge* forced to look to Jews for help simply felt confused and helpless.

When the youthful Hannah Klewansky went to the Gestapo office on the November morning after *Reichskristallnacht*[136] in 1938 to inquire where the Nazis had taken her Jewish father Eugen, a sign informed her that the Jewish Community Center was processing such inquiries. She went there and waited in a long line of anxious people looking for loved ones. When her turn arrived, the Jewish secretary got out her family's file. "Is your father Christian?" Hannah answered that yes, he was a converted Jew. Then the official asked if she was Jewish. She answered that her mother was not Jewish and that she herself had been raised Christian. The secretary then sent

Hannah away saying, "We don't deal with your kind." Hannah then boldly returned to the Gestapo to ask how she could locate her father. The officer took her to a back room where two SS men were playing cards. The officer asked the men if they liked what they saw and left. They raped her.[137]

Young *Mischlinge,* as Hannah's traumatic story illustrates, did not know where to seek help. This feeling of helplessness was strongly enforced when they had to deal with relatives who were convinced Nazis. Dieter Bergmann's aunt, Valerie von B. née Bergmann, a Party member, told him one day in 1941, "My dear boy, I think people like you must be exterminated if our fatherland is to remain pure and victorious against the Marxist-Jewish conspiracy. Sorry, my dear boy. You know I love you."[138] When Hans-Geert Falkenberg had dinner with his godmother, Dora Rogoszinsky née Elmer, in March 1940, she asked him about his grandmother and he replied, "Haven't you heard? . . . She's been deported with the Jews from Stettin to the East." When she asked why he had not told her, he simply said because she was a Nazi. "Geert, naturally I believe that the Jews are Germany's misfortune, but that has nothing to do with Grandma." Geert claims that such was the German schizophrenia back then.[139] Beate Meyer notes that such situations in families caused severe problems.[140]

This feeling of helplessness stemmed largely from suddenly being forced to come to terms with their "new" identity. In general, they had problems adjusting to the situation in which they suddenly found themselves. Graf Wolf von Bredow wrote his wife about their son's desire to get Hitler's approval to become an officer: "If I were in his place, I would say to the Nazi officials handling the case, 'Do what you like. I couldn't care less. I know who I am and that's enough. Period. *Finito.*'"[141] Many parents of *Mischlinge* were bewildered by their children's frustrations. Bredow's twenty-four-year-old son, Achim, could not have said what his father wanted him to because the son was still discovering who he was. Even teenagers growing up in stable environments have enough trouble making the transition to adulthood. It was not surprising that the identity crisis many young *Mischlinge* suffered was a highly amplified version of standard growing pains. Half-Jew Heinz Puppe wrote in 1997, "Individuals have the desire, the need, to belong, belong to an identifying group of some sort, family, ethnic group, a country, a school, etc. The problem is that anyone not belonging to my group becomes 'them.' . . . Being branded as a

Mischling by Globke[142] and associates has been that I don't feel I belong anywhere."[143] The alienation the Nazis forced *Mischlinge* to experience was painful, especially since most, until Hitler became chancellor, were accepted by mainstream German society. Many still feel a sense of loss — a permanent estrangement.

The Struggle to Be Aryan

Many *Mischlinge,* despite their troubles and feelings of abnormality, tried to be considered as Aryans and labeled as normal. They knew that the Nazis scrutinized *Mischlinge* to determine whether the Aryan or the Jewish side dominated.[144] Consequently, most fought a constant battle to prove that their Aryan side had completely eclipsed their Jewish side. Since Nazi ideology declared *Mischlinge* inferior, they strove to be better than the Aryans around them, hoping they might be accepted back into society. Young *Mischlinge* tried hard to excel, particularly in athletics. Hans-Geert Falkenberg's teachers from school taught that *Mischlinge* and Jews were inferior. In response, he "compensated. . . . I was the best long-distance runner, the best boxer, the best swimmer, the best goalie, whatever they wanted. Not because I was a natural athlete; only to prove that everything they taught was absolute nonsense. . . . I've not lost this drive to be the best even until now."[145] Rolf von Sydow did the same in school and sports, but doubted his success. "Sometimes I'm scared," he wrote, "because I know that I'm not supposed to be so good. However, if I'm so good, then they must make an exception for me."[146] In December 1940, Sydow faced an Aryan opponent in a boxing match and beat him into a "bloody pulp." He wanted to prove that he was not a coward as the Nazis described *Mischlinge* and Jews. Sydow explained that during his boxing match he reasoned, "The harder I hit, the less likely it is that anyone might think I'm a *Mischling.* Because *Mischlinge* are cowards. They're worse than full Jews."[147] These *Mischlinge* internalized Nazi standards even as they tried to fight them.

Their desire for acceptance took on a new twist when they entered the Wehrmacht. Many believed that the armed forces gave them an opportunity to prove their "Aryanhood." For example, Helmut Krüger wrote that as a soldier, he always had Nazi opinions ringing in his ears, such as their description of Jews as flat-footed cowards. "By some dumb logic, I felt I had to prove them wrong, so at the beginning of the war, I volunteered for reconnaissance missions." Krüger's officers awarded him the EKII for his bravery.[148] Jürgen Krackow remembered telling his father in 1943 that "being good isn't enough. I have to be sharper, tougher, faster, braver . . . than all the others."[149] Krackow tried even harder after Lieutenant Wierhyn-Pesch accused him of choosing the Panzer corps because the infantry had previously rejected him for having Jewish flat feet.[150] Later, Hitler granted him the *Genehmigung* and his commanders decorated him several times for his successes as a tank officer. He did all he could to prove his loyalty to Germany by showing his bravery in battle. He won the EKII, the EKI, and the Golden Wound Badge.[151] His brother, Reinhard, claimed that he was a brave soldier only because he was a *Mischling* fearing to be called a "cowardly Jew *(feiger Jude)*."[152]

Most believed their meritorious service would convince their comrades and society to accept them as "normal." Half-Jew Wilhelm Dröscher wrote in 1940 that he wanted to serve on the front to prove that he was "a great guy *(Kerl)*" and worthy German. He would prove his desire to be a "worthy German" by receiving Hitler's *Genehmigung,* being promoted to first lieutenant and receiving both Iron Crosses and the German-Cross in Gold.[153] Many did more than required, and thus one can safely assume that several died premature or unnecessary deaths attempting to prove their worthiness. Out of 1,671 Jewish and *Mischling* soldiers documented in this study, 7 Jews, 80 half-Jews, and 76 quarter-Jews died in battle. Some 244 received the Iron Cross,[154] 1 the German-Cross in Silver,[155] 19 the German-Cross in Gold,[156] and 15 the Knight's Cross (Ritterkreuz) of the Iron Cross,[157] one of Germany's highest military honors.

To receive the Ritterkreuz, one had to perform valorous and significant acts during battle. For example, according to the famous fighter-ace and later Bundeswehr General Johannes Steinhoff, three fellow pilots were partial Jews and won the Ritterkreuz. They were Captain Siegfried Simsch (95 kills), First Lieutenant Oskar "Ossi" Romm (92 kills), and Feldwebel Rudolf Schmidt (51 kills). Keeping in mind that well-known American fighter-aces had only 20 kills, the accomplishments of men such as Simsch, Romm, and Schmidt are quite impressive.[158]

Field Marshal Walther Model, commander of the Ninth Army in 1943, recommended half-Jew Lieutenant Colonel Walter Hollaender[159] for the

Ritterkreuz on 14 July 1943. Hollaender had successfully led his Storm *(Sturm)* Regiment 195 south of Orel near Dmitrowski on 5–6 July six kilometers into a heavily defended enemy position. This event occurred during the Battle of Kursk, also called Citadel *(Zitadelle)*. Personally fighting in the front lines, Hollaender and his men broke the enemy's resistance. His regiment destroyed twenty-one enemy tanks and several enemy positions. Model claimed that through Hollaender's actions, he secured the Ninth Army's left flank and cut off lines of supplies and replacements for the Soviets. Hollaender was awarded the Ritterkreuz on 20 July 1943.[160]

Quarter-Jew Admiral Bernhard Rogge even received the oak leaves[161] to his Ritterkreuz for his activities as a surface raider captain where he sank and captured almost two dozen enemy ships. Rogge may have even had a significant impact on the manner in which Japan conducted its invasion of the British possessions in Asia in 1942. Before sinking the U.K. steamship *Automedon* on 11 November 1940, Rogge and his men were able to capture "highly confidential" documents drawn up by the war cabinet for the British "Commander-in-Chief, Far East." These documents detailed the British military strength in the Far East, including the number of Royal Air Force units, the number and type of ships, an assessment of Australia and New Zealand's military roles, copious notes on the Singapore fortifications, and an assessment of the feasibility of Japan entering the war. Rogge turned these documents over to the Japanese,[162] who awarded him a samurai sword for his contribution to their success. Besides Rogge, only Reichsmarschall Göring and Field Marshal Rommel received swords from the Japanese emperor.[163]

Men who received the Ritterkreuz played significant strategic roles during the war. They shot down many enemy airplanes, destroyed numerous enemy tanks, sank several enemy ships, and killed hundreds of men in action to earn this medal, of which most were very proud. Although the vast majority of *Mischlinge* in uniform were simple soldiers, there were some whose contributions to the war effort made it into the history books.

Many behaved the same way as Aryans: out of loyalty to Germany, belief in the Nazi government, because they were scared to act otherwise, for opportunistic reasons, or, most commonly, out of a mixture of all four. Heinz Gerlach wrote on 11 May 1941 to Minister Rust, "My parents have raised me as a true German and to love the Führer and Fatherland."[164] This study has documented four full Jews, fifteen half-Jews, and seven quarter-Jews who were Party members.[165] Others were not Party members, but nonetheless believed in the Nazi ideology and even voted for Hitler.[166] The Jew and Wehrmacht soldier Shlomo Perel said, "To survive, I must disguise, to be someone else. A Nazi . . . and so, I began to be a German soldier. . . . And I began to react as I was taught by the Nazis. Like a Nazi, and true, I was one [*sic*]"[167] One day, when Hitler arrived at the Berlin Opera House, half-Jew Dieter Bergmann rushed up to see him in person, got caught up in the enthusiasm, greeted him with the characteristic outstretched arm, and yelled "*Heil* Hitler."[168] First Lieutenant Heinz Dieckmann, a 75 percent Jew,[169] said that back then, "I was a small Nazi. . . . I was fascinated with Hitler. I found him wonderful. . . . Today, we only see the devil, but back then, we did not see it." Dieckmann claimed that the ideology had made them blind and that they could not discern good from evil.[170] Although Peter Schliesser had been expelled from school, called a Jew, and beaten up, he generally believed in Hitler's ideals and felt impressed by what Hitler had done "in pulling Germany out of the recession and virtually eliminating poverty."[171] However, his fascination with Hitler quickly ended when the Nazis deported his Jewish father, Otto, an Austrian World War I decorated first lieutenant, to Auschwitz in August 1944 and Peter himself two months later to an OT (Organization Todt)[172] forced labor camp at Weissenfels, Saxony.[173] Moreover, many became good actors and played "Nazi." Half-Jew Hans Mühlbacher wrote, "To survive [the Nazi Reich] and not be a victim of denouncers it was necessary to save yourself and fly into a second 'I.' The first, the real 'I' could only exist secretly or when speaking with reliable friends."[174] Mühlbacher convinced many around him that he was a committed Nazi.[175] But these men just described may have been rare cases.

For a time, the Wehrmacht offered many *Mischlinge* and some Jews a way to prove their patriotism and escape discrimination, and most accepted military duty without reservation. When the Wehrmacht drafted them, most felt that they belonged and were somewhat in control of their lives. Half-Jew Hans Meissinger said that being a soldier "gave me a sense of not being the 'outcast' that I had experienced in civilian life."[176] They wore the same uniform, ate the same food, and fought a "common enemy." They could prove that they were not *Untermenschen* (subhumans). Serving in the army, Ernst Ludwig said, "gave me the opportunity to prove to myself and others that as a half-Jew, I was not inferior."[177] Half-Jew Otto Lüderitz said, "I volunteered. I wanted to be a normal German. I wanted to prove I was a German. . . . I did not want to be an outsider."[178] Lüderitz's desire to be a soldier was reinforced by his Jewish family, who were proud that he could serve.[179] Half-Jew Dieter Bergmann wrote that in the army, "I sensed the solid comfort of being 'one of the guys' and being accepted."[180] Half-Jew Oberschütze Hugo Freund said that he experienced an "honest camarade-rie" in his unit and that he preferred to stay with his comrades in 1940 when the army discharged him because of the racial laws. "It was my family," Freund simply said.[181] Waffen-SS soldier and Jew Heinz-Günther Löwy claimed that he felt connected with his men, especially since they had saved each other's lives so many times.[182] They also quickly came to realize that during war, there was no difference between themselves and the so-called Aryans. Quarter-Jew Fritz Binder said, "It's a joy for me even today to have seen how the wonderful supermen *(Herrenmenschen)* shat in their pants when a battle started. Death doesn't discriminate between Jews and supe-rior races."[183] During war, Binder could feel equal to those around him, and this validated his self-worth. Many had similar experiences as Binder; how-ever, this sense of equality and belonging quickly faded when their com-manders failed to promote them or had to discharge them for racial reasons. They also felt that their Wehrmacht service protected them from the Gestapo. Ilse Körner wrote of her deceased husband, half-Jew and Lieutenant Hans-Joachim Körner, "He wanted to distinguish himself through his bravery and willingness to fight as a soldier and thus, escape the persecution of the Nazis."[184]

Mischlinge *Come to Terms with Their Situation during and after the War*

Many came from the middle class and resented that their status in society decreased significantly after the Nazis labeled them *Mischlinge.* For some, the Wehrmacht offered them a chance to regain some of their lost prestige. Yet, this had its price. During the war, many felt torn between the desire to belong, regain some of their lost pride, and protect themselves and their families through military service and the realization that to do so, they had to serve Hitler. As half-Jew Gefreiter Richard Riess said, "What I was doing was actually against my interest and my family. I had to serve. I had to serve my mortal enemy. I rationalized that I did so to help my father, but that was definitely not how it felt and ultimately my service didn't help. . . . I always asked myself why I am serving a criminal — evil Hitler."[185] This dilemma plagued many *Mischlinge.* Many describe feeling as if their soul or heart were torn in two.[186] On the one hand, they felt secure in the army, but on the other hand, they felt that they were betraying their Jewish family. Many felt guilty that while they lived securely in the Wehrmacht, their Jewish families suffered Nazi persecution. Some rationalized their actions by convincing themselves that they were serving to save their Jewish family. Many provided temporary protection for their family members through their service until the Wehrmacht discharged them throughout 1940 and 1941. Half-Jew Hans Meissinger said that "being a soldier in the army of the Third Reich naturally gave me a bad feeling. The conflicting emotions are hard to reconstruct today. Naturally, I had some confidence that doing what other Germans had to do gave some shielding to my mother [Rosa] from the ever-present threat around her. After I was dismissed from the army, that shield was gone."[187] Self-protection and protecting their families in any way they could was only human, but in doing so, ironically, many *Mischlinge* felt they were betraying the very people they wanted to protect. Moreover, they felt that they were not being true to their own convictions by serving Hitler, who many knew hated them because of their Jewish ancestors. It was a paradox, but their sense of pride made them seek every opportunity to be like everyone else. At the time, however, many did not dwell on the ironies involved in their service. Only with time and reflection did many of these paradoxes become clearer to them.

In retrospect, many say that being forced out of mainstream society, especially when the Wehrmacht discharged them, made them look at Hitler and his policies more critically. Helmut Krüger feels fortunate that he had a Jewish mother because it helped him see things more clearly. Had he not had a Jewish mother, he claims, he probably would have joined the Party or SS.[188] Former German Chancellor Helmut Schmidt, a Luftwaffe first lieutenant during World War II, echoed Krüger when he admitted that without his Jewish grandfather, he could have become a Nazi.[189] Because of the persecution they and their families suffered, many grew to hate the

Nazi regime. In 1936, Hans Koref felt irritated to discover that his grandfather was a Jew, but later, his Jewish past helped him hate Hitler, who labeled him "nonhuman."[190] The majority of *Mischlinge,* knowing that they descended from Jews and were being persecuted because of that ancestry, became critical of Hitler and his regime. However, several have expressed that had it not been for their Jewish ancestry, they probably would have become Nazis.[191]

Interestingly, *Mischlinge* had a knack for finding each other. Most had contact with other *Mischlinge.* When asked how, many echo the answer one half-Jew gave: "We could smell one another."[192] Neither religious beliefs nor nationality nor heritage united *Mischlinge.* Rather, their common fate created this community. In time, they started to take on similar characteristics. These behavioral changes, however, were so subtle that usually only other *Mischlinge* could recognize them.

Some did not learn of their Jewish past until after the war. Heinz Dieckmann, a highly decorated first lieutenant, recalled that shortly after the war's conclusion, his grandfather told him he was Jewish. His family had kept the information hidden to guard him, but the Allies had different attitudes. His grandfather decided it was now time to tell Dieckmann he was a "bastard." He explained that Dieckmann's mother was a half-Jew and that his real father had been a Communist Russian Jew. The revelation that he belonged to the people he had been taught to hate overwhelmed Dieckmann. A few months before the war ended, a grenade splinter had taken off Dieckmann's foreskin in battle. A sense of irony came over him as he realized that his "circumcision had been appropriate."[193]

After the war, the Allies and many Jews had a hard time understanding the *Mischling* concept or that some German Jews had served in the Wehrmacht. Some half-Jews freed from OT forced labor camps by Allied troops were handled like POWs[194] because the Allies considered OT a paramilitary organization and therefore *Mischlinge* were OT "soldiers."[195] Many discovered it was more trouble than it was worth to try to explain to impatient Allied authorities what a half-Jew was and the persecution half-Jews suffered under Hitler. Since most of the Allies only understood Nazi and Jew, the half-castes were ignored. Egon Bossart said, "We didn't belong to the Nazis, but we were also German. I was always scared what would happen."[196] When half-Jew Alfred Bütow told an American interrogator that he was a Jew and ex-soldier, the interrogator told him that "you must've betrayed your Judaism." Bütow was not released earlier as he had hoped.[197] Hermann Lange tried to explain to a Russian soldier that he was a half-Jew and not a soldier anymore and that his mother and grandmother both died in concentration camps. Not interested in explanations, the Russian held a pistol to his head and pulled the trigger. Luckily, the Russian had run out of bullets. Later, a Russian officer told him that he did not understand what a half-Jew was and that a German was either a Jew or a soldier. From then on, Lange told everybody he was a Jew.[198] Lange was lucky. When half-Jew and ex-soldier Karl Helmut Kaiser tried to explain his situation to impatient Russian soldiers, they shot him in cold blood.[199]

After his discharge, the Jew Günther Kallauch, while trying to return home, met a group of freed Jewish concentration camp prisoners *(KZ-Häftlinge)* on the road. Kallauch tried to explain his survival and that he was a Jew, but the people, not believing a Jew could be wearing a Wehrmacht uniform, beat him horribly.[200] Half-Jew Helmuth Kopp tried to emigrate to South America after the war. He told everybody he met that he was Jewish and recited the Shema to prove it. He went to a rabbi in Berlin who had contacts in Colombia to ask for help. When Kopp entered the rabbi's office, he saw other *Mischlinge* and Jews there. When the rabbi asked about Kopp's experiences during the war, Kopp told him honestly that he was a Gefreiter and had served as a driver of a *Selbstfahrlafette* (self-propelled artillery piece) from 1941 to 1944.[201] Shocked, the rabbi said that Kopp must have shot Jews if he served so long. Kopp said, "This rabbi was a fanatic. I was more goy than Jew for him. All he cared about were full Jews or religious ones. He couldn't bring himself to believe that I didn't shoot Jews. I told him, 'You think that since I served in the army, I suddenly started hating Jews, that's crazy!' Then I left."[202] Unfortunately, the rabbi Kopp met held the view of many — namely, that all Wehrmacht soldiers were Nazis and "Jew killers."[203] Such a view is historically wrong. On meeting Kopp, the rabbi's opinion about how the war was conducted was challenged and he could not bring himself to change the way he felt about German soldiers, regardless of their ancestry or true military activities. For Kopp, turning to Jews for help turned into a humiliating experience. He quickly learned that many would never understand his situation and that regardless of Halakah, many Jews would not consider him Jewish and would always reject him. Jewish organizations refused to help ex-soldier Alfred Bütow, a half-Jew, after the war because he had converted to Christianity.[204]

Some half-Jews were more successful in convincing the Allies of their difficult situation. After ex-Unteroffizier Karl-Arnd Techel explained his case to Allied authorities in charge of the POW camp he was incarcerated in, they released and sent him home.[205] A few years after the war, many half-Jews received official documents from the Allies and other agencies founded throughout Germany (e.g., the Bavarian State Office for Reparations)[206] claiming that the Nazis had persecuted them.[207] Some received compensation for the atrocities committed against them and their families.[208]

Aryans who had rejected their *Mischling* relatives did an about-face after the war. Suddenly, most Germans claimed they had not supported Hitler and had not been involved in any of the atrocities. Often, the Allies believed only those claims that a Jew would confirm. Since the Allies later came to view *Mischlinge* as Jews, *Mischling* relatives became a significant asset. Heinz Puppe wrote, "The Aryan part of my family ostracized me during the Third Reich, . . . [but] they were eager to meet me after the demise of the thousand-year Reich. 'Oops, we made a little mistake. Forgive and forget now, dear Heinz.' I have forgotten nothing and forgiven nothing. The pain of my experience will not go away. . . . I cannot amputate my memory."[209] What Puppe experienced with Aryan relatives was common; this study found that many did not help their Aryan relations. They saw through their repentance and once again viewed their opportunistic relatives with disdain.

Although most *Mischlinge* had little or no contact with Judaism before Hitler and after the war were not embraced as fellow victims by Jewish survivors, since 1945 many have tried to rediscover their Jewish roots. After the war, many have read extensively about Judaism, traveled to Israel, and researched their Jewish ancestors. Books about Jews, Jewish philosophy, Israel, and Judaism line their bookshelves, and it is common to see a menorah[210] somewhere in their homes.[211] Many take pride in their Jewish heritage now through the state of Israel, although most do not agree with the fundamentalist religious movement there, often comparing it with Nazism.[212] Some, on the other hand, have even converted to Judaism and been circumcised.[213]

Some families of these men have shown even more interest than the *Mischlinge* themselves in their Jewish past. Countless children and grandchildren enjoy going to Israel, studying about Judaism, and even learning Hebrew. Half-Jew Werner Eisner's son Mijail (Michael) not only immigrated to Israel but also served in the Israeli army.[214] He must have converted, since his mother was not only not Jewish, but was a daughter of an SS man.[215]

Israel has helped many *Mischlinge* deal with the pain they experienced during Hitler's tyranny. For many of them, Israel's military achievements concretely refute the stereotype of the cowardly Jew.[216] Many *Mischling* veterans looked for a country that would accept them and their patriotism. Some transferred their old German pride and military values to Israel. A few *Mischlinge* and Jews who had served in the Wehrmacht even traveled to Israel after 1945 to fight in Israel's War of Independence and later conflicts.[217]

Some tried to establish contact with their Jewish relatives in Israel and the United States after 1945, but several were rejected because they had served in the Wehrmacht and had fought for Hitler. Helmuth Kopp explained, "I couldn't leave Germany. I didn't have the money — both my parents were dead. I didn't want to serve in Hitler's army, but I had to. Now my relatives call me the Jewish Nazi. They don't really like to have contact with me at all."[218] Protests by *Mischlinge* and "hidden" Jews that the Wehrmacht drafted them fell, in most cases, on deaf ears. Karl-Heinz Löwy, raised in a religious home, hid his Jewishness and was drafted into the Waffen-SS and served as a Sturmmann[219] (under the assumed name of Werner Grenacher). He feels it was by God's grace that he survived the war.[220] He complained that many Jews do not understand him or consider him Jewish, and are not willing to acknowledge his suffering. He says he wants to have contact with his Jewish relatives but claims they have rejected him.[221]

Such allegations also come from many *Mischlinge* who have felt discriminatd against by Jewish relatives or other members of the Jewish faith. Many *Mischlinge* who after the war tried to establish contact with Jews have experienced unpleasant reactions. When half-Jew Anton D. tried to worship in Mannheim's synagogue, the Jews there kicked him out when they learned about his Wehrmacht service. Referring to the extreme religious beliefs of some Orthodox Jews, quarter-Jew Karl Partsch said, "Some Jews are just as bad as the Nazis."[222] Many *Mischlinge* and people living in mixed marriages feel that Orthodox Jews are prejudiced against them. Prominent Frankfurt banker and 37.5 percent Jew Michael Hauck said that Jews in the academic world do not like *Mischlinge*. He claimed that they "don't like people not of their group. They exclude us from their history. We are outcasts."[223] After the war, when Adolf Blum and his wife Lenni met the rabbi of Frankfurt at the train station and Lenni told him she only survived the war because Adolf, an Aryan and veteran Wehrmacht soldier, chose to remain married to her, the rabbi told them she had sinned by marrying a non-Jew and left the Blums standing there.[224] From such experiences, one can understand why half-Jew Walter Schönewald said, "A Jew is only a religion; everything else is Hitler; everything else is racism." Schönewald claimed that Israel has its own "racial laws" in that the rabbinical courts prevent marriages between Jews and non-Jews and do not recognize the Reform or Conservative movements.[225] Since the Nazis persecuted *Mischlinge* because they were products of mixed marriages, many resent the fact that religious Jews also condemn such mixed marriages. Ironically, many *Mischlinge* maintain that their existence actually helped mitigate the Holocaust by making it difficult for the Nazis to exterminate Jews married to non-Jews and those with *Mischling* children.

Because of their experiences with some religious Jews, many *Mischlinge* blame Orthodox Jews for anti-Semitism. Quarter-Jew Fritz Binder claimed that Orthodox Jews, by maintaining they are the only ones who have found the "truth" and that their "lifestyle is the best, are just as bad as the Nazis."[226] Half-Jew Bergmann said, "The fact that the religious Jews pray each day and thank God that He did not make them gentiles is disgusting."[227] Quarter-Jew Horst von Oppenfeld, a descendant of the Jewish Oppenheim family,[228] who was a captain and an adjutant to Stauffenberg,[229] said that Orthodox Jews experience so many problems because they do not assimilate. "Their problem," he claims "is due to the fact that they want to be different."[230] Consequently, many *Mischlinge* avoid contact with very religious Jews.

After 1945, most *Mischlinge* put their unpleasant experiences behind them and started to live normal lives. They hate the word *Mischling,* but many still secretly do everything they can to prove they do not fit the Nazi stereotypes. Most strove to be the best in their respective fields after the war, and most have been successful. Many make it a point that they are not *Mischlinge.* However, they always use this word in their description of the past to describe their *Webfehler* (ancestral defects)[231] or *falscher Makel* (wrong blemish).[232] Many make light of their "racial situation" to show they

have come to terms with it, such as calling themselves *Mampe,* a term derived from the name of a popular cocktail in Berlin at the time "*Mampe
Half-and-Half.*"[233] Many had never talked about their experiences until
interviewed for this study. Most still struggle with identity issues and where
they belong. Their experiences under Nazism have been a source of inse-
curity throughout their lives. For example, after the war Hans Günzel told
his first wife that he was of Italian rather than Jewish descent because he was
afraid that she would not marry him.[234] Reinhard Krackow, still afraid
after the war, asked his fiancée Edith whether she would marry him, knowing he was a quarter-Jew. She told him it did not matter. They now have
been married for over fifty years. He has never discussed his Jewish ancestry with his children.[235] Many *Mischlinge,* especially in Vienna, refused to
meet, stating that they had not discussed their past even with their own
families and saw no reason to do so with a stranger. Some still fear that
people will reject them once they learn they are "partially" Jewish. For example, Rolf Zelter, whose 75 percent Jewish father Obergefreiter Joachim
Zelter fought on the Russian front, found out about his Jewish past after the
war. When he confronted his mother, she quickly told him, "Don't let your
children know. It can only cause them problems." For the Zelters, like many
families documented in this study, Jewish ancestry should simply be concealed and forgotten.[236]

After I interviewed half-Jew Heinrich Hamberger[237] in Munich, his girlfriend recommended that he take me with him that evening. He immediately tried to hush her, but she insisted, saying, "The young American
would find it interesting." He explained that his army buddies met in a pub
once a month.[238] After discussing the matter, he agreed to take me there, but
only on two conditions: first, under no circumstance would I tell anyone
about his Jewish descent, and second, I would tell them I studied something
else besides *Mischlinge* who fought in the Wehrmacht. I agreed.

A few hours later, we entered the pub. Loud voices greeted us, and the
smell of smoke smarted our nostrils. I felt odd sitting among these old men
singing, drinking, and telling war stories. I watched the years melt away as
they relived the "good old days." After a while, Hamberger left me alone
and I started to talk with his former company commander. He wanted to
impress upon me how honorable the Wehrmacht had been. I just listened.
During our conversation, I told him that during my studies I had come

across an anomaly that Jews and men of Jewish descent had fought in the Wehrmacht. "Have you ever heard about this?" I asked. The commander looked around, spotted Hamberger on the other side of the room, and nodded his old, scarred head. He lowered his raspy voice to a conspiratorial tone: "Don't tell Hamberger, but we know he's a Jew." I acted surprised and promised not to tell. This event illustrates the universal fear present among many *Mischlinge* who feel insecure about their "Jewishness" and cower at being labeled "Jewish."

Moreover, Hamberger's comrades did not appear to have cared that he was Jewish. To them, he was simply a member of the unit; he was a comrade. This story highlights the irony inherent in the fact that most *Mischlinge*'s fellow soldiers viewed them as brothers-in-arms, which created strong bonds of friendship. Many non-Jewish Wehrmacht soldiers did not view Aryan and *Mischling* unit members differently. This fact, with time, greatly influenced the way *Mischlinge* came to view themselves and their time in the armed forces. Whether they felt their comrades knew about their "problem" or not, they started to feel like they were among close friends who were loyal and dedicated to one another regardless of circumstances. This bond is quite common among men-of-arms, but for the *Mischlinge,* who had experienced years of persecution, this bond was welcomed and desired.

Claiming that a person who was either 25 percent or 50 percent Jewish was a *Mischling* under Nazi law does not explain a *Mischling*'s problems. That person, more often than not, was plagued by uncertainty and persecuted for being different. Many still do not know how to describe themselves. Are they primarily Jewish or German? Do they share guilt with the perpetrators or solely belong to the victims? A *Mischling,* in both the past and the present, has been forced to come to terms with who he was and is. It involved more than just having a certain percentage of "Jewishness" according to Nazi laws. Being a *Mischling* was a nightmare for them — a nightmare of uncertainty regarding their identity which, in most cases, is still present today.

Assimilation and the Jewish Experience in the German Armed Forces

Although it is incredibly difficult to determine definitively the actual number of *Mischlinge* who served in the Wehrmacht during Hitler's rule, I estimate that at least 150,000 did so. As illustrated in the tables in this chapter, previous estimates varied and future scholars may devise more advanced computations to produce a more precise figure. All such efforts should lead to the same significant conclusion: the number of *Mischlinge* in the Wehrmacht was far greater than anyone previously imagined. To understand this fact, one needs to consider briefly the assimilation of Jews in Germany and Austria, which began almost two hundred years before Hitler's ascent to power.[1] German Jews were so successful in assimilating into society that they became, according to some historians, more German than Jewish by 1933.[2] For example, a Gestapo report claimed in 1935 that Jews in the non-Zionist camp, especially assimilationists, were "more German than the Germans."[3] Efforts by generations of German Jews to assimilate led to mixed marriages and mixed offspring. The Nazis were unable to find a satisfactory method of dealing with them, especially since there were so many.

Assimilation of Jews in Germany and Austria

Between 1800 and 1900, around seventy thousand Jews converted to Christianity in Germany and in the Austro-Hungarian Empire.[4] These numbers do not include those Jews who left Judaism and did not embrace another religion. Ruth Gay writes that by 1871, three generations after the philosopher Moses Mendelssohn lived, who was a famous proponent for German-Jewish assimilation, the German Jews "had become Germans in speech, outlook, and culture, as well as their patriotic feelings."[5] In 1890, the philologist Hermann Steinthal said, "Today we can be good Jews only if we are good Germans, and good Germans only if we are good Jews. . . . Together with the prophets, it is Lessing, Herder, Kant, Fichte, Schiller, and Goethe and the two Humboldts who arouse our enthusiasm — and they could not have emerged from any other people."[6] For some Jews, assimilation into German society was completely consonant with being a "good Jew." They did not feel a need to leave Judaism because they did not see a conflict between being both German and Jewish. For many others, their "super patriotism"[7] and desire to be accepted as fellow Germans led German Jews to leave Judaism in considerable numbers in spite of Steinthal's opinion that good Jews would be good Germans.

At the turn of the nineteenth century, conversion rates began to increase (see table 1).[8] Between 1880 and 1920, some 29,000 Jews converted to Christianity in Germany (an average of 725 per year).[9] Between 500 and 700 Jews in Vienna converted to Christianity annually during the same period. The sociologist Arthur Ruppin[10] estimates that between 1868 and 1929, some 28,777 left Judaism in Vienna primarily to marry non-Jews.[11] No other city in Europe had conversion and dissident rates as high as Vienna (see table 1).[12] The movement to convert largely came from the younger generation of Jews, but it was not uncommon for Jewish parents to have their children baptized in the hope of easing their plight in a society hostile to Jews.[13]

Some German Jews were simply dissidents[14] and did not adopt another religion once they left Judaism.[15] The demographer Felix Theilhaber predicted in 1911 that because of conversion, intermarriage, and dissidents, no Jews would be left in Germany by the year 2000: "[T]he modern Jew no longer knows why he should remain a Jew."[16]

Many Jews converted because they desired more honor, freedom to marry whomever they wanted, better social standing, and better positions at work. Christianity was the predominant religion, and thus many Jews followed it to become better Germans.[17] Christian-German society seemed willing to accept converts. The journalist Sebastian Haffner points out that "religious anti-Semitism" did not focus on the "extermination of the Jews but [on] their conversion; the moment they were baptized all was well."[18] Christians set up organizations in Germany to convert Jews.[19] However, Theilhaber notes that few Jews converted because they were seduced by the Christian message. The majority of Jews who converted did so solely to assimilate. For example,

Table 1. Dissidents and Converts among Jews in Germany and Austria

Years	Location	Number	Source
Dissidents			
1868–1929	Vienna	28,777	Ruppin, *Modern World,* p. 332
1873–1908	Berlin	2,209	Theilhaber, *Untergang,* p. 96
1873–1922	Berlin	4,953	Behr, p. 98
1912–1923	Vienna	10,429	Behr, p. 98
1924–1925	Vienna	1,698	Grunwald, p. 527
1919–1937	Vienna	17,000	Meyer, *German-Jewish History,* vol. 4; Barkai, p. 33; Robertson, p. 386
Converts			
1770–1830	Berlin	1,582	Lowenstein, p. 120
1800–1847	Germany	5,200	Lea, p. 31
1800–1900	Germany	22,520	Gay, p. 139
1800–1870	Germany	11,000	Deut.jüd. 1871–1918, p. 20
1822–1840	Prussia	2,200	Fischer, p. 138
1825	Prussia	396	Behr, p. 104
1828	Prussia	400	Behr, p. 104
1831	Prussia	356	Behr, p. 104
1834	Prussia	391	Behr, p. 104
1837	Prussia	345	Behr, p. 104
1840	Prussia	312	Behr, p. 104
1880	Vienna	110 incl. Freethinkers	Frankel and Zipperstein, p. 237; Rozenblit, p. 237
1880–1928	Prussia	18,705	Behr, p. 105
1880–1910	Germany	12,000	Gay, p. 202
1880–1919	Germany	25,000	Deut.jüd. 1871–1918, p. 20–21
1886–1889	Vienna	165	Ruppin, *Jews of Today,* p. 165
1900–1903	Austria	2,700	Ruppin, *Jews of Today,* p. 186
1880–1925	Germany	22,695	Ruppin, *Modern Jews,* p. 330
1900	Vienna	599	Frankel and Zipperstein, p. 237; Rozenblit, p. 237
1901–1905	Vienna	3,543 incl. Freethinkers	Ruppin, *Jews of Today,* p. 190
1911–1925	Germany	5,775	Marcus, p. 246
1910	Vienna	512	Oxaal, "Jews of Vienna," p. 32[a]
1912–1923	Vienna	10,429	Behr, p. 98

[a]See Ivar Oxaal, "The Jews of Young Hitler's Vienna," in *Jews, Antisemitism, and Culture in Vienna,* ed. Gerhard Botz, Ivar Oxaal, and Michael Pollak (New York, 1987).

when the famous German Jewish poet and writer Heinrich Heine converted, he claimed he had bought "an entry ticket to European culture."[20]

Some Jews took this belief further and maintained that marrying an Aryan would make a German Jew more German. The 37.5 percent Jew Michael Hauck's Jewish grandfather, Henry Oswalt, forbade his daughter to marry a Jew. She obeyed. The grandfather, whose mother was a cousin of Heinrich Heine's, wanted the family to be more German and accepted by society. He was tired of the stigma that followed them and wished above everything else to "get away from the ghetto."[21] As historian Dietz Bering wrote, "[T]he [German] Jews were . . . a minority who sought to be admitted to a majority."[22] The quickest way for a Jew to enter the dominant German society was to marry a non-Jew. Theilhaber writes that mixed marriages brought on the death of the German-Jewish population,[23] noting that mixed marriages showed that German Jews no longer were "racially conscious."[24]

A natural outcome of these unions was that children were born in Austria and Germany who were partially Jewish. If one looks at the continued increase in intermarriage and conversion rates in Germany, a logical conclusion is that tens of thousands of children resulted from these marriages, especially since Germany at the turn of the century had the highest birthrate among countries of northwestern and central Europe.[25] True to Theilhaber's predictions, just before World War I, more than 30 percent of German Jews who married, married non-Jews.[26] Between 1901 and 1929, over 36,000 mixed marriages occurred in Germany.[27] In Vienna alone,[28] between 1919 and 1937, probably close to 17,000[29] mixed marriages occurred.[30] From this number, one gets an average of at least 895 mixed marriages transpiring annually in Austria.[31] Extrapolating from this average, one can assume that between 1901 and 1929, around 25,000 mixed marriages occurred in Austria.[32] Since the average family during this time period had two to three children, at least 122,000 half-Jewish children likely were born from these combined 61,000 unions in Germany and Austria (see table 2).[33] Mixed marriages between 1900 and 1929 probably produced the majority of half-Jews of military age during Hitler's rule.[34]

An estimated 20,000 mixed marriages occurred in Germany between 1870 and 1900.[35] In Prussia alone, over 8,000 mixed marriages occurred between 1875 and 1900.[36] A conservative estimate of mixed marriages occurring in Austria between 1870 and 1900 is 3,000.[37] Thus, in accordance with the average German family size, 46,000 to 69,000 half-Jewish children likely resulted from these combined 23,000 unions in Germany and Austria.[38] From these half-Jews, another 92,000[39] to 197,000 quarter-Jewish children could have come into the world by 1929, according to the recorded data (see tables 2 and 3). This assumes that half-Jews all married non-Jews. Mixed marriages from 1870 to 1900 accounted for most of the quarter-Jews of military age during the Third Reich.

The number of *Mischlinge* under Hitler's rule has been underestimated because of registration procedures in Germany and Austria. Many marriages were registered solely as Protestant or Catholic and, thus, it has been difficult for sociologists to know whether one partner was previously of the Jewish faith. In other words, just looking at identified mixed marriages does not account for converted Jews who married Christians, although the Nazis classified children from such marriages as *Mischlinge*. It suffices to say that by 1933, there were tens of thousands of people in Germany and Austria who did not call themselves Jews, but were of Jewish descent because of the conversions and intermarriages that had taken place for decades in these countries.

When the Nazis came to power, they attempted to solve the problems they perceived years of Jewish assimilation had created. Jews and *Mischlinge*, no matter how loyal they were to Germany, were no longer seen as German. Their assimilation, or that of their ancestors, would no longer be honored. Hitler saw all forms of assimilation as a long-term plot to destroy society.

Hitler argued that assimilated Jews were the most dangerous because they remained hidden,[40] and corrupted the Aryan people's purity through intermarriage.[41] Hitler wrote in *Mein Kampf* that the Jews "contaminated" the *Volk:* "Systematically these black parasites of the nation defile our inexperienced young blond girls, and thereby destroy something which can no longer be replaced in this world."[42] Hitler feared that the Jewish *bacillus,* a predatory agent, would infect Aryan women and take away their ability to produce purely Aryan progeny. Hitler was determined to end these sexual abuses.

Reversing assimilation proved difficult. Most German Jews and *Mischlinge* looked, acted, and dressed like Aryan Germans. Many Jews not only had changed their names, but also had married into the dominant culture and converted to the dominant religion. Identifying such Jews and their *Mischling* offspring was laborious. Some Germans discovered they had Jewish ancestry after 1933. Ruppin explained this phenomenon in 1939:

Table 2. Intermarriage in Germany and Austria

Years	Location	No.	Source	ESTIMATED NO. OF HALF-JEWISH CHILDREN[a]				ESTIMATED NO. OF QUARTER-JEWISH CHILDREN			
				Theilhaber (1.4)[b]	Lenz (2–3)	Rigg (2.8)[c]	Naval Intelligence (2.96)[d]	Theilhaber (1.4)	Lenz (2–3)	Rigg (2.6)[e]	Naval Intelligence (2.96)
1874–1900	Prussia	8,091	Meiring, p. 91	11,327	16,182–24,273	22,655	23,949	15,858	32,364–72,819	58,903	70,889
1875–1908	Prussia	7,270	Theilhaber, Untergang, p. 103–4	10,178	14,540–21,810	20,356	21,519	14,249	29,080–65,430	52,926	63,696
1876–1900	Prussia	7,814	Behr, p. 112	10,940	15,628–23,442	21,879	23,129	15,316	31,256–70,326	56,885	68,462
1876–1900	Bavaria	502	Behr, p. 112	703	1,004–1,506	1,406	1,486	984	2,008–4,518	3,656	4,399
1870–1930	Germany	50,000	Meyer, German-Jewish History; Barkai, p. 252	70,000	100,000–150,000	140,000	148,000	N/A			
1881	Austria	51	Cohen, Jewish Life, p. 304	71	102–153	143	151	99	204–459	372	447
1881–1906	Austria	2,488	Ruppin, Jews of Today, p. 166	3,483	4,976–7,464	6,966	7,364	4,876	9,952–22,392	18,112	21,797
1881–1907	Vienna	1,824	Ruppin, Jews of Today, p. 167	2,554	3,648–5,472	5,107	5,399	3,576	7,296–16,416	13,278	15,981
1900–1908	Germany	7,088	Theilhaber, Untergang, p. 104	9,923	14,176–21,264	19,846	20,980	N/A			
1901–1908	Germany	6,222	Ruppin, Jews of Today, p. 165	8,711	12,444–18,666	17,422	18,417	N/A			
1901–1924	Prussia	21,694	Behr, p. 112	30,372	43,388–65,082	60,743	64,214	N/A			
1901–1924	Bavaria	1,575	Behr, p. 112	2,205	3,150–4,725	4,410	4,662	N/A			
1901–1933	Germany	42,326	Meiring, p. 91	59,256	84,652–126,978	118,513	125,285	N/A			
1902–1914	Germany	14,644	Kahn, Der Jude, Jahr I 1916–1917, p. 856	20,502	29,288–43,932	41,003	43,346	N/A			
1900–1927	Germany	33,800	Bienenfeld, p. 99	47,320	67,600–101,400	94,640	100,048	N/A			
1901–1925	Germany	30,171	Behr, p. 112	42,239	60,342–90,513	84,479	89,306	N/A			
1901–1929	Germany	36,257	Berman, p. 123	50,760	72,514–108,771	101,520	107,321	N/A			
1901–1930	Germany	36,168	Noakes, "Nazi Policy," p. 291	50,635	72,336–108,504	101,270	107,057	N/A			

1906–1930	Germany	33,000	Marcus, p. 246	46,200	66,000–99,000	92,400	97,680	N/A
1909	Vienna	216	Cohen, Jewish Life, p. 304	302	432–648	605	639	N/A
1910	Vienna	155	Oxaal, "Jews of Vienna," p. 33	217	310–465	434	459	N/A
1914	Austria	212	Bloch and Taubes, p. 10	297	424–636	594	628	N/A
1914–1918	Prussia	4,000	Deut.jüd. III, p. 19–20	5,600	8,000–12,000	11,200	11,840	N/A
1919–1937	Vienna	17,000[f]	Meyer, German-Jewish History; Barkai, p. 33	23,800	34,000–51,000	47,600	50,320	N/A
1926–1929	Austria	1,667	Bloch and Taubes, p. 10	2,334	3,334–5,001	4,668	4,934	N/A
1921–1930	Germany	15,288	Noakes, "Nazi Policy," p. 291	21,403	30,576–45,864	42,806	45,252	N/A
1920–1926	Germany	12,422	Lenz, Menschliche, p. 228–29	17,391	24,844–37,266	34,782	36,769	N/A

[a]Since the birthrates are applied to different years from which these averages are taken, they are intended to give readers a general impression of the potential number of children that could have been born, instead of the exact birthrate for the time period between 1870 and 1930. According to Behr's estimates, mixed marriages produced more children before the turn of the nineteenth century than during the early 1900s.

[b]Theilhaber apparently focused only on marriages in which the Jewish spouse remained Jewish, which may have resulted in lower birthrates. The average of 1.4 children per mixed marriage comes from statistics taken from 1900 to 1908 (Theilhaber [1911], p. 113). In his study "Die Juden in Deutschland von 1935–1939," Bruno Blau found that in 1939, 31.8 percent of mixed marriages were childless (Blau, "Die Juden in Deutschland," p. 279). Stefan Behr found an average of 1.22 children per mixed marriage between 1875 and 1926 for Prussia (Behr, p. 114). These figures are probably not reliable to use for this study because most parents of Mischlinge in this study did not remain religiously Jewish, and thus would not have been included in Theilhaber's, Blau's, and Behr's studies, which focused on Jewish partners who remained religiously Jewish. Furthermore, the percentage of childless marriages Blau gives in 1939 would have been higher because of the oppression during the Third Reich, during which these couples would have been discouraged from having children.

[c]This average was taken from the 174 families of half-Jews documented in this study. Since this average was determined by talking to the children of mixed marriages, this study was not able to document those marriages without children. When possible, aunts and uncles who were in childless mixed marriages were included in the final tally.

[d]These figures are extrapolated from data compiled in 1944 by the U.S. Naval Intelligence Division. According to Behr, the average number of children of Jewish families in Prussia from 1875 to 1926 was 2.8. Theilhaber puts the average of 2.8 children per Jewish family in 1900 and 2.7 in 1904. Theilhaber puts the average for Christian couples at 4.1 for both 1900 and 1904 (Theilhaber, p. 113). Since most of the half-Jews in this study had Christian parents, they would have fit into the Christian category rather than the interfaith marriage category that Theilhaber was fond of using.

[e]This average was taken from the 75 families of quarter-Jews documented in this study.

[f]Barkai claims that the majority of these 17,000 who were dissidents left Judaism to marry non-Jews. As a result, the 17,000 has been left alone as if all of them "seceded" (Ruppin's words) from Judaism to marry non-Jews, especially since Jews could only marry Christians in Austria when there were either converted to Christianity or konfessionslos (without confession).

Table 3. Mixed Marriages and the Number of Their Possible Offspring in
Germany and Austria, 1870 to 1929

Years	No. of Marriages	Average No. Children per Marriage	Total No. of Children	Total No. of Grandchildren
1870–1900	23,000	2–3	46,000–69,000	92,000[a]–197,000
1900–1929	61,000	2–3	122,000–183,000	N/A

Source: Bryan Rigg's estimates using various assimilation records (see tables 2 and 4).

[a]This number has been left according to a pure mathematical model. Although some of these half-Jews did not marry or married other *Mischlinge* and Jews, the Naval Intelligence Division figures from 1944 show that the net reproduction rate from 1870 to 1929 (with a few gaps) would have produced at least 92,000 children. See Naval Intelligence Division, ed., *Germany*, vol. 3, *Economic Geography*, p. 73.

[T]he Jew, if indifferent, tends to conceal the fact that he is a Jew, even from his own children. For these, and still more for their children, the connection with Jewry is completely broken, and they freely intermarry with non-Jews, and often do not even know about their Jewish extraction. This is why the hunt after the 'Jewish grandmother,' officially launched in Germany in 1933 has produced numerous surprises.[43]

Ruppin articulated well the quandary many *Mischling* families faced after 1933. Many did not have the faintest idea what it meant and even less what it would mean to be Jewish in such a hostile environment. When the Nazis confronted those families who did not know about their Jewish ancestors with the truth about their backgrounds, many reacted in disbelief, anger, and despair. The new racial definitions confused not only *Mischlinge* but also many German Jews who had converted to Christianity and no longer felt Jewish. Mathilde Blanck said half seriously and half ironically, "We no longer knew that we were Jews."[44] Consequently, they felt it was unlawful to treat them like Jews. On 15 May 1935, Reinhard Heydrich, head of the SS Reich Main Security Office, took issue with this "problem" in an article titled "The Visible Enemy" in the SS's organ, *Das Schwarze Korps:*

The assimilationists deny their Jewish race, based on their many years of life in Germany, claim to be Germans, and after baptism claim to be Christians. Those assimilationists are the very ones who are trying to subvert and abrogate the principles of National Socialism by means of various declarations of loyalty typical of this race, protestations that make them despicable in the eyes of others.[45]

Heydrich's description of how "assimilationists" responded to racial policy depicts how desperate many had become. Most converted Jews and *Mischlinge* felt German, and being labeled "Jewish," and, thus, enemies of the government and un-German, made many panic. Some became desperate to prove to the Aryans around them that they were faithful German patriots. Others did nothing, paralyzed with fear.

When Hitler took power, he officially abolished the civil equality granted to Jews by the emancipations of 1812[46] and 1871,[47] and the hunt for "hidden Jews" commenced. Hidden Jews were those fully assimilated Jews and people of Jewish descent who did not claim to be Jewish. The targets of this witch-hunt numbered in the tens of thousands. In 1939, 328,176 Jews remained in Germany, down from 600,000 in 1933.[48] The Nazis documented 30,000 Jews married to non-Jews.[49]

On 17 May 1939, the Nazis published the first "official" numbers of *Mischlinge:* 72,738 half-Jews and 42,811 quarter-Jews.[50] Since the term *Mischlinge* had not applied to Germans of Jewish descent until 1933, the results were highly inaccurate. The office that began these statistics in late 1935 or early 1936 not only failed to identify all the *Mischlinge* in Germany, but also overlooked the many German *Mischlinge* living in the lands Germany occupied from 1935 to 1940. The population under German control increased from 67 to 90 million.[51] The Saarland was returned to Germany in 1935 after the plebiscite, and Germany regained control of the Rhineland in 1936 and annexed Austria in March of 1938 *(Anschluß).*[52] An additional 220,000 Jews[53] and tens of thousands of *Mischlinge* lived in Austria.[54] Occupying the Sudetenland in 1938 added another 27,374 Jews and thousands of *Mischlinge.* The Nazis later occupied the rest of Czechoslovakia on 15 March 1939 with its additional 300,000 "full-blooded or nearly full-blooded" Jews.[55] The historian Raul Hilberg estimates the number of *Mischlinge* in the Protectorate[56] at 30,000.[57] On 23 March 1939, the Nazis reoccupied Memelland with its unknown number of Jews and *Mischlinge.* When Germany successfully conquered Poland in 1939, they joined the free port city of Danzig[58] once again to Germany proper and in May 1940, when Germany defeated France, they reoccupied the provinces of Alsace-Lorraine[59] with its 30,000-

plus Jews[60] and its unknown number of *Mischlinge*. However, the authorities did not include in the May census the numbers from Memelland, Danzig, and the newly acquired eastern and western territories taken after May 1939.[61] No one knows how many of the 40,000 Baltic Germans, 120,000 Valhynian Germans, 40,000 Lithuanian Germans, 80,000 to 100,000 Bukovinian Germans, and 100,000 to 130,000 Bessarabian Germans also had some Jewish ancestry.[62] The Nazis attempted to include the numbers from Austria and the Sudetenland, but those results must be considered with skepticism, since officials had only a little over a year to document over seven million people in Austria and a little over six months to document three and a half million people in the Sudetenland. Furthermore, Nazi bureaucrats did not exhibit the same sense of urgency in locating *Mischlinge* as they did with Jews.

The statistics on *Mischlinge* were compiled by asking people to classify themselves as Jews, Jewish *Mischlinge*, or Aryan. Many did not know their true status, and many lied. Nonetheless, many told the truth. However, family trees were not usually researched, and the data compiled were incomplete. Dr. Achim Gercke, an expert in racial research in the RMI, claimed in 1935 that "to ascertain the Jewish blood of [all the] people in Germany, it would take one thousand family researchers working for thirty years."[63] In fact, the understaffed team of civil servants had only three and a half years to work on this census during a stressful and eventful time. Their 1939 figures significantly underestimated the number of German *Mischlinge* in the Reich.

In 1935, overwhelmed by his task, Gercke wrote that because of the emancipations of 1806,[64] 1812, and 1871, there were too many *Mischlinge*. He warned that attempting to eliminate *Mischlinge* from German society would cause several problems, because so many officers, professors, and politicians had married Jews. In 1935, Gercke believed that there were a minimum of 600,000 *Mischlinge*.[65] Historian Leni Yahil wrote, "[T]hose loose definitions [of the *Mischlinge*] and the absence of statistical data prevent us from citing definitive information on how many people were considered full- or partial-Jews."[66] Some writers estimate the number at two to three million *Mischlinge*, which is not unrealistic.[67] Lösener in the RMI claimed on 30 October 1933 that the number of *Mischlinge* must be high because so many prominent people had been affected.[68] On 8 October 1935, he believed there were 40,000 to 45,000 half-Jews of military age out

of a total half-Jewish population of 200,000. Lösener believed that an additional 30,000 would soon be of military age.[69] State secretary in the RMI,
Hans Pfundtner, wrote to Hitler's Wehrmacht adjutant, Friedrich Hoßbach,
on 3 April 1935, asserting that assimilation records indicated there were
roughly 150,000 half-Jews and quarter-Jews of military age out of a total
Mischling population of 750,000.[70] Historian Werner Cohn estimates that
there were at least 500,000 partial Jews in Nazi Germany.[71] According to the
RMI, in June of 1943, there were 16,000 half-Jews and 3,200 men married to
half-Jews who were of military age. These numbers were apparently based on
the census of May 1939, which significantly underestimated the total number of *Mischlinge* (see table 4).[72] Local military offices and police stations
initially registered half-Jews who reported for military service. Apparently
they did not keep complete lists of *Mischlinge* turned away as ineligible
after Hitler prohibited half-Jews from military service in April 1940. Such
records would have provided a much more accurate estimate of the total
number of half-Jews of military age than did the census of 1939. The reason why a half-Jew was discharged from military service was registered in
his personnel file, military service book, and in most local police stations,
but not recorded anywhere else. No central database existed.

The assimilation figures clearly indicate that the statistics of 70,000 half-
Jews and 40,000 quarter-Jews the Nazis presented in 1939 were inaccurate.
There should have been more quarter-Jews than half-Jews. The Central
Association of German Citizens of Jewish Faith[73] had the mathematical
proportions right when it estimated there were 47,695 half-Jews and 71,543
quarter-Jews in Germany in May 1935.[74] From the recorded assimilation numbers, there should have been at least two to three times more *Mischlinge* in 1939
than the Nazi census counted.[75] The numbers reported in the census of 1939
were low because of people's ignorance, lack of interest, or dishonesty, as well
as the Nazis' inexperience with such census taking. Sociologist Bruno Blau
wrote in 1949 that such a census had never been taken and probably will never
be conducted again.[76] Lösener wrote in May 1939 that the actual number of
Mischlinge had not been determined because so many hid the truth.[77]

As these statistics demonstrate, tens of thousands of *Mischlinge* lived in
Germany, many unknown to the Nazis. Strangely enough, thousands of
these *Mischlinge*, though by definition Hitler's enemies, found themselves
serving in Germany's armed forces. The Nazis originally allowed half-Jews

Table 4. Estimates of the Number of *Mischlinge* during the Third Reich

Date	Source	No. of Half-Jews	No. of Quarter-Jews	Total No. of *Mischlinge*	NO. OF *MISCHLINGE* AGED 18–45 ELIGIBLE FOR WEHRMACHT SERVICE		
					Half-Jews	Quarter-Jews	Total
June 1943	RMI	Unknown	Unknown	Unknown	16,000		
May 1939	Nazi census	72,738	42,811	115,549	18,185[a]	10,703	28,888
1935	Dr. Achim Gercke, head of the Reich Ministry of the Interior for Racial Research	Unknown	Unknown	600,000			150,000
October 1935	Dr. Bernhard Lösener in the RMI	200,000	Unknown	200,000	40,000–45,000		
April 1935	Hans Pfundtner, state secretary in the RMI	Unknown	Unknown	750,000		150,000	150,000
May 1935	Central Association of German Jews	47,695	71,543[c]	119,238	11,924	17,886	29,810
1939	Bruno Blau in Judaica 5 and 7	69,943	40,060	109,003	17,486	10,015	27,501
	This study (see this chapter and table 2)[b]	122,000–183,000	92,000–197,000[c]	214,000–380,000	61,000–91,500	46,000–98,500	117,000–190,000

[a]Since half of the 72,738 half-Jews were women, this number has been subtracted, leaving a total of 36,369 males. From this group, probably around 50 percent were within the draft age of eighteen to forty-five years. As a result, probably 18,185 were able to serve. This method was also used to determine the number of quarter-Jews in this table and the figures for Bruno Blau and the Central Association of German Citizens of Jewish Faith.

[b]Data here do not take into account children born out of wedlock.

[c]This number has been left according to a pure mathematical model. Although some of these half-Jews did not marry or married other *Mischlinge* and Jews, the Naval Intelligence Division figures from 1944 show that the net reproduction rate from 1880 to 1929 (with a few gaps) would have produced at least 92,000 children. See Naval Intelligence Division, ed., *Germany*, vol. 3, *Economic Geography*, p. 73.

to serve, but in 1940 discharged many not qualified for exemptions.[78] Yet, how many *Mischlinge* Wehrmacht personnel were there?

Through documents and personal referrals, this study has documented 967 half-Jews, 607 quarter-Jews, and 97 full-Jews who served in the Wehrmacht and/or the SS, or Waffen-SS. The ranks of the Jews were as follows: 71 soldiers, 4 NCOs, 15 lieutenants, 3 captains, 2 majors, 1 colonel, and 1 admiral. The ranks of the half-Jews were as follows: 808 soldiers, 77 NCOs, 38 lieutenants, 9 captains, 5 majors, 15 colonels, 11 generals, 3 admirals, and 1 field marshal.[79] The ranks of the quarter-Jews were as follows: 423 soldiers, 55 NCOs, 63 lieutenants, 20 captains, 10 majors, 24 colonels, 9 generals, and 3 admirals. Altogether, this study has documented 1,671 German soldiers of Jewish descent (see table 5).[80]

These figures are not representative, since during the first few years of research, this study focused strictly on full- and half-Jews. Once quarter-Jews were documented with the same energy as half-Jews, it soon became apparent that since quarter-Jews had to serve the entire war, a greater percentage of them had died than half-Jews. For this study, 10 full-Jews, 146 half-Jews, and 75 quarter-Jews who served in the German armed forces during World War II were interviewed (see table 6).

If between 92,000 and 197,000 quarter-Jewish and between 122,000 and 183,000 half-Jewish children were born who were of military age during World War II, then there must have been tens of thousands of *Mischling* Wehrmacht personnel. Since 50 percent[81] of the children would have been female, between 46,000 and 98,500 quarter-Jewish and between 61,000 and 91,500 half-Jewish males would have been eligible for military service during the Third Reich.[82]

Taking into consideration Lösener's data, recorded mixed marriages, estimates of mixed marriages not on record, and estimates of *Mischlinge* in lands Germany occupied between 1936 and 1940, at least 60,000 half-Jews served in the Wehrmacht from 1935 to 1945 (see tables 2 and 4). This is an extremely conservative estimate. Even Lösener, who had very incomplete information, estimated in 1935 that 40,000 to 45,000 half-Jews were of military age and 30,000 would soon be of military age. Moreover, retired Bundeswehr Colonel Otto Wolters, who worked in OKH (army high command),[83] estimated that at least 70,000 half-Jews were discharged in 1940.[84]

Table 5. Ranks of Jews and *Mischlinge* Who Served in the Wehrmacht, Waffen-SS, and SS during the Third Reich, according to Rigg's findings

Rank	No. of Jews	No. of Half-Jews	No. of Quarter-Jews	Total No.
Soldiers/Sailors	65	799	421	1,285
Waffen-SS Men	5	5	1	11
SS Men	1	4	1	6
NCOs	4	77	55	136
Lieutenants (Wehrmacht)	13	38	63	114
Lieutenants-Untersturmführer/Obersturmführer (SS)	2	0	0	2
Captains	3	9	20	32
Majors	2	5	10	17
Lt. Colonels/Colonels (Wehrmacht)	1	15	23	39
Lt. Colonels/Colonels Obersturmbann-/Standartenführer (Waffen-SS)	0	0	1	1
Generals	0	11	9	20
Admirals	1	3	3	7
Field Marshal (Five Star General)	0	1	0	1
Total	97	967	607	1,671

Note: Except for admirals, all naval ranks have been converted to army ranks. The data in tables 5–6 are not representative. They could not be prepared by a random sampling technique. They are a convenience sample. Consequently, they are only meant to show numbers accumulated during this study.

To ascertain how many quarter-Jews served, one must use records of mixed marriage in Germany between 1870 and 1900 as well as consider all those quarter-Jews who lived in other lands Germany occupied from 1936 to 1940. From this data, this study estimates that at least 90,000 quarter-Jews served from 1935 to 1945 (see tables 2 and 4). This is also a conservative estimate. Wolters estimated that quarter-Jews were "twice as plentiful" as half-Jews, putting their number at 140,000. These figures are much larger than previously believed, but when put into perspective with intermarriage trends, they make sense (see table 2). Since roughly 17 million soldiers served in the Wehrmacht,[85] a conservative number of possible *Mischling* soldiers, according to this study's estimate (150,000), represents less than 1 percent of the total manpower of the Wehrmacht.

Table 6. Places Where *Mischlinge* and Jews Were Interviewed for
This Study Who Served in the Wehrmacht or in OT Camps

Interview Location	No. of Half-Jews	No. of Quarter-Jews	No. of Jews	Total No.
Berlin	45	8	2	55
Bremen	0	1	0	1
Brandenburg	0	1	0	1
Austria	13	4	0	17
Bavaria	25	11	1	37
Hessen	29	10	2	41
Hamburg	8	5	1	14
Schleswig-Holstein	1	1	0	2
Baden-Württemberg	22	10	0	32
Niedersachsen	2	7	1	10
Nordhein-Westfalen	10	13	0	23
Rheinland-Pfalz	0	3	0	3
Sachsen-Anhalt	1	0	0	1
Sachsen	3	0	0	3
Canada	2	0	1	3
Israel	0	0	1	1
United States	11	0	1	12
Switzerland	1	1	0	2
Total	173	75	10	258

Note: Interviews were conducted between 1994 and 1998.

One does not know how many full Jews served. If the ratio of 97 full Jews
for every 967 half-Jews can be applied from the data collected for this study,
and given the estimate that 60,000 half-Jewish soldiers served, then one
could assume that at least 6,019 full Jews also served in the Wehrmacht. The
numbers presented here are insignificant relative to the Wehrmacht's size,
but are startling in light of the Holocaust. The idea that at least 150,000 men
of Jewish ancestry served in the Wehrmacht is hard to accept. Nevertheless,
the evidence strongly suggests that was the case.

History of Jews in the German and Austrian Armies

One cannot understand how thousands of men of Jewish descent served in
the Wehrmacht without knowing that others of that descent had served in
German armies for almost two hundred years prior to Hitler (see table 7).[86]

Table 7. Number of Jews Who Served in the Prussian, German, and Austrian Armies from 1756 to 1918

War	Soldiers	Officers	Casualties
Prussia's War from 1756 to 1763	Unknown	At least 3	Unknown
Prussia's War of Independence, 1813–1815	At least 731	23	At least 55
Prussia 1815–1827	1,100	Unknown	N/A
Prussia 1827–1844	2,200	Unknown	N/A
Austria between 1798 and 1821	35,000	Unknown	Unknown
Austria 1855	Unknown	157	Unknown
Prussia's War of 1864 against Denmark	194	Unknown	Unknown
Prussia's War of 1866 against Austria	At least 1,025	26	Unknown
Austria 1872	12,471	Unknown	Unknown
Austria 1893	40,669	2,181	Unknown
Austria 1897	Unknown	1,993	Unknown
Austria 1898	52,282	Unknown	Unknown
Austria (around 1900)	Unknown	2,180	Unknown
Austria 1904	Unknown	1,662	Unknown
Austria 1911	44,016	1,871	Unknown
Germany 1914–1918	100,000	3,200	12,000
Austria 1914–1918	300,000	Unknown	25,000

Note: Austria is used to denote the Austro-Hungarian Empire.

The history of German Jews who served in their country's armies reveals that they felt German and wanted to participate in the development of Germany's international prestige and in the enlargement of her territorial holdings. Some historians have wrongly claimed that Jews could not become officers in Germany.[87] In reality many did, but most often had to convert to do so. German Jews displayed their willingness to make the supreme sacrifice for their country time and time again when Germany went to war. Accurate figures are difficult to find because Germany was split into so many states until 1871, but the examples of Prussia, Bavaria, and Austria will give an indication of military policy occurring in German-speaking lands that later would be unified under Hitler's rule.

FREDERICK THE GREAT'S RULE

In 1760, the "enlightened despot" Frederick the Great promoted the Jew Konstantin Nathanael von Salémon to general for his bravery in battle.

Salémon's son also became a Prussian officer. One does not know how many Jews fought in Frederick's army, but if Prussia's king promoted a Jew to general, there is no reason to doubt that Frederick allowed some of his Jewish population to serve. In fact it had been a law since 1701 that all Prussian inhabitants were defenders of the state (whether Jews were included in this law is not known).[88] Because of the dire nature of Frederick's situation between 1756 and 1763 (the Seven Years' War), one can assume that he would have drafted every able-bodied man regardless of ethnicity or religion.[89] Most likely, the Jews who served as officers under Frederick were baptized Jews. For example, baptized Jews seemed to have had no problem serving in the Austrian army during this time.[90] Although many Jews served under Frederick, the Prussian state did not officially recognize their service.

Frederick also employed some *Schutzjuden*,[91] who had become court Jews, as general purveyors to his army. For example, Frederick commissioned Marc Raphael and Jacob Wolff to buy horses for his army from the Tartar Khan in the Crimea. The king also encouraged the Jews under his rule to build factories to supply his army.[92] Veitel Ephraim and Daniel Itzig possibly "helped Fredrick avoid defeat" during the Seven Years' War by supplying and equipping his troops.[93] In recognition for his intelligence and contribution to society, Frederick granted the German-Jewish philosopher Moses Mendelssohn exemptions from some of the laws restricting Jews' freedom.[94] However, this should not imply that Frederick liked Jews — he in fact detested them.[95] But it seems his hatred did not cloud his reason. He knew he needed some Jews to ensure the smooth running of his country. It would be fifty years later, however, before Jews could officially serve in Prussian armies.

WAR OF INDEPENDENCE (1812–1815) AND THE NINETEENTH CENTURY UNTIL 1870

On 11 March 1812, Prussia's first prime minister *(Staatskanzler)*, Karl August von Hardenberg, emancipated the Jews and allowed them to perform military service.[96] Chief of the General Staff and Minister of War Gerhard von Scharnhorst had pushed the agenda of having a nation-in-arms after the disastrous defeat at Jena and Auerstedt of 1806. He wrote, "In the future every subject of the state, without regard for birth, will be obligated to perform military service. . . ."[97] During Prussia's War of Independence from 1813 to 1815, a conservative estimate of 731 Prussian Jews[98] served in the war against Napoleon. Five hundred and sixty-one of them were volunteers.[99] One German Jew wrote, "[W]ho doesn't rejoice to hear the honorable call to fight and conquer for the Fatherland. . . . Oh Death for the Fatherland, you're the most beautiful fate to befall any mortal."[100] Luise Grafemus (real name Esther Manuel) decided to join the Prussian army after she lost her Jewish husband in battle. She served during the battles of 1813 and 1814 and later became a Wachtmeister.[101] She was wounded twice in battle and received the Iron Cross.[102] During the battle at Belle-Alliance (Waterloo) in 1815 alone, 55 Jewish soldiers of the reserve militia died in combat.[103] Prussia decorated 82 Jews with the Iron Cross, and one received the Pour le Mérite decoration[104] between 1813 and 1815.[105] Moritz Oppenheim depicts these valorous German-Jewish soldiers in his famous painting of a Jewish soldier returning home to his traditional family after the Wars of Liberation with an Iron Cross.[106] Moses Mendelssohn's youngest son, Nathan, reported for duty in 1813 and later became a lieutenant.[107] According to the records, 23 of these Prussian Jewish soldiers became officers: one major and 22 lieutenants.[108] After the war, all of the Jewish officers except one were allegedly forced to leave the army. The authorities did not think it advantageous to their establishment to maintain Jewish officers during peacetime. The army allowed only Major Meno Burg, called the "Jewish major," to remain. He taught at Danzig and Berlin's Artillery Officer schools. Although an officer, he also found time to be a board member of Berlin's Jewish Community Center.[109] Hardenberg praised German Jews, both male and female, for their service in the War of Independence despite the fact that many in the Prussian military establishment did not want to retain the Jewish officers (or common soldiers for that matter).[110] German Jews continued to serve in the Prussian army despite such opposition. From 1815 to 1827, 1,100 Prussian Jews served in the armed forces, and from 1827 to 1844, 2,200.[111]

Jews also served in Bavaria at the same time. Bavaria showed more tolerance than Prussia, and many Jews actually left Prussia to join the Bavarian army.[112] Jews had more of a chance to advance through the ranks in that army than in the strict, *Junker*[113] controlled Prussian army, despite the fact that hundreds of *Junker* families had intermarried with Jewish families.[114]

Officers often married Jewish women not only in Prussia, but in Austria as well.[115]

Hitler condemned this, stating that it endangered the armed forces: "[A]s soon as it became fashionable for individual officers, especially of noble descent, to pair off with, of all things, department-store Jewesses, a danger arose for the old army."[116] It was common throughout the nineteenth century for aristocratic but poor Prussian officers to marry into rich Jewish families; he got the money, and her family gained social acceptance. Chancellor Otto von Bismarck even advocated marriages between the nobility and Jews.[117] As German writer Theodor Fontane claimed in 1893, "[T]here are very few aristocratic generals who do not have Jewish blood flowing in their veins."[118] The marriages of Prussian officers with Jewish women must have also helped many Jews to enter the army.

Although Prussia and Bavaria had Jews in their armies, they did not integrate them into their armed forces as successfully as Austria did. Joseph II of Austria, with his Toleration Patent of 1782, required Jews to perform military service. Joseph hoped that this policy would make the Jews "more useful to the state,"[119] and many Jews willingly served in the hope of improving their social status.[120] By 1821, some 35,000 Jews had fought in Austria's wars against Napoleon.[121] Austrian Jews enjoyed more success in the armed forces during the nineteenth century than their counterparts in Prussia or Bavaria. For instance, in 1829, Gustav von Heine-Geldern, brother of Heinrich Heine, enlisted in the Austrian cavalry (an elite military service) and attained the rank of first lieutenant.[122] By 1855, the Austro-Hungarian armed forces had 157 Jewish officers, most of them in the medical corps. In 1893, there were 40,344 Jewish soldiers and as many as 2,179 Jewish officers in the Austro-Hungarian army.[123] By 1898, the number of Jews who served in the Austro-Hungarian armed forces increased to over 52,000.[124]

A Jew in the Prussian army had to show remarkable talent like Burg, convert, or gain the favor of the ruling classes before he could become an officer. For example, in 1848, the German Jew Jakob Wilhelm Mossner helped the prince of Prussia flee to England to escape the revolution.[125] In 1860, the prince, then king of Prussia, commissioned Mossner's son Walther into the most "feudal" of cavalry regiments. The son served in three wars (1866, 1870–1871, and 1914–1918) and became a general. Emperor Wilhelm II eventually ennobled the family.[126]

In 1864, 194 Jews fought in the army in Prussia's war against Denmark. In 1866, a conservative estimate of 1,025 Jews fought in Prussia's war against the Austrian Empire. Prussia's army employed two Jewish generals, four Jewish colonels, and twenty Jewish staff officers in its medical corps.[127] Although the exact number is not known, between 10,000 and 20,000 Jews served in the Austrian army at this time.[128]

FRANCO-PRUSSIAN WAR (1870–1871) UNTIL WORLD WAR I

In Prussia's war against France from 1870 to 1871,[129] 12,000 Jews served: 120 were officers and 373 received the Iron Cross;[130] 483 died or were wounded during the war.[131] The army even allowed the Jews to observe their Yom Kippur[132] services in the field. Near Metz, 1,200 German Jews took part in the service there.[133] After the war's victorious conclusion, many Jews felt their service now entitled them to enter the ranks of the German elite.

Between 1870 and 1899, 5 Jews were promoted to active officers in Prussia, and between 50 and 100 were made reserve officers in the Bavarian army. In 1872, out of 135 Prussian general staff officers, one was a Jew.[134] Prussian officials cited religious traditions and holidays, keeping Jewish soldiers from their military duties, to explain why Prussia did not promote more Jews.[135] For example, in 1897, German Admiral Eduard von Knorr refused to accept a Jew because he refused to be baptized and required kosher food.[136] The armed forces repeatedly used this argument about the difficulty of providing soldiers special food to deny Jews promotions, admission to certain units, or permission to serve,[137] although most German Jews at this time did not keep strictly kosher. One historian wrote that the army feared that "Jews might not be able to command the respect due a superior officer [because of their strange habits and ethnicity]."[138] Yet thousands of Jews continued to serve in the German armed forces, although the authorities denied the majority of them opportunities of advancement.

From 1885 to 1914, the Prussian army trained some 30,000 Jews as soldiers but gave none of them a reserve officer's commission.[139] However, out of the 1,200 to 1,500 Jewish soldiers who had converted, the army promoted 300 to reserve officers. By 1906, out of 33,067 active German officers, only 16 were Jews.[140] In contrast, at that time, the Austro-Hungarian Empire had 2,180 Jewish officers including one field marshal.[141] Even Dr. Sigmund Freud served as a reserve medical officer in the Austrian army.[142] Although Jews numbered only about 4.5 percent of the population in the Austrian Empire in 1900, they made up 8 percent of the officer corps.[143] Among the Jewish officers, there were 6 generals, 17 colonels, and 1 admiral. Three Austrian warships were commanded by Jewish captains.[144]

In the Prussian army, converted Jews or Christians with Jewish ancestry were usually treated just like other Prussian soldiers.[145] But conversion did not guarantee total acceptance. As the historian Holgar Herwig wrote, "[A] few baptized Jews were allowed to enter the executive officer corps, but this did not *ipso facto* signify social acceptance of the Jews by the executive officers."[146] Jews, whether converted or not, still had difficulties becoming Prussian officers during peacetime.[147]

Yet the German armed forces' aversion to promoting Jews to officers did not prevent them from doing business with Jewish businessmen. Historian Jonathan Steinberg states that executive naval officers, "unlike their Prussian counterparts, belonged to clubs and mingled freely with prominent Jews, especially in Hamburg. Mutual respect and social relations between naval officers and members of the Jewish community arose naturally from common interest." For example, the great Jewish industrialist Albert Ballin mingled freely with executive officers in Hamburg and had contact with the kaiser. The kaiser even received Ballin at court and made sure that officers of his retinue danced with Ballin's daughter.[148]

Those Jews who served had a profound sense of duty. The Prussian war minister, General Karl von Einem, stated publicly on 22 March 1904 that the Jews did not serve badly. He said they fulfilled their military duties in peace and felt they would do the same in war.[149] However, as in the past, many Jews in Prussia decided to serve in the Bavarian army because it proved more tolerant.[150]

World War I

During World War I, German Jews would prove their patriotism and willingness to fight for Germany. When war broke out, the Central Association of German Citizens of Jewish Faith issued this statement on 1 August 1914:

> During this deciding hour of history, the Fatherland calls all its sons to the flag. That every German Jew is willing to give his life for Ger-

many, to do his duty, is a foregone conclusion. Religious comrades! We urge you to go beyond the call of duty in devoting your strength to the Fatherland. Hurry up and volunteer. All of you, men and women, do everything within your power to aid the Fatherland with both your deeds and your money.[151]

German Jews were largely loyal and dedicated patriots. The famous German-Jewish philosopher Hermann Cohen passionately expressed this loyalty and patriotism well in 1916: "Thus, in these times of epoch-making fatefulness for our people, we, as Jews, are proud to be Germans. For we are conscious of our task to convince all our co-religionists the world over of the religious significance of Germandom, of its influence, of its rightful claim over the Jews of every nationality, in religious developments as in general culture."[152] About 10,000 volunteered for duty, and over 100,000 out of a total German-Jewish population of 550,000 served during World War I. Some 78 percent saw frontline duty, 12,000 died in battle,[153] over 30,000 received decorations, and 19,000 were promoted. Approximately 2,000 Jews became military officers, and 1,200 became medical officers. An estimated 30 Jewish chaplains served in the German army, one of them being the famous rabbi Dr. Leo Baeck (Baeck even received the EKI). Out of the 10,000 German pilots of the Great War, 120 were Jews.[154] One Jewish pilot, Lieutenant Wilhelm Frankl, died in action and received the prestigious Pour le Mérite.[155] He was credited with sixteen kills.[156] The youngest Jewish volunteer of the war was thirteen-year-old Joseph Zippes. He lost both legs during combat.[157] Among the oldest of those who fought for Germany was Reichstag deputy Ludwig Frank, who died in battle in 1914 at the age of forty.[158] A poem written by a German Jew expressed how many Jews felt in 1914:

We are united, one people, one army.
In love and loyalty we get along.
We stand together! All differences disappear
Wherever they had been;
Whether of high or low birth, whether Jew or Christian,
There is only one people in our land!
We fight together for the kaiser and the Reich.[159]

The sense of camaraderie and duty seemed to override previous prejudices, and the symbiosis between the two groups appeared complete during this hour of national struggle. The Central Association of German Citizens of Jewish Faith wrote in 1914: "[W]e cannot turn anyone away who sacrifices his all for the Fatherland, Christian or Jew, Aryan or Semitic. The Fatherland supersedes everything else, the holy Fatherland . . ."[160] Another Jew closed an article in 1914 with these words: "The German Jews stand shoulder to shoulder with their Christian comrades without anyone asking about ancestry or religion."[161] Master Sergeant Fritz Beckhardt, a Jew, flew a plane with a swastika[162] on its side to display his German pride.[163] Another pilot, Lieutenant Josef Zürndörfer, wrote, "[A]s a German, I took to the field to defend my endangered Fatherland. But, also as a Jew, to fight for complete equal rights and for my religious brothers."[164] Jews fought not only because they were patriots but also because they felt their service would open the door to social equality.

Jews exhibited their support for Germany's war not only through military service but also through other skills. Professor Fritz Jacob Haber, a baptized Jew, helped in the manufacture of munitions and explosives.[165] He also organized the chemical warfare service and personally directed gas operations on the field of battle. In addition, he and Professor Richard Willstätter "designed the first gas mask used by the German army."[166] Banker Max Warburg and industrialist Walther Rathenau helped design and carry out the financial plans that enabled the army to conduct operations for the four long years.[167] At the end of the war, Warburg implored the high command to keep fighting when quartermaster general of the general staff, General Erich Ludendorff, suffered a mental breakdown during the crisis.[168] These Jews felt German and believed in Germany's destiny.

In the Austro-Hungarian Empire, of the 300,000 Jews who served in World War I,[169] 25,000 were officers;[170] 25,000 died in battle.[171] There were 76 Jewish chaplains, all holding the rank of captain.[172] During the war, 24 Jews attained the rank of general,[173] 76 received the Gold Medals for bravery,[174] and 22 the Orders of the Iron Crown Third Class.[175] General Baron Samuel Hazai, a baptized Jew, was "practically the most important officer in the whole monarchy" besides the general staff "commanding recruiting and supplies."[176] In Vienna's Jewish cemetery alone are buried 160 lieutenants, 40 captains, 40 colonels, 16 majors, and 20 generals.[177]

The Austro-Hungarian armed forces were more tolerant of Jews than Germany's armed forces. Its ranks included men from thirteen nationalities and twelve religious groups.[178] Both the German Reich and the Austro-Hungarian Empire's willingness to allow Jews to serve in their armed forces for years show how integrated these Jews were.

Thousands of German and Austrian *Mischlinge* had generations of family members who had served in the armed forces when Hitler came to power. Applicants for clemency often cited this ancestry. Half-Jew Ulrich Engelbert, a Wehrmacht soldier, wrote Hitler that his father had served as a World War I officer and was decorated with both Iron Crosses, that his grandfather had served in the war of 1870–1871, and that his great-grandfather had volunteered in the War of Independence from 1813 to 1815.[179] Gert Dalberg, who volunteered for the Wehrmacht, mentioned in his application to the University of Berlin that his Jewish father had been a World War I officer and had been decorated with both Iron Crosses, the House of Hohenzollern's Knight's Cross with swords, Turkey's Iron Half-Moon Medal, and Silver Wound Badge. Dalberg's father also had fought against the Communists after World War I in the Freikorps.[180]

After World War I, General von Deimling urged all Germans to remember "that thousands of Jews went to the war voluntarily — that thousands died heroes' deaths for the fatherland — that thousands were crippled for life. In my corps, the Jews fought as bravely as their Christian comrades and to many of them I presented the Iron Cross."[181] However, during the war and after, many of these Jews were treated with contempt by some of their officers and fellow comrades.[182] Ironically, many of these Jewish soldiers (those from Prussia) had sworn an oath to Emperor Wilhelm II, an anti-Semite.[183] Despite this treatment, many Jews believed that this war would prove to their countrymen once and for all that they, the Jews, were true Germans. Many hoped to gain equal rights not only in theory, but now in practice through their service. One Jew explained, "Our mission will be successful when we have convinced the reader that Jews are people too just like any other people, not Devils and not Angels, but just people with noble and unnoble, with good and bad, and that their religion and ancestry never prevent them from being good citizens or from performing their duty for the Fatherland."[184] The challenge for German Jews to prove to society that they exhibited the same range of character traits as most other humans came to the forefront during the war.

The war provided many Jews with the opportunity to prove their loyalty to Germany. These Jews fought faithfully for Germany in World War I and showed that they felt fully German in everything they did. However, one must not forget that the *Judenzählung* (Jewish census) carried out by the Prussian War Ministry in October 1916[185] provided proof that Germany did not yet consider Jews equal to Aryans even if they fought on the front lines.[186] The Reichstag followed up on the War Ministry's statistical inquiry to ascertain how many Jews worked "in the offices and agencies of the war economy."[187] The German government and army conducted this research to document how many Jews had been "shirking" military service.[188] Ironically, in proportion to their numbers in society, they were overrepresented among the frontline troops. German Jews did not shirk their duty to the Fatherland. Although disillusioned and hurt by the *Judenzählung,* most Jews continued to serve Germany loyally and fight next to their Christian comrades.[189] Unlike the Jews under Hitler, in 1916 the Jews in Germany had more opportunities to serve their country and prove their patriotism. Unfortunately, Germany would forget them after Hitler came into power. With the knowledge that thousands of *Mischlinge* came from families with proud military traditions, one can understand why many did not find their Wehrmacht service as abnormal as many might think today.

ADOLF HITLER

Nach Vortrag des Chefs der Kanzlei des
Führers der NSDAP. habe ich auf dem Gnaden-
wege entschieden, daß Ihre sowie Ihrer Ge-
schwister Nachkommen trotz nicht einwandfrei
geklärter Abstammung als arisch im Sinne der
Vorschriften der NSDAP. sowie der reichsge-
setzlichen Bestimmungen zu gelten haben.

gez.

Herrn
Dr.August G a n g h o f e r
Berlin - Charlottenburg 9
Stallupöner Allee 45)

ohne Adresse

Aryan declaration for half-Jew Dr. August Ganghofer and his siblings' children.
"After the presentation made by the head of the Kanzlei des Führers der
NSDAP [Bouhler], I have generously decided that you and the children of
your siblings are classified as Aryan for purposes of NSDAP regulations and
federal laws, although your ancestry is not completely clear. Signed: Adolf
Hitler." Ganghofer had several nephews who served in the Wehrmacht.

Half-Jew Werner Goldberg (last rank Gefreiter) in a photograph used in a Nazi propaganda newspaper with the caption "The Ideal German Soldier," taken in 1939; modern photo (*facing page*) taken on 17 November 1994, around 8:30 P.M.

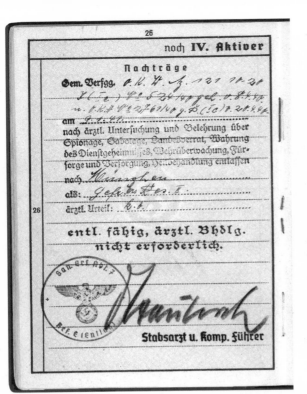

noch **IV. Aktiver**

Nachträge

Gem. Verfgg. O.K.H. Az. 121 12.31
2(50) u. 5 34 Nr. gel. v. 8.4.40
u. O.K.H. Az. 2761409. P(50).20.4.40

am 9.1.41

nach ärztl. Untersuchung und Belehrung über
Spionage, Sabotage, Landesverrat, Wahrung
des Dienstgeheimnisses, Wehrüberwachung, Für-
sorge und Versorgung, Heilbehandlung entlassen

nach München

als: Gefreiter II

ärztl. Urteil: k.v.

entl. fähig, ärztl. Bhdlg.
nicht erforderlich.

Stabsarzt u. Komp. Führer

Military service book (*top and bottom*) of half-Jew Hermann Aub. Note the laws of 8.4.1940 and 20.4.1940 discharging half-Jews cited plus the handwritten "n.z.v." (*nicht zu verwenden—not to be used*) in the top line of the page (*bottom*). Most discharged half-Jews had similar entries. Unless one knew that these laws from April in addition to "n.z.v." were clear indications that the person in question was a half-Jew, then the half-Jew was just looked upon as being a part of the reserves.

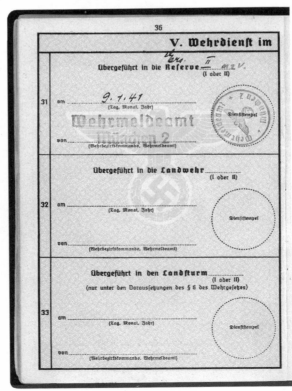

V. Wehrdienst im

Übergeführt in die Reserve II M.R.V.
(I oder II)

31 am 9.1.41
(Tag, Monat, Jahr)

Wehrmeldeamt
München 2

von
(Wehrbezirkskommando, Wehrmeldeamt)

Übergeführt in die Landwehr
(I oder II)

32 am
(Tag, Monat, Jahr)

Dienststempel

von
(Wehrbezirkskommando, Wehrmeldeamt)

Übergeführt in den Landsturm
(I oder II)
(nur unter den Voraussetzungen des § 5 des Wehrgesetzes)

33 am
(Tag, Monat, Jahr)

Dienststempel

von
(Wehrbezirkskommando, Wehrmeldeamt)

Example of the oath being administered.

Picture taken in 1939 by half-Jew Hermann Aub showing orthodox Jews pushing a German army wagon. This was typical harassment of the Jews by Wehrmacht personnel.

Achim von Bredow (last rank Gefreiter), a 37.5 percent Jew. (Military awards: EKI, EKII, Panzer Assault Badge in Silver, and Eastern Campaign Medal 1941–1942.)

Half-Jew Edgar Francken (last rank first lieutenant); he received Hitler's *Genehmigung.* (Military awards: EKII and Silver Wound Badge.)

Half-Jew Horst Geitner (last rank Obergefreiter). (Military awards: EKII and Silver Wound Badge.)

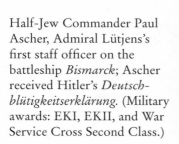

Half-Jew Commander Paul Ascher, Admiral Lütjens's first staff officer on the battleship *Bismarck*; Ascher received Hitler's *Deutsch-blütigkeitserklärung.* (Military awards: EKI, EKII, and War Service Cross Second Class.)

Half-Jew Michael Günther (last rank Obergefreiter). (Military awards: EKII.)

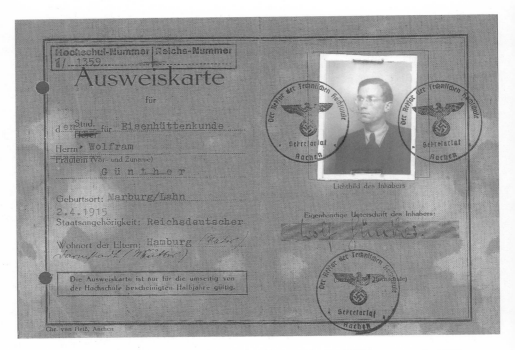

Half-Jew Wolfram Günther (last rank Obergefreiter). (Military awards: EKI, EKII.)

Lieutenant and Jew Paul-Ludwig (Pinchas) Hirschfeld. (Military awards: Wound Badge and War Service Cross Second Class with swords.)

(*Below*) Paul-Ludwig (Pinchas) Hirschfeld holding his War Service Cross Second Class with swords in a military cemetery outside Hanover in 1996. (Photo credit: Ian Jones, *London Telegraph*)

Hitler and General Werner Blomberg.

Hitler and Hermann Göring (*right*), head of the Luftwaffe and second in command after Hitler. In the middle is President Gömbös.

Dr. Hans-Heinrich Lammers, secretary of state and head of the Reichskanzlei.

Hitler and Paul von Hindenburg, field marshal and Reich's president.

Captain and Jew Edgar Jacoby, company commander of Propaganda Company 696 in France. (Military awards: EKI, EKII, and Wound Badge.)

With his children Barbara Jacoby (*left*) and Hans Edgar Jacoby (*right*), in a photograph taken after a military parade in Berlin in 1941.

Quarter-Jew Hans-Christian Lankes (last rank Gefreiter).

Half-Jew Anton Mayer (last rank Gefreiter) in a typical series of photographs that accompanied a "*Mischling*'s" application for clemency.

Half-Jew Richard Riess (last rank
Gefreiter).

Half-Jew Christoph-Michael Salinger
(last rank Gefreiter).

Quarter-Jew Klaus von Schmeling-Diringshofen (last rank captain); he
received Hitler's *Deutschblütigkeitserklärung*.

Half-Jew Kurt Zeunert's picture taken for Organisation Todt forced labor.

Example of an Organisation Todt registration book.

Hitler's army adjutant major, Gerhard Engel (*right; person on the left is unknown*). (Photo credit: Charles Hamilton, courtesy of R. James Bender Publishing)

Half-Jew Dietmar Brücher (last rank Kanonier). (Military awards: EKII and Wound Badge.)

Half-Jew Peter Gaupp (last rank Soldat).

Half-Jew Dieter Fischer (last rank Obergefreiter); he received Hitler's *Genehmigung*. (Military awards: EKII, Wound Badge, Assault Badge, and Eastern Campaign Medal 1941–1942.)

Erklärung

gem. § 10 Abs. 1 der Verordnung über das Erlaßungswesen vom 15. Februar 1937.

—

Mir sind nach sorgfältiger Prüfung keine Umstände bekannt, die die Annahme rechtfertigen könnten, daß ich Jude bin. Über den Begriff des Juden bin ich unterrichtet worden.

Mir ist bekannt, daß ich die sofortige Entlaßung aus dem Reichsarbeitsdienst und dem aktiven Wehrdienst zu gewärtigen habe, falls dieſe Erklärung ſich als unrichtig erweiſen ſollte.

Wuppertal, den 14. XII. 193 9

....
(Eigenhändige Unterſchrift des Dienſtpflichtigen)

Declaration of ancestry that most Wehrmacht soldiers had to sign.

Oberkommando der Wehrmacht

Az. 12 i 10—20 J (Ic)

Nr. 524/40 geh.

II 12 i

10/36

2001248

Geheim!

Berlin, den 8. April 1940

Betr.: Behandlung jüdischer Mischlinge in der Wehrmacht

Der Führer und Oberste Befehlshaber der Wehrmacht hat nachstehende Entscheidung getroffen:

1. 50%ige jüdische Mischlinge oder Männer, die mit 50%igen jüdischen Mischlingen oder Jüdinnen verheiratet sind, sind je nach Lebensalter (§§ 10 und 11 des WG) der Ersatzreserve II bzw. der Landwehr II zu überschreiben, jedoch mit dem jeweiligen Zusatz »n. z. v.« (nicht zu verwenden), um sie von den übrigen Wehrpflichtigen dieser Kategorien grundsätzlich zu unterscheiden.

Ausgenommen bleiben hiervon die Offiziere, die auf Grund der Führerentscheidung (OKW — WZ (II)/J — Nr. 651/39 vom 13. 3. 39) in der Friedenswehrmacht verblieben sind.

In besonders gelagerten Fällen behält sich der Führer Ausnahmen vor, die über OKW zu beantragen sind.

2. 25%ige Mischlinge und Wehrmachtangehörige, die mit 25%igen Mischlingen verheiratet sind, verbleiben in der Wehrmacht und können während des Krieges ausnahmsweise befördert und als Vorgesetzte verwendet werden, wenn eine besondere Bewährung erwiesen ist.

Außerdem können ehemalige Unteroffiziere, Beamte und Offiziere, die 25%ige Mischlinge sind, oder solche, die mit 25%igen Mischlingen verheiratet sind, bei ausreichender Begründung während des Krieges in der Wehrmacht verwendet werden.

Jeder Beförderungs- bzw. Wiedereinstellungsantrag ist dem Führer über OKW zur Entscheidung vorzulegen.

Um beschleunigte Durchführung der angeordneten Maßnahmen sicherzustellen, wird um umgehende Bekanntgabe vorstehender Verfügung gebeten.

Die Verfügungen OKW Nr. 190/40 J (I c) vom 16. 1. 40 und OKW Nr. 280/40 J (I c) vom 20. 1. 40, letztere mit Ausnahme der für Freimaurer geltenden Bestimmungen, werden hiermit aufgehoben.

Der Chef des Oberkommandos der Wehrmacht

Keitel

The 8 April 1940 order discharging half-Jews from the Wehrmacht.

Half-Jew Karl Henle (last rank captain); he received Hitler's *Deutschblütigkeitserklärung*.

A platoon in the Panzer Abwehr Regiment 23: Potsdam Sans Souci for the taking of the oath to Hitler. Out of the twenty-two soldiers in the Nachrichten (communications) platoon, three were half-Jews: Karl-Heinz Scheffler (*middle row, fourth from right*), Rudolf Sachs (*front row, third from right*), and Hannes Bergius (*front row, far right*).

Half-Jews and brothers Johannes (*above*) and Karl (*facing page*) Zukertort
(last rank for both general); both received Hitler's *Deutschblütigkeitserklärung*.

4

Racial Policy and the Nuremberg Laws, 1933–1939

The Beginning of Racial Policy in 1933

In 1942, an ex-Wehrmacht soldier entered SS headquarters in Berlin. He walked slowly, uneasy in those surroundings. On his civilian jacket, he wore the EKII and EKI ribbons he had earned in battle. An SS officer asked what he wanted. Hugo Fuchs asked where they had taken his father. The SS man looked shocked and said, "If you didn't have those medals, I would send you straight to where your father is!" Fuchs never saw his father; he had been killed in the Sachsenhausen concentration camp.[1] That a man could have served bravely while the Nazis imprisoned and murdered his Jewish father seems impossible.

But Fuchs was not alone. During World War II, hundreds, if not thousands of Jews and tens of thousands of *Mischlinge,* not only served in the Wehrmacht but also held some of its highest positions. Any full Jew who served in the Wehrmacht or SS during the Third Reich did so with false papers. As far as his superiors knew, he was an Aryan. The Nazi conscription laws required *Mischlinge* to serve. However, they could not hold positions of authority or be promoted past the rank of corporal without an exemption from Hitler. The laws affecting *Mischlinge* became increasingly restrictive throughout the Third Reich, ultimately pushing them down the same bloody road as the Jews.

To comprehend how *Mischlinge* served, one must know about the German armed forces' racial policies. Hitler's racial theory was simple: Jews destroyed German (i.e., Aryan) society; therefore, they must be removed. The Nazis first stumbled onto the difficulty of determining exactly who was Jewish enough to be dangerous when considering the civil service.

Soon after Hitler's "seizure of power" on 30 January 1933, Jews began to lose their jobs, although by then no law had been enacted that required them to leave their posts. On 1 April 1933, the Nazis enacted a nationwide boycott against converted and nonconverted Jews alike.[2] This boycott of Jewish firms, including retail outlets, lawyers, and doctors, affected thousands.[3] Sometimes the boycott became violent and Jews were injured and even a few murdered.[4] Many wrote letters of protest to several government offices. In response to letters that field marshal and Reich's president Paul von Hindenburg received from several of these distraught men and their families, he wrote Hitler on 4 April 1933:

> [C]ivil servants, judges, teachers, and lawyers who were wounded in the war or were soldiers at the front, or are sons of those who died or had sons who died in battle must — insofar as they have not given cause to be treated otherwise, be allowed to continue in their profession. If they were prepared to bleed and die for Germany, they deserve to be treated honorably by the Fatherland.[5]

Hitler confidentially informed Hindenburg the next day that "a law has been in preparation for about a week which will take into consideration those Jews who are veterans who suffered in the war, who served in some capacity, or who after long civil service do not warrant dismissal."[6] Although the Enabling Act of March 1933 gave Hitler almost unlimited power, his willingness to grant Hindenburg's request showed that Hitler did not feel fully secure in his new position.[7] Hitler knew that without Hindenburg's support, he would not have the army's backing, which he desperately needed if he wanted to remain in power.[8] Hitler felt only contempt for the "Old Man." Hindenburg distrusted the "Bohemian corporal." But placed in a position of power under him, Hitler had to take Hindenburg's "middle-of-the-road anti-Jewish arguments"[9] seriously, especially since their relationship had been less than friendly throughout 1932.[10]

The Law of Restoration of the Civil Service (known later along with its supplementary decrees as the *Arierparagraph*), enacted on 7 April 1933, ordered the dismissal of all non-Aryan civil servants. They were not defined as Jews, contrary to what some historians claim.[11] As Hindenburg had requested, the law granted exemptions for those who had entered the civil service before World War I, for World War I veterans, and for those whose fathers or sons had died in action.[12] The first supplementary decree to this law, issued on 11 April, defined a non-Aryan as anyone with at least one Jewish parent or grandparent. The Nazis assumed that a parent or grandparent of the Jewish faith was non-Aryan.[13] At the time, this decree actually allowed some Jews and *Mischlinge* to hold onto their jobs and livelihood. Peter Gaupp's Jewish grandfather, Dr. Sammy Ascher, a retired World War I medical officer,[14] was allowed to retain his medical practice.[15] Gaupp felt that the Nazis had "some kind of heart" to make exemptions for these officers.[16] But in general, this new law adversely affected thousands of non-Aryans.[17] In a few years, the Hindenburg exemptions would no longer help full Jews.

Many did not understand why these laws were enacted. Professor Klemperer wrote on 25 April 1933, "The destiny of the Hitler movement lies without a doubt on the Jewish question. I cannot understand why the Nazis have made this such a central issue. It will be their downfall."[18] As the Nazis discovered, these racial policies caused many problems.

Some civil servants were fired who should have been protected by the exemptions specified by the 1933 supplementary decrees to the *Arierparagraph*. Arthur Partisch, a civil servant of Jewish descent, wrote Hermann Göring on 8 July 1933 to protest his dismissal: "It's certainly not the Führer's will to treat a person who served the Fatherland faithfully for eighteen years, including service at the front in World War I, so cruelly. . . . I see myself as the victim of the personal desires for revenge of some of my co-workers who don't like me."[19] Thousands of complaints like this were filed. Many protested vehemently, demanding to know the real reason for their dismissal. They could not believe non-Aryan descent was reason enough to lose their jobs. With such problems coming to Hitler's attention, he remarked on 14 July that "one could make an exception only for those who had taken part in direct combat. Only participation in combat, and not mere presence in the combat zones, was decisive. A commission to check the roles of the various units was necessary."[20] Such orders created more work for a bureaucracy already confused as to how to implement the *Arierparagraph*. More guidelines were needed.

On 1 September 1933, Frick issued the second supplementary decree to the April laws:

> In defining the concept of Aryan descent in accordance with section 3 of the Law for the Restoration of the Civil Service, it is not religion which is decisive, but rather descent, race, blood. It is in particular not only those of whom a parent or grandparent belonged to the Jewish religion who are non-Aryan. . . . Thus, the Law by no means excludes the possibility of non-Aryan descent, even if none of the parents or grandparents belonged to the Jewish religion, in the event that non-Aryan descent can be established by other means.[21]

Frick failed to specify what these "other means" were. Subsequently, civil servants were dismissed for any suspicion of non-Aryan descent. This extreme decree would later prove impractical. The only reliable way to prove non-Aryan descent was through religious records.

General Werner von Blomberg, minister of defense, brought the racial laws one step closer to affecting soldiers when on 27 May 1933 he approved the decree that fired non-Aryan civil servants dependent on the armed forces (for example, workers in munitions factories).[22] Perhaps in response to protests from officers who resented this politicization of the armed forces, in June 1933, Blomberg commented that the Reichswehr could not ignore the new racial regulations adopted in the civil service.[23] During the tumultuous Weimar years, the Reichswehr had participated in political maneuvering, but never was controlled by one Party, much less one politician.[24] However, when Hitler came to power, the armed forces increasingly showed its support for the Nazi Party until it was ultimately controlled by the politician, Hitler. According to historian James Corum, "Hitler won the admiration and gratitude of the military for instituting rearmament on a scale beyond the military's wildest dreams, restoring Germany to a major military power."[25] For example, the later First Lieutenant Paul-Ludwig Hirschfeld said, "[A]s a Jew, I hated Hitler, but I have to give the man respect for some of the things he did. . . . He had a smart mind and accomplished many things [especially for the army]."[26] Military personnel of all ranks welcomed Hitler's government, his policies, and his dreams of a new, powerful Reichswehr.[27] Traditionally, soldiers held positions of honor in their communities. Consequently, most non-Aryan military personnel believed that the racial policies would not affect them as long as they remained in the Reichswehr. However, a few felt the walls of Nazi Germany slowly closing in on them.

During 1933 and 1934, reports about soldiers' racial backgrounds and their protests that such men were still serving poured into the government. Many non-Aryan soldiers started to get nervous. Lieutenant Ernst Prager informed his superiors of his Jewish father when he was considered for promotion in 1933. He felt bound "to report my ancestry even though officers aren't affected by the laws." On 21 July 1933, Blomberg reassured him that "nothing stood in the way of his promotion."[28]

Hitler and high-ranking officials apparently did not realize how many non-Aryans wore the military uniform in 1933. Hitler had assured Hindenburg on 5 April 1933 that the officer corps had remained "[racially] pure,"[29] perhaps because it embodied most directly the Aryan honor and fighting spirit. However, Hitler probably knew differently. He had had personal experience with Jews serving in the German army and had received his EKI during World War I because of the nomination given by a Jew.[30] Hitler had even told his army adjutant captain, Gerhard Engel, that he knew about several Jews who fought valiantly during World War I.[31] But Blomberg declared officially to a periodical in November 1933 that no Jews served in the armed forces.[32] Both men publicly adhered to Nazi ideology, while privately they knew non-Aryans served in the armed forces.

On 17 January 1934, the Association of High-Ranking Civil Servants' public relations office asked Blomberg to comment on the rumor that over eight hundred non-Aryan officers served in the Reichswehr. The authors of the letter wanted Blomberg to provide them with facts refuting such allegations and to punish those spreading these rumors.[33] Although he had no statistics to offer, Blomberg denied these claims. On 28 February 1934, Blomberg issued the *Arierparagraph* for the Reichswehr, perhaps to prevent more speculation regarding non-Aryan service members.[34] This military racial regulation, like the civil servant laws, did not apply to World War I veterans or children of veterans. All other non-Aryans were to be discharged. Non-Aryans not protected by the Hindenburg exemptions were to be reported by 31 May. Historian Manfred Messerschmidt described this introduction of racial laws into the armed forces as "a major break with the tradition of the officer corps."[35] With this decree, Blomberg sent a clear message that Nazi ideology would serve as the guiding force behind military policy. He had relinquished the Reichswehr's cherished independence from political affairs. Blomberg emphasized this shift in policy throughout 1933 and 1934, often in small ways. On 19 September 1933, he ordered military personnel to salute uniformed SA members.[36] He gave permission "for the Reichswehr music corps to play National Socialist tunes."[37] Similarly, on 25 February 1934, he ordered the addition of the Nazi emblem[38] to all uniforms.[39] According to historian Ian Kershaw, Blomberg introduced the racial laws and Nazi emblem into the Reichswehr in a "conscious attempt" to gain Hitler's support to act against the SA, an organization perceived as a grave threat to the Reichswehr's autonomy as the nation's bearer of arms.[40] Although Blomberg ordered the *Arierparagraph* for political reasons, he did not have to sacrifice his ideological beliefs to do so. As Hitler would later say of Blomberg, "That the troops could be brought to adopt the National Socialist *Weltanschauung* is due to the understanding and the boundless loyalty of the Minister of War."[41] These racial laws dramatically changed the way Reichswehr personnel were handled and screened.

Under the *Arierparagraph*, a conservative estimate of how many the Reichswehr discharged was between seventy and one hundred men.[42] Blomberg felt that the benefit he would gain with Hitler outweighed the few soldiers he would lose, since the majority of the valuable non-Aryans would remain in the service because of the Hindenburg exemptions.[43] Most likely, since most dismissed were young and inexperienced, Blomberg did not feel the Reichswehr would suffer much because of their loss. Since the numbers of dismissals were published in April and May 1934, one does not know how many the armed forces released under this law in late 1934 and throughout 1935. Several were discharged because of the *Arierparagraph* between 1935 and 1938.[44] Later laws should have been stated as the reason for these discharges instead of the *Arierparagraph*, but the bureaucrats were either used to citing this law as the reason for the discharge of *Mischlinge* or did not know about the other laws. The number dismissed because of the *Arierparagraph* is difficult to determine. Messerschmidt concurred that "it will never be determined how many 'non-Aryan' officers served in the Reichswehr."[45] Since it applied not only to officers but also to all soldiers, one can safely assume hundreds were discharged because of the *Arierparagraph*.[46] Most have assumed that the majority discharged were full Jews, but out of the almost thirty men documented in this study discharged because of this law, only two were full Jews; the rest were half- or quarter-Jews. Most felt shocked that their ancestry suddenly disqualified them from serving.

Lieutenant Hans-Heinrich Lebram was discharged from the navy in 1934. He wrote, "[W]hen in early March 1934 the commander[47] of the [cruiser] *Königsberg* ordered all officers to prove our 'Aryan descent,' it was as if a lightning bolt hit me from the heavens."[48] Bitter and disillusioned, Lebram tried to see the commander in chief of the Kriegsmarine, but Admiral Erich Raeder avoided him. "Raeder was too much of a coward to tell me himself why I was being discharged," Lebram claimed after the war.[49] One of Lebram's commanding officers, Captain Günther Lütjens, who later was the fleet commander of the battleship *Bismarck* and heavy cruiser *Prinz Eugen*, explained that Raeder could not bear to see Lebram because this matter "had affected him so deeply."[50] Raeder wrote to Lebram that he "greatly regretted" having to discharge him, but he had to follow orders.[51] Lütjens probably empathized with Lebram. His wife and her brother, Admiral Otto Backenköhler, were half-Jews. Lütjens's two sons were naval officers and thus risked discharge on the same grounds.[52] Lütjens told the angry Lebram that the *Arierparagraph* "is the Führer's wish."[53] When Lebram pressed him for a better explanation, Lütjens acknowledged that this was hard to understand but told Lebram that "we cannot change anything."[54] The Kriegsmarine discharged Lebram on 31 July 1934.[55] His brother, Lieutenant Walter Lebram, was so distraught over his coming discharge that he committed suicide.[56]

In the navy, many officers viewed the *Arierparagraph* as an unjust measure. Some came to the aid of discharged non-Aryan naval personnel and helped them find positions in civilian life. For example, Hans-Heinrich Lebram was transferred to the merchant marine, where he served out the war transporting military goods to different sectors of the German front along the Atlantic.

Other naval officers accepted the new racial laws. Ironically, 12.5 percent Jew and Blomberg's naval adjutant Captain Hans-Georg von Friedeburg, the future commanding admiral of U-boats, accepted the *Arierparagraph* as "necessary . . . in order to act within the sense of our Führer."[57] Friedeburg, a fervent supporter of Hitler's,[58] may have been a quarter-Jew and thus risked being discharged himself.[59] He was spared the humiliation and discrimination families like Lebram's had to suffer.

Lebram's family was not alone in its distress. Quarter-Jew Lieutenant Klaus von Schmeling-Diringshofen, discharged in June 1934 under the *Arierparagraph,* lamented that he would no longer "be allowed to serve Germany."[60] The night before his discharge, 31 May 1934, the dramatic Schmeling-Diringshofen reflected on his situation:

> I'm sober and alert. . . . It's the last hour that I'll be a lieutenant. Do you see how I sit and write and spend this last hour in which I'm something still for Germany. . . . I put on my army coat. I'm still allowed to wear it and I'll do so until the end. . . . This is like a slow death for me. What will become of me? What did I do before? . . . For four years and two months, I've lived this life, which will be destroyed in ten minutes [it was 11:50 P.M.].[61]

Although Colonel Erich von Manstein (later field marshal and one of Germany's finest army commanders),[62] chief of staff of Wehrkreis III Berlin,[63] tried to help him, Schmeling-Diringshofen still had to leave the army.[64] Schmeling-Diringshofen wrote Manstein that "perhaps Germany will need us later, and if so, we [he and his brother] will be there for her."[65] Discharge was the worst disgrace soldiers like Schmeling-Diringshofen could face both professionally and socially. Bewildered about what he should do with his life, Schmeling-Diringshofen viewed his demise as an officer as though his life were over. The disintegration of all his hopes and dreams destroyed the young man's self-confidence. Most discharged non-Aryans did not understand why they were discharged. The rules of the game had changed suddenly, and they could not clearly comprehend why they no longer could serve in a profession of their choosing, a profession where most had performed well.

After his discharge, Schmeling-Diringshofen went to China, where he helped Chiang Kai-shek train his Nationalist army.[66] Apparently, General Ludwig Beck, head of the troop office in 1934 and chief of the army's general staff from 1935 to 1938, helped several discharged non-Aryan officers get military posts in China as advisers under the leadership of General Hans von Seeckt,[67] and later, General Alexander von Falkenhausen.[68] For example, Beck had already sent Major Robert Borchardt, a half-Jew and later recipient of the Ritterkreuz, to China a few months before he sent Schmeling-Diringshofen there.[69] Borchardt was in charge of training the Chinese Nationalist Army's first mechanized units. He would actually engage in combat with Chinese troops against the Japanese.[70] Most *Mischlinge* in China wanted to return to Germany and serve the fatherland. Before Schmeling-Diringshofen left for China, he told his good friend, the later General Dietrich Beelitz, "[W]hen war comes, and it will come, you do everything you can to get me back here so I can serve. You have the connections." "I couldn't believe that he was discharged. He didn't look Jewish at all," Beelitz said. "Schmeling looked just like an Aryan. His nickname was *Blubo,* after the phrase of *Blut und Boden* [blood and soil].[71] If any soldier looked German, it was Schmeling-Diringshofen."[72] Strangely enough, before war broke out, Germany allowed most of the *Mischling* soldiers in China to return to the Wehrmacht in 1938.[73] But until war looked like a distinct possibility and the alliance with Japan strengthened, most of these soldiers spent several years in China in "forced exile."

On 23 March 1934, retired captain Dr. Leo Löwenstein,[74] president and founder of the Jewish Frontline Soldier Federation,[75] wrote Hindenburg criticizing the *Arierparagraph* for depriving Jews of military service. He felt that Jews had an honorable place in the armed forces despite the National Socialist government.[76] The following day, Löwenstein wrote Major Hermann Foertsch in the Reichswehr Ministry, "It's of course impossible for German Jews to accept this fundamental denial of their rights as German citizens."[77] In 1934, German Jews felt German and could not understand why the privileges they had enjoyed for decades were suddenly revoked. They felt offended as Germans deprived of their basic rights.

Although public relations officer in the Bundeswehr's[78] Ministry of Defense, Colonel Gerd Schmückle, acknowledged in 1961 that the *Arierparagraph* opened a dark chapter in German military history in which the Wehrmacht's leadership forgot to stand by their comrades,[79] only Colonel von Manstein dared to protest in 1934.[80] Manstein wrote Beck on 21 April 1934 and explained that the Schmeling-Diringshofen case had made him think about the racial policy. He wrote, "The honor of these young [men] is all our honor."[81] Manstein argued that if the Reich was ready to require soldiers to sacrifice their lives, it could not legally say to those same soldiers that suddenly they were "no longer true Germans."[82] Manstein believed anyone willing to sacrifice his life for the *Volk* had proven himself Aryan regardless of his grandmother's racial status.[83] Manstein assured Beck that he welcomed Nazism and admitted that Germans no longer wanted to serve under non-Aryans, even though it had never mattered before. Although Party officials might not like it, Manstein maintained that no common officer would ask to see his lieutenant's family tree as long as that lieutenant had earned his respect.[84]

Manstein wanted the army to retain the right to judge its own rather than abdicate that power to Party civil servants.[85] Manstein saw the *Arierparagraph* as a plot by "certain elements" to destroy the officer corps and gather this power in their hands.[86] Manstein's commanding officer, General Erwin von Witzleben, supported Manstein's protest "with all his authority."[87] Manstein's letter reached head of the ministerial office and Blomberg's chief of staff, Colonel Walter von Reichenau, who then showed it to Blomberg. Blomberg in turn ordered the army commander in chief, General Werner von Fritsch, to take disciplinary action against Manstein. Fortunately for Manstein, Fritsch did nothing.[88] The intelligent Fritsch, although anti-Semitic,[89] disliked Hitler and "his cronies"[90] and thus probably empathized with Manstein's position vis-à-vis the government. Nonetheless, Manstein's protest accomplished nothing.

Manstein agreed that Jewish influences should be removed from society, but his letter in 1934 showed he understood Jewishness to mean something other than what Nazi ideology claimed. Manstein thought of Jewishness as part of a cultural rather than racial identity. Any non-Aryan, Manstein believed, who adopted German culture and beliefs by serving in the army was German. Manstein probably felt motivated to write Beck such a letter because he wanted to help not only his subordinate Schmeling-Diringshofen, but also his two great-nephews, both of whom were soldiers and *Mischlinge*.[91]

Manstein was not alone in having different priorities when implementing Nazi ideology. Interestingly, Göring privately told his wife that he really did not believe in all this racial ideology. He said that the Jews were just like other people, "'a bit smarter,' he would say grinning, 'and they have their good and bad, just like every other race.'"[92] On the one hand, he allowed half-Jews to serve in some of the Luftwaffe's highest positions, alleging that he could tell whether they were Jewish. In other words, Göring was notorious for his struggle to maintain as much power as possible over the organizations under his control.[93] Only Hitler could tell him whom he could or could not have in positions of authority regardless of their ancestry. On the other hand, he issued orders and authorized actions that exterminated Jews. For Göring and many others, personal relationships sometimes overrode Nazi ideology. But in general, he fully supported Nazi policies regardless of what he said in private.

From 1934 to 1935, Blomberg, who praised Hitler's "strategic genius,"[94] aligned the armed forces more closely with Hitler's ideology. Naturally, Hitler welcomed this shift. Hitler knew he could not control society or dominate Europe without military support. He demonstrated his gratitude for Blomberg's loyal service by sacrificing his SA in June 1934 ("Night of the Long Knives") to ensure the Reichswehr's primacy.[95] The ailing Hindenburg wrote Hitler soon thereafter and thanked him for saving "the German nation," which provided Hitler with "legitimation from the head of state."[96] On 29 June, Blomberg wrote in the *Völkischer Beobachter* that the Reichswehr "stands behind Hitler . . . who remains one of ours." After Hindenburg's death on 2 August 1934, Hitler took over the office of president as well as chancellor, placing all executive power in his hands.[97] Now holding both offices, Hitler's "power had effectively shed formal constraints on its usage."[98]

The Reichswehr would help Hitler in his quest for total domination. Not obligated or prompted, the Reichswehr implemented policies to honor Hitler and his newly acquired power. General von Reichenau, a Nazi sympathizer[99] and nicknamed the "Nazi General,"[100] drafted a new military oath to swear allegiance to Hitler as the supreme commander of the armed forces.[101] The ambitious Reichenau took this new draft to Blomberg, who enthusiastically took it to Hitler. Hitler approved it, and from then on, military personnel swore allegiance to the person of Hitler rather than to Germany. The oath read: "I swear by God this holy oath, that I will render to Adolf Hitler, Führer of the German Reich and People, Supreme Commander of the Armed Forces, unconditional obedience, and that I am ready, as a brave soldier, to risk my life at any time for this oath."[102] Before 1918, soldiers took an oath to the kaiser and Germany, and during the Weimar Republic, they swore allegiance to the constitution and the presidency.[103] The new oath of 1934 demanded obedience to one specific person and established a personal connection between every soldier and Hitler. The Führer could not have asked for a better act of subservience or a clearer vote of confidence from the armed forces than this oath. The new oath confirmed, more emphatically than anything else, that Hitler had established a level of control over the armed forces unparalleled since the kaisers. Hitler was now the highest authority in the land. Quarter-Jew Colonel Christoph von L'Estocq later wrote that "it was a horrible burden to have this obligation to want to live or die for . . . Hitler."[104] Beck called this day a "black day" for the army but did not refuse to take the oath.[105] When a *Mischling* or any other soldier had the courage to refuse to take this oath, like Walter Falk, his resistance did not last long. Falk stated that he could not give the oath because he had a Jewish father. He was arrested, brought to court, and sentenced to six months of imprisonment. After hearing Falk's appeal, Berlin's high military court *(Oberkriegsgericht)* reduced his sentence by four months. After he had served his time, the army returned him to his unit. His comrades and superiors warmly welcomed him back. However, before war broke out in September 1939, he was forced to take the oath. He was threatened with deportation to a concentration camp if he did not. With tears in his eyes, Falk swore his loyalty to Hitler.[106]

Many have claimed that the oath was administered during a public ceremony, and as a result, since they were standing alongside many others, they claim, they did not say the words; consequently, they freed themselves, they allege, from feeling bound to it.[107] This new oath followed the precedent Hitler established in 1930 when he assumed the post of SA supreme leader and demanded "an oath of unconditional allegiance to his person, as an assurance against future insubordination" from every SA leader.[108] Blomberg sped up the process by which Hitler gained control over the armed forces. By giving this oath to Hitler, the Reichswehr "symbolically marked its full acceptance of the new order."[109] Also during August, Blomberg suggested that all soldiers address Hitler as *"Mein Führer* (my leader)."[110] Acknowledging that the Reichswehr had placed its collective head in his hands, on 19 August 1934 Hitler pledged to make it his "highest priority to maintain and preserve the armed forces."[111] By the end of the summer of 1934, Hitler's "popular standing had never been higher."[112] Reichenau wrote that the armed forces now "loved him because he has shown himself a true soldier" in murdering Röhm and doing away with the SA threat.[113]

Hitler's military, political, and social successes between 1933 and 1935 made it easier for military leaders to accept this major power shift.[114]

On 16 March 1935, Hitler made it mandatory for every young man in Germany to serve in the armed forces, now called the Wehrmacht,[115] and set the goal of establishing a peacetime army of twelve corps and thirty-six divisions. With these moves, Hitler put an end to the military restriction of the Versailles treaty,[116] making him even more popular with the German people.[117] Hitler believed that military training would bond Germans to each other and to the Nazi regime. Young, fully Jewish men also had to report to draft stations, but not surprisingly, the Wehrmacht only registered them and did not allow them to serve.[118] Hitler required some non-Aryans (i.e., half- and quarter-Jews) to serve, but they could not hold positions of authority.[119] Ironically, some non-Aryans who wanted to emigrate with their families because they feared Hitler and Nazism could not do so because the Wehrmacht drafted them.[120] The inclusion of *Mischlinge* in the draft contradicted the rule set by the *Arierparagraph* a year earlier that prohibited non-Aryans from serving at any rank. Hitler and Blomberg may have backed down from the harsh position taken in the *Arierparagraph* to avoid the hassle of complaints or because they did not want to deny the Wehrmacht so many potential soldiers.[121] Hitler did say in 1935 that he favored the assimilation of *Mischlinge* "to avoid any weakening of the German potential for war."[122]

Since enough full Jews wanted to serve in the armed forces, Löwenstein wrote state secretary and head of the Reichskanzlei, Dr. Hans-Heinrich Lammers, in March 1935 to argue that Jews had the right to serve.[123] A few months later, he pleaded with Hitler to give German Jews the right to wear the gray army uniform which they had so "proudly" worn in the past.[124] Dr. Max Naumann, head of the Association of National German Jews, also wrote Hitler in March 1935 and promised that every German Jew would prove that "he is just as good as an Aryan" if Hitler gave them the chance to serve in the armed forces as they had in World War I.[125] Hans Joachim Schoeps, leader of Jewish organization called the German Vanguard, also wrote the government a letter similar to Löwenstein's and Naumann's in March of 1935.[126] In response to such letters, the SS organ, *Das Schwarze Korps,* "advised Jews to give up their efforts to enlist in the armed forces."[127] Even in 1940, Jews were still trying to enter the Wehrmacht. On 4 March

1940, OKW[128] again issued a statement that "Jews, just as in peacetime, are not allowed to serve."[129] Jews would never receive approval to serve in the Wehrmacht.

As the Wehrmacht enforced the racial laws, Aryan officers started to report non-Aryans and used Nazi terminology in their reports on subordinates — a practice relatively new to the armed forces. For example, in 1935, General Heinrich Doehla wrote in a routine performance review that he felt Major Karl Helwig, a half-Jew, could not effectively train officers because of his ancestry.[130] Such accusations became increasingly common, most likely because some Aryan officers truly believed in Nazi ideology or wanted to remove someone whom they disliked (or both).

Efforts to purify the Wehrmacht racially were not confined to military personnel. Several minor orders attempted to ensure that soldiers only interacted with Aryans. On 21 December 1934, Fritsch, usually tolerant of *Mischling* soldiers, commented that "it must be a matter of course that an officer seeks his wife only in the Aryan groups of the nation."[131] A Defense Law was issued on 21 May 1935 banning marriages between Wehrmacht personnel and people of "non-Aryan origin."[132] On 15 July 1935, Blomberg prohibited all Wehrmacht soldiers from shopping "at non-Aryan shops."[133]

In 1935, Reichenau commented that in principle, non-Aryans could not hold positions of authority, but if war broke out, the Wehrmacht would use special regulations to handle these cases, and Hitler would give final approval.[134] Although the armed forces had a clear policy on what to do with non-Aryan soldiers, it did not have an efficient way to identify them. The armed forces routinely had their soldiers report their religion, but had never inquired about the religion of their soldiers' parents or grandparents. Now officers had to submit their and their wives' family trees, and soldiers had to sign Aryan declarations.[135] Most officers identified themselves truthfully, and many who lied were often subsequently denounced. The Wehrmacht relied on soldiers to sign the mandatory Aryan declarations truthfully, since investigating so many family documents was practically impossible. Fear kept most soldiers honest. Despite harsh penalties, some risked the lie. For example, half-Jew Richard Cohn claimed on his papers that he was Aryan. No one verified his ancestry, although his name was clearly Jewish in origin.[136] If the authorities caught a Jewish or *Mischling* soldier lying about his ancestry, they usually imprisoned him for making a false report. For example, when officials discovered that half-Jew Lieutenant Hans-Joachim Körner had lied about his ancestry, the military court of the 408th Division in Breslau sentenced him to four months in prison. The Party's Ortsgruppenleiter of his hometown had informed the army that Körner was a half-Jew after Körner's grandmother was deported to Poland, where she was murdered.[137] Captain Edgar Jacoby, stationed in France as the company commander of Propaganda Company 696, was only identified as a Jew after his sister, Käthe Himmelheber, attended a Nazi *Frauenschaft* meeting. The Ortsgruppenleiter Alfred Krömer of Pinneberg stated that when questioned, Käthe had said she had been invited and added that her brother was an officer. Krömer immediately wrote the local Wehrmacht authorities about this incident describing Käthe's "insolence *(Frechheit)*."[138] When Jacoby's commander informed him that his lie about his ancestry had been discovered, Jacoby suffered a heart attack. Thanks to his sister, his true ancestry was revealed and his false documents would no longer hide him as an Aryan. Despite the fact that he was a World War I officer decorated with the Iron Cross and in poor health, Jacoby was brought before a military court, discharged, and deported to a forced labor camp.[139] Quarter-Jew Rolf von Sydow also lied about his ancestry and became an officer. When the Wehrmacht learned of his trickery, he was demoted and thrown in jail.[140]

Many felt that they deserved more than the army had given them, and lied to get it. Sydow felt he had been wrongly imprisoned and vowed to fight "until my honor is restored — that is until I'm an officer."[141] In a letter to his parents, he expressed outrage at his fate: "I can hardly deal with the monstrosity of this decision. . . . I want finally to have what I deserve based on my abilities."[142] The authorities later released Sydow, and he returned to the army as an Obergefreiter.[143] He never attained a higher rank. He was one of the lucky ones. Most guilty of lying remained in jail or were sent to concentration camps.

Sometimes when the authorities caught a *Mischling* lying, loyal comrades in positions of power protected him. For instance on 19 August 1939, the commander of the Seventeenth Army Corps, General Werner Kienitz, wrote the OKH Personnel Office asking it to discharge half-Jew Captain Robert Colli. Kienitz had received proof from the Gestapo that Colli was "not Aryan." Colli's commanders and probably someone in the OKH

Personnel Office (most likely the later General Seegers)[144] ignored these allegations. Colli remained a soldier and eventually received the *Deutsch-blütigkeitserklärung* (German blood declaration). He reached the rank of colonel and received both the German-Cross in Gold and the Ritterkreuz. He lost one of his legs in combat.[145] The quarter-Jewish Marine-Oberbaurat and Nazi Party member Franz Mendelssohn was hounded throughout the 1930s, but like Colli, his superiors protected him. Ultimately, the authorities could not prove Mendelssohn's Jewish ancestry, although the name should have been evidence enough (Mendelssohn was a great-great-great grandson of Moses Mendelssohn). Many encouraged him to change his name as his brother Alexander had done. He refused. Luckily, Commodore Ernst Wolf and Admiral Eugen Lindau protected Mendelssohn, and he continued to build torpedo boats and submarines.[146]

What Wolf and Lindau did for Mendelssohn was not uncommon. Others in the Wehrmacht personnel offices sometimes hid non-Aryan officers simply by not reporting them. When Colonel Karl-Heinrich Fricke took over Section 5 (Army Corps of Engineers and Communication Units)[147] in Army Personnel Group Office[148] 1 (P1)[149] from Colonel Rolf Menneking, Menneking gave him the files of three officers and said, "[T]hese three commanding officers are non-Aryans. No one knows this except me. I've allowed these three to remain at their post and to be promoted despite the racial laws. . . . It's now your responsibility."[150] Admiral Patzig, in charge of the Navy Personnel Office as well as Hitler's Army Adjutant Engel, did the same thing as Menneking and Fricke did. In dealing with military personnel files, one could easily help a non-Aryan remain in the armed forces by not reporting his racial status.

Others successfully hid their Jewish ancestry without the help of those in the personnel office. The later First Lieutenant Paul-Ludwig Hirschfeld, a Jew, moved to another town before the war and registered himself as an Aryan.[151] Like Mendelssohn and Jacoby, he falsified his papers, but unlike the Jew Jacoby, he severed all ties with his family except his Jewish fiancée. Soon thereafter, he entered the army and rose up through the ranks. He did his duty and even saved his whole regiment on several occasions, of which he is still proud. For his tactical abilities, he was nicknamed the "wise Jew" by his comrades.[152] He claims that he was also able to use his position to help Jews: "I often secretly gave Jews who had been rounded up by the SS and military police special permits *(Passierscheine)* [to get extra food or to travel home]. I did all this as my unit marched east into Lithuania, Latvia, and Russia. I could do more for those persecuted Jews than those Jews who ran away to foreign countries!"[153] Later in the war, Hirschfeld was able to falsify the papers of his fiancée and married her, fitted out in his full dress uniform. Hirschfeld claims that he was not alone in surviving the war as he did:

> The fact remains that several educated Jews decided to escape the concentration camps and death by changing their religion and [by serving in the Wehrmacht as officers]. One who wore a uniform in Germany back then was safe. . . . Who could present himself as a Jew back then? No one! So they carried their Jewish secret around with them and weren't permitted to share it with anybody.[154]

Hirschfeld asserted that he feels fortunate that he served because it allowed him to survive: "Service in the Wehrmacht was my salvation. . . . My brother, sister, family all died in the Holocaust. The whole family."[155] Hirschfeld claimed that he remained religiously Jewish as best he could while serving in the Wehrmacht. He recited his Shema every day and did his best to say his prayers. He testifies that without God, he would not be alive today. When confronted with the fact that Jews served in the Wehrmacht, New York Orthodox Rabbi Chaskel Besser said, "It may seem strange at first glance [that these Jews served]. However, I can understand how one may have done it to survive."[156] Many tried to hide their ancestry, some successful like Hirschfeld and Mendelssohn, others unsuccessful like Jacoby and Sydow. They all wanted to live a better life under Hitler, and to do so, they needed to hide their Jewish past.

The fact that the Wehrmacht either relied on the men themselves to report their racial status or waited for someone to denounce them showed that the Wehrmacht, perhaps understandably, did not want to look too hard for non-Aryan soldiers, especially officers. With war in the air in the mid-1930s, the Wehrmacht needed all the experienced officers it could get. Most non-Aryans documented in this study were loyal and good soldiers.

Ironically, when the Nazis wanted to prove that a non-Aryan served in the Wehrmacht, they sometimes enlisted the help not of a Nazi organization but of a Jewish one. The director of the Central Archives of German

Jews, Jacob Jacobson, helped the Nazis in their racial research. At the Central Archives, the Nazis were able to document many people's Jewish ancestry, including some who served in the armed forces. For example, one day, probably in the late 1930s, a "Jewish looking army officer" was sent to Jacobson "by his superiors to inquire whether he had Jewish ancestry."[157] Although Jacobson did not really want to help this officer, he found no evidence of Jewish ancestry. The officer left, evidently relieved by the result. By chance, the next day, Jacobson discovered that both the soldier's parents had been buried in the Jewish cemetery.[158] Although no record of what happened to this particular soldier exists, he was probably dismissed. This soldier's "ignorance" of his Jewish past was common among non-Aryan soldiers. Even though many full Jews did indeed feign ignorance, several *Mischlinge*, especially quarter-Jews, really did not know about their ancestry until after 1933.

Many first learned of their Jewish heritage when civil servants proved it to them. For example, Unteroffizier Kreuzer harassed one of his subordinates, quarter-Jew Reinhard Krackow, by calling him a *Judenbengel*[159] and other anti-Semitic names until Kreuzer suddenly learned that he himself was also a quarter-Jew. The army demoted him to Obergefreiter and he became deeply depressed. He even had the audacity to ask Krackow's father, Hans, for help.[160] Surprisingly, the Krackows decided to counsel the unfortunate man. If one could prove complete ignorance of one's Jewish heritage, the authorities were often more lenient.[161]

Some reported non-Aryans to the authorities because they believed in the need for a "racially pure" Wehrmacht while others reported non-Aryans because they saw racial laws as an opportunity to depose someone who stood in their way of a promotion, to settle old scores, or to be sadistic.[162] Enough people joined the witch-hunt that most non-Aryan soldiers and officers worried about their positions. Even if they were not discharged, many non-Aryans were passed over for promotion or sent to undesirable posts.

One did not have to be non-Aryan to have problems. It was enough to be married to one. For example, in July 1935, an anonymous letter arrived at a Munich police station which claimed that Dr. Zeise, a military psychologist, was married to a Jew. The police turned this information over to the army, and by March 1936, General Wilhelm Keitel had decided it was not wise to retain Zeise.[163] This case was then passed to Reichenau, now commander of the Seventh Army Corps. Although Reichenau wanted Zeise out of the army, he told the authorities to continue allowing Zeise to collect his salary for the next three months to help him in his search for another job. It is not clear from the documents what ultimately happened to Zeise.[164] In 1937, Lammers appealed to government officials to stop their denunciations because he was overwhelmed with reports.[165] Whether disillusioned with their lives, anti-Semitic, or morally depraved, quite a few Germans derived gratification from seeing others overtaken by tragedy by denouncing them.[166] Once someone was denounced, like Zeise, or exposed, like Schmeling-Diringhofen, the Wehrmacht usually dismissed that person.

THE NUREMBERG RACIAL LAWS OF 1935 AND THEIR AFTERMATH

The Nuremberg Laws enacted on 15 September 1935 marked a major step in clarifying racial policy and removing Jewish influences from Aryan society.[167] Interestingly, these laws, on which the rest of Nazi racial policy hung, were written hastily. In September 1935, Hitler decided that the time was ripe for more restrictions on Germany's Jews, especially since many Party militants had expressed their disappointment with the *Arierparagraph*. He outlined new laws for the protection of German blood and honor. These laws would "regulate the problems of marriage between 'Aryans' and 'non-Aryans.'"[168] On 13 September 1935, he called on Lösener in the RMI, and others, among them state secretaries Hans Pfundtner and Dr. Wilhelm Stuckart, to formulate the legal language.[169] Hitler wanted to present these new laws at the Nuremberg Party rally on 15 September, leaving only two short days to write them. During these two days, several of the men involved in the drafting process did not sleep. A lot of preliminary work had been done for the drafting of such laws prior to 13 September, but they still had to agree on their severity and language. They wrote notes at mealtimes on menu cards as they threw together the laws that would decide the fate of millions. Hitler had asked these men to translate racial ideology into law. Remarkably, the head of Reich Office for Genealogy Research, Dr. Kurt Meyer, heard about these new laws for the first time when they were officially announced. He openly expressed his anger, humiliation, and surprise at not having been consulted during the drafting process.[170] Hitler made no pretense of basing these laws on any "scientific truths" discovered by his "racial scientists." His driving force was not reason but rather the need for an enemy. Hitler had said that if the Nazis had not had Jews, they would have had to invent them.[171] Since Hitler believed he was the sole authority on racial policy, he had the final say about what the law stated.

The laws issued on 15 September 1935, approved by Hitler personally, deprived Jews of citizenship, prohibited Jewish households from having German maids, forbade any German from marrying a Jew, and outlawed sexual relations between Jews and Germans. These laws enforced a new morality on Germans. Hitler claimed during a Reichstag session that the Nuremberg Laws would actually help the Jews by creating "a level ground on which the German people may find a tolerable relation with the Jewish people."[172] Hitler's statement was a "blatant deception, aimed at the outside world."[173] Regardless of what Hitler said, he implemented these laws to ostracize, discriminate, and expel Jews from society.[174] This was quickly gleaned from his speech when he next said that if this "tolerable situation" was not found and if the Jewish agitation both within Germany and abroad continued, then the position must be reexamined.[175] In other words, Hitler would then implement further laws and policies to persecute the Jews. The Nuremberg Laws, according to Hitler, were just a precursor to other more degrading decrees. To create his homogenous and harmonious Aryan society, Hitler had first to discard the Jews, a "people" incompatible with "true Germans." The Nuremberg Laws helped Hitler to take the first step toward getting rid of "these parasites"[176] and imposing racial conformity on society.

The Nuremberg Laws issued on 15 September 1935 prohibited marriages between Jews and Germans but failed to specify who counted as a Jew. Years of German-Jewish assimilation made this a difficult question to answer. The debate raged for the next several months. Hitler wavered between declaring half-Jews the same as Jews or keeping them separate as half-Jews.[177] Many issues about *Mischlinge* and intermarriage were discussed. For example, Nazi hard-liners thought the *Arierparagraph* had been too lenient. Dr. Gerhard Wagner, Reichsärzteführer (Reich doctors' leader) and a fanatical anti-Semite, had many talks with Hitler during the drafting of the racial laws. He wanted to equate all half-, quarter-, and even one-eighth-Jews with full Jews.[178] Such extremists argued that partial Jews were more dangerous than full Jews because their mix of German and Jewish blood would enable them to lead the state's enemies with the skill of Aryans.[179]

The racial theorist Dr. Achim Gercke in the RMI introduced another argument when he wrote in September 1935 that *Mischlinge* could really be disguised Jews. Anyone who mathematically defined "50 percent, 25 percent, 12.5 percent, 6.25 percent, etc., *Mischlinge*" had not understood Mendel's laws of genetics, Gercke maintained. Gercke warned that *Mischlinge* could also "mendel out pure Jews."[180] At this time, Hitler refused to give his decision on whether to declare half-Jews as Jews. Hitler's wavering was typical of his style of rule. He often avoided giving a final decision that involved choosing different options proposed by two or more of his trusted underlings.[181] And being the good politician he was, Hitler probably did not declare half-Jews as Jews because he did not want to alienate the Aryan families of *Mischlinge* too much.

The Nazis not only persecuted people of Jewish descent, but Aryan Germans with Jewish spouses as well. Stuckart in the RMI argued that anyone who married a Jew was an inferior German. Any children born to such parents did not deserve any better treatment than Jews, since their German half was not really worth protecting.[182] Streicher tried to convince Frick that Jewish semen permanently polluted an Aryan woman to such an extent that later, although married to an Aryan, she could not bear "pure-blooded Aryan babies."[183] Luckily men like Lösener, who were responsible for drafting these laws, did not take Gercke's or Streicher's beliefs too seriously.[184]

Throughout this process of defining Jewishness, Lösener realized the problems inherent in labeling as un-German people who felt German, thereby marking them for persecution. Lösener feared the disastrous social repercussions that would result from branding as Jews several highly decorated half-Jewish World War I veterans (one a Pour le Mérite recipient) and distinguished supporters of the Nazi movement.[185] Lösener argued that since most felt German and rejected Judaism, their suicide rate would climb dramatically if the government labeled them as Jews.[186] Lösener also cautioned that if they treated half-Jews as Jews, the armed forces would probably lose 45,000 soldiers.[187] He felt that the "laws transformed dissimulation into an established fact [and] would minimize hatred," and he "stressed that legal segregation meant legal protection."[188] After the war, Lösener explained his reasoning: "One could no more achieve any movement on the Jewish question in the narrow sense, i.e. the full-Jews, than one could move a mountain. It would also have been tactically the most stupid thing I could possibly have done because it would have removed any further possibility of making use of my position [in helping half-Jews]."[189] He knew the Jews were doomed but felt that he could save the *Mischlinge* from meeting the same fate if he could prevent the authorities from labeling them as Jews. In this battle between the Party, led primarily by Wagner, and the RMI, led by Stuckart and Lösener, the RMI won. Hitler had been content to let these two factions fight it out.[190] Hitler apparently allowed the RMI to enact its version of the law because he feared the unrest in society that the harsh law of the Party fanatics would cause. According to historian Nathan Stoltzfus, Hitler was only concerned "for his popularity" in permitting RMI to get its way.[191]

On 14 November 1935, the RMI issued a supplement to the Nuremberg Laws of 15 September 1935 which created the racial categories of German, Jew, half-Jew (Jewish *Mischling* first degree), and quarter-Jew (Jewish *Mischling* second degree), each with its own regulations.[192] Apparently, Hitler decided for the time being to keep half-Jews as such rather than treating them as full Jews. Full Jews had three to four Jewish grandparents.[193] According to Hitler, when someone was more than 50 percent Jewish, he was beyond the point of saving and was evil *(übel)*.[194] Half-Jews had two Jewish grandparents, and quarter-Jews had one Jewish grandparent.[195] The Nazis had to resort to religious criteria to define these racial categories,[196] ultimately determined by birth, baptismal, marriage, and death certificates. Often stored in churches and courthouses, these records indicated what religion one adhered to or had left. When a *Mischling* belonged to the Jewish religion or was married to a Jew, the Nazis counted him as a full Jew. Jews could only marry Jews or half-Jews, and half-Jews could only marry Jews or other half-Jews. Quarter-Jews could only marry Aryans, although in practice they experienced difficulties in doing so. Marriages between a Jew and an Aryan that had occurred before 1935 were called "privileged mixed marriages" and provided some protection for the Jewish spouse.[197] Most Jews who survived the Holocaust in Germany were married to non-

Jews.[198] At the same time, Hitler allowed some *Mischlinge* to apply for exemptions under section 7 of the supplementary decrees of November 1935. In some cases, if Hitler approved, the *Mischling* was allowed to call himself or herself an Aryan.

The Nuremberg Laws of 1935 laid the foundation for the next ten years of racial policy. Subsequent official documents usually replaced the term non-Aryan[199] with the more specific "Jewish *Mischling* first or second degree" and Jew. Although by 1938 Hitler felt the Nuremberg Laws had been too "humane,"[200] he never changed them.

As Lösener had predicted, these laws calmed many individuals of Jewish descent by clarifying their situation somewhat. Half-Jew Peter Gaupp, who called the time from 1933 until the racial laws of 1935 the "lawless years,"[201] said:

> In 1935, the laws came out, the Nuremberg Laws. That was the first time you knew where you stood legally. . . . Before it was all guesswork. You could meet a Nazi in some office and he could exterminate you or you could meet a Nazi that was very human and he could help you. . . . Before 1935, before the laws came out of Nuremberg, you swam your way through. . . . You know, there was no regulations. The laws of Nuremberg was the first, ah, form, legal shape where you knew where you stood.[202]

Mischlinge felt oppressed, but at least they knew where they belonged. Some Jews welcomed the laws because they felt that now they could live an "orderly existence."[203] Moreover, for a few years after these laws, most *Mischlinge* continued to live fairly "normal" lives — that is, they were able to study, date, serve in the armed forces, and so on. Most felt pleasantly surprised that the majority of their Aryan friends and acquaintances did not treat them differently after the issuance of these laws. Kershaw wrote, "Between the promulgation of the Nuremberg Laws and the summer of 1938, it would not be going too far to suggest that the 'Jewish Question' was almost totally irrelevant to the formation of opinion among the majority of the German people."[204] Many people did not take the new laws seriously. As Kershaw claims, "[The Nuremberg Laws] appear to have passed by much of the population almost unnoticed."[205] It seems that those who did know about these laws, including *Mischlinge*, accepted them without objection.[206] Quarter-Jew

Hans Koref claimed that he looked upon these laws as the "biggest heap of shit in world history"; however, he acknowledged them as binding.[207]

In 1936, Stuckart and his assistant, Dr. Hans Globke in the RMI, claimed that Nazi racial laws differed little from Jewish law: "The German people want to keep their blood pure and together just like the Jews have done since the prophet Ezra ordered them to do so."[208] Regardless of what Nazi officials said, these laws inflicted humiliation and suffering on Jews and *Mischlinge*. Quarter-Jew Hans Ranke said, "I was shocked [by these laws]. I no longer felt like a worthy German."[209] The Reichstag felt it had secured the purity of blood essential for the German people's future existence.[210] Lammers wrote Frick on 20 February 1936 that Hitler's goal in *Mischling* politics was to make the "mixed race disappear" and to force *Mischlinge* to lose their citizenship rights.[211] The Nazis used these Nuremberg Laws to define, control, and dehumanize *Mischlinge* and eventually to expel them from Aryan society. Germans had already experienced three years of Nazi rule and had come to accept anti-Jewish regulations. The average citizen also had a high respect for the law in general and would not have questioned its legitimacy. Those who might have objected privately feared reprisals enough to hold their tongues. Protest would have been suicidal folly.

The Wehrmacht quickly implemented regulations based on these laws. Blomberg, now minister of war, did not wait a whole year to implement the Nuremberg Laws[212] in the armed forces as he had done with the *Arierparagraph*. In the many conflicts that resulted from the increasing Party control over the Wehrmacht, Blomberg almost always sided with the Party. This case was not different.[213] On 12 November 1935, Blomberg stated that every "soldier is without a doubt a National Socialist, even if he isn't a card carrying Party member."[214] Such a declaration from the war minister could easily disconcert the average *Mischling* soldier. On 27 November 1935, a few days after the first supplementary decree to the Nuremberg Laws was issued, Blomberg ordered all officers and military civil servants to prove their Aryan descent.[215] Blomberg issued this order to identify the racially unreliable. If there was any doubt about a grandparent, then the great-grandparents were to be researched. Officers who had been protected by the Hindenburg exemptions until then no longer enjoyed this clemency. On 31 December, the Wehrmacht discharged most who had been protected by the *Arierparagraph* exemptions.[216] Their number remains unknown.

Only one officer protested these new racial decrees of 1935 through official channels. No less a figure than World War I Field Marshal August von Mackensen wrote Hitler on 3 December 1935 and argued that one should take care of Jewish war veterans who had been severely wounded and disabled and, because of the new laws, were vulnerable to financial hardships. But as far as Jews in general were concerned, he welcomed Nazi persecution.[217] Although he respected Mackensen, Hitler ignored his request. Unlike his reaction to Hindenburg's similar request in 1933, Hitler did not revise the laws. Mackensen, not receiving the desired action from Hitler, wrote Blomberg on 11 January 1936 with the same request. These exemptions, Mackensen argued, were in the army's interest.[218] Mackensen's request was still not granted. Jewish war veterans would not be helped.

After the Nuremberg Laws, several *Mischling* army officers were encouraged to transfer to the Luftwaffe, where many believed Göring would protect them from further discrimination.[219] Several officers stayed at their posts by falsifying their papers or by finding a commanding officer who would protect them (or both).[220] For example, when civil servants started chasing the later Marine-Oberbaurat Franz Mendelssohn, he falsified his documents and informed his superiors about his situation so that they could protect him. Then he became a Nazi Party member.[221] Officers like Mendelssohn took the precautions they felt necessary as *Mischling* restrictions multiplied, especially after World War I service no longer mattered. Some got lucky because their commanding officers still followed outdated laws. For example, the Tenth Army Corps commander wrote OKH in 1936 that he would not discharge the quarter-Jew Captain Peter Sommer (later Waffen-SS Obersturmbannführer) because his father had died in World War I.[222] This confusion in the Wehrmacht only increased as Hitler issued more stipulations on how to deal with *Mischlinge*.[223] During this time, Hitler and some of his associates left several *Mischling* officers at their posts without subjecting them to any persecution.

Throughout the first half of 1936, the Wehrmacht worked diligently along with the Reichskanzlei to find and process Jewish officers. Considering the work involved, one wonders whether these officials did anything besides thinking about how to handle Jews and *Mischlinge*. Yet, since the catalyst for making racist policy was Hitler, who according to associates could not talk ten minutes without discussing the Jews,[224] one should not find it surprising that the Nazis devoted so much time to formulating and applying racial laws. Blomberg argued against the laws that denied *Mischlinge* citizenship, saying that "anyone permitted to serve the State in the Wehrmacht must have the right to citizenship."[225]

Besides the citizenship issue, officials and officers argued whether *Mischlinge* should hold any positions of authority. From March to June 1936, Blomberg argued with Lammers and Frick whether the racial laws, when applied to the armed forces, should say that *Mischlinge* "should not" or "cannot" hold positions of authority. The debate stemmed from how the Reich should handle *Mischlinge* who warranted special treatment. Blomberg probably favored a more flexible position based on his experience with the implementation of both the *Arierparagraph* in 1934 and the draft law in 1935. Blomberg claimed that NCOs, not officers, actually held most positions of authority in the armed forces, and that the Wehrmacht should handle the racial requirements for officers and career soldiers.[226] He was not ready to relinquish total control over the Wehrmacht. In May of 1936, Hitler reached a compromise with Blomberg. The new racial policy read: "Jewish *Mischlinge* cannot hold positions of authority in the Wehrmacht: exemptions require the Führer's consent."[227] Although Hitler allowed loopholes to be written into the laws, his public comments would never have led one to believe he endorsed such exemptions.

On 13 May 1936, Hitler admonished the Wehrmacht to learn and teach the racial principles and the laws designed to convert those principles into reality:

> The National Socialist concept of state demands the nurturing of the idea of race, and of a specially selected group of leaders from people of pure German or similar blood. It is therefore a natural obligation for the Wehrmacht to select its professional soldiers, hence its leaders, in accordance with the strictest racial criteria above and beyond the legal regulations, and so to obtain a selection of the best of the German people in the military school of the nation.[228]

Hitler's next paragraph included instructions on how to select soldiers racially.[229] Taking such statements of Hitler's seriously, Blomberg ensured that Nazi "teaching covered all instructional institutions, especially officers."[230] Yet Hitler contradicted the hard line he advocated publicly by making exemptions behind closed doors for *Mischlinge*.

In the summer of 1936, Field Marshal von Blomberg and Hitler enforced the policy that half- and quarter-Jews had to do military service, but that they could not hold positions of authority without Hitler's approval.[231] Interestingly, the Wehrmacht did not distinguish between half- and quarter-Jews with these initial policies — they were only *Mischlinge*.[232] Nonetheless, despite the laws, many *Mischling* officers remained unknown to the authorities because it was difficult to document every person's ancestry.

During this time, Wehrmacht officials received letters from worried parents, angry Party members, and demoralized soldiers. Since the Nuremberg Laws affected the entire society rather than just the civil service, the numbers of complaints and petitions for exemptions increased dramatically. The *Arierparagraph*, introduced in the civil service in 1933 and in the armed forces in 1934, caused the number of cases dealt with by the Party Genealogy Office to increase from 4,887 to 7,692 from 1933 to 1934. The staff grew accordingly from 27 in 1933 to 126 in 1934.[233] The number of personnel would continue to grow in genealogy offices. Experts estimated that it would take 80 million Reichsmarks to check every German's ancestry.[234] This estimate was made before the *Anschluß* of Austria and the incorporation of the Germans living in the Sudetenland and Memelland, which significantly increased the number of people involved.[235] When the exemption clause in the 1935 Nuremberg Laws became known, it prompted thousands of *Mischlinge* to write the government for help. Likewise, many Aryans wrote letters of condemnation and defamation against *Mischlinge*.

The Party often took it upon itself to help the armed forces identify *Mischlinge*. For example, the Kreisleiter[236] in Mannheim, Dr. Reinhard Roth, wrote Baden Gauleiter[237] Robert Wagner in Karlsruhe on 8 January 1936:

> It's absolutely incomprehensible to us how such a politically questionable person [Captain Hans von Schlebrügge] who's not purely Aryan and whose anti–National Socialist sentiments have been clearly expressed on many occasions can become an army officer. . . . His bank in Berlin has even told us that it's obvious from his business transactions that he's of Jewish descent.[238]

This information was sent to the Wehrmacht and ended up on Reichenau's desk. Luckily for the half-Jew Schlebrügge, the army did not take action against him. Reichenau wrote Wagner on 20 March 1936 that the army along with the political police *(politische Polizei)* had found nothing incriminating in Schlebrügge's papers.[239] On 13 June 1936, Wagner's deputy reminded Reichenau of Schlebrügge's Jewishness, this time including detailed data about his ancestry.[240] Even so, Schlebrügge's file shows that he remained with his unit and ended the war as a colonel decorated with the Ritterkreuz.[241] His superior described him in 1944 as a "National Socialist in attitude and action."[242] Many officers resented the Party's attempt to diminish their authority, as Reichenau's cool response demonstrated. In this case, Reichenau valued Schlebrügge's abilities more than the racial laws.

Most officers had to document not only their own ancestry but also that of their wives. Much to the surprise of their superiors, hundreds of men had married *Mischlinge.* During a conference of the Abwehr[243] on 27 January 1936, Abwehr personnel argued that future officers and their wives had to be Aryan, but present officers should not be punished for their wives' ancestries.[244] However, on 1 April 1936, Blomberg ordered all personnel to prove their wives' Aryan descent.[245] When an officer had a Jewish or *Mischling* wife, the Wehrmacht sometimes told the man to choose between his wife and his career. In one case, Göring protected General Bernhard Kühl's Jewish wife and half-Jewish sons for several years. One son served as an officer. Finally in 1938, Göring gave Kühl an ultimatum, probably forced by Hitler, either to divorce his wife or leave the service. Kühl divorced his wife. She left for the United States, and he stayed on as a general. His son, Lieutenant Heinz-Jürgen Kühl, remained an officer and received the *Deutschblütigkeitserklärung* from Hitler. Heinz-Jürgen died in Rommel's Deutsches Afrika-Korps in 1942.[246] Kühl was not the only one given an ultimatum. Navy Captain Arnold Techel, a friend of Raeder's, refused to leave his Jewish wife, Paula née Pick, and was consequently discharged in 1938.[247] Although most soldiers felt such racial laws had no place in military policy, all had to take them seriously. Fritsch sent a letter to the various Wehrmacht offices on 15 January 1936 saying, "I expect from the spirit of brotherhood within the officer corps that officers will refrain absolutely from any conjectures or spreading of rumors about the non-Aryan ancestry of a comrade or his wife. . . . Any correspondence regarding the non-Aryan ancestry of an officer is to be treated as a secret matter."[248] Apparently, rumors had been

spread. *Mischling* officers or their wives' racial flaws became a popular topic
of conversation.

On 11 October 1936, the War Ministry announced that *Mischlinge* could
not volunteer for military service;[249] however, this was not widely enforced.
Many *Mischlinge* volunteered between 1936 and 1940. The Wehrmacht
would have drafted them later anyway, but they wanted to serve the required time sooner so they could enter the university earlier or choose
which military branch they fought in. Also, a good military record increased a young man's chances of being accepted for his desired course of
study. With the scent of war already in the air, the Wehrmacht did not
reject many volunteers. Even so, sometimes the armed forces made it
difficult for *Mischlinge* to volunteer. For example, when half-Jew Felix
Bruck volunteered in 1938, the Wehrmacht forced him to go through a
racial test. He had to strip in front of three officials, who then measured
various body parts. "It was incredibly humiliating," Bruck said. The
Wehrmacht rejected him then, but drafted him a year later.[250]

On 19 October 1936, OKH issued an order to distinguish between half-
and quarter-Jews. It specified that commanders could promote half-Jews no
higher than Oberschützen;[251] quarter-Jews could be promoted in special
cases to higher ranks.[252] Klemperer knew about this order. In 1939, he wrote
about the Meyerhof family, whose half-Jewish son served and "was even
allowed to become a Gefreiter."[253] Klemperer went on to explain, however,
that the Wehrmacht would not promote Meyerhof any higher because of
the laws.[254] Once these racial laws were issued, many newspapers printed
them. Ironically, although *Mischlinge* could serve and hundreds of *Mischling* officers remained in the Wehrmacht, OKH ordered officers on 15
December 1936 not to associate with civilians of Jewish descent. If officers
had already developed such relationships, OKH encouraged them to break
contact with such persons gracefully and respectfully.[255] This order, however, did not take into consideration that many enforcing it were either
Mischlinge themselves or Aryans who had daily contact with *Mischling*
soldiers. On 28 March 1938, OKW advised Wehrmacht personnel not to
rent apartments from Jewish landlords. On 16 July 1938, the Wehrmacht
even issued an order that no soldier could spend the night in a Jew's home.[256]
The law did not specify whether *Mischlinge* were permitted to stay with
their Jewish parents when home on leave.

Yet, many *Mischlinge* did not know about the racial regulations. Moreover, although the government had issued several laws on how to deal with *Mischlinge,* not every commanding officer knew about the new racial laws. For example, on 24 January 1938, the general command of the Seventh Army Corps chastised Munich's War School for promoting soldiers without checking their ancestry. The authorities instructed the school to revoke immediately any reserve officer status granted to anyone proven to be a *Mischling.* The letter further stated that even "Jewish *Mischlinge*" who had permission to remain Party members through a *Gnadenakt* (act of mercy) could not become NCOs or officers.[257]

Many *Mischlinge* were identified after the military racial laws had been issued. The Wehrmacht sometimes gave them the choice between discharge and demotion to the enlisted ranks. First Lieutenant Karl Henle, a half-Jew, refused to return to the rank of private and left the army. Yet, on 30 August 1941, when the Wehrmacht needed trained soldiers, Hitler reactivated Henle as an active army officer. Eventually, Hitler declared him *deutschblütig* on 30 August 1941. Henle thought that his service might protect his Jewish father. For his valor in combat, his superior awarded him the EKII. On 18 August 1942, he died in battle as a captain.[258] Several *Mischling* soldiers, however, were not identified and discharged in the 1930s like Henle. They continued to serve and were promoted as usual.

By February 1938, nothing on the macro level of Wehrmacht policy could happen without Hitler's approval. Hitler removed Blomberg on 4 February 1938 because his second, considerably younger wife, Margarethe Gruhn,[259] had reportedly been a prostitute and had posed for pornographic photos. Hitler was furious with his war minister.[260] Blomberg left in disgrace. Although Blomberg supposedly had not known about his bride's sordid past, he refused to leave her. Soon thereafter in March 1938, Fritsch was accused of homosexuality and also had to leave his post in disgrace, though a military court later found the charge to be false. Most military personnel welcomed these moves, and those who thought the dismissals unorthodox simply accepted Hitler's reorganization of the Wehrmacht as a fait accompli. They did not realize at the time that this reshuffling of the command structure had left Hitler holding all the aces.[261] On 4 February 1938, Hitler declared that "henceforth, I exercise personally the immediate command over the whole armed forces."[262] Historian Wilhelm Deist writes that the

Wehrmacht no longer was a "part of the foundation of the state but rather merely its instrument."[263] It was now a "National Socialist Wehrmacht."[264] Hitler had total control over the armed forces,[265] allowing him to "decide over war and peace."[266] Indeed, people in authority took Hitler's new position seriously. For example, Admiral Wilhelm Canaris explained on 3 March 1938 at an Abwehr conference that "today, every German officer should unconditionally be a National Socialist" and feel bound by his oath to Hitler.[267]

After taking control of OKW, Hitler turned his attention to Austria, where he flexed his new military muscles. On 11 March 1938, Hitler ordered the Wehrmacht to invade Austria, which many Austrians welcomed most heartily.[268] As of 15 March 1938, the Nuremberg Laws applied to all Austrian military personnel to be integrated into the Wehrmacht. Keitel, Blomberg's replacement, officially issued the order on 23 March 1938 to discharge Jews from the formerly Austrian army.[269] Generally speaking, the Austrians, who were more passionately anti-Semitic than the Germans, welcomed this change.[270] By the end of 1938, the Wehrmacht discharged at least 238 Austrian military personnel, most of them officers, for racial reasons. Possibly as many as sixty-six high-ranking officers were discharged because of their racial backgrounds.[271] These sixty-six high-ranking officers did not fare well as civilians. One general was allegedly murdered in 1938. One lieutenant colonel was sent to Mauthausen, where he committed suicide. Another lieutenant colonel was sent to Buchenwald, where he died. Four other officers were sent to prison; one of the men, a general, died there.[272] One can be sure that many more than sixty-six high-ranking officers were discharged from the Austrian Bundesheer for political reasons.[273] Some officers did not wait for the Nazis to deport them. Fearing the worst, a retired Jewish colonel first shot his wife, then himself.[274] He was not alone. Over five hundred Austrian Jews committed suicide, fearing the worst from their new Nazi government.[275]

Many Austrians accepted the racial laws with indifference. However, some Austrians, now known as Germans from the German state Ostmark, did not understand some of the Wehrmacht's racial policies. One Austrian Jewish soldier, Josef Getreuer, wrote:

As soon as the Austrian army received the insignia of the Wehrmacht, I was asked not to train any longer. German soldiers who

were billeted in our garrison were very good. Nobody bothered me,
I would speak freely and disagree with the Führer. (I spoke in front
of thirty soldiers one evening), and I received expressions of sympathy from German soldiers. My Austrian Nazi buddies even put
me under their protection.[276]

Most of Getreuer's comrades would not have minded keeping him in the
unit. He was an assimilated Jew and was just as German as the next man.

As in Germany, officials had trouble enforcing the racial laws in the
newly acquired Ostmark.[277] Keitel, chief of OKW, reminded OKH,
OKM,[278] and OKL[279] of the importance of the racial laws by repeating his
order to discharge officers, NCOs, and soldiers who were Jews, Jewish
Mischlinge, or married to Jews or Jewish Mischlinge on 3 November 1938.
Keitel added that those married to quarter-Jews could remain at their jobs
in special cases. He specified that only career-enlisted soldiers had to leave.
Young Austrian Mischling males, like their German counterparts, still had to
perform their mandatory military service.[280] For example, when Dr. Robert
Braun received his draft notice in 1938, he wrote the Wehrmacht several times
telling them of their apparent mistake because he was a half-Jew. The
Wehrmacht ignored his letters and drafted him, and he served as a medical
Unterarzt until his discharge for racial reasons in 1940.[281] Perhaps because
of the confusion illustrated by Braun's case, on 23 November 1938, Keitel
issued an additional decree repeating that racial laws only affected career
soldiers. Mischlinge and those married to Jews and Mischlinge had to perform compulsory military service, but they could not choose to remain
soldiers or expect promotions after their time was up.[282] In 1938, Keitel took
this policy of not allowing Mischlinge positions of authority one step further and ordered that they could not perform sentry duties because the job
implied a degree of authority.[283]

From 1938 to 1939, Mischling soldiers experienced many social difficulties with Reichskristallnacht, the issuing of Jewish identification cards to
their relatives, and the ever-present feeling of uncertainty. In a generous
mood, Hitler instructed Field Marshal Göring to write a decree in late 1938
preventing families in which the father was Jewish and the mother Aryan
from being moved to Jewish districts. Their children would have to perform
Wehrmacht service and, thus, should not have to experience such persecu-

tion. If the mother was Jewish, the exemption did not apply.[284] Hitler believed that Aryan women who had intercourse with Jews should not be as persecuted as Aryan men who slept with Jews.[285] This decree was rare in that Hitler seemed to acknowledge the paradox inherent in a policy that forced men to risk their lives for a regime that discriminated against their families. This decree protected some Jews temporarily.

In 1939, the Wehrmacht continued to increase its Jewish persecution. On 20 January 1939, Hitler ordered the discharge of officers married to Jewish wives.[286] One does not know how many discharges resulted. Also, the army started discharging *Mischlinge* from munitions factories. During this time, the Kriegsmarine seemed to ignore many *Mischling* decrees. On 26 August 1939, the Kriegsmarine clarified its position on employing *Mischling* civilian contractors: "Since *Mischlinge* must serve in the armed forces and are supposed to be integrated into German society, they shouldn't be hindered in their economic pursuits. Consequently, there's no reason not to employ *Mischlinge* in military industries as long as they aren't classified as Jews and don't hold special or leadership positions."[287] The Kriegsmarine always seemed to lag behind the army in implementing racial policies. It is not known whether they dragged their heels intentionally, but this policy aided hundreds if not thousands of *Mischlinge* to stay in the Kriegsmarine.

Several powerful men, such as Raeder and Göring, enforced the racial laws inconsistently. They chose to ignore the fact that certain officers had non-Aryan wives, and both knowingly left several high-ranking *Mischling* officers at their posts. Although Raeder and Göring helped some *Mischlinge,* they did so while avidly supporting the Nazi government. For example, on 12 March 1939, Raeder, who just a few months previously had seemed relatively sympathetic to the Jews' plight, gave a virulently anti-Semitic speech on German Hero's Day. He said in part, "National Socialism, which originates from the spirit of the German fighting soldier, has been chosen by the German people as its ideology. . . . This is the reason for the clear and unsparing summons to fight Bolshevism and international Jewry, whose race-destroying activities we have sufficiently experienced in our own people."[288] In 1939, Göring instructed Heydrich to "solve" the Jewish question by forcing Jews to emigrate.[289] But by 1941, the methods of "solving" the Jewish question had radically changed, and Göring now charged Heydrich with the responsibility of exterminating all Jews in Europe.[290] In setting the priorities for their respective organizations, Raeder and Göring felt that protecting their *Mischling* comrades outweighed racial policy in certain cases. Their behavior typified the enforcement of racial policies throughout the military chain of command.

WORLD WAR II BEGINS, 1939

Just as many Nazis felt unsure or acted in contradictory ways when dealing with *Mischlinge*, many *Mischlinge* often reacted in bizarre ways when dealing with Jews or issues of Jewishness. *Mischlinge* often felt the same anti-Semitic emotions that non-Jews expressed. Many today have a tendency to believe that racism somehow applied only to non-Jewish Germans, but such attitudes had been passed on to *Mischlinge* as well, especially after living with Nazi anti-Semitic propaganda for six years. In 1939, when Germany invaded Poland, most *Mischlinge* felt just as horrified and disgusted by the appearance, habits, and living conditions of the *Ostjuden* as many German-Jewish soldiers of World War I had been.[291] Obergefreiter Heinz-Günter Angreß, a half-Jew, described that as his unit moved deeper into Poland, he felt *Der Stürmer* (a virulent anti-Semitic newspaper) had not exaggerated. The Jews there "looked simply horrible."[292] The later Unteroffizier Hans Mühlbacher wrote in his diary:

> The Jews are dressed better on Saturday and go outside the ghetto (Ropczyce, Poland). I walk through the ghetto. It's awful what horrible people I see there. With grimacing faces they lean against the doors of their homes and businesses and stare amazed at the tall officers walking by. . . . Truly two worlds stand opposite one another. . . . The Jews give the impression of being the eternal Ahasverus.[293] . . . The Jews make a much more decadent impression probably due to centuries of inbreeding.[294]

Although Mühlbacher had a Jewish mother, he did not see any connection with the Orthodox Jews in the ghetto. He depicts them as weak and lacking self-respect by not carrying themselves upright like the Germans. His description of these Jews as "decadent" and products of "inbreeding" shows his utter contempt for them. He calls them the anti-Semitic name "Ahasverus." Ironically, Mühlbacher's Jewish family had "wandered" from the East before finally settling in Vienna.

Most *Mischlinge* could not believe that any of their ancestors ever looked like *Ostjuden* and found their poverty and archaic customs embarrassing. While a Landser[295] during the invasion of Poland in 1939, half-Jew Gefreiter Friedrich Schlesinger was appalled to think that his ancestors looked like the *Ostjuden* he saw.[296] Many veterans interviewed showed pictures or told stories of soldiers cutting off Jews' beards, forcing Jews in traditional garb to push military wagons, or cruelly prodding Jews with guns.[297] Unfortunately, most *Mischlinge* did nothing to help Polish Jews they saw mistreated by fellow soldiers. Most claim today that such actions would have been foolish and unproductive, but their statements also betray some prejudice on their part. Quarter-Jew Hans Bernheim,[298] who today feels strongly Jewish and attached to his Jewish family *(Mischpoke)*, "shamefully admits" that he stood by while German soldiers beat and cut the beards off Polish Jews. He especially regrets that he did nothing when his staff doctor leaped out of the marching column and shot a Pole, probably a Jew, in cold blood for no apparent reason. Bernheim continued to march.[299] A few did have the courage to intervene on behalf of certain Polish Jews, but these people were rare. For example, Gefreiter Helmut Krüger, a half-Jew, when he witnessed several soldiers vandalizing a synagogue, reminded them that they were in God's house. Surprisingly shamed, the men stopped and left.[300] Krüger's intervention was uncommon. Most *Mischling* soldiers celebrated the German victories with their comrades and hoped that their service would alleviate their discrimination back home. They worried little about the persecution of Jewish-Polish civilians by their countrymen.[301] Some *Mischling* soldiers mistakenly believed that the anti-Semitism directed toward *Ostjuden* would not be directed at them or their families. They underestimated Hitler's true intentions.

Many half-Jews distinguished themselves in Poland in 1939. For example, when the Poles attacked their position near Tomaszow, half-Jew Kanonier[302] Dietmar Brücher bravely removed several wounded comrades from the battlefield to the rear echelons. He witnessed how in fits of rage, some of his fellow soldiers committed "horrible acts" of violence. One of the few who had remained uninjured, Brücher continued to help wounded comrades in need of medical attention. While busy on the battlefield, he suddenly was forcefully knocked to the ground. He had been shot through the leg. He saw the enemy nearby and feared the worse, having heard rumors of what Poles did to wounded Germans. The Poles noticed Brücher but left him alone. One actually stopped and helped him dress his wound. They shook hands, and Brücher said, "War sucks *(Krieg ist Scheiße)*."[303]

Eventually, Brücher was found by his own troops and was sent back to Vienna to recover from his wound. While in a military hospital, his Jewish aunt, Gretel Florey née Pick, visited him. Brücher worried about her son, Klaus Florey, who had served in the unit next to Brücher's during the campaign. She was happy to report that he had survived and was also in a military hospital in Vienna.[304]

For his "bravery in the face of the enemy," his commander First Lieutenant Schlike awarded Brücher the EKII. He also received the Wound Badge. Schlike ended his letter wishing Brücher a quick recovery so that "we can see you once again in our ranks."[305] Not all *Mischlinge* reaped the benefits of official recognition as Brücher did.

By October 1939, the fighting in Poland had ended. The time had come for promotions and medals, a process made more intricate by racial policy. Several *Mischlinge* have reported their officers' regret over not being able to award them the EKII or EKI because they were half-Jews. Also, when a *Mischling* deserved a promotion, the racial policy of not allowing *Mischlinge* to serve as NCOs or officers often meant that a potentially less qualified Aryan would get the job. For example, Fritz Steinwasser's commander told him that although he was a "good soldier," he regrettably could not promote him to sergeant because he was a quarter-Jew. When Steinwasser was still a Stabsgefreiter[306] after five years of service, his rank had become a bad joke. During the war, people who did not know the reason for his rank often wondered why such a good soldier remained unpromoted. Many thought only an idiot could get stuck as a Stabsgefreiter for five years and therefore treated him offensively. His military pay, significantly smaller than it would have been if he had received promotions, remained a constant reminder of his discrimination.[307] Obergefreiter Michael Günther's letter of 28 February 1940 to his half-brother, Gefreiter Konrad Schenck, illustrates the frustration felt by so many half-Jews[308] who could not be promoted:

I can't be promoted, which is a real hardship, as only someone who has served in the army for a long time can really understand. If I were an idiot *(Depp)*, then all this wouldn't be so hard to take. But, my captain tells me all the time how truly sorry he is that he cannot promote me to Unteroffizier, and I'm continually asked [by my comrades] why I've not been promoted.[309]

Although Günther had served commendably for years and was an *Abiturient*,[310] he had to resign himself to the fact that no matter how well he performed, his ancestry prevented him from being promoted. Günther's officer had sent an application on Günther's behalf to Hitler. After one year, the officer received a reply from Hitler's headquarters saying that the Führer had "not yet decided" Günther's case. Günther's officer tried again later with the same result. Although his officer had the mental fortitude to apologize for this mistreatment, Günther felt inadequate and abused. Being asked by his comrades about why he was not promoted only added to his feelings of inferiority and frustration. Many *Mischlinge*, like Günther, resented that they did not receive the rewards their intelligence and actions deserved.

The reason why many *Mischlinge* were not being promoted quickly became common news among the troops. Achim von Bredow, a 37.5 percent Jew, was never promoted because of his racial background. He wrote his sister Ada: "[T]he only unpleasant thing is that soon the whole regiment will know my embarrassing situation [apparently most in his platoon knew about his case]. Life is awful here. I had resigned myself to playing the eternal Gefreiter. . . . If it [the application for clemency] doesn't work out, I want to change regiments to get away from it all."[311] Two days later, Bredow wrote his parents: "Unfortunately, my situation has made the rounds here."[312] Often, *Mischlinge* described their fellow soldiers as sympathetic and somewhat understanding of their situation; however, they also felt that many of their comrades looked on them as cripples. The fact that the men in their units knew about their situation was embarrassing. They struggled to maintain a sense of dignity and self-respect in an organization that often reminded them that they were inferior.

Most *Mischlinge* not only felt upset about the military treatment they received, but also were disturbed by how the Nazis treated their Jewish family members. *Mischling* soldiers home on leave felt outraged by the persecution their parents suffered. Traditionally parents of soldiers were honored by their communities, but Jewish parents of soldiers were excluded from such praise and glory in 1939 and 1940. After the war in Poland, thousands of

Mischlinge returned home in the winter of 1939–1940 and found that their mothers and fathers had lost their jobs, could not shop in certain stores, and that Nazis spit on some of them in public. The laws enacted on 17 August 1938 required Jews to add either Israel or Sara to their first names by 1 January 1939, and on 5 October, they were required to have their passports marked with the letter *J* (*Jude* — Jew).[313] German Jews and *Mischlinge* could not walk in parks or a city without seeing benches marked "Only for Aryans" or signs outside restaurants saying "Jews Not Welcome." These decrees and others added insult to injury for *Mischling* families and soldiers who had risked their lives fighting for Germany.[314] Although *Mischling* soldiers' families did enjoy some protection from persecution in the late 1930s and early 1940s, they felt they deserved more. Many *Mischling* soldiers complained to their commanders about the mistreatment of their parents. Complaints also poured into military offices from families whose sons fought in the Polish campaign. Clara von Mettenheim, a Jew with three sons in the Wehrmacht, wrote army commander in chief General Walther von Brauchitsch on 8 December 1939 on behalf of all half-Jewish soldiers, asking him to work with the Party to alleviate the problems they and their families experienced:

> I speak to you as the mother of three soldiers, and as an old soldier's wife [of Lieutenant Colonel Erwin Fischer].[315] . . . My boys are soldiers from head to toe. The godfather of one of my boys is Germany's crown prince,[316] and my old friend [General von] Seeckt held the other one at his christening. My sons are *Mischlinge* because of me. During the war, when my sons were fighting in Poland, we were tortured here on the home front as if there were no more important tasks to be done during the war. . . . Please [stop this mistreatment of half-Jewish soldiers and their parents].[317]

Frau von Mettenheim felt desperate and did not understand why a family of their social standing had to endure such persecution. She felt guilty for the misfortune that had visited her family and pleaded with Brauchitsch to remove the obstacles her sons faced. She described how angry it had made one of her sons when he returned from the war in Poland to find that his sister had been expelled from certain organizations and his mother was constantly being persecuted. For example, Obergefreiter Dieter Fischer accompanied his mother to the Office for Jewish Affairs on the street Hermes

Weg to pick up her Jewish identification papers.[318] He wore his uniform with his EKII, Wound Badge, and Assault Badge. He did so not to provoke anyone but because he was about to return to his unit, never imagining how this would shock those in that office. He returned to the front deeply upset and worried about his mother. Frau von Mettenheim enclosed her son's picture in this letter

> to prove that my son does not degrade the Wehrmacht racially. . . .
> I beg you to use your influence to make sure the Party leaves those [Jewish *Mischlinge* and their relatives *(jüdisch Versippte)*] alone. . . . These men already have it bad enough being treated as second-class soldiers, they shouldn't also have to worry about their families at home while they are fighting a war.[319]

Frau von Mettenheim's request was logically argued, and one would think that the Wehrmacht should have anticipated such predicaments; however, this was obviously not the case. Before the army could answer her request though, they had to complete her racial dossier. OKH wrote her back on 16 December asking exactly how non-Aryan she was.[320] She answered, and on 24 December, probably because of her connections with Seeckt, Keitel informed her that the offices responsible for such cases would look into what they could do to help Jewish parents of soldiers.[321] On 16 January 1940, Frau von Mettenheim received a letter from chief of the general Wehrmacht office,[322] General Hermann Reinecke, stating that the RMI rather than OKW was responsible for these issues.[323] Apparently, Frau von Mettenheim then sent her request to the RMI after being brushed aside by OKW.

Perhaps annoyed by such protests, on 16 January 1940, Hitler ordered the Wehrmacht to ascertain how many *Mischling* soldiers there were to "get a clear picture of the situation."[324] Keitel informed the government that this number could not be determined before April.[325] On 16 January, Hitler, in an OKW decree, decided that anyone married to a quarter-Jew could be used in war but could not become an active officer.[326] On 20 January, OKW confirmed the rule that men married to Jews or Jewish *Mischlinge* could remain in the Wehrmacht but not hold ranks higher than sergeant,[327] which in practice did not happen.

At the beginning of 1940, the armed forces and government continued to entangle themselves in unclear policies regarding *Mischlinge*. Although Hitler had drawn the lines of enforcement, he issued new decrees regarding *Mischlinge* at a frequency that made it difficult for government agencies to avoid implementing outdated, and thus conflicting, policies. As Ian Kershaw wrote, "The character of Hitler's decisions was guaranteed to lead to continuing uncertainty. . . . The open-ended nature of some decrees, bestowing extensive power which conflicted with those of other authorities, could create serious problems of implementation."[328] It proved difficult for a *Mischling* family to keep abreast of the new decrees that controlled their lives. For example, Hans Schenck wrote his friend, the lawyer Dr. Ferdinand Bang, on 12 January 1940 complaining that Konrad, his third son, presently in the army, had been rejected by the university's medical school. The father complained that his son's commander wanted to help Konrad and had promoted him to Unteroffizier. Before the paperwork went through, the commander found out Schenck was a *Mischling*, and the promotion was canceled. The father was perplexed because his other son had been promoted to Unteroffizier without difficulty.[329]

On 14 February 1940, Admiralstabsarzt Dr. Fikentscher turned to OKW on behalf of a half-Jew and retired navy staff doctor, Ferdinand Rohr, brother of the famous World War I storm battalion commander, Willy Rohr.[330] Rohr had described the adversity *Mischlinge* experienced,[331] having not only himself and his siblings in mind, but all their children as well. It is significant that Fikentscher listened to Rohr and took his grievances directly to OKW, and it may have had some influence on Hitler. It was noted after this conference that Hitler would consider protecting half-Jewish parents of those soldiers who had proven themselves in battle and who had been declared *deutschblütig*.[332] Rohr had two nephews (Heinz and Joachim Rohr) who would receive this highly sought after exemption in December 1939, but any protection that it may have given their half-Jewish father, Willy Rohr, was for naught because he was the only one of Ferdinand Rohr's siblings who had already died.

5

The Policy toward *Mischlinge* Tightens, 1940–1943

Mischling *Policy in the Wehrmacht Becomes Stricter, 1940*

In March 1940, the military future for half-Jews looked bleak. The famous Evangelical theologian Heinrich Grüber, an enemy of Hitler and a good friend of Clara von Mettenheim, tried to discuss her sons' cases in March 1940 with some OKW contacts he had: "I tried to describe the difficult situation these young men found themselves in, but I didn't find the officers very understanding."[1] According to a memorandum written on 26 March 1940 for deputy head of the KdF, Viktor Brack,[2] the chief Wehrmacht adjutant, Colonel Rudolf Schmundt, had told Hitler about Frau von Mettenheim's embarrassing experience when her son Dieter accompanied her to acquire her Jewish identification card. Schmundt told Hitler that the son had been decorated in Poland for bravery and was shocked at how his mother had been treated. Hearing this story, Hitler pronounced such events intolerable. Either all half-Jews must immediately leave the Wehrmacht, Hitler stated, or the government must protect their Jewish parents. Hitler did not want to protect full Jews, so he ordered the half-Jews discharged.[3] The Nazis felt *Mischlinge* were overly ambitious to distinguish themselves in battle to protect themselves and their families. The Nazis did not like this attitude. Klemperer wrote that from what he had heard, the half-Jews had been dismissed because the army wanted to advance these brave soldiers, an idea that the Party would never tolerate.[4]

On 28 March 1940, Brack's deputy in Section IIb of the KdF, Oberbereichsleiter Werner Blankenburg, responsible for *Mischling* applications, discussed the problems that half-Jewish soldiers' families experienced. He wrote Hitler's army adjutant major, Gerhard Engel, that Jewish parents could not go into cinemas with their soldier sons; they had problems with ration cards, despite their sons' military service; and they lost their jobs. Blankenburg complained that such treatment could affect troop morale. Furthermore, he explained, the half-Jews could turn into a liability. If they became enemies of the state, then they could use their military training and possible military secrets against the Nazis. Therefore, Blankenburg supported the proposal to discharge all half-Jews.[5] If the half-Jews were not discharged, then Blankenburg argued it was important to know what residual benefit such combat service would have for their parents. Blankenburg informed Engel that the chief of the KdF, Philipp Bouhler, was willing to meet Keitel if he wanted. If such a meeting did take place, Blankenburg also recommended to have Lammers there. Blankenburg felt that the total number of half-Jews would play a vital role in what the regime would decide.[6] That number was still not forthcoming, although Hitler had ordered a *Mischling* census on 16 January. It remains unknown if OKW ever gave Hitler an answer. The Wehrmacht adjutants shared Blankenburg's concerns, and consequently they welcomed the KdF's willingness to take the initiative to get the half-Jews discharged.[7]

On 8 April 1940, under Hitler's direct order, OKW issued the directive requiring the dismissal of half-Jews and soldiers married to Jews and half-Jews. Keitel signed the decree.[8] This order was passed down the chain of command to the company level.[9] Blankenburg believed that his letter of 28 March 1940 about *Mischling* problems influenced Hitler to dismiss the half-Jews.[10] Blankenburg may have influenced Hitler, but more likely Hitler had already decided to discharge the half-Jews on 26 March after hearing about the Mettenheims' problems.

This order explicitly stated that exceptional half-Jews could apply for exemptions. Hitler allowed half-Jews who filed such petitions to remain with their units until the authorities and he decided their cases. *Mischling* officers who had received Hitler's clemency before the 8 April decree could remain at their posts. Hitler allowed quarter-Jews and men married to quarter-Jews to stay, but they could not become NCOs or officers unless they had Hitler's approval, which they would only receive by demonstrating exceptional service in battle. Furthermore, quarter-Jews and men married to quarter-Jews who were retired NCOs, officers, or civil servants could be reinstated only if their talents proved absolutely indispensable. Hitler would personally decide on all applications.[11] Anyone less than "25 percent Jewish" was not officially affected by the laws. But that did not mean men less than 25 percent Jewish were left alone. For example, when brothers Tycho and Prosper Du-Bois Reymond tried to become officers, the Wehrmacht rejected them because they were "12.5 percent Jewish."[12]

On 20 April 1940, OKH passed on the OKW decree from 8 April. OKH repeated the definitions of a Jew, half-Jew, and quarter-Jew and reinforced the edict that every soldier had to sign an ancestry declaration. As is often the case with *Mischling* policy, it is important not to confuse formal pronouncement with results. Because of war preparations, the Wehrmacht did not have enough time or personnel to locate, document, and discharge all half-Jews then serving. The Wehrmacht was unable to discharge any half-Jews who served with units that had invaded Norway and Denmark on 9 April 1940. Most in units preparing for the French campaign also remained untouched because of bureaucratic mishaps or the secrecy surrounding the plans for the attack on France and the fact that many were not known to be half-Jews.[13]

Not all who remained did so because of the Wehrmacht's inability to locate them — many units simply did not enforce the new decree. And, of course, when many half-Jews were asked to sign ancestry declarations, they simply lied about their racial backgrounds.[14] For instance, Obergefreiter Heinrich Bamberger's sergeant called him to headquarters and asked him whether he was a half- or quarter-Jew. Bamberger lied and said he was a quarter-Jew. Then the sergeant had him sign a statement declaring he was a 25 percent Jew. The Wehrmacht would tolerate his presence, but he could not be promoted or receive medals even if he deserved them.[15] Moreover, the document warned Bamberger that if he gave the army any reason to take disciplinary action against him, he would be subject to more severe punishment than normal. Bamberger wrote, "I signed the document and returned to my company, and I was totally depressed and downcast. I almost cried."[16] Had Bamberger's commander looked into his case, he would have found that Bamberger had lied. After Bamberger signed his ancestry declaration, his unit dropped the issue. Some half-Jews, if asked about their background, simply told their commanders that they were Aryans, and most officers did not doubt them. Unlike Bamberger, unless someone researched their ancestry, these *Mischlinge* were left alone and remained in their billets.

Why did many units not properly enforce Hitler's decree? Several half-Jews remained because their commanders wanted to keep experienced soldiers in their units. Interviewees stated repeatedly how their commanders expressed total disregard for the April laws, and thus, they stayed with their companies. For example, Obergefreiter Horst Geitner, whom the Luftwaffe had honored with a position on Göring's special guard battalion, always feared what would happen to him if someone discovered he was a half-Jew. When he told his company commander, First Lieutenant Ladach, about his concerns, Ladach just winked at him and said he had nothing to fear. Geitner remained at his post. Later, while fighting on the Russian front, he was the first in his battalion to receive the EKII for his bravery, although the officer who gave him this award knew about his ancestry.[17]

Many interviewees have described how their superiors explained that they knew about their Jewish past but respected their abilities and would allow them to stay. Their commanders often warned them not to do anything careless that would draw the attention of the authorities. Some commanders simply said they would discuss the matter after the campaign in France, which seemed a much more pressing concern than the new racial decrees. For example, Dieter Fischer's commander decided he would ignore Hitler's decree until hostilities ceased. This extra time before Fischer's inevitable discharge would give him the opportunity to distinguish himself and thereby help his plea for equality. Maybe commanders like Fischer's also held on to their half-Jewish soldiers because they wanted the unit to perform as well as possible in the upcoming battle, and the more trained men they had familiar with each other, the better chance they had of achieving their objectives. The commanders may also have felt loyalty to soldiers who had trained for months or years in their unit. When one works with a group of soldiers during trying circumstances, that group usually becomes a close-knit surrogate family.[18]

After the quick victory in France, commanders no longer could say they needed the half-Jews to fight or claim they were too busy fighting a war to deal with the matter. Fischer's commander had to discharge him. When Fischer left his unit, all his comrades and unit commander accompanied him to the train station to see him off.[19] No matter how strong the bonds of comradeship or how clearly the commanders saw the common humanity of half-Jews, after the war was over, most obeyed the law to dismiss them. Surprisingly, almost all half-Jews in this study describe their officers as sympathetic to their situation and say they were treated decently.[20] Karl-Arnd Techel said, "My officer told me that I was a good soldier and that he did not care that I was a half-Jew. He told me that such a term was only used by that 'madman Hitler.'"[21] Half-Jew Gefreiter Otto Lüderitz claimed that "my superiors were incredibly nice to me and made sure that I received the EKII. I'm still amazed at how kind and understanding they were with my situation."[22]

Many officers asked the half-Jews whether they wanted to apply for permission to stay in the Wehrmacht. Most opted to apply for clemency. The few who did not were immediately released. For instance, Gerd zu Klampen was asked in June 1940 whether he wanted to remain in the Wehrmacht. He refused, and a few days later was sent home.[23]

Since the racial status of many was unknown, commanding officers had to rely on these soldiers to answer questions honestly. Sometimes officers asked all half-Jews in the company to step forward during roll calls or report later. The roll call technique allowed several half-Jews to lie about their situation. In this situation, lying was as simple as standing still. Many were honest during roll calls, but several lied, afraid they would be persecuted if they reported themselves. Unteroffizier Hans Günzel said, "When our sergeant asked for half-Jews to step forward during our roll call, I remained still and thought, 'God help me.' Another man reported himself. We never saw him again."[24] Others were identified when asked to sign an "ancestry declaration," which in most cases simply stated that a person was either a non-Jew or Jew. Some were honest and wrote "half-Jewish" or told the bureaucrats that they could not truthfully sign the document. Yet, just as in the roll call situation, many "truthfully" signed that they were non-Jews according to their understanding and, thus, remained in their units.

Half-Jews reacted in many ways to the 8 April decree. Some felt lucky about the discharge order. Unterarzt Robert Braun remembered feeling "happy that I didn't have to serve that idiot anymore."[25] Most felt loyal to Germany despite their disgust at having to serve under Hitler's command. Unteroffizier Karl-Arnd Techel, who had parachuted onto Crete, said, "I felt honored to be a paratrooper [an elite branch of the Luftwaffe] and serve

Germany, but I hated the fact that I had to serve Hitler to do so. When I was discharged, I no longer had to struggle with this dilemma."[26] Some hated military life. When Schütze[27] Joachim Le Coutre's girlfriend informed him about the decree, which she had read in a newspaper, he immediately told his company commander his situation and demanded his discharge. He abhorred the Wehrmacht and thought his officers were "big assholes." The officer replied, "Everybody could come here with such a story and say he wants to go home." Le Coutre then told him to look into the matter, and a few days later he was discharged.[28] Le Coutre was not alone in reporting his ancestry. Others did the same thing, although for different reasons. They felt tired of not being promoted, tired of war, tired of being treated like second-class citizens, and tired of serving a cause many did not believe in. So some welcomed the new racial decree.

Many have said that their comrades congratulated them on being able to go home.[29] Some envied the half-Jews this freedom.[30] One comrade, who was a quarter-Jew, wished Wolfgang Spier luck and remarked wistfully, "If only I could've had one more Jewish grandmother!"[31] Peter Gaupp had grown up with many of his fellow soldiers and considered his company and comrades "family." They knew he was half-Jewish, but apparently, most did not seem bothered by it.[32] Gaupp sought permission to stay in the army but was rejected. When Gaupp left, his comrades threw him a party.[33] However, not every comrade of a discharged half-Jew was as friendly as the men in Gaupp's unit. After Gefreiter Michael-Christoph Salinger's reason for his discharge became known, a comrade, who he thought was a friend, approached him, spat in his face, and called him a "Jewish pig." When Salinger was asked how he felt, he replied, "Strangely enough, I was not offended. . . . At that moment, I thought, 'I hope there's no bacteria in his spit,' and then I thought, 'Forgive them, for they know not what they do.'"[34]

Fortunately, Salinger's case was rare. The majority of *Mischlinge* recalled their commanders and comrades as being sympathetic when their discharge order was issued. Unterarzt Robert Braun remembered his commander calling him "one of the best soldiers" as he left.[35] Some commanders even apologized for discharging their half-Jews. For example, Gerd Grimm's officer treated him with respect and told him he regretted what he had to do, but the Wehrmacht required him to discharge half-Jews.[36] Most still think fondly of their comrades, although they hated war and military life. Fellow soldiers had usually treated them respectfully. When Friedrich Schlesinger's comrades started talking about the Jews, one of them said, "You know, there's something wrong with the Jews. But not you, Schlesinger. You're all right."[37]

Many commanders wrote a positive recommendation for their discharged half-Jews.[38] A standard recommendation read as follows: "Hans Cornely, a *Mischling* first degree, wasn't promoted because of his ancestry, although he was a decent and dutiful soldier. His Jewish ancestry also prevented him from being awarded the EKII."[39]

A half-Jew's discharge could be traumatic. A few suffered severe humiliation. Wolfgang Jordan's commander singled him out as the entire company waited at attention and explained that Jordan was being discharged because he was racially inferior. The commander completed the paperwork, and Jordan left his unit a few hours later, devastated by the public humiliation.[40] Richard Riess was sent home to Vienna. There he first had to go to an SS office, where they measured his head and other body parts. The SS then issued him an official half-Jew certificate. Riess was scared. He had seen the SS blow the heads off black French colonial POWs and feared what the SS would do to him, another "racially inferior" person. The SS merely told him that he was unworthy to serve in the Wehrmacht and sent him out saying, "*Mazel tov!*"[41] Karl-Heinz Scheffler saw the treatment of black POWs as an indication of what half-Jews should expect.[42] Many had witnessed the way Polish Jewry had been treated in 1939 and feared they would be treated similarly. A few half-Jews did not survive the announcement of their racial status long enough to be formally discharged. When Wilhelm Vielberth reported his racial status, his officer pulled out his pistol and shot Vielberth dead.[43]

After the April 1940 decree, some officers worried that they might be punished for having half-Jews among their troops. They saw the presence of half-Jews as a threat to their prospects for advancement. Other officers felt betrayed when they learned that soldiers under their command were *Mischlinge*. These officers often threatened them with disciplinary action because they believed they had been deceitful. However, in most cases, the officers found that the soldiers had honestly reported their ancestry. The authorities, and not the half-Jews, had overlooked, concealed, or omitted this information. For example, Gefreiter Heinz Bleicher was called to his company commander sometime during the fall of 1942. The commander yelled at him, "Why haven't you told us that you're a Jew?" Bleicher calmly explained that he had always written "*Mischling* first degree" in all his papers. The commander, not being satisfied with his answer, had Bleicher brought before a court because he, as a "Jewish person," had been training Aryans. After the hearings, Bleicher was absolved of all wrongdoing because his superiors, and not he, had failed to follow the regulations. Bleicher had not known that half-Jews were not allowed to serve. Soon thereafter, the army discharged Bleicher and he returned home.[44]

Later, Party or Gestapo officials (or both) identified many *Mischlinge* when they found out they were the sons or grandsons (serving in the Wehrmacht) of Jews they had deported or put in jail. Most of these soldiers were not found until late 1941 and early 1942 when the deportations started in earnest. Apparently, not much coordination between the Wehrmacht and Party existed.

Despite such complications, many half-Jews wanted to remain in the Wehrmacht. They claimed that on the one hand, they wanted to leave, but on the other hand, they felt that in the Wehrmacht they were safe from Nazi persecution. They maintain that only in the Wehrmacht could one escape the Nazis. Funker[45] Ferdinand Lichtwitz wrote, "In the army everything was different. In the army, you were . . . guarded [i.e., from the Gestapo]."[46] Many knew that the only way to improve their lot was to remain soldiers and get a medal. For example, on 6 August 1940, Dieter Bergmann wrote that he longed to prove himself in a great battle and show he was worthy to serve the fatherland.[47] Many distinguished themselves in battle, and thousands received the Iron Cross.[48] Sometimes the desire to distinguish themselves ended in tragedy; many *Mischlinge* went beyond the call of duty to earn medals that cost them their lives. Out of the 967 half-Jewish soldiers documented in this study, 80 died in battle,[49] and out of the 607 quarter-Jewish soldiers, 76 died in battle.

Many half-Jews remained soldiers to help their families. Unteroffizier Egon Bahr claimed that because he was in uniform, he was able to obtain normal ration cards for his Jewish mother, who had to wear the Jewish star and feared leaving her home.[50] Since the government prohibited Jews from eating certain foods rich in nutrients, such as fish, milk, and poultry, and limited where and when Jews could shop,[51] Bahr's efforts on his Jewish mother's behalf helped maintain her health. When on leave in Munich, Walter Hamburger would visit the Gestapo and Gauleitung[52] dressed in his uniform to ensure that his parents would be allowed to remain in their apartment and that his father would not be persecuted. According to Hamburger, his efforts helped his family. Hamburger also described a time when the Gestapo did not arrest his father because when they entered the house, his mother pointed to a picture of him in uniform. They challenged the Gestapo, who were about to arrest the father of a soldier. When a Gestapo official asked his mother how that was possible, she answered that they "must ask the Führer" to find out. The Gestapo then left.[53] Several have claimed that they thought the only way to safeguard their Jewish loved ones was to serve and receive honors. Helmut Krüger believed that by receiving the EKII, he had secured protection for his siblings and Jewish mother.[54]

Finally, some fought, even gave their lives, because they believed in the war. They got caught up in the excitement of victory. On 1 September 1939, half-Jew Dietmar Brücher wrote in his diary, "The old injustice of Versailles must be erased."[55] Quarter-Jew Hans-Christian Lankes wrote in his diary in late September 1939, "[T]he most beautiful report today is that German troops are in Warsaw!"[56] On 9 June 1940, Unteroffizier Bergmann wrote in his diary, "We're conquering! The greatest slaughter of all times ended on 4 June."[57] Bergmann wrote on 2 August 1940 that he "believed with my whole heart" that Germany would win the war. He continued, "I must believe in this victory, because I've sacrificed so much for it. I also believe in it because of my burning love for the Fatherland."[58] Many *Mischlinge* wanted to fight, and knew they might die, just as their forefathers had done for Germany in the past. They fought to return Germany to her place of honor among nations and felt proud to be soldiers. Bergmann seemed to believe Nazi propaganda when he wrote on 22 August 1940 that England was controlled by "Jewish capitalistic pigs *(jüdische Kapitalistenschweine)*."[59] As historian Marion Kaplan wrote, "[M]any who disliked or opposed the Nazis were confused or infected by the atmosphere."[60] Bergmann, like many *Mischlinge*, did not see himself as Jewish and was caught up in the war fever. That was the difficult position many *Mischlinge* found themselves in — they were German and felt personally involved in Germany's war. Some felt excited about battle, which is quite common among young men. For example, half-Jew Unteroffizier Emil Lux said that it was "a great feeling to be a great warrior *(Kämpfer)*." Lux described how exhilarating it was to see how the Russians ran away when they engaged them in battle.[61] Dieter Bergmann said, "[A]s a soldier, you felt powerful. You felt strong and German. You could threaten people."[62] In April 1941, when Luftwaffe paratrooper Karl-Arnd Techel, a half-Jew, received live ammunition he wrote in his diary, "It's finally here [the attack of Crete]. The time that we've waited for so long. The deployment! The 'jump' against the enemy!"[63] Many not only felt that it was their duty to serve, but also found themselves caught up in the enthusiasm of going to war. Some residing in foreign countries when war erupted in 1939 quickly returned to Germany to enlist.[64] They did not want to miss the fight. A few even did everything they could to return to Germany once taken into captivity. For example, once the pocket battleship *Graf Spee* was scuttled after the Battle of River Plate, chief gunnery officer and half-Jew Paul Ascher was interned in Argentina. He soon escaped and returned to Germany. In 1941, he became the fleet operations officer on the battleship *Bismarck*.[65]

Most did not find their situation paradoxical until later, usually after the war in France when the Wehrmacht dismissed many of them. In August 1940, Bergmann started to recognize his true situation: "I cannot be entirely optimistic about the outcome of the war. The Nazis want to get rid of me."[66] Bergmann knew that the Nazis had many reasons to do away with him; namely, he was not only Jewish but also a homosexual. In 1940, his family started to experience obvious signs of discrimination. Although his brother, Schütze Ulrich Bergmann, had died in battle on 18 May 1940, his family's racial status prevented them from being as honored as others who had fallen sons and brothers. Ulrich's commander had claimed that they had to keep his name out of the local newspapers because of his "racial mistake."[67]

Another example of this lack of respect shown to the family of a fallen Landser happened to Hans Meissinger and his mother Rosa when they met a comrade of his dead brother, Ernst. The "friend," Plorin, wanted to pay his respects to his comrade's family. Plorin praised Ernst for his camaraderie and described how he had bravely died in battle. During the conversation, Frau Meissinger told Plorin it was agonizing to have lost her son in "Hitler's army" because she was a Jew. Plorin had not known this about Ernst. Shocked, he cursed the Jews as the cause of all that had befallen Germany. She tried to contradict him by describing her honorable brothers, World

War I veterans. Hans and his mother then left "the scene of that explosive encounter." Frau Meissinger broke down and cried. Later, Plorin's wife called Frau Meissinger and taunted her, saying that she would soon be deported.[68] With each passing day, any illusions that half-Jews may have had before April 1940 about their military service helping them were slowly eaten away by the proliferation of anti-Jewish measures. Yet, during this atmosphere of growing intolerance, many still remained soldiers.

Hitler seemed to understand the difficulty of locating and discharging *Mischlinge* during the war in France. When Schmundt informed the victorious Führer that most half-Jews had remained with their units during the French campaign and that many had been decorated, Hitler did not erupt in anger. He certainly was not prepared for this, but believed there was nothing they could do about it.[69] These men had served, but they were now to be found and dismissed.

After the war in France, many half-Jewish veterans felt the government was obligated to honor them as citizens and protect their families. They were sadly mistaken, but their experiences as soldiers bolstered their will to fight for equal rights. Even Hitler agreed somewhat with their position. On 2 October 1940 Schmundt wrote to chief of the KdF, Philipp Bouhler, saying that Hitler had said that half-Jewish veterans had rendered the Reich and the National Socialist state a great service, even if only by accident. Hitler admitted that many had been decorated, and he agreed that second-class treatment of them was unworthy of the Nazi state. As a result, Hitler told Schmundt that such decorated soldiers were to be immediately declared *deutschblütig*. Hitler stated that this *Ausnahmebehandlung* (exceptional treatment) applied only to *Mischlinge;* the soldiers' relatives would not enjoy any residual benefit.[70]

This Hitler decree was repeated in various ministries. For example, on 18 December 1940, Blankenburg wrote Lösener that according to Hitler, *Mischlinge* who had received combat medals were to be declared *deutschblütig*.[71] In addition, Hitler ordered that these brave *Mischlinge* should have no problems with their university studies.[72] But in practice, many courageous *Mischlinge* did not receive any form of clemency.

From 8 April of 1940 to December 1940, the Wehrmacht discharged thousands of half-Jews.[73] One officer in OKH has stated that over seventy thousand were discharged.[74] Unfortunately, the exact total cannot be ascertained. That thousands were being discharged did not seem to bother OKW, still celebrating the quick victory over France, a feat that Germany had been unable to accomplish during the four years of World War I. As of June 1940, the Wehrmacht had almost 5.8 million soldiers.[75] The loss of thousands if not tens of thousands of men apparently did not worry the military command. Now that the war on the continent was over, many felt it would just be a matter of time before England surrendered. Immediately after the French campaign, the Wehrmacht started to downsize anyway.[76]

Officially, most in the Wehrmacht accepted their discharge although they had served loyally. Had OKW known what awaited Germany in Russia, they might have protested the dismissal of thousands of well-trained, battle-hardened troops. Even so, no documents have yet surfaced that indicate the Wehrmacht lobbied for the return of these soldiers.

A protest against the discharge of thousands of half-Jews was unlikely to have any effect during the summer of 1940. Generals, many of whom had just received another promotion,[77] did not openly protest on moral grounds, especially after Hitler had won one of the greatest battles of history[78] and "stood on the pinnacle of his popularity in Germany."[79] "Humanitarian" arguments did not impress Hitler. As army chief of the general staff, General Franz Halder, said during the Nuremberg trials, "The thing that most impressed me about Hitler was the complete absence of any ethical or moral obligation."[80] Hitler clearly did not foster an intellectual climate that valued morality. With their official dismissal from the armed forces, half-Jews took one step closer to sharing the fate of full Jews. The Wehrmacht turned a blind eye.

On the other hand, the armed forces found it impossible to discharge all half-Jews or to prevent their conscription. Since the armed forces had never dealt with *Mischlinge,* it did not have the experience, the personnel, or the time to check the ancestry of every soldier before they entered the Wehrmacht. It was nearly unthinkable to research the family trees of everyone serving before 1940. Hitler had created a witch-hunt, a task the Wehrmacht seemed neither overly enthusiastic about nor capable of carrying out, especially during war times. Over 50 percent of the half-Jews documented in this study were still serving in 1941. Many were later identified, and several would never be located.

During 1941, the Wehrmacht repeated the 1940 decrees to remind the bureaucrats how to deal with *Mischlinge.* Perhaps the Wehrmacht did so because people were perplexed by the laws and did not enforce them. The Luftgaukommando 6[81] issued the following decree on 8 January 1941: "[T]he promotion of half-Jews to Gefreite and higher ranks is prohibited because . . . half-Jews who are still found in the Luftwaffe were already to have been discharged . . . and they are not to be drafted anymore."[82] The document also outlined policies for quarter-Jews that differed little from what Hitler had specified in September of 1940.

Many Nazis viewed *Mischlinge* to be just as "unknowingly" dangerous as Jews, if not more so, because they had "German blood." Many wanted to treat half-Jews as Jews. It seemed that the only redeeming factor for German half-Jews was that they had half "German blood," making them still "half good." Lösener repeatedly made this point with members of the Reichskanzlei and the Party to deter them from exterminating half-Jews along with the Jews.[83] In spring 1941 when Göring heard about the possibility that the government was going to treat half-Jews as Jews, he wrote Stuckart not to make any decisions about half-Jews during the war.[84] In February 1941, Field Marshal Keitel met with Hitler after Keitel found out that the head of the department that dealt with the Jewish question within the Reich Security Head Office, SS-Obersturmbannführer Eichmann, wanted to include half-Jews in the *Endlösung*.[85] The anxious Keitel argued against it, stating that many quarter-Jewish soldiers would be burdened if their parents were treated as Jews. For troop morale, this action needed to be avoided.[86] Keitel's reaction showed that he believed that such a policy at this stage was irrational. But Eichmann was not alone in his desire to classify half-Jews as Jews. On 5 April 1941, Generaloberstabsarzt Dr. Anton Waldmann, head of the army's medical corps, wrote in the magazine *Deutsches Ärzteblatt* that "half-Jews must be treated like full-Jews."[87] In March 1941, Dr. Walter Groß, chief of the Party's Race-Political Office, said it was necessary to equate half-Jews with Jews because they were just as undesirable. He argued that if they did not eliminate them, then undesirable Jewish racial elements would remain in Europe. If his plan was adopted, Groß claimed, then the number of quarter-Jews could be kept to an absolute minimum.[88] During his postwar trial, Eichmann said that in September 1941, the SS debated classifying German half-Jews as Jews. However, the army blocked the measure because of the reaction quarter-Jewish soldiers would have when the government started to treat their parents like Jews "in the full sense of the word." "The matter went right up to Hitler himself," Eichmann said, "and he rejected the proposal for widening the scope of the law."[89] Hitler did this against the counsel of many advisers.

But such opposition did not kill the issue. The debate resurfaced often before the end of the Third Reich. Perhaps many SS and Party personnel acted aggressively because they saw how a *Mischling*'s service helped his Jewish family, thereby causing confusion among the authorities and more paperwork for them. Also, many Party and SS officials simply wanted half-Jews exterminated along with the full Jews. However, certain people in the RMI under Lösener's leadership and in the armed forces continued to rally against SS and Party moves to treat half-Jews as Jews. In December 1941, Lösener argued again that redefining what constitutes a Jew would only create more difficulties for an already overburdened bureaucracy, exacerbate the confusion surrounding the Jewish question, and unnecessarily affect thousands of families.[90] The fact that many half-Jews served in the Wehrmacht made finding a solution to this problem more complicated.

Military service often benefited Jewish relatives. In March 1941, Hitler issued a decree protecting the parents living in a privileged mixed marriage whose only son had died in action. Hitler believed that the son's "hero-death" granted his parents special privileges.[91] This document proves that privileged mixed marriages were not enjoying the protection they had in the past and that a half-Jew's military service protected his parents, in this case, only when he died and had no siblings. Interestingly, Hitler issued this decree in March 1941, almost one year after he had ordered half-Jews out of the Wehrmacht. One wonders why Hitler gave families of fallen half-Jews additional protection when these men, most of whom had died between May and June 1940 in France, died while serving illegally. As late as 1945, the Nazi bureaucrats seemed to honor this decree. For example, in 1945 when a Gestapo agent came to arrest Marianne Gärtner, a Jew, she showed him a letter from the army announcing the death of her son, Rainer. The man turned his back on her and said, "Your son has saved your life." He left without her.[92]

Divorced or widowed parents, formerly protected by a mixed marriage, sometimes also received clemency because of a son's service. For instance, Jewish widow Olga Mühlbacher heard in 1943 that a Jewish parent of a fallen soldier no longer had to wear the Jewish star.[93] It seems that during the first part of the war, Jews who had Aryan husbands or half-Jewish sons in the Wehrmacht were granted certain privileges, and if their spouse or child died in battle, they were given the same support an Aryan wife or mother received.[94] However, although Frau Mühlbacher benefited from her son's service, she did not feel that her protection would last long: "I know that it was all for nothing to rely on the war performance of my son. It wouldn't have helped. . . . There was only one way to help myself — not to have been a full-Jew. . . . My son's application for an *Arisierung*[95] has been submitted a long time ago; however, that is a mistake if I am deported to Theresienstadt!"[96] Frau Mühlbacher had an amazing presentiment of the coming horror. Although a half-Jew's service may have helped protect a parent, it would have stopped had Hitler won or prolonged the war.

Hitler must have bewildered several Nazi hard-liners when he allowed Jewish mothers and fathers to send their sons to war, and afterward, protected these parents because of their son's service. But as Hitler had reminded a group of his generals on 30 March 1941 after discussing the coming war with Russia, "I cannot demand that my generals should understand my orders, but I demand that they follow them."[97] Hitler held his high-ranking Party members and government officials to the same standard. When Hitler ordered his government to treat *Mischlinge* a certain way, he expected his government to obey, no matter how contradictory his new policies seemed. Hitler often displayed such erratic behavior, not just with racial policy, but with military, political, and economic policy as well.[98]

As the Parteikanzlei, Reichskanzlei, KdF, RMI, and OKW processed *Mischling* applications for exemptions, it became evident that many half-Jews were still serving without Hitler's approval. When reprimanded for allowing these *Mischlinge* to serve, most units claimed that they had had no idea that they had these Jewish soldiers. In response, on 2 April 1941, OKH ordered that soldiers who had not filled out their "ancestry declarations" must sign them as an attempt to identify remaining half-Jews.[99] As before, the military authorities relied on *Mischlinge*'s honesty. One can only imagine the flood of papers that poured in through all levels of the Wehrmacht. Tens of thousands, if not millions, of soldiers had to be called into their commanders' offices, sometimes for the second time, to sign papers declaring that they were of "Aryan descent" or "not Jewish" (or both). Many half-Jews were identified this way because they answered honestly. Obergefreiter Wolfgang Voigt was the first in his unit to see this order because he worked in the officers' duty hut. He did not know what to do. After several days of contemplation, he went to sign the ancestry declaration. As he filled out the form, his first sergeant[100] was watching over his shoulder. At the sight of the words "half-Jew," the sergeant burst into tears. Voigt does not know why his sergeant reacted this way. Perhaps he cried because his clerk had to leave or because he knew that Voigt's future looked bleak. In May 1941, Voigt received his discharge papers and returned home.[101]

Most *Mischlinge* claim they answered truthfully because they feared what would happen to them or their families if they were caught lying. Yet, once again, a war launched in the Balkans on 6 April 1941 prevented the Nazis from tracking down several *Mischlinge* for months. Many half-Jews say that during the spring of 1941, a year after Hitler issued his April decree of 1940, they still did not know that they were not allowed to serve. Many had been illegally promoted and decorated in the meantime. During a summer morning inspection in 1941, Unteroffizier Felix Bruck's company commander informed his men that one of them had betrayed and misused the army. He had learned about Bruck's ancestry. When the army discharged Bruck a few days later, they not only forced him to leave but also retroactively took away his rank, claiming that they should have never promoted him in the first place.[102]

Mischling *Life and Policy, 1941–1943*

By 22 June 1941, however, a large majority of the half-Jews who had entered France in 1940 with the Wehrmacht had been discharged. Interestingly, the Kriegsmarine was two to three years behind relative to the army and Luftwaffe in discharging its *Mischlinge*, although all services apparently issued the same decrees. Allegedly, Raeder prevented some racial laws from affecting the Kriegsmarine because of his relationship with Hitler.[103] The only place in the army where one might find a place of refuge was in the Deutsches Afrika-Korps (DAK) under the leadership of the "Desert Fox," Field Marshal Erwin Rommel. According to this study's files, his half-Jews were not as affected by the racial laws as most others serving on the European continent.[104] It remains unclear whether Rommel was directly responsible for this. According to quarter-Jew Captain Horst von Oppenfeld, the staff officer to Colonel Claus von Stauffenberg, Rommel did not concern himself with the racial decrees. Although Rommel never acted on behalf of Oppenfeld personally, Oppenfeld never experienced any trouble because of his ancestry while he served in the DAK.[105] However, this study's research is not conclusive on Rommel's DAK. According to historian Beate Meyer, Nazi authorities searched for one soldier in the DAK, but before they could apprehend him, he had become a POW.[106] Perhaps Rommel failed to enforce the order to discharge half-Jews because he was unaware of it. Rommel spent two years fighting a war in the desert, where he, unlike many generals, was given freedom to conduct operations largely without Hitler's interference. Many viewed the African campaign as a sideshow,[107] especially after the invasion of Russia in 1941. Thus, it is more likely that orders based on racial policies never reached Rommel, rather than that he actively decided not to enforce them. Although Rommel knew about the persecution of the Jews, he seemed not to allow Nazi racist policy to affect the running of his DAK. Oppenfeld believes that Rommel blocked orders to have Jews in their area of operations deported.[108] In June 1942, Hitler had supposedly ordered Rommel through the OKW to exterminate all German Jews (political refugees taken prisoner who were fighting on the side of the free French). However, Rommel apparently ignored this order and turned the prisoners over to the Italians, "who treated them like all other prisoners of war."[109]

Most half-Jews discharged from 1940 to 1941 returned home. At first, they felt scared about what would happen. Richard Riess felt as though he suddenly faced what he labeled a "great vacuum" and was unsure of his fate.[110] Most quickly found work or studied until they entered Organization Todt's forced labor camps in 1944. Hans Mühlbacher and Hans Meissinger worked as rocket scientists.[111] Mühlbacher, already an engineer, worked at Peenemünde on the guided rocket program designed to sink enemy ships (HS293294).[112] Meissinger worked at the DVL (Deutsche Versuchsanstalt für Luftfahrt)[113] on guidance and control theory of aircraft and on air-to-ground missiles.[114] Kurt Hohenemser worked in an armament factory. He remembered playing the game Battleship with his coworkers to pass the time.[115] Helmut Krüger built U-boat bunkers at Brest. He even had a group of forced Jewish laborers under his control.[116] Many started to live a normal life again after their discharge. Besides studying or working, some went skiing, played tennis, had girlfriends, and socialized.[117] Many encountered uncomfortable situations when military police, as well as common Germans, challenged them as to why they were not in uniform. But by and large, they avoided any further trouble by telling those who questioned them truthfully that they were members of the reserves[118] as recorded in their military service books *(Wehrpaß).*[119] Most half-Jews' service books had *"n.z.v."* (*nicht zu verwenden* — not to be used) written on their discharge page with a citation to the law of 8 or 20 April 1940 dismissing half-Jews from active service. Some had *wehrunwürdig* (unworthy of military service) written in their service books. Nonetheless, discharge papers did not necessarily protect a half-Jew from the SS. After the Gestapo arrested a half-Jew for suspicion of going AWOL,[120] he tried to explain to them that half-Jews could not serve. The SS did not believe him. They sent him to Theresienstadt.[121] However, this was the exception rather than the rule.

In May 1941, Hitler turned his attention to the sexual behavior of *Mischlinge.* Although Hitler had a war in the Balkans and one coming up with Russia, he desired, as State Secretary Pfundtner reported on 7 May 1941, an extension of the racial laws to prohibit sexual relations between Aryans and half-Jews.[122] Possibly Hitler turned his attention to private matters of *Mischlinge* in connection with his sharpening of policy against full Jews. For instance, on 7 June 1941, Lammers informed Bormann, head of the Parteikanzlei, that the Führer wanted no more Jews in Germany after the war.[123] Hitler had no misgivings about including parents of half-Jewish soldiers in the Holocaust. It was just a question of timing.

The Wehrmacht's willingness to work with the Party and SS foreshadowed a murderous future for Jews and *Mischlinge.* Already in March of 1941, Keitel issued a Wehrmacht directive that Reichsführer-SS Heinrich Himmler had full responsibility to prepare the political administrations in conquered areas. Keitel knew that the directive meant the murder of thousands of defenseless people, especially Jews. On 28 April 1941, Heydrich signed an agreement with General Eduard Wagner, army quartermaster, that the SD[124] would operate behind army lines when Germany invaded Russia.[125] The war with Russia was to be ideological. A guideline approved by OKH and sent out to the Wehrmacht services in mid-May 1941 explained how the armed forces should act in the upcoming war: "This struggle demands ruthless and energetic action against *Bolshevik agitators, guerrillas, saboteurs, Jews,* and the complete elimination of every active or passive resistance."[126] The Wehrmacht also ordered that all Soviet political officers (commissars) should be exterminated when captured because they were the "exponents of the Jewish-Bolshevik world outlook" and not accepted as "genuine soldiers."[127] These military directives fell under the "Führer decree" and *Kommissarbefehl* (commissar order) that came into being throughout the spring and summer of 1941.[128] Halder wrote that many in the army felt confused about the Barbarossa[129] plans and the strategic purpose of the war. He started to realize that military objectives might be "subordinated to ideological ones," and the destruction of the Bolshevik system and the extermination of the Jews would take priority over the goal of weakening the enemy's will to fight.[130] Halder was right. However, such conduct of war did not encounter any opposition from military leaders[131] or prevent Halder from turning Hitler's racial ideology into functioning decrees in preparation for the attack on Russia.[132]

No one in the Wehrmacht officially complained about the "Führer decree" or the *Kommissarbefehl.* General Alfred Jodl, chief of OKW operations and Hitler's principal military adviser,[133] explained that after Hitler's successes in Poland and France, the Führer "required nothing more than the technical support necessary to implement his decisions, and the smooth functioning of the military organization to carry them out."[134] In other words, had anyone complained on moral grounds against these directives, they would not have found Hitler or any high-ranking Nazi officials willing to listen, especially if that complaint came from a *Mischling* officer.

Most Germans had become accustomed to and even accepted Hitler and his regime and, thus, would never have thought to protest against anything Hitler decreed. After his military successes in Poland and France, Hitler had become even more popular among the German population.[135] Most generals did not argue with the Barbarossa plans on political, economic, or ideological grounds. Rather, most were intoxicated with Hitler's triumph. Reflecting the mood of many at this time, Field Marshal von Mackensen wrote a few months after Barbarossa that "as long as God gives me life, in thanks I'll remain faithfully bound to . . . Hitler, the Führer and savior of my German Fatherland. He's the German man I've searched for since 1919."[136] If Germans disapproved of Hitler in 1941, they were either doomed to die or knew they had to keep their mouths shut. If they wanted to live or remain at their posts, they had to adhere to the state's policy.

During the initial weeks of Barbarossa in June and July 1941, ideological goals seemed to override the strategic objectives. Hitler's Einsatzgruppen[137] exterminated Jews at a phenomenal rate during the opening weeks of Barbarossa.[138] Hitler's chief Wehrmacht Adjutant Schmundt claimed on 5 July 1941 that the extermination of Jews was part of "a necessary mopping up operation."[139] Schmundt wrote his friend, Irmgard Böhrne, on 11 July 1941, "Thank God we attacked the Asiatic East before they attacked us. We're saving Western culture." Then on 20 October 1941, he wrote her again, telling her that they fought for a new Europe against "Jewish anarchy."[140]

More Jews died in the first month of Barbarossa than in all of the previous eight years in Germany.[141] Without the Wehrmacht's help, the SS would not have been able to murder so many. In September 1941, Keitel continued to help the SS by ordering replacements for Jews who worked in the General Government so these Jews could be deported.[142] On 21 October 1941, Hitler explained that by exterminating this "pest [the Jews]," he would render humanity a great service.[143] Yet, during this slaughter of Jews, Hitler made some surprising decrees for *Mischlinge*. On 10 July 1941, Hitler announced that quarter-Jews would become "German-blooded" citizens after the war. Manfred Messerschmidt writes that this "tactic" of Hitler's "relieved those *Mischlinge* to some extent."[144] Hitler told some of his associates that he wanted to show battle-tested *Mischlinge* that the Nazis were not ungrateful to brave *Mischling* soldiers.[145] Hitler said he wanted to prevent unpleasant situations both in Germany and abroad created by unhappy decorated veterans. Thus, he intended to treat quarter-Jews as *deutschblütig* after the war. More extraordinarily, Hitler allowed some discharged, "worthy" half-Jews to return to the Wehrmacht and gave them an opportunity to become officers.[146] Influential military or civil connections (or both) played a significant role in selecting those invited to return. Perhaps Hitler also believed these experienced soldiers deserved a second chance to demonstrate their Aryan qualities. This is a good example of the inconsistency in *Mischling* policy.

During the fall of 1941, the Nazis took *Mischlinge* down another evil path when they threw sterilization onto the worktable of extermination.

Sterilization was not a new idea; it had been used throughout the century. The Germans had had a lot of practice with these techniques. In the 1920s, German authorities had sterilized some 225,000 people.[147] The Nazis used and expanded this technique, performing hundreds of thousands of sterilizations throughout the Third Reich.[148] On 2 October 1941, Groß held a discussion with Lammers in which they discussed the sterilization of *Mischlinge*, which they both favored. To implement sterilization, Lammers contended, they needed Wehrmacht cooperation. Lammers felt that Keitel would approve the measure and, thus, would ensure military support. Once agreement was reached, Lammers felt that they could then inform Hitler and ask that the plan be approved.[149]

Throughout 1941, the Nazis placed the destruction of Jews as a top objective but still debated the *Mischling* question. The Nazis did not know whether to treat them as Germans, sterilize them, or annihilate them. But most seemed to forget the connection between Jews and their *Mischling* children when discussing the Jewish question. As the Nazis deported Jews, thousands of *Mischlinge* lost their loved ones. The *Mischlinge* were being pushed further down the Holocaust road. Even the Wehrmacht implemented harsher policy for those *Mischlinge* they still let serve.

Although no official OKW documents surfaced during this study, a few half-Jews were documented as having been drafted by the Wehrmacht into penal battalions. According to these men, the Wehrmacht drafted them for petty offenses or simply because they were *Mischlinge* (or both). For example, Hugo Friedländer was sent to a Frontbewährungseinheit[150] in 1942 because he was a half-Jew. In 1943, he died in action.[151] Half-Jew Heinz Schindler was sent to one of these units because he had offended a Nazi. He lost his arm in battle after only a few months serving in a Bewährungsbataillon[152] in Russia.[153] Most who entered such battalions never came back. These units were known as Himmelfahrtskommandos — "straight to heaven detachments." Beate Meyer documented that a half-Jew became a Bewährungssoldat for two months to prove his worthiness to marry an Aryan.[154] The majority of such soldiers did not survive. Half-Jew Dieter Fischer, who had received Hitler's *Genehmigung,* was sent into Russia in October 1941 in a Bewährungsbataillon with one thousand men. On 9 December, when he was wounded and sent back to the rear echelons, the Bewährungsbataillon had only thirty-five men left.[155]

Friedländer's, Schindler's, and Fischer's experiences were not surprising, considering the great vigor with which German high-ranking officers pursued Hitler's anti-Semitic crusade. Although Keitel had helped his quarter-Jewish friend Colonel Felix Bürkner acquire the *Deutschblütigkeitserklärung*[156] and argued against classifying half-Jews as Jews,[157] he still issued a murderous decree to military commanders on 12 September 1941. It read, in part, that "the struggle against Bolshevism demands ruthless and energetic measures, above all against the Jews, the main carriers of Bolshevism."[158] In order to eliminate the "Jew," Hitler felt that "Jewish Bolshevism" must be annihilated.[159] With such public messages coming from OKW and the Reichskanzlei, many *Mischlinge* wondered why they served when they at the same time were the targets of persecution.

The Wehrmacht asked itself similar questions. To find those serving illegally, on 30 September 1941, OKH again issued a decree that soldiers who had not signed the "Aryan declaration" must do so.[160] Military authorities repeated this order probably because they felt officers were either not getting the government-issued decrees or simply not enforcing them. For example, half-Jews were not banned from reserve police units until October 1942.[161] Often, new laws were not widely known, particularly at the front. For example, when quarter-Jew Hans-Christian Lankes's officer informed him that he was promoting him to officer-cadet, Lankes explained that this was illegal. The officer seemed confused. Lankes spent the next thirty minutes explaining the racial laws to his bewildered officer.[162] Other times, officers knew how to circumvent the racial decrees. Johannes Heckert wrote:

[D]uring the invasion of Russia in 1941, I was promoted to Unteroffizier. Since we didn't receive any mail from Germany, I had no papers to present. And since there was little tolerance in the army for Hitler's persecution of the Jews, my superior told me, "All you have to do is sign a declaration that you only had a great-grandmother who was a Jew, OK?" "Yes sir," I replied. The next day I was an Unteroffizier.[163]

Heckert's superior valued him more than Nazi ideology and knew how to falsify Heckert's papers to retain him. With his commander's help, Heckert no longer had to concern himself with his racial status. Interestingly, in

Heckert's opinion, most in the Wehrmacht did not condone Hitler's persecution of the Jews. As historian Jonathan Steinberg wrote, "Hitler's
rabid anti-Semitism . . . seemed irrelevant to the Wehrmacht."[164] The help
that Aryan officers rendered to countless *Mischlinge* in this study proves
Steinberg's claim. They treated *Mischlinge* in their care surprisingly well.
Many Aryan officers felt the racial decrees were absurd and wasted valuable
time diverting them from their duties. After all, *Mischlinge* were either half-
or three-quarters German.

Another telling document illustrating that the decrees were not being
followed was a letter that Wolfram Günther wrote to his half-brother Konrad
Schenck in January 1943:

> Father tells me that you find it painful that you can no longer be
> promoted. Now you have become a Gefreiter, and that's the first
> step out of the "primordial soup." I congratulate you warmly. You
> must understand a few things regarding further promotions. Under
> normal conditions, we will not be promoted and must deal with that
> fact. That's often bitter and I can tell you that many times during my
> five years of service, I would've gladly thrown everything away and
> given up. However, that's no solution to this problem. You must
> adopt an attitude that allows you to live in this situation without re-
> sisting it or hating life. . . . I also wanted to tell you that, from my
> experience [with the company] with only one exception, all my
> commanders and comrades who knew about my situation not only
> treated me with respect, but were also especially friendly and will-
> ing to help. I've told most of my comrades what my situation is in
> a manner suited to each situation and man. . . . You don't have to be
> afraid to talk about it.

Wolfram added that exceptional courage might lead to more promotions
if the commanding officer was so inclined.[165] Günther's letter explains the
frustration many half-Jews felt with the racial laws. The best coping mechanism Günther found was to have an apathetic attitude. Interestingly, Günther
felt he could trust most Aryans in his unit and even confided his racial background to many of them. Talking about their problems, according to
Günther, was one of the best ways to deal with their situation. Günther's
letter also showed that even in 1943, some half-Jews found ways without

much difficulty to continue serving. For instance, on 13 July 1943, First Lieutenant Schlesremkämber reported that the "intelligent" and "brave" Gefreiter Friedrich Schlesinger had received the EKII and the Assault Badge in battle against tanks. Schlesremkämber noted that had Schlesinger not been half-Jewish, he would have been "promoted to Unteroffizier a long time ago."[166] Apparently, Schlesremkämber did not know about or was ignoring the April 1940 decrees discharging half-Jews. Several half-Jews like Günther and Schlesinger remained with their units throughout the entire war although they should have been discharged back in 1940.

When the Nazis persecuted Jews at home and increased the rate of deportation of German Jews, they traumatized thousands of *Mischling* soldiers. During his trial in Israel, Eichmann said that between 1941 and 1942, Hitler and Keitel had expressed concern that when *Mischlinge* went on leave, they would become distressed to discover that their parents had been deported.[167] Lösener also worried about the deleterious effect deportations would have on half-Jewish soldiers. On 4 December 1941, Lösener wrote that the government should grant special consideration to *Mischlinge* and their families, especially during the war. According to Lösener, it would be illogical to let *Mischlinge* serve while the government persecuted their parents. Lösener described Ernst Prager's situation as an example of this problem. Even after Prager had received Hitler's *Deutschblütigkeitserklärung*, the police arrested his father Heinrich (World War I veteran with the EKII and Wound Badge), and threatened him with months of imprisonment if the authorities saw him talking with an Aryan in public. The Nazis also required him to wear the Jewish star and made him perform forced labor.[168] Prager was lucky, though, in some respects. Many soldiers learned that a parent or grandparent had been deported and possibly murdered. At least Prager knew where his father was and that he was still alive.

Other *Mischling* soldiers were not so fortunate. Bundeswehr General Johannes Steinhoff reported that when he went to receive the oak leaves for his Ritterkreuz, Field Marshal Milch asked him if there was anything he could do for him. Steinhoff first requested more ammunition for his planes. Milch said this would be done and then asked if there was anything else. Steinhoff inquired if something could be done to help the half-Jew Feldwebel Rudolf Schmidt, whose Jewish mother and grandparents had been deported. "You, of all people, should know how difficult it is to fly missions against Russia all day fearing the Gestapo might be waiting to interrogate you when you land," Steinhoff told Milch. It is unknown what happened to Schmidt's relatives. Later, Schmidt was reported missing in action when he failed to return from a mission.[169] While in the Jewish hospital in Berlin, Jenny Lux told another patient about her son, half-Jew Emil Lux, who had been a Wehrmacht soldier. The other woman agreed that it was paradoxical that she wore a star while her son the fighter-ace wore the Ritterkreuz.[170] Perhaps Jenny Lux had met Rudolf Schmidt's mother.

Sometimes, when a soldier served on active duty, he could assist a relative by eliciting help from a high official. For instance, in the spring of 1941, the Nazis deported Helene Krüger to the east. Her three grandsons served in the Wehrmacht. Fortunately, their Aryan father was a friend of Engel's, Hitler's army adjutant. After hearing about the case, Engel agreed to help. "One of the main arguments Engel used with Hitler to get my grandmother free," Bernt von Helmolt said, "was that we grandsons all had the EKII and other medals."[171] The grandmother was freed, and Helmolt remembered being threatened by the Gestapo that they would all disappear if anyone ever found out what had happened.[172] The Helmolt family's situation showed how important personal politics and access to Hitler could be in helping people in need during the Third Reich.

Mischling soldiers sometimes could help a family member directly. Jürgen Krackow went with his father to the deportation station in his black Panzer uniform. When Krackow informed the officer in charge that he was the son of this half-Jew, the civil servant looked confused and asked him to prove it. Krackow insisted that no further proof was necessary. The man said that they could not deport a front officer's father. "Your father's a half-Jew," the civil servant said, "that means that you must be . . . at least . . ." "A quarter-Jew. Correct," Krackow blurted out. Then Krackow announced that he had a document personally signed by Hitler that allowed him to serve as an officer. Krackow's father was not deported.[173] Krackow would save his father from deportation three times. The last time he rescued his father, the icy SS man said to him, "Alright then, take your good little thing (*gutes Stück*) with you, Lieutenant."[174] Lieutenant H. Ruge,[175] who had received Hitler's *Genehmigung*, was able to arrange the release of his brother, Jürgen, from an OT forced labor camp in France.[176] It caused much resentment among other half-Jews there because they did not have an older brother to help them escape.[177]

Often soldiers were not able to prevent the deportation of family members. Moreover, once relatives were put in camps, getting them out — especially if they were full Jews — became almost impossible unless they had good connections like the Helmolt family. Some could visit their loved ones in the camp, but not secure their release. For example, a horrible situation developed when Lieutenant Joachim Cohen[178] visited his Jewish father at Sachsenhausen in 1943 while on leave. The perplexed camp commander could not understand how Cohen could be a decorated Panzer officer. When the commander implied that Cohen must have inherited his "blood" from his mother to have accomplished so much in the army, Cohen replied that his father was a World War I veteran and had been wounded in battle. Then the son asked the commander if his father would remain protected. The commander stated that just as long as the "Jewish professor" continued to clean his clothes and boots, he could stay there with him. During the five minutes he was allowed to talk with his father, Cohen said, "When the war's over, Papa, you'll leave this place. We'll live together in freedom and if I survive at the front, Hitler said he would consider declaring us Aryans. . . . Papa, you can count on that. I'll do everything I can at the front and elsewhere, Papa. It'll all be ok, when the war's over."[179] Cohen showed immense courage by visiting his father. He capitalized on the psychological advantage he had by being an officer and felt comfortable enough to see and encourage his father in Sachsenhausen. Cohen's conversation with his father conveys Cohen's hope that his service would protect them. Whether he believed that his father would truly survive or reassured him only to ease his fear of the death that probably awaited him is unknown. Nonetheless, Cohen concluded that if he performed well militarily, not only he, but possibly his father, could be "Aryanized." Both of their fates remain unknown.

Some *Mischlinge,* uncertain of where to turn or what to do for their relatives, asked their superiors for help. In 1940, after half-Jew Werner Goldberg had received news of the persecution his sick father was experiencing, he approached his commander. He reasoned that it was absurd that a father of a soldier should be humiliated in his neighborhood, given reduced food ration cards, and now threatened to report for forced labor.

Goldberg's superior, in turn, passed the matter up the chain of command. Eventually, "through a colleague who was a nephew of their general," Goldberg was able to meet with the general of the Potsdam garrison, Count Erich von Brockdorff-Ahlefeldt. During the meeting, Goldberg explained his situation. Afterward, the general promoted Goldberg, gave him permission to wear a pistol, and instructed him to go to the proper authorities "to arrange things as they should be for a German soldier."[180] Goldberg was able to convince the Berlin officials that sending a father of a soldier to forced labor was unacceptable. Without General von Brockdorff-Ahlefeldt's help, Goldberg would have been unable to help his sick father.

In 1943, Obergefreiter Heinrich Schlepegrell tried to get people to help his Jewish grandmother, who had been bombed out of her home twice. Captain Ehrlich, his officer, wrote the authorities on 29 December 1943 that because of Schlepegrell's bravery and medals, the Nazis should help his eighty-year-old Jewish grandmother.[181] Schlepegrell later said, "[U]nfortunately, it didn't help. My grandmother killed herself in March 1944."[182] Another case involved Obergefreiter Ludwig Reinhard, who was informed while he was in France that the Nazis had deported his grandmother, Johanna Broell née Bendeix. Reinhard asked for leave at headquarters but was denied. Reinhard was at the point of tears when an officer in his unit took him outside and comforted him for at least thirty minutes until he regained his self-control. Unfortunately, Reinhard could do nothing for his grandmother. He "cried like a baby" when he realized that he "couldn't save her."[183] The traumas of Prager, Helmolt, Krackow, Cohen, Goldberg, Schlepegrell, and Reinhard exemplify what thousands of *Mischlinge* had to endure. Most never saw their relatives again after the Nazis deported them.

Lösener argued that since half-Jews who remained soldiers and proved themselves in battle would, according to Hitler, be declared *deutschblütig* after the war, their relatives should not be persecuted.[184] Unfortunately, only a few bureaucrats heeded Lösener's advice. As a result of the problems surrounding *Mischlinge,* several bureaucrats suggested that they should deal with them after the war.[185] However, many did not want to wait that long. On 2 October 1941, Groß reopened the discussion of sterilizing half-Jews to prevent the birth of more quarter-Jews. Over the course of a generation, this would eliminate *Mischlinge* from society.[186] Lammers and other officials supported Groß's plan.[187]

To further control *Mischlinge,* the Nazis also wanted to regulate their marriages. Many Nazis felt that the control and elimination of marriages with *Mischlinge* was crucial to preventing the birth of future *Mischlinge.* Groß denounced marriages of quarter-Jews with Aryans. He believed it prudent to allow quarter-Jews only to marry among themselves, and when an unfavorable child resulted, then the Nazis should exterminate it.[188] In practice, some quarter-Jews experienced problems marrying Aryans, but others had no trouble.[189] Although Wehrmacht personnel were prohibited from marrying quarter-Jews by a decree issued on 15 February 1939,[190] many successfully did so.[191] The only problem Rosa Taraba and her husband Karl experienced was that they did not receive Hitler's *Mein Kampf* when they married, because Karl was a *Mischling.*[192]

Hitler agreed that they needed to be careful with *Mischlinge* and prevent them from procreating. He remarked on 1 December 1941: "[W]hat's amazing is that Jewish *Mischlinge* in the second and third generations quite often resemble Jews."[193] However, he felt that if they continued to procreate, evolution would ensure that the stronger Aryan blood would finally triumph over the inferior Jewish. He claimed: "Nature, however, removes harmful elements in the end. The Jewish elements are eventually mendeled out by the seventh, eighth and ninth generations and the purity of the blood is apparently restored."[194] Perhaps Hitler allowed *Mischlinge* to serve and marry Aryans, because he had faith that a *Mischling* who mentally and physically resembled an Aryan would produce, by the family's seventh generation, Aryan progeny. Yet, since the Nazis had not created laws to document people to the seventh generation, and since Hitler wanted the *Mischling* race to disappear, a *Mischling* family had little hope of ever reaching this safe generation. Hitler said in the same context that by enforcing racial laws, he would save future generations numerous problems.[195]

Many Nazis wanted to eliminate *Mischlinge* by late 1941. Most agreed that although sterilization offered one solution, the easiest resolution would be equating half-Jews with Jews. However, a few officials wanted this discussion to cease. Lösener felt appalled that Party hard-liners once again wanted half-Jews treated like Jews. He believed the Party had enough difficulties with half-Jews and their parents without taking this step.

Keitel insisted in February 1941 that to equate half-Jews with Jews would disrupt the lives of numerous quarter-Jewish soldiers. Lösener expanded this argument when on 4 December 1941 he wrote that the government planned to declare almost all quarter-Jews *deutschblütig* after the war. He explained that almost every quarter-Jew had a half-Jewish parent.[196] Lösener concluded that "one shouldn't sterilize, defame or deport the parents or even relatives of people one wants to treat like full-blooded Germans. This would create a new class of enemies of the State."[197] Lösener also warned that one should not turn half-Jews into enemies because they were more dangerous than Jews. They had above-average intelligence, good educations, and "German blood," all of which made them "born leaders." Their "German heredity shouldn't be abandoned to the Jews, but used for our purposes."[198] Lösener gained the support of some bureaucrats to allow half-Jews to retain their separate status. He was not able to secure support for protecting their Jewish relatives. Given the atmosphere in which Lösener worked, that would have been impossible.

Unable to bear the burden any longer, Lösener submitted his resignation to Stuckart on 19 December 1941. He told Stuckart that the SS had deported German Jews to Riga, and once there, the authorities had brutally murdered them. Lösener said he no longer would work as an expert on Jewish matters. Stuckart tried to convince Lösener to stay by reminding him "that all this takes place by the highest order [i.e., Hitler]." Lösener pointed to his chest and replied, "I have a judge within myself who tells me what to do."[199] Stuckart accused Lösener of not being "dynamic enough" in handling the Jewish question and sticking too "rigidly" to the letter of the Nuremberg Laws. That was why, Stuckart explained, Lösener had no longer been promoted. Stuckart did not accept Lösener's resignation. Lösener stayed on in the RMI under Stuckart, but stopped taking an active role in racial politics. He did the "bare minimum" required of him, and soon after his talk with Stuckart, went on an unusually long vacation. He was eventually granted a transfer in March 1943.[200] When Lösener's influence dwindled after 1941, the *Mischlinge* lost their strongest and most vocal advocate. Simultaneously, they gained more attention from their worst enemy, head of the Parteikanzlei, Martin Bormann.[201] With Bormann dealing with the *Mischlinge*, their situation could only worsen. Not surprisingly, the ability of certain Wehrmacht personnel to help *Mischlinge* also decreased at this time.

On 19 December 1941, after the last offensive near Moscow had ground to a halt and the Russian counteroffensive gained momentum, Hitler re-

lieved Army Commander in Chief Brauchitsch of his command and formally announced that he would assume command of the army.[202] On dismissing Brauchitsch, Hitler said, "It is the task of the Supreme Commander
of the Army to educate the Army in a National Socialist sense. I know no
army general capable of doing this. Therefore, I have decided to assume
supreme command of the army myself."[203] As Claus Hermann wrote, "This
was the last step taken to complete the ideological integration of the Wehrmacht."[204] Hitler bent the whole military structure to his supreme will. As
General Jodl said about 1942, the war then attained the ultimate in irratio-
nality, "with Germany's commanding generals reduced to the status of
highly paid NCO's."[205]

Hitler continued to propagate his anti-Semitic ideology. On 30 January 1942, he said at Berlin's Sports Palace that "the war will not end as the
Jews imagine it will, namely with the uprooting of the Aryans, but the result
of this war will be the complete annihilation of the Jews."[206] The fate that
awaited the *Mischlinge* could only be equally murderous.

Surprisingly, the Wehrmacht was still calling up half-Jews. If it were not
for the efforts of some *Mischlinge* themselves and their family members,
several would have served when it was against the law. They viewed the
racial decrees as saving them from going to the "meat grinder" in the East.
Many interviewees expressed gratitude toward the Führer that he had issued
a law that prevented them from having to go to Russia. Many described that
once the recruiter knew about their ancestry, they were released from military service throughout 1941 to 1944. For example, in 1943 when the draft
letter arrived for half-Jew Wolfgang Ebert, his mother Sonja did not wait
for her son to report at the appointed time but decided to go directly to the
Potsdam recruiting station herself. The impulsive Sonja Ebert née Himel-
stein, a Russian Jew, did not want to lose her son in battle. She proved to the
recruiters that she was Jewish and, consequently, they should not draft her
son. One of the men wrote "*n.z.v.*" (*nicht zu verwenden* — not to be used)
in Ebert's *Wehrpaß* and assigned him to the reserves. According to Ebert,
his mother, "whose life defined chutzpah," left the confused officers saying, "and besides, the war is over so you should just write my son sick."[207]
Sonja was lucky that the recruiters did not report her insolence and that she
was married to an Aryan. Many half-Jews were not as fortunate as Ebert.
Several were called up between 1941 and 1944 and served on the murder-

ous battlefields of Russia. Even so, the authorities continued to try to correct their mistakes by discharging those half-Jews who were serving illegally. Busy conducting the largest war in modern history, the Wehrmacht experienced some understandable difficulties in finding these men. Over seventeen million men served in the Wehrmacht before the war ended.[208] Consequently, the Wehrmacht found it impossible to test whether all were racially pure. Officials succeeded in filtering out many *Mischlinge* during the in-processing stage, but the odds of identifying and discharging them after they had joined combat units following the spring of 1941 were low.

Even the SA had problems keeping half-Jews out of its ranks.[209] Blankenburg wrote SA-Gruppenführer[210] Girgensohn's office on 12 February 1942 that *Mischlinge* who had been rejected for an exemption often claimed that they had completed their premilitary training with the SA. Blankenburg asked Girgensohn, who served as the SA adjutant to the SA chief of staff in the Reichskanzlei, to send an order out to the different SA offices to inform them that this was not allowed.[211] Half-Jew Walter Scheinberger, a SA member during the whole war, claimed that his superior knew about his ancestry but did not care.[212] Half-Jew Werner Seldis claimed that he knew not only of *Mischlinge* but also of several Jews in the SA in Berlin. They often entered the SA to help protect their family. According to Seldis, the SA personnel told him that they would "protect their Jews" and "fight to keep them in the SA."[213] Bormann even complained in December 1943 that ex-colonel and quarter-Jew Felix Bürkner had taken on a position in the SA leadership. The SA claimed that it had not known of Bürkner's racial makeup.[214] If the SA had such problems without a war to fight, removing half-Jews from the Wehrmacht during the war posed an enormous challenge for the authorities.

Many Aryan Wehrmacht personnel did not concern themselves with *Mischling* policy. After fighting on the Russian front in 1941, Edgar Francken's commander told him, "A good soldier like you . . . needs to go to officer school." Edgar told him he could not because he was a half-Jew. "Nonsense," replied the officer, "you're going."[215] Francken later received Hitler's *Genehmigung* and became an officer, but not before his family was drawn into the ordeal. Before the Nazis could approve Edgar's case, an SS racial office measured his father Hermann's body. On the basis of Hermann's physical features (he was tall and had a high forehead) and his mother's false testimony,[216] the SS decided that he was not a full Jew but rather a half-Jew. Consequently, Edgar was a quarter-Jew and, thus, did not have difficulties receiving clemency.[217]

By 1942, several civil servants had grown increasingly lax in their enforcement of *Mischling* policy. Lammers wrote Bormann on 16 January 1942 that the government needed to handle the half-Jews more competently.[218] Also, Bormann, Lammers, and others were becoming restless about how to handle the Jewish question officially. The Nazis had been using methods of extermination, such as gas vans and execution firing squads, that had proved inefficient and cumbersome.[219] The firing squads also took a psychological toll on the perpetrators.[220] Although these methods helped the Nazis murder hundreds of thousands, the Nazis wanted a faster and more efficient procedure.[221] Moreover, the Nazis still did not know whether to include *Mischlinge* in their murderous plans. On 20 January 1942, Heydrich gathered several high-ranking officials such as Stuckart, Eichmann, and head of the Foreign Ministry's "Jewish Desk" *(Judenreferat)*, Franz Rademacher, to discuss the Jewish question at a villa in Berlin-Wannsee.[222] Heydrich did not invite the armed forces, because he and others thought the Wehrmacht might cause problems.[223] Göring's infamous letter of 31 July 1941 to Heydrich had been a major turning point in the Nazi handling of the *Endlösung*. This letter, as well as the problems the Nazis had with *Mischlinge*, may have motivated Heydrich to call this meeting. Göring's letter gave Heydrich plenipotentiary powers to conduct the "overall solution of the Jewish question in the German sphere of influence in Europe."[224] The following conference was crucial in planning how this "solution" was to be conducted, although the systematic murder of Jews had been going on for a while. Heydrich had already concluded that the eleven million European Jews should be destroyed, but did not know what was to be done about the *Mischlinge*.[225]

Later known as the Wannsee Conference (or first Final Solution conference), this meeting was devoted in large part to the dilemma surrounding the *Mischlinge*. During the deliberations, most agreed that quarter-Jews in general should later be declared *deutschblütig*. Only those quarter-Jews who had two quarter-Jewish parents, inferior racial characteristics, police records, engaged in undesirable political activities, or "acted or felt like Jews" would not be treated as Aryans.[226] Regarding the *Endlösung*, most agreed that half-Jews should be treated like Jews. Exemptions conceivable for half-Jews included those married to Germans, those who had children, and those with clemency; however, half-Jews with exemptions would have to go through further racial tests after the war. Most agreed that half-Jews who remained in Germany would be sterilized.[227] Stuckart preferred sterilization because killing them would create too much paperwork and too many problems.[228] The meeting ended with most agreeing that the Jews would be exterminated, but left the issue of the treatment of half-Jews unresolved.

During this round of the ongoing debate about whether to declare half-Jews Jews, Hitler surprised his government again. The Führer wanted Jewish *Mischlinge* who had proven themselves in battle and who had been discharged recalled to active duty. If they continued to prove themselves, Hitler would declare them *deutschblütig*. It remains unknown how many Hitler recalled or declared *deutschblütig*.[229] Moreover, Hitler had sanctioned a decree that allowed Jewish *Mischlinge* who had died in battle to receive the *deutschblütig* declarations posthumously. This decree also awarded severely wounded *Mischlinge* the *Deutschblütigkeitserklärung*. These two new stipulations to the racial laws added thousands to the final number whom Hitler declared *deutschblütig*.[230]

In March 1942, Nazi officials again debated the pros and cons of defining half-Jews as Jews. This meeting held on 6 March 1942, referred to as the second Wannsee Conference (or second Final Solution conference), picked up where the first Wannsee Conference left off. Those involved agreed that the Nazis should sterilize half-Jews. After sterilization, the Nazis would transport them to one place in order to control them. The concentration camp Theresienstadt, where most older Jews were sent, was used as a model.[231] Lammers's office reported that when they considered half-Jews who had performed military service, they would have to divide this group into Jews and Germans for sterilization purposes. The Nazis decided that they should separate these people according to their physical characteristics because they did not want "*Mischlinge* permanently existing" as a third race.[232] Lammers's office argued that sterilizing half-Jews and then allowing them to live where they wanted negated Nazi goals. If they did not isolate them in a single city, Stuckart warned, then sterilization would neither solve the racial dilemma nor lessen the administrative problems surrounding them.

Sterilization and deportation were regarded as a "gracious favor" because they allowed *Mischlinge* to remain alive.[233]

Nazis also discussed giving half-Jews a choice between sterilization and deportation. Many believed that they would prefer sterilization to deportation, and, as Stuckart argued, such a policy toward half-Jews would ensure their disappearance.[234] Nothing was decided. Just as after the first meeting at Wannsee, the question of the *Mischlinge* was not resolved. Most in the Party still wanted to treat half-Jews like Jews, but Hitler remained indecisive. Perhaps Hitler did so because of the problems such a policy would cause in society. For example, Goebbels wrote on 7 March that eliminating the Jews "of course raises a large number of exceedingly delicate questions. What is to be done with the half-Jews? What with those related to Jews? In-laws of Jews? Persons married to Jews? Evidently we still have quite a lot to do and undoubtedly a multitude of personal tragedies will ensue within the framework of the solution of this problem."[235] For the present, many wanted to prevent such tragic, not to mention labor intensive, problems from developing.

Stuckart relied on Lösener's former arguments when he wrote several of the ministries (especially Himmler's office) to convince them of the necessity of not treating half-Jews as Jews. He argued in March 1942 that after Hitler had granted half-Jewish status to approximately three thousand *Geltungsjuden*, it would be "incompatible with the Führer's authority if we re-branded them as Jews."[236] He continued:

> I may point out that the Führer has, in addition to normal acts of grace, granted the status of racial Germans to a large number of officers and officers' wives who were [half-Jews] and that he'd promised to a large number of [half-Jews] who had remained in the Wehrmacht, the same status after the war, if they prove their worth during the war. . . . These cases show that those half-Jews whose activities take place within the Reich's territory aren't necessarily and always harmful to the German people.[237]

Declaring half-Jews as Jews would force Hitler to deport high-ranking officers or their wives, and would cause severe morale problems in the Wehrmacht and unrest in society. Stuckart further argued that one needed to remember the Aryan relatives of these half-Jews and the "50 percent of their blood which was German." Stuckart reasoned that half-Jews had above-average intelligence and that their talents should be used for the Reich rather than relinquished to her enemies, especially since most half-Jews were loyal to Germany.[238] Half-Jews were lucky that the bureaucrats and, most important, Hitler, remained indecisive on this topic.[239] Stuckart implored others to remember that Germany's highest authority, Hitler, had already decided what policy should govern the treatment of half-Jews. He warned that changing the status of them would cause bureaucratic chaos. Stuckart felt puzzled by those who wanted to exterminate half-Jews because most presented no threat.

Perhaps the bureaucrats felt irritated by the fact that many young half-Jews did not have to share the risk of battle. This may have contributed to the desire to treat half-Jews more severely. According to this study's interviewees, half-Jews forbidden to serve had a much more comfortable life between 1940 and 1944 compared with the life of hunger, cold, disease, and death that faced soldiers in Russia. Their Aryan comrades had the "honor" of going to Russia and dying for Germany, while half-Jews stayed home and studied or worked. For example, Helmut Krüger, who the army discharged in 1940, later learned that his entire company was decimated fighting outside Moscow in 1941.[240] Back home, plenty of lonely girlfriends, wives, and widows kept *Mischlinge* company during their free time.[241] The SD expressed its indignation in April 1942 that half-Jews slept with German women, while their "German-blooded" boyfriends and husbands fought. The SD stressed that if they caught a half-Jew with a married woman, they would send him to a concentration camp.[242] Surprisingly, several Aryan girlfriends documented in this study remained loyal to their half-Jewish boyfriends although they knew it was dangerous.[243]

The Wehrmacht still searched for *Mischlinge* who remained in the Wehrmacht illegally. On 14 March 1942, Hitler ordered that *Mischling* officers, NCOs, and army civil servants who had received the *Genehmigung* could remain in the army, but *Mischlinge* who had not received his approval were to be immediately discharged. However, the *Mischlinge* in question could apply for clemency if they had performed exceptional service. Applicants would remain in the service until Hitler decided their cases.[244]

These decrees did not solve the problem. Thousands of *Mischlinge* remained in the Wehrmacht. When OKH found *Mischlinge* illegally in the ranks, their commanders usually claimed ignorance about their subordinates' racial backgrounds. In June 1942, OKH demanded that all units obey the 8 April 1940 and 16 July 1941 decrees that required everyone to sign Aryan declarations. OKH discovered that many units still used the old declarations that required a soldier only to state whether or not he was a Jew. Thus many *Mischlinge* had truthfully stated that they were not Jews.[245] To catch those Jewish *Mischlinge*, OKH now commanded everybody to state they were 100 percent Aryan on new declarations. The longer the updated declarations were not completed, OKH claimed, the more work the Personnel Office would have in the future.[246]

In May 1942, Hitler told Lammers that he was tired of the *Mischling* problems and that he would deal with them after the war.[247] Hitler's change of heart, combined with Heydrich's death in June 1942, probably brought the discussion over whether to treat half-Jews as Jews to a halt for a few months.[248] Although Hitler wanted to defer the half-Jewish question until after the war, he had issued too many racial laws and subsequent decrees to enable civil servants to ignore the *Mischlinge*.[249]

For example, head of the KdF, Bouhler, wrote Bormann, head of the Parteikanzlei, on 10 July 1942 to say he could tolerate the delays in resolving the *Mischling* issue if he knew that the goal of eliminating half-Jews from the *Volk* would be achieved. However, Bouhler told Bormann that "you know yourself that this isn't the case." Bouhler was disturbed by the Racial Office's figures on the high rate of illegitimate children born to half-Jews. He complained that the Party (i.e., Bormann) had done nothing to combat this problem. Bouhler had suggested several measures that would stop "these unfortunate creatures" from being born, but apparently they had been ignored.[250] Finding a solution to the *Mischling* problem was hampered by Bouhler and Bormann's hostility toward one another.[251] Nonetheless, both believed that eliminating half-Jews would be far easier to manage than regulating them, especially since, as Bormann claimed, they occupied valuable government time. Yet, the Wannsee Conferences had shown that such a policy was impossible to implement at that time.

On 11 June 1942, Rademacher summarized the Wannsee Conferences by saying that the equalization of half-Jews with Jews was undesired but that the majority of the Nazis welcomed the sterilization program. Yet, to sterilize the half-Jews would require almost a million hospital days, which was impossible while medical resources were devoted to the war. Not only were more time and training needed, but the sterilization technique also required further development. The Nazis had experimented with plant poisons, X rays, and physical removal of the genitals, but they were not satisfied with the results. Furthermore, more trained surgeons would be required to implement a mass sterilization program.[252] Plans for mass sterilizations of *Mischlinge* were postponed because of events at Stalingrad.[253] Himmler actually wanted to deport half-Jews to a separate city.[254]

Based on the documents, the Nazis did not discuss the problems they would encounter if they started to sterilize and/or deport *Mischling* soldiers who had received clemency. Although somewhat illogical, many *Mischling* soldiers with exemptions would not have been spared this fate. Such plans to dispose of loyal soldiers only mirrored Hitler's growing fanaticism.

According to Halder, Hitler became extreme in many areas during this time. On 24 September 1942, on being dismissed by Hitler, Halder wrote that Hitler spoke about the necessity for educating the General Staff in "fanatical faith in the idea [of National Socialism]." "He is determined to enforce his will also on the Army," Halder wrote.[255] Halder was a little late in drawing this conclusion, but the fact that he started to feel Hitler's presence more in 1942 demonstrated Hitler's increased radicalism. Perhaps Hitler had the *Mischlinge* in mind when he talked about the army becoming more devoted to Nazism. On 25 September 1942, OKW reported that Hitler ordered the discharge of half-Jews still serving.[256] Many times when these men were located, they were sent to concentration camps for violating one or more laws, such as lying to the authorities, drawing extra pay from an illegal promotion, having an Aryan girlfriend, and so on.

Half-Jewish veterans caused a new type of problem when Nazis deported them. When half-Jew Werner Eisner was caught sleeping with an Aryan, who was pregnant with his child, the SS sent him to Auschwitz on 7 December 1942 for *Rassenschande*. After he got off the train at Auschwitz and stood in line for the gas chamber, he pulled out a picture of himself in uniform and screamed, "Now you'll exterminate a Wehrmacht soldier." After inspecting the photo, an SS man saved his life by pulling him out of the line. These SS guards did not feel comfortable gassing a veteran.[257]

Mischlinge still on active duty became increasingly nervous as rumors circulated about new plans to sterilize or deport half-Jews. Many feared that if discharged, they would face deportation. Some decided to desert before they could be discharged.[258] Half-Jew Matrose[259] Kurt Schinek left his unit in 1942 for Switzerland but was caught. On 7 October 1942, his officer, Lieutenant Berlling, actually wrote in his defense that he was a good soldier and that extenuating circumstances existed. He explained that Schinek's first fiancée, Liselotte Steinbrech, who had a daughter by him, had left him for racial reasons. Berlling asked the court to release Schinek and tried to convince the authorities that Schinek's Jewish ancestry troubled him so much that it caused him to have a lapse in judgment.[260] Schinek's new fiancée, Thea Liebe, wrote a letter to the authorities on 8 October 1942: "This news has shocked me horribly, especially since I know that my fiancé didn't try to cross the border because he was a coward. Since the Wehrmacht refused to grant us permission to marry, we wanted to marry in Switzerland [where it was allowed]. . . . As the daughter of an officer, I would've never gone with a deserter. . . . "[261] The open admission that she wanted to marry him, thus committing *Rassenschande,* proved either her disregard for or her ignorance of the racial laws. Unfortunately, her passionate plea did not help. Schinek should not have been serving in the first place, but he apparently did not know this. The court ruled that he should not have left his unit without permission. He was executed.[262]

Gefreiter Werner Kohn, who was born out of wedlock,[263] also left his unit because of a woman and because he feared what the Nazis planned to do with the half-Jews. He wrote the court on 9 June 1942 that he liked the Wehrmacht and had lied about his ancestry to remain a soldier. Although several comrades suspected that he was Jewish because of his name, he explained that only people who spelled Kohn with a *C* were Jewish. His comrades apparently accepted this reasoning. While Kohn served, he "heard several times that *Mischlinge* were supposed to be discharged. . . . I naturally thought deeply about such things." "I left my unit," Kohn continued, "because I worried about my pregnant bride [Maria Hempfling], my future and because the decrees for *Mischlinge* were becoming stricter."[264] The court was unsympathetic. Despite Kohn's Party membership (he had been expelled in 1934 because of his ancestry) and military service, he was sent to prison. For months thereafter, he petitioned to serve on the front lines in a Bewährungs unit, but the court rejected his requests.[265] He remained in prison until the war's end. Perhaps since Kohn had been a Party member, the court was not as harsh as it had been with Schinek. The documents are unclear on this point.

A tragic case was that of Gefreiter Anton Mayer. He left his unit in 1943 not only to be with his fiancée, but also because he worried about what would happen if the authorities discovered he was a half-Jew.[266] The court condemned him to death. Anton wrote a desperate plea on 23 July 1944 to Admiral Karl Dönitz:

> [I only left my unit] because I was afraid. . . . I ask to serve on the front immediately to prove my worthiness. . . . I'll prove that I can atone for the stupid thing I did out of fear. . . . I beg you to believe me that I've always been a good German. I was always proud to be German, even when I was persecuted for it while I lived in Romania. . . . I plead with you, Herr Großadmiral, to think about the fact that I'm the only son of my parents. . . . Long live our Great Führer. Long live Greater Germany.[267]

Mayer's ordeal revealed how little he understood his position in society and the options left open to him. Had he truly been trying to dodge suspicion in the Kriegsmarine, then he should never have left his unit. Evidently, Mayer was too frightened to report his ancestry, too scared to stay in the navy, and too short-sighted not to realize that he could not run away to his fiancée to escape his fears and duties without dire consequences. Dönitz ignored Mayer's letter and the court condemned him to death. Mayer, however, was not shot by a firing squad. He was beheaded. Admiral Walter Warzecha, chief of the Allgemeines Marineamt,[268] made sure that Mayer received this cruel punishment.[269]

Ironically, only after December 1942, when quarter-Jew Admiral Martin Baltzer took over the Navy Personnel Office from Admiral Conrad Patzig, did the discharge of *Mischlinge* in the Kriegsmarine begin. Until then, Patzig had been able to help and hide most *Mischlinge* within the Kriegsmarine.[270] Possibly Baltzer feared what would happen if he did not enforce racial policies vigorously, since his superiors knew about his ancestry. Perhaps Baltzer acted harshly against people in a position he could fully relate to because he did not wish to deal with them.

As the debate over the Jewish question intensified, General Schmundt issued a decree on 31 October 1942 that required every soldier to acknowledge that the Jewish influence had forced Germany to fight a war in which its best sons died. Therefore, Schmundt argued, "There's no difference between so-called respectable Jews and the others. . . . The present war against the Jewish Bolshevistic arch enemy shows with clarity Jewry's true face. Thus, the officer must, from inner conviction, reject Jewry and all contact with it. Whoever doesn't follow this unrelenting attitude is no longer fit to be an officer."[271] Although he had helped some *Mischlinge* earlier in his career, he seemed now to toe the Party line and to become less tolerant of anybody or anything Jewish. Schmundt's statement expressed the growing intolerance of Jews among the military leadership.

Bureaucrats pushed the sterilization program again in October. On 27 October 1942, a third Final Solution conference took place. Karl Klingenfuß of the Foreign Office submitted a memorandum advocating the sterilization of half-Jews wanting to remain in Germany and the deportation of those who refused. The attitude was that this measure was a "gracious favor."[272] This proposal gained support among the civil servants, but Hitler refused to act.[273]

Although Hitler did not feel ready to order the sterilization of half-Jews, he continued to make decisions that restricted both their freedom and the freedom of those affiliated with Jews. For example, Hitler rejected a soldier's application on 2 November 1942 to marry a woman who had previously been married to a Jew. Engel wrote Commander Frey, who worked in the General Wehrmacht Domestic Office,[274] that Hitler had reasoned that "the fact that this woman, regardless of the circumstances, was willing to marry a Jew is a sign of a weak character that shouldn't be overlooked."[275] Shortly thereafter, Hitler issued a decree in December 1942 that no soldier could marry any woman who had previously been married to a Jew. In certain cases, Hitler allowed soldiers to submit an application for an exemption, but in most cases, such a woman was unworthy of a Wehrmacht soldier.[276] Streicher had taken this a step further and believed that just having sex with a Jew could poison the body, but he did admit that a vaccination might exist.[277]

6

Turning Point and Forced Labor, 1943–1944

Forced Labor and the Worsening Situation for Mischlinge

The year 1943 was a turning point for the "*Mischling* Question."[1] During this time, several Nazis recognized that a harsh policy against *Mischling* veterans was unwise. Bureaucrats in Berlin debated whether to recall previously discharged half-Jewish soldiers, a group they believed to number 8,330.[2] The OKW had reported that these men were good soldiers. Reichsreferent Dr. Gussmann said, "It could be argued that by letting them fight, they're being given the opportunity to prove whether the Nordic blood in their veins outweighs their Jewish blood."[3] From this document, one can infer that the Wehrmacht was interested in using this reservoir of men.

However, the Party disapproved. Ernst Kaltenbrunner, Heydrich's successor, wrote on 3 March 1943 that traitors, homosexuals, half-Jews, men married to Jews, and Gypsies could not serve in special military units.[4] When Gussmann wrote "Herrn Leiter" at the Hauptverbindungsamt on 10 February 1943, he suggested the government form *Mischling* work battalions instead. Men married to Jews were to be included. By forming such battalions, they could remove several *Mischlinge* from their positions and thereby appease Aryans who had protested their employment. Also, the Nazis could bypass the discussion of whether to treat half-Jews and Jews married to Aryans as full Jews if they sent them to forced labor battalions. Kaltenbrunner and a civil servant who worked on *Mischling* policy, Sachbearbeiter Heinrich Dietz[5] in OKW, supported the forced labor proposal. Dietz objected to letting Jewish *Mischlinge* perform military service because this meant that they would later be declared *deutschblütig*. Dietz believed that these men should not wear uniforms and should work only in particularly "unhealthy swamps and other dangerous locations."[6] In other words, Dietz wanted to start a slow but nonetheless systematic eradication of this group. On 17 July 1943, Gussmann echoed Dietz's plan and wrote that according to a Hitler decree, half-Jews and men married to Jews or *Mischlinge* should be fired from their jobs and drafted into forced labor battalions, especially to help clean up bombed-out regions. Wehrmacht personnel would guard them.[7] OKW would work with the labor offices to organize the battalions, and the Reichskanzlei would give Bormann the responsibility for the project.

Göring feared that these new decrees would negatively affect some of his subordinates. Göring had expressed to Bormann that he should be able to make exemptions and wanted to discuss everything with Hitler.[8] Apparently Göring got the concessions he wanted because, during the same month, Göring decreed that OT would draft half-Jews and Aryans married to Jews who did not work in important military related installations into forced labor battalions.[9] Evidently, the people Göring had helped protect would remain at their posts, or else he would not have changed his position on OT so quickly.

On 13 October 1943, Fritz Sauckel, plenipotentiary for labor mobilization, decreed on Hitler's orders that civilian half-Jews and Aryans married to Jews be drafted into OT.[10] Hitler decided that only those Jewish *Mischlinge* who worked for installations providing support for the war effort could be exempted from OT.[11] Most had to prove they were indispensable to their companies. For example, Gerhard Wundermacher remembered his boss Dankbardt telling him that in the name of Siemens, he would protect him.[12] However, most half-Jews would eventually have to leave for OT camps. Many could not get important jobs after their military discharge because of their racial status. Consequently, their bosses could not justify keeping them in 1943 and 1944. Furthermore, many were college students, and studies did not exempt one from OT. However, some were exempted from OT duty because of their war service.[13] (Table 8 shows the ages of all *Mischlinge* in this study.)

As with earlier policies, implementation often proved more challenging than anticipated. Albert Speer, head of armaments production, wrote

Table 8. Years of Birth of *Mischlinge* Who Served in the SS and the Wehrmacht, Documented in This Study

Year of Birth	No. of *Mischlinge* First Degree	No. of *Mischlinge* Second Degree	Total No.
1875		1	1
1878	1		1
1880	1		1
1881		2	2
1882	1		1
1883	1		1
1885		1	1
1886	1	2	3
1887		2	2
1888	2		2
1890	2	1	3
1892	1	1	2
1893	1	2	3
1894	3	2	5
1895	2	1	3
1896	4	1	5
1897	2	2	4
1898	6	1	7
1899	5	3	8
1900	6	2	8
1901	3	1	4
1902	2	3	5
1903	9	1	10
1904	5	2	7
1905	5	3	8
1906	4		4
1907	8	5	13
1908	7	2	9
1909	6	3	9
1910	11	5	16
1911	17	4	21
1912	10	11	21
1913	26	6	32
1914	29	7	36
1915	25	11	36
1916	45	5	50
1917	40	14	54
1918	55	17	72
1919	71	18	89
1920	69	22	91
1921	49	14	63

continued

Table 8. *continued*

Year of Birth	No. of *Mischlinge* First Degree	No. of *Mischlinge* Second Degree	Total No.
1922	35	15	50
1923	23	9	32
1924	8	17	25
1925	14	16	30
1926	9	5	14
1927	8	11	19
1928	10	4	14
1929	1	1	2
1930	1	0	1
1931	2	0	2
Total	646	256	902

Note: Birth dates were available for only 902 of the 1,574 *Mischlinge* identified by Bryan Mark Rigg.

Himmler a year later on 16 October 1944 that Hitler's order to send half-Jews and men married to Jews to OT camps had caused problems. Speer protested the loss of skilled workers at several munitions factories who would be difficult to replace. Speer asked that the deportation of highly skilled half-Jews and men married to Jews or half-Jews be deferred until he could find qualified replacements.[14]

As 1943 progressed, the Party aggressively attacked *Mischlinge* still on active duty. On 18 December 1943, Bormann, now Hitler's personal secretary, claimed that *Mischlinge* used the Wehrmacht as a hiding place and implied that they were not concerned with their duties. Bormann used the quarter-Jew Colonel Felix Bürkner, former head of Krampnitz's Cavalry School and Keitel's friend and old comrade, as an example. Bürkner trained soldiers in a military school, a position Bormann claimed Bürkner received because of his relationships with Keitel and General Fritz Fromm. Despite the noteworthy support, Bormann said Bürkner's Jewish blood continued to reveal itself. When the army discharged Bürkner, Bormann wrote that his fellow officers felt relieved because of his Jewish character. Bormann ended his circular proclaiming that declaring *Mischling* soldiers *deutschblütig* endangered the *Volk* by allowing them to hide in the Wehrmacht. The Reich would suffer later when this concealed Jewishness reared its ugly head, Bormann wrote. For Bormann, the idea that *Mischlinge* could be employed as soldiers was asinine from the outset. Keitel felt that since Schmundt was also against Bürkner, he could not take his case to Hitler, so he did nothing for his friend. Bürkner was discharged.[15] Bormann tried to ensure that the paramilitary organization, called the Deutscher Volkssturm,[16] in which he was responsible for political and organizational matters,[17] would not encounter similar problems that the Wehrmacht had with its *Mischlinge* as illustrated by Bürkner's case.

At a time when Germany needed every man, Bormann wrote on 9 December 1944 that Jews, Gypsies, and half-Jews could not serve in the Volkssturm; quarter-Jews could serve as long as they did not hold positions of authority. Bormann stipulated that the Parteikanzlei would review applications for exemptions.[18] However, racial policies proved harder to enforce during late 1944 because of the war's chaos. Despite Bormann's racial restrictions, many *Mischlinge* served in the Volkssturm. Others used these restrictions to avoid serving. For example, when the Volkssturm drafted Hermann Nast-Kolb, he went to his Gauleiter and claimed he could not serve because he was a half-Jew and his mother was in a concentration camp. The Gauleiter freed him from Volkssturm duties.[19] However, many were forced into the Volkssturm regardless of their racial status, and many met their deaths in these units. For example, discharged half-Jew Colonel Ernst Bloch[20] not only served in the Volkssturm but also trained men to fight in it. He died in the Volkssturm near Berlin in 1945.[21]

Although Sauckel had already ordered the deportation of half-Jews and Aryans married to Jews to OT in 1943, the first major action to implement this in force happened in the spring of 1944,[22] during "*Aktion Hasse*"[23] and "*Mitte.*"[24] These men would be called "OT-men" or "B-men."[25] Himmler joined the chorus of voices and ordered that half-Jews and men married to Jews or *Mischlinge,* who were not active soldiers, be sent to OT.[26] These "conscripts" also included criminals, homosexuals, and Gypsy *Mischlinge*. Apparently, some Jews not married to Aryans were also sent. Ex-Gefreiter Herbert Beyer remembered having Jews with the yellow star in his OT camp, Rositz near Altenburg in Thüringen.[27] Many deported to OT were Wehrmacht veterans. The Wehrmacht forgot their loyal service. On 21 March 1944, Sauckel repeated his order that half-Jews and men married to Jews be deported to OT.[28] Most half-Jews could not escape it. Only a few who could prove that their jobs were invaluable to the war effort were exempted from deportation. Others prevented their own deportation by falsifying papers from their work, claiming that they were needed at their jobs.[29] Sometimes, half-Jews outran the orders sent out by the SS. Friedrich Schlesinger avoided the Gestapo by moving around to three different cities where he had three different girlfriends to hide him. [30]

Besides *Hasse* and *Mitte*, OT conducted the deportations under the call sign *Aktion Barthold* in the region of Glogau (today Głogów, Poland) at Ost Linde. Along with their male counterparts, female half-Jews were deported to this camp, where they were forced to perform hard manual labor. Christoph-Michael Salinger recalls that their number was close to 250.[31] However, it appears that in general most women conscripted by OT were not deported to camps like Ost Linde but simply deployed in local work details.[32] In March 1944, between two thousand and three thousand Jewish and Gypsy *Mischlinge* and men married to Jews were sent from the province of Baden to the West to perform forced labor.[33] Between May and October 1944, 820 half-Jews and 127 men married to Jews were deported to such camps from Hamburg.[34] Thousands of half-Jews and men married to Jews must have been deported to OT from Vienna, Berlin, Frankfurt, and Munich.

Most received draft cards from the local police or Gestapo offices informing them that they had a few days or weeks to report to a certain train station with a change of clothes and toiletries.[35] Sometimes, employment offices would print official notices in the local newspapers under the title of "Registration of *Mischlinge*," which notified half-Jews of when and where they were required to report.[36] Though most had lost several relatives in the Holocaust, only a few tried their luck as "U-boats" (a term used for people who went into hiding with false papers) or tried to escape to Switzerland. However, hiding a *Mischling* fugitive was as dangerous as hiding a hardened criminal, and the chance to escape to another country was slim at best. For example, Helmut Rehfeld tried to escape to Basel, Switzerland, from Breslau, a distance of approximately seven hundred miles. Every twenty miles, police questioned him at checkpoints as to why he was not in uniform and where he was going. After traveling only a few miles, he decided that he would never reach the border and gave up.[37] Half-Jews had few options left open to them other than to obey the OT draft order. Most reported at the appointed time. For all they knew, the SS could have used OT to disguise an "extermination action." Although Gerhard Guttstadt's father had been murdered in 1939 in Sachsenhausen, Guttstadt still reported to his deportation station.[38] Many stated that they had no real options. Herbert Beyer remembered that he almost committed suicide before his deportation;[39] other half-Jews killed themselves to avoid going to OT.[40] Some feared *Sippenhaft,* a process whereby not only the person who disobeyed orders was punished, but his family as well.[41] Hermann Steinthal explained:

> I don't know what I feared more: to obey the order or not to obey the order. Both were probably dangerous, and it was impossible to know which one was more dangerous. We didn't know where they were taking us or what awaited us. . . . Perhaps, we could've hidden, but where and with whom? There were brave people who hid Jews back then, but, first of all, I didn't know any of them, and second, we knew that the Nazis sometimes took revenge on the family if they couldn't find the person they were looking for *[Sippenhaft].* One could've committed suicide like a few people among family and acquaintances had done, but I didn't think about that.[42]

Steinthal expresses eloquently the dilemma half-Jews faced. Events swept them along and they felt powerless to influence them. Although Steinthal thought about hiding, he, as most half-Jews, had few choices other than to obey the OT draft order. Steinthal showed up at his deportation location and was sent to the OT camp Wolfenbüttel.

Often relatives accompanied them to their deportation stations. Once there, most half-Jews were loaded into cattle cars and had to endure their journey without water or food for days.[43] Others were deported in normal passenger trains.[44] Surprisingly, most in OT camps survived the war, probably because they had to endure only a few months in these camps, as compared with the many months or years that concentration camp victims had to endure. Moreover, OT camps were not as nefarious as death camps as long as the inmates worked long and hard.

Those *Mischlinge* still serving in the Wehrmacht experienced increased restrictions during 1944. On 4 September 1944, Hitler ordered that half-Jews still serving could no longer receive medals.[45] Bormann also pushed for high-ranking officers who had received Hitler's *Deutschblütigkeits-*

erklärung to be discharged. In late 1944 and early 1945, Hitler discharged several high-ranking officers who were either *Mischlinge* themselves or had *Mischling* wives. On 2 November 1944, Hitler also ordered Jewish *Mischling* civil servants discharged.[46] Many of the discharged half-Jews would find themselves in OT camps, a humiliating experience for these battle-tested officers. For example, the *Neue Zürcher Zeitung* reported on 15 January 1945 that it was hard for discharged officers to bear the humiliation of working in an OT camp.[47] Herbert Beyer remembered that a captain was sent to the OT camp one week after he had been discharged, and "one could see he was destroyed because of it."[48] Heinz Wollenberg remembered one officer who broke down into tears when he entered the OT camp at Wolfenbüttel/Braunschweig.[49] Several half-Jews wore their Iron Crosses,[50] and Beyer remembered a fellow prisoner wearing the Ritterkreuz in the OT camp Rositz.[51] Several quarter-Jews, some highly decorated, had to endure the uncertainty about their older half-Jewish fathers laboring away in OT camps while they still served on the front.[52]

By 1944, thousands of concentration camps and forced labor camps sprinkled the landscape of Nazi-dominated Europe.[53] Many camps incarcerated half-Jews. Speer claimed ignorance after the war about what type of manpower had been recruited.[54] Speer acknowledged that OT camps built concrete dugouts, roads, and railroads, but explained little about where his labor came from or how those workers were treated.[55] By May 1944, OT camps were no longer controlled by Speer's organization, but by the SS Building Administration. Even then, the treatment of half-Jews in these OT camps varied greatly.

Many OT camps provided prisoners decent shelter, good food, and normal working hours. Sometimes the OT units had weapons at their disposal in case they had to defend their camp.[56] According to Kurt Einstein, his camp allowed prisoners to leave their barracks on Sundays for church or the cinema or just to take a stroll in town.[57] Other camps allowed girlfriends or sisters of OT men to bring them food.[58] Some in certain camps received OT uniforms.[59] Ernst Ludwig said that at the Zerbst camp, where around three hundred half-Jews worked, they performed hard labor day and night, but that the Luftwaffe guards there treated them decently. They built a large airport for the new Messerschmitt Me 262 fighter jets. They did not have much to eat, but nonetheless, Ludwig described it as survivable.[60]

Dieter Bergmann said that he felt "good" in his OT camp. He worked hard but felt energized by the outdoor work. Called up with another eight hundred half-Jews, they had to build launchpads in France for V-1 flying bombs.[61] There were many OT camps in the Harz Mountains in central Germany where several mines and gasoline production faculties were located.[62] Ex-Funker Hermann Rath was deported with a group of one hundred other half-Jews to a mine near Zeitz where they worked close to fourteen hours a day. Rath lived with "an indescribable fear" and felt that he might die soon.[63] Peter Schliesser experienced hard labor, and the half-Jews in his camp in Saxony had little food, usually of poor quality, and lived in dilapidated shelters.[64]

Some OT camps had, instead of guards, just a foreman to whom the half-Jews reported.[65] Sometimes, the interned half-Jews provided their own guards.[66] However, sometimes these camps resembled a concentration camp in their brutality.[67] People were beaten and died of hunger and hard labor. Some committed suicide because of the trauma and stress. Sometimes SS personnel guarded these camps as at Weissenfels/Halle, Derenburg/Harz, Rositz, and the OT barracks in Casernes Mortier near the metro station Porte des Lilas in Paris.

Whether OT camps were lenient or brutal, prisoners feared deportation to a concentration camp. Christoph-Michael Salinger, at the Ost Linde OT camp, remembered that those *Mischlinge* who misbehaved were sent to Auschwitz.[68] At Derenburg, the SS threatened the *Mischlinge* constantly with deportation to a concentration camp if someone tried to escape. Many OT camp commanders warned that if any of them tried to escape, not just the offender but all who lived in his barracks would be deported to a death camp. Consequently, inmates often policed themselves. When Robert Schindling escaped from Derenburg, some of the other inmates in the camp searched for him, found him at a train station, and brought him back to the camp. Then Heinz-Herbert Karry, brothers Ernst and Heinz Scheinberger, Aristoteles Trembelis, and several others brutally beat Schindling out of fear and anger until he lay dead. According to Peter Cahn, another prisoner who witnessed this awful act: "[I]t wasn't murder, it was a *Totschlag* (manslaughter)."[69] Other OT escapees were sent directly to concentration camps when found. Ex-Funker Ferdinand Lichtwitz successfully escaped with three other inmates (he remembers two of their names as being Fleischmann and

Claus Cohen) from Rositz. After one month of hiding in Munich, Lichtwitz was denounced by Frau Einstein and deported to Dachau. While there, he was reunited with Fleischmann and Cohen.[70]

Others were more successful with their escapes. Hans-Geert Falkenberg escaped along with several others from his OT camp at the Casernes Mortier in Paris in 1944. He obtained false papers and masqueraded around France and Germany as an OT officer until the end of the war. He believes his escape saved his life.[71]

As the war drew to a close, *Mischlinge* stood at the edge of the Holocaust's gaping jaws. At the close of 1944, Himmler ordered the execution of *Mischlinge* in camps near the enemy before the enemy overran their position and liberated them. Harald Etheimer claimed that a fellow half-Jewish inmate discovered in camp documents after the war "Himmler's order" that the SS should have executed them.[72] Luckily for them, it was not obeyed. If such an order was indeed given, SS commanders of OT camps did not enforce it.[73] Contrary to normal Nazi camp behavior, *Mischlinge* were free after their guards typically deserted their posts.

At the war's end, control over the OT camps disintegrated, leaving each camp commander at liberty to decide what to do with his prisoners. Some in OT were offered the opportunity to fight in the Wehrmacht against the invading Allied armies. Horst Schmechel remembered that probably three out of approximately two hundred half-Jews in his camp decided to do this when their commander, OT-Frontführer[74] Bauer, presented this option to them.[75] Klaus Budzinski remembered his SS camp commander gave the half-Jews weapons, addressed them as "my dear *Mischlinge*," and then told them that they would fight the Allies.[76] This last-ditch effort by the Nazis was not uncommon. Gypsies and Gypsy *Mischlinge* were drafted at the beginning of 1945 into the ill-famed SS Special Regiment Dirlewanger and given weapons to fight at the front.[77]

On 3 January 1945, probably under Party pressure, the Wehrmacht issued one of its last orders regarding *Mischlinge*. It ordered that employing "Jewish-*Mischling*" officers, even those who had exemptions, in key positions and promoting them past colonel should be avoided.[78] This last order showed that the Party was probably tired of "discovering" so many *Mischling* generals, most of whom had been discharged throughout the fall of 1944.

Discharging such men in high positions negatively affected both morale and the Wehrmacht's ability to fight efficiently.

It seems that only active officers were discharged. Most reserve *Mischling* officers served until the war's end. Roughly half of the half-Jews documented in this study spent the last months of the war in concentration or OT forced labor camps. The others, whether because they were not found or had received exemptions, continued to work, study, or serve.

Hitler's preoccupation with race, particularly his desire to discharge high-ranking and experienced officers from their posts, targeted not only *Mischlinge* but also those married to *Mischlinge*. Few active officers escaped Hitler's discharge order. An exception was General Gotthard Heinrici, who was left alone by Hitler because of his exceptional military acumen. Heinrici finished the war as an army commander and conducted the final battle of the Oder and the defense of Berlin.[79] In January 1945, Himmler repeated the order to send half-Jews to forced labor battalions.[80] Hitler at this time was a physically sick man. Although he was only in his mid-fifties, his head and hands shook visibly (probably from Parkinson's disease), his eyes were bloodshot, and saliva sometimes trickled from his lips.[81] In this state of poor health, he still obsessed about the Jews. His decision to send thousands of half-Jews, many of whom were Wehrmacht veterans, to forced labor units instead of the front, showed again Hitler's obsession with race and destructive policies. These thoughts were still on his mind just a few hours before he shot himself on 30 April 1945 when he said, "Above all, I charge the leadership of the nation, as well as its followers to a rigorous adherence to our racial laws and to a merciless resistance against the poisoner of all people — international Jewry."[82] A few days later, the war ended.

What Would Have Happened to Mischlinge *If Germany Had Won the War*

The Nazis' "mechanism of destruction" would also have engulfed the half-Jews if Hitler had continued or won the war. Büttner wrote, "It was only a question of time when [half-Jews] too should share the fate of the 'full Jews.'"[83] Quarter-Jews would also have suffered further discrimination, selective sterilization, as well as possible extermination. The elimination of

Mischlinge had already been conceived in the 1930s. According to the first supplementary decree of 14 November 1935 to the Nuremberg Laws, Article 5, section 2, paragraph (c), any half-Jews born after 15 September 1935 would be considered Jews in violation of the law.[84] Also, as Stuckart and Globke wrote in 1936 in their commentary about the racial laws, the disappearance of the "*Mischling*" race was the aim of the legal solution to the "*Mischling* Question."[85]

The Nazis continued to betray their true plans about how to treat *Mischlinge*. For example, when the Nazis discovered that a half-Jew had not left the Jewish community and had tried to marry his pregnant Aryan fiancée, the SS sent him to Auschwitz. The SS wrote, "We'll do everything we can so that not only the full-Jews, but also the *Mischlinge* will disappear."[86] The Nazis planned to handle the *Mischlinge* as they had the Jews. They believed this would eliminate the disguised Jew, considered the most dangerous of all Jews.[87]

In 1943, Himmler informed Lammers that the *Endlösung* would include half-Jews.[88] Dr. Richard Hildebrandt, head of the SS Main Office for Race and Resettlement, wrote Himmler on 17 March 1943 about the Final Solution of the "Jewish *Mischling* Question" ("*Endlösung der Judenmischlingsfrage*"). He said that SS-Standartenführer[89] Dr. Bruno Kurt Schultz in the Main Race Office recommended further testing of quarter-Jews in the future to see if they looked racially inferior. One that "looked Jewish" should be treated like a half-Jew. To justify this policy, he argued that a quarter-Jew could have inherited more than 25 percent "Jewish blood" from his half-Jewish parent.[90] Himmler wrote Bormann on 22 May 1943 that he wished that children of *Mischlinge* would in the future be tested "just like plants and animals," and that those racially inferior would be sterilized. Such a policy would safeguard the German gene pool.[91] Himmler believed "*Mischlinge* . . . were particularly unpleasant occurrences" and implied that *Mischlinge* were "freaks" of nature.[92] Had Himmler had his way, he would have included half-Jews in the *Endlösung* from the beginning. By the summer of 1944, Himmler's office issued the statement that in one hundred years, if any *Mischlinge* were still alive, they would be only "*Mischlinge* of the third, fourth and fifth degrees." The office hoped that half-Jews and quarter-Jews would be extinct by then. "The removal of Judaism from our German Reich," the memorandum continued, "and the purification of our German

Volk from Jewish-*Mischling* blood is the greatest racial-political task presently."[93] But before systematic deportation and total expulsion of *Mischlinge* from society could be executed, German society would have to be desensitized to *Mischling* persecution. The decision to deport half-Jews to OT forced labor camps in 1944 was a big step in this direction. Until then, the plan to deport and exterminate *Mischlinge* had been largely theoretical.

However, German *Mischlinge* were fortunate compared with their non-German *Mischling* counterparts. Already in the eastern territories, non-German *Mischlinge* were marked for extermination.[94] The Reich Security Main Office for the Eastern Territories wrote in the summer of 1941: "In view of the Final Solution . . . it appears necessary both from a political and a racial standpoint, in order to avoid a later recovery of the Jews, to define the concept of a Jew as broadly as possible. . . . Anyone who has one parent who is a Jew will also count as a Jew."[95] This policy for the occupied areas was clear: all half-Jews would be deported to death camps along with Jews. There would be no segregation of half- and full-Jews as in Germany. Hans Frank, the governor general of occupied Poland, included *Mischlinge* in his scheme of extermination in a report on 16 December 1941:

> The Jews are for us also very parasitical eaters. We have in the General Government an estimated 2.5 million, maybe together with *Mischlinge* and all that hangs on, 3.5 million Jews. We can't poison them, but we will be able to take some kind of action which will lead to an annihilation success and I am referring to the measures to be discussed in the Reich. The General Government will be just as *judenfrei* as the Reich.[96]

Frank felt that the Nazis would be free of the "Jewish disease" only when the *Mischlinge* were also exterminated. The policy implemented in Poland and other areas would follow this line of thinking. For example, already in the summer of 1940, *Mischlinge* in Poland were pushed into ghettos.[97] Half-Jews there were also included in plans for deporting Jews to concentration camps.[98] Some *Mischlinge* from Greece, Hungary, and even Italy were also deported.[99] Klemperer had met *Mischlinge* from the Protectorate who had to wear the Jewish star in accordance with a law decreed after Heydrich's assassination on 4 June 1942.[100] Half-Jewish Danes felt the need to escape from Denmark. Out of the 5,919 refugees of Jewish ancestry who fled

Denmark for Sweden, 1,310 were half-Jews.[101] The Nazis also forced half-Jews to identify themselves as Jews in Luxembourg, Holland, northern France, Denmark, Vichy France, Belgium, Poland, the Baltic states, and Russia.[102] One can safely conclude that hundreds of thousands of non-German *Mischlinge* ultimately died in the Holocaust.

The Nazis treated German *Mischlinge* better than non-German *Mischlinge* to maintain popular support among Aryan Germans, particularly relatives of *Mischlinge*. Non-German *Mischlinge,* especially in the East, had no such lobby group.[103] From the racial scientists' point of view, a German half-Jew was still half-Aryan. Since all things Aryan were to be preserved and encouraged, policy regarding German *Mischlinge* was problematic at best. This ideological dilemma took so long to resolve that the war ended before the Nazis could deport the German half-Jews to the death camps.

Nonetheless, Himmler wanted German half-Jews and Jews married to Aryans destroyed.[104] Several brutal acts against German *Mischlinge* had already been committed. An institution had been set up specifically to exterminate *Mischlinge*.[105] Wilhelm Kube, general commissar for Belorussia, wanted to know in 1941 whether German Jews and *Mischlinge* should be given exemptions. Apparently, he felt uncomfortable exterminating "part-Jews *(Mischlinge)*, Jews with war decorations, or Jews with 'Aryan' partners."[106] From the documents, it seems that these Germans of Jewish descent were not given any preferential treatment. They were earmarked for extermination. In 1942, Gestapo Chief Heinrich Müller issued an order that Jewish and half-Jewish patients in hospitals and sanatoriums be sent to the extermination camps.[107] In 1943, some German half-Jews and Jews married to non-Jews had been sent to the Warsaw ghetto.[108] Hauptsturmführer[109] Alois Brunner, a deportation expert, deported some German *Mischlinge* to the East in 1942–1943. During one investigation of a *Mischling*'s papers, he crossed out the word *Mischling* and wrote "Jew," saying: "What? Y'er a *Mischling*? . . . Y'er a dirty Jew."[110] Between 1943 and 1944, *Mischling* children from welfare institutions were sent to Hadamar's euthanasia center, where they were poisoned.[111] On 9 November 1944, an article in *Der Stürmer* stated: "The Jews that we still have aren't as dangerous as the half-Jews because these half-Jews can mix in with the German population. . . . Hopefully the time will quickly come, when this dangerous pack of people won't be allowed to do what they want to. If the half-Jews aren't taken care of, then the Jewish-question will only be partially solved."[112] The article reflected what many Nazis desired. They believed that the destruction of European Jews would be final only when half-Jews were eliminated.

By late 1944 and early 1945, the Nazis deported some *Mischlinge* from the Reich to Theresienstadt.[113] During the evacuation of Auschwitz in late 1944, the SS transferred the *Mischlinge* there to Ravensbrück.[114] Hans Kirchholtes, who served in an OT camp near Hamburg, remembered that many half-Jews were interned in the Neuengamme concentration camp.[115] Wolf Zuelzer's mother, a half-Jew who, though married to an Aryan, had to wear a Jewish star, was forced to work in a munitions factory and was later deported to Theresienstadt.[116] This study has documented some German half-Jews who were deported to Auschwitz, Buchenwald, Minsk, Groß-Rosen, Sachsenhausen, and Dachau.[117] Many were sent to such camps presumably because they had acted against Nazi orders such as escaping from OT camps.

The alternative to exterminating half-Jews was to sterilize them. The Nazi regime sterilized some four hundred thousand people during its twelve years in power.[118] It had developed techniques that would make mass sterilizations possible. Hans-Oskar Löwenstein de Witt, a *Geltungsjude*, claimed he knew a couple of *Mischlinge*, a young man and woman, ages eighteen and nineteen, respectively, whom the Nazis had forcibly sterilized.[119] Half-Jew Gerhard Bier remembered one half-Jew who was told that if he volunteered for sterilization, he would not be deported. Because he did not want to take any chances, he became sterilized.[120] Holocaust historian Yehuda Bauer wrote that while "no clear policy was adopted, experiments in sterilization were made and undetermined numbers of *Mischlinge* were thus crippled."[121] Fritz Steinwasser, a quarter-Jew, claimed that his uncle found SS documents that spoke of plans to sterilize the Jews and *Mischlinge* in their family and then send them to the East.[122] However, it never came to a universal sterilization of German *Mischlinge* because Hitler never gave his approval.

Mischlinge ultimately owe their survival to Hitler's inability to decide on how to deal with them — whether to execute them like Jews, sterilize them, or to deport them. Hitler probably feared social unrest if he also exterminated half-Jews. Backlashes against the government such as after *Reichskristallnacht*[123] in 1938, the euthanasia program[124] after it became known to churches throughout 1939–1941, and during the Rosenstraße protest[125] outside Goebbels's office in 1943 indicated that unrest was likely if too many Germans were personally affected by the persecution. As Eichmann said in Jerusalem, "*Mischlinge* were protected by a forest of difficulties because of their non-Jewish relatives and because there was no effective means of sterilization."[126] As a result, Hitler repeatedly said he would deal with the half-Jews after the war. Many *Mischlinge* today have little doubt about what would have happened to them if Hitler had continued his rule. Reiner Wiehl said, "[Had Hitler won], my mother, my sister, myself — all dead!"[127] Robert Braun asked, "After Hitler killed six million Jews, what would it mean to him to kill several thousands of *Mischlinge* to keep German blood pure?"[128] Wilhelm Dröscher wrote in 1946 that had Germany won the war, "that would have meant the end of me."[129]

Interestingly, Hitler condemned softness on the Jewish question and rejected those who treated anyone of Jewish descent leniently. Yet he practiced what he ultimately condemned and often made exceptions to his own ideology. Nonetheless, the *Mischlinge* situation was on the verge of turning into a nightmare, and looking at Hitler's track record, it is now clear where he was going with the *Mischlinge*.

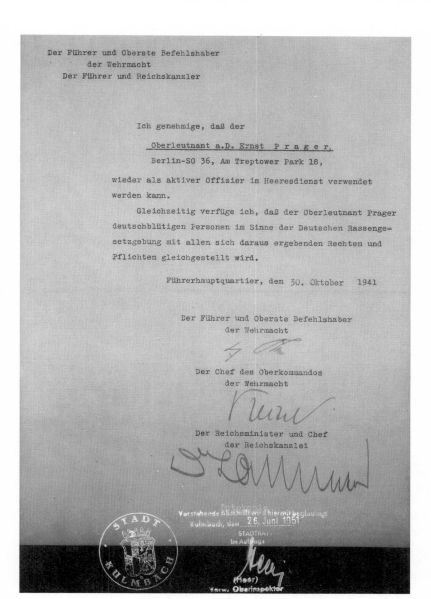

Der Führer und Oberste Befehlshaber
der Wehrmacht
Der Führer und Reichskanzler

Ich genehmige, daß der

Oberleutnant a.D. Ernst P r a g e r,

Berlin-SO 36, Am Treptower Park 18,

wieder als aktiver Offizier im Heeresdienst verwendet

werden kann.

Gleichzeitig verfüge ich, daß der Oberleutnant Prager
deutschblütigen Personen im Sinne der Deutschen Rassenge=
setzgebung mit allen sich daraus ergebenden Rechten und
Pflichten gleichgestellt wird.

Führerhauptquartier, den 30. Oktober 1941

Der Führer und Oberste Befehlshaber
der Wehrmacht

Der Chef des Oberkommandos
der Wehrmacht

Der Reichsminister und Chef
der Reichskanzlei

Vorstehende Abschrift wird hiermit beglaubigt
Kulmbach, den 26. Juni 1951
STADTRAT
Im Auftrag:

(Heer)
terw. Oberinspektor

Half-Jew Ernst Prager's *Deutschblütigkeitserklärung.* "I approve that retired First Lieutenant Ernst Prager (Berlin-So 36, Am Treptower Park 18) may be used again as an active officer in the service of the army. At the same time, I declare that First Lieutenant Prager is of equal status with German blooded persons with respect to German racial laws with all of the consequent rights and obligations. Führerhauptquartier, 30 October 1941. Signed: The Führer and Supreme Commander, Adolf Hitler; the Commander in Chief of the Wehrmacht, Keitel; the Secretary of State and Head of the Reichskanzlei, Lammers."

Marriage of quarter-jew Lieutenant Wolfgang Beindorff (*kneeling with wife, middle row*); he received Hitler's *Deutschblütigkeitserklärung.*

Half-Jew Ernst Bloch (last rank colonel); he received Hitler's *Deutsch-blütigkeitserklärung.* The horrible scar was from taking a bayonet through the face during hand-to-hand combat in World War I. (Military awards: EKI, EKII, Wound Badge, War Service Cross Second Class, and War Service Cross First Class.)

Quarter-Jew Fritz Steinwasser (last rank Stabsgefreiter) standing in the foreground, France 1940 (*above*) and in 1949 (*right*) after he returned from POW camp in the Soviet Union. (Military awards: Recommended for the War Service Cross with swords in 1945, but the paperwork did not go through because it was at the war's end.

Half-Jew Robert Borchardt (*right*) (last rank major) wearing the Ritterkreuz.
Left of Borchardt is Major von Loeffelholz. July 1942. (Military awards:
Ritterkreuz, German-Cross in Gold, EKI, EKII, Assault Badge, and Wound
Badge.) (Photo credit: Dal McGuirk)

Half-Jew Eberhard Fischer (last rank Unteroffizier). (Military award: EKII.)

Quarter-Jew Wihelm von Gwinner (last rank second lieutenant); he received Hitler's *Genehmigung*. (Military award: Wound Badge.)

Half-Jew Rainer Gärtner (last rank Unteroffizier) in the summer of 1943 on the island of Crete. (Military award: EKII.)

Quarter-Jew and First Lieutenant Helmut von Gottberg (*third from right*); he received Hitler's *Deutschblütigkeitserklärung*. (Military awards: EKII, War Service Cross Second Class with swords, Wound Badge, and Eastern Campaign Medal 1941–1942.) Below is his military pay book.

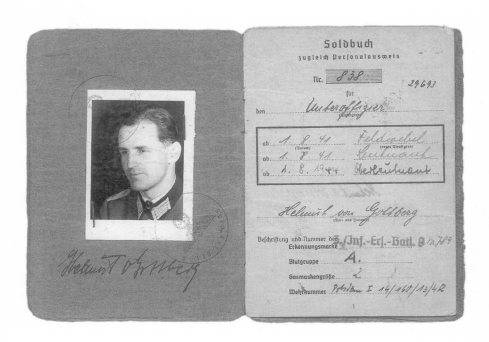

Half-Jew Wilhelm von Helmolt (last rank Feldwebel). This picture was taken several months after Helmolt lost his leg in combat. (Military awards: EKII, Silver Wound Badge, Assault Badge, and Eastern Campaign Medal 1941–1942.)

Quarter-Jew Hartmut Heinrici (last rank captain); he received Hitler's *Deutschblütigkeitserklärung.* (Military awards: EKI, EKII, Wound Badge, Assault Badge, and Eastern Campaign Medal 1941–1942.)

General Gotthard Heinrici (*far left*), who was married to a half-Jew, meeting Hitler in 1937. Hitler would award Heinrici's wife and children the *Deutsch-blütigkeitserklärung*. He received the Ritterkreuz with oak leaves and swords.

General Gotthard Heinrici.

Hitler's working style.

Hitler and General Karl Litzmann, Staatsrat and Nazi Party member.
Litzmann had two grandsons who were quarter-Jews according to Nazi law.
He granted the family an exemption allowing Frau Litzmann, the daughter of
General Litzmann, to remain in the Party and for her sons to serve in the
Wehrmacht.

Ich genehmige ausnahmsweise die Wiedereinstellung

der Leutnante a.D.

      Joachim   R o h r   und

      Heinz   R o h r .

Document granting approval by Hitler for the quarter-Jews and brothers Joachim and Heinz Rohr to return to the army. "I approve the reinstatement of the retired lieutenants Joachim Rohr and Heinz Rohr. Signed: Adolf Hitler."

Half-Jew Emil Lux (*far left*) (last rank Unteroffizier), with his company commander, First Lieutenant Müller. The other two (*on the right*) are unknown. (Military awards: EKII, Assault Badge, Silver Wound Badge, and the Eastern Campaign Medal 1941–1942.)

General and half-Jew Werner
Maltzahn; he received Hitler's
Deutschblütigkeitserklärung.
(Military awards: EKI, EKII, and
War Service Cross Second Class.)

Quarter-Jew Helmut Meyer-
Krahmer (last rank first lieu-
tenant); he received Hitler's
Deutschblütigkeitserklärung.
(Military awards: EKII.)

Half-Jew Ernst Prager (*standing, in uniform*) and wife Hella's wedding in 1941 (last rank captain); he received Hitler's *Deutschblütigkeitserklärung*. (Military awards: EKI, EKII, and the Golden Wound Badge.)

Quarter-Jews and siblings Lieutenant Heinz Rohr (*left*), Margot Rohr (*middle*), and Lieutenant Joachim Rohr (*right*), 1934. (Military awards for Heinz Rohr: German-Cross in Gold, EKI, EKII, Panzer Assault Badge in Silver, and Golden Wound Badge. Military awards for Joachim Rohr: German-Cross in Gold, EKI, EKII, and Eastern Campaign Medal 1941–1942.)

Half-Jew and later Luftwaffe General Helmut Wilberg; Hitler declared him Aryan in 1935. (Military awards: Knight's Cross with Swords of the Royal House Order of Hohenzollern, Military Service Cross Second Class of the Grand Duke of Mecklenburg-Schwerin, Commemorative Flier Badge, EKI, EKII, and many others.)

Philipp Bouhler, head of the KdF (Kanzlei des Führers, the Führer's chancellery; not to be confused with the same abbreviation used for Kraft durch Freude of the German Labor Front). (Photo credit: Charles Hamilton, courtesy of R. James Bender Publishing)

Martin Bormann of the Parteikanzlei. (Photo credit: Charles Hamilton, courtesy of R. James Bender Publishing)

Dr. Wilhelm Stuckart, state secretary in the RMI (Reichsministerium des Innern; Reich Ministry of the Interior). (Photo credit: Charles Hamilton, courtesy of R. James Bender Publishing)

Half-Jew Friedrich Gebhard (last rank major); he received Hitler's *Deutschblütigkeits-erklärung*. (Military awards: EKI, EKII, War Service Cross First Class with swords, War Service Cross Second Class with swords, and Eastern Campaign Medal 1941–1942.)

Quarter-Jew Felix Bürkner (last rank colonel). He was commanding officer of Krampnitz Calvary School and received Hitler's *Deutschblütigkeitserklärung*.

Quarter-Jew Major
Heinz Rohr's wedding
in 1944 (wife Stefanie);
he received Hitler's
*Deutschblütigkeits-
erklärung* and was
decorated with the
EKI and German-Cross
in Gold.

Quarter-Jew and SA
Sturmführer (Lieutenant)
Hans Sander in 1935; he was
also a Party member and
was awarded the Gold Party
Badge; he later received
Hitler's *Deutschblütigkeits-
erklärung* and served in the
army (last rank lieutenant).
(Military award: EKII.)

ADOLF HITLER

BERLIN, DEN **30. Juli 1935**

    Herrn
    H. S a n d e r ,
    S.A.- Sturmführer,
    M e i n i n g e n .

        Der Chef der Kanzlei des Führers der
N.S.D.A.P. hat mir über Jhren Fall Vortrag gehalten.

        Jch gebe Jhrem Gesuch,soweit es sich
auf Sie persönlich bezieht, mit Rücksicht auf Jhre
lange Zugehörigkeit zur N.S.D.A.P. und auf die Ver-
dienste, die Sie sich um die Bewegung erworben haben, hiermit statt.
        Gegen Jhr Weiterverbleiben in der NSDAP.
als deren Mitglied und in der S.A., unter Beibehal-
tung Jhrer Führerstellung, bestehen somit keine Be-
denken.

                              [signature]

Document from Hitler allowing quarter-Jew SA Sturmführer (Lieutenant) Hans Sander to remain in the Party. A loose translation reads: "Adolf Hitler, Berlin, 30 July 1935. To H. Sander, S.A.-Sturmführer, Meiningen. The head of the KdF [Kanzlei des Führers] of the NSDAP has presented your case to me. I approve your petition insofar as it regards you personally in consideration of your long membership in the Party and because of your noteworthy service to our movement. There is no reason why you should not remain in the Party or the SA and retain your leadership position. Signed: Adolf Hitler."

Half-Jew Ernst Prager a few days after he was shot seven times while fighting on the Russian front (last rank captain). A few months after this photo was taken, he met Eichmann about his Jewish relatives.

Clara von Metteheim, mother of half-Jews Obergefreiter Deiter Fischer and Unteroffizier Eberhard Fischer.

Half-Jew Werner Eisner; he later was deported to Auschwitz. (Military award: Wound Badge.)

Half-Jew Martin Bier (last rank Gefreiter) (*left and right*).

Quarter-Jew Helmut Schmoeckel (last rank captain of *U-802*); he received the *Deutsch-blütigkeitserklärung.* (Military awards: Silver U-Boat Badge, Battleship Badge, EKI, and EKII.)

Der Führer hat entschieden, daß der

Hauptmann

Walter H o l l a e n d e r ,

Infanterie-Regiment 46,

geboren am 15.10.1903 zu Verden als deutschblütig
im Sinne der deutschen Rassengesetzgebung und der
hierzu erlassenen Gesetze mit allen daraus sich
ergebenden Rechten und Pflichten zu gelten hat.

Berlin, den 31.August 1939

Der Reichsminister und Chef
der Reichskanzlei

Der Chef des Oberkommandos
der Wehrmacht

Deutschblütigkeitserklärung for half-Jew Captain Walter H. Hollaender. It
reads: "The Führer has decided that Captain Walter H. Hollaender, Infantry
Regiment 46, born on 15 October 1903 in Verden, is of German blood in
accordance with the German racial laws with all the corresponding rights and
obligations. Berlin, 31 August 1939. Signed: Secretary of State, Dr. Lammers.
Signed: Chief of OKW, Keitel."

7

Exemptions from the Racial Laws Granted by Hitler

Why Hitler Granted Exemptions

Throughout Hitler's political career, he made several exemptions from his ideology. Whatever Hitler had written into decrees was always subject to alteration at his discretion. Hitler granted thousands of *Mischlinge* exemptions from the provisions of his racial laws.

Some have claimed that Hitler made exemptions for *Mischlinge* because of his own "Jewish" past.[1] Since this issue was raised frequently during discussions of this study, it is explored in some detail.[2] The facts seem to indicate that Hitler feared his paternal grandfather was Jewish.[3] As Dr. Fritz Redlich, psychiatrist and author of *Hitler: Diagnosis of a Destructive Prophet,* said, "Hitler was mixed up about his descent. He was definitely scared about the possibility that he had a Jewish grandfather."[4] However, no documents have survived to confirm or deny this allegation.

In general, Hitler was very secretive about his origins.[5] He tried to conceal many embarrassing stories about his relatives and forbade that anything about his family or youth be published.[6] Hitler invented his own history, changing his origins and ethnicity. He even had people murdered who knew too much about his past.[7] According to Hitler's nephew, Patrick, Hitler claimed that the public "mustn't be allowed to find out who I am. They mustn't know where I came from and who my family is."[8] Several plausible explanations for Hitler's discomfort exist: his family had a history of mental illness[9] and incest;[10] his mother and father were second cousins;[11] his niece and possible lover, Geli Raubal, had committed suicide allegedly because of his domination of her;[12] his half-brother, Alois Jr., had an extensive criminal record;[13] Hitler may have had a son;[14] one of his relations married a Jew;[15] his Aunt Johanna was a hunchback;[16] his father was illegitimate;[17] his father beat him, as well as his mother and his dog;[18] his father was promiscuous;[19] his father was a drunkard;[20] Hitler feared that his father may have been half-Jewish.[21] Rumors spread throughout the 1920s and 1930s about Hitler's "Jewish past,"[22] but they were mainly "fostered by sensationalist journalism of the foreign press."[23] Only a few sources exist that refer to Hitler's potential Jewish heritage: one is a book written by Hansjürgen Koehler, an ex-Gestapo man who emigrated to England in the 1930s; another is the memoirs of Hans Frank, Hitler's notorious lawyer, written while awaiting the hangman in Nuremberg in 1946. Neither source is particularly reliable.[24]

Koehler's book was published during 1940, a time when several "spurious books" were being published about the Führer.[25] Koehler reported in 1940 that he had come across information in SS files that proved that Hitler's grandmother had been impregnated by a Jew for whose family she worked as a domestic servant in Vienna.[26] The fact that Koehler's book was published in 1940, and that articles about Hitler's past had already been printed in the 1930s, shows how widespread such rumors were about Hitler. Thus, they could not have escaped his notice.

Frank's book, published in the 1950s, is full of mistakes. Frank's son, Niklas, warned that his father "lied about everything" and his memoirs must therefore be looked at skeptically.[27] Ian Kershaw wrote that Frank's memories were "dictated at a time when he was waiting for the hangman and plainly undergoing a psychological crisis, [and] are full of inaccuracies and have to be used with caution."[28] Even so, the "psycho-historian" Robert Waite, author of *The Psychological God Adolf Hitler*, found "reason to believe [Frank's] story. He wrote his memoirs as a condemned man who had converted to Catholicism. He had no reason to misrepresent Hitler or to invent a story."[29]

In 1946, Frank's memoirs substantiated allegations like Koehler's. In 1930, Hitler had asked him to research his family's past in light of some unpleasant rumors. Frank did so and allegedly found that Hitler's grandmother, forty-two years old and unmarried, became pregnant while working in the Jewish Frankenberger (perhaps Frankenreiter) household in

Graz.[30] It was unclear whether the head of this Jewish home or his teenage son was the father of the child, although based on the documents, Frank assumed it to be the youth. According to Frank, letters he found proved the Frankenberger family was responsible, since they paid child support to Hitler's grandmother for several years. The child in question was Alois Schicklgruber, Hitler's father, who later changed his name to Hitler. When Frank reported these findings, Hitler told him to keep quiet. Frank claimed that Hitler confirmed the facts that Frank found except one. Hitler maintained that his grandmother had been impregnated by Georg Hiedler rather than the Jew, and had only pretended the father was Frankenberger to extort money from them. But as psychotherapist George Victor wrote, "Hitler's version [via Frank] is doubtful on its face. It implies Maria was engaging in sex with Georg and the Frankenberger youth at the same time. If so, she could not have been sure who the father was, and Hitler could not have been sure, although he said he was."[31]

If this story is true, it might help explain Hitler's actions in Austria after the annexation of 1938. Supposedly, Hitler had the whole town of Döllersheim, where possible secrets about his family were, turned into an artillery field.[32] However, according to Redlich, Waite is wrong in assuming that the Döllersheim documents about Hitler's family were destroyed by this "hostile act."[33] A more likely scenario was that Hitler took away whatever documents he thought were incriminating from the Döllersheim parish archives and had them destroyed. We do know that Hitler's "frantic efforts" to locate the documents about his evasion of the Austrian draft were futile because they had been removed from the archive and hidden.[34] But the fact that he looked for them proves that Hitler was searching out documents that might have harmed the identity he had created for himself.[35] Hitler probably found most of the documents he wanted. His past occupied much of his time; Hitler had his origins repeatedly investigated (nine times in total) and reportedly had incriminating documents destroyed.[36]

We can assume that Hitler believed that his grandmother had been "taken advantage of" while working in a Jewish home. This belief may have intensified his already anti-Semitic writings, statements, and policies. Even before Frank told Hitler this story about his grandmother, Hitler feared that Aryan women might be "misused" as servants in Jewish homes. *Mein Kampf* often refers with horror to Jews sexually abusing Aryan women.

Perhaps hearing the stories of his grandmother confirmed his fears and probably intensified his reactions to this sensitive subject.[37] Hitler often flew into a rage when he heard about Aryan chambermaids in Jewish homes.[38] This may explain why Hitler falsely accused Matthias Erzberger,[39] a staunch Republican and representative of Weimar democracy, of being the illegitimate son of a servant girl and a Jewish employer. The fact that Hitler considered this kind of heritage a vile insult speaks volumes on how he felt about his father. Later, Hitler had a law implemented to prevent the situation he feared. The Nuremberg Laws of 1935 forbade Aryan women under forty-five years of age as of 31 December 1935 to work in Jewish households.[40] Concerning these policies, Redlich wrote that they were "possibly motivated by Hitler's concern that his paternal grandmother was impregnated by a Jew when she worked in a Jewish household."[41]

The SS also investigated Hitler's ancestry. Usually the SS only looked for Jews in a person's family tree. In 1944, Himmler wrote Bormann about Hitler's dubious past: "It's rumored that some of the Führer's relatives live in Graz-St. Peter, some of whom are half-idiots or insane. . . . The Schicklgruber line seems to have several abnormal people, as demonstrated by the mentally retarded ('*idiotische*') descendants."[42] Hitler probably knew about mental illness in his family; namely, one cousin had committed suicide, another lived in an insane asylum, and two others were mentally retarded.[43] The SS report did not mention any Jewish stains in his "bloodline." The race office had researched his ancestry with the "predictable outcome" that they found him to be 100 percent Aryan.[44] Two facts emerge from this mass of rumor and inference. First, no one will ever know with certainty whether Hitler had Jewish ancestry unless new documents surface. Second, Hitler feared that the rumor about his Jewish past could have been true. He had expressed this implicitly to Captain Schuh in his regiment during World War I and later, during the Third Reich, voiced certain doubts about his ancestry to Speer.[45] This personal identity crisis may have led him to make so many exemptions to the Nazi racial laws.

Hitler may have given exemptions to *Mischlinge* because of his own experiences with them and Jews. Hitler spent time and possibly was romantically involved with quarter-Jew Gretl Slezak.[46] He had met the Austrian Jew Dr. Eduard Bloch, who took care of his mother during her battle with cancer. Hitler respected Bloch. After the *Anschluß* in 1938, Hitler made sure that Bloch was protected until the proper documents had been procured for his emigration. Hitler saw to it that Bloch, whom he called a "noble Jew," could leave Germany unharmed.[47] Hitler may also have given exemptions to *Mischling* soldiers because of his contact with Jews during World War I, through which he learned how brave many of them had been.[48] Hitler received his EKI on the nomination of Hugo Gutmann, his regiment's adjutant, a Jew.[49] Such firsthand experiences may have motivated Hitler to give exemptions to some *Mischlinge*.

Hitler had shown from the beginning of his political career a tendency to make exemptions. Between 1920 and 1933, he usually granted them because of political necessity. He allowed Ernst Röhm to command the SA even though Röhm was a homosexual.[50] Although those who were homosexual were later marked for persecution, at this stage Hitler believed matters "purely in the private sphere" should be left alone.[51] Perhaps the most famous exemption was given to Heydrich, the "Blond Beast," head of the SD Reich Security Main Office and one of the architects of the *Endlösung*. Because so many have argued about Heydrich's possible Jewish past, his case, like Hitler's, is described in detail.

When Heydrich was a child in Halle, neighborhood children made fun of him, calling him "Isi" (Izzy), short for Isidor, a name with a Jewish connotation.[52] This nickname upset Heydrich.[53] When he served in the navy, many of his comrades believed he was Jewish.[54] Some called him the "blond Moses."[55] Others who lived in Halle have claimed that everybody believed that his father, the musician Bruno Heydrich, was a Jew. Half-Jew Alice Schaper née Rohr, who took piano lessons from Bruno, claimed, "We all knew he was Jewish. . . . He looked just like a typical Jew."[56] In town, Bruno was called Isidor Suess behind his back.[57] With such rumors going around, it was not surprising that Heydrich felt continually burdened by these allegations, especially when he served as an SS general. One will never know whether Heydrich was truly of Jewish descent unless more documents are found, but it is possible that Himmler and Hitler may have believed he was. In the early 1930s, according to Himmler's masseur Felix Kersten (if he can be believed), Hitler had told Himmler, "Heydrich was a highly gifted but also dangerous man, whose gifts the movement had to retain. Such people could still be used so long as they were kept well in hand and for that purpose his non-Aryan origins were extremely useful; for he would be eternally grateful to us that we had kept him and not expelled him and would obey blindly."[58] According to Speer, Hitler often used flaws of men in positions of authority to control them. In this case, Heydrich's possible flaw was "Jewish ancestors."[59] Heydrich often took those who claimed he was Jewish to court for slander. He did so as late as 1940[60] and sent another man to a concentration camp.[61] Admiral Canaris, head of the Abwehr, presumably had a large dossier on Heydrich's Jewish past and threatened to reveal what he had if the SS tried to infringe on Abwehr activities.[62] Heydrich was definitely haunted by stories of his Jewish past.

Hitler's actions with Röhm and Heydrich show that he had the ability to ignore "defects" in men who, he felt, could serve his political cause. In this respect, Hitler bent his ideological principles to meet political needs.

Hitler granted exemptions for military necessity. Two examples of those who received such exemptions were Field Marshal Erhard Milch and General Helmut Wilberg. The accomplishments of these two men show that Hitler needed them to organize and develop his cherished new service, the Luftwaffe.

Milch became one of the most powerful men in the Luftwaffe and the Third Reich. In 1933, when Hitler wanted to hire the half-Jew Milch to help build an air force, he told him, "Now look, I haven't known you for very long, but you're a man who knows his job, and we have few in the Party who know as much about the air as you. That's why the choice has fallen on you. You must take the job. It's not a question of the Party, as you seem to think — it's a question of Germany and Germany needs you."[63] Milch admitted later that this talk with Hitler convinced him to take the job.[64] Milch noted in his diary on 1 November 1933 that Göring had discussed his ancestry with Hitler, Rudolf Heß (deputy head of the Party), and Blomberg and that "everything was in order."[65] Milch "possessed tremendous drive, a thorough knowledge of the production capabilities of the German aircraft industry, a detailed understanding of its managers and designers, and perhaps most importantly, excellent connections within the political leadership" of the Third Reich.[66] According to James Corum, the greatest contribution Milch made "to the Luftwaffe was organizing the massive program of aerial rearmament" begun in 1933.[67] By 1936, under Milch's leadership, "the German air industry had become a first-class organization" and the rearmament program was producing modern aircraft that were reaching Luftwaffe flying units.[68] Hitler had claimed in 1936 that "two names are . . . linked with the birth of our Luftwaffe," Göring and Milch.[69] In April 1940, when the Norwegian campaign was running into several difficulties, Milch's skills as an excellent organizer and administrater helped lay the "foundation for the success of airpower in Norway."[70] Hitler eventually was victorious in Norway, thanks to the solid leadership that generals like Milch displayed. If the Germans had not secured their northwest flank in Norway, Hitler would probably have been unwilling and even possibly unable to launch his invasion of France one month later. Hitler presented Milch with the Ritterkreuz for his efforts during the Norwegian campaign.[71] A few months later, with the successful conclusion of the war in France, Milch was one of three Luftwaffe generals Hitler promoted to field marshal.[72] Over two years later, when the battle for Stalingrad was going poorly, Hitler called on Milch in January 1943 to save the situation. Hitler put Milch in "charge of the entire airlift operation" to relieve the Sixth Army.[73] However, the situation was beyond saving and Milch was unable to achieve the goals Hitler had set for him.[74] Nonetheless, it is important to note that when the situation became critical, Hitler called on Milch. Milch was an ardent and enthusiastic Nazi who strongly believed in Hitler. By 22 February 1944, Milch ranked seventh among Hitler's subordinates.[75]

Wilberg was an intelligent general who also received Hitler's "Aryanization." Wilberg was a first-rate commander who developed the important groundwork for the Luftwaffe operational concept later known as Blitzkrieg.[76] During World War I, Wilberg was the first German air commander who organized and employed whole air groups in the ground attack role. He was one of the senior Luftstreitkraefte (air service in World War I) officers and commanded over seven hundred planes in the great Flanders campaign of 1917, one of the high points of German airpower during the Great War. The army regarded him as one of the pioneers of "ground-support tactics."[77] He was good friends with Milch and had given Milch a squadron to command in World War I.[78] General von Seeckt had hand-picked him to serve as the aviation commander of the secret Luftwaffe from 1920 until 1927. Wilberg became the Reichswehr's leading air theorist[79] and was quite successful getting around most of the Versailles treaty restrictions on training German pilots.[80] He was a serious airpower thinker during the interwar period and was respected by everyone in the aviation field. When the Luftwaffe came into being in 1935, he prepared the operations manual that served as the Luftwaffe's "primary expression of . . . battle doctrine into" World War II.[81] Later in 1935, he commanded the War College.[82] Hitler allowed him to be the staff officer for the Condor Legion[83] during the Spanish Civil War in 1936. He was responsible for the whole operation.[84] Luftwaffe General Erwin Jaenecke wrote that "Wilberg, owing to his abilities and career, was the obvious choice to command the Luftwaffe, a position given . . . to Göring because of party politics. He was tall, good-looking and an officer who was a pleasure to work for, but, unfortunately, he was 50 percent Jewish."[85] Wilberg was an old professional soldier who was unpolitical and clearly did not like the Nazis. Nonetheless, he remained loyal to the Luftwaffe and did all he could to make it a first-rate military organization. He would die in a flying accident on 20 November 1941.

Both Milch and the lesser known Wilberg played crucial roles in developing the Luftwaffe. Hitler probably found it easy to make exemptions for men like Milch and Wilberg because of their abilities. Looking at these men's military records, Hitler had no reason to regret his decision of allowing them to serve although they were *Mischlinge*.

Hitler also allowed *Mischlinge* to serve because they had an important sponsor or relative. Many *Mischlinge* looked for influential people to support their application for exemptions. For example, on 24 October 1941, the "37.5 percent Jew" Gefreiter Achim von Bredow wrote his mother about his application and explained that "it's whom you know that matters here, especially in my situation, and it's quite obvious that I don't have anybody to stand up for me. Doesn't father know anybody in the high ranks of the Panzers?"[86] The later Lieutenant Wilhelm von Gwinner, a quarter-Jew, had received Hitler's exemption because of his military accomplishments. Perhaps the fact that his uncle was General von Studnitz also helped him receive the *Genehmigung*.[87] Gwinner firmly believed that everybody in his situation needed "a guardian angel."[88] Usually friendship played the biggest role in motivating someone in a high position to help a *Mischling*. For example, half-Jew Commander Georg Langheld approached Admiral Hermann Boehm for help in 1934 because of the *Arierparagraph*. "You've been my comrade for many years and to me that's what you will remain," Boehm told him.[89] Thanks to Raeder and others like Boehm, Langheld received the *Deutschblütigkeitserklärung* as soon as his case was brought to Hitler's attention.[90] While in command of the destroyer Z-8 *Bruno Heinemann* from 4 December 1939 until 14 May 1940, Langheld conducted several mine-laying operations off the British coast and embarked troops at Trondheim during the invasion of Norway. From 1942 until the end of the war, he commanded a series of destroyer flotillas.[91]

Throughout government, many in high places were willing to help *Mischlinge* by petitioning Hitler directly. Göring was a good example of a high-ranking official and officer willing to help *Mischlinge*. In 1937, when Göring told Hitler that Arthur Imhausen, a famous chemist and industrialist, was a half-Jew, Hitler announced that if he had really discovered so many amazing things such as synthetic soap, then "we'll declare him Aryan." The next day, Göring informed Imhausen that because of his own efforts, Hitler had declared Imhausen Aryan.[92] Other scientists were also helped. In 1941, Otto Warburg, who had conducted significant cancer research that Hitler valued, was reclassified a quarter-Jew on Göring's orders to mitigate his situation.[93] Göring not only helped distinguished generals and scientists but also assisted common people. He supported half-Jew Walbaum, a Gefreiter, and took his case personally to Hitler.[94] Göring brought the case of the Jew Lieutenant H. Fränzel to Hitler's attention after General Bruno Lörzer[95] recommended this man to him (the authorities believed he was a *Mischling*).[96] He remained an officer in the Luftwaffe. Göring also protected the half-Jewish test pilot, Melitta Gräfin Schenk von Stauffenberg, who would receive the *Deutschblütigkeitserklärung* and EKII for her service.[97] Göring was probably able to help so many people because he "had independent access to Hitler."[98]

Göring was not alone in helping people receive clemency. For example, Oberfüsilier[99] Rüdiger von Briesen, a half-Jew, was only considered and finally approved after General Kurt von Tippelskirch and Rüdiger's cousin, General Kurt von Briesen,[100] wrote letters on his behalf. Consequently, Engel took his case personally to Hitler.[101] After several months, Hitler gave Briesen the *Genehmigung*.

Raeder was another example of a powerful man who helped several people of Jewish descent. Perhaps Raeder was so predisposed because his own son-in-law was a *Mischling*.[102] Raeder wrote after the war, "When individual cases came to my notice, I made use of my right to approach Hitler and various high Party authorities."[103] Certainly cases existed in which Raeder turned a blind eye, but he helped more than one would have expected. For example, Raeder personally helped retired Admiral Karl Kühlenthal, who was a half-Jew married to a full Jew. Based on Raeder's briefing, Hitler allowed Kühlenthal, his wife, and their two sons to remain in Germany and for the admiral to retain his rank and pension. Hitler ordered that he and his family suffer no defamation.[104] After the war, Kühlenthal claimed that without Raeder's help, his family would have been sent to a concentration camp.[105] Raeder also helped the children of Admiral Wolf Wegener, the famous naval strategist, stay in the navy. He was even the godfather of one of Wolf's sons, Edward,[106] a man that his comrades called the best "racial mix" of Prussian charm and Jewish modesty.[107] Although a quarter-Jew, he became a lieutenant commander, winning the German-Cross in Gold.[108] Retired naval logistics officer (Verpflegungsamtsvorsteher) Erich Katz, a Jew, also owed his survival to Raeder. Raeder wrote Katz on 6 January 1940: "I can see from the letter you sent me on 17 December 1939 your difficult situation. . . . In order to support you, I've included a separate letter of recommendation which you may use to help in certain situations. I wish you good success."[109] Furthermore, Raeder pleaded with those who might harm Katz to refrain from doing so.[110] Katz claimed that the Gestapo later informed him that Raeder's letter saved his life.

Not everyone was so fortunate. Retired Lieutenant Field Marshal[111] Johann Friedländer,[112] an Austrian half-Jew, refused to divorce his Jewish wife, Leona Margarethe née Abel, and thus, according to the laws, was also considered Jewish (Geltungsjude). He wrote many officers for assistance, but some ignored him and others were not powerful enough to help. He had tried to become an "honorary Aryan" with the help of lawyers, but without success. He also attempted to prove that his real father had been an Aryan, and not the Jewish husband of his mother, but was not successful. Unfortunately, Friedländer did not have a high-profile personality looking out for him. The Nazis deported him and his wife to Theresienstadt. She would die there. In 1944, the SS deported him to Auschwitz. On 20 January 1945, during a death march,[113] Friedländer could no longer walk, so an SS man pulled out his pistol and shot him in the head.[114]

Government employees also took advantage of their proximity to Hitler to help out Mischlinge in their chain of command. When Hitler's foreign minister, Joachim von Ribbentrop, brought a *Mischling* in his department to Hitler's attention, the Führer quickly gave Ribbentrop permission to retain the man.[115] Ribbentrop claimed in 1946 that he believed "the Führer was not at all uncompromising in those years and I thought he would go on in that direction."[116]

High-ranking officials and officers such as Sauckel, Lammers, Bormann, Canaris, Oster, Heydrich, Engel, Schmundt, Dönitz, Kesselring, Manstein, Baldur von Schirach, Curt von Gottberg, and Kaltenbrunner helped *Mischlinge* by taking their cases to Hitler or to the proper authorities who submitted them to Hitler.[117] At one stage, Hitler claimed that Party members had brought so many cases to him for review that apparently "they [Party members] seem to know more respectable Jews than the total number of Jews in Germany. That is scandalous!"[118] Himmler described this phenomenon during a speech at Posen on 4 October 1943 when he said, "It is hard to talk about [extermination of the Jews], and then they come, 80 million Germans and each one has his decent Jew. Of course, the others are vermin, but this one is an A-1 Jew."[119] Even Himmler helped a Jew, Professor Fritz Pringsheim, leave a concentration camp and escape Germany.[120] Several officials had old comrades of Jewish ancestry. They had seen the common humanity of German-Jewish soldiers who fought bravely and died in World War I. Moreover, many had grown up with Jews and *Mischlinge* and had come to view them as friends and colleagues — some were even relatives or lovers — and they valued these relationships more than they did their anti-Semitism.[121] Hitler seemed to respect the opinions of these men when they endorsed a particular *Mischling* for an exemption. For example, throughout the early 1930s, several people brought the Litzmann family's situation to Hitler's attention. Hitler quickly granted exemptions to the grandchildren of the famous General Karl Litzmann, Staatsrat and Nazi Party member.[122] Litzmann had two grandsons who were quarter-Jews according to Nazi law.[123] Hitler allowed their mother to stay in the Party and her children to remain officers although her husband was a *Mischling*.[124] One of the grandsons, Walter Lehweß-Litzmann, attained the rank of colonel in the Luftwaffe, served as the Luftflotte 5 (Air Fleet 5) operations adjutant to General Hans-Jürgen Stumpff in Norway, and successfully flew 160 missions with the Ju-88 twin-engine medium bomber. For his accomplishments, he received the German-Cross in Gold and the Ritterkreuz.[125]

But not every high-ranking official helped a *Mischling* because he was a friend or family member. Sometimes they did so for material gain. Unteroffizier and quarter-Jew Friedrich Rubien claimed that his cousins (soldier Johann-Christoph Beindorff, Unteroffizier Günther Friedrich, and First Lieutenants Klaus and Wolfgang Beindorff) received the *Deutschblütigkeitserklärung* only because they paid hundred of thousands of Reichsmarks to a Reichskanzlei official who in exchange made sure the applications reached Lammers with favorable reports.[126] According to Rubien, his cousins had to pay over one million Reichsmarks.[127] Goebbels reported such corruption in the KdF: "Appeals for clemency have in part been taken care of by bribery; . . . the Fuehrer blames Bouhler for not having intervened in time."[128] Since a *Mischling* seeking an exemption depended on the goodwill of those handling his case, many felt it worth several thousand Reichsmarks to ensure the application arrived at the proper office with the necessary stamps of approval. Sometimes a *Mischling* would pay off a local civil servant in order to receive his "certificate of Aryan descent." After half-Jew Werner Bujakowsky did this, he entered the army. In 1941, he would die in battle.[129]

Political and international pressure motivated Hitler to grant exemptions. The 1936 Olympics presented Hitler with a dilemma. He wanted an Aryan team, but several well-known athletes were half-Jews. If he refused to let them compete, he would face an international scandal. As a result, in 1935 the half-Jew Helene Mayer was invited to compete for Germany. Mayer, who lived in California at the time, wrote the Reich's sport leader, von Tschammer und Osten, that she would fence for Germany only if the government granted her full citizenship.[130] When the American press got word that Mayer was considering competing for Germany, several American Jews became angry and called her a traitor. Mayer felt that she did not deserve such insults, especially since she was German.[131] Klemperer expressed bewilderment at the insults Mayer received: "I don't know where the great shame is when [Mayer] comes as a German to perform for the Third Reich."[132] The American Olympic team told Germany that if they did not allow Mayer to participate, the United States might boycott the Games.[133] In December 1935, Tschammer informed Mayer that the government had given her and her two brothers full rights as citizens.[134] Mayer won the silver medal in fencing for Nazi Germany.[135]

Mayer was not alone in the Olympics. The government also granted hockey star Rudi Ball, a Jew, permission to represent Germany[136] and Captain Wolfgang Fürstner, a half-Jew, permission to erect and organize the Olympic village.[137] The half-Jewish commissioner of the Games, Theodor Lewald, continued to perform his duties unofficially.[138] Tschammer, who had officially replaced Lewald, addressed a meeting of German sport officials and said, "You are probably astonished by the decision in Vienna, but we had to consider the foreign political situation." He declared that Jewish athletes would not be discriminated against.[139]

Hitler's ideas of racial purity caused political problems not only at the Olympics, but also in dealing with his allies. Hitler could argue that his Italian allies were heirs to the ancient Roman legions and a southern type of Aryan.[140] Justifying the alliance with the Japanese, who fit into the Nazi category of "Asiatic barbarians" and whom Hitler had degraded in *Mein Kampf*, called for a more creative rationalization.[141] Speer called Germany's alliance with Japan "from the racist point of view a dubious affair."[142] Strict Party members disapproved of the association with "barbarians," and the Japanese did not appreciate being called inferior "non-Aryans."[143] Particularly because of the strategic importance of the 1936 Anti-Comintern Pact with Japan, creating a unified front against Communism, Hitler needed to ease the racial tension both internally and externally.[144] Consequently, Hitler "officially" labeled the Japanese "honorary Aryans" because they possessed Germanic qualities,[145] although in private, he felt they posed a grave danger to the white race.[146] Nonetheless, Japanese residents of the Reich were not subject to the racial laws and were allowed to intermarry with Aryans.[147]

Likewise, Hajj Amin el-Husseini, the grand mufti of Jerusalem and leader of the Palestinian Arabs, left the Middle East for Germany in 1941 because of political upheavals and surprisingly the Nazis treated him as an ally.[148] He lived comfortably in an elegant Berlin villa "in the pay of both the Foreign Office and the SS."[149] And once again, the Nazis had to compromise their racial views by approving racial "inferiors" as allies.[150] The Arabs were declared "honorary Aryans" because "the term anti-Semitic did not apply to them" and because Nazism was strictly anti-Jewish and the Arabs were not Jewish.[151] Hitler was impressed with the blond-haired, blue-eyed mufti and was "mildly interested" in the leader.[152] After Hitler met with him in November 1941, Hitler said, "Despite his sharp physiognomy resembling a mouse, he's a person who has among his ancestors more than one Aryan with probably the best Roman heritage."[153]

The central figure in Christianity, the Jew Jesus, presented Hitler with a dilemma: either make an exemption from his racial ideology or face millions of angry Christians if he condemned their savior. Hitler dubbed Jesus an Aryan, and Nazi Christianity revised images of Jesus to look more Nordic and described him no longer as the advocate of love but as the bearer of the sword focused on the rebirth of the *Volk*.[154] Hitler believed Jesus was the greatest early fighter in the war against the Jews and that he did not practice Judaism. Jesus was not, according to Hitler, the apostle of peace. Hitler believed Jesus preached against capitalism, and this was why the Jews, his archenemies, killed him. Hitler had boasted that what Christ had started, he would finish.[155] Hitler approved the Institute for the Research and Elimination of Jewish Influences on Christian Living in Eisenach,[156] headed by Dr. Walter Grundmann. This institute stated that Jesus was Aryan, and published a translation of the Bible that was "de-Jewified." This Bible was written by the poet Lulu von Strauß und Thorney. Hitler "Aryanized" Christianity to make it conform to his *Weltanschauung*. To do so, Hitler had to declare that "Jesus was not a Jew." Thus, Hitler Aryanized Jesus.[157]

Hitler may have allowed exemptions to maximize the number of soldiers available for war. Right before and during the Polish campaign, Hitler allowed many previously discharged *Mischlinge* to reenter the service as officers. He had also included them in the draft, though he generally did not permit half-Jews to serve after 1940. From Hitler's experience in World War I, he knew how many could die in one battle and may have believed that the war would bring him high casualties. However, after his tremendous success in Poland, Hitler may have changed this opinion after seeing Blitzkrieg in action. A few thousand half-Jewish soldiers would not make a difference in the war's outcome. Although most served in the western campaign, Hitler had decided to discharge half-Jews by March 1940. The need for sheer numbers was greatest during the Russian campaign. Germany invaded Russia with 3.6 million soldiers on 22 June 1941. By January 1942, 214,000 German soldiers had died. Casualties had reached over one million by March 1942. In only nine months, almost 30 percent of Germany's soldiers had been put out of action, and by March 1942, 250,000 had fallen.[158] Throughout

1941 and 1942, 809,310 German soldiers died on the eastern front alone.[159] In 1942, Hitler could have recalled thousands of half-Jews. Many felt that the Wehrmacht would indeed draft them back because of the casualties.[160] However, except for a few hundred who received exemptions, Hitler did not allow half-Jews to return en masse to active duty. In 1939, Hitler may have believed that he needed every soldier possible, but by 1942, this conviction had disappeared.

Hitler placed great emphasis on applicants' physical appearance. Photographs seemed to have played a decisive role in Hitler's decision to grant an exemption or not.[161] For example, Admiral Werner Ehrhardt wrote in 1956 that he pressured Navy Adjutant Karl-Jesko von Puttkamer (probably in 1939), to bring the cases of five half-Jews to Hitler's attention. Only after Hitler had personally reviewed their applications, giving special attention to the photos of the men and their families, did he grant them the *Arisierung*.[162] Every application had to have profile and side shots of the *Mischling*, and when the required photos were not enclosed, Hitler would not decide. If the applicant looked stereotypically "Jewish," Hitler apparently rejected him out of hand.[163] For two men, photos played a pivotal role in their applications. They were Commander Paul Ascher, Admiral Lütjens's first staff officer on the battleship *Bismarck*, and General Gotthard Heinrici. During the late 1930s, half-Jew Ascher had to send professional photographs to get Hitler's approval. He was later told that because of these photos, Hitler awarded him the *Deutschblütigkeitserklärung*.[164] Heinrici had a similar ordeal. Several of Heinrici's commanders encouraged him to leave his half-Jewish wife, Getrude née Strupp, but he refused. Consequently, he was "forced" to apply for the *Deutschblütigkeitserklärung* not only for his wife but also for his son, the later Captain Hartmut Heinrici, and daughter, the later Gisela Petersson. All three were photographed extensively to prove, as one family member described, "that they didn't look Jewish, and their features were in fact typically Nordic."[165] In due course, Frau Heinrici and her children became "honorary Aryans."[166] Even later in the war, Hitler's obsession with photos did not abate. On 17 June 1942, Engel wrote Blankenburg and told him that Hitler needed photos of six *Mischlinge* to decide their cases and that Hitler had rejected three because they looked "racially inferior."[167]

A *Mischling* could improve his odds by knowing exactly how to prepare the application and which channels to send it through. For example, Engel wrote on 19 November 1940 to retired navy captain Jochen Vanselow and explained exactly how he should submit an application on behalf of his half-Jewish son. Engel gave more details and helpful advice than the decrees from April 1940 had done: "You should send your application immediately to the Führer and ask to be granted active service for the war's remainder. It's wise first to send the application with a short note to me. What's further absolutely necessary is a complete CV [curriculum vitae] as well as any further documentation like ancestry documents and front and profile photographs of your son."[168] It is surprising that Engel took so much time to help this man, but he seemed to do this for many. Not only did Hitler approve Vanselow's son, but he also gave his daughter clemency.[169]

Beginning in 1941, *Mischlinge* not only had to send in photos, family backgrounds, and military records but also a full portfolio about their political convictions and activities. Throughout 1941, Hitler slowly started to be more influenced by what a *Mischling* had done politically rather than militarily, even when the applicant wanted to remain in the Wehrmacht rather than in the Party. For example, Engel wrote the KdF on 26 September 1941 that for Hitler to decide Gefreiter Alfred Käferle's case, Hitler needed to know if he had been politically active, how he behaved after his discharge, if he had perpetrated any actions against the Nazis, and what the Deutsche Arbeitsfront[170] thought about him. The Baden Gauleiter's report on Käferle had not provided the information necessary for Hitler to make a decision.[171] If a *Mischling* could prove that he had been loyal to the Party, he usually got clemency.

Hitler did not want seriously wounded *Mischling* veterans to suffer discrimination. On 4 May 1941, OKW issued a directive stating that severely disabled *Mischling* veterans (*Stufe* III)[172] who had received their wounds because of actions "above and beyond the call of duty" should apply for the *Deutschblütigkeitserklärung*.[173] In February 1942, the RMI wrote that Hitler had decided that half-Jews severely injured in war should be declared *deutschblütig*, but since the decree was not supposed to be enacted until after the war because of the small number,[174] these wounded men had not yet been awarded such clemency.[175] On 29 September 1943, Dietz in OKW confirmed in a memorandum, probably for Blankenburg, that for a while now, Hitler had declared gravely wounded *Mischlinge deutschblütig*.[176] As OKW wrote in a circular on 16 September 1942, Hitler did not want such soldiers to experience further difficulty, since they had rendered the Reich such service.[177] Although it appeared that this declaration was automatic, most *Mischlinge* still had to apply before Hitler granted them clemency.[178] For example, on 17 August 1943, Obergefreiter Heinrich Bamberger received Hitler's exemption in the mail only after applying for it in August 1941. The certificate said that Hitler had declared him *deutschblütig*, but that the exemption would not allow him to become a Party member. Max Gsell, a friend who was with him when the letter arrived, commented, "Man, you're lucky. You don't even have to join the assholes."[179] Bamberger received this award because of wounds suffered in Russia, two of which were the loss of sight in his left eye and severe head trauma.

However, Hitler did not grant all severely wounded *Mischlinge deutschblütig* status.[180] Unteroffizier Emil Lux, a half-Jew who had lost his arm in battle, applied for the *Deutschblütigkeitserklärung* in 1943 but was rejected because of his political convictions. Even though he had received the EKII and the Silver Wound Badge, he was labeled anti-Nazi and thus unworthy of an exemption.[181] Of several *Mischlinge* in this study who had lost legs, arms, or eyes in the war, only a few were declared *deutschblütig*, although one would think that their wounds qualified them for clemency. The way applications were processed depended on whether the *Mischling* in question was still on active duty. OKW processed those severely wounded *Mischlinge* still on active duty and then sent them to Schmundt for Hitler's decision. KdF handled those who had already been discharged before reaching Hitler.[182] It seems Field Marshal Keitel rerouted the severely wounded veterans to KdF.[183] Wounded *Mischlinge* still on active duty probably had a better chance of receiving clemency, since they did not have to obtain Party recommendations or go through Bouhler's department.

Hitler did not want to be "ungrateful to those *Mischlinge* who had bled for Germany." He sanctioned a decree that allowed those killed in battle to receive the *Deutschblütigkeitserklärung* posthumously. Yet, Hitler issued two stipulations. If a fallen *Mischling* had a wife or children, he would not receive this honor. Furthermore, Hitler's policy stated that after the war, their names would likely be left out of commemorations for fallen soldiers and off war monuments.[184] That meant Hitler subsequently gave, or should have given, thousands of fallen *Mischlinge* the *Deutschblütigkeitserklärung*.[185] In a memorandum, Dietz in OKW explained on 29 September 1943 that during the war, *Mischlinge* who had died had already been declared *deutschblütig*.[186]

Late in the war the criteria for receiving an exemption had significantly changed. Hitler granted exemptions only to *Mischlinge* who had directly worked for the Party. Furthermore, he allowed only those who had not known about their Jewish ancestry until 1933 and had fought for the Party during the *Kampfzeit*[187] to apply. Hitler's reasons for granting exemptions late in the war seemed based less on military necessity and more on ignorance of one's ancestry and loyalty to the Nazis.

Hitler sometimes granted exemptions for no apparent reason other than sympathy or "goodwill" and without distinction in the armed forces or Party. They were people to whom Hitler realistically should not have paid any attention. Engel wrote on 13 August 1938 that Hitler felt sorry for some of these "Jewish" soldiers because, as Hitler said with rare generosity, "Regardless of what people nowadays say, there were brave Jewish soldiers, even Jewish officers during World War I. With such individuals, one can make an exception, because the children cannot help it who their parents were." Engel explained the tragic circumstances surrounding most of these cases: "I noticed that Hitler didn't like to hear this, but he promised he would look at each case."[188] Indeed, Hitler did review thousands of ordinary soldiers, and perhaps his sympathy for them motivated him to grant some exemptions.

How Many Exemptions Were Granted during the Third Reich?

The evidence does not permit a definite determination of how many *Mischlinge* received some form of clemency. Although this study has documented hundreds of *Mischlinge* with exemptions, the Nazis did not keep complete records about these men, and the few documents that do list statistics must be looked at skeptically. Tables 9 to 11 illustrate the statistics given by different offices at different times during the Third Reich and this study's findings. These numbers do not correspond probably because of the different sources

Table 9. Conflicting Reports of Number of Exceptions (Half-Jews)

Source	Date	APPLIED		GENEHMIGUNG		DEUTSCHBLÜTIGKEITSERKLÄRUNG		PENDING	
		Half-Jews	Married to Half-Jews	Half-Jews	Married to Half-Jews	Half-Jews	Married to Half-Jews	Half-Jews	Married to Half-Jews
BA-B DZA, Bl. 29–32 Reichskanzlei	31 Dec. 1940–30 Sept. 1943	1,563	113	130	24	14	2	81	20
BA-B DZA, Bl. 43 Blankenburg's office	28 Oct. 1943	845		126[a]		N/A	N/A	101	
BA-B DZA. Bl. 147–48 Blankenburg's office	9 June 1942	310	21	139	21	11	1	225	
BA-B DZA Bl. 136–137. Letter from Bormann to Bouhler	1940–1942	Unknown	N/A	262	N/A	N/A		Unknown	
IfZ, N 71–73 Anträge und positive Entscheidungen gemäß §7 der Ersten Verordnung zum Reichsbürger-gesetz	1935–22 May 1941	9,636[b]		260		N/A		Unknown	
IfZ, N 71–73, Zahl der Gnadenentscheidungen nach dem Reichsbürger-gesetz	10 Sept. 1942	Unknown		258[c]		394[c]		Unknown	
BA-MA, BMRS, Bryan Mark Rigg Collection	N/A	Unknown		69	Unknown	74	20	Unknown	

[a]Including the OKW figures, the number would be 213.
[b]Includes Jews and quarter-Jews.
[c]Degree of *Mischling* not stated.

Table 10. Conflicting Reports of Number of Exceptions (Quarter-Jews)

Source	Date	APPLIED		GENEHMIGUNG		DEUTSCHBLÜTIGKEITSERKLÄRUNG		PENDING	
		Quarter-Jews	Married to Quarter-Jews	Quarter-Jews	Married to Quarter-Jews	Quarter-Jews	Married to Quarter-Jews	Quarter-Jews	Married to Quarter-Jews
BA-B DZA, Bl. 29–32 Reichskanzlei	31 Dec. 1940 –30 Sept. 1943	288	80	167	62	19	3	152	21
BA-B DZA, Bl. 43 Blankenburg's office	28 Oct. 1943	239		139		N/A		173	
BA-B DZA. Bl. 147–48 Blankenburg's office	9 June 1942	62	4	55	4		0	109	
BA-B DZA Bl. 136–37 Letter from Bormann to Bouhler	1940–1942	Unknown	N/A	186	N/A	N/A		Unknown	
BA-MA, BMRS, Bryan Mark Rigg	N/A	Unknown	Unknown	20	Unknown	137	15	Unknown	

Table 11. Conflicting Reports of Number of Exceptions (Jews)

Source	Date	APPLIED		GENEHMIGUNG		DEUTSCHBLÜTIGKEITSERKLÄRUNG		PENDING	
		Jews	Married to Jews	Jews	Married to Jews	Jews	Married to Jews	Jews	Married to Jews
BA-B DZA, Bl. 29–32 Reichskanzlei	31 Dec. 1940– 30 Sept. 1943	33	35	0	0	0	0	0	0
BA-MA, BMRS, Bryan Mark Rigg	N/A	Unknown	Unknown	4	0	2	3	0	0

these bureaucracies used, the indifference with which some of these bureaucrats approached the task, and the lack of coordination between the various offices that worked on exemptions.

On 10 August 1940, Wehrkreis VII Munich, one of seventeen military districts, made a list of officers with special status. This list counted 2,269 officers who had received special permission to enter the Wehrmacht. The document does not indicate how many of the 2,269 were "quarter-Jews or married to quarter-Jews."[189] According to an officer who worked in OKH Personnel Office in 1944, most of these 2,269 were probably quarter-Jews. He also speculated that combining the *Mischling* officers with exemptions from all seventeen military districts would raise the number by a factor of five to seven, for a total of between 11,000 and 16,000 *Mischlinge* serving as a result of exemptions.[190]

The RMI stated that from November 1935 to 27 May 1941, Hitler had approved 260 out of 9,636 petitions under section 7 of the supplementary decree to the Nuremberg Laws.[191] As Beate Meyer rightly notes, this number of 9,636 is low.[192] Several tens of thousands of applications must have been submitted. On 2 June 1942, Bormann reported to Bouhler that between 1940 and 1942, 262 half-Jews and 186 quarter-Jews had received Hitler's *Genehmigung*. On 16 June 1942, Engel clarified to Blankenburg that 134 half-Jews and 115 quarter-Jews of the group Bormann reported were in the Wehrmacht.[193] On 9 June 1942, Blankenburg compiled a list stating that Hitler had granted the *Genehmigung* to 139 half-Jews and 55 quarter-Jews and the *Deutschblütigkeitserklärung* to 11 half-Jews and 4 quarter-Jews out of 331 half-Jewish and 66 quarter-Jewish male applicants. A further 225 half-Jewish and 109 quarter-Jewish applicants were still in process.[194] In September 1942, the government reported that 258 had been given *Genehmigungen* and 394 had received *Deutschblütigkeitserklärungen*.[195]

In September 1943, a certain H. Politz in the Reichskanzlei compiled statistics for Sachbearbeiter Dietz on *Mischling* exemptions. From January 1940 to September 1943 according to this document, Hitler approved 130 half-Jews out of 1,560 applications and 165 quarter-Jews out of 288 applications for the *Genehmigung*. The Reichskanzlei also reported that from January 1940 to September 1943, Hitler declared 14 half-Jews and 19 quarter-Jews *deutschblütig*. Decisions were pending for a further 81 half-Jewish and 152 quarter-Jewish cases.[196]

KdF put a list together on 28 October 1943 stating that out of 859 applicants who went through their office between 1940 and September 1943, 126 half-Jews or Aryans married to half-Jews received *Genehmigungen.* The KdF added that if the applicants approved by OKW who received Hitler's approval were included, then the number of those who received *Genehmigungen* would be 213. The KdF was still working on a further 101 applications. The document commented that the number of applications received represented less than 5 percent of a possible 21,800 of half-Jews and men married to half-Jews eligible for military service. The document also stated that between 1940 and June 1942, cases involving 139 of 239 quarter-Jews or men married to quarter-Jews had received exemptions. A further 173 cases were pending.[197] These statistics were probably made hastily and were incomplete. Government documents did not include those people Hitler exempted between 1933 and 1935, such as Field Marshal Milch or General Wilberg. Cases approved after 1944 were also not included.

This study has documented 4 Jews, 69 half-Jews, and 20 quarter-Jews who received Hitler's *Genehmigung,* and 2 Jews, 74 half-Jews, and 137 quarter-Jews who received Hitler's *Deutschblütigkeitserklärung,* most granted by 1941. These numbers total 306, and the majority were military officers.

This study's evidence indicates that statistics from the RMI were off by almost one hundred people in 1939. Hitler approved more people than previously believed. This was especially the case, since many *Mischlinge* who died in battle were posthumously granted the *Deutschblütigkeitserklärung.* According to the Reichskanzlei, only 33 received the *Deutschblütigkeitserklärung* between January 1940 and September 1943. According to this study's findings, between 1940 and 1943, 54 received it. Perhaps the Reichskanzlei or OKW tried to hide the real figures from certain people in the Parteikanzlei, such as Bormann, or just did not keep accurate records. Lammers claimed after the war that the number of *Mischlinge* granted exemptions ran into the thousands.[198] Most of the data sheets made by Bouhler's office under Blankenburg's supervision were to prove to Bormann that KdF had not been too lenient with *Mischlinge.* Consequently, their findings must be looked at with skepticism. Bouhler's office most certainly made the figures smaller to prove to Bormann that his department had not helped *Mischlinge.* Moreover, since the government had never planned to count all of them, as Colonel Georg Erdmann's experience (as head of Group IV in the P2 Group Office) in OKH indicates (see chapter 8), the Reichskanzlei, KdF, OKW, and the Parteikanzlei did not have complete databases from which to draw accurate figures.

Although the numbers vary widely, it is clear that thousands applied for racial exemptions. Quarter-Jews faced better odds than half-Jews. Hitler approved over 60 percent of quarter-Jewish applicants while approving only 10 percent of half-Jewish applicants from the Reichskanzlei files. For example, in July 1942, at a time when no half-Jews were being approved, Hitler approved over half of the quarter-Jews who came to his attention.[199] We will never know exactly how many received some form of clemency from Hitler, but the fact remains that there were thousands, especially since most *Mischlinge* who died in war were supposed to receive the *Deutschblütigkeitserklärung*.

How Did Those Who Received Exemptions View Their Effect?

Most described receiving the exemptions as a momentous event in their lives. They still feel a sense of importance when they talk about it. When Wilhelm von Gwinner received Hitler's *Genehmigung* on 5 March 1941, he remembered: "I had a problem with Hitler because of my Jewish past. My problem was solved by the *Genehmigung*. My salvation. With the *Genehmigung*, I was no longer a *Mischling*." Even today, Gwinner feels a sense of accomplishment in receiving this exemption.[200] Walter Hamburger felt "pleased and relieved" about the success of his efforts in getting clemency, which allowed him to return to the army. Although he knew he would have to put himself in danger if he received the exemption, he felt this was the only way to protect himself and his father. In 1994, he still believed that he was the only one who received such an honor.[201] Hamburger's belief that his award was unique was common. Ernst Prager thought he was one of only a few because of the seven years Hitler spent reviewing his case before awarding him the *Deutschblütigkeitserklärung*.[202]

Many felt that Hitler's exemption restored their self-respect. On 15 October 1942, Dr. Gerhard Koken wrote Engel that after his half-Jewish son Lutz was promoted to Unteroffizier, "much of his depression and inhibitions" had disappeared.[203] However, the Koken family felt unsure whether Lutz should stay in the army. Engel answered Dr. Koken's letter on 19 October and gave him the "friendly advice" that Lutz should remain in the army and concentrate on his duties because he needed to distinguish himself further to receive the *Deutschblütigkeitserklärung*. Engel told the family they were lucky, because for a long time half-Jews had been denied exemptions regardless of their combat service. "We should be thankful to Providence," Engel wrote, "that Hitler gave his signature" for Lutz's *Genehmigung*.[204] Some felt a *Genehmigung* saved their lives. Half-Jew Arnim Leidoff felt that without it, he would have been deported to a concentration camp.[205]

Others were encouraged by their relatives to get an exemption. When the officer and quarter-Jew Georg Meyer wanted to marry, his future father-in-law, General Hans Rühle von Lilienstern, expressed his reservations to his daughter, Margot, about the fact that she would be marrying a quarter-Jew. Both he and his wife, Lisa, liked Georg and approved of the marriage, but felt that they could encounter problems later because of his ancestry. Nonetheless, Margot and Georg were married on 1 April 1939 in the chapel of the Königsberg[206] castle. Margot's family was shocked that Georg had any "Jewish blood" because he "looked so Aryan" with his blond hair and blue eyes. In 1942, thinking that Meyer might experience career difficulties, Rühle von Lilienstern suggested that Meyer apply for the *Arisierung*. Meyer's wife, Margot, maintained, "We had heard that Hitler had said, 'Who's Jewish and not, I'll decide.'"[207] Georg had little faith in the Aryanization process, but he complied with his father-in-law's wishes. On 4 March 1942, Georg and his cousin, First Lieutenant Helmut Meyer-Krahmer, received the *Deutschblütigkeitserklärung* without much trouble. In 1944, his superior wrote that Meyer, a lieutenant colonel and general staff officer, was a "passionate officer" and "convinced National Socialist."[208] He had been decorated with the EKII and the War Service Cross Second Class. He proved that he was worthy of this clemency. He and two of his three brothers, Lieutenant Ulrich Meyer and Unteroffizier Rolf Meyer, died fighting in the war.[209]

Many felt that Hitler's exemptions would protect them and their families. Exemptions did indeed help, but often not as much as the *Mischlinge* thought. As pointed out earlier, although Prager could marry his fiancée and

return to the army, his exemption did not prevent the Nazis from deporting his uncle to Theresienstadt and forcing his father to wear the star and
perform forced labor.[210] In 1941, Prager had hoped his award would save
his family, but two years later, this hope proved unrealistic.

Some Jewish relatives did not want a Hitler exemption in the family.
They feared what could happen to their loved ones in battle. Mrs. Elisabeth
Maria Heard née Borchardt wrote that she and her Jewish father, Philipp
(who had been sent to Dachau in 1938),[211] both felt ashamed that her brothers, Major Robert Borchardt and Lieutenant Ernst Borchardt, got "Aryan
declarations" and continued to fight. The father was "furious" with his sons,
and the family felt upset that the brothers had wanted an exemption from
Hitler. Their sister argued that the dangers of war heavily outweighed the
benefits of clemency. She cited the case of her younger brother, Ernst, who
was incapacitated by battle wounds and shot himself after several years in
constant pain. She said her family never understood why her older brother,
Robert, felt proud of his Ritterkreuz even after the war. Borchardt had
received this prestigious medal on 23 August 1941 for holding a strategic
position near Uman with his Panzer company that ultimately saved hundreds of German soldiers.[212] His superior, Colonel Menton, wrote in a
review that "Borchardt's extraordinary bravery was praised in the official
army news letter." Menton then recommended him for the General Staff
School, a very high honor.[213] During one discussion after 1945, Borchardt
told his sister, "I served because I wanted to prove Hitler's racial nonsense
wrong. I wanted to prove that people of Jewish descent were indeed brave
and courageous soldiers."[214]

As the war progressed, many *Mischlinge* realized that no piece of paper
could make them truly *deutschblütig*. Lieutenant Eike Schweitzer, half-Jew
and descendant of Moses Mendelssohn, received the *Genehmigung* in 1941
and wrote his Aunt Dorle on 11 January 1942:

I see that I've deceived myself. Instead of making things clearer, sim-
pler, all that I've experienced just makes things more confusing. I
only understand a few things clearly; everything else is chaos. . . . My
situation is so impossible and always up in the air, observations of
it sound delusional. My position as a soldier is such a paradox that
there is no rational explanation. It would be good if I could talk to

someone about these things, yet there's no one with whom I am ever really honest. That's a horrible position to be in. I've often feared that in the heat of the moment I would say more than I should. I'm not afraid of the truth but once I started, I would have to tell everything. . . . I've become lonely. Many good friends are dead. If only it would all end soon.[215]

Schweitzer realized his hope for equality was an illusion and felt unsure about why he actually served. His family was being persecuted and his father had already immigrated to the United States.[216] He longed for someone to confide in who could provide him with at least some sympathy if not understanding. In his loneliness, Schweitzer became fatalistic about his future. Schweitzer died in battle in 1945. Many felt cheated, especially after years of hoping that their service would bring equality to them and their families.

Many could serve and retain their rank, self-respect, and pay, but were passed over for promotion and disdained in most social circles. As with General Wilberg, even if a *Mischling* officer had received Hitler's *Deutschblütigkeitserklärung,* he was often denied responsibilities equal to his capabilities.[217]

As previously stated, Hitler played an active role in evaluating *Mischling* applicants for racial exemptions. In the summer of 1941, before one of the greatest battles of modern history, Hitler continued to review applications. Did he have nothing better to do than to analyze applications from *Mischlinge,* sometimes with a rank no higher than private, to see whether they were worthy to be declared *deutschblütig?* Hitler took racial hygiene very seriously. He felt that only he could decide whether one was really a *Mischling* or an Aryan. Even during Stalingrad, one of the most decisive battles of the war, Hitler turned his attention to the problems of *Mischlinge.* He often busied himself with policy minutiae during times when one would think that other matters of greater importance required his attention.[218] As is often the case with Hitler, finding rational explanations for his behavior is difficult.

Instead of worrying about the war, Hitler turned his attention on 15 January 1943 to half-Jew Renate Schiller. Hitler declared her and her daughter Christa *deutschblütig.* He also decided that since her longtime lover, Captain Ludwig Eitel, had died, they could retroactively be declared husband and wife. She would have been married to Eitel had the laws allowed this union. She had to send in photos of their child with her application to prove that they had no unpleasant racial characteristics. Hitler also granted her a widow's pension. Frey wrote her on 10 February 1943 to tell her the good news.[219] The attention Hitler gave to Schiller's case, even if only a few minutes, showed Hitler's inability to prioritize his duties during a time when Germany was about to lose one of its most important battles — Stalingrad. But Hitler often gave his time and energy to "trivial matters" such as horse racing, architecture, art, and history.[220] Hitler became quite adept at turning a blind eye to reality when much more pressing issues were at hand.

Hundreds of *Mischlinge* continued to submit applications throughout 1943 and 1944 during a time when the Holocaust was reaching its apex and the Wehrmacht was suffering frightful defeats in Russia. Hundreds of Aryan officers showed surprising understanding and sympathy for these *Mischlinge,* writing them recommendations and giving them counsel. The fact that *Mischlinge* sent applications for exemptions demonstrated that some still believed Germany would win the war. Even those who thought Germany would lose the war sought to protect themselves in the interim, since no one could predict its end.

It is understandable why *Mischlinge* would want to obtain Hitler's exemption. Receiving an exemption made life easier. The inordinate amount of time that Hitler took to examine these applications not only seems bizarre but also indicates that he truly believed in his racial doctrine and that he alone could decide whether a soldier was worthy to enter the ranks of the Aryans.

8

The Process of Obtaining
an Exemption

The Process of Granting Exemptions from the Racial Laws

The process by which Hitler granted exemptions as well as the criteria he used to make decisions evolved throughout the Third Reich. *Mischling* policy remained in a state of permanent improvisation. One thing was certain: Hitler took his responsibility to grant exemptions seriously. He personally decided every case, and when he did consider someone for an exemption, it took him weeks, often months, to decide.[1] Sometimes Hitler decided in a single day, as in the case of Georg Langheld, a destroyer commander and later a winner of the German-Cross in Gold.[2] Other times Hitler took several years to make a decision, as in the case of Captain Ernst Prager.[3] Normally, he looked through photos, curricula vitae, family histories, military records, and military and Party recommendations to decide whether a soldier deserved immunity.

Hitler could not be "bypassed or ignored" on key issues, and the government relied on his decisions.[4] His ad hoc style was characterized by spurts of activity punctuated with long spaces of inactivity. He gave much of his time to analyzing the *Mischling* applications. Where decisions were awkward for him, for whatever reasons (as the Prager case and the extermination of ex-*Mischling* soldiers apparently were), he avoided action.[5] He often acted quickly and favorably when faced with apparently difficult decisions, such as declaring generals and admirals *deutschblütig*. One thing is for certain: when a *Mischling* was considered for clemency, Hitler knew about it.

Before Hitler took power in 1933, political importance was the standard used to determine whether a person deserved clemency. In Hitler's eyes,

Röhm's and Heydrich's abilities to forward his movement outweighed their offensive characteristics of being homosexual or of Jewish descent. If a person was deemed to have political importance, Hitler apparently ignored the other issues, and the person was allowed to remain at his post.

When Hitler took power in 1933, people of Jewish descent immediately started to experience problems. This increased after Hitler issued the *Arierparagraph* for the Civil Service in 1933 and after Blomberg issued the same decree for the Reichswehr in 1934. As far as the laws were concerned, a legal process had not yet developed by which someone could apply for exemptions. Non-Aryans either fell under the Hindenburg provisions, were granted immunity by Hitler, or were dismissed. Despite the claim by some historians, the Hindenburg exemptions continued to be used throughout late 1934 and 1935 and were not totally "abolished after his death" in August 1934.[6]

During 1935, the issuing of exemptions became more formalized as more people were involved and procedures became more complicated. Hitler and several of his ministers discussed how to deal with this new and convoluted field. For instance, in May 1935 Blomberg asked Lammers, secretary of state and head of the Reichskanzlei, whether non-Aryans who trained soldiers should remain in the service.[7] Reichenau, Blomberg's assistant, provided the answer on 22 May. He maintained that on principle, non-Aryans could not hold positions of authority, but if war broke out, the Wehrmacht would use special regulations to handle these cases, and Hitler would give final approval.[8]

Hitler made exemptions for the Party as well. To illustrate, when Fritz Sauckel, the Reich's governor of Braunschweig, brought SA-Sturmführer (Lieutenant) Hans Sander's case to Hitler's attention, Hitler responded quickly and favorably. On 30 July 1935, Hitler awarded quarter-Jewish Sander, who was a passionate Nazi and had the Gold Party Badge, the approval to remain in the Party and the SA.[9] Hitler allowed several *Mischlinge* like Sander to remain in the Party, but as Hitler wrote Minister Frick, these men "cannot hold positions of authority" because of the danger if they suddenly started acting like Jews.[10]

Section 7 of the first supplementary decree of November 1935 to the Nuremberg Laws allowed for exemptions officially.[11] Hitler specifically put in this safety clause that allowed him to grant exemptions from the restrictions placed on Jews and *Mischlinge*.[12] Probably based on his previous experience with non-Aryans, Hitler recognized that he should not tie his prestige to a law that might later serve to restrict his power. The historian Karl Schleunes called these loopholes "Hitlerian afterthought[s]."[13] As Hitler had claimed in 1937, "[W]hat matters constantly is not to take any step forward that I would have to retract."[14] With his signature, Hitler could declare someone *deutschblütig*. Petitions for exemptions based on Party service, civil or military importance, or exceptional distinction in some field of study could be sent to the RMI. If the RMI approved it, the Ministry sent the application to Hitler for final authorization. At this initial stage, Blomberg and Frick seem to have been responsible for examining whether a *Mischling* deserved an exception *(Ausnahme)*[15] for the armed forces before it reached Hitler for a final decision.

After this supplementary decree and both General Milch and Helene Mayer's cases became public knowledge, thousands started to send in their applications.[16] Sometimes *Mischlinge* wanted to remain officers, at other times they wanted to keep Jewish or Aryan maids, and still other times to marry Aryans or *Mischlinge*.[17]

Before November 1935, Hitler usually had a specific letter of exemption drawn up for the *Mischling* in question. After the adoption of the Nuremberg Laws, he had standard forms printed. When the individual in question received Hitler's *Deutschblütigkeitserklärung,* the Reichskanzlei would send this former *Mischling* a form letter signed by Hitler, often accompanied by Keitel's and Lammers's signatures.[18] A month or so after the individual received this letter, he would then receive an official green "German blood" certificate from Dr. Kurt Meyer, the director of the Reich Office for Genealogy Research, allowing him to describe himself as *deutschblütig* in official documents.[19]

Hitler's exemptions did not permit certain privileges unless explicitly stated. For example, "Aryanized people" could not become Party members or farmers.[20] Also, unless specifically mentioned, the racial status of the approved applicant's children did not change. If a *Mischling* married a *Mischling,* then there seemed to be no hope of altering the children's racial status unless the children received some form of clemency directly.[21] In the Wehrmacht, one could not be promoted above colonel unless the exemption stated otherwise.[22] For example, when half-Jew Colonel Walter

Hollaender, who had won the German-Cross in Gold and the Ritterkreuz, was up for promotion to general, he was rejected because of his Jewish father, although he was described as a "convinced National Socialist" and had been friends with Reichenau. Hollaender was devastated.[23] Moreover, Hitler had expressed his desire that no Aryanized wounded *Mischling* veteran could settle in the eastern territories without additional approvals. The report stated that although these *Mischlinge* had been severely wounded (which might have meant that they had received an exemption), that did not give them special rights to live in the East.[24]

From 1935 through 1940, Hitler had Lammers, his closest legal adviser, formulate more elaborate exemption documents. Hitler still ultimately decided each case personally, with little advice from others,[25] except from the unimaginative Lammers. On 4 October 1937, Hitler ordered that all applications go through Lammers. On 25 October 1937, Lammers wrote important civil and military offices to inform them about Hitler's decision that Lammers would present applications for exemptions from the race-related provisions of the Nuremberg Laws to Hitler personally. Apparently, different offices had been sending their applications without any systematic order. In response to this confusion, Lammers assured all offices that he would take special care to observe each applicant's importance for Germany.[26] It is difficult to trace exactly who processed the applications and how they eventually ended up in Hitler's office because the Nazi administration had a very "fluid character."[27] There was no chain of command but rather nominal bosses and deputies one had to approach before reaching Lammers, who was Hitler's gatekeeper at this time.[28] The highly acclaimed Nazi coordination of political, social, and public life, called *Gleichschaltung,*[29] was not as polished or organized as one would think. Hitler often created "new offices and agencies without establishing clear lines of demarcation of responsibility with existing government departments."[30] Nonetheless, although applications continued to reach Hitler's office through most government channels open to him, the majority, especially during the late 1930s, were sent to Lammers before traveling on to the Führer.

The bald, shy, and one-eyed[31] Lammers reviewed most letters sent to Hitler on matters of state. By 1936, Lammers's office was handling six hundred communications daily. Consequently, Lammers held a position approximately equivalent to "Vice-Chancellor"[32] because he prepared state matters for Hitler and added his own evaluations. He became the unofficial coordinator between the ministries and the Reichskanzlei. With the exception of Bormann, he achieved more importance than other ministers because he had the Führer's ear. Lammers often knew what was happening throughout the top levels of the government, especially from 1935 to 1941. Hitler often left it up to him to carry out an order and to select the means and the personnel to do it.[33] Kershaw writes that "the only link between government ministers and Hitler was through Lammers."[34] Only with the rise of Bormann's power in 1941–1942 and when military considerations assumed paramount importance in the summer of 1941 did Lammers's importance as Hitler's adviser dwindle. By 1943, Bormann had usurped all essential power of the Reichskanzlei. Out of the several *Deutschblütigkeitserklärungen* and *Genehmigungen* collected for this study (mostly done between 1936 and 1941), Lammers almost always cosigned them. As Lammers said at Nuremberg, "I was responsible for seeing to it that the Führer's wishes were properly and suitably formulated." Lammers was in control of the legal formulation of Hitler's will, and such orders were, as Lammers said, always "co-signed by me."[35] Speer mockingly called Lammers the Reich's "notary."[36]

The vast majority of full Jews were not included in Hitler's exemption process after 1935. However, a few Jews did receive some form of clemency from the racial laws. Goebbels, Göring, and Hitler protected some who, because of their usefulness scientifically or politically, served their purposes. These Jews were called *Schutzjuden* (protected Jews), and in Berlin alone, there were some two hundred of them.[37] As far as the armed forces were concerned, it seems that most Jews were not given clemency.

Most Jewish World War I veterans received no help. The majority were abandoned, had their pensions reduced, and were later deported to concentration camps. In 1939, when Field Marshal von Mackensen asked Hitler to help some German-Jewish veterans, Hitler said that in principle, "any application for exemption concerning a Jew must be rejected."[38] During the war, Hitler apparently did not make an exception to this policy. For example, Schmundt brought the case of the German Jew Captain Erich Rose, who was a liaison officer between the Wehrmacht and the Spanish Blue Division,[39] to Hitler's attention sometime in 1942. Hitler reportedly said that Rose was a good officer, and "had he been a half-Jew, I would have given him the *Arisierung . . .* but a 75 percent Jew must be rejected." Hitler felt that the Blue Division was a good place for Rose.[40]

Between 1935 and 1939, most *Mischlinge* who did not hold a rank higher than Gefreiter had no problems — they were allowed to serve. Especially after 1935, most *Mischlinge* usually had no problems performing their mandatory two-year military service. Only those who aspired to become or were already NCOs or officers had difficulties.

From 1934 to 1939, Hitler reviewed many *Mischling* officers. He allowed several to remain at their posts. For example, the Fifth Division wrote OKH on 6 September 1937 that quarter-Jew Captain Alfred Simon deserved help to get a job in the Civil Service after his discharge. The Nuremberg Laws canceled the provision in the *Arierparagraph,* which previously allowed non-Aryans who had served in World War I to remain officers.[41] This stipulation had protected Simon until 1935. Reichenau wrote the Army Personnel Office on 3 August 1937 that both Simon's ignorance about his ancestry and good military record warranted that the army retain him or find him a civilian post. Reichenau argued that this proven comrade should not be treated poorly.[42] OKH wrote Göring on 11 September 1937 for his assistance.[43] Eventually, Reichenau and others' efforts produced the desired result. On 15 June 1938, Hitler gave Simon an exemption citing that his World War I service entitled him to remain in the army.[44] The following year, Hitler declared Simon *deutschblütig.* Simon later attained the rank of colonel and earned both Iron Crosses and the War Service Cross Second Class during World War II. His commander described him as a good soldier and "positive about National Socialism."[45]

Simon was lucky that he was not one of the several *Mischlinge* the Wehrmacht discharged between 1934 and 1939. However, many of those discharged were told that if war broke out, they would be drafted back. For example, in 1936 the army discharged lieutenants and quarter-Jewish brothers Heinz and Joachim Rohr. At the time, Heinz felt sad. The commander of Dresden's Kriegsschule,[46] General Joachim Lemelsen, took Heinz into his arms, shook his head, and said, "How could they do this to your father?" Rohr's father, Willy, was a famous World War I officer, commander of Storm Battalion Rohr. Before Rohr left, Lemelsen told Heinz to call him if he ever needed any help.[47] Rohr knew he could do nothing other than obey the laws, so he decided to start his university studies. But before leaving, his superior told him to apply for an exemption. Not Rohr, but his mother Elisabeth, who still had several contacts among the military elite, started the difficult process to obtain exemptions for her sons.

These applications included pictures, military records, records of his family's military past, ancestry information, and recommendations. For example, Lieutenant Klaus von Schmeling-Diringshofen, a soldier Manstein had unsuccessfully tried to retain in 1934, filed an application for exemption before he left for China, where he worked under Seeckt training the Chinese National Army. In 1938, Ursula von Knigge, Klaus's sister, said Engel came to her home to gather family documents and photographs to convince Hitler to declare the family *deutschblütig*. She humored Engel but did not hope for much. After several days, she sent him off with a large stack of documents. Engel told her that the applications of several men were being filed away in case of war.[48]

Engel was willing to help many *Mischlinge* get the coveted *Genehmigung* or *Deutschblütigkeitserklärung*. Engel became Hitler's army adjutant after the Fritsch-Blomberg crisis in 1938. He immediately was thrust into Hitler's presence and accompanied him on many trips and was present at several meetings when Hitler outlined his policies.[49] Engel's responsibility was to facilitate communication between Hitler and OKH.[50] He often went on private walks with Hitler, which was a coveted honor.[51] During these walks as well as during their trips and meetings, Hitler discussed many matters with Engel,[52] among them the *Mischling* question. Engel spent a lot of his time helping *Mischlinge* prepare their applications.[53] After Bouhler and Blankenburg approved an army applicant politically, the applicant's file was sent on to Engel to present to Hitler. Engel's responsibilities enabled him to bring several cases to Hitler's attention, and this study supports his claim that he helped *Mischlinge* when he could. He also had constant contact with his boss, Schmundt,[54] with whom he frequently discussed *Mischling* cases.[55] Hitler met regularly with both Engel and Schmundt, and often told them how to handle *Mischling* personnel.[56] Engel was joined by Hitler's navy adjutant, Karl-Jesko von Puttkamer, and his Luftwaffe adjutant, Nicolaus von Below. According to Below, petitions for clemency *(Bitt- und Gnadengesuche)* for Wehrmacht personnel first went through Bouhler's office. Below described that Hitler's military adjutants worked closely with KdF and that Bouhler's "nice and congenial" staff encouraged this cooperation.[57] The adjutant from the branch of service where the *Mischling* in question served was needed to process the case.[58] Below reports spending about one hour each day handling petitions for clemency for soldiers and their family members.[59] Since the majority of those who applied for clemency came from the army, simply because it was the biggest service, one can assume that Engel spent more than an hour a day on exemption cases.

Between 1938 and 1939, Hitler brought several of the *Mischlinge* he had discharged back into the ranks, declaring them along with those *Mischlinge* who had remained on active duty *deutschblütig*.[60] Hitler had complete dossiers on these men, as the Rohr and Schmeling-Diringshofen cases illustrate, thanks in part to Engel. On 2 September 1939, OKH reported that Hitler had declared a group of officers *deutschblütig* who were either 50 percent Jewish or married to 50 percent Jewish women and who were World War I veterans. There were others, such as half-Jew Colonel Karl Zukertort, whom Hitler had not yet decided on. Men in Zukertort's situation were simply told that they were to remain at their posts until Hitler had reviewed their applications.[61] Those who had not applied or had been rejected were to be discharged. Hitler had already declared as *deutschblütig* officers who were 25 percent Jewish or married to 25 percent Jewish wives and who were World War I veterans.[62] Hitler gave three out of four officers and NCOs whom the Kriegsmarine had discharged between 1934 and 1939 the *Deutschblütigkeitserklärung*.[63] Hitler also declared several *Mischlinge*, all admirals, *deutschblütig* during this period.[64] Evidently in every case, Hitler agreed with Raeder's assessment of the *Mischling* in question.[65] For example, quarter-Jew Admiral Bernhard Rogge experienced great personal hardships until Raeder took his case to Hitler. Soon thereafter, Hitler declared him *deutschblütig* in 1939. This change of status saved Rogge from utter despair. Earlier in 1939, several Party officials[66] had made Rogge's life a "living Hell," and both his beloved Jewish wife and his mother-in-law had committed suicide because of this persecution. Rogge received Hitler's *Deutschblütigkeitserklärung* soon after war broke out, which prevented Nazi bureaucrats from further attacking him.[67] Rogge accepted this "privilege" and went about his duties as a typical Prussian officer. He was the most successful surface raider commander of the war, sinking or capturing twenty-two ships for a combined displacement of 150,000 tons with his ship *Atlantis* while being at sea for 655 straight days and traveling over one hundred thousand miles.[68] At war's end, Rogge was in charge of battle group "Rogge," which included the old battleship *Schlesien,* the heavy cruiser *Prinz Eugen,* the light cruiser *Leipzig,* and escorts.[69] His flag flew on the *Prinz Eugen.*[70] Rogge was just one of hundreds of *Mischlinge* who received the *Deutschblütigkeitserklärung* from 1938 to 1940. For example, Colonel Werner Schmoeckel took his quarter-Jewish son and half-Jewish wife's cases *(Gnadengesuch)* to the proper authorities in the late 1930s. His son, Helmut, had been discharged from the Kriegsmarine in 1936 as a Fähnrich z. S.[71] because of the *Arierparagraph.* Yet through his father's efforts, Hitler declared Helmut and his mother *deutschblütig* on 2 September 1939. Helmut Schmoeckel would become a U-boat captain in 1943 *(U-boat 802)* and would earn the EKII and EKI. He successfully conducted four patrols off the Canadian coast and in the North Atlantic for a total of 247 days.[72] A fellow U-boat captain, Thilo Bode *(U-858),* said of Schmoeckel, "I could not believe that he was Jewish. He was more blond than any Aryan I had ever seen. It was no wonder that Hitler Aryanized him."[73]

Quarter-Jews Heinz and Joachim Rohr received Hitler's *Deutschblütigkeitserklärung* and reentered the service in 1939. Heinz wrote in 1994: "I was proud and happy to be allowed once again to put on the Wehrmacht uniform."[74] Field Marshal von Brauchitsch's family had promised that when war came, they would do everything in their power to get the Rohr brothers back into the service. They made good on their promise. In 1939, Engel personally met with Heinz in the Reichskanzlei and told him that Hitler had declared him *deutschblütig.* Engel told him, "The Führer has approved your reactivation. . . . I hope this is good news for you?" Heinz replied that "he was very happy that Hitler had decided to do this for him." Then Engel asked him if he wanted to finish his studies before he returned to the army. Heinz replied, "No . . . we already missed the war in Poland and we don't want that to happen again."[75] Heinz believed that the reason Hitler gave him this *Arisierung* resulted from his father's World War I service.[76] Rohr viewed the racial laws with disdain and regarded this exemption simply as allowing him to return to his rightful place in society: "I thought the Nuremberg Laws were total nonsense, and I never viewed myself as a quarter-Jew. We were Germans just like everybody else and more than willing to serve our Fatherland."[77] Coming as they did from a strong military background, they felt pleased to return to the army. They were warriors at heart. Heinz's brother, Joachim, would pay the ultimate price for this honor. He died in Russia in 1944.[78] Both received the EKII, the EKI, and the German-Cross in Gold for their bravery and attained the rank of major.[79] Heinz's superior wrote that he was a "good National Socialist," and Joachim's superior reported that he "advocated the ideas of National Socialism."[80] They had proved their political and military worthiness.

Hitler reactivated several hundred *Mischling* officers between 1938 and 1940. In 1938, Hitler reactivated Klaus von Schmeling-Diringhofen as a captain and granted him the *Deutschblütigkeitserklärung*.[81] Klaus's friend, General Beelitz, explained that Engel had secured the *Deutschblütigkeitserklärung* for Klaus. Engel reported that he brought Schmeling-Diringhofen's case to Hitler's attention while Engel and Hitler took a walk together. Hearing Klaus's story, Hitler told Engel he wanted Schmeling-Diringhofen back in the army.[82] Unfortunately, soon after war erupted in 1939, Schmeling-Diringhofen died in action in Poland while leading his company into battle.[83] His sister Ursula wrote her mother on 24 September 1939 in anger after his funeral saying, "[W]e can thank the Führer for this!" Schmeling-Diringhofen was praised on the radio for his "hero's death."[84] With full military honors, his coffin draped with the swastika flag, he was buried next to his comrades in Poland.[85]

In addition to low-ranking officers such as Schmoeckel, the Rohrs, and Schmeling-Diringhofen, Hitler granted some high-ranking officers the *Deutschblütigkeitserklärung* between 1938 and 1940. General Günther Blumentritt helped two comrades get Aryanizations in 1939. One was the quarter-Jew and later German-Cross in Gold and Ritterkreuz recipient General Hans-Heinrich Sixt von Armin,[86] commander of the 113th Infantry Division. The other was the half-Jew and later German-Cross in Gold and Ritterkreuz recipient General Günther Sachs, commander of the Twelfth Flak Division.[87]

Beginning in 1940, more *Mischlinge* experienced difficulties receiving official approval. After an OKW conference on 14 February 1940, a government memorandum stated that in principle, all applications from half-Jews were to be rejected. Applications were no longer to be sent to Keitel, who apparently used to review them and forward them to Lammers. He evidently did not want to deal with half-Jews anymore. Applications of *Mischlinge* now went directly to Lammers's office before Hitler received them.[88] Alternately, Engel, Puttkamer, or Below took applications to Hitler for his decision and then passed them to the Reichskanzlei or OKW for processing. If Lammers did not present cases himself, he was definitely informed about them. If a *Mischling* was approved, it was Lammers's responsibility to ensure that he received the certificates he needed to change his documents.

However, on 8 April 1940, after officially discharging half-Jews from the Wehrmacht, Hitler gave them the opportunity to apply for exemptions to remain in the armed forces. OKH outlined the stipulations for the petitions on 20 April 1940 when it reissued the OKW decree of 8 April. This decree seemed to reverse Hitler's government memorandum of February, which had called for the cessation of exemptions for half-Jews. The new decree now required an applicant to show proof of meritorious service. He also had to include his racial status, curriculum vitae, whether his Jewish parent or grandparents were alive, his frontal and profile photos, and his commander's recommendations. Many hired lawyers to help them put together their applications, which sometimes cost a few thousand Reichsmarks.[89]

Since *Mischlinge* had a hard time being heard themselves, letting Aryan lawyers speak on their behalf often proved to be a more effective strategy. Many approached their applications as if they were on trial. For example, the half-Jew Wolfram Günther's lawyers, Dr. Alfred Holl and Dr. Fritz Hamann, wrote Hitler that Günther's racial status deeply troubled him and that it would be a pity for the *Volk* if Günther did not receive clemency. The lawyers argued that Günther's commander did not promote him to reserve officer "because of his ancestry." They noted that he was the only one in his battery to be promoted to Oberkanonier,[90] were convinced of Günther's Germanness, and felt he would work only for the betterment of Germany. General Freiherr von Maltzahn, commander of the Fifty-sixth Infantry Division, wrote a report on Günther's father. The lawyers added pictures of Günther and his two brothers to his *Gnadengesuch* as the state required and explained that one could clearly see that these men were Aryans.[91] That Günther fought in a dangerous Sturmgeschütz (assault gun) unit also could only help him in his quest for Aryanization.[92] Although he was awarded both Iron Crosses, he felt that some of his actions warranted his receiving the Ritterkreuz (for instance, he destroyed several Russian tanks in one day with his self-propelled gun).[93] Had he been awarded the Ritterkreuz, he probably would have received clemency.

Normally, approved applications for personnel from the armed forces eventually came to Hitler's office through Hitler's Wehrmacht adjutants (Engel, Below, Puttkamer, and Schmundt), after being approved of by KdF, and later in 1942 and 1943, by the Parteikanzlei. Once approved, it seems that the Reichskanzlei and the RMI's Office for Genealogy Research[94] would send the *Mischling* his new documents. Apparently, if one of the bureaucrats in any of these organizations felt that a *Mischling* had no chance of receiving Hitler's approval, then his application was rejected before it ever reached Hitler. Thousands applied for exemptions. Many commanders of *Mischlinge* offered to write letters on their behalf to see if they might be eligible for an exemption. For example, between 1939 and 1941, Captain Wecker worked diligently on behalf of half-Jew Obergefreiter Martin Bier. Bier had "strongly requested" to stay with his unit and asked his superior for assistance. Because Bier had shown himself a leader and had set a good example for the whole company of how a soldier should conduct himself, Wecker decided to retain Bier and apply for clemency on his behalf.[95] During the winter of 1939–1940, Wecker contacted deputy Gauleiter Otto Nippold of Munich to discuss Bier's case. Wecker reported that after hearing about Bier's exploits in Poland and how he had received the EKII,[96] Nippold said, "If a man has proven himself like Bier has in Poland, then he has shown that he is German in his thoughts and actions and has earned special consideration in the future."[97] Nippold promised Wecker that he would look into the possibility of getting Bier an exemption from the Nuremberg Laws.[98] Bier wanted this exemption because he felt that with it, he could protect his family. He reasoned that the Gestapo would not harm a family with a son on the front.[99] Bier admits today that this was a naive thought, but nonetheless, he truly believed his service would save his Jewish relatives and himself. Bier's previous regiment commander, General Hubert Lanz, and his divisional commander, General Ludwig Kübler, supported his application for a *Genehmigung,* which would allow him to be promoted to Gefreiter and Obergefreiter.[100] Although Bier had all this support and had been decorated in battle, it still was not enough. In fall of 1940, he was discharged.[101]

Most half-Jewish soldiers, like Bier, asked their units to write such request letters for an exemption. Most of these "feelers," like Bier's, were rejected. Until a decision was reached, the inquiry allowed a half-Jew to remain with his unit for weeks, if not months. Only after a preliminary inquiry was approved, probably by the personnel office of either the army, navy, or Luftwaffe, did a *Mischling* start the involved process of applying for Hitler's exemption. Bier never got past this first stage even though his commander, Captain Wecker, explored several possibilities to support Bier's bid for clemency.

Three types of exemptions from the racial laws allowed a half-Jew to stay in the Wehrmacht. One form allowed him simply to remain in the armed forces. The next allowed him to remain and be promoted. These forms were generally called *Genehmigungen.* The third allowed him to describe himself on official documents as *deutschblütig.* The *Deutschblütigkeitserklärung* gave the recipient all the rights of an Aryan except the right to join the Party or own farmland. Several quarter-Jews tried for the second and third types just as aggressively as the half-Jews. However, almost all of the *Genehmigung* forms (first and second types) had a clause written in the award letter saying that Hitler would decide after the war if the person was worthy to receive the third and highest form of being classified as *deutschblütig.* Such clauses gave many *Mischlinge* the hope that they would regain their rights as full citizens.

Many who received the *Genehmigung* strove to attain the final level and be declared *deutschblütig.* Their superior officers often guided these *Mischlinge* through this difficult process. For instance, General Friedrich Sixt gave Colonel Hans-Wolfgang Schoch, the quartermaster for the Seventh Army, permission to write Engel on behalf of the half-Jewish Unteroffizier Karl Cadek on 10 November 1942. Although Cadek had received Hitler's *Genehmigung,* Schoch sent him to the front, where he could distinguish himself to improve his chances of being declared *deutschblütig.*[102] Schoch wrote: "Cadek has an irreproachable character and he's altogether German with soldierly values . . . and Cadek's the opposite *(Gegentyp)* of the typical Jew who served in the offices *(jüdischer Etappenschreiber)* during World War I — he's honorable, dutiful, German and thoroughly a militarist."[103] Schoch recognized that to procure a higher level of clemency for Cadek, he needed to show that Cadek did not exhibit any Jewish behavior. In Schoch's opinion, Cadek's valor and militaristic bearing proved that his Aryan blood dominated his personality. Cadek's fate remains unknown. Many officers, like Schoch, did all they could within the boundaries of the law to help worthy *Mischlinge* subordinates. General Heinrich Eberbach, commander of the Fourth Panzer Division, tried to promote Obergefreiter Georg Struzyna to Unteroffizier and to get him Hitler's *Deutschblütigkeitserklärung*. Although decorated with the EKI and severely wounded (*Stufe* III), Hitler refused to declare Struzyna *deutschblütig*.[104] Several high-ranking officers, like Schoch and Eberbach, did all they could to help brave and honorable *Mischlinge* soldiers who, in their opinion, warranted Hitler's *Deutschblütigkeitserklärung*.

The RMI reported on 22 May 1940 that *Mischling* applications were proving difficult to process as long as Hitler demanded that he personally decide each case.[105] An RMI document stated that it was receiving too many applications to process. Many applicants felt desperate and awaited the outcome as if it were a matter of life and death *(Sein oder Nichtsein)*.[106] For example, the half-Jew A. R.[107] wrote the RMI, "My daughter and I cannot help it that my father married a Jew. Should I forever continue to do penance for this fact?" The RMI rejected his application. Before the army completed his discharge, he died in battle.[108]

In response to the 8 April 1940 decree, thousands of family members of *Mischlinge* began the application process for one of Hitler's exemptions on behalf of a loved one. For example, on 19 June 1940, Dr. Adam Carl Maier wrote Hitler saying:

> My Führer! . . . My nephew, Walther Hofmann, lost his mother twelve days after he was born. His mother was a Jew who had converted to Christianity. . . . In order to keep away any Jewish influence on the child, my wife . . . and I decided to adopt him. . . . Walther thus remained in my Aryan family. . . . He has never been with his Jewish family. . . . While in the army, he would have become an Offiziersanwärter,[109] but that was dropped as soon as [they found out he was a *Mischling*]. And although his half-Aryanhood became public knowledge, his comrades still liked him. . . . As a result, I plead with you . . . that you will grant my nephew . . . the rights of a full Aryan so he can continue to fight at the side of his comrades and belong fully to his German homeland.[110]

Maier believed that Jewishness was cultural and, since his nephew was not raised as a Jew, he should not be considered Jewish and should be given the *Arisierung*. Moreover, since Gefreiter Hofmann was raised as an Aryan, then, according to his uncle, he should be treated with the rights an Aryan deserved. Maier noted that in addition to his upbringing, his nephew's physical characteristics and military performance added further evidence that displayed Aryan qualities. Despite Maier's passionate plea, he received no response. Hofmann wrote OKW on 7 June 1940, declaring that he had not been polluted by the "Jews" and passionately requested to return to the "sides of my comrades."[111] Hofmann's application was probably rejected.

During the spring of 1940, Hitler still awarded soldiers dismissed between 1934 and 1939 *Deutschblütigkeitserklärungen*. For example, on 27 February 1940, Brauchitsch wrote Frau Irmgard von Brockhusen, daughter of Field Marshal von Hindenburg, regarding Wilhelm von Gottberg, a family friend whose application she had supported: "I'm especially pleased to be able to inform you that the Führer and Supreme Commander of the Wehrmacht has approved that Oberfähnrich[112] Wilhelm von Gottberg can once again serve. . . . [He] is to be declared *deutschblütig*. However, the Führer doesn't wish that his *Arisierung* will be used to help other relatives."[113] Brauchitsch honored the fact that Brockhusen had worked hard for the Gottberg family, friends of her family, to get Wilhelm clemency. Apparently, Brauchitsch shared in her celebration of Wilhelm's reinstatement. Brauchitsch and Brockhusen had not been alone in their support of Gottberg. Wilhelm's uncle was the notorious SS general, Curt von Gottberg,[114] who helped not only him but also his brother and six cousins receive Hitler's *Deutschblütigkeitserklärung* in the spring of 1940. His cousin Helmut von Gottberg had personally asked Curt in the late 1930s for assistance. Curt told Helmut that he would talk to the appropriate authorities.[115] Obviously, the family's reputation and connections with distinguished personalities had impressed the government to take the Gottbergs' situation seriously.

Unlike the Gottbergs, siblings or cousins of one who received clemency would not automatically receive their own exemptions. In fact, it could prove difficult to get clemency for all of one's children. For example, Elisabeth Rohr, mother of Heinz and Joachim Rohr, wrote Brauchitsch on 14 January 1940 that now that her sons had received Hitler's *Deutsch-blütigkeitserklärung,* maybe Brauchitsch could help her daughter get the *Arisierung.* She thanked Brauchitsch for his help in taking her sons' cases to Hitler and reported that they were "once again free and happy people because of you." She now felt they were no longer labeled as inferior human beings. Her concerns had now turned toward her daughter, Margot.[116] Not Brauchitsch but someone in OKH answered Frau Rohr on 29 January 1940 to inform her that Brauchitsch deeply regretted that he could not help her. The army was not responsible for this particular kind of *Gnadengesuch.* She would have to send her request through the Party.[117] However, Engel did step in and assisted her through the difficult process. Eventually, Engel informed Elisabeth Rohr on 26 November 1940 that Margot had received the *Deutschblütigkeitserklärung.*[118] By the length of time it took to Aryanize her daughter, Hitler showed that he did not believe siblings were created equal and, consequently, each had to be analyzed separately.

The issue about siblings not being racially equal was discussed by the government and Wehrmacht in 1942. Engel wrote Blankenburg on 28 April 1942 that after discussing the issue of siblings with Commander Frey and Schmundt, he had decided that siblings could differ racially, and the proven performance of one did not give his sibling any rights. Consequently, Hitler had to examine every case.[119] Perhaps the sibling dilemma was discussed again because of the Haller family's situation, although similar cases must have been known to the authorities at this time.[120] The three quarter-Jewish Haller sons were being considered for the *Deutschblütigkeitserklärung.* On 13 May 1942, Schmundt answered a letter from Martha Haller, the mother of the boys. She had tried for years to get the Aryan declaration to free her sons from the feeling of inferiority.[121] Schmundt was surprisingly kind and showed great understanding for the family's situation. He wrote that her children's applications awaited Hitler's decision. Schmundt expressed his regrets that one of her sons was missing in action and probably had died a "hero's death."[122] On 25 May, Frey wrote Schmundt that they had to clarify how one of the brothers had become an officer without Hitler's permission, but Frey added, since he had earned both Iron Crosses, he apparently had proved himself worthy of being an officer. Since the Haller boys had distinguished themselves in battle and the governor of Hamburg had given the family his approval, he believed they would receive exemptions.[123] Hitler eventually gave them *Genehmigungen*. Schmundt informed Frau Haller that Hitler intended to declare the boys *deutschblütig* after the war — if they continued to prove themselves. The one who later turned out to have died was probably declared *deutschblütig* posthumously because of his soldier's death. Hitler examined each brother separately before he gave them *Genehmigungen*. The Haller family was lucky. Sometimes within one family, one brother received an exemption, whereas another, because of unpleasant physical characteristics or poor military performance, did not. This policy led to confusion and strife in many families.

Applications sent to OKW and the Reichskanzlei by half-Jews increased dramatically throughout 1940. After the war in France, the government and Wehrmacht realized that the *Mischling* regulations laid down in April 1940 were not being followed. To limit the number of applications, the government announced on 28 July 1940 that applicants should be soldiers with a distinguished military record.[124] The announcement specified that the Iron Cross alone did not justify an application.[125] This medal was awarded quite frequently, so many received it. Out of the 967 half-Jews in this study, 127 (13.1 percent) received the EKII, and 40 (4.1 percent) also received the EKI.[126] By extrapolation, out of the 60,000 half-Jewish soldiers estimated in this study, at least 7,880 probably received the EKII, and 2,460 should have also received the EKI. All these half-Jews could have applied for exemptions under the original requirements. It seems that if a half-Jew was promoted, this also could demonstrate that he had proven himself in battle.[127]

However, even *Mischlinge* who did not have sufficient proof that they had distinguished themselves in battle applied for exemptions. For example, although he had no military awards, Schütze Heinrich Levin wrote OKW on 9 November 1940 to protest his discharge. "During my time as a soldier," Levin wrote, "I conducted myself in a correct, soldierly manner and had a perfect record. I volunteered for service in March of 1940. This didn't benefit me at all economically." Levin explained that he had had a good business, but left it to serve as a volunteer when he was thirty-three years old. By law, he did not have to serve. "I'm a half-Jew, but I have a pure German appearance. . . . Because of all these reasons, I plead with you to let me serve my Fatherland."[128] OKW rejected his application. Although Levin should never have applied, he, like most *Mischlinge*, felt that his case was special. For example, Kanonier[129] Viktor Mendel, a Jew (officially classified a half-Jew), wrote on 23 February 1941 that it was his wish "once again to be a soldier . . . and serve the Fatherland." He sent in his résumé, a copy of his military service book, photographs of himself, military reports written by his commander, and a description of his Jewish ancestors. With such a large file, it took several days to cross-check Mendel's information before the rejection was processed. He did not meet the requirements.[130]

Based on the supplementary decrees issued after 8 April 1940 concerning *Mischlinge*, one can conclude that the Nazis had no idea how many *Mischling* soldiers existed. Although Hitler had specified that previously discharged quarter-Jewish officers and officers married to quarter-Jews could apply to reenter the Wehrmacht, OKH added on 12 September 1940 that only men who had also performed an outstanding act in World War I or who had served the Party admirably as a member could apply for reinstatement.[131] Criteria probably were made more restrictive to reduce the number of *Mischling* applications. Once again, only Hitler could give the final word.

Since Hitler sometimes took years to decide on someone's application, a *Mischling* could feel quite distressed about his uncertain fate and status. For example, General Karl Zukertort, who had been on active army duty since 1909, applied for the *Deutschblütigkeitserklärung* in 1939. He was allowed to remain at his post at the Army Weapons Development Office until Hitler decided his case. In 1941, he still had not heard anything about his application. His performance reviews markedly changed from 1939 to 1941. On 21 April 1939, General Erich Stud wrote that Zukertort was an excellent officer and "performs his job as department head very well."[132] On 10 July 1939, Colonel Adolf von Schell in Göring's Office of the Four-Year Plan wrote that Zukertort had performed "excellent work" and that he was an exceptionally qualified officer for the Army Weapons Department.[133] Nonetheless, on 3 July 1940, it was noted in his review that Hitler would not decide on his case until after the war.[134] In February 1941, his superior, General Emil Leeb, wrote that although Zukertort ran his headquarters in Paris with skill and caution, he was shy and lacked a common bond with his fellow officers. Most likely, because of the uncertainty and the lack of recognition because he was a half-Jew, Zukertort had probably become apathetic or even angry. He resigned, probably because he was upset that he had not received the *Deuschblütigkeitserklärung.*[135] General Zukertort is the only high-ranking officer documented in this study who most likely resigned because of the racial nightmare in which he found himself. Field Marshal von Brauchitsch accepted his resignation, and Zukertort was scheduled to leave on 31 July 1941.[136] Eventually, Hitler declared Zukertort and his sons *deutschblütig* in April 1942, but he did not return to the army.[137] Both his sons, Soldat Kurt Dagobert and Gefreiter Karl Adolf, served in the army at the end of the war. Karl Adolf would die in battle fighting in Poland in 1944. Retired general Karl Zukertort spent the last three and one-half years of the war, according to his son Dagobert, selling jams and jellies in his hometown.[138] Ironically, his brother, General Johannes Zukertort, remained on active duty. Hitler also declared him *deutschblütig,* and by 1944, he was the highest ranking artillery officer in the commanding area of Commander in Chief "West."[139]

Some half-Jews tried several times for an exemption. A few who had previously been rejected were later granted exemptions. For instance, OKW informed Walter Hamburger on 17 April 1941 that Hitler had allowed him to reenter the army even though he had been discharged on 2 December 1940. His special approval was under the title of *Gnadengesuch.* Hamburger felt that the only way to protect his father, who almost died in Dachau during his imprisonment there from 1938 to 1939, was to serve. As a result, he sent in an application in December 1940, which had the standard items: profile head shots, his résumé, recommendations from his officers, and a report about his father's military career. During that very month, the Reichskanzlei informed Hamburger that his application was sent on to OKW for further review. Although he had not performed any exceptional military acts, OKW sent his petition on to Hitler, which he approved. In May, OKH informed Hamburger that he was to return to his old army unit. The document stipulated that Hitler would consider declaring Hamburger *deutschblütig* after the war if he proved himself in battle.[140] Perhaps a high-ranking personality who knew Hamburger helped push his case. General Gustav Freiherr von Perfall wrote Hamburger's sister on 31 May 1941 and extended his congratulations on her brother's success. The general believed that Hamburger's reactivation was rare.[141] Why he may have helped the family remains unknown, but since he wrote a young half-Jewish woman about the case, he must have cared about her and her brother.

The army discussed the policy of giving half-Jews exemptions on 4 June 1941 at Zossen.[142] Here, General Bodewin Keitel, head of the Army Personnel Office[143] and brother of Wilhelm Keitel, informed field commanders that presently the *Arisierung* cases for those who had proven themselves in battle were being treated "in a liberal manner."[144] It was reported that *Mischling* officers who had proven themselves in the face of the "enemy" would be "100 percent approved" for an *Arisierung*.[145] The notes taken from the minutes of this meeting show that B. Keitel was referring to the possibility of declaring *Mischlinge* in the army *deutschblütig*.[146] It is difficult to ascertain what effect this meeting had on overall policy concerning exemptions, but the fact that field commanders were discussing the *Mischling* exemption issue showed that this subject matter was widely known and debated, and that the army was in favor of allowing worthy *Mischlinge* to be declared *deutschblütig*.

On 16 July 1941, Hitler repeated his April 1940 directives through OKH again with a few changes. The directive defined the distinctions between a Jew, half-Jew, and quarter-Jew. It reiterated that soldiers needed to sign "ancestry declarations," and emphasized that half-Jews and those married to half-Jews were to be immediately discharged. However, half-Jews who had exhibited "meritorious war service" and who had medals[147] to prove it could apply. Now it seemed that an EKII was indeed enough to warrant a *Mischling* sending in an application that contradicted the decree of July 1940. This new decree gave the same guidelines as those set in 1940 for quarter-Jews and stated that only under special circumstances could a soldier marry a quarter-Jew. Although the Nuremberg Laws allowed quarter-Jews to marry Germans, this new directive held soldiers to a higher standard. Again, Hitler stated that only he could approve applications for exemptions.[148]

The criteria by which Hitler judged applications for exemptions had significantly changed since the OKH decree of 20 April 1940. Whereas previously a soldier had to prove meritorious war service, now he was required to have medals. He also had to obtain a recommendation from his commander rather than just a statement from any other officer that the soldier in question had performed valorous acts. Now a half-Jew had to send in a copy of his military service book or an official list of battles in which he had taken part. Hitler also required OKH to ask each *Mischling* applicant to provide proof of Party affiliations or honors. Previously, Hitler had not required such proof. Finally, OKH wanted to know whether the *Mischling's* Jewish relatives were still alive and what type of relationship he had with them. Previously, they had simply requested the address of the Jewish parent or grandparent. Hitler probably made the requirements more difficult to reduce the number of applications submitted for his review.

As the war worsened, Hitler became less generous with his exemptions. He told General Jodl during an afternoon tea session on 10 May 1942 that he regretted giving exemptions to so many half-Jewish soldiers. "For experience showed," Hitler said, "that from these Jewish offspring four, five or six generations of pure Jews keep Mendeling out."[149] Only when a *Mischling* was exceptional would Hitler consider him worthy for an exemption. On 1 July 1942, as part of a discussion of the danger of intermarriage, Hitler referred to Herr von Liebig, considered a commendable Nazi, to prove that Jewish "blood" was very dangerous. Hitler was stunned when he met Liebig because he looked Jewish.[150] Many assured Hitler that "there wasn't a drop of non-Aryan blood" in him. However, after some research, racial experts discovered that one of Liebig's ancestors had married a Jewish woman in 1616. Hitler claimed that Liebig's Jewish appearance proved his point. Even if there was a tiny drop of Jewish blood in someone, over several generations, a racially full Jew could still "Mendel out." Hitler believed Jewish blood was simply stronger.[151] This contradicted what he had said in December 1941, when he claimed that after several generations, German blood would eventually weed out the unwanted Jewish portion. Six months later Hitler felt that Jewish blood was tougher and would dominate well into future generations, regardless of whether the progeny married Aryans.

Hitler wanted the Party and KdF to play a larger role in deciding who was worthy to serve. A shift toward emphasizing Party service also reduced the pool of applicants. Beginning in 1942, the Party played a more active role in deciding which applications reached Hitler's office. Oberbereichsleiter Blankenburg wrote Engel on 23 May 1942 that the "hard cases" should go through his boss, Reichsleiter Bouhler, chief of the KdF, with comments from OKW. Normally, Bouhler gave applications to Engel to be reviewed by Hitler, but now with these hard cases, Engel would examine them first and then send them to KdF. If approved, Bouhler would then present these applicants to Hitler personally. These hard cases included illegitimate children, those who never knew their Jewish parent, and those who grew up with Aryan stepparents and step-siblings and were totally oblivious of their Jewish past.[152] These cases had better than average chances of approval because the Party felt that Judaism had not affected them.

Engel wrote in his diary on 28 and 30 May 1942 that the armed forces had received new criteria for processing applications.[153] That probably meant that the Wehrmacht would have to work more closely with the Party to approve an individual before his dossier reached Hitler. The Party's role did not please Engel. Throughout Engel's diary, he complained about Bormann's intrusions and observed how he was always around Hitler, making Engel's own efforts to help *Mischlinge* more difficult.[154] Engel often argued with Bormann, whom he clearly loathed.[155] He feared that his ability to help *Mischlinge* would now decrease. He claimed that he had been able to help "hundreds of 25 percent, 50 percent, and in some cases 75 percent Jews" to remain in the Wehrmacht.[156] However, Party officials in the Gauleitungen[157] and Kreisleitungen[158] had been finding out that some of these *Mischlinge* Engel had been helping had received exemptions under false pretenses. In other words, Engel probably deleted harmful information about an applicant before Hitler reviewed his case to ensure that the *Mischling* would receive an exemption (for example, Engel helping one falsify his documents to make it look like he was a *Mischling* rather than a Jew).[159] When different Party functionaries asked about these cases, Engel and Frey claimed that they were approved because of an oversight or mistake *(Versehen)*. Possibly some people, such as Bormann, knew about Engel's and Frey's generosity (mistakes) toward *Mischlinge* and thus encouraged Party involvement to make it harder for *Mischlinge* to get exemptions,[160] which in fact happened. Engel wrote on 30 May 1942 that he now had to get applications approved by the Parteikanzlei.[161] Neither Schmundt nor Engel nor Frey welcomed Party interference.[162] It would now be harder to get *Mischling* cases reviewed by Hitler because Party members, like Bormann, prevented them from reaching him.[163] The "sinister guttersnipe" (Guderian's words) Bormann was chomping at the bit to get rid of officers surrounding Hitler and "replace them with his creatures."[164] Bormann also knew of Hitler's growing irritation with the Wehrmacht and probably capitalized on this to make Engel's position more precarious.

On 30 May 1942, Engel felt Hitler was in a sour mood about the *Mischlinge*. Hitler told Engel that he suspected several people of going behind his back *(Mogeleiversuchen)*[165] in matters regarding *Mischlinge*. Just as he had told Jodl a few days earlier, he believed that the Wehrmacht (i.e., Engel and Frey) were treating the *Mischlinge* too leniently. He told Engel that he had discussed this matter with Bormann and Keitel. Engel felt helpless. He wrote that he thought about approaching Göring, who had been "generous" to *Mischlinge*,[166] but knew that Göring could do only so much, now that the Party was involved. With Bormann around, Engel would be restricted in what he could do for *Mischlinge*. Hitler seemed to welcome such conflicts. Problems with implementing Nazi ideology "intensified personal rivalries and enmities immeasurably," which Hitler encouraged.[167] Bormann was winning such a struggle against Engel. By 1942, Bormann had more contact with and responsibilities from Hitler than Engel, who was slowly being pushed aside regarding the *Mischlinge*. By July 1942, according to Bouhler's deputy, Viktor Brack, Engel had expressed that he had lost the desire to present half-Jews to Hitler,[168] probably because of the problems he had encountered with Hitler's changed mood about and Bormann's increased involvement with them.

Bormann took over Rudolf Heß's responsibilities and became head of the Parteikanzlei in May 1941 when the dim-witted Heß made his quixotic flight to Scotland in his insane hope to secure peace and to form a German-English alliance against Russia. Then on 12 April 1943, Bormann became Hitler's personal secretary.[169] The pot-bellied, disagreeable, colorless Bormann was called Hitler's "evil genius" and was described at the Nuremberg trials in 1946 as "an evil archangel at the side of the devil Hitler."[170] Hitler valued Bormann tremendously. He once remarked to an aide, "I need him to win the war."[171] By 1942–1943, Bormann held almost complete control of the Party machinery. Bormann was responsible for laying down the guidelines for those who deserved promotions and government positions. Kershaw wrote of Bormann, "His talent lay not in demagoguery and agitation but in organization, where he combined ideological fanaticism with bureaucratic skill, Machiavellian deviousness, indefatigable energy and a remarkable capacity for hard work."[172] By late 1942, *deutschblütig* declarations that allowed recipients to remain on or return to active duty now had to go through Bormann before reaching Hitler. By 1942, Lammers's access to and influence on Hitler had declined sharply, and he was required to submit the points about which he wished to talk to Hitler through Bormann, who was now the Führer's gatekeeper.[173] During the war, Bormann "controlled in good measure not only which persons were admitted to Hitler's presence, but also what information reached the Führer."[174] As Bormann said, cynically altering Jesus' words, "No one can come to the Führer but through me!"[175] Almost all high-ranking Party, government, and military personalities feared or hated Bormann. When Göring was asked at Nuremberg in 1946 whether Bormann was still alive, Göring replied, "If I had my say in it, I hope he is frying in Hell, but I don't know."[176]

Bormann was a rabid anti-Semite and detested *Mischlinge*. The *Mischlinge* lost their most loyal ally when Lösener significantly curtailed his activities as RMI's desk officer for racial matters in December 1941. They gained their worst enemy in Bormann, who took more control over policy affecting them in 1942. This danger became more acute when Hitler made Bormann his personal secretary in 1943, permitting him to assert his power in every department. When he was with Hitler almost every day from 1942 to 1945,[177] racial policies affecting *Mischlinge* became more restrictive.

On 1 June 1942, Hitler said the *Volk* would be endangered by the *Mischlinge* still serving. He felt that it would be bad "if *Mischlinge* are allowed to serve in the Wehrmacht, because it opens a door for them to be declared *deutschblütig*."[178] Ironically, Hitler was the one who had allowed them both to serve and to apply for exemptions. On 2 June 1942, Hitler expressed his irritation to Bormann about the lenient handling by KdF of *Mischlinge*. Hitler felt an exemption was justified only for those who never knew about their ancestry and who had served the Party during the *Kampfzeit*.[179] One can be sure that Bormann, always armed with his pad and pencil, took copious notes of what the Führer had discussed with him. Bormann then funneled what Hitler had said into "directives for action."[180] Although many bureaucrats followed these new criteria from Hitler, several *Mischlinge* who did not meet these guidelines were still reviewed.

On 1 July 1942, Hitler decided it would be a shame if the government allowed *Mischlinge* to serve and thereby allowed them "the possibility of equal treatment with those of German blood." Hitler believed that the number of exemptions should be reduced.[181] To this end, on 1 July 1942, the Parteikanzlei issued another decree signed by Bormann stating that henceforth, before Hitler would consider their applications, all *Mischlinge* required a recommendation from the Gauleiter where they lived, stating the special reasons why they should receive an exemption. Hitler still favored *Mischlinge* who had not known about their ancestry and who had served the Party during the *Kampfzeit*. Bormann wrote that Hitler no longer wanted to consider those who had just fulfilled their duty to the state, were members of some minor Nazi organization, read Nazi literature, were army volunteers, or were sons of World War I veterans. The bar had been raised.[182]

The next day, Bormann wrote Bouhler complaining that Bouhler had continued to send applications to Hitler that did not meet the criteria. Bormann explained that Hitler had expressed his indignation at the handling of *Mischling* cases. He explained that only men who had performed special service to the Party during the *Kampfzeit* should be considered. Party membership alone was not enough. Hitler warned that if they were not careful, the *Mischlinge* would create a new Jewish race. One needed to exercise caution, Hitler had told Bormann, because it had been proven that *Mischlinge* always "Mendeled" out Jews. Hitler pointed to Cripps[183] and Roosevelt[184] to support his claim. Bormann reminded Bouhler that Hitler had asked the bureaucrats to be careful, because keeping a *Mischling* in the Wehrmacht with only a *Genehmigung* was basically the same as declaring him *deutschblütig*.[185]

On 3 July 1942, Bormann again complained that regional Party offices (Gauleitungen)[186] were being too lenient with *Mischlinge,* and he warned officials not to take *Mischlinge*'s statements at face value. Many claimed that they had fought for the Party before 1933. Bormann also complained that *Mischlinge* often lied about the identity of their fathers, claiming their real fathers were not their mothers' Jewish husbands, but rather "gold blond Aryans." Only those who had not known about their Jewish ancestry or suffered injury or imprisonment because they were a Party member would now be considered. Bormann informed everyone through the *Reichsverfügungsblatt*[187] that from now on, the Führer "will personally and thoroughly look over" every case.[188] It seemed that Bormann was implying that if the civil servants (e.g., Bouhler) wanted to keep their jobs, they should enforce the decrees.

Although Bormann disliked Bouhler and wanted his responsibilities, he also truly believed that Bouhler was not being tough enough with the

Mischlinge. Bouhler felt that he had obeyed the laws and that Bormann was unfairly representing his actions to Hitler. On 10 July 1942, he wrote Bormann and complained that approving *Mischlinge* for the *Deutsch-blütigkeitserklärung* who had proven themselves on the battlefield did not result from his support alone, but had been done according to Hitler's instructions.[189] Bouhler complained to Bormann that his office had incessant workloads created by the Nuremberg Laws, the *Mischling* classifications, and pertinent decrees. Moreover, the infighting between offices and the necessity to keep track of the *Mischling* decrees made his job difficult. For seven years, an unbelievable number of *Mischlinge* had come to Bouhler daily in the quest for Hitler's signature. "Nobody else except Lammers knows what I've endured." The number of applications Bouhler (with Blankenburg) had rejected was "legion." He denied the majority without forwarding them to Hitler.[190] Bouhler vigorously defended himself to Bormann to prove that he was not guilty of lenience toward *Mischlinge.* Bouhler told Bormann in this cantankerous letter that his office (Blankenburg's letter of March 1940) had originally encouraged and ultimately persuaded Hitler to issue the 8 April 1940 decree, since apparently "your office didn't or couldn't (which can be construed from a conversation that took place with Dr. Blome[191] at the end of 1939) do anything about [the *Mischling* problem]."[192] Because Bouhler felt that *Mischlinge* would do everything in their power to enter the armed forces so that they could be declared *deutschblütig,* he supported the discharge of half-Jews from the Wehrmacht. As a result, he had his department write Hitler in March 1940 about this problem. Bouhler argued that the fact that Hitler had given some form of exemption to "quite a number" of half-Jews should not be blamed on him, since most serving in the Wehrmacht in 1940 were not discharged before the campaign against France started. Consequently, they had the opportunity to prove themselves in battle.[193] Even so, Bouhler said that when Blome had visited his office, he was stunned that the number of exemptions was much smaller than he had expected.[194] Bouhler felt that this fact should have been known before Bormann talked with Hitler about his actions. Bouhler reminded Bormann again that he had started the process of discharging the *Mischlinge* from the Wehrmacht.[195] Until now, it had been his understanding that he only had to verify that a soldier was politically sound and not that he had performed exceptional service for the Party.

Bouhler welcomed the Party's new responsibility to approve cases before they reached Hitler. Bouhler ended his letter saying "that any support for *Mischlinge* is the farthest thing from my mind." If this was the case, Bouhler wrote, then he would not have given Himmler so much support for exterminating the Jews (*Lösung der Judenfrage*[196]). Most likely, Bouhler meant that he had given Himmler the information he had collected while conducting the euthanasia program from 1939 to 1941.[197]

Apparently after not getting a reply, on 13 July Bouhler wrote Bormann's brother, Albert, chief of Hitler's private chancellery (a subdivision of KdF),[198] requesting that he set up a meeting for him with Hitler. Bouhler had sent a copy of the letter he had sent Martin Bormann on 10 July. Bouhler expressed that Hitler needed to hear his side of the story, knowing as he did that Martin Bormann had already briefed Hitler on what he thought Bouhler had been doing. Bouhler felt that if he met with Hitler, Hitler could then tell him personally how he should deal with *Mischlinge*. And of course, such a meeting with Hitler, Bouhler felt, would clear his name of any wrongdoing.[199] However, such a meeting probably did not take place.

By 10 July 1942, Hitler was becoming tired of *Mischlinge*. Hitler emphasized again that Party service was more important than military service when granting exemptions. Consequently, although they were at odds with each other, Bouhler and Bormann took over more responsibility from Engel.[200] At the beginning of July, Engel felt that Hitler had become stricter in handling *Mischlinge*. For example, Engel had brought to Hitler's attention twenty applicants who had already been approved by the KdF but were not yet approved by OKW. After Hitler reviewed the twenty applications, he told Engel that if OKW approved the nine he had selected, then he would grant the men clemency. When Engel returned on 2 July 1942 to get Hitler's decision on the men, Hitler did not approve any of them. Instead, he told Engel that he would have to discuss them with Bormann.[201] The armed forces were being increasingly pushed aside in their handling of *Mischlinge*. On 16 July 1942, Blankenburg instructed Frey to stop inquiring directly with the Gauleitungen concerning support for *Mischling* applications. Such inquiries were to be funneled through him.[202]

At this time, Hitler seemed eager to include Bormann more in the discussion of the "*Mischling* Question."[203] Bormann claimed on 21 August

1942 in a letter to Heydrich that Hitler "was fundamentally in agreement with classifying half-Jews as Jews,"[204] which would have immediately terminated pending applications from half-Jews and theoretically revoked those already approved. When Lösener heard about the possibility that half-Jews were going to be declared Jews or sterilized, he protested to Himmler on 10 September 1942 using the same arguments he had before and "consoled" Himmler, writing that "one cannot rectify errors and sins committed during the last two hundred years in one day."[205] Lösener urged that the matter be submitted to Hitler for a final decision. On 24 October 1942, Bormann passed on an OKW regulation from 25 September 1942 to the Party which stated that Hitler now prohibited half-Jews from applying to stay in the Wehrmacht. If they had been discharged, they could not return to active duty. Applications in process had to be returned, and it was repeated that if the Wehrmacht found a half-Jew illegally in the ranks, he was to be discharged.[206] Several applicants were informed in 1942 that according to the new decrees, they could no longer be considered for exemptions. For example, Frey wrote the father of several half-Jews in September 1942 that he should stop trying to obtain exemptions for his sons because, according to the new laws, they did not have the necessary credentials. Frey firmly asked him to stop sending in more information.[207]

In late March 1943, the *Mischlinge* lost one of their last lobbyists. Engel left his position as Hitler's army adjutant and went to the battlefield. Hitler had ordered Engel to leave. Engel found this dismissal difficult and was "completely surprised" by it.[208] Now the Party dominated *Mischling* policy, although it still needed Wehrmacht cooperation. On 13 March 1943, Albert Bormann answered Blankenburg's letter of 17 February 1943 about several *Mischlinge* who were being considered for clemency. Albert Bormann said out of ten cases under review, he felt positive about five describing their Party service. Three had shown service "above and beyond the call of duty for the movement." The other two had been Party and SA members. Albert Bormann viewed the remaining cases as going either way — "borderline cases" in which Hitler would have to decide personally. Some had shown Party service, but nothing exceptional. Others had not served the Party, but were good soldiers.[209] Although the soldiers were to be used for the armed forces, according to Albert Bormann, Party service was the determining factor as to whether they would receive Hitler's clemency.

Blankenburg wanted to receive Albert Bormann's opinion before he sub-mitted these *Mischlinge* to the Wehrmacht. Interestingly, Blankenburg felt positive about nine of them.[210] Blankenburg's letter to Albert Bormann shows that Blankenburg (probably with Bouhler's approval) did not take Martin Bormann's decree of 1 July 1942 about how to judge *Mischlinge* seriously.[211] Blankenburg was not following Bormann's strict criteria when he recommended at least two of the nine on the list. Although Bormann had decreed in October 1942 that Hitler no longer wanted to review half-Jews, Blankenburg and Albert Bormann's discussion of these *Mischlinge* (most of whom were half-Jews) showed that Bormann's *Rundschreiben*,[212] which originated from OKW, was not being followed.[213]

It was clear from some Nazi officials' comments that they were con-fused about how to implement Hitler's measures affecting *Mischlinge*. On 3 June 1943, Dr. Kurt Blome, deputy to the chief Reich physician in the Parteikanzlei, Dr. Leonardo Conti,[214] answered the KdF (probably Bouhler) that he believed half-Jew Wachtmeister[215] Ernst Liebscher should have been declared *deutschblütig* back in 1940 because of his bravery. However, Blome said that since Hitler had changed the criteria by which to handle *Mischlinge* in 1941, Liebscher was rejected from getting a *Deutschblütigkeitserklärung,* although the Gauleitung and his military superiors had supported his case. Nonetheless, Blome said that Liebscher belonged to the group that Hitler would declare *deutschblütig* after the war, and as a result, he gave his approval for Liebscher to marry. Because of Hitler's new regulations, Blome also believed that Liebscher could remain in the Wehrmacht.[216]

OKW and KdF also showed in their dealings with each other that they were confused about how to handle exemptions. In August 1943, OKW asked Blankenburg for clearer statements of approval or rejection from Bouhler in order to know how to deal with the *Mischlinge* being reviewed. This was especially the case, since the Party now played a role in who would be reviewed for clemency.[217]

But the confusion between OKW, KdF, and the Parteikanzlei in how to handle the *Mischlinge* up for clemency only mirrored the confusion many *Mischlinge* and their commanding officers felt in how to submit applications for exemptions. For example, Göring issued a Luftwaffe decree in Novem-ber 1943 that OKW had explained in October 1943 that *Deutschblütigkeits-erklärung* applications had often been sent to the RMI. OKW explained that such applications should come to them and not the RMI.[218] In November, OKH also sent out a decree that RMI had been receiving applications from *Mischlinge* in the army. OKH instructed its personnel offices that such applications were supposed to come to OKH and not the RMI.[219] Obviously, many *Mischlinge* and their superiors still did not know where to submit clemency applications.

Even in late 1943, while working in his windowless, air-conditioned bunkers with reinforced concrete walls, Hitler continued to review *Mischling* cases despite his desire to stop. Bormann wrote Bouhler on 27 September 1943 that on the previous day, Hitler had given him the files of ten *Mischlinge.* It was reiterated that applications would be accepted only when accompanied by a Party's statement of approval. Bormann requested that Bouhler also send him any other related files with approved applications.[220] On this date, Bouhler's department lost the right to submit applications to Hitler, although in practice it continued to do so. Bormann informed his rival, Bouhler, that Hitler had decided that only Bormann could present *Mischling* cases to him with a recommendation from the Parteikanzlei.[221] According to Jeremy Noakes, with this action Bormann "usurped the right of submission from his brother, Albert." Bormann was now able to "enforce the hard line towards *Mischlinge*" that he had long desired.[222]

Party service was the primary criterion in 1943 and 1944 for granting exemptions. As General Guderian wrote about Party interference in Wehrmacht affairs, "[T]he Party was less interested in the military qualifications than in the political fanaticism of the men it appointed to fill the responsible posts."[223] However, some *Mischlinge* being reviewed were simply too young to have served the Party before they entered the Wehrmacht. On 12 October 1943, Dr. Vogtherr at OKW asked Dietz if they could use alternate criteria to judge *Mischlinge* who, because of their age, had not served the Party.[224] On 19 October 1943, Dietz drew up a memorandum for Blankenburg which explained that Hitler had decided that in the future, the Parteikanzlei and not KdF should consider the applications because present political considerations were now more important when considering acts of clemency.[225] That was probably the answer to Vogtherr's question.

Schmundt had helped several men between 1938 and 1942, but in 1943, his attitude toward *Mischlinge* had become more intolerant. On 3 November 1943, his friend Irmgard Böhrne wrote Schmundt again about helping *Mischlinge*, this time on behalf of the Röper family. Schmundt advised that Dr. Röper should contact him directly and explain his situation. "However," Schmundt finished his letter, "[i]t's a pity that you continue to ask for help in this area. This contradicts my personal view during this time when the pack of Jews *(Meute der Juden)* is attacking us from everywhere. It is hard for individuals but matters of State take precedence. . . . Because I care for you so much, I will look into this case."[226] Schmundt's letter demonstrated the growing impatience the government had with *Mischlinge*. However, during this time, Hitler still reviewed cases of *Mischlinge* widows and orphans of fallen soldiers once they passed through KdF.[227] If Hitler's goal was to ultimately remove half-Jews from the *Volk*, this was a counterproductive move.[228]

In 1944, Germany might be collapsing, but "purity of the blood" was still hotly debated. On 2 January 1944 Hitler ordered Schmundt to put together a list of active army *Mischling* officers or officers married to Jews or *Mischlinge* who had received Hitler's *Deutschblütigkeitserklärung*. Hitler had the list made, according to Schmundt's order, to locate and discharge these officers. Schmundt wrote that the Personnel Office[229] needed to prepare their discharge orders now, especially for the older ones.[230] Personnel P1 (General Linnarz)[231] and P2 (Lieutenant Colonel Seegers)[232] Group Offices *(Amtsgruppen)* put together the list.[233] On its completion on 11 January 1944, Colonel Georg Erdmann, head of Group IV[234] in P2, sent the list to P5 (Colonel Hessemann).[235] Erdmann complained that tabulating the list had been difficult, because in previous years neither OKH, OKW, nor apparently the Reichskanzlei had put together a catalog of such officers. Consequently, Erdmann wrote, this "list cannot be accepted as complete." He was absolutely correct. On this list, Erdmann identified seventy-seven officers. Erdmann documented twelve *Mischling* generals and twelve generals married to *Mischlinge* or Jews. He documented thirty-seven other *Mischling* officers and sixteen officers married to *Mischlinge*. Most had received the *Deutschblütigkeitserklärung* by early 1940.[236] Some were put on the list although they had died in battle or had been taken prisoner. Several officers should have been on the list, but were either purposely excluded or simply not found. For example, Captain Klaus von Schmeling-Diringshofen and his brother, Lieutenant Joachim von Schmeling-

Diringshofen,[237] along with Major Ernst Prager, were just a few who were not listed. Moreover, Erdmann had difficulties determining the officer's blood percentage, since Hitler's *Deutschblütigkeitserklärungen* had not stated their degree.[238]

Before Erdmann sent this list to other offices, he showed it to his nephew, Captain Otto Wolters, who worked in his department. When Wolters saw the names of over twenty generals, he told his uncle, "If we discharge these men, it'll cause so many problems in the army. We need every man in the war, especially if they're generals!" His uncle agreed, shook his head, and walked away.[239] Erdmann had to send in the list. However, for months thereafter, nothing happened to these officers. Most remained at their posts, and the army even promoted a few.

Other lists of *Mischlinge* and *Mischehen* (mixed marriages) were compiled during 1944. Bormann made a list of high-ranking civil servants under Hitler's direct orders on 7 November 1944. There were eighty-three men on this list: ten half-Jews and twenty-one men married to half-Jews, fifteen quarter-Jews and twenty married to quarter-Jews, and seventeen married to full Jews.[240] However, Luftwaffe and Kriegsmarine lists have not been found. It is doubtful that such lists were ever drawn up, since the Aryanized officers documented in this study from these military branches remained at their posts until the war's end. Ironically, during this time, Hitler continued to evaluate applications for exemptions. In this study, three cases have been documented that received Hitler's clemency in 1944.

On 18 February 1944, OKW wrote KdF and complained that the Gauleiter political reports necessary to process *Mischlinge* were taking forever. The Wehrmacht complained that even in regions not being bombed, it took over three months to get the necessary political references. The armed forces would write KdF after four months, and even then they did not receive an answer. The Wehrmacht told KdF that the longer the Party made them wait to complete a *Mischling*'s file, the longer he had to distinguish himself since, by law, he was allowed to remain with his unit until his case was decided.[241] Blankenburg explained to OKW on 11 March 1944 that their office had been bombed, thus delaying the reports. Blankenburg wrote that OKW would soon receive the Gauleiter reports they needed.[242]

On 20 February 1944, Hitler issued a decree that henceforth only he and Bormann would consider *Mischling* applications.[243] Hitler believed that only

Bormann could solve the *Mischling* problem.[244] According to Göring, toward the end of the Third Reich, only Bormann was admitted to Hitler's tea sessions where important matters were decided.[245] By 1944, Lammers was hardly consulted about the *Mischlinge*. His influence had apparently peaked by 1941, probably about the time Bormann took over the Parteikanzlei, which gave Bormann unlimited access to Hitler. He now had to receive Hitler's orders through Bormann.[246] Despite Bormann's increased responsibility in dealing with *Mischlinge*, other offices besides his Parteikanzlei, such as OKW and KdF, surprisingly continued to process cases. However, the chaos continued. On 3 March 1944, OKW wrote KdF returning twenty-five *Mischling* memoirs from KdF and their request for updates on various applications. OKW expressed its irritation at KdF for implying that OKW had not worked hard enough on the applications. OKW explained that they just could not ask the Führer and his men to work as fast as KdF would like and besides, the memoirs they sent OKW served no purpose. OKW asked KdF to stop sending letters asking for updates because such work wasted time and paper and created more work for OKW.[247]

In June 1944, under pressure from the Parteikanzlei, the Wehrmacht was ordered to discharge all quarter-Jews.[248] Although the Wehrmacht decreed this discharge, only one quarter-Jew, possibly dismissed because of this decree, has been documented.[249]

After the 20 July 1944 bomb plot failed to kill Hitler, he and many of his cronies declared *Mischlinge*, among many others, the scapegoats.[250] In general, Hitler now no longer deemed *Mischlinge* worthy of his time or of living in the Reich. They were to be earmarked for extermination. Ironically, Field Marshal Milch sent Hitler a telegram immediately after the bomb blast: "[I cannot express my] heartfelt joy that a merciful Providence has protected you from this cowardly murder attempt and preserved you for the German *Volk* and its Wehrmacht."[251] Perhaps Milch really believed what he said, or perhaps he was protecting himself, knowing as he did that Hitler knew about his Jewish father and that the events on 20 July made a *Mischling*'s situation, like his, more precarious.

On 26 July 1944, Himmler's office issued a lengthy decree about *Mischlinge*.[252] This document suggested that the Party use not only the categories *Mischlinge* first and second degrees, but also those of third, fourth, fifth, and higher.[253] During 1944, Himmler focused on purging the Wehrmacht of

Mischlinge. Himmler's staff argued that those Jewish *Mischlinge* who had distinguished themselves in battle should not expect automatically to receive the *Deutschblütigkeitserklärung.*[254] Exemptions should be made only for unique cases.[255] Himmler's staff argued that declaring a Jewish *Mischling deutschblütig* or giving him the *Genehmigung* enabled him to disappear and camouflage himself. Although such a person may have been proclaimed *deutschblütig,* he still was Jewish in a biological sense. Consequently, the Party should "be very reluctant to recommend someone for aryanization."[256] Himmler's staff warned that *Mischlinge* tended to want more privileges. After they received an exemption, they wanted to study, to become officers, to marry, and to enter the Party.[257] They warned that every chance a *Mischling* had to prove himself in battle gave him a better bargaining position to improve his lot after the war.[258] The document echoed Hitler's earlier decree claiming that *Mischlinge* who died in action could be declared *deutschblütig,* but reiterated that clemency would be granted only when they did not have any children.[259] Himmler's staff mentioned that OKW was basically the only organization still processing applications for *Ausnahmebehandlungen.*[260] The document strongly implied that this should cease. They forbade any marriages between Aryans and *Mischlinge* except when a half-Jewish veteran was so disabled (*Stufe* IV)[261] that he could not live without a wife's care.[262]

On 29 July 1944, Himmler ordered the army to replace General Karl Sachs, a quarter-Jew, German-Cross in Gold bearer, and accomplished divisional commander, with General Hoernlein.[263] Sachs's Aryanization would no longer be honored,[264] although he was highly decorated and had fought bravely "protecting Germany," as he phrased it, from the "terror of the Bolsheviks."[265] Sachs was one of the seventy-seven soldiers on the list drawn up by Erdmann. It was just a matter of time before the others would also be discharged, especially since the SS and Party had the list.[266] On 9 September 1944, General Wilhelm Burgdorf dismissed Sachs on Hitler's orders.[267] Burgdorf had replaced Schmundt, who would die in October from wounds he sustained in the explosion on 20 July 1944 in Hitler's headquarters. Sachs was one of the most distinguished officers on the list, and since Hitler decided that he should go, one can assume that Hitler also ordered most of the others on the list to be discharged.

During this purge, Bormann wrote Lammers on 2 November 1944 that the "event of 20 July has shown the necessity to remove all people in positions of authority, who, owing to their ancestry, could be seen as a liability to the National Socialist ideology and its *Weltanschauung.*" Bormann said that these individuals could become a dangerous liability in times of stress, and explained that because of *Mischlinge*'s convictions, they could never be trusted. Although these *Mischlinge* had been declared *deutschblütig,* Bormann believed they should not enjoy the rights of Aryans.[268] Hitler ordered the armed forces on 26 October to discharge officers who were half-Jews or married to half-Jews and who had received some form of clemency by 31 December 1944.[269] During the war's final days, Hitler discharged almost two dozen battle-tested generals who had proven their loyalty and been awarded clemency.

Discharging such accomplished officers showed Hitler's detachment from reality. The more Hitler realized that he could not change the war's outcome, the more irrational he became, which had a catastrophic effect on the conduct of government.[270] The release of two dozen generals was counterproductive at a time when Hitler needed every experienced general available. Hitler discharged only active officers who were on Erdmann's list. *Mischling* officers who had reserve commissions were not on the list. Most of them and *Mischling* soldiers remained at their posts.[271]

The hopes that Hitler's clemency had given many were now dashed. Half-Jew Werner Maltzahn had been promoted to general one month before Hitler discharged him. His dismissal depressed him.[272] Many discharged *Mischlinge* felt demoralized and dishonored. Half-Jew Major Friedrich Gebhard wrote Hanover's General Command on 21 October 1944 complaining about his upcoming discharge:

> [M]y discharge is especially hard, because the reasons stated are nothing I was responsible for. Considering my service to Germany in two world wars, and that I have to leave the army despite good evaluations as the result of unusual circumstances, I ask you to grant me the rank of Lieutenant Colonel. . . . This higher rank will open more doors to me in civilian life, which I'm now forced to enter sooner than anticipated.[273]

Mischlinge like Gebhard still could not understand why their ancestry prevented them from serving. A mixture of anger, bewilderment, and depression possessed them, and they did not know where to turn for help.

The SS also did their part to hunt down *Mischlinge* on the list. Himmler had already removed Sachs, and he wanted others. On 15 September 1944, SS-Obersturmbannführer[274] Suchanek of Himmler's office wrote General Burgdorf, informing him that Himmler requested the dismissal of the half-Jew Colonel Ernst Bloch and asked that he be sent to a forced labor battalion.[275] On 26 September 1944, Burgdorf responded to Himmler's office, confirming that Bloch had been dismissed, but added that in 1943 Bloch had asked to be "sent to the front despite his several World War I wounds."[276] Burgdorf's halfhearted protest did not succeed in easing Bloch's plight. It also did not seem to matter that Bloch was described as a "positive National Socialist."[277] Bloch left his post on 27 October 1944. On 15 February 1945, Hitler signed the official order discharging him because of his Jewish past. Burgdorf officially informed Bloch of his discharge: "The Führer has decided as of 31 January 1945 to discharge you from active duty. It is an honor to thank you on behalf of the Führer for your service rendered during war and peace for our people and fatherland. I wish you all the best for the future. *Heil* Hitler."[278] Most discharged *Mischlinge* received the same dismissal letter. Bloch was flabbergasted because he knew Hitler had personally declared him *deutschblütig.*[279] However, Bloch probably did not know the particularities behind his discharge. He was simply ordered to leave, and he obeyed without questioning. Walther Brockhoff, a close friend of Bloch's, wrote to Bloch's wife, Sabine, on 31 October 1945 to ask why his friend had been discharged. Brockhoff wrote, "One doesn't dismiss a brave and battle-tested officer away from the front during the hour of the greatest danger. There have been and will be few officers of his caliber."[280]

Most *Mischling* officers dismissed did not know about each other and believed that they were one of a handful of men who had to leave the Wehrmacht. Probably most were not told that they were discharged because of their Jewish heritage, although they probably suspected that that was the reason.

Most returned home and looked for employment. Some were sent to OT camps or to the makeshift Volkssturm units. Burgdorf saw the idiocy of discharging these proven officers. Since he knew he could not prevent their discharge, he informed the authorities that these men should stay at their posts during the three-month period after they were informed of their discharge. It was crucial that Germany use all its resources during the *Totaler Krieg* (Total War).[281] Burgdorf was able to hold on to a few officers until late 1944 or early 1945, but others were immediately sent home.

With the discharge of high-ranking *Mischling* officers, and those married to *Mischlinge,* the process of granting exemptions ended. Although this study has documented one person who supposedly received the *Deutschblütigkeitserklärung* in 1945[282] after the July 1944 bomb attack on Hitler, almost no more exemptions were granted. The discharge of these high-ranking officers foretold what would ultimately happen to all *Mischlinge* had Germany won or continued the war. They were not wanted.

Case Studies of the Exemption Process

To help readers gain a better understanding of what a person had to undergo to receive an exemption, a few cases are described in detail.

CASE STUDY I: HANS-GÜNTHER VON GERSDORFF

The army discharged Lieutenant Hans-Günther von Gersdorff on 30 September 1935 in accordance with the *Arierparagraph.*[283] Yet Gersdorff and his mother did everything they could to get him back into the Wehrmacht by proving his Aryanhood. This proved difficult since, according to Nazi law, his grandmother was a Jew. On May 1935, a civil servant from the Office for Racial Affairs instructed the army that Aryan ancestry "isn't the religion, but the ancestry, the race, the blood."[284] Consequently, the fact that Gersdorff's grandmother, Henriette Seligmann,[285] was not of the Jewish faith and that her parents had converted "doesn't satisfy the criteria to pronounce Gersdorff Aryan."[286]

Although Gersdorff may have resigned himself to his fate, his impulsive mother refused to let this shame fall on their family. She could not believe that the army discharged Hans-Günther because of his ancestry, but felt that someone wanted to harm him. Her husband had died and she had remarried, but she still had several well-known relatives in the army.

On 30 August 1935, General Viktor von Schwedler, head of the Army Personnel Department, answered her letter of 25 August 1935: "I'm very sorry. . . . The laws explicitly state that your son cannot remain in the army. Despite his ancestors' meritorious service for the Fatherland, an *Ausnahme-behandlung* is not possible. I regret, my dear Lady . . . not being able to give you a better answer."[287] The fact that Schwedler wrote such a sympathetic reply showed how much influence the family had. Schwedler had to enforce the law, but could not afford to dismiss this woman's protests lightly.

Frau von Gersdorff apparently had a nervous breakdown, but refused to give up. On 2 September 1935, she wrote to Schwedler again:

> It's not fair that the same blood-mixes *(Blutmischungen)* are handled so differently. . . . My son is considered non-Aryan while the sons of the daughters of my sisters-in-law, who have the same blood mix are Aryan. The only difference is that my son has a non-aristocratic mother. . . . I found out that my nephews' papers had been checked again and everything was fine with them. . . . Only hateful people could have brought my son's case to your attention.[288]

Since Schwedler still did not give her what she wanted, she took her case directly to the minister of war, General von Blomberg, on 5 September 1935. She wrote that if Blomberg reviewed the papers, he would see that the Jewish grandmother was christened at birth, and that her parents had already converted before she was born, thus making Hans-Günther an Aryan. She went on to list the officers of the family. Frau von Gersdorff closed her letter saying, "I cannot believe . . . that my son, who's with his whole soul and being a soldier deserves to have his life and mine destroyed because of denunciations."[289]

Blomberg replied on 18 September 1935 that he regretted having to discharge her son, but that he could not make an exception despite the family's distinguished military service: "I regret that I cannot spare you this difficult destiny."[290] Again, it was quite remarkable that she got a reply from Blomberg, even a courteous one.

Frau von Gersdorff wrote to Blomberg again on 2 October 1935 with her second argument, following the same strategy she had tried unsuccessfully with Schwedler. "The fact that my nephews [Horst and Wilhelm von Gottberg] can stay in the army shows that the grandmother is no problem for them. . . . I'm an Aryan. . . . This is definitely not the will of our Führer." She pleaded with Blomberg to help her in this matter of "life or death."[291]

Blomberg did not yield. Neither her suicide attempt nor more passionate letters to both Schwedler and Hitler did anything to help Hans-Günther. All Frau von Gersdorff achieved was the discharge of her two nephews in January 1936.[292]

Yet three years later, Frau von Gersdorff's dream was realized for her son, but not because of her efforts. Hitler declared the two Gottberg brothers and Hans-Günther *deutschblütig,* and the army recalled them to active duty.[293] Walther von Brauchitsch, army commander in chief, wrote to a friend of the Gottberg family, Hindenburg's daughter, Irmgard von Brockhusen, on 29 February 1940 about the case: "It's a special pleasure to be able to inform you that the Führer . . . has approved the re-call to active duty of . . . Wilhelm von Gottberg. . . . [He] will be declared *deutschblütig.* "[294] Brockhusen also received a friendly letter from Dr. Otto Meissner, head of the presidential chancellery: "I'm delighted to be able to give you this news about this special exemption *(Ausnahmebewilligung)* [made for Wilhelm von Gottberg]."[295] Hans-Günther must have received similar treatment as his cousin had.

Gersdorff fought with Artillery Regiment 156 during the western campaign in 1940 and received the EKI in May 1940. However, in 1942, First Lieutenant von Gersdorff, now married, spent three months and one week in military prison for taking his Russian lover, Shura, and her sister along with his unit and showing them the equipment under his control. The court ruled that he set a bad example and endangered his men by having women of the enemy in close quarters.[296] When Gersdorff was released, he returned to the fighting troops. He continued to have troubles, bombing his own troops with artillery in 1944. However, throughout 1943–1945, he was described as a "National Socialist" and continued serving until the war's end.[297]

CASE STUDY 2: ERNST PRAGER

The army discharged half-Jew Ernst Prager in 1934, but it was not until 1941 that Hitler awarded him the *Deutschblütigkeitserklärung.* The fiery, clear-headed, and deliberate Prager had started his application process in 1934, and three years later was still sending photos of himself and lengthy historical reports about his family, seven generations back, to the Wehrmacht and to Berlin's police headquarters.[298]

Prager's Jewish uncle, Stephan (retired World War I army major with both the EKII and EKI), helped him with his application. The family believed that if Ernst could get Hitler's *Deutschblütigkeitserklärung,* they could be protected. On 19 July 1937, Prager wrote his uncle that his case had been sent to the RMI,[299] but by the end of August, he still had heard nothing.[300] Although this news was disheartening, Prager's family still worked on his case by writing governmental officers, gathering new documents, and seeking advice where they could (i.e., from lawyers and officers).

Luckily for Prager, as with many *Mischling* applicants Hitler considered, he had a high-profile personality supporting him. Wilhelm Haehnelt,[301] a well-known retired Luftwaffe general and a friend of Lammers, repeatedly wrote Lammers and the Wehrmacht to help Prager.[302] On 22 December 1937, Prager told his uncle Stephan that Haehnelt had heard that the bureaucrats had started to review his case.[303] He informed Stephan on 14 February 1938 that his application, like most others, had been filed away because the government was not in a hurry to deal with such cases.[304] Possibly one reason why Prager had to wait so long was because the authorities were being bombarded with applications. Prager continued trying throughout 1938–1941 for an exemption, but without success.

When the war in the Balkans broke out in the spring of 1941, Prager tried again to be reinstated. He wrote OKW on 24 May 1941 and emphasized his family's Christian values and military tradition and asked to be sent immediately to war: "I chose the career of a soldier due to my deepest conviction and with a firm desire to be the best that I could be."[305] Prager also wanted to marry his fiancée, Hella, which he could do only if proclaimed *deutschblütig.*[306] Without Hitler's approval, Prager could not legally get married to an Aryan or have children with one. Prager wrote his uncle that he had talked the matter over with his friend, Jürgen Roth, one of Göring's adjutants. Roth claimed that it all depended on whether Hella could continue to fight with Prager.[307] He had already lost one fiancée (Ruth) because of his racial status, and he did not want to lose another.[308] Roth suggested that if he did not get clemency, then he and Hella could learn to "live for one another" instead of having children. Prager explained that such a position "contradicts the natural inclination of a woman. Hella loves children."[309] A few months later, Prager met with Amtsrat Hitze working in Lösener's office to discuss his options. As he entered his office, Hitze said, "[Y]ou came here, First Lieutenant, because of marriage? You're making things difficult for yourself."[310] Hitze explained that only when he had done some-

thing noteworthy as a soldier could he expect to get an exemption. Ironically, since Prager could not serve, he could not receive it. The meeting
ended. "I then went to the district court," Prager wrote, "totally consumed
by my worries, nervous, and held together only by my will and ability to pull
myself together in the hope of finding out whether I could again serve."[311] In
the court, the civil servant told Prager, "Hopeless. We all had to fight, and
the service of your ancestors will be considered, but I don't think it's enough
for a *Genehmigung.*"[312] Despairing, Prager believed he would not be able
to pursue a career he so desired, would never marry the woman he so dearly
loved, and would not be able to protect his cherished family. However,
on 26 June 1941, he informed his uncle Stephan that his application had
reached Hitler's adjutant, Engel. Prager had heard that his and another half-
Jew's applications had been sent on, and if approved, they would be the first
half-Jews to reenter the army.[313]

Four months after the invasion of Russia, Hitler granted Prager the
Deutschblütigkeitserklärung. When Haehnelt heard about Prager's
award, he said, "Finally some good news during these shitty times *(in
dieser beschissenen Zeit).*"[314] Prager wrote that Haehnelt cried because he
was so happy for him.[315] In his diary, Prager wrote, "I finally belong to the
army again."[316] Prager legally could serve, get married, and have children.
He wrote Stephan after his wedding and said, "[T]hank you for your good
wishes. . . . I know that you rejoice with me, and that a large stone has been
removed from your heart."[317] Prager's uncle could not travel to the wedding
because of the ban on Jews traveling inside Germany.[318] Prager wrote his
uncle that the people at his wedding were truly happy about his Aryanization.[319] Prager believed his *Deutschblütigkeitserklärung* was unique.[320] This
was a customary response of most who received Hitler's award — most
thought their case was special: "We can once again hold up our heads with
pride. . . . This decision shows, especially during this particular time, the
special handling of this case. . . . This exemption would've been impossible
without grandfather's, your and father's attitudes and convictions. This fact
should always maintain you and father when you have problems."[321] On
26 November, he learned that at least two other *Mischlinge* had also received the *Deutschblütigkeitserklärung:* "[A]nother lieutenant with the
same situation has been approved. A third one, whose percentage I don't
know, was in China as an instructor . . . then he was in Spain and now he's

a captain who received the Ritterkreuz (Borchard[t]!).[322] So, a well-deserved equalization *(Gleichstellung)* [of a Jewish person with an Aryan]!"[323] Prager continued to talk to his uncle about his Aryanization:

> Hella seems now to dream the most. That poor child has suffered so much. She could really only believe what had happened when Hitler's letter came in the mail. Along with the documents came the news that the Office for Racial Research[324] will send me a certificate concerning my equality with Aryans. The letter further stated that I'm allowed to say I'm *deutschblütig* in questionnaires, as can my children.[325]

It was ironic that Prager's Jewish uncle had to continue to wear the Jewish star while Hitler's clemency gave his nephew permission to declare himself non-Jewish and to wear the army uniform with the swastika. Stephan, a convert to Christianity and strong German patriot, probably felt relieved that his nephew could enter his rightful place in society. Prager felt proud to once again serve in the Wehrmacht, but he was exhausted. By December 1941, he claimed that he was a nervous wreck.[326] The process to get the exemption had taken its toll.

It was unclear exactly why Hitler gave Prager the exemption. Possibly Hitler allowed him to reenter the army because of the heavy officer casualties Germany had experienced or because Lammers had recommended this case for his friend Haehnelt. However, Hitler really had no intention of protecting Prager's Jewish relatives, contrary to Prager's hopes. Prager's father would have to perform forced labor from 1941 until the end of the war, and his uncle Stephan would be sent to Theresienstadt in June 1942. Had Germany won the war or prolonged it, the Nazis would have deported Prager's father, although Prager's service did indeed prevent his deportation for years. Prager's father rightly said to his daughter-in-law after Ernst had been shot seven times in one day in March 1942 in Russia that "if he dies, I'm finished."[327] One bullet had grazed his head, another went through his neck, and two others had hit his shoulder. Remarkably, Prager crawled back through hundreds of yards of enemy territory to his own lines. During this amazing feat, Prager thought about his Jewish family. He knew if he died, they would die also. He had to survive.

But alas, his *Deutschblütigkeitserklärung* and his devout service since 1941 did not prevent his family from being persecuted. Haehnelt again wrote

Lammers to help Prager, since several of his relatives had been deported in June 1942 and his father required to perform forced labor since 1941. On 2 April 1943, Haehnelt wrote Lammers that Prager, an "outstanding soldier," who had been wounded several times and had proven his bravery, had experienced several problems. Haehnelt asked that Prager's father, Heinrich, remain protected, though his Aryan wife had died: "The son shouldn't have to continually worry about his father."[328] Lammers answered Haehnelt on 8 April 1943 and told him that he had long been aware of Prager's case. Lammers assured him that he would help within the realm of possibilities.[329] Prager's case should have seemed hopeless when officers were being discharged because they were seen in public with a Jew or wrote a Jewish friend a birthday card.[330] Fortunately, his father was not deported for a second time and was only required to continue to perform forced labor in his hometown of Kulmbach. Prager, with the help from his friend Major Eberhard von Hanstein in OKW, was able to get support from the Wehrmacht to protect his father in 1943. Prager's position as a distinguished army officer who had received Hitler's *Deutschblütigkeitserklärung* also allowed him to prevent the deportation of his uncle Stephan from Theresienstadt to a death camp in 1942. Unfortunately, several other relatives did not benefit from Prager's unique status as an officer with the Führer's clemency.[331] Prager ended the war as an army commander of a replacement battalion in Bayreuth.[332]

CASE STUDY 3: RAINER GÄRTNER

The third case is that of the unassuming, youthful playboy Rainer Gärtner. It all started on 5 January 1942 when a man claimed at a Luftwaffe Unteroffizier meeting that one of them was Jewish. He demanded that the person reveal himself. After minutes of silence, Gärtner's first sergeant (Spieß) nodded to Gärtner to talk. Most were dumbfounded because Rainer was blond, blue-eyed, and looked like a "true Germanic man." Rainer lied and told them that he "was only 25 percent," thinking this would not shock them as much as being "50 percent Jewish." He later feared what would happen when his commanders found out the truth. A depressing mood fell upon Gärtner's comrades. Then his Spieß took Gärtner aside and told him they would apply for Hitler's clemency.[333] "It has to work, because if it doesn't, I'm finished; I don't know what else to do," Gärtner wrote his parents on 5 January 1942.[334]

As with most *Mischlinge,* his family rallied to his cause. During 1942,

Rainer's father, Dr. Robert Gärtner, met with officers in the Reichskanzlei and wrote letters to OKW. In February 1942, Dr. Gärtner finally found a "nice and humane" and "competent man," Commander Frey in OKH, who told them what they needed to do to receive clemency. Frey told Dr. Gärtner that to prevent Rainer's discharge, they should apply for Hitler's *Genehmigung* immediately. Frey added that Rainer's regiment needed to submit his application and send it through Göring to Hitler, who then would personally decide the case. Frey instructed Dr. Gärtner that until it reached Hitler, he (Frey) would process the application. He added that Rainer might face difficulties if he did not have combat medals. Only those cases, Frey claimed, got approved without difficulties. Since Rainer worked in a general staff office, his father reported that he "hasn't had contact with the enemy and thus hasn't . . . received any military honors. However, Frey told me that we shouldn't lose hope. . . . He said that the decision made for or against the applicant depended also on Rainer's and his parents' personalities."[335] The family felt that Rainer's application would not be delayed forever, and delay might even prove useful (giving him an opportunity to receive combat honors).[336] Rainer needed the exemption to find work and marry. Dr. Gärtner felt that his son's Jewish mother's early conversion and World War I service as a nurse would help him. He also felt that Rainer's participation in the youth Stahlhelm and in the SA would show Rainer's Aryan convictions. And last of all, Dr. Gärtner believed his own service, for which he had also volunteered, and which eventually resulted in his becoming a decorated World War I officer, would aid Rainer.[337] Yet, Rainer experienced troubles from the start. His superiors should never have promoted him to Unteroffizier, and thus, his unit started to experience difficulties from the higher-ups. Consequently, Rainer experienced complications getting the recommendation from his superior, who felt perturbed that he had promoted a non-Aryan illegally. Rainer worried about what his officer would write to OKL. But Rainer and his father did not let this setback discourage them, and they continued working on Rainer's application.

A few weeks later, Rainer's friend and teacher, Dr. Hans-Harder Biermann-Ratjen, wrote Rainer a recommendation. He had observed Rainer's development for years, never noticing anything particularly Jewish: "[H]e looks like a typical Aryan, and Rainer was raised German." He described how Rainer loved his fatherland and that he should not be discharged because "he's the typical soldier type . . . [and] can be totally re-lied upon politically due to his ancestry and education."[338] Frau Marianne Gärtner also asked friends for recommendations. In February 1942, she wrote Professor Risshon: "Today, I come to you for your help. We're worried sick for our boy. For 3.5 years he has been a soldier and for the last 1.5 years he has been an NCO, and now, suddenly his ancestry has become problematic." She explained that Rainer had never lied, but that suddenly in the last year, half-Jews were no longer allowed to serve with-out special permission. With such a statement, she either was consciously lying or was repeating what Rainer had told the family. She pleaded for help. The professor granted them assistance and wrote a letter similar to Biermann-Ratjen's.

Rainer worried about his mother and had written his father to watch after her. He knew that she would feel unsettled: "[P]lease explain to mother diplomatically that she shouldn't talk about this with certain people."[339] On 5 January 1942, Rainer wrote his parents for certificates of his mother's and father's World War I medals,[340] and on 7 March 1942, Rainer wrote an urgent letter to his father and requested photos of himself and his family.[341] The father sent them and continued to pursue other people for recommen-dations. Dr. Gärtner wrote Rainer on 15 March 1942 that they would get a recommendation from Uncle Emil, who was a World War I officer and Rainer's boss during civilian life. Frey had informed him that "recommen-dations from officers are especially important and mean much more than recommendations from civilians."[342] Two days later, Dr. Gärtner ex-pressed his surprise that not only did Rainer have to send front and profile photos of himself, but photos of his parents as well.[343] Frey also informed Dr. Gärtner that Rainer needed to report for frontline duty. Frau Gärtner strongly disagreed, but the father insisted that Rainer "must show that he has no fear."[344]

The family worked on their genealogy for weeks and gathered the ap-propriate pictures. Rainer even wrote a twenty-page résumé.[345] Frey em-phasized the need for good photos, so on 27 March 1942, Dr. Gärtner wrote his son: "I've sent you all the photos, a small shot from when you were a recruit, the Norway photo, which I don't particularly like, but your mother thought it was important to include, and the picture from Italy which I think is the best. It's also half-profile and that's what counts —

the nose." Then Dr. Gärtner informed Rainer to stress that his Jewish family were honorable citizens.[346] A few days later, Rainer's old SA officer, Schwenn Lindemann, wrote a recommendation in which he described Rainer as "neither Jewish in his looks nor behavior. . . . [H]e's positive about Nationalistic matters . . . and I know how much he suffers from this ancestry business."[347] In August 1942, depressed, Rainer confided his situation to Hannerle, one of his girlfriends. Later, she described the event: "Your situation is now my situation. . . . You had no one you could trust. . . . You came to me in my room and laid your head on my shoulder and said, 'They want to destroy me.' . . . then that evening you told me everything."[348]

The family continued to gather data for the next year and a half. Then the situation turned tragic. A report about Rainer's death reached Dr. Gärtner in 1944. Rainer's commander, Captain Giese, sent him the official notification on 14 January 1945:

> [Rainer] did his duty and received the praise and respect of his commanders. During the terrible weather these last few months, he proved that he had a tough and soldierly spirit. . . . He never took his frustrations out on anybody. I knew all about his problems. . . . His death is a sacrifice for his Fatherland. . . . You should be proud of your only son, Rainer, who knew why we must all do our duty to the very end.[349]

On 10 February 1945, Dr. Gärtner thanked Giese and explained how disappointed he felt because a few weeks before Rainer's death, OKW had rejected Rainer's application. Hitler no longer reviewed such cases. Dr. Gärtner thought that God may have spared Rainer from being discharged and sent to an OT forced labor camp, which would have destroyed him.[350] Rainer's case was probably not abnormal. Thousands of families probably experienced the same process as Rainer's did, and most were disappointed.

CASE STUDY 4: THE METTENHEIM FAMILY
The last case involves the ordeal of the Mettenheim family. The family experienced several problems throughout the Nazi regime. By summer 1941, they had sons in the army. In July 1941, one son would die in battle in Russia. The strong-willed Clara von Mettenheim asked her husband to

write OKW on 9 September 1941 on behalf of their boys. After discussing one son's difficulties, he wrote:

> [W]ill the *Mischlinge* recalled to active duty be treated the same as
> other soldiers? Does this mean they have all their civil rights back (like
> permission to marry)? Or will they be told to wait until after the war?
> Will a department be created for them like it was for the old Foreign
> Legion? My sons don't need to "prove themselves" *(bewähren)*, as one
> secret decree said they would have to. They have been decorated for
> their duty in battle. One with the EKII, the other got his a week after
> he was discharged. My third son, whose unworthiness to be a soldier
> due to his Jewish ancestry was not known by the authorities, was pro-
> moted and awarded the Iron Cross and died in battle in Russia. His
> commander wrote, "[H]e was an exemplary front line soldier with
> regard to his willingness and readiness for action. His ambition, espe-
> cially during difficult times, will never be forgotten."351

Professor Heinrich von Mettenheim lobbied for equal rights for his sons on
the basis of their meritorious service. Obviously irritated with the authorities, he could not understand the double standard the Wehrmacht followed.
He found it incomprehensible that Germany could treat loyal soldiers with
such disrespect. On 13 September 1941, Frey answered that since their sons
had proven themselves, exemptions were possible. To move their applications on to Hitler, Frey needed their names, ranks, and units. Moreover, he
requested photos of them showing front and side shots. "If the Führer
decides to approve the applications of your sons to reenter the Wehrmacht,
they'll be handled just like every other soldier. . . . If your children continue
to prove themselves, the Führer reserves the right to decide after the war
whether or not half-Jews will be declared *deutschblütig.*"352 On 21 October 1941, Frey informed the family that one of the sons, Dieter, had received
Hitler's *Genehmigung* to reenter the army.353 Hitler had rejected the other
son.

On 22 March 1943, Professor von Mettenheim wrote OKW and requested exemptions from the Gestapo measures against Jews that prevented
his wife from using Aryan doctors or leaving her house when she wanted.
He pleaded with OKW to free from the debilitating laws a mother of a fallen
soldier and of a son who had received Hitler's *Genehmigung* and been

wounded.[354] No reply was forthcoming. During this time, relatives continued to disappear. They were being deported to concentration camps throughout Europe.[355] These events had taken their toll on the family. Frau von Mettenheim felt responsible for Eberhardt's death, her eldest son, especially after she heard how he died. He had seen a wounded comrade on the battlefield and decided to rescue him. While helping the man, he was killed. Frau von Mettenheim wrote that "he didn't have to stay out there . . . he only did it because he wanted to compensate with a medal for his blemish (me!), or possibly he wanted to die to escape everything."[356] After not hearing anything for months, Professor von Mettenheim wrote OKW on 4 November 1943 that he realized they were not willing to protect the mother of a fallen soldier. He wanted his letters returned. OKW finally responded that it could do nothing. This only added to the family's trauma.[357] On 29 January 1944, Professor von Mettenheim died during a British air raid on Frankfurt. Consequently, Frau von Mettenheim lost the protection of her privileged mixed marriage. With the help of one of her sons, she went into hiding on 10 February 1944 and survived the Holocaust. Three of her four sons survived the war.

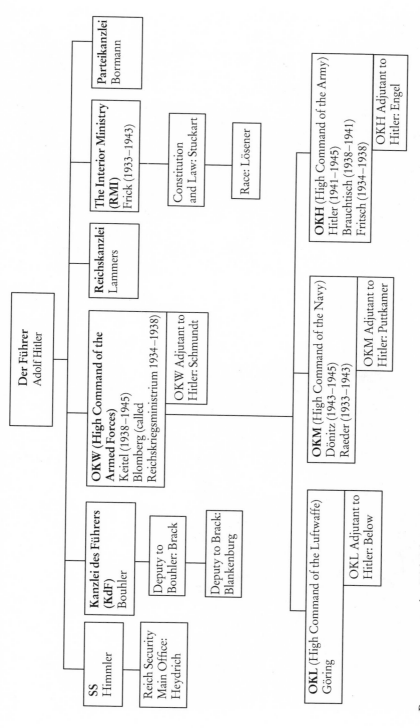

Power structures under Hitler, late 1941.

Execution of Jews in Lemberg, Russia, in a photograph taken by half-Jew Funker Friedemann Lichtwitz when he was a soldier. He was later deported to Dachau.

Half-Jews and brothers Werner (*left*) and Rudolf (*right*) Sachs (last rank for both Obergefreiter).

Bryan Mark Rigg and Chancellor Helmut Schmidt in 1995.

Quarter-Jew Helmut Schmidt
(last rank first lieutenant).

Half-Jew Hans Günzel in Russia (last rank Unteroffizier). (Military awards: EKI, EKII, Assault Badge, and Eastern Campaign Medal 1941–1942.)

Quarter-Jew Horst von Oppenfeld (last rank captain); he was Stauffenberg's adjutant in Africa. (Military awards: EKI, EKII, Panzer Assault Badge in Silver, and Wound Badge.)

Half-Jew Rolf Schenk (last rank Oberschütze), who was later deported to Buchenwald.

Above: Jewish professor and medical doctor Alexander Czempin (29 October 1861–1 March 1943), the grandfather of half-Jew and Unteroffizier Robert Czempin. He committed suicide before his deportation.

Half-Jew Robert Czempin (last rank Unteroffizier). (Military awards: EKII, Wound Badge in Gold, Assault Badge, and German-Italian Campaign Medal.) He lost a leg in battle.

What Did *Mischlinge* Know about the Holocaust?

Most soldiers in war have enough trauma "with physical hardships, the psychological burden, and the often crushing anxieties of death and killing that constitute the everyday life"[1] of combat without worrying about their families' and their own persecution at the hands of their countrymen. Jewish and *Mischling* soldiers not only served in armed forces controlled by a government hostile to them as racially inferior beings, but many also witnessed the disappearance and occasionally the death of their relatives. This chapter discusses how *Mischling* and Jewish soldiers experienced the persecution of the Jews. The question that will be looked at most closely is, Did these men know about the Holocaust (i.e., the systematic murder of Jews by the Nazis)?

Mischlinge became accustomed to seeing not only themselves but also their family members persecuted. For example, on 7 August 1935, several Nazi hooligans broke into the home of the half-Jew Hans Krackow. His son Jürgen remembered his mother, Ursula, asking the crowd what they had done. One man answered her, "You should've thought about that before you went to bed with a *Judenlümmel.*"[2] Another yelled, "Does the Jew fuck better?" They all laughed and tore up the whole house. Hans locked his family in a room and called a World War I comrade who now commanded troops in the area. Eventually, the troops arrived and dispersed the hooligans. The Krackows tried to leave Germany, but could not find overseas support, so they stayed.[3] Throughout 1944, Hans anxiously expected the Nazis to deport him to a concentration camp. The Krackows' dilemma mirrored the plight of many *Mischling* families.

Mischlinge often remained in Germany because they did not feel as threatened as their Jewish relatives, still had to finish their military service, or could not find overseas support. Quarter-Jew Ludwig Reinhard could have left for New York but did not do so because he did not feel at risk.[4] Peter Scholz tried to leave, but his Jewish mother, Olga (Olli) Gertrud Scholz née Samuel, reminded him, "You cannot leave, you have to serve." This in fact was true.[5] Most who wanted to emigrate, especially to the United States, experienced difficulties because of red tape, basic immigration restrictions, and lack of financial support. Many faced obstacles because the immigration authorities dealt with *Mischlinge* as with other German nationals.[6] Half-Jew Hans Pollak, living in the United Kingdom in 1937, tried to enter the English army to remain in England, but was rejected and returned to Germany, where the Wehrmacht drafted him. He served the entire war as an Obergefreiter and was decorated with the EKII and the Golden Wound Badge.[7] Tragically, a few half-Jews would later face emigrated Jewish relatives in combat who had entered Allied armies.[8] In the late 1930s, Gefreiter Hans-Geert Falkenberg's Jewish father, Richard Albert, immigrated to England and changed his name to Mountfalcon. After the war, Falkenberg learned that his father's British unit had fought against his Wehrmacht unit during the French campaign in 1940.[9]

Many started to awaken to the danger of their situation after *Reichskristallnacht* on 9–10 November 1938 when the Nazis carted off some of their Jewish parents to concentration camps. For example, the Nazis deported the Jewish father of Heinz-Georg Heymann to Buchenwald. A few months later, after his release, Heymann's father, Georg-Jakob, left for England. Gefreiter Heymann had to endure this while he served in the Luftwaffe.[10] Dietrich Moll had to swear the oath of loyalty to Hitler while his father, Leonard, was in Sachsenhausen concentration camp. Moll later became an Obergefreiter. He said that "the situation drove you crazy" but that he still did not consider leaving Germany.[11] After the Nazis arrested his Jewish father, Walter Hamburger went to the Gestapo jail to see him, only to find out that his father had been sent to the Dachau concentration camp. During this time of turmoil, Hamburger decided to volunteer for the army. He thought his service might help his family.[12]

The Nazis mistreated not only many *Mischlinge*'s parents during *Reichskristallnacht,* but many *Mischlinge* also suffered humiliation and persecution. For example, a group of SA men noticed half-Jew Dieter Bergmann watching the Jewish buildings in Leipzig go up in flames and accused him of being Jewish. Bergmann "stammered, 'I'm not Jewish.'" "I felt like Judas," Bergmann later recalled. The SA men, unsatisfied with this halfhearted answer, said, "All right, shithead, if you aren't Jewish, you must have a cute little bit of skin down there. Let's see it." They forced Bergmann to remove his pants. On seeing his uncircumcised penis, one of the SA men said he was "lucky" tonight and then kicked him on the "behind so that I slid into the street." Bergmann quickly dressed himself and disappeared into the night.[13]

After 1939, the situation worsened for *Mischlinge* and their families, but most still failed to foresee the coming danger. For example, Hans-Geert Falkenberg corresponded with and sent money to his Jewish grandmother Ida Klein née Löwe, who had been deported to the Glusk ghetto, south of Lublin, on 12 February 1940. She remained there until 1943, when she was murdered.[14] She wrote Falkenberg on 8 July 1940:

> The hopelessness makes me so unbelievably sad. . . . It's cruel one has to die soon. . . . If there's a God, a Higher-Being, how can He allow such horrible things to happen? . . . Most of the people now have no conscience or else all this horribleness wouldn't happen. . . . [I write this] letter to say goodbye to you with a bleeding heart because the world is so beautiful. The distant view of the fields, the forest . . . the magnificent colors of the sky, the beautiful sunset fills me with wonder. At the same time it's sad to think I have to leave all this without seeing my loved ones again. I will die a cruel death, sacrificed to someone's mania.[15]

Falkenberg thought his grandmother had exaggerated her situation.[16] In response to one of his letters, she wrote him on 5 April 1942 that "no one has a clue what beastly things are going on here."[17] On 10 May 1942, she described how a man in the ghetto was shot because he did not wear his Jewish star.[18] Soon thereafter, her letters stopped. Not hearing from her, Falkenberg decided to leave for Glusk in September 1943 to visit her. After he arrived in this village, he found out that all the Jews there had been deported to an unknown destination. After the war, Falkenberg realized that the Nazis had murdered his grandmother and that her letters were not written by a "delusional old woman." But by then he had read about the Nuremberg trials, and the facts were clear about what had happened to Jews under Hitler. *Geltungsjudin* Rita Kuhn echoed Falkenberg when she said, "It was not until 1945, after I had seen the liberation of the concentration camp at Buchenwald on a movie screen and learned of other death camps that I knew that many members of my family and all those friends who had disappeared after 1942 would never return."[19]

Another person who failed to see the Holocaust was General Werner Maltzahn, who commanded Celle's mortar rocket school and had led regiments in Russia. He lost his Jewish mother, half-sister, and two nieces in the *Endlösung.*[20] According to the files, he did nothing to prevent his family's deportation and ultimate death. His lover, who wishes to remain anonymous, said Maltzahn did not know until after the war what had happened to his family.

Many officers, like Maltzahn, were simply passionate soldiers and confined their thoughts and actions to the military realm. For example, half-Jew General Richard Metz wrote in June 1946 that he would like "to remember the German soldier once again with respect and thankfulness" for his "heroic deeds throughout the war." Metz commented that they remained true to their oath and bravely fought for "*Volk* and Fatherland." Metz ended his report with: "To have been the leader of such soldiers will always be the thankful and proud memory of every German officer."[21] There was no mention of the devastation European Jewry suffered under Hitler. The omission is striking, since he was a half-Jew and the Nuremberg trials had just happened. Although the evidence is not conclusive, he probably lost several relatives in the Holocaust.

Like most other Germans, many *Mischlinge* knew about deportations, but did not equate them with systematic murder. Wolfgang Lennert, a quarter-Jew, had a Jewish girlfriend, Marie Händler. While in the army, he wrote his mother on 17 January 1941 that he would continue to aid Marie.[22] While Lennert fought in Russia, Marie was deported on 13 June 1942.[23] Lennert wrote his mother on 28 July 1942 that the knowledge of Marie's uncertain destiny depressed him.[24] On 12 October 1942, Wolfgang again wrote his mother and wondered how Marie was. He trusted that "God would give her strength."[25] Marie was murdered shortly after her arrival at Majdanek in June 1942,[26] but Lennert never learned of her fate. He died in battle in 1943.

The cause of the denial or ignorance (or both) of Falkenberg, Maltzahn, Metz, and Lennert of the atrocities committed against their loved ones could have stemmed from their disbelief or lack of understanding of the mechanism of death operating under Hitler. Whatever they thought, their actions demonstrate that they did not comprehend what was happening to their loved ones. Most claim that they learned what had befallen their relatives only after the war.

Some might think that had Falkenberg, Maltzahn, Metz, and Lennert witnessed their loved ones' deportation, they might have behaved differently. This study's evidence suggests the opposite. For example, Feldwebel[27] Georg-Friedrich Müller, who had received Hitler's *Genehmigung,* visited some of his family on the night of their deportation. He claims he did not know until after the war what fate awaited them. While on leave from the front and in full uniform, he went to his Jewish cousin's house in Berlin. After he knocked on the door, a relative hesitantly opened it. The entire house was empty except for about ten people. Müller alleged that he could feel the fear. Three generations waited in the room, from a toddler who played among the baggage to an old, gray-haired grandmother who nervously twisted her handkerchief. All wore the Jewish star. Müller never saw them again after he left their home that night.[28] At the time, he did not think they would be killed. Only after the war did he learn that they had all been murdered.

In 1943, Dieter Bergmann secretly visited his Jewish grandmother, Elly Landsberg née Mockrauer. He knew it was dangerous to visit her but decided to see her although he had been ignoring her because she was a Jew.[29] As Bergmann talked with his grandmother, the SS came. His grandmother introduced her grandson, the army Unteroffizier. Bewildered, the SS left. Unfortunately, the next day, the SS took his grandmother away. The Nazis deported her first to Theresienstadt and then later to Auschwitz. "That was the last time I saw her," Bergmann said sadly. It did not enter Bergmann's mind that she was being sent to her death.[30]

Even if a *Mischling* was in a ghetto, he did not necessarily know what awaited those in it. Half-Jew Gefreiter Alfred Posselt fell in love with a Jew, Helene (Halina) Göldner, in the ghetto at Rzeszów, Galicia.[31] He worked at a nearby airport with his unit. Posselt claimed that he would sneak into the ghetto and bring her family food. While there, he witnessed Jews being executed and heard about deportations to the Belzec death camp. One day when he went to see Helene, she was gone and the ghetto had been liquidated. Posselt continued to serve for several more years while his own family disappeared.[32] The significance of what he witnessed did not escape him, but he felt that he could do nothing but continue serving. He believed the evil he had witnessed was an exception and not the rule.[33]

Not only did men like Müller, Bergmann, and Posselt witness deportations, but many knew about the suicides of relatives who did not want to be deported. Ex-Obergefreiter Heinz Günther Angreß' two great-aunts took the barbiturate Veronal before they would have been deported in February 1942.[34] In 1942 Obergefreiter Hans Pollak lost his father, who committed suicide before he could be deported to the Stutthof concentration camp near Danzig.[35] Another man who wishes to remain anonymous remembered coming home and finding no one to greet him at the front door. As he walked into the house, he called for his Jewish grandmother. There was no reply. As he entered the kitchen, he saw her legs dangling. She had hanged herself, and the corpse had started to decay. The young man pulled her down and held her in his arms. Tears welled up in his eyes as he sat there saying softly, "No. No. No." Later, he found her suicide note. She apologized for leaving this world and regretted having caused her dear grandson so many worries. She was tired of living with fear.[36]

Hermann Schucht's Jewish mother, Luise née Friedenthal, committed suicide on 15 October 1942 before she would have been deported to Theresienstadt. She wrote, "My dear Son! Don't be upset with me that I left this life without telling you goodbye. I believe this decision is best for both of us. You have enough problems of your own to deal with, and your dear wife will stand by you when hard times come. . . . Times now are horrific and there's no way out for me. . . . An eternal kiss I send you. Love, your Mommy."[37] Frau Schucht had abandoned her illusions of living unharmed under Nazi rule, painfully concluding that she would soon have to die. Instead of giving the Nazis the gratification of murdering her, she decided to take her own life.

Robert Czempin's Jewish grandfather, Alex Czempin, also committed suicide. Robert was an Unteroffizier who lost a leg in battle and was decorated with the EKII and Silver Wound Badge. He recalled his grandfather standing over his bed one evening in 1943, saying the holy Jewish Kaddish prayer for the dead. Robert Czempin alleged "that it was his goodbye, a goodbye forever." He pretended to sleep. He admired his grandfather's courage. His grandfather did not want to be taken to a concentration camp. That night the grandfather took poison. He left a note to his grandson:

> If I'd not killed myself, your worries would've only increased, and you may have faced unimaginable tortures. Believe me, this is best for all of us. I'm old and this way I can die in my own bed. That's much better than to be driven to some horrible death by inhumane persons. This way maybe a rabbi (if there still is a rabbi alive in Berlin) will say Kaddish at my grave. I've tried all my life to be an honorable person. . . . Although it sounds very strange, I was more Prussian than Jew. . . . However, I did do my best to live by God's laws. . . . The Nazis have almost taken everything I have. . . . Think of your grandfather occasionally, who loved you dearly. God protect you! Alex.[38]

Czempin's grandfather knew what awaited him after deportation. Consequently, just as Frau Schucht had done, Czempin's grandfather chose to die on his own terms. "And once again Hitler had a small victory — one less Jew!" Czempin later wrote. He knew that deportation was horrible, but states today that he did not know Hitler had decided to systematically murder the Jews.[39]

Most did not believe deportation would turn out to be murderous. For example, Joachim Gaehde said that after his eighty-four-year-old grandfather, Carl Pick, and his great-aunt, Else Pick, committed suicide in March 1942, he was "angry and grief-stricken, but I don't remember drawing any conclusions as to the impending danger."[40] Most felt that their relatives who committed suicide were most often quite old and did not want to suffer further humiliation and persecution. Death camps were unimaginable.

Most had heard rumors that Jews were being sent to Madagascar (which the Nazis actually had planned to do before the war)[41] or to a colony in the East. Some had heard about shootings and gassings, but most had no evidence for such accusations. Hans Schmechel, who lost both grandparents, Emma and Wilhelm Gotha, at Theresienstadt, manned a flak gun in 1944 while the Nazis deported his brothers, Horst and Heinz, to an OT forced labor camp. They found it quite ironic that two of them had to perform forced labor in an OT camp while the other served in the Luftwaffe. Schmechel's family had only heard about the atrocities when his Aryan uncle, Walter Schmechel, a guard at Auschwitz, came home in 1943 and reported what he had seen. The family believed the uncle but still did not know that systematic extermination of millions was under way.[42]

An even more bizarre case was that of Horst Reinhard's[43] family. While Reinhard served with false papers to make the authorities think he was a quarter-Jew, his father was forced to serve as an army staff sergeant in the SS guard unit at the concentration camp Flossenburg. Reinhard's Jewish mother, Marie, even lived with her husband in the camp's staff housing and thus survived. Reinhard said that although he wrote letters to his parents at this camp, he did not know about the Holocaust until the 1950s. He knew about deportations but, like most other Germans, never thought the Jews were systematically murdered.[44] The Schmechel and Reinhard families had more information than most families, but they still failed to either understand or believe the signs they received.

Most profess that they did not see anything that revealed the genocide. Only a few witnessed atrocities. The actions of men who witnessed atrocities differ little from those who did not. Most did not defy the Nazis because they knew it was useless and suicidal.

Fritz Steinwasser witnessed the SS murder a group of Jews in Latvia. "I looked into the eyes of my people. There in the last minutes of their life. I was shocked. My heart bled."[45] During their invasion of Latvia, near the city of Dünaburg (Dugavpils) while stopped on a bridge two hundred meters away, Steinwasser observed the Latvian SS drive a group of naked Jews into a trench. "There were even babies still sucking on their mothers' breasts," Fritz said. The SS shot them all. Steinwasser, with a sick stomach and tears in his eyes, did think of his family. "That could have been my grandfather!"[46] However, he believed that what he had witnessed was uncommon. Yet, Steinwasser's grandfather would later be deported to Theresienstadt and his uncle would die in Buchenwald.[47]

In their unique status as both soldiers and partial Jews, some *Mischlinge* witnessed Jewish persecution at crucial sites of the Holocaust. But shocked as they were, they were unable to prevent it. The highly distinguished Ritterkreuz recipient Colonel Walter Hollaender, a half-Jew, when asked by his wife, Hertha-Barbara, in the 1970s whether he wanted to see Dachau, replied, "Ah, I saw enough of that when I had to go through the Warsaw ghetto in 1943."[48] According to Frau Hollaender, he did not see the larger picture of what was happening to Jews in general and continued to serve with distinction. Robert Braun, a half-Jew and ex-Unterarzt who worked in a pharmaceutical plant in Hamburg, visited the Neuengamme concentration camp with an SS officer whom Braun had helped conduct research for his doctorate in medicine.[49] Although Braun helped the SS officer study how certain medicines could help "the poor creatures in the concentration camp" who had dysentery, Braun did not draw any conclusions about the Holocaust from his time there.[50] Throughout 1943, Dieter Bergmann worked in a rubber factory in Litzmannstadt, today Lodz. He had to travel through the Jewish ghetto on his way from his home to the factory. Bergmann "saw so much suffering." However, he eventually "decided to bury my face in a newspaper like everybody else on the streetcar, and so participated in the world-wide conspiracy not to see the inhumanity."[51] Bergmann admits that he lived a "normal" life in Lodz. He acknowledges that he did not try to help any Jews, something for which he feels guilty today. However, he claimed in 1996 that his experience there would never have led him to conclude that a systematic extermination of the Jews was under way elsewhere.[52]

A few have claimed they knew quite a lot about the Holocaust. For example, the ex-Obergefreiter Klaus Florey, a half-Jew, had heard rumors from returning soldiers about the death camps in Poland. He claimed that he knew by 1942 about the systematic murder of the Jews because of how many relatives and friends had disappeared, and because by 1944, strong rumors about the gas chambers had become commonplace.[53] When asked why he did not investigate these rumors, he simply said, "I knew that some of the deported Jews were killed. The gas chambers were rumors, hard to believe. How could I investigate? Go up to an SS officer and ask him? That probably would have been the end of me!"[54] Gefreiter Heinz Bleicher, who trained troops in the region of Belci in Rumania, claimed that during the summer of 1941, he observed what the Einsatzgruppen did to Jews. He witnessed the "bestial" manner in which the SS shot hundreds of Jews in cold blood. Later, the brother and sister of his Jewish mother, Helen Bleicher née Wolff, were sent to Buchenwald and Riga, respectively. Both were murdered in these camps.[55] Half-Jew Hanns Rehfeld knew the Nazis murdered most people they deported and heard about Auschwitz and all its horror during the Christmas of 1942 from friends of his in a mixed marriage.

In "hidden terms," some of his acquaintances knew about it, but then added "perhaps not in every detail." Former classmates of Rehfeld's showed him photos from their brothers on the front, where naked Jews had been shot in ditches.[56] During the last days of the war, Rehfeld was in Breslau and heard from the soldiers defending the city that they feared that the Russians would do to them what Germany had done to the Jews. At the very end, when Rehfeld was in the protective care of nuns in a monastery, the nuns told him of the stories that dying soldiers in their care had told them about the murder of Jews.[57] Florey, Bleicher, and Rehfeld's accounts are the exception rather than the rule among Mischling interviewees. Their knowledge of the systematic murder was rare. The Waffen-SS soldier Günter Löwy lost his entire family at Minsk, with the exception of his mother, who escaped to Switzerland. Löwy knew about the concentration camps at Drancy and Auschwitz and that people were being gassed. He claimed he continued to serve to survive.[58] However, while in the Waffen-SS, he does not remember any of his comrades talking about the Holocaust.[59] Löwy firmly believed that his Waffen-SS comrades did not know about the Holocaust. However, he added, had his comrades known he was a Jew, they would have "hung me up on the first tree."[60] That even Waffen-SS soldiers remained unaware of the Holocaust, in the opinion of a Jew who did know about it, shows how difficult it was to grasp the deadly fate of the Jews. Florey claimed that the general population had enough to worry about (their husbands and sons in the war and air raids at home) to be concerned about the Jews.[61]

Some were asked to participate in the killings, but none documented in this study admitted to taking part. Half-Jew Alfred Catharin's superior ordered him to take part in the execution of Jews. Catharin knew that disobedience would be punished with imprisonment. Fortunately for him, he found another comrade who was willing to take his place. Later, his comrade told him how they had taken the Jews to a field and shot them.[62] Scared as Catharin was, he felt that as long as he wore his uniform, he and his family would remain protected. Like many others, Catharin did not draw any sweeping conclusions from what he had heard from his comrade as to what was happening to Jews in general.

In this study, some of the nine Mischling veterans deported to concentration camps failed to fully comprehend what was going on.[63] Most testified that until they were sent to the camps, they had no idea about the extreme persecution there and, even then, had no knowledge of the systematic extermination of Jews going on in the death camps. Ex-Funker Friedemann Lichtwitz was sent to Dachau, where he was prisoner number 144724, because he tried to escape from his OT forced labor camp. He contends that although he lived in Dachau and saw all its horror, he still did not know about the systematic extermination of Jews until after the war.[64] Ex-Oberschütze Rolf Schenk was sent to Buchenwald, where he was prisoner number 134658, because he was a half-Jew and a political enemy of the regime. Although he experienced one of Hitler's camps, he said he did not know about the true extent of the Holocaust until after the war.[65] One must realize that reports on the systematic extermination of Jews were *Geheime Reichssachen* (top secret operations), and indiscretions about it were severely punished, making it difficult to obtain concrete evidence about the industrialized mass murder. Moreover, the experiences of Lichtwitz and Schenk, although horrible, did not take place in extermination camps like Auschwitz or Treblinka.

Contrary to expectations, this study has documented that some people of Jewish descent participated directly in the Holocaust as perpetrators, primarily because of their rank and responsibilities. Like most high-ranking Nazi officials at the Nuremberg trials, Field Marshal Erhard Milch, a half-Jew, lied when he swore that he did not know about the Holocaust.[66] He had read reports from Dr. Sigmund Rascher, the notorious doctor at Dachau who conducted brutal experiments.[67] Milch wrote the head of Himmler's personal staff, SS General Karl Wolff, on 20 March 1942 about the "interesting" experiments at Dachau.[68] On 31 August 1942, Milch also wrote Himmler to express his interest in Rascher's tests.[69] Besides knowing about and approving of these horrific experiments, Milch also served as co-chairman with Speer on the Pursuit Plans Staff, which needed about a quarter-million slave workers. Milch knew of about one hundred thousand Hungarian Jews expected in Auschwitz who could be utilized for his project.[70] With respect to slave labor, Milch (probably in 1942) told General Carl-August von Gablenz that he wanted him "to get in touch with [General Hermann] Reinecke concerning the French POW's. I demand that if the people refuse to work they immediately be placed against the wall and shot."[71] As historian Georg Meyer asserted, Milch can be considered a "German Jewish war criminal."[72] Unfortunately, Milch was not alone.

Ministerialrat[73] in the Reichskanzlei Dr. Leo Killy, a quarter-Jew who had a half-Jewish wife and who received Hitler's clemency in 1936,[74] was a paradox. He should have been grateful that Hitler had saved his immediate family and should have refrained from harming others in the same situation. Instead, as Raul Hilberg writes, he "performed significant functions" in the destruction of the Jews.[75]

Even more detestable was the notorious doctor at Dachau, Dr. Hans Eppinger, a quarter-Jew, possibly a half-Jew, who performed horrible experiments on inmates. Like Milch, he not only knew about but also participated in evil medical studies.[76] Some people claim that he may have been 75 percent Jewish and was able to obtain false papers.[77] He killed himself awaiting his trial in 1946.[78]

Stella Goldschlag, a Jew, helped the Gestapo hunt down hidden Jews in Berlin to deport to the East.[79] She was a beautiful woman, with blue eyes and blond hair. The Gestapo told her that they intended to declare her Aryan.[80] Called the "blond poison," she was responsible for several, if not hundreds, of people's deaths.[81] She claims that her only crime was survival.[82] Stella was not alone. The Jew Günther Abrahamsohn, another "catcher (Greifer)," as they were called, also helped the Gestapo locate Jews in hiding. He claimed after the war that he did so to survive.[83] Stella and Abrahamsohn were two of around fifteen to twenty "catchers" working in Berlin.[84]

Some ran concentration camps. SS-Obersturmführer[85] Fritz Scherwitz (real name Eleke Sirewiz), a Jew and Nazi Party member, controlled the concentration camp at Lenta[86] outside of Riga and was responsible for sending Jews to their deaths.[87] Witnesses claimed that he personally took part in the killing of two hundred Jews in Riga on 31 October 1942 and raped several women.[88] After the war, he worked in a Munich organization that helped Jews recover their property until someone recognized him and reported him to the authorities. Scherwitz was brought to trial as a war criminal.

Yet the cases of Milch, Killy, Eppinger, Goldschlag, Abrahamsohn, and Scherwitz were rare. Few people of Jewish descent attained the rank, positions, and responsibility that these people did. Perhaps they behaved as they did to show the Nazis that they truly believed in Hitler's Weltanschauung. Possibly they felt that the more brutal they acted, the more Aryan they appeared. However, unlike the others, the Nazis did not know about

Scherwitz's Jewishness. Perhaps he was "a pathological killer,"[89] as one rabbi claimed. Why Scherwitz acted as he did is puzzling, but what he did was no less pathological than the actions of Milch, Killy, and Eppinger, as well as some others, although one would think their Jewish ancestry should have prevented them from acting as they did.

Many *Mischlinge* heard wild rumors but did not want to investigate for fear of jeopardizing their own lives. When asked why he continued to serve despite all he knew, half-Jew Hans Pollak replied, "I had to put my teeth together and bite down. Somehow, life must continue, I thought."[90] In other words, Pollak saw little else he could do realistically. Many living as civilians did not want to draw undue attention to themselves. Most just wanted to survive. Half-Jew Peter Gaupp said he knew about concentration camps, but not about the Holocaust. He claimed it was easy to ignore what was happening to the Jews. Such a reaction, according to Gaupp, was only natural, only "human" under the circumstances.[91]

Many who heard about the atrocities did not believe the reports. Half-Jew Peter Schliesser said that "it was hard if not impossible to imagine that the Jews were deported to be killed." Even when his father told him about this in 1944, he did not believe it.[92] Others did not concern themselves with the atrocities, although they knew about them. Captain Horst von Oppenfeld, a quarter-Jew and adjutant of Stauffenberg, received news in 1942 that Jews were being shot and that the executioners were removing the gold teeth from the corpses around Jelnya, Russia.[93] "I even heard the shooting myself," Oppenfeld claimed, but "I lived for the day and did not pay much attention to all of it."[94] Some men like Oppenfeld quickly adapted to the surrounding situations and did what was expected of them.

Many who are unfamiliar with the realities of Nazi Germany feel puzzled by the fact that these men did not oppose the regime when they knew about Nazi persecution. Most who knew about or suspected Nazi atrocities declare that they would have been killed if they had acted against the Nazis. Obergefreiter Rudolf Sachs, a half-Jew, said, "What should I have done? Gone to the Gestapo and say, 'Please don't deport my relatives?' Impossible . . . that would've just hastened my death."[95] Half-Jew Fritz Kassowitz echoed Sachs, saying, "What was I supposed to do? In protest tell the authorities that I disapproved of the murder of Jews because I was a half-Jew? That would've accomplished nothing, especially at the war's end." Kassowitz finished the war as an Unteroffizier and was decorated with the EKII and Wound Badge.[96] Both Sachs and Kassowitz's dilemmas illustrate what most have claimed about their situations during the ruthless dictatorship of the Third Reich. The feeling of helplessness is almost universal among *Mischlinge*.

A few *Mischling* officers were able to help their relatives in danger, either through the weight of their military rank or through connections to influential people. First Lieutenant Ernst Prager, who had received Hitler's *Deutschblütigkeitserklärung* and was decorated with both Iron Crosses and the Golden Wound Badge, met with Eichmann two and a half months after being injured and was sent home. Although his doctors warned that traveling might kill him because of his wounds, he decided to leave Nuremberg for Berlin anyway. Prager's wife, Hella, accompanied him to several SS departments because of his serious war wounds. When SS personnel learned that he had received Hitler's *Arisierung* and that he was a decorated frontline officer, they treated him with the utmost respect and greeted him properly for his rank and status. Eventually, he was told to visit Eichmann's office. Surprisingly, Eichmann admitted him. Wrapped in bandages, Prager marched into Eichmann's office with only a subtle hint of lameness. After they exchanged formalities, Prager explained the situations of his father, who was performing forced labor, and of his uncle Stephan Prager and aunt Mathilde Blanck, who had both been deported to Theresienstadt. According to Prager and his wife, Eichmann responded by describing Theresienstadt very positively as a new home for Jews, where they were well treated and could decide their own fates. Prager became so irritated with Eichmann that he jumped up and said sarcastically, "[N]ext you'll tell me you regret not being Jewish so you could spend a holiday in Theresienstadt." Eichmann then became serious and admitted that he could do nothing for Prager's father, but assured him that his uncle would be moved to the "Prominent Jews" barracks, where he would receive better food and would not be deported to a death camp.[97] Eichmann claimed he could not do anything for Prager's father, since he had not been deported yet and thus fell outside Eichmann's jurisdiction. Eichmann's promise to help Prager's uncle was carried out.[98] Nothing was said about the aunt, whom the Nazis later murdered.[99]

Captain Georg Langheld, destroyer commander and German-Cross in Gold winner, wrote that Admiral Walter Gladisch helped him protect two of his female relatives for a while. Eventually the SS murdered both, one eighty-six and the other sixty years old.[100] Admiral Raeder's intervention for Langheld's Jewish mother (Frau Langheld née Gerson), who was threatened with deportation, successfully protected her.[101]

Only a few *Mischlinge* who were not officers tried to help Jewish relatives. Klemperer described a case in which the soldier Horst Siegfried Weigmann went to Dresden's Gestapo headquarters to free his Jewish mother. After some negotiations and claiming he was an SS officer, he freed his mother. However, as they were leaving, an SS man recognized them and prevented their escape. The Gestapo deported the mother to Theresienstadt and threw him in jail. Soon thereafter, the son hung himself in his cell.[102] After the Nazis deported Camilla Krüger to Theresienstadt, her sons and Wehrmacht veterans Helmut and Answald Krüger went to an SS office in Berlin to inquire about their mother. On their way in, they met Eichmann's deputy, SS-Sturmbannführer[103] Rolf Günther, at the entrance. He asked them both what they wanted. They explained their situation and said they wanted to see if they could get their mother back. They then told him they were both ex-Gefreite decorated with the EKII. Surprised, Günther looked at them and hatefully said, "Every criminal is courageous *(Mut hat jeder Verbrecher),*"[104] and then left. Helmut and Answald also tried to reenter the Wehrmacht to help their mother, but were rejected.[105] Camilla would remain in Theresienstadt until the war's end.

Sometimes the knowledge of what the Nazis were doing to one's relatives was too painful to live with. Captain Erich Rose,[106] a liaison officer between the Spanish Blue Division and the Wehrmacht, told his comrade, Albert Schnez (the later Bundeswehr general), in 1942, shaking his head and depressed, that his Jewish father[107] and half-Jewish mother had been deported to Theresienstadt. He also knew of several Jewish relatives who had been deported and feared that they had all been murdered. He expressed his desire to die. "I'm torn apart. I've nothing to live for. My family has all been murdered," he told Schnez. Schnez, who worked in OKH General Staff at the time, told Rose that he would try to get the *Arisierung* for him. A comrade of theirs, Major Eberhard von Hanstein in OKW, had contact with Schmundt and explained Rose's situation to him. Soon thereafter, Schmundt brought Rose's case to Hitler. Rose did not agree with Schnez's desire to get this exemption for him and told him, "I'm a *Schwein.*[108] The Nazis murder my family (which I have to assume), and at the same time, I fight for them."[109] Hanstein's and Schmundt's efforts to get Rose clemency failed.

Rose saw that the sands of his life had begun to run out. Experiencing several problems with his unit because of his criticism of Hitler and Nazism and because of his Jewish ancestry, Rose became depressed. Soon thereafter, he exposed himself in battle and died.[110]

An important question is if half-Jews knew about the Holocaust, why did they report to their OT deportation stations? The answers to this question are complex. Since most reported to their OT deportation stations when ordered, it seems obvious that most did not know about the Holocaust. If everyone knew about the Holocaust, most would have tried to hide, escape, or possibly commit suicide, rather than report at the OT gathering point. However, few foolproof hideouts existed. The Swiss border was heavily patrolled on both sides. Sweden was difficult to reach, being separated from Germany by the Baltic Sea. Nonetheless, although the odds were stacked against those who attempted to hide or escape, if half-Jews had known what eventually awaited them, they likely would have tried their luck no matter what the cost. Most had the time to make a quick getaway. A few were actually arrested and sent to OT,[111] but most received their deportation notices from either the Gestapo or local government employment offices, which gave them several days, if not weeks, to report. Usually most reported as ordered because they did not fear for their lives. Karl-Arnd Techel claimed he knew about Nazi atrocities, but still reported to his OT deportation station. He did not know where he was going and why half-Jews were being "really" drafted. He heard about Auschwitz only after the war and did not fear for his life at the time. He does not know why he was not scared, "but that's the truth of the matter — I simply did not think it was dangerous."[112] When Dieter Bergmann was deported to an OT camp, he recalled another train parked near his own where people cried and groaned, "a true sound from Hell."[113] However, he still did not think his own life was in danger.[114] If they had known that their deported relatives had probably been murdered, their survival instinct would have taken over and most of them would have tried to flee Germany or go underground. Today, most respond to such propositions that they had nowhere to flee or to hide. Nonetheless, the majority were unaware of what lay beyond the OT camps. Peter Schliesser said that "very few knew or even assumed [that their Jewish relatives had been murdered] at that time."[115] Many did not see that OT was the first step on the path to systematic murder. Thus, the majority reported when called to OT.

Only a few, with the knowledge they had, risked hiding or escaping to Switzerland. The few men who did "know" received privileged information or were told by those in higher positions not to report for OT. When half-Jew Franz Calvelli-Adorno heard about the true reality of OT, a friendly physician committed him to an insane asylum, where he would survive the war.[116] The three Bier brothers (Georg, Gerhard, and Martin) decided to act because many in high positions encouraged them to try and flee. A World War I comrade of their father, Gustav, who served on the General Staff, informed them in 1943 that half-Jews were going to be sent to "special units." This friend encouraged them to escape. Also, U-boat Captain Heinz Sternberg *(U-473)*, after hearing about the Biers' problems, encouraged Gerhard Bier and his brothers to leave Germany for Switzerland.[117] Gerhard Bier felt that if they stayed around and were deported to OT, they would have to clear minefields and perform other dangerous work that would eventually kill them. They did not think they would be systematically exterminated and did not know about the extermination of the Jews. Although Martin Bier had heard about Jewish executions by firing squads in Russia, he could not comprehend that such a thing had really taken place. He especially did not think that a systematic annihilation of the Jews was under way.[118] Eventually, the three Bier brothers successfully jumped out of a moving train traveling inside the border of Switzerland. They were able to remain in that neutral country.[119]

Historians have hotly debated the question for the past fifty years whether Germans knew about the Holocaust. Perhaps a better way to phrase this question is, Did Germans understand what was happening to Jews during the war? This study has shown that the answer is no. Maybe many *Mischlinge* did not want to know and denied what they could not or would not believe, but this is something difficult to prove. From the hundreds of cases documented, it is evident that most did not know nor understand what was going on in the extermination camps.

Most *Mischlinge* did know that relatives disappeared, but what actually happened to them was beyond their imaginations. The knowledge that the Nazis deported a Jewish relative differed dramatically from understanding that this often meant annihilation. As half-Jew Hans Meissinger said, "Neither Hannah [née Gerber, his wife, who is also half-Jewish] nor I knew anything about the Holocaust during wartime (nor did any of our friends), but [we] had fears for the Jewish relatives who were deported. We didn't even hear of Auschwitz! No one could imagine the monstrous genocide that was underway. . . . Poor ignorant sheep that we were."[120] Meissinger simply could not imagine that "Germany could do a thing like that."[121] He lost four relatives, and his wife, Hannah, lost two relatives in the Holocaust (Bergen-Belsen and Auschwitz).[122]

And even if *Mischlinge* did imagine the worst, most did not believe what their consciences told them. The average person lacked the imagination to process the signs that warned a *Mischling* that not only his Jewish relatives but he himself was in mortal danger. Each of the men in this study lost an average of eight relatives in the Holocaust. Unteroffizier Hans Günzel, a half-Jew, lost fifty-seven relatives. He and his brother, Unteroffizier Peter Günzel, were decorated soldiers who served the entire war and did not believe until after 1945 that their relatives had been systematically murdered.[123] Hans Herder said he did not know about the systematic extermination of the Jews, although he lost two uncles in concentration camps and lived near Mauthausen.[124] Heinz Dieckmann, a 75 percent Jew, said that during training, they often marched by Bergen-Belsen. "We all thought that the people in there were a-socials and should be removed from society," Dieckmann commented, "but we didn't know that in places like that murder was going on. . . . We actually didn't want to know what the truth was. That was the problem. . . . Ideology had made us inhuman." Dieckmann explained that witnessing the Nazis discriminate against Jews became commonplace and that they did not give the persecution much thought because it did not seem out of the norm. However, at the time, Dieckmann never thought the Jews were being systematically murdered.[125] Rolf von Sydow, who lost his grandfather in a Gestapo prison in 1943 and fourteen other relatives in the camps, said he did not believe until after the war that Germany had killed millions of Jews.[126] Even the Jew Max Mannheimer, who was sent to a concentration camp, professed that he had no idea about the Holocaust before he was deported. "I didn't think it was possible. Too many rumors," he said.[127] As the former German chancellor and quarter-Jew Helmut Schmidt wrote, "I never knew about the horrible crimes [of the Nazis]. . . . I learned of the concentration camps, but I imagined they were used very differently. . . . I thought they were a kind of prison where people under investigation were held."[128] Only after the war did Schmidt learn about

Auschwitz, the final Solution, gas chambers, and the systematic killings. Only then did Schmidt realize that he had served as an officer for a government that was responsible for the criminal murder of millions.[129] Even Hugo Fuchs, who lost his father in Sachsenhausen, claimed that he only knew after 1945 about the systematic destruction of the Jews by the Nazis.[130]

From the evidence, one would think that most Germans should have been aware of what today is called the Holocaust. This assertion applies even more to the *Mischlinge* who had opportunities to find out about the Holocaust. But most refused to believe or failed to assess the incriminating evidence they heard about or witnessed. Although many doubted the accuracy of the death certificates of relatives that stated they had died of "natural causes in the camps," they did not believe their relatives had been systematically murdered. Many could not understand why the people they had grown up with would want to kill them or their families. Deported Jews often led their *Mischling* relatives to believe that their deportation was not serious. When Harald Etheimer's aunt left for her deportation, she told him not to worry because she would soon return.[131]

Since the victims themselves, according to the Holocaust historian Lucy Dawidowicz, alleged that it was beyond their imagination they would be gassed and killed,[132] one should not expect ordinary Germans to know much more. Steinberg wrote, "Holocaust records show that Jews themselves often refused to believe what was happening in spite of the evidence of their own eyes."[133] Another Holocaust historian, Leni Yahil, claimed that systematic murder was beyond anyone's imagination.[134] Marion Kaplan wrote, "But a far more effective barrier to their comprehension was the sheer inconceivability of the genocide. Even those who received information frequently reacted with disbelief or repressed it."[135] If Jews did not believe what was happening to them, it follows that most *Mischlinge* also could not believe the Holocaust was happening, because they had less direct exposure to persecution. Almost all the interviews conducted for this book support this conclusion. The average German, who had even less contact with those who were persecuted, was highly unlikely to suspect the extent of the Holocaust. As Kershaw wrote:

During the war years interest in the "Jewish Question" declined still further. The deportation passed off apparently little heeded by the population. Most people seem to have asked little and cared less about the fate of the Jews. The war, its worries and deprivations, dominated opinion. The Jews were out of sight and out of mind. Knowledge of shootings and atrocities in occupied territories was widespread, and rumors about extermination circulated. Details in particular about the systematic gassing programme in the camps, appear, however, to have been largely unknown.[136]

Initially, this study expected to find that *Mischlinge* knew and understood what was going on in the camps. While *Mischling* and Jewish soldiers did know more than the average German, in the end their actions and testimonies prove that most soldiers of Jewish descent failed to grasp what was happening to the Jews. Similarly, most half-Jews did not realize what would have happened to them beyond the OT camps. As Sigmund Freud said, "At bottom, nobody believes in his own death."[137]

CONCLUSION

Many historians and writers have mentioned *Mischlinge* or described some of the policies that affected their lives during the Third Reich. This book builds on the foundation laid by Jeremy Noakes in his essay about *Mischlinge* published in the 1989 *Leo Baeck Yearbook,* which explored their history in the Wehrmacht for the first time.

The predicament of people fighting for a regime that did not recognize their basic human rights is not new. Throughout the American Civil War, thousands of free blacks and slaves, as well as some mulattoes ("half-" and "quarter-blacks") fought for the Confederate States of America.[1] A few mulattoes even served as Confederate officers.[2] Some of these African-Americans were slave owners "willing to fight for the protection of their slave property."[3] Historians estimate that some forty thousand African-Americans served in the Confederate armed forces.[4] These men fought to preserve a social order that sought to keep the majority of southern African-Americans as slaves. African-Americans also fought in the armed forces during World War I and II, long before the civil rights movement gained popular support in the United States.[5] Japan conscripted Koreans for the Japanese army during World War II.[6] A few hundred Japanese-Americans *(Nisei)* served in the American armed forces in World War II, although the U.S. government interned some of their families.[7] Many returned home in 1945 to find their property sold and anti-Japanese sentiment rampant.[8] In these cases too, soldiers fought on behalf of their oppressors.

Despite the obvious similarities, the story of Jews and *Mischlinge* who served in the Wehrmacht is fundamentally different. Unlike African-Americans in the United States and Koreans in the Japanese army, German Jews and *Mischlinge* had enjoyed many years of equal rights in Germany before Hitler came to power. In 1933, the majority of them did not feel Jewish; consequently, they did not feel threatened by Hitler's anti-Semitic diatribes. It was not until the 1935 racial laws that some of them started to associate themselves with the Jews. Even so, the *Mischling* segment of society remained loyal and served Germany obediently. Hitler excluded most *Mischlinge* from positions in society and the armed forces where they could have better served his military goals. *Mischlinge* fought for a government that had not only taken away their human rights, but also murdered many of their relatives.

This book offers several historical insights. It reminds many that the Third Reich cannot be understood in extremes of black and white. Not everyone who wore a uniform with a swastika was a Nazi as we use that word today. Not everyone who had Jewish ancestry was a victim of the death camps. Not every German officer was a pure Aryan, and not every Aryan officer was a rabid anti-Semite. It proves that at least 150,000 *Mischlinge* could have served in the Wehrmacht. It also proves that several *Mischlinge* were high-ranking officers, some of whom reached general and admiral rank. The *Mischling* experience clearly demonstrates the complexity of life in the Third Reich. Nazi policy toward them was a maze of confusion and contradictions, which reflected the regime's uncertainty about how to deal with Germans of partial Jewish descent.

Mischling policy was difficult to enforce for many reasons. One reason, as Nathan Stoltzfus argues in his book *Resistance of the Heart,* was that the Nazi ideology of "race" came into conflict with the goal of maintaining power.[9] If Hitler had treated the *Mischlinge* too harshly in the 1930s and early 1940s, he might have lost support from thousands of Aryans in key positions in the economy, armed forces, and government who had *Mischling* relatives. Another reason for the difficulty of enforcing *Mischling* policy was that since they did not exist as a category of people before 1935, bureaucrats had to rely on church and city or county registry records, denunciations, and honest confessions to identify *Mischlinge*. In the Wehrmacht, enforcement, particularly of discharge orders, was often hindered by officers who valued trained soldiers more than the racial laws. The fact that Hitler reserved the right to grant exemptions from these laws reinforces the perception that even he recognized how impractical these laws and how contradictory his goals were. However, as Henry Turner wrote, Hitler was driven by "the unshakeable conviction that reality would eventually conform to his will."[10] Hitler had complete faith in his abilities to change reality to suit his irrational philosophy. Diplomatic and military triumphs from 1933 to 1940 reinforced his belief in his own infallibility as a leader, prophet, and racial hygienist. Hitler perverted Germany's legal system and forced it to implement his racial ideas as laws.

It is important to note that when racial discrimination affected *Mischling* Wehrmacht personnel, some Aryan officers were willing to help them. Many did so while avidly supporting Hitler and his ideas. Field Marshal von Reichenau was sympathetic and helpful to several *Mischlinge*. He even protested the killing of Jews in Poland in 1939.[11] Perhaps because of this action, Hitler claimed in 1939 that Reichenau was not reliable.[12] But in general, Reichenau supported the regime and its racial policies. Hitler recognized this by giving him command of the Sixth Army in 1939 and then Army Group South in 1941. One must also not forget that Reichenau on 10 October 1941 issued one of the most murderous orders of any field commander, directing his men to annihilate "Jewish-Bolshevism," emphasizing that "the soldier must have complete understanding for the necessity of the harsh, but just atonement of Jewish subhumanity."[13] Hitler described Reichenau's initiative as "excellent."[14] Likewise, Field Marshal von Manstein, who helped some *Mischlinge* and wrote a protest against the *Arierparagraph* in 1934, also issued an order on 20 November 1941, as commander of the Eleventh Army, calling for the destruction of the "Jewish-Bolshevik system" and explaining that "the soldiers must show understanding for the harsh atonement of Judaism, the spiritual carrier of the Bolshevik terror."[15] Like many in Germany, these generals did not equate *Mischlinge* with Jews. For them, getting rid of "Jews," as former army commander in chief General von Fritsch said in December 1938, was a goal to be achieved.[16] These generals could make exceptions for *Mischlinge* they viewed as Germans and comrades-in-arms. Nonetheless, after Manstein received no response to his protest in 1934, and after Reichenau's last efforts in 1938 to help a *Mischling*, according to this study, neither man took further action to prevent the persecution of *Mischlinge*. On the contrary, their dastardly orders of 1941 probably helped sanction the deaths of thousands of innocent Jews,[17] and diminished the redeeming value of the acts of "benevolence" they had performed for a few *Mischlinge* in the 1930s. Although they felt certain *Mischlinge* were worth saving, they agreed that Jews should be exterminated, especially the "Asiatic" and Communist *Ostjuden*. One must not forget that even Hitler helped many *Mischlinge* at the same time he ordered Jews to be exterminated.

In light of how aggressively Hitler pursued the extermination of the Jews, it is surprising how much time he spent reviewing applications for exemptions from the racial laws submitted by *Mischlinge*. One can understand his careful analysis of the pros and cons of removing a *Mischling* general from his post, but many to whom Hitler granted these coveted exemptions were common soldiers with the ranks of private or NCO. Hitler's exemptions and the actions of thousands of Aryan officers, including men close to Hitler, such as Army Adjutant Engel and Commander Frey, in helping *Mischlinge,* and even occasionally Jews, contradicted the Nazis' *Weltanschauung.*

Though it is hard to believe, documents prove that Engel and Frey went beyond the scope of their job responsibilities to help *Mischlinge.* Perhaps these men did so, and this is purely speculation, because this was a way they could rationalize not doing anything for the Jews. Both Frey and Engel, because of their positions and activities, knew more than the average officer about the Holocaust. This rationalization and the desire to help comrades and brave soldiers may have motivated Frey and Engel to do so much for *Mischlinge.* What is particularly difficult to believe is that the arch-anti-Semite Hitler himself granted even one exemption from the racial laws. But he personally issued many. As Kershaw wrote, "[N]othing was as it seemed in the Third Reich."[18]

Some of his actions suggest that Hitler believed Jewish "blood," even in minute amounts, could ruin a person. Other actions suggest that Hitler believed Mendel's theory of genetics by which a *Mischling* could be 100 percent Aryan if he inherited all his blood from the Aryan parent. But Hitler consistently wavered on facts about race. Some of his own decisions did not reflect the pure categories of race so central to Nazi rhetoric and philosophy.

Mischling policy also demonstrated the triumph of ideology over reason. OKW discharged tens of thousands of half-Jews on Hitler's orders throughout his regime. If winning the war had been his top priority, Hitler could have easily recalled all these soldiers to active duty on the Russian front. But even in the winter of 1942, when Germany needed every able-bodied German to fight as the intensity of the war increased, Hitler still ignored the thousands of *Mischlinge* previously discharged from the Wehrmacht.[19] Instead, Hitler focused on whether a few hundred *Mischlinge* deserved exemptions.

Hitler gave thousands of *Genehmigungen* and *Deutschblütigkeitser-klärungen* during his rule,[20] even as his regime crumbled before his eyes. If the war were more important than the destruction of the Jews, then Hitler could have allowed thousands of *Mischlinge* and Jews to serve in the Wehrmacht. The vast majority would have fought bravely for their homeland, and even the worst soldier would have been useful as cannon fodder. Hitler apparently valued a pure Aryan society more than victory. The subtleties of *Mischling* policy and exemptions absorbed Hitler as late as 1944. Hitler took this exemption process seriously and believed he had the power to discern a person's true racial makeup. For Hitler, carrying out racial policy was more important than winning the war. Hitler once said, "The Jewish question takes priority over all other matters."[21]

Even if Hitler did not consider racial purity more important than winning the war, he may have realized the inevitability of defeat and preferred to deal with matters he could still control. In 1939, he had promised that if war came, he would destroy the European Jews. By 1944 and early 1945, the deportation of Hungarian Jews to Auschwitz and hardened measures against *Mischlinge* showed that this was one of the only promises he could still keep.

After the attempt on his life in July 1944, Hitler revoked many of the exemptions he had granted earlier. He needed to blame someone for this attack, and *Mischlinge* and their Aryan spouses presented an easy target. To order the discharge of so many high-ranking officers late in 1944 — even generals who had received the Ritterkreuz — simply because they were partially Jewish or had partially Jewish wives, did not make strategic sense.

Initially, the Wehrmacht seemed not to have been bothered by *Mischling* soldiers. But as the Holocaust gained momentum and the Party pressured the Wehrmacht to comply with racial policies, the Wehrmacht as a whole forsook its non-Aryan comrades. It failed to protest against the deportation and gassing of Jewish World War I veterans. In 1944, when Hitler started pushing the half-Jews down the road of the Holocaust, the Wehrmacht again watched passively. As Karl Dietrich Bracher wrote, "[T]he Army closed its eyes to the reality and the consequences of the war rule, limited itself to the efficient conduct of its trade, and avoided all strategic and political disputes."[22] In individual cases, many officers did all they could unofficially to help *Mischlinge,* but stopped short of disobeying direct orders.

It seems that the only person who officially tried to help *Mischlinge* through the proper chain of command was Dr. Bernhard Lösener in the

RMI. He consistently lent his support and "expertise" to protect *Mischlinge* in a climate where such behavior was not politically advantageous for him. For his activities, according to Lösener, several people in the Party called him a "Friend of the Jews *(Judenfreund),*"[23] a highly derogatory term then.[24] Unfortunately, Lösener's influence diminished dramatically after December 1941 when *Mischlinge* needed him the most. It is doubtful that Lösener would have been able to change significantly the worsening situation of *Mischlinge* had he continued actively to protect them from further persecution. This was especially the case, since Bormann's influence dramatically increased when he became head of the Parteikanzlei in May 1941.

As the war worsened, Hitler's persecution not only of Jews but also of *Mischlinge* dramatically escalated. The number of exemptions granted to *Mischling* soldiers between 1941 and 1943 sharply decreased from what it had been between 1938 and 1940. By 1944, Hitler regretted having treated *Mischling* soldiers leniently. He expressed his change of heart by discharging many who had exemptions and deporting them and other half-Jewish veterans to OT forced labor camps.

Mischlinge often found themselves the losers in a game where the rules changed at the whim of their opponent. These men, who had served loyally and had been awarded some of Germany's highest honors, would eventually have been subjected to the same fate as World War I German-Jewish veterans. Had the war continued, or had Germany won, most half-Jews would have been exterminated. Quarter-Jews would have suffered further discrimination and probably selective extermination.

Hitler's extensive personal participation in *Mischling* matters supports the theory that nothing could happen on the Jewish question without his knowledge. He had quickly established dictatorial control over the sophisticated government apparatus that administered the Holocaust. Hitler's retention of personal control over the *Mischling* problem indicates that he would not have relinquished any of his power to decide the fate of European Jewry.[25] For instance, during a meeting in 1937, discussing measures against the Jews with district Party leaders, Hitler vehemently said, "Who can give the order? Only I!"[26] He thrived on wielding all of his instruments of domination even until the last minutes of his life. By design, the different departments and organizations of the regime were unified under Hitler's leadership. Hitler's power "derived from his position as the fulcrum, linchpin and mediating element of the differing interests."[27] Since Hitler spent so much time on the *Mischlinge,* one wonders how much more time he must have spent planning the destruction of the Jews. Hitler ordered the Holocaust and oversaw its implementation, though no written directive ordering the extermination of the Jews bearing his signature has been found to date.[28] Just as Hitler gave verbal orders to Engel, Schmundt, Lammers, and Bormann about how to handle *Mischlinge,* he likewise gave orders to Himmler (whom Hitler often met in private), Heydrich, and others on how to annihilate the Jews.[29] He knew what was going on because he ordered it. As Hitler said in 1942, "No matter how long the fight lasts, the Jew will be exterminated."[30]

NOTES

NOTE ON SOURCES

Although oral testimonies are subject to fallible human memories, they have nonetheless proven invaluable in explaining several documents collected for this study. Documents never before seen by historians, found in people's closets, basements, and desk drawers, created a much fuller and complex history, especially when their owners supplied the background and history of the documents as well. These sources helped re-create the unique and tragic history of the *Mischlinge,* which is still so little understood over half a century later. The thousands of pages of documents and oral testimonies (on 8 mm video and VHS video) in this study are now part of the permanent collection at the Bundesarchiv-Militärarchiv in Freiburg, Germany, as the Bryan Mark Rigg Collection. Although interviews need to be treated with some skepticism, they have repeatedly shown that oral history often enriches rather than contradicts historical documents. All too often, history is written without the human element, that is, without knowing what these people thought, felt, and believed. Oral history helps reconstruct many of these people's thoughts, feelings, and beliefs through their diaries, letters, interviews, and photographs. In this way, a healthy combination of hard documents or primary sources and secondary sources and testimonies expands our sense of this history. Often one reads about men and women but feels no human connection with them. The interviews were done to try to bridge this gap and to provide readers with the means to enter these men's and women's thoughts and feelings to understand them better and to deepen readers' knowledge of this history.

INTRODUCTION

1. Some loose translations of *Mischlinge* are "half-breeds," "hybrids *(Zwischenrasse),*" or "partial Jews."
2. Wehrmacht was the German word for the German armed forces from 1935 to 1945.
3. See chapter 3 on German-Jewish assimilation.
4. Since Austria was united with Germany under Hitler's rule, discussion of German-Jewish assimilation here often includes Austrian-Jewish assimilation.
5. See chapter 9, "What Did *Mischlinge* Know about the Holocaust?" The term "Holocaust" only came into general use in the 1960s as the full scope and impact of Nazi Jewish policy became clear. "Holocaust" is used throughout this section to mean the Nazi genocidal policy.
6. To read about the sources used in this book, see "Note on Sources."

CHAPTER I: WHO IS A JEW?

1. Asher Maoz, "Who Is a Convert?" *International Association of Jewish Lawyers and Jurists,* 15 (December 1997): 11.
2. B.C.E. (before the common era) is used where B.C. was used in the past. C.E. (common era) is used for A.D. Karen Armstrong, *A History of God: A Four-*

thousand-Year Quest of Judaism, Christianity, and Islam (New York, 1993), p. 12.

3. The *Ivrim*, or Hebrews, were members of any group of Semitic peoples who lived in ancient Palestine and claimed descent from the biblical patriarchs Abraham, Isaac, and Jacob. The literal meaning of the word *Hebrew* is the people "who crossed over" or the people "from the other side of the river." Max I. Dimont, *Jews, God, and History* (New York, 1994), pp. 30–31; Uri Kaploun, ed., *Likkutei Dibburim: An Anthology of Talks by Rabbi Yosef Yitzchak Schneersohn of Lubavitch*, vol. 3 (New York, 1990), pp. 46–47.

4. Leo Trepp, *The Complete Book of Jewish Observance* (New York, 1980), p. 2.

5. Dimont, p. 33; Armstrong, p. 72. Interestingly, *Ivri*, or Hebrew, from the root *avar*, meaning "cross over," also connotes one who crosses over the bounds of propriety accepted by common culture. Abraham lived in a polytheistic world. By affirming his faith in one God, he crossed over the line. He became an iconoclast, an idol smasher. However, some believe that Abraham simply returned to the pure faith. Maimonides holds that monotheism was only reinitiated by Abraham, not discovered. See Baruch Frydman-Kohl, "Covenant, Conversion, and Chosenness: Maimonides and Halvei On 'Who Is a Jew'?" *Judaism* 41, no. 1 (winter 1992): 69.

6. Dimont, pp. 43–47; Matthew Black and H. H. Rowley, eds., *Peake's Commentary on the Bible* (New York, 1963), p. 74. *Torah* (rendered "law") literally means "direction" or "teaching." The Torah is the five books of Moses, or Pentateuch.

7. Dimont, p. 39; BA-MA, BMRS, File Dovid Gottlieb, Gottlieb to Rigg, 05.07.2001; Lecture given by Rabbi Cordoza at the *Yeshiva Ohr Somayach*, 27 December 1993; information given to the author by Henry Soussan (former president of Heidelberg's Jewish community) in December 1997 and by Rabbi Avraham Laber, rabbi of Congregation Beth Tephilah, Orthodox Synagogue of Troy, New York, January 2001; Herman Wouk, *This Is My God: The Jewish Way of Life* (New York, 1959), p. 35. In academic circles, there is no historical validation of the revelation at Sinai.

8. Trepp, p. 1.

9. From the tribe of Dan, one of the twelve tribes of Israel.

10. Leviticus 24:10–12 New International Version (NIV); Yisrael Isser Zvi Herczeg, ed., *The Torah: With Rashi's Commentary* (Brooklyn, 1994), pp. 309–11; Black and Rowley, *Peake's Commentary*, pp. 251–52. Another interpretation says that this Danite was rejected not because he had an Egyptian father but because he had rejected God. Still another interpretation says that he only wanted to belong to a certain tribe to inherit land. Thus, the tribes rejected him because of his motivation for trying to join them.

11. Genesis 41:45 NIV; Nosson Scherman and Meir Zlotowitz, eds., *The Artscroll Series Torah with Rashi's Commentary: Genesis* (Brooklyn, 1997), pp. 459–60; *Enger's Dictionary*, p. 606; Jack Miles, *God: A Biography* (New York, 1995), p. 83. On was an ancient city in northern Egypt. The city was also known as Heliopolis.

12. Numbers 12:1 NIV; *The Artscroll Series with Rashi's Commentary,* pp. 135–36; Black and Rowley, *Peake's Commentary,* p. 259; Dimont, pp. 38, 42; Miles, p. 101. Interestingly, Moses' brother Aaron and sister Miriam disapproved of Moses' marriage to this Ethiopian. Numbers 12:1–2 NIV; Miles, p. 101; Trepp, p. 260.

13. BA-MA, BMRS, File Rabbi Dovid Gottlieb, Gottlieb to Rigg, 05.07.2001.

14. The Tanach according to Christians is the Old Testament.

15. The Talmud is the rabbinic codification of the oral tradition. It was codified around 500 C.E.

16. Halakah is the body of Jewish scriptural law. Jacob Immanuel Schochet, *Who Is a Jew? Thirty Questions and Answers about This Controversial and Divisive Issue* (Brooklyn, 1987), p. 32. Often, the term *Din Torah* is interpreted as being tantamount to Halakah. See Maoz, "Who Is a Convert?" p. 12.

17. Hayim Halevy Donin, *To Be a Jew* (New York, 1991), p. 8; Howard M. Sachar, *A History of Israel,* vol. 2, *From the Aftermath of the Yom Kippur War* (Oxford, 1987), p. 139; Lawrence H. Schiffman, *Who Was a Jew? Rabbinic and Halakhic Perspectives on the Jewish-Christian Schism* (New Jersey, 1985), pp. 9–11; Trepp, pp. 247–54, 299; Dimont, p. 272; Schochet, *Who Is a Jew?* pp. 18, 28; Norman Lamm, "Who Is a Jew? The Supreme Court and The Supreme Judge," in *Who Is a Jew?* pp. 83–84; Nissim Rejwan, "Who's a Jew? Two Famous Non-Questions Answered," in *Who Is a Jew?* p. 95; Asher Cohen and Bernard Susser, *Israel and the Politics of Jewish Identity: The Secular-Religious Impasse* (London, 2000), p. 33; Federal Research Division, ed., *Israel: A Country Study* (Washington, D.C., 1990), p. 107.

18. Schochet, p. 18.

19. BA-MA, BMRS, File Rabbi Dovid Gottlieb, Gottlieb to Rigg, 05.07.2001.

20. Alfred Kolatch, *The Jewish Book of Why* (New York, 1981), pp. 13–14.

21. *Israel: A Country Study,* p. 107; Rejwan, "Who's a Jew?" in *Who Is a Jew?* p. 97; Donin, p. 9.

22. Nissim Rejwan, "Who's a Jew?" in *Who Is a Jew?* p. 97.

23. Lecture given by Rabbi Gottlieb at the *Yeshiva Ohr Somayach* on 24 December 1993.

24. See Wouk, p. 35.

25. BA-MA, Bryan Mark Rigg Sammlung (BMRS), interview Shlomo Perel, 10.09.1994, T-16; Sally Perel, *Ich war Hitlerjunge Salomon* (Berlin, 1992), p. 82.

26. Saul Friedländer, *Nazi Germany and the Jews,* vol. 1, *The Years of Persecution, 1933–1939* (New York, 1997), p. 172.

27. Nicholas De Lange, *Judaism* (New York, 1986), p. 4.

28. Rabbis N. Scherman and M. Zlotowitz, eds., *The Complete Artscroll Siddur* (Brooklyn, 1984), pp. 90–91. The Shema is the Jewish profession of faith. Armstrong, p. 52.

29. De Lange, p. 20.

30. H. G. Adler, *The Jews in Germany* (London, 1969), p. 100.

31. There is really no race besides the human race. There are different ethnicities, but race is almost impossible to define scientifically. See Schochet, p. 15.

32. This is a derogatory term by which Ethiopian Jews do not like to be called. A literal meaning of *Falashas* is "outsiders," depicting how the Ethiopians treated their Jewish minority. Sachar, p. 108.

33. Sachar, p. 108; David Kessler, *The Falashas: A Short History of the Ethiopian Jews* (London, 1996), p. 154.

34. The Hebrew term *giyur* is used for conversion to Judaism. The Hebrew word *lechumra* means that if there are two views, one stringent and one lenient, then the stringent one must be followed. Rejwan, "Who's a Jew?" in *Who Is a Jew?* p. 93.

35. Maoz, "Who Is a Convert?" p. 12.

36. Sachar, p. 108. See also Kessler, pp. 154–57.

37. Sachar, pp. 109–10, 139.

38. Cohen and Susser, 34–36; Schochet, p. 32; Sachar, pp. 137–39. Many religious Jews want this secular definition changed to read "has converted to Judaism Halakically," meaning they have gone through an Orthodox conversion. Philip S. Alexander, *Textual Sources for the Study of Judaism* (Manchester, 1984), pp. 166–67; David Bleich, "The Proposal for a 'Neutral' Beis Din," in *Who Is a Jew?* p. 101; *Israel: A Country Study,* pp. 109, 389.

39. BA-MA, BMRS, interview Major Yoav Delarea, 05.07.1998. See also Sachar, pp. 109, 139.

40. Within all these movements, there are different denominations. For example, within the Orthodox movement, there are the Modern, Mizrachi, Sefards, Shas, Traditional, and Hasidic Orthodox.

41. Sometimes this definition can be difficult to enforce. For example, when Oswald Rufeisen (also known as Brother Daniel), a Holocaust survivor and convert to Christianity, applied to the Israeli government to be defined as a Jew in his papers, he was denied. Although he was born of a Jewish mother, the Israeli court did not recognize him as a Jew because he had changed his religion. Israel recognizes a Jew only as a Jew if he or she is not a member of another religion. Maoz, "Who Is a Convert?" p. 13; Alexander, pp. 168–71; *Israel: A Country Study,* p. 108.

42. *Israel: A Country Study,* p. 110.

43. See Maoz, "Who Is a Convert?" pp. 11–19; Schochet, pp. 31, 73–75; Lamm, "Who is a Jew? The Supreme Court and the Supreme Judge," in *Who Is a Jew?* p. 87; Israel Religious Action Center, "Assaults against Reform Continue" (www.irac.org) 10 September 1997.

44. Sachar, pp. 139–40.

45. BA-MA, BMRS, File Rabbi Dovid Gottlieb, Gottlieb to Rigg, 05.07.2001. See also Frydman-Kohl, p. 64.

46. Maoz, "Who Is a Convert?" p. 17.

47. Schochet, p. 14.

48. Ibid.

49. As Raul Hilberg notes, the term "Aryan" "is not even a race designation. At best, it is a term for a linguistic-ethnic group." Raul Hilberg, *Destruction of the European Jews* (New York, 1961), p. 45, n. 6. The Nazis used the term to describe a people they believed were Germanic, blond, and blue-eyed.

50. A local Party leader of the Nazi Party.

51. *Die Nationalsozialistische Deutsche Arbeiterpartei* (NSDAP) was the name of the Nazi Party.

52. BA-MA, BMRS, interview Helmut Krüger, 27, 31.08.1994, T-13; Helmut Krüger, *Der Halbe Stern. Leben als deutsch-jüdischer Mischlinge im Dritten Reich* (Berlin, 1992), p. 88.

53. *Jeckes* is a derogatory Yiddish term meaning "jackets" and was used to describe German Jews who usually wore nice-fitting suits—hence, the term "jackets." This term was most commonly used for German Jews who lived in Palestine, but now has come into popular use among many Israeli and American Jews.

54. Steven E. Aschheim, *Brothers and Strangers: The East European Jew in German and German Jewish Consciousness, 1800–1923* (Wisconsin, 1982), p. 3; BA-MA, BMRS, File Peter Noa, Bl. 9.

55. Aschheim, pp. 3–5, 13–14.

56. Ibid., p. 152.

57. Wouk, p. 240.

58. Erwin A. Schmidl, *Juden in der K.(u.) K. Armee, 1788–1918, Studia Judaica Austriaca, Band XI* (Eisenstadt, 1989), p. 145.

59. Friedländer, pp. 27, 39; Yehuda Bauer, *A History of the Holocaust* (New York, 1982), p. 101; Hilberg, p. 19.

60. Ian Kershaw, *Hitler, 1936–1945: Nemesis* (New York, 2000), p. 136; Wolfgang Benz, *The Holocaust: A German Historian Examines the Genocide* (New York, 1999), p. 28; Ian Kershaw, *The Nazi Dictatorship* (New York, 1985), p. 93; Marion A. Kaplan, *Between Dignity and Despair: Jewish Life in Nazi Germany* (New York, 1998), p. 121; Norbert Frei, "Die Juden im NS-Staat," in *Das Dritte Reich im Überblick*, ed. Martin Broszat and Norbert Frei (Munich, 1989), p. 125. See also Nathan Stoltzfus, *Resistance of the Heart: Intermarriage and the Rosenstrasse Protest in Nazi Germany* (New York, 1996), p. 62; BA-MA, interview Werner Goldberg, 17.10.1994, T-42.

61. Wolf Zuelzer, "Keine Zukunft als 'Nicht-Arier' im Dritten Reich," in *Der Judenpogrom 1938: Von der >Reichskristallnacht< zum Völkermord*, Walter H. Pehle (Frankfurt am Main, 1988), pp. 147–48.

62. Ruth Gay, *The Jews of Germany* (New Haven, 1992), p. 234.

63. Aschheim, pp. 31, 221–24.

64. Leni Yahil, *The Holocaust* (Tel Aviv, 1987), p. 79.

65. *Weltanschauung* means "worldview." Naumann's group was dissolved by the Gestapo in 1935. He died in 1939 of cancer.

66. David Vital, *A People Apart: The Jews in Europe, 1789–1939* (Oxford, 1999), p. 814; Karl A. Schleunes, *The Twisted Road to Auschwitz: Nazi Policy toward German-Jews, 1933–1939* (Illinois, 1970), pp. 188–89.

67. Vital, p. 815. Schoeps would leave Germany for Scandinavia. He would survive the war.

68. Adler, *Jews in Germany*, pp. 107–8.

69. Schleunes, p. 101.

70. See Sarah Gordon, *Hitler, Germans, and the "Jewish Question"* (Princeton, 1984), p. 8; Aschheim, p. 231; Peter Wyden, *Stella: One Woman's True Tale*

of *Evil, Betrayal, and Survival in Hitler's Germany* (New York, 1993), p. 22;
Yahil, p. 23.

71. Aschheim, p. 15.

72. BA-MA, BMRS, interview Robert Braun, 10–14.08.1994, T-10; BA-MA,
BMRS, interview Robert Braun, 07.01.1996, T-190.

73. Manfred Messerschmidt, "Juden im preußisch-deutschen Heer," in *Deutsche
Jüdische Soldaten, 1914–1945,* ed. Militärgeschichtliches Forschungsamt (Bonn,
1984), p. 127; Messerschmidt, p. 42.

74. Aryan Paragraph.

75. For more information on the Aryan Paragraph, see chapters 4–6. Readers must
keep in mind always that for the Nazis, the Aryans were a race.

76. The phrase *Blut und Boden* (blood and soil) should not be confused with the
way the Nazis used it to depict agrarian romanticism (after Walter Darré, "the
Blut und Boden guru" [Kershaw, *Hitler, 1936–1945,* p. 374]). Benary used this
phrase before it had Nazi connotations attached to it, to show how German
he thought he and his family had become.

77. BA-MA, RW 6/ v.73, Oberstlt. a.D. Benary an Reichsleitung der NSDAP,
25.09.1933.

78. The Maccabees was the name of a priestly Jewish family who ruled Judea during
the first and second centuries B.C.E. The books Maccabees 1 and Maccabees 2,
describing the history of the Maccabees, are part of the Apocrypha. It is also
the name of the Jews "who engaged in a seemingly hopeless yet successful
struggle against Greek rule in 168 B.C." (Kaplan, p. 56).

79. BA-MA, RW 6/ v.73, Oberstlt. a.D. Benary an Reichsleitung der NSDAP,
16.10.1933.

80. The Reichswehr was the name of the German armed forces until March 1935.
Afterward, with the introduction of the draft with the new law, *Gesetz für den
Aufbau der Wehrmacht,* from 16 March 1935, the name of Reichswehr was
replaced by Wehrmacht to denote German armed forces. The Reichswehr was
a small armed forces made up of 100,000 soldiers, 4,000 army officers, 15,000
sailors and navy officers, and 3,040 civil servants with office rank. James S.
Corum, *The Luftwaffe: Creating the Operational Air War, 1918–1940* (Kansas, 1997), p. 85.

81. BA-MA, RW 6/v.73, Schreiben v. 20.11.1933.

82. Sebastian Haffner, *The Meaning of Hitler* (Cambridge, 1997), p. 9. Ironically,
the man who coined the word "anti-Semitism," Wilhelm Marr, and who established the League of Anti-Semites in 1879, had a Jewish father, the famous
artist Heinrich Marr of Hamburg. Yahil, p. 36; Marvin Lowenthal, *The Jews
of Germany: A History of Sixteen Centuries* (Philadelphia, 1936), pp. 295–96;
Dimont, p. 321.

83. Werner Maser, *Adolf Hitler. Legende Mythos Wirklichkeit* (München, 1971),
pp. 95, 268; Fritz Redlich, *Hitler: Diagnosis of a Destructive Prophet* (Oxford, 1998), p. 259; George Victor, *Hitler: The Pathology of Evil* (Dulles, 1998),
pp. 124–25.

84. Brigitte Hamann, *Hitlers Wien. Lehrjahre eines Diktators* (München, 1997).

85. Victor, pp. 124–25, 187. See also Henry Picker, *Hitlers Tischgespräche im Führerhauptquartier, 1941–1942*, ed. Percy Ernst Schramm (Stuttgart, 1976), p. 340; *The Speeches of Adolf Hitler*, vol. 1, pp. 733–35; John Keegan, *The Mask of Command* (New York, 1987), p. 255.

86. Adolf Hitler, *Mein Kampf* (Boston, 1971), p. 556.

87. Ian Kershaw, *Hitler, 1889–1936: Hubris* (New York, 1999), pp. 109, 112–13; Gordon A. Craig, *The Politics of the Prussian Army, 1640–1945* (New York, 1955), p. 344.

88. Enzo Traverso, *The Jews and Germany* (Nebraska, 1995), p. 30.

89. Richard M. Watt, *The Kinds Depart. The Tragedy of Germany: Versailles and the German Revolution* (New York, 1968), pp. 325–28. It seems that Arco-Valley's motivation for killing Eisner was to prove to a local racist group called the Thule Society, who had rejected his application for membership because of his Jewish mother, that he was "braver than they were." Watt, pp. 292–93; Bernt Engelmann, *Deutschland ohne Juden* (Köln, 1988), p. 352.

90. Hitler, *Mein Kampf*, p. 207.

91. An official Parteikanzlei document from 1944 stated that "5/8-Jews" would be considered only half-Jewish because they only had two full Jewish grandparents. See *Akten-NSDAP*, 107-00389, Reichsführer-SS/Persönlicher Stab an SS-Wirtschafts-Verwaltungshauptamt, Hauptsturmführer Dr. Volk, 26.07.1944. This study has indeed found some "five-eighths Jews" who were handled like half-Jews; however, many were classified as full Jews. It seems that the Nazi civil servants were very confused about what to do with this small group of partial Jews.

92. Hitler, *Mein Kampf*, p. 300. This translation of *Mein Kampf* used for this book follows the first version that came out in 1925.

93. Jonathan Steinberg, "Croatians, Serbs, and Jews, 1941–5," in *The Final Solution: Origins and Implementation*, ed. David Cesarani (New York, 1994), p. 190. See also Lucy S. Dawidowicz, *The War against the Jews, 1933–1945* (New York, 1988), p. 21.

94. Hamann, *Hitlers Wien*, p. 239.

95. Hamann, p. 95; Redlich, pp. 27, 259; Kershaw, *Hitler, 1889–1936*, pp. 23, 616 n. 110; Maser, p. 268; Werner Jochmann, ed., *Adolf Hitler Monologe im Führerhauptquartier, 1941–1944* (Hamburg, 1980), p. 294. Mahler converted to Catholicism in the same year in which he became director of the Wiener Hofoper. He never could have obtained this post without conversion.

96. Robert Payne, *The Life and Death of Adolf Hitler* (New York, 1973), p. 71.

97. Dawidowicz, p. 21. For an in-depth look at Hitler's anti-Semitic development, see Kershaw, *Hitler, 1889–1936*.

98. Hitler, *Mein Kampf*, p. 325. Hitler was probably influenced by Theodor Fritsch in his beliefs about Jews abusing Aryan women. See Kershaw, *Hitler 1889–1936*, p. 151.

99. Yahil, p. 43. See also Redlich, p. 324.

100. Dawidowicz, *War against Jews*, p. 18; Hitler, *Mein Kampf*, p. 232.

101. Jeremy Noakes, "The Development of Nazi Policy towards the German-Jewish 'Mischlinge,' 1933–1945," *Leo Baeck Yearbook* 34 (1989): 298.

102. G. Warburg, *Six Years of Hitler: The Jews under the Nazi Regime* (London, 1939), p. 41.

103. BA-B, R 40, Bl. 280, SS-Standartenführer Prof. Dr. B. K. Schultz, Chef des Rassenamtes /Rasse-u.Siedlungs-Hauptamt-SS, Gutachten zur Frage weit zurückreichenden fremden (jüdischen) Rasseneinschlags, 12.11.1943.

104. BA-B, R 15.06/ 64–65, Bl. 8–9, Oberstes Parteigericht der NSDAP an Reichsstelle für Sippenforschung, 24.11.1936.

105. SA stands for Sturmabteilung (storm detachment), a Nazi Party paramilitary formation. By 1933–1934, the SA membership numbered 1.5 million, which was fifteen times larger than the German army. Craig, *Prussian Army, 1640– 1945*, p. 474.

106. BA-MA, BMRS, interview Rudolf Sachs, 20.11.1995, T-168.

107. The Gestapo dealt "with all political opponents and 'enemies'" of the Third Reich. Benz, p. 53.

108. Friedländer, *Nazi Germany*, p. 138. See also Kaplan, p. 34.

109. *Deutsche Juristen-Zeitung*, Heft 1, Jahrgang 39, 01.01.1934, Dr. Wilhelm Frick, "Die Rassenfrage in der deutschen Gesetzgebung," p. 3.

110. After 1871, Germans had to register themselves (birth, weddings, and deaths) throughout Germany with the city or county register's office (Standesamt). During this registration, the religion was noted. The hundreds of documents collected for this study indicated that a person was registered as Jewish if *mosaisch, hebräisch,* or *israelitisch* was written next to the religion line.

111. Hitler claimed that Jewry was not a religion but a race. Maser, p. 176; Adolf Hitler, *Hitler's Secret Book*, introduction by Telford Taylor (New York, 1961), p. 212. However, almost all racial policies relied on religious documents to prove a person's "race."

112. Hilberg, p. 19; George L. Mosse, *The Crisis of German Ideology: Intellectual Origins of the Third Reich* (New York, 1964), p. 308.

113. Hilberg, p. 52; Stoltzfus, p. 273. This study documents a few cases of individuals who converted to Judaism, but who were not treated as full Jews. Half-Jew Peter Schliesser remembered that there were two Aryans who had converted to Judaism who were handled like half-Jews in his forced labor camp. BA-MA, BMRS, File Peter Schliesser.

114. A *Geltungsjude* was the Nazi term for a *Mischling* who had been raised Jewish or had converted to Judaism or a half-Jew who was married to a Jew. See *Akten-NSDAP*, 107-00393; Stoltzfus, p. 102; Kaplan, p. 75.

115. The Nazis used the word *Volk* to mean "folk and folkdom." In the Nazi philosophy, it embodied the "totality of the German people and the German race." Peter Adam, *Art of the Third Reich* (New York, 1992), p. 9.

116. *Akten der Parteikanzlei der NSDAP: Rekonstruktion eines verlorengegangenen Bestandes,* Bundesarchiv (Akten-NSDAP), Microfiches, hrsg. v. Institut für Zeitgeschichte (Munich, 1983), 101-28808, Der Reichsminister der Justiz, Führerinformation 1942 NR. 59. See also Friedländer, p. 152. However, some-

times the Nazis would turn a blind eye to those who adhered to Judaism but could claim non-Semitic ancestors. General Ernst Köstring and Field Marshal Ewald von Kleist were able to prevent the Jewish Mountaineers in the Caucasus, called the Tats, from being exterminated because they convinced the authorities that the Tats were only of the Jewish religion but free of Jewish "blood." The SD was "forced to desist" and spared the Tats. The SS spared the Crimean Karaimes, who practiced Judaism but were not "racially" Jewish. These two groups were the only exemptions found for this study where the Nazis made allowances for those who practiced Judaism but were not of Jewish descent. See Alexander Dallin, *German Rule in Russia, 1941–1945* (New York, 1957), p. 247; BA-MA, BMRS, File Jackobschwilli, Bl. 10. See also Hans von Herwarth, *Zwischen Hitler und Stalin. Erlebte Zeitgeschichte, 1931–1945* (Frankfurt, 1982); BA-MA, BMRS, interview Hans von Herwarth, 12.09.1994, T-17; Karl Dietrich Bracher, *The German Dictatorship* (New York, 1970), p. 424.

117. Reichsleiter was the highest rank in the Nazi Party under Hitler, the Parteichef (chief of the Party).

118. BA-B, NS 6/342, Bl. 64, Rundschreiben Nr. 124/43 von Bormann v. 02.09.1943. For more information about Hitler's relationship to Islam, see Albert Speer's *Inside the Third Reich* (New York, 1970), pp. 114–15. Also, Hitler seemed not to mind organizing military units with Muslims in them. See *Germany and the Second World War*, vol. 4, *The Attack on the Soviet Union*, ed. Militärgeschichtliches Forschungsamt (Oxford, 1998); Jürgen Förster, "Securing 'Living-space,'" p. 1,223; Dallin, pp. 244–46, 267–70, 600–601; Joachim Hoffmann, *Kaukasien 1942/43. Das deutsche Heer und die Orientvölker der Sowjetunion* (=Einzelschriften zur Militärgeschichte, 35; hersg. V. Militärgeschichtlichen Forschungsamt) (Freiburg, 1991); George Lepre, *Himmler's Bosnian Division: The Waffen-SS Handschar Division, 1943–1945* (New York, 2000).

119. Geoffrey Hartman, ed., *Holocaust Remembrance: The Shapes of Memory* (New York, 1994); David Tracy, "Christian Witness and the Shoah," in *Holocaust Remembrance*, p. 83; Martin Gilbert, *The Second World War* (New York, 1989), p. 351; Engelmann, p. 197; Aleksandar-Saša Vuletić, *Christen Jüdischer Herkunft im Dritten Reich. Verfolgung und Organisierte Selbsthilfe, 1933–1939* (Mainz, 1999), p. 6. In 1934, Edith Stein entered the Carmelite convent at Köln and took the religious name Teresa Benedicta of the Cross. On 9 August 1942, she and her sister died in Auschwitz. On 1 May 1987, Pope John Paul II beatified her.

120. Gilbert, *Second World War*, p. 351.

121. A convenient sample collected from this study found that out of 459 half-Jews documented, 267 had Jewish mothers and 192 had Jewish fathers. Out of 160 quarter-Jews documented, only 51 were Halakically Jewish.

CHAPTER 2: WHO IS A *MISCHLING*?

1. Special thanks to Christa Brunner for information on this event recorded on 29 February 1998.

2. *HarperCollins German Dictionary* (New York, 1990), p. 201; *Pocket Oxford German Dictionary* (Oxford, 1975), p. 229.

3. Joachim C. Fest, *The Face of the Third Reich* (Vermont, 1970), p. 98.

4. Walter Laqueur, ed., *The Holocaust Encyclopedia* (New Haven, 2001), p. 420; Wolfgang Eckart, "Biopolitical Seizure of Power and Medical Science in Germany, 1933–1945. Law for the Prevention of Genetically Diseased Offspring of July 14, 1933" (University of Heidelberg, 2000). The "Rehoboth Bastards" were originally called "colored" or "bastards." They got their name from the hot-water spring at Rehoboth, Namibia, in Africa where many of them lived.

5. According to one study from 1927, France had three hundred thousand "colored soldiers under arms" in the Rhineland. Hermann Stegemann, *The Struggle for the Rhine* (London, 1927), p. 425.

6. Hitler, *Mein Kampf,* p. 624; Maser, p. 226. See also Hitler, *Hitler's Secret Book,* p. 163.

7. Victor, pp. 134, 140, 175; Reiner Pommerin, *Sterilisierung der Rheinlandbastarde. Das Schicksal einer farbigen deutschen Minderheit, 1918–1937* (Düsseldorf, 1979); Friedländer, pp. 207–8; Robert Gellately, *The Gestapo and German Society: Enforcing Racial Policy* (Oxford, 1990), p. 215.

8. BA-MA, BMRS, File Helmut Wilberg, Heft II, Tagebuch, 26.09.1933.

9. BA-MA, BMRS, File Hermann Lange, "Jüdische Mischlinge: Als die Nationalsozialisten eine neue Rasse erfanden," Bl. 2.

10. Bruno Blau writes that 80 percent of half-Jews and 90 percent of quarter-Jews in his study were Christians. Bruno Blau, "Die Christen jüdischer und gemischter Abkunft in Deutschland und Österreich im Jahr 1939," *Judaica, Yearbook 5* (1949), p. 276.

11. Hans Globke and Wilhelm Stuckart, *Kommentare zur Deutschen Rassengesetzgebung* (München, 1936), p. 18.

12. For example, see *Akten-NSDAP,* 107-00398, 107-00407-408; Stoltzfus, p. 54; Vuletic, p. 21.

13. Hilberg, p. 49; Stoltzfus, p. 54; Vuletić, p. 21; BA-MA, BMRS, H. Lange. For example, three men had to leave the SS because they were 1/256 Jewish. See BA-B, NS 19/453; BA-B, NS 19/3857; BA-B, NS 19/1194.

14. BA-MA, BMRS, File Hans-Geert Falkenberg, Veranstaltung zum 08.05.1945 im Bergischen Kolleg, Wuppertal, 10.05.1995, Bl. 55. See also Friedländer, p. 167.

15. Hitler, *Mein Kampf,* pp. 248–49.

16. Ibid., pp. 400–402.

17. Hilberg claims that these records were often quite difficult to get. See Hilberg, p. 49. Stoltzfus maintains the opposite, saying that churches made "their records freely available." See Stoltzfus, p. 10.

18. Hitler, *Mein Kampf,* p. 120.

19. Joseph Walk, ed., *Sonderrecht für den Juden im NS-Staat. Eine Sammlung der gesetzlichen Maßnahmen und Richtlinien. Inhalt und Bedeutung* (Heidelberg, 1981), Gesetz v. 04.10.1936.

20. SS lieutenant colonel.

21. Hannah Arendt, *Eichmann in Jerusalem* (New York, 1984), p. 159; Robert Wistrich, *Who's Who in Nazi Germany* (New York, 1982), p. 62.

22. Interestingly, Göring's ancestry had Jews in it a few centuries back. See Wolfgang Paul, *Wer war Hermann Göring* (Esslingen, 1983), p. 33; W. R. Staehelin, ed., *Wappenbuch der Stadt Basel. 1 Teil. 1 Folge* (Basel, 1934), Familie Eberler gennant Grünenzweig.

23. Karl-Heinz Janßen, *30 Januar. Der Tag der die Welt veränderte* (Hamburg, 1983), p. 24; Karl Demeter, *The German Officer Corps, 1650–1945* (New York, 1965), p. 228; *Der Judenpogrom 1938*, Beitrag von Zuelzer, p. 147; Bracher, p. 254; Hamann, pp. 416–17. This phrase originally came from Dr. Karl Lueger, mayor of Vienna from 1897 to 1910. He would say, "*Wer a Jud ist, bestimm i!*" See also Willi Frischauer, *The Rise and Fall of Hermann Goering* (Boston, 1951), p. 151.

24. BA-MA, BMRS, from database of documented Wehrmacht soldiers of Jewish descent, "50 percent Jew" Field Marshal Erhard Milch, "50 percent Jew" General Günther Sachs, and "50 percent Jew" General Helmut Wilberg.

25. Jobst Frhr. von Cornberg, and John M. Steiner, "Willkür in der Willkür. Hitler und die Befreiungen von den antisemitischen Nürnberger Gesetzen," *Vierteljahreshefte für Zeitgeschichte*, Heft 2 (1998), p. 161.

26. Das Reichsbürgergesetz vom 15.09.1935, RGBl. 1935, Teil I, Nr. 100, p. 1146; Gesetz zum Schutz des deutschen Blutes und der deutschen Ehre vom 15.09.1935, RGBl. 1935, Teil I, Nr. 100, p. 1146; Erste Verordnung zum Reichsbürgergesetz 14.11.1935, RGBl., Teil I, 1935, Nr. 125, pp. 1,333–34. See also *Akten-NSDAP*, 107-00387-388.

27. After the Nuremberg Laws of 1935, *Rassenschande* was declared a crime. Gellately, *Gestapo and German Society*, p. 160.

28. BA-MA, BMRS, interview Eduard Hesse, 30.10.1998, T-430; BA-MA, BMRS, interview Susi Byk, 23.11.1995, T-176.

29. Martin Gilbert, *The Holocaust: A History of the Jews of Europe During the Second World War* (New York, 1985), p. 50.

30. BA-MA, BMRS, interview Dieter Bergmann, 19.09.1996, T-218.

31. BA-MA, BMRS, interview Margot Braun, 07.01.1996, T-191; BA-MA, BMRS, interview Braun, 07.01.1996, T-190; Bracher, p. 253. For example, after the authorities found out that an SS man had fallen in love and had relations with a Jewish woman, both were immediately executed. Gilbert, *Holocaust*, p. 681. A more extreme handling of a *Rassenschande* case happened to Lehmann Katzenberger, president of the Jewish community in Nuremberg, who was sentenced to death for kissing the Aryan Irene Seile. Hilberg, p. 111. See also BA-MA, BMRS, File Dieter Fischer, Bl. 72.

32. BA-MA, BMRS, interview Rudolf and Traute Sachs, 20.11.1995, T-168. See also BA-MA, BMRS, interview Otto Lüderitz, 28.03.1997, T-334.

33. Noncommissioned officers.

34. Unteroffizier is a corporal. Often Obergefreiter and Unteroffizier are translated as corporal; however, Unteroffizier was a higher rank and was given more responsibility than Obergefreiter (acting corporal).

35. BA-MA, BMRS, File Gerhard Fecht, Fecht an Professor Dr. Lev Kopelev, 31.01.1986 Bl. 3.
36. "Gesetz-und Verordnungsblatt der Evangelischen Landeskirche, 1942," p. 4 Zit[iert]. nach Amelis von Mettenheim, *Die zwölf langen Jahre, 1933–1945;* BA-MA, BMRS, File Dieter Fischer, Bl. 29. See also Kaplan, pp. 160, 225.
37. Institut für Zeitgeschichte (IfZ), München, N 71–73, Vermerk an Herrn Minister, Anwendung der Arierbestimmung auf Abkömmlinge aus Mischehen, 30.10.1933; Bernhard Lösener, "Als Rassereferent im Reichsministerium des Innern" (in: Das Reichsministerium des Innern und die Judengesetzgebung, *Vierteljahreshefte für Zeitgeschichte*, Heft 6 [1961]), p. 269; Noakes, "Development of Nazi Policy," pp. 304–5.
38. BA-MA, RW 6/v. 73, "Dennoch treudeutsch"—Ansprache des Vorsitzenden der Bezirksgruppe Stuttgart im Reichsverband der Christlicher Nichtarier [Erwin Goldmann] am 19.11.1934 (p. 6).
39. IfZ, N 71–73, Reichs- und Preußisches Ministerium des Innern, Abt. I Referent: Ministerialrat Dr. Lösener, 11.10.1935; Lösener, *Vierteljahrshefte*, p. 280.
40. IfZ, N 71–73, 11.10.1935.
41. IfZ, N 71–73, 11.10.1935; Lösener, p. 280.
42. Half-Jew Hans Leipelt was part of the White Rose resistance group. Quarter-Jews Hans von Dohnanyi, Helmut von Gottberg, and General Fritz Lindemann were members of the 20 July 1944 plot to kill Hitler.
43. BA-MA, BMRS, File Erik Blumenfeld. Blumenfeld would later be sent to Buchenwald; remarkably, he survived the war. After the war, he played an active role in the German political party CDU and was president of the German-Israeli Society (Deutsch-Israelische Gesellschaft).
44. IfZ, N 71–73, 11.10.1935; BA-B, R 18/5514, Bl. 30–31.
45. BA-MA, BMRS, interview Hans Pollak, 07.12.1994, T-72.
46. BA-MA, BMRS, interview Hofrat Hans Herder, 05.01.1996, T-186. *Mensch* is German or Yiddish for "human being."
47. Unterarzt (equivalent of a Sanitätsoffizier-Anwärter or medical officer-cadet).
48. BA-MA, BMRS, interview Braun, 10–14.08.1994. This phenomenon has happened among other groups with children of mixed marriages. For example, during the eighteenth and nineteenth centuries in Haiti, mulattoes quickly came to bitterly despise "Negroes." As the historian of this period, C. L. R. James commented, "[I]t all reads like a cross between a nightmare and a bad joke." C. L. R. James, *The Black Jacobins* (New York, 1989), pp. 38–43.
49. BA-MA, BMRS, File Joachim Gaehde, Bl. 18.
50. BA-MA, BMRS, interview Bergmann; Dieter Bergmann, *Between Two Benches* (California, 1995), p. 99.
51. BA-MA, BMRS, interview Felix Bruck, 18.04.1998, T-422.
52. Marine-Oberbaurat was the engineer rank equivalent to a commander (Fregattenkapitän) in the Kriegsmarine.
53. BA-MA, BMRS, interview Barz-Mendelssohn, 17.03.1995, T-120.
54. Rolf von Sydow, *Angst zu atmen* (Berlin, 1986), p. 63.
55. Hauptgefreiter was an administrative corporal.

56. The literal translation of *Genehmigung* is "approval" or "authorization." The *Genehmigung* was a form of clemency that allowed one to continue serving in the Wehrmacht. Most *Genehmigung* award letters stated that Hitler would decide after the war whether the *Genehmigung*'s recipient had proved himself sufficiently in battle to be declared *deutschblütig*.

57. Kriegsmarine was the official name of the German navy during the Third Reich.

58. The Kanzlei des Führers (Führer's chancellery) was set up in 1934 to handle written correspondence from Party members to Hitler. It was designed to keep Hitler in touch with "the concerns of his people." These letters dealt with complaints, grievances, and personal squabbles. By the late 1930s, around a quarter of a million letters for Hitler poured into the KdF. Kershaw, *Hitler 1936–1945*, p. 257. Bouhler's Führer's chancellery was also in charge of clemency petitions and from 1939 to 1941 was in charge of the euthanasia program.

59. BA-MA, BMRS, File Herbert Lefévre, Bl. 15, 61, 80.

60. Rust was thought an idiot by many in the Nazi government. According to Lochner, Rust had been an inmate in an insane asylum as a young man. *The Goebbels Diaries, 1942–1943*, ed. and trans. by Louis P. Lochner (New York, 1948), p. 378 (Goebbels's diaries must be looked at critically, since he wrote them in the hope of publishing them as an "official Nazi document" in the future). Dr. Georg Meyer of the *Militärgeschichtliches Forschungsamt* (Military Research Center) Potsdam/Freiburg claims that Rust's wife was Jewish.

61. BA-B, R 21/10875, Heinz Gerlach an Rust, 11.05.1941, Bl. 45–46.

62. On 24 September 1940, this anti-Semitic film appeared in theaters around Germany and in occupied Europe. Goebbels had been very involved in its production. The film depicted the Jews as being extremely dangerous. Gilbert, *Second World War*, p. 128.

63. Sydow, *Angst zu atmen*, p. 74.

64. BA-MA, BMRS, File Hans Mühlbacher, Teil V, Tagebuch, 30.07.40, Bl. 50.

65. Viktor Klemperer, *Ich will Zeugnis ablegen bis zum letzten, 1933–1945* (Aufbau Verlag, 1996), Buch I, 10.01.1939, p. 457.

66. BA-MA, BMRS, interview Bergmann.

67. BA-MA, BMRS, interview H.A., 18.11.1997.

68. BA-MA, BMRS, File Dr. Dieter Bergmann, Tagebuch, 14.08.1940, Heft II, Bl. 25.

69. Ibid., 31.05.1941, Heft II.

70. Klemperer, Buch II, 30.05.1942, p. 105.

71. Moses Mendelssohn, *Jerusalem: Or on Religious Power and Judaism* (London, 1983), p. 44.

72. An interesting side note here is that this study has documented one Jew, eleven half-Jews, six 37.5 percent Jews, fifteen quarter-Jews, and six 12.5 percent Jews who served in the Wehrmacht who were all descendents of Moses Mendelssohn.

73. Sachverständiger für Rassenforschung im Reichsinnenministerium. After 5 March 1935, this office was called Reichsstelle für Sippenforschung. Rudolf Absolon, *Die Wehrmacht im Dritten Reich. Band III, 3. August 1934 bis 4.*

Februar 1938, "(=*Schriften des Bundesarchivs 16/III*) (Boppard, 1975), p. 104, n. 452.

74. BA-B, R 15.09/52, Bl. 45, p. 5, "Die Lösung der Judenfrage" (Grundsätzliches zur Mischlingsfrage) von Dr. Achim Gercke. See also BA-B, R 15.09/58, Bl. 27–28; Alison Owings, *Frauen: German Women Recall the Third Reich* (New Brunswick, 1995), pp. 111–12.

75. SS captain.

76. *Akten-NSDAP,* 107-00404. See also Hilberg, pp. 49–50; BA-MA, BMRS, interview Herbert Frank, 27.06.1995, T-152; BA-MA, BMRS, File Heinrich Bamberger, Bl. 25; Stoltzfus, p. 122. See also BA-MA, BMRS, File August Oestreicher, Bl. 2.

77. Alfred, Richard, and Oskar were names of Anton Milch's cousins. Anton Milch was Erhard Milch's Jewish father. These names came from the Wehlau family, sons of Sigmund and Fanny Wehlau née Milch (sister of Anton Milch).

78. BA-MA, BMRS, File Erhard Milch, Heft III, Heinz Fahrenberg (ex-major in the Generalstab der Luftwaffe) an Bryan Rigg, 18.04.1997 and 22.06.1997, and Walter Frank to Rigg, 18.04.1997, and proof of Walter Frank's duties on Generalfeldmarschall Milch's stationery, 24.07.1945, and Dr. Ludwig Spangenthal (distant relative of Milch) an Rigg, 04.07.1997; BA-MA, File Erhard Milch, Heft II, Prof. Klaus Herrmann to Rigg, 14.10.1994, and 30.03.1995; BA-MA, N 179, Bl. 46, Milch's Tagebuch, 01.11.1933. See also John Wheeler-Bennett, *The Nemesis of Power* (New York, 1980), p. 342; Manfred Messerschmidt, *Die Wehrmacht im NS-Staat* (Hamburg, 1969), p. 46; Klemperer, Buch I, 18.10.1936, p. 317; BA-MA, BMRS, interview Bergmann; BA-MA, Pers 6/11, Bl. 4, "Milchs Vater Anton Milch, Marine-Oberstabsapotheker"; BA-MA, Pers 8-385; Ronald Smelser and Enrico Syring, eds., *Die Militärelite des Dritten Reiches* (Berlin, 1995), Horst Boog, "Erhard Milch"; Gerhard L. Weinberg, *Germany, Hitler, and World War II* (New York, 1996), p. 66; *Hitlers Tischgespräche im Führerhauptquartier,* Notiz von Picker, p. 277; Friedländer, p. 153.

79. *Leiter der Reichsstelle für Sippenforschung.*

80. BA-B, R 15.09/90, Bl. 2, Göring an Meyer, 07.08.1935.

81. Conversation with the Honorable John E. Dolibois on 22 July 2001. BA-MA, BMRS, File John E. Dolibois, Dolibois to Rigg, 23.07.2001. Dolibois was part of the Ashcan program (Ashcan was the military code word for CCPWE32). CCPWE32 was the Central Continental Prisoners of War Enclosure 32, where Göring and many other Nazi officials were incarcerated from May to August 1945. Dolibois was working for the Nazi War Crimes Commission, headed by Justice Robert H. Jackson.

82. Konrad Heiden, *Der Fuehrer: Hitler's Rise to Power* (London, 1967), p. 500.

83. Wistrich, p. 210. In a letter to the author, Professor Wistrich mentioned that he did his research on Milch twenty years ago in the Wiener Library in London. Wistrich to Rigg, 18.06.2001. In author's private collection. Louis L. Snyder also claims that Milch's mother was Jewish, but he, like Milch, does not provide evidence to prove this. Louis L. Snyder, *Encyclopedia of the Third Reich* (New York, 1989), pp. 229, 378.

84. BA-MA, BMRS, File Erhard Milch, Dr. James Corum an Michael Briggs, March 2001.
85. Matthew Cooper, *The German Air-Force, 1933–1945* (New York, 1981), p. 13.
86. BA-MA, BMRS, File Erhard Milch, Prof. Klaus Herrmann an David Irving, 26.10.1997; BA-MA, ZA 3/648, Personal-Nachweis über Erhard Alfred Richard Oskar Milch; BA-MA, RL 3/3271, Personal-Nachweis über Erhard Milch; Gilbert, *Second World War*, pp. 11–12, 20, 32, 70, 105; Michael Burleigh, *The Third Reich: A New History* (New York, 2000), p. 383.
87. BA-MA, BMRS, File Klaus Menge, Bl. 3–7, Martin Bier, "Klaus Hugo Menge. Zum Gedenken an unseren Klassen-Kameraden," 26.09.1995, and Bl. 8, Vortisch an Rigg, 09.04.1997, and Bl. 10–12. Vortisch an Ursula, 04.12.1995, and Bl. 13–14; DDS, Bescheinigung über Klaus Menge, 07.08.1996, and Bl. 15–16, Vortisch an Jorge Volberg, 10.10.1996.
88. *Rassenbiologisches Institut der Hansischen Universität Hamburg.* BA-MA, BMRS, File Wolfgang Spier.
89. BA-MA, BMRS, interview Wolfgang Spier, 06.12.1994, T-70.
90. For examples, see BA-MA, BMRS, File Wilhelm Hollaender, Bl. 8, 19; BA-MA, BMRS, File Alfred Marian, Bl. 4–5; BA-MA, BMRS, File Horst Geiger, Bl. 4; BA-MA, BMRS, interview J. L., 09.11.1994; Hilberg, p. 50; Jobst Frhr von Cornberg and John M. Steiner, "Willkür in der Willkür," pp. 163–66.
91. Not his real name—the interviewee requests that he remain anonymous.
92. Waffen-SS sergeant.
93. BA-MA, BMRS, interview J. L.
94. Beate Meyer, *Jüdische Mischlinge. Rassenpolitik und Verfolgungserfahrung, 1933–1945* (Hamburg, 1999), pp. 114–15.
95. Meyer, p. 114. See also BA-MA, BMRS, File Anton Paul Rengers, Bl. 2–3.
96. Meyer, pp. 113–17. See also BA-MA, BMRS, File Spier; BA-MA, BMRS File Helmuth Jacobsen, Bl. 3–5.
97. Not his real name—the interviewee requests that he remain anonymous.
98. BA-MA, BMRS, interview J. G., 05.01.1995. Grün would later be deported to an OT forced labor camp. He would survive the war.
99. *AWA (I)= Allgemeines Wehrmachtsamt (Inland).*
100. BA-B, DZA (Potsdam) 62 Ka. 1 83, Bl. 96.
101. Ibid., Bl. 96–96b.
102. BA-MA, BMRS, File Bernhard Rogge, Heft III, Bl. 123, "Die Antwort der Geschichte."
103. Hitler started declaring *Mischlinge deutschblütig* (of German blood), giving them an official *Deutschblütigkeitserklärung* sometime after the Nuremberg Laws in 1935. This form of clemency was given to those whom Hitler judged to look and act like persons of "German blood." Such a declaration freed a *Mischling* from most racial laws and allowed him to call himself *deutschblütig* in identification papers.
104. Perhaps they did so not because of religious reasons but because parents of these sons did not want them to be different from their fathers. See BA-MA,

BMRS, interview Rolf Gottschalk, 01.12.1994, T-67; See also Stoltzfus, p. 104.

105. BA-MA, BMRS, interview Wolfgang Behrendt, 21.11.1994, T-58.

106. BA-MA, BMRS, interview Reiner Wiehl, 17.05.1996, T-205; BA-MA, BMRS, interview Günther Voelsen, 20.02.1997, T-308; BA-MA, BMRS, interview Peter Dröscher, 27.10.1997, T-405; BA-MA, BMRS, File Ernst Prager; BA-MA, BMRS, File Heinz Puppe; BA-MA, BMRS, interview Spier; BA-MA, BMRS, interview Karl-Arnd Techel, 29.05.1997, T-355; Bergmann, pp. 225–26; BA-MA, BMRS, File Gerhart von Gierke; Bergmann, pp. 225–26; BA-MA, BMRS, interview Bergmann; BA-MA, BMRS, interview Goldberg; Stoltzfus, p. 62; BA-MA, BMRS, interview Braun; Kaplan, p. 83.

107. BA-MA, BMRS, File Wilhelm Dröscher, Tagebuch, 7.05.1938.

108. BA-MA, BMRS, interview Dröscher.

109. BA-MA, BMRS, interview Hamburger; BA-MA, BMRS, interview Hellmut Arndt, 25.05.1997, T-351; BA-MA, BMRS, interview Walter Brück, 12.07.1997, T-371; BA-MA, BMRS, interview Arno Spitz, 17.06.1996, T-211.

110. *Privilegierte Mischehe* gave the Jews in the marriage special rights not allowed to Jews who were not married to Aryans. These couples were protected if they had not raised their children as Jews and if their marriage had happened before the Nuremberg Laws. For example, they did not have to wear the star and were not deported. One must remember, though, that if an Aryan married a Jew after 1935, he or she usually did so outside of Germany, since the Nuremberg Laws prohibited mixed marriages. Meyer, pp. 20–21, 92; Gellately, *Gestapo and German Society,* pp. 190–91; H. G. Adler, *Der Verwaltete Mensch. Studien zur Deportation der Juden aus Deutschland* (Tübingen, 1974), pp. 280–81; Vuletić, p. 8; Kaplan, pp. 148–49.

111. See Stoltzfus, pp. xxvi, 85, 92–93.

112. BA-MA, BMRS, interview Braun, 10–14.08.1994, T-10. See also Stoltzfus, pp. 106–7; Kaplan, pp. 190, 231.

113. Ursula Büttner, "The Persecution of Christian-Jewish Families in the Third Reich," *Leo Baeck Yearbook* 34 (1989): 279; Stoltzfus, p. 12.

114. Kaplan, pp. 90–91, 182.

115. For example, Julius Scholz took his ex-wife to court and explained to the authorities that he did not have to pay alimony to a Jew. The court ruled that Julius did have to continue the alimony, but they reduced it from 1,500 Reichsmarks to 110 Reichsmarks per month.

116. BA-MA, BMRS, interview Peter Scholz, 07.01.1995, T-85.

117. BA-MA, BMRS, interview Karl Heinz Scheffler, 09.03.1995, T-113; BA-MA, BMRS, interview Karl Heinz Scheffler, 19.05.1996, T-208; BA-MA, BMRS, interview Günther Scheffler, 10.03.1995, T-115; BA-MA, BMRS, interview Günther Scheffler, 14.12.1996, T-273; BA-MA, BMRS, File Karl Heinz Scheffler; BA-MA, BMRS, File Günther Scheffler.

118. Iron Cross Second and First Classes are like Bronze and Silver Stars in the U.S. armed forces.

119. BA-MA, BMRS, interview G. Scheffler, 10.03.1995; BA-MA, BMRS, interview G. Scheffler, 14.12.1996; BA-MA, BMRS, File G. Scheffler. Interestingly, after

the war, Max Scheffler saw the advantage of having a Jewish wife. Helena took him back and they were remarried after the war. Their son, Karl Heinz Scheffler, said, "[W]hat a load of crap *(Solch ein Scheiß)*." BA-MA, BMRS, interview K. H. Scheffler, 09.03.1995; BA-MA, BMRS, interview K. H. Scheffler, 19.05.1996.

120. Kaplan, p. 87.

121. *Goy* is Yiddish for "gentile."

122. A Bris is a Jewish ritual circumcision. It is a sign of the covenant all Jews have with God. This mark displays that a Jew is linked to every other Jew and stands with them in primordial relation to God. Trepp, p. 2.

123. BA-MA, BMRS, interview Helmut Kopp, 27.09.1994, T-20.

124. Forschungsstelle für die Geschichte des Nationalsozialismus in Hamburg, Auszug aus 040 G, Alfred Bütow. Special thanks to Beate Meyer for her help in obtaining these files for the Bryan Mark Rigg *Sammlung* (collection) (BMRS). See also BA-MA, BMRS, File Hans Hiefner, Bl. 16; BA-MA, BMRS, interview Döppes.

125. Friedländer, p. 167; Primo Levi, *Moments of Reprieve: A Memoir of Auschwitz* (New York, 1986), p. 91; BA-MA, BMRS, general impressions gained from interviewees.

126. *Shiksa* (sometimes spelled *schike* or *shikse*) is a derogative Yiddish word to denote a non-Jewish young woman.

127. BA-MA, BMRS, File Hanns Rehfeld, Rehfeld an Rigg, 07.12.1996, Bl. 2–3.

128. Today, Breslau is Wroclaw, Poland.

129. In Breslau, the Gestapo offices adjoined the Breslau prison.

130. BA-MA, BMRS, File Hanns Rehfeld, Rehfeld an Rigg, 07.12.1996, Bl. 2. See also Hans J. Auman, *Mein Leben als Mischmosch* (München, 1977), p. 23.

131. IfZ, N 71–73, 11.10.1935. See also Kaplan, pp. 112–113.

132. BA-MA, BMRS, interview Hanns Rehfeld, 16.11.1996, T-239.

133. IfZ, N 71–73, 11.10.1935.

134. BA-MA, BMRS, File Hans Mühlbacher, "1941–1945. Im Zeitalter der Gestapo," Erinnerungen von Olga Mühlbacher, Teil II, Bl. 16.

135. See Kerstin Meiring, *Die Christlich-Jüdische Mischehe in Deutschland, 1840–1933* (Hamburg, 1998), pp. 120–25, for a discussion on this subject; BA-MA, BMRS, general impression gained from this study.

136. *Reichskristallnacht* was the name given to the Nazi pogrom of 9–10 November 1938. Its literal meaning is "Reich Crystal Night," or as it was later termed in English, the "Night of Broken Glass." Benz, p. 31. Around one hundred Jews were murdered, hundreds of synagogues were burned, and some thirty thousand male Jews were deported to concentration camps. Ian Kershaw, *Profiles in Power: Hitler* (London, 1991), p. 149.

137. BA-MA, BMRS, interview Hannah Leopold, 11.11.1996, T-232. Eugen Klewansky had been a Stabsarzt during World War I. For another example of extreme abuse of power, see Kaplan, p. 20.

138. Bergmann, pp. 179–80.

139. BA-MA, BMRS, File Hans-Geert Falkenberg, Bl. 59.

140. Beate Meyer, *Mischlinge*, p. 18.

141. BA-MA, BMRS, File Achim von Bredow, Heft III, Bl. 37.

142. Dr. Hans Globke was a Ministerialrat in the RMI who headed its international law section. He, along with state secretary Dr. Wilhelm Stuckart, wrote a commentary on the racial laws in 1936. After the war, he worked in the Bundeskanzleramt under Adenauer.

143. BA-MA, BMRS, Heinz Puppe to Rigg, Bl. 1.

144. Ursula Büttner also talks about this dilemma in her essay in the 1988 *Leo Baeck Yearbook*. See Büttner, "Persecution," pp. 274–75.

145. BA-MA, BMRS, File Hans-Geert Falkenberg, Veranstaltung zum 08.05.1945 im Bergischen Kolleg, Wuppertal, 10.05.1995, Heft I, Bl. 55. Falkenberg puts the sentence, "I've not lost this drive to be the best even until now" at the beginning of this quote. The author thinks it reads better at the end of this section. Falkenberg has been shown this change.

146. Sydow, p. 66.

147. Ibid., pp. 77–78; BA-MA, BMRS, interview Rolf von Sydow, 17.12.1994, T-82.

148. Helmut Krüger, *Der Halbe Stern. Leben als deutsch-jüdischer Mischlinge im Dritten Reich* (Berlin, 1992), p. 67.

149. Jürgen Krackow, *Die Genehmigung* (München, 1991), p. 213.

150. BA-MA, BMRS, interview Jürgen Krackow, 14.11.1994, T-50; BA-MA, BMRS, interview J. Krackow 18.11.1994, T-56; Krackow, p. 145.

151. BA-MA, BMRS, File Jürgen Krackow, Bl.1, Photo 1, and Genehmigung Hitlers an Jürgen Krackow, 28.01.1943, and II./Panzer-Regiment 23: Beurteilung über Lt. Jürgen Krackow, 20.02.1945. The Gold Wound Badge was issued to a soldier who was wounded at least five times. In Krackow's case, he was wounded nine times, so his Wound Badge would be the equivalent of earning nine Purple Hearts in the U.S. armed forces. He still has a metal splinter in his head and has been classified as 100 percent disabled. His Iron Crosses were for such actions as destroying sixteen enemy tanks and disabling several others. BA-MA, BMRS, interview J. Krackow.

152. BA-MA, BMRS, interview Reinhard Krackow.

153. BA-MA, BMRS, File Wilhelm Dröscher, Tagebuch, 16.11.1940. One could compare the German-Cross in Gold with the Navy Cross in the U.S. Navy and U.S. Marine Corps.

154. BA-MA, BMRS, information gathered from the database of the collection. By early 1944, over half a million Iron Crosses First Class, and three million Iron Crosses Second Class had been awarded. BA-K, R 22/4003.

155. Nine hundred men were awarded this medal during the war. "50 percent Jew": Gen.-Arzt Dr. Helmuth Richter.

156. Apparently, 16,876 men were awarded this medal during the Third Reich. Horst Scheibert, ed., *Die Träger des Deutschen Kreuzes in Gold* (Friedberg/H.), 1981, p. 15. "Jew": (1) Lt. Heinz Dieckmann; "50 percent Jew": (1) Lt. Harder, (2) Oberst Robert Colli, (3) Oberst Walter Hollaender, (4) Generallt. Wilhelm Behrens, (5) Gen. Maj. Günther Sachs, (6) Major Robert Borchardt, (7) Kapt. Georg Langheld; "25 percent Jew": (1) Oblt. Wilhelm Dröscher, (2) Korv.Kapt. Walter Jacobson, (3) Hptm. Heinz Rohr, (4) Hptm. Joachim Rohr,

(5) Oberstlt. Alfred von Rosenberg-Lipinsky, (6) Waffen-SS-Obersturmbann-führer (SS Lt. Colonel) Peter Sommer, (7) Oberst Hans Viebig, (8) Kapt.z. See Edward Wegener, (9) Gen. d. Pi. Karl Sachs, (10) Hptm. Wilhelm von Gottberg.

157. About 7,300 men were awarded the Knight's Cross during the war; Angolia, *For Führer and Fatherland: Military Awards of the Third Reich* (New York, 1976), pp. 351–57. One could compare this medal with the Medal of Honor in the U.S. armed forces. "25 percent Jew": (1) Uffz. Arthur Becker, (2) Major Wilhelm Goriany, (3) Oberstlt. Walter Lehweß-Litzmann, (4) Vizeadmiral Bernhard Rogge, (5) Gen. Hans-Heinrich Sixt von Armin, (6) Oberst Hans Viebig; "50 percent Jew": (1) Oblt. Gerhard Simon, (2) Major Robert Borchardt, (3) Oberst Robert Colli, (4) Oberst Gustav Hertz, (5) Oberst Walter Hollaender, (6) Oberstlt. Hans von Schlebrügge, (7) Gen. Lt. Wilhelm Behrens, (8) Gen. Maj. Günther Sachs, (9) Generalfeldmarschall Erhard Milch.

158. Interviews conducted by Colin Heaton with General Johannes Steinhoff from 26–28 January 1984.

159. Walter Hollaender was a nephew of Frederick Hollaender, the famous composer of *Falling in Love Again,* a song immortalized by Marlene Dietrich in the 1930 movie *The Blue Angel (Der Blaue Engel).*

160. BA-A, Pers 63210 Walter Hollaender, Fernschreiben von Model, 14.07.1943; BA-A, Pers 63210 Walter Hollaender, Beurteilung zum 01.03.1944.

161. Six hundred received this award during the war. Angolia, pp. 351–57. "25 percent Jew": (1) Vizeadmiral Bernhard Rogge.

162. Ulrich Mohr and A. V. Sellwood, *Ship 16: The Story of the Secret German Raider Atlantis* (New York, 1956), pp. 152–58; Wolfgang Frank and Bernhard Rogge, *The German Raider Atlantis* (New York, 1956), p. 117.

163. Karl August Muggenthaler, *German Raiders of World War II* (London, 1977), p. 55; BA-MA, BMRS, File Bernhard Rogge; Mohr and Sellwood, p. 158.

164. BA-B, R 21/10875, Gerlach an Rust, 11.05.1941, Bl. 47.

165. BA-MA, BMRS, information gathered from the database of the BMR Collection. Party members: "25 percent Jew": (1) Herr Bergbohn, (2) Marine-Oberbaurat Franz Mendelssohn, (3) Hptm. Hans Joachim Nischelsky, (4) Lt. Hans Sander, (5) Oblt. Karl Weigel, (6) Eberhard Rogge, (7) Dr. Leo Killy; "50 percent Jew": (1) Lt. Kurt Erdmann, (2) Matr. Herbert Lefévre, (3) Hptm. Iva Lissner, (4) GFM Erhard Milch, (5) Dr. Heinz Neumann, (6) Obgfr. Werner Pollak, (7) Gefr. Karl Reinschmidt, (8) von Ribbentrop's Adjutant, (9) Obgfr. Herbert Schlögl, (10) Gefr. Günther Treptow, (11) Martin Wronsky, (12) Frau Reichshandwerkmeister Schmidt, (13) Rittmeister a.D. Wickel. This study was unable to identify the names of the last two. "Jew": (1) Matr. Werner Kohn, (2) SS-Obersturmführer (SS First Lt.) Fritz Scherwitz, (3) SS-Obersturmbannführer Vivian Stranders, (4) Grandfather Föppel. See also Beate Meyer, *Mischlinge,* pp. 252–59.

166. BA-MA, BMRS, interview Alfred Catharin, 04.01.1996, T-185; BA-MA, BMRS, interview Horst. G. (Reinhard).

167. BA-MA, BMRS, lecture given at Yale by Shlomo Perel, 22.04.1994, T-2.

168. Bergmann, pp. xvi–xvii; BA-MA, BMRS, interview Bergmann.

169. Dieckmann did not know about his ancestry until after the war.

170. BA-MA, BMRS, interview Heinz-Dieckmann, 19.09.1994, T-24.

171. BA-MA, BMRS, File Peter Schliesser.

172. OT camps were forced labor camps. Organization Todt (OT) was named after Dr.-Ing. Fritz Todt (1891–1942), Hitler's minister of armaments and munitions. OT was the German public construction agency.

173. BA-MA, BMRS, interview Peter Schliesser, 28.04.1996, T-200. Tragically, after the war when Peter Schliesser returned to Czechoslovakia, he narrowly escaped being sent to a Czech forced labor camp. Unfortunately, his father was caught and put in a Czech concentration camp. Their "crime" was that they were German. BA-MA, BMRS, File Schliesser. Schliesser's situation was not unique. Half-Jew and ex-soldier Franz Margold's mother experienced problems from the Czech authorities after the war because she had had two sons in the Wehrmacht. BA-MA, BMRS, interview Franz Margold, 18.05.1996, T-206.

174. BA-MA, BMRS, File Hans Mühlbacher, Mühlbacher to Rigg, 03.03.2001.

175. BA-MA, BMRS, File Hans Mühlbacher, Teil V, Tagebuch, 30.07.40, Bl. 50; BA-MA, BMRS, File Hans Mühlbacher, Mühlbacher to Rigg, 03.03.2001.

176. BA-MA, BMRS, File Hans Meissinger, Meissinger an Rigg, 08.11.1996, Bl. 10.

177. BA-MA, BMRS, File Ernst Ludwig, Ludwig an Rigg, 05.02.1997, Bl. 22.

178. BA-MA, BRS, interview Lüderitz.

179. Ibid.

180. Bergmann, p. 113.

181. BA-MA, BMRS, interview Hugo Freund., 30.11.1994, T-66. See also BA-MA, BMRS, interview Krüger; Krüger p. 72.

182. BA-MA, BMRS, File Heinz-Günther Löwy, Bl. 7.

183. BA-MA, BMRS, File Fritz Binder, Bl. 80, Binder an Rigg, 01.10.1994; BA-MA, BMRS, interview Fritz Binder, 02.10.1994, T-34.

184. BA-MA, BMRS, File Hans-Joachim Körner, Brief Frau Ilse Körner-Völker, 29.03.1997, Bl. 1.

185. BA-MA, BMRS, interview Richard Riess, 15.10.1994, T-39. Riess's father, Ernst, had to perform three years of forced labor in Vienna.

186. See BA-MA, BMRS, interview Lüderitz; BA-MA, BMRS, interview Bergmann; BA-MA, BMRS, interview J. Krackow.

187. BA-MA, BMRS, File Meissinger, Meissinger an Rigg, 08.11.1996, Bl. 10.

188. BA-MA, BMRS, interview Krüger.

189. *Kindheit und Jugend unter Hitler.* Mit Beiträgen von Helmut Schmidt u.a., Berlin, 1992, hier: Helmut Schmidt, *Politischer Rückblick auf eine unpolitische Jugend*, p. 188 ff; BA-MA, BMRS, interview Helmut Schmidt, 22.11.1995, T-174; BA-MA, BMRS, interview Helmut Schmidt, 15.10.1996, T-225.

190. BA-MA, BMRS, interview Hans Koref, 06.01.1996, T-189.

191. BA-MA, BMRS, interview Reinhard; BA-MA, BMRS, interview J. Krackow; BA-MA, BMRS, interview Krüger.

192. BA-MA, BMRS, interview Heinz-Karl Scheffler, 09.03.1995, T-113; BA-MA, BMRS, interview Heinz-Karl Scheffler, 19.05.1996, T-208; BA-MA, BMRS, interview Sachs.

193. BA-MA, BMRS, interview Dieckmann. Interestingly, Dieckmann's stepfather, who was a Party member and had adopted Dieckmann, protected him throughout the entire Third Reich.
194. POWs are prisoners of war.
195. BA-MA, BMRS, File Gaehde, Bl. 13.
196. BA-MA, BMRS, interview Egon Bossart, 05.12.1994, T-69.
197. Forschungsstelle für die Geschichte des Nationalsozialismus in Hamburg, Auszug aus 040 G, Alfred Bütow. Special thanks to Beate Meyer for her help in attaining these Files for the Bryan Mark Rigg Collection; BA-MA, BMRS, File Bütow, Bl. 4.
198. BA-MA, BMRS, interview Hermann Lange, 01.10.1994, T-33.
199. BA-MA, BMRS, File Du Bois Reymond, Bl. 5.
200. BA-MA, BMRS, interview Günther Kallauch, 06.08.1994, T-9; BA-MA, BMRS, interview Günther Kallauch, T-35.
201. A *Selbstfahrlafette* was a self-propelled artillery piece mounted on a tracked chassis. It was a modified version of the *Sturmgeschütz* (assault gun). Kopp and his comrades destroyed over twenty Soviet tanks with their *Selbstfahrlafette*.
202. BA-MA, BMRS, interview Kopp.
203. Such views were expressed in the Wehrmachtausstellung that toured Germany a few years ago. The Wehrmachtausstellung's information is documented in Hannes Heer and J. P. Reemtsma, eds., *Vernichtungskrieg: Verbrechen der Wehrmacht* (Hamburg, 1995). See also Ben Hecht, *Perfidy* (New York, 1961), p. 94.
204. BA-MA, BMRS, File Bütow, Bl. 5.
205. BA-MA, BMRS, interview Techel.
206. *Bayerisches Landesamt für Wiedergutmachung.*
207. They would receive certificates that they were either racially, religiously, or political persecuted *(Amtlicher Ausweis für rassisch, religiös und politisch Verfolgte).*
208. See BA-MA, BMRS, File Dietmar Brücher; BA-MA, BMRS, File Eugen Frank; BA-MA, BMRS, File Alfred Catharin; BA-MA, BMRS, File Heinz Eder; BA-MA, BMRS, File Dieter Effenberg.
209. BA-MA, BMRS, Heinz Puppe to Rigg, Bl. 1.
210. A menorah is a nine-branched candelabrum used during the Jewish festival of Hanukkah.
211. For examples, see BA-MA, BMRS, interview Emil Lux, 30.05.1997, T-356; BA-MA, BMRS, interview Gerhard Fecht, 18.11.1997, T-410; BA-MA, BMRS, interview Hansotto Goebel, 07.12.1996, T-254.
212. BA-MA, BMRS, interview Bruck; BA-MA, BMRS, interview Binder; BA-MA, BMRS, interview Karl Partsch, 14.12.1994, T-81; BA-MA, BMRS; interview Walter Schönewald, 06.01.1996, T-188; BA-MA, BMRS, interview Bergmann.
213. BA-MA, BMRS, interview Scholz.
214. Landgericht München I, Akten Werner Eisner, Heft IV, Report given by Dr. Jose Maria Alvarado, 3 June 1965, La Paz, Bolivia, Bl. 455.
215. Ibid., Protokoll aufgenommen in öffentlicher Sitzung des Einzelrichters des 17. Zivilsenats des Oberlandesgerichts München, Bericht von Zeuge Walter

Julius Eisner, 3 July 1968, Heft IV, Bl. 649, and Zeuge Frau Emma Hummel, Heft IV, 11 November 1968, Bl. 684.

216. BA-MA, BMRS, interview Richard Ohm, 11.02.1995, T-91; BA-MA, BMRS, interview Bruck; BA-MA, BMRS, interview Ettheimer.

217. BA-MA, BMRS, data list: Schlomo Perel, Karl-Heinz Maier, Bob Winter, Siegfried Behrendt, Ephraim Glaser, Nachemia Wurman, and Günter Kallauch.

218. BA-MA, BMRS, interview Helmut Kopp, 3–4.09.1994, T-15, and 29.09.1994, T-31; BA-MA, BMRS, interview Helmut Kopp, 06.02.1997, T-299. For a similar case, see BA-MA, BMRS, interview Sachs.

219. Sturmmann is a Waffen-SS private. Löwy was stationed with the Sixth SS Mountain Division in Salzburg.

220. Through Löwy's experiences in World War II, he became religious. When he dies, he plans on being buried in a Jewish cemetery and having Kaddish said for him.

221. BA-MA, BMRS, interview Karl-Heinz Löwy, 12.01.1996, T-195.

222. BA-MA, BMRS, interview Partsch.

223. BA-MA, BMRS, interview Michael Hauck, 24.11.1994, T-61.

224. BA-MA, BMRS, interview Adolf Blum, 22.04.1995, T-147; BA-MA, BMRS, interview Lenni Blum, 22.04.1995, T-148.

225. BA-MA, BMRS, interview Schönewald. See V. D. Segre, *Israel: A Society in Transition* (New York, 1971), p. 196; De Lange, p. 144.

226. BA-MA, BMRS, interview Binder.

227. BA-MA, BMRS, interview Bergmann. This saying comes from the traditional liturgy: "Blessed are You *Hashem,* our God, King of the universe, for not having made me a gentile." *The Complete Artscroll Siddur,* p. 19. The blessing is one of three that reflect that a Jewish male has more commandments from God (a privileged status) than a female Jew, a gentile, or a slave.

228. Christoph fischer and Renate Schein, eds., *O ewich is so lanck. Die Historischen Friedhöfe in Berlin-Kreuzberg. Ein Werkstattbericht* (Berlin, 1987).

229. Colonel Count Claus von Stauffenberg was one of the leading members of the conspiracy to kill Hitler that culminated in the 20 July 1944 bomb plot.

230. BA-MA, BMRS, interview Horst von Oppenfeld, 05.01.1995, T-84.

231. *Webfehler* literally means "weaving flaw." It means that someone has abnormal ancestry.

232. *Falscher Makel* literally means that one is stained or polluted. During the Third Reich, these words were used to describe the "racial problem" of *Mischlinge.*

233. *Mampe* was the name of a well-known brand of brandy *(Kräuterlikör),* which was half sweet and half bitter.

234. BA-MA, BMRS, File Hans Günzel, Bl. 3.

235. BA-MA, BMRS, interview Reinhard Krackow, 20.05.1996, T-209.

236. BA-MA, BMRS, R. Zelter; BA-MA, BMRS, interview Joachim Zelter, 27.10.1997, T-166. Joachim Zelter's great-great-grandfather was Karl-Frederick Zelter, who was a distinguished man of letters and a friend of Goethe.

237. Not his real name.

238. Many *Mischlinge* documented in this study still meet with their comrades or have

contact with old comrades. For a few examples, see BA-MA, BMRS, File Peter Gaupp; BA-MA, BMRS, interview A. Spitz; BA-MA, File Werner Maltzahn; BA-MA, BMRS, File Helmut Schmoeckel. Even the Jew Shlomo Perel went to a large meeting of veterans from his division in 1987. See Perel, p. 63.

CHAPTER 3: ASSIMILATION AND THE JEWISH EXPERIENCE IN THE GERMAN ARMED FORCES

To make sure this chapter would be statistically and mathematically sound, it was reviewed by Dr. Stan Stephenson, professor of business statistics in the Department of CIS and QMST at Southwest Texas State University; Dr. Monnie McGee, assistant professor of statistics at Hunter College in New York City; Sybille Clayton, instructor of mathematics at Louisiana State University (LSU); and (USMC) Lt. Edmund Clayton, Ph.D. in physics from LSU.

1. Because Austria was united with Germany under Hitler, this study includes data on Austrian assimilation.
2. Gay, *Jews of Germany*, pp. 165, 182–84; Haffner, *Meaning of Hitler*, pp. 92, 103. See also Kershaw, *Hitler, 1889–1936*, pp. 32, 78.
3. Gellately, *Gestapo and German Society*, p. 108.
4. Arthur Ruppin, *The Jews in the Modern World* (London, 1934), p. 329; Gay, p. 139; Michael A. Meyer, ed., *Deutsch-Jüdische Geschichte in der Neuzeit. 1871–1918: Band III* (München, 1997), p. 20.
5. Gay, p. 165.
6. Adler, *Jews in Germany*, p. 98.
7. Haffner, p. 93.
8. Ibid., p. 9.
9. Meyer, *Deutsch-Jüdische Geschichte: Band III*, pp. 20–21; Ruppin, *Modern World*, p. 330; Stephan Behr, *Der Bevölkerungsrückgang der deutschen Juden* (Frankfurt, 1932), p. 105; Gay, p. 202.
10. Arthur Ruppin, also called the "father of Jewish sociology," was the most noted Jewish statistician and demographer of his time. He was a Zionist and the "first professor of Jewish sociology at the newly established Hebrew University of Jerusalem in the twenties." Alex Bein, "Arthur Ruppin: The Man and His Work," *Leo Baeck Yearbook* 17 (1972): 117.
11. Ruppin, *Modern World*, p. 332.
12. Avraham Barkai, "Population Decline and Economic Stagnation," in *German-Jewish History in Modern Times*, vol. 4, ed. Michael A. Meyer (New York, 1998), pp. 32–33; Meyer, *Deutsch-Jüdische Geschichte: Band III*, pp. 21–22; Behr, *Der Bevölkerungsrückgang*, pp. 100–107; Marsha L. Rozenblit, "Jewish Assimilation in Habsburg Vienna," in *Assimilation and Community: The Jews in Nineteenth-Century Europe*, ed. Jonathan Frankel and Steven J. Zipperstein, (Cambridge, 1992), p. 237.
13. Gay, p. 198; Meyer, *Deutsch-Jüdische Geschichte: Band III*, p. 20; Felix A. Theilhaber, *Der Untergang der deutschen Juden* (München, 1911), pp. 95–96; BA-MA, BMRS, File Peter Noah, Bl. 12; Stoltzfus, *Resistance*, pp. 30–31, 57–58, 71; BA-MA, BMRS, interview Goldberg.

14. The word *dissidents* is used in this study to describe those Jews who separated themselves from the Jewish community without conversion. They simply became *konfessionslos* (without confession).
15. Meyer, *Deutsch-Jüdische Geschichte: Band III*, p. 21.
16. Theilhaber, *Der Untergang*, p. 93. See also Lowenthal, p. 270; Engelmann, p. 54; Kaplan, p. 12.
17. Theilhaber, *Der Untergang*, pp. 94, 160.
18. Haffner, p. 91. See also Edward Crankshaw, *Bismarck* (New York, 1981), p. 380; Bracher, pp. 25, 36; Marsha Rozenblit, *The Jews of Vienna, 1867–1914* (New York, 1983), p. 127; Heinrich Walle, "Deutsche jüdische Soldaten, 1914–1945. Ein Rundgang durch die Ausstellung," in *Deutsche Jüdische Soldaten, 1914–1945*, ed. Militärgeschichtliches Forschungsamt (Bonn, 1984), p. 19. BA-MA, BMRS, interview Rolf Zelter, 14.05.1996, T-201.
19. Behr, p. 102.
20. Vuletic, p. 15; Gay, p. 141; Lowenthal, p. 234. Of course there were some Jews, like Edith Stein, mentioned earlier, who earnestly believed in the Christian message, but they were a minority.
21. BA-MA, BMRS, interview Hauck.
22. Dietz Bering, *Stigma of Names* (Michigan, 1992), p. 14. See also Friedländer, p. 80.
23. Theilhaber, *Der Untergang*, pp. 116–17, 148.
24. Ibid., p. 153.
25. Robert E. Dickinson, *Germany* (New York, 1953), p. 100. From 1815 to 1925, Germany's population grew from twenty-eight million to eighty million. Dickinson, p. 104.
26. Adler, *Jews in Germany*, p. 107. See also Ritchie Robertson, *The "Jewish Question" in German Literature, 1749–1939: Emancipation and Its Discontents* (Oxford, 1999), p. 286; Lowenthal, p. 270. By 1933, over 44 percent of German Jews who married, married non-Jews. Blau, "Die Mischehe im Nazireich," *Judaica: Beiträge zum Verständnis des jüdischen Schicksals in Vergangenheit und Gegenwart*, Bd. 4 (1948), p. 46; Stoltzfus, *Resistance*, p. xxvi; Gordon, p. 17.
27. Meiring, p. 91; Louis A. Berman, *Jews and Intermarriage: A Study in Personality and Culture* (New York, 1968), p. 123; F. R. Bienenfeld, *The Germans and the Jews* (London, 1939), p. 99; Blau, "Die Mischehe im Nazireich," pp. 46–57; Ernst Kahn, "Die Mischehen bei den deutschen Juden," *Der Jude, Eine Monatsschrift, Erster Jahrgang, Berlin (1916–1917)*, pp. 855–56; Behr, p. 112. See also Fritz Lenz, *Menschliche Auslese und Rassenhygiene (Eugenik)* (München, 1932), pp. 228–29; BA-B, 15.09/36, C. V. Zeitung, 16.05.1935, Bl. 28; Theilhaber, *Der Untergang*, p. 104; Uriah Zevi Engelman, "Intermarriage," *Jewish Social Studies* 2 (1940): 157–67; Werner Cohn, "Bearers of a Common Fate? The 'Non-Aryan' Christian 'Fate-Comrades' of the Paulus-Bund, 1933–1939," in *Leo Baeck Yearbook* 33 (1988): 327–68; Arthur Ruppin, *The Jews of Today* (New York, 1913).
28. At the time, 201,513 of Austria's 220,000 Jews lived in Vienna. Chajim Bloch and Löbel Taubes, eds., *Jüdisches Jahrbuch für Österreich* (Wien, 1932), p. 8.

29. The remaining areas of Austria would have added a few thousand to the seventeen thousand possible mixed marriages from Vienna.

30. Avraham Barkai, "Population Decline and Economic Stagnation," in *German-Jewish History in Modern Times,* vol. 4, pp. 32–33; Robertson, *"Jewish Question,"* p. 386. Austria prohibited marriages between Jews and Christians. If a Jew and a Christian wanted to marry, one of the partners had to convert so that both would be of the same religion. If one became *konfessionslos* (without religious affiliation), then he or she could marry a Jew or a Christian under Austrian law, unlike in Germany where couples could, since 1875, have a civil ceremony regardless of their religions (Israel Cohen, *Jewish Life in Modern Times* [New York, 1914], p. 305). Although Barkai estimates that these seventeen thousand dissidents probably did so to marry, these mixed marriage figures are low because only those Jews who married people who were *konfessionslos* were recorded. Marsha Rozenblit wrote that accurate figures cannot be recorded because "all those Jews who converted to Christianity or became *konfessionslos* prior to their marriage with gentiles elude statistical discovery" (Rozenblit, *The Jews of Vienna, 1867–1914,* p. 129). See also Ruppin, *Jews of Today,* pp. 166–67; Bloch and Taubes, p. 10.

31. The number derived from Ruppin's sources for the possible average of mixed marriages occurring in Vienna from 1921 to 1924 is 979 per year (Ruppin's records indicate that dissidents were numerous because "marriages with non-Jews contribute[d] to them considerably" [Ruppin, *Modern World,* p. 332]). If one assumes that the majority of dissidents Behr lists between 1912 and 1923 in Vienna (10,429) did so to marry non-Jews, then that would yield an average of 869 mixed marriages per year in Vienna (Behr, p. 98). The number stated in this study (895) is between Ruppin's and Behr's averages.

32. Barkai, "Population Decline and Economic Stagnation," in *German-Jewish History in Modern Times,* pp. 32–33; Ruppin, *Modern World,* pp. 331–32. Ruppin gives the figures of dissidents in Vienna as 2,900 from 1901 to 1905, 3,914 from 1921 to 1924, and 2,692 from 1927 to 1929. If the average from 1901 to 1905 (580) is applied to 1906–1920, there could have been 8,700 who left Judaism in Vienna during this period. If the average between 1921–1924 (979) is applied to 1925–1926, there could have been 1,958 who left Judaism during this period. According to these calculations, around 16,644 Jews "seceded" (Ruppin's word) from Judaism from 1901 to 1929. Since most did so to marry non-Jews according to Ruppin, then one can assume that at least 16,000 mixed marriages occurred during this time in Vienna. However, since people of Jewish descent who were Christians were not recorded when they married, the number of mixed marriages must have been much higher than this estimate of 16,000.

33. Statistics about the number of children in each family come from Ruppin, Behr, Theilhaber, Lenz, a U.S. Naval Intelligence study done on Germany in 1944, and the average number of siblings of the hundreds of people interviewed for this study. Ruppin, Behr, and Theilhaber had political agendas to prove. They believed that assimilation of Jews with non-Jews was not healthy for the Jewish people. As a result, one must look at their findings carefully, because it was in their interest to show that mixed marriages did not produce the same num-

ber of children as Jewish or non-Jewish unions. Moreover, it seems that their data focus only on marriages where the Jewish partner remained religiously Jewish and not those unions where the Jewish partner had converted to Christianity. Marriages where one of the partners remained religiously Jewish did indeed produce fewer children according to the national average. Lenz also must be looked at carefully because being a Nazi, he naturally wanted to present the data in such a way as to show the danger that Jewish assimilation had for German society. As a result, the data heavily relied on come from *Germany,* vol. 3, *Economic Geography,* ed. Naval Intelligence Division (Washington, D.C., 1944), pp. 67–78, and this study documenting *Mischlinge* in the offspring generation. Since many of the Jewish parents of the *Mischlinge* documented in this study did not remain Jewish, they would have not been included in the statistics given by Theilhaber and Ruppin, but rather included in the birthrates of couples who were either Protestant or Catholic. Given that the average number of children per Catholic family was 4.33 and per Protestant family was 3.06 (Meiring, p. 91), the numbers found in this study are more accurate for children of mixed marriages. See also *Statistical Year-Book of the League of Nations 1936/37,* ed. League of Nations Economic Intelligence Service (Geneva, 1937), pp. 35, 41.

34. Military age ranged from eighteen to forty-five years of age. IfZ, N 71–73, Pfundtner an Hoßbach, 03.04.1935.

35. Meyer, Avraham Barkai, "Jewish Life under Persecution," in *German-Jewish History, in Modern Times,* p. 252; Behr, p. 112; Berman, p. 123; Bienenfeld, p. 99. Most sources put mixed marriages from 1900 to 1930 at just over 30,000. Barkai estimates that between 1870 and 1930, 50,000 mixed marriages occurred. From this figure, roughly 30,000 has been subtracted for the years of 1900 to 1930 to yield an estimate of 20,000 between 1870 and 1900.

36. Behr, p. 112 (Behr writes that between 1876 and 1900, 8,316 mixed marriages occurred); Meiring, p. 91 (Meiring writes that between 1874 and 1900, 8,091 mixed marriages occurred). The number of 8,000 does not take into account the mixed marriages happening between 1870 and 1875, as well as those in other German states such as Saxony, Baden, Württemberg, Hessen, and so on.

37. Ruppin, *Jews of Today,* p. 166. Ruppin states that 2,488 mixed marriages occurred in Austria between 1881 and 1906 (an average of 99.52 mixed marriages per year). Taking this average and applying it to the years 1870 to 1900 gives one a total of 2,985.6 mixed marriages. Since only mixed marriages where a Jew married someone who was *konfessionslos* (without religious affiliation) were recorded, the numbers Ruppin gives are very low. However, this is the only source found that indicates how many mixed marriages were occurring during this time. For more data on mixed marriages in Austria, see Max Grunwald, *History of Jews in Vienna* (Philadelphia, 1936), p. 527; Bloch and Taubes, p. 10; Cohen, p. 304.

38. These figures do not take into consideration the children who were born out of wedlock. They would have added to the numbers presented here.

39. This number has been left according to a pure mathematical model. Although some of these half-Jews did not marry or married other *Mischlinge* and Jews, the Naval Intelligence figures from 1944 show that the net reproduction rate from 1880 to 1929 (with a few gaps) would have produced at least 92,000 children. See *Germany*, vol. 3, *Economic Geography*, p. 73.

40. Michael R. Marrus and Robert O. Paxton, *Vichy France and the Jews* (New York: Basic Books, 1981), p. 42.

41. Schleunes, pp. 4–5; Hitler, *Hitler's Secret Book*, pp. 100, 212–14.

42. Hitler, *Mein Kampf*, p. 562.

43. Ruppin, *Modern World*, p. 4. Ruppin even traveled to Germany during the Third Reich and talked with the Nazi race theoretician, Dr. Hans Günther (Friedländer, p. 64), where apparently he collected some of the data he used to write his above-mentioned book.

44. BA-MA, BMRS, File Ernst Prager, S. Prager to Rigg, 05.07.2001. See also Kaplan, p. 78.

45. Yahil, p. 80; Schleunes, pp. 193–94.

46. When Prussia regained its autonomy in 1812 from Napoleon, it emancipated the Jews under the leadership of Hardenberg and Stein. However, this did not mean that Jews enjoyed equal rights. Although they received more rights than before, they were still excluded from some professions and had difficulty becoming officers in the armed forces. The partial emancipation of 1812 was rescinded after the Congress of Vienna in 1815. Unconverted Jews could not hold elective office and by law could not become officers according to the 1812 law. See Vital, p. 62.

47. In 1871, Bismarck followed in the footsteps of Hardenberg and Stein, and emancipated the Jews in all of the newly unified German Reich (Gay p. 161). However, this emancipation was still imperfect (e.g., baptized Jews could not be judges). Only with the Weimar Republic would full civil and political rights be granted to the Jews. See Kaplan, p. 67.

48. Most of these six hundred thousand "declared themselves Jews and viewed themselves as a religious minority." Benz, p. 14. Had the people who declared themselves Christians who were of Jewish descent been included, this number would have been significantly larger.

49. Hilberg, p. 115.

50. IfZ, N 71–73, Die Juden und jüdischen Mischlinge im Deutschen Reich, Vorläufiges Ergebnis der Volkzählung vom 17.05.1939.

51. Martin van Creveld, *Fighting Power* (New York, 1982), p. 65. By 1942, the population of Greater Germany would be 112 million people. Naval Intelligence Division *Germany*, vol. 3, p. 341; *Hitlers Tischgespräche im Führerhauptquartier*, Einführung v. Picker, p. 9.

52. *Anschluß* means "annexation."

53. Federal Research Division, ed. *Austria: A Country Study* (Washington, D.C., 1994), p. 46; Karl Renner, *Österreich von der Ersten zur Zweiten Republik, II. Band* (Wien, 1953), pp. 94–95; IfZ, N 71–73, Westdeutscher Beobachter, No. 159, 29.05.1940; Militärgeschichliches Forschungsamt, ed., *Das Deutsche*

Reich und der zweite Weltkrieg. Kriegsverwaltung, Wirtschaft und Personelle Ressourcen, 1939–1941, vol. 5/1, (Stuttgart, 1988), Rolf-Dieter Müller, "Die Mobilisierung der Deutschen Wirtschaft für Hitlers Kriegführung," p. 283; Bloch and Taubes, p. 5.

54. According to his figures, E. H. Buschbeck estimates that there were 300,000 people of Jewish descent in addition to the 190,000 adherents of the Jewish faith in Austria in 1938. E. H. Buschbeck, *Austria* (London, 1949), pp. 16, 149. Barkai puts the number of *Mischlinge* in Austria at 24,400, which is very low looking at the data on birthrates (*German-Jewish History in Modern Times,* vol. 4, Barkai, p. 252) (see also table 2). Blau puts the *Mischling* figures for Austria at 16,938 half-Jews and 7,391 quarter-Jews in 1939 (Blau, "Die Christen jüdischer," p. 273). Many of the Austrian *Mischlinge* documented in this study were filed as *Mischlinge* only when they were discharged from the Wehrmacht in 1940.

55. George F. Kennan, *From Prague after Munich: Diplomatic Papers, 1938–1940* (Princeton, 1968), pp. 42–43; *Das Deutsche Reich und der zweite Weltkrieg,* vol. 5/1, Rolf-Dieter Müller, p. 284.

56. The Protectorate was the Czech lands of Bohemia and Moravia.

57. Hilberg, p. 268, n. 43. See also Picker, ed., *Hitlers Tischgespräche im,* p. 70, n. 16; Adler, *Der Verwaltete Mensch,* p. 281.

58. Present-day Gdansk in Poland.

59. Known also as Elsass and Lothringen in Germany. These provinces had a long history of being under different sovereigns and countries.

60. Kaiserliches Statistisches Amt, ed., *Statistisches Jahrbuch für das Deutsche Reich* (Berlin, 1903), p. 7; Robert Gellately, *Backing Hitler: Consent and Coercion in Nazi Germany* (Oxford, 2001), p. 31.

61. For example, this study has documented eleven *Mischlinge* from Czechoslovakia, six from Danzig, and six from Alsace-Lorraine who served in the Wehrmacht.

62. Christopher R. Browning, *Nazi Policy, Jewish Workers, German Killers* (Cambridge, 2000), pp. 10–12.

63. BA-B, 15.09.1952, "Die Lösung der Judenfrage," von Dr. Achim Gercke, Sachverständiger für Rassenforschung beim Reichsministerium des Innern, Bl. 48.

64. In 1806, when Napoleon took over German lands, he gave Jews living there equal rights and ordered them to take on last names. See Gay, pp. 125–27.

65. BA-MA, 15.09/52, Bl. 47, pp. 9–10.

66. Yahil, p. 73.

67. Veit Valentin, *Geschichte der Deutschen* (Berlin, 1947), p. 691; George E. Sokolsky, *We Jews* (London, 1935), pp. 35, 118; Victor, p. 181.

68. Lösener, p. 269.

69. BA-B, R 18/5514, Bl. 3, 29; IfZ, N 71–73, 11.10.1935; Edward Peterson, *The Limits of Hitler's Power* (New Jersey, 1969), p. 140.

70. BA-B, 15.09/43, Bl. 53–55; BA-B, 25.09/39, Bl. 13; IfZ, N 71–73, Pfundtner an Hoßbach, 03.04.1935. Bruno Blau disputes this figure of 750,000 *Mischlinge,* saying it was an exaggeration. Blau, "Die Christen jüdischer," p. 272.

71. Cohn, *Jewish Life,* pp. 327, 330.

72. BA-B, DZA 62 Ka. 1 83, Bl. 83–84.
73. *Centralverein deutscher Staatsbürger jüdischen Glaubens.* In 1893, some German Jews banded together to fight for their rights "in the face of anti-Semitic attacks." Kaplan, p. 13.
74. BA-B, R 15.09/36, Bl. 28; BA-B, R 18/ 520; Lösener, p. 300. Ursula Büttner recognizes this problem and believes that the number of quarter-Jews the Nazis gave in their census of 1939 should have been larger because some quarter-Jews were able to conceal their ancestry. Büttner, "Persecution," p. 271.
75. Some people have suggested that many *Mischlinge* may have emigrated. Although this study has documented a few who did emigrate during the 1930s (see BA-MA, BMRS, File Hans Schmitt), the vast majority of *Mischlinge* remained in Germany.
76. Blau, "Die Christen jüdischer," p. 273.
77. Lösener, p. 282; Adler, *Der Verwaltete Mensch*, p. 281. Theilhaber had already encountered some of the problems the Nazis now faced when recording statistics about German-Jewish assimilation. He admitted the numbers he compiled were smaller than in reality because people moved, did not report their new faith, or had never officially changed their religion. Theilhaber, *Der Untergang*, pp. 95–96.
78. From this study's data collected, half of the half-Jews were still serving in the Wehrmacht one year after this decree.
79. A field marshal is the U.S. equivalent of a five-star general (general of the army).
80. This study has done its best to record the accurate rank and Nazi "racial percentage" of every soldier, but because of the uncertainty of some of the data, there may be a few discrepancies whether one was "50 percent" or "25 percent Jewish."
81. Actually, according to Dr. Monnie McGee, for every one hundred babies, an average of 49 percent of them are female. Consequently, the number of possible *Mischling* Wehrmacht personnel would be slightly higher. For the sake of simplicity, however, the numbers have been split evenly.
82. This study has documented a couple of female *Mischlinge* who served in the Wehrmacht, but their number remains unknown. For example, quarter-Jew Bettina Fehr worked in a munitions factory in Dippach bei Berka. She was employed by the armed forces and worked for a captain. Her station was 12 Hülsenkart. D.I.F.H.18. (BA-MA, BMRS, File Bettina Fehr, Bl. 3–5). The total number of female *Mischling* Wehrmacht personnel was probably around a few hundred, but this study has found no documentation to help give a clear picture about this facet of the history.
83. Oberkommando des Heeres.
84. BA-MA, BMRS, interview Wolters. See also Krüger, p. 75, n. 30.
85. Rolf-Dieter Müller and Hans-Erich Volkmann, eds., *Die Wehrmacht. Mythos und Realität* (Stuttgart, 1999). Wilhelm Deist, "Einführende Bemerkungen," in *Die Wehrmacht. Mythos und Realität*, p. 39; Jürgen Förster, "Wehrmacht, Krieg und Holocaust," in *Die Wehrmacht. Mythos und Realität*, p. 948; Friedrich Hoßbach, *Zwischen Wehrmacht und Hitler, 1934–1938* (Göttingen, 1965),

p. 125; Angolia, *For Führer and Fatherland,* p. 366; data from the Deutsche Dienststelle, Berlin; information from Dr. Georg Meyer of the Militärgeschichtliches Forschungsamt (Military Research Center) Potsdam/Freiburg, March 1998; Englemann, p. 202; Creveld, p. 65.

86. Since Austria was united with Germany during Hitler's rule, the history of Jews in the Austrian armies is also included. Also, before Bismarck united all the German states in 1871 as the Deutsches Reich (German Empire), there were separate states (e.g., Prussia, Bavaria). As a result, these states will be named as they were, but readers must keep in mind that also under Hitler, all these states were united as Germany.

87. Bauer, p. 39.

88. Charles Edward White, *The Enlightened Soldier: Scharnhorst and the Militärische Gesellschaft in Berlin, 1801–1805* (New York, 1989), p. 133.

89. Walle, pp. 75, 86, n. 85a, in *Deutsche Jüdische Soldaten, 1914–1945.*

90. Schmidl, p. 97.

91. *Schutzjuden* were "protected Jews" during the eighteenth and nineteenth centuries. They paid a yearly tax to live and trade in a particular town or city. Some became court Jews, but the majority remained *Schutzjuden.*

92. Gay, p. 96.

93. Eda Sagarra, *A Social History of Germany, 1648–1914* (New York, 1977), p. 161.

94. Gay, pp. 99–102; Sander L. Gilman, *Jewish Self-Hatred* (London, 1986), p. 87; *The Encyclopedia Americana,* vol. 18 (Danbury, 1984), p. 690.

95. Jonathan Steinberg, *All or Nothing* (New York, 1991), p. 230.

96. Manfred Messerschmidt, "Juden im preußisch-deutschen Heer," in *Deutsche Jüdische Soldaten,* p. 109; Rolf Vogel, *Ein Stück von uns* (Bonn, 1973), pp. 28–30; Bering, p. 9.

97. White, pp. 133, 148. Craig, *Prussian Army,* p. 48. Besides wanting to have an army with loyal Prussian subjects, Scharnhorst probably wanted to get away from an army of foreigners. By 1804, mercenaries accounted for 50 percent of the army's manpower. Craig, *Prussian Army,* pp. 22–23.

98. The Jewish population in Prussia at the time was 123,938.

99. Messerschmidt, in *Deutsche Jüdische Soldaten,* p. 110; Vogel, pp. 27–28, 31; Bering, p. 85.

100. Vogel, p. 29.

101. Wachtmeister is the U.S. equivalent of a staff sergeant.

102. Vogel, p. 51.

103. Vogel, p. 52; Nachum T. Gidal, *Die Juden in Deutschland von der Römerzeit bis zur Weimarer Republik* (Könemann, 1997), p. 146.

104. Pour le Mérite is the U.S. equivalent of the Medal of Honor. It was created in 1740 by Frederick the Great. During World War I, it was associated with German fighter-aces. The British gave the medal the popular name "Blue Max," which referred to the color of the medal and to Max Immelmann, the first German ace to receive the award. By 1918, a soldier had to have shot down eight planes to receive this medal. Until 1918, this was the highest medal given for bravery for the German armed forces.

105. Vogel, pp. 31, 52; Gidal, p. 146.

106. The painting is called *The Return of the Jewish Volunteer from the Wars of Liberation to His Family Still Living in Accord with Old Customs*. It was painted between 1833 and 1834.

107. Kartine Lauer, *Schicksale: Leben des Nathan Mendelssohn*, p. 1; *Studien: Beiträge zur neueren deutschen Kultur- und Wirtschaftsgeschichte, Band 8* (Berlin, 1993), pp. 59–84, Ilse Rabien, "Nathan Mendelssohn als preußischer Offizier im Befreiungskrieg 1813," in Lauer, *Schicksale*, pp. 59–84.

108. Vogel, pp. 31, 52; Gidal, p. 146; Sidney Osborne, *Germany and Her Jews* (London, 1939), pp. 71–72; Militärgeschichtliches Forschungsamt, ed., *Handbuch zur deutschen Militärgeschichte, 1648–1939 Bd. IV, 2: Militärgeschichte im 19. Jahrhundert, 1814–1890* (München, 1976), pp. 202–4; Werner T. Angress, "Prussia's Army and the Jewish Reserve Officer Controversy before World War I," *Leo Baeck Yearbook* 17 (1972): 20–21.

109. Messerschmidt, in *Deutsche Jüdische Soldaten*, pp. 109–10; Gidal, p. 146; Joachim Schoeps, *Bereit für Deutschland* (Berlin, 1970), pp. 213–15; Vogel, pp. 32–33; Engelmann, p. 207.

110. Vogel, p. 32.

111. Messerschmidt, in *Deutsche Jüdische Soldaten*, pp. 112–13; Horst Fischer, *Judentum, Staat und Heer in Preußen im frühen 19. Jahrhundert* (Tübingen, 1968), pp. 135–40.

112. Walle, in *Deutsche Jüdische Soldaten, 1914–1945*, p. 20.

113. Prussian aristocrat who owned land.

114. *Weimarer historisch-genealogisches Taschenbuch des gesamten Adels jehudäischen Ursprunges* (München, 1912); *Semigothaisches Genealogisches Taschenbuch aristokratisch-jüdischer Heiraten* (München, 1914). (Both these books were brought out by the anti-Semitic Kyffhäuser Publishing House. Although much of the data within these books is accurate concerning the genealogy of certain families, they need to be used with caution.) BA-B, 15.09/52, Bl. 46; BA-MA, BMRS, interview Hornstein; BA-MA, BMRS, interview Schmidt-Pauli; Kitchen, p. 47; Günther Martin, *Die bügerlichen Excellenzen* (Düsseldorf, 1976), pp. 58–59; Engelmann, pp. 136–38; Lamar Cecil, *Albert Ballin: Business and Politics in Imperial Germany, 1888–1918* (Princeton, 1967), p. 102; Holgar H. Herwig, *The German Naval Officer Corps* (Oxford, 1973), pp. 80–81. According to Herwig, young, single Jewish ladies placed advertisements in some newspapers. See also William Godsey, "The Nobility, Jewish Assimilation, and the Austro-Hungarian Foreign Service on the Eve of the First World War," *Austrian History Yearbook*, vol. 27 (1996): 155–80.

115. Schmidl, *Juden*, p. 134.

116. Hitler, *Hitler's Secret Book*, p. 26. See also *Speeches of Adolf Hitler*, vol 1, p. 27.

117. Emil Ludwig, *Bismarck* (Boston, 1927), p. 320; Vital, p. 177. Interestingly, Bismarck's son, Herbert, married a half-Jew, Marguerite Gräfin Hoyos. Engelmann, p. 171.

118. Martin, p. 59.

119. James J. Sheehan, *German History, 1770–1866* (Oxford, 1989), p. 51; Schmidl, p. 98.
120. Grunwald, pp. 177–81; George E. Berkley, *Vienna and its Jews* (Maryland, 1988), pp. 30–31.
121. Grunwald, p. 178; Berkley, p. 32; Schmidl, p. 112. If the number of Jews is included from Hungary, the total was 36,200.
122. Grunwald, p. 179.
123. Osborne, p. 72. See also BA-MA, BMRS File Klaus Florey. Florey's grandfather, Franz Pick, born in 1863 in Theresienstadt, was a reserve officer in an exclusive Austrian cavalry regiment. He was already an officer when he converted to Christianity in 1894.
124. Schmidl, p. 184.
125. Jakob Wilhelm Mossner was baptized on 16 April 1836.
126. Karl Demeter, *The German Officer Corps, 1650–1945* (New York, 1965), p. 398, n. 1; Engelmann, p. 208; Günther Martin, *Die bürgerlichen Excellenzen*, pp. 12–13.
127. Vogel, p. 34; Messerschmidt, in *Deutsche Jüdische Soldaten*, p. 116.
128. István Deák, *Beyond Nationalism: A Social and Political History of the Habsburg Officer Corps, 1848–1918* (New York, 1990), p. 174.
129. In the English-speaking world, this war has been called the Franco-Prussian War, but in Germany it is called the German-French War *(Deutsch-französischer Krieg).* Although Prussia's government and military conducted the war, all the German states, except Hannover and Kurhessen, participated in the conflict.
130. Messerschmidt, in *Deutsche Jüdische Soldaten*, p. 116; Vogel, pp. 35–37; Militargeschichtliches Forschungasmt, *Handbuch IV, 2*, p. 210; Gidal, p. 230; Gay, p. 161; Bering, p. 85. Angress, p. 21, n. 13; Osborne writes that "no less than 411 [Jews] were decorated for conspicuous gallantry." Osborne, p. 71.
131. Osborne, p. 71; Messerschmidt, in *Deutsche Jüdische Soldaten*, p. 116.
132. Yom Kippur is the Jewish holiday called the "Day of Atonement." On this day, those who observe it fast all day and ask forgiveness for all their sins committed during the past year.
133. Gidal, p. 231.
134. Walter Goerlitz, *The German General Staff, 1657–1945* (New York, 1971), p. 96.
135. Vogel, p. 25.
136. Herwig, p. 43.
137. Martin Kitchen, *German Officer Corps, 1890–1914* (Oxford, 1968), p. 44.
138. Demeter, pp. 224–25; Vogel, p. 43. See also Kitchen, *German Officer Corps*, pp. 40–44.
139. Deák, pp. 174–75. See also Angress, pp. 32–33; Messerschmidt, in *Deutsche Jüdische Soldaten*, p. 116; Volker Rolf Berghahn, *Germany and the Approach of War in 1914* (New York, 1993), p. 18.
140. Messerschmidt, in *Deutsche Jüdische Soldaten*, p. 116; Vogel, p. 38; Bering, p. 28; Angress, p. 33, n. 57.
141. Berkley, p. 38.

142. John Keegan, *The Second World War* (New York, 1989), p. 20.
143. The Jews were underrepresented among active officers, but overrepresented among reserve officers. The Jews represented 18.3 percent of the reserve officer corps in 1900. Deák, p. 133. During this time, it was still difficult for Jews to get augmented and become active officers in the Austro-Hungarian armed forces. See Schmidl, pp. 183–89.
144. Berkley, p. 38.
145. Vogel, pp. 22–23. During this time, being a *Mischling* was not even an issue in the armed forces. For example, the commander and chief of the military mission in Turkey who masterminded the Allied defeat at Gallipoli in 1916, General Otto Liman von Sanders (1855–1929), was a half-Jew. He was not alone during World War I. Admiral Felix von Bendemann, a half-Jew, was the commanding officer of the navy station on the North Sea, and General Johannes von Hahn, a quarter-Jew, commanded the Thirty-fifth Infantry Division in 1914. Engelmann, pp. 208–9; Martin, p. 59.
146. Herwig, p. 95.
147. Kitchen, p. 43; Max J. Loewenthal, *Das jüdische Bekenntnis als Hinderungsgrund bei der Beförderung zum preussischen Reserveoffizier* (Berlin, 1911), p. 31.
148. Jonathan Steinberg, "The Kaiser's Navy," *Past and Present* 28 (24 July 1964): 106; Engelmann, pp. 231–32; Adler, *Jews in Germany*, p. 113; Cecil, *Ballin*: Engelmann, pp. 44, 231. His skills enabled him to form the first transatlantic shipping conference. In 1918, when the kaiser fled Germany, Ballin killed himself.
149. Vogel, p. 40; Angress, p. 34.
150. Vogel, p. 61; Angress, opp. p. 24.
151. Vogel, p. 70.
152. Adler, *Jews in Germany*, p. 117.
153. Interestingly, the number of Jews who died fighting in the German army during World War I—twelve thousand—is more than all Jews who died in Israel's wars of 1948, 1956, 1967, 1973, and 1982. Vogel, p. 139; statistics compiled during *Marva* training in the Israeli army.
154. Osborne, pp. 71–72; Adler, *Jews in Germany*, pp. 114–15; Bauer, p. 54; Demeter, p. 227; Gilbert, *Holocaust*, p. 21; Walle, in *Deutsche Jüdische Soldaten*, pp. 23, 38–39, 65; Messerschmidt, in *Deutsche Jüdische Soldaten*, pp. 119–20; Gidal, p. 312; BA-MA, RW 6/v. 73, BA-B, R 43 II/1273; Julius H. Schoeps, "Mußte die Emanzipation mißlingen?" in *Juden in Deutschland*, ed. Ludger Heid and Julius H. Schoeps (München, 1994), p. 15; Engelmann, pp. 206–8. According to Ian Kershaw, after the 1916 *Judenzählung*, the Prussian army stopped promoting Jews as officers. Kershaw, *Hitler 1889–1936*, p. 100.
155. Vogel, pp. 169, 345.
156. Walle, in *Deutsche Jüdische Soldaten, 1914–1945*, p. 49.
157. Adler, *Jews in Germany*, p. 114.
158. Ibid., p. 114.
159. Vogel, p. 75.
160. Ibid.

161. Ibid.
162. Beckhardt probably displayed this symbol because he was a patriotic German and believed the swastika to exemplify his German loyalty, not because he had anti-Semitic tendencies. Only when the Nazis took over power in Germany in 1933 did this symbol universally become equated with anti-Semitism. However, many anti-Semitic associations had used the swastika long before 1933 to symbolize their belief in German superiority.
163. Felix A. Theilhaber, *Juedische Flieger im Weltkrieg* (Berlin, 1924), p. 49.
164. Vogel, p. 9.
165. He was responsible for developing ammonia synthesis (method of manufacturing synthetic ammonia gas), which made Germany independent from outside sources in making fertilizers and high explosives. Without his inventions, some claim, the war would not have lasted as long as it did.
166. Walle, in *Deutsche Jüdische Soldaten, 1914–1945*, p. 30; Jacob R. Marcus, *The Rise and Destiny of the German Jew* (Cincinnati, 1934), p. 82; Goerlitz, pp. 169–70; Fritz Klein, *Verlorene Größe* (München, 1996), pp. 216, 241; Vital, p. 649. Fritz Haber was a reserve NCO when World War I started. He also was a member of the Volunteer Automobile Service, which was made up of wealthy individuals who put themselves and their automobiles at the service of the army. After a few weeks of the war, he was given a commission as an active duty captain. This was a very high honor. Bismarck was made a reserve major for his role in creating the German Empire. When the Nazis came into power, Haber fled to Switzerland. He would die there as a refugee.
167. Friedländer, p. 74; Bauer, p. 78; Christhard Hoffmann, "Between Integration and Rejection: The Jewish Community in Germany, 1914–1918," in *State, Society, and Mobilization in Europe during the First World War*, ed. John Horne (Cambridge, 1997), p. 95; Marcus, p. 82; Goerlitz, p. 169.
168. Adler, *Jews in Germany*, pp. 113–14; Speer, *Third Reich*, p. 249; Engelmann, p. 231; Jehuda L. Wallach, *The Dogma of the Battle of Annihilation: The Theories of Clausewitz and Schlieffen and Their Impact on the German Conduct of Two World Wars* (London, 1986), p. 193. Ludendorff was chief of operations for the army after 1916. According to Ian Kershaw, Ludendorff was "in effect Germany's dictator during the last two war years." Kershaw, *Hitler, 1889–1936*, p. 186.
169. Martin Senekowitsch, "Ich hatt' einen Kameraden," *Der Soldat* 12 July 1995, p. 6; Nathaniel Katzburg, *Hungary and the Jews: Policy and Legislation, 1920–1943* (Bar-Ilan Univ.), 1981, p. 203; Martin Senekowitsch, *Gleichberechtigte in einer grossen Armee: Zur Geschichte des Bundes Jüdischer Frontsoldaten Österreichs, 1932–1938* (Wien, 1994), p. 1; Schmidl, pp. 5, 144; In 1910, the Austro-Hungarian Empire's Jewish population numbered 2,258,013. Deák, p. 13.
170. Deák, p. 196. See also Marsha L. Rozenblit, *Reconstructing a National Identity: The Jews of Habsburg Austria during World War I* (Oxford, 2001).
171. Osborne, p. 71.
172. Schmidl, pp. 140–41.

173. Deák, p. 196. Some of the Jewish generals remained Jewish while others had converted to Christianity.

174. Until 1918, the Austro-Hungarian Empire awarded the Gold Medals for bravery *(goldene Tapferkeitsmedaille)* to NCOs during times of war. In 1917, it was also awarded to officers.

175. Deák, p. 196. Until 1918, the Austro-Hungarian Empire awarded the Orders of the Iron Crown Third Class *(Orden der Eisernen Krone 3. Klasse)* to officers and government ministers during times of war and peace.

176. Schmidl, p. 128.

177. Data gathered from statistical sheets compiled by Walter Pagler, director of *Oder Shalom* of the Central Jewish graveyard in Vienna.

178. Schmidl, p. 130.

179. BA-B, R 21 (76)/874, Bl. 284–85.

180. BA-B, R 21 (76)/874, Bl. 139; for information on the Freikorps, see Keegan, *The Second World War*, pp. 27–30; Albert Seaton, *The German Army, 1933–45* (New York, 1982), p. 2.

181. Adler, *Jews in Germany*, p. 114.

182. Gay, p. 221.

183. During World War I, those Germans serving in the Bavarian, Württemberg, and Saxony army swore an oath to their *Landesherren* (kings). Those from Baden swore an oath to the *Groß Herzog* (grand duke) from Baden. Those men from Prussia swore an oath to King Wilhelm II, who was also the German kaiser (emperor). However, those in the navy (Kaiserliche Marine) and the colonial troops (Kaiserliche Schutztruppe) swore an oath only to the emperor, even though they may have come from Bavaria or Baden or other states. See also Cecil, *Ballin*, p. 100; Michael Balfour, *The Kaiser and His Times* (Cambridge, 1964), p. 386; Lamar Cecil, *Wilhelm II: Prince and Emperor, 1859–1900* (Chapel Hill, 1989), pp. 141–42, 226; John C. G. Röhl, *The Kaiser and His Court: Wilhelm II and the Government of Germany* (New York, 1994), pp. 190–212.

184. Vogel, p. 46.

185. Prussian war minister, Adolf Wild von Hohenborn, ordered on 11 October 1916 that all military commands conduct a census of Jews serving in the armed forces on active duty, those not drafted yet, and those found temporarily or permanently unfit for active service. The intent behind the order was to find out whether their participation in battle was commensurate with their numbers in society. This decree showed that the long tradition of anti-Semitism within the Prussian army, especially within the officer corps, was still very real. Hoffmann in *State, Society, and Mobilization,* p. 98.

186. Friedländer, pp. 73–74; Jürgen Förster, "Wehrmacht, Krieg und Holocaust," in *Die Wehrmacht. Mythos und Realität,* p. 949; Bauer, p. 54.

187. Kershaw, *Hitler, 1889–1936,* p. 100.

188. David Welch, *Germany, Propaganda and Total War, 1914–1918: The Sins of Omission* (New Brunswick, 2000), p. 200.

189. Hoffmann in *State, Society and Mobilization,* pp. 99–101; Ruth Pierson, *German Jewish Identity in the Weimar Republic* (New Haven, 1970), pp. 248–50.

CHAPTER 4: RACIAL POLICY AND THE NUREMBERG LAWS,
1933–1939

1. BA-MA, BMRS, interview Hugo Fuchs, 08.07.1995, T-159.
2. Bauer, pp. 114–15; Dieter Rebentisch, *Führerstaat und Verwaltung im Zweiten Weltkrieg. Verfassungsentwicklung und Verwaltungspolitik, 1939–1945* (Stuttgart, 1989), p. 434.
3. Gellately, *Gestapo and German Society*, p. 102.
4. Kaplan, p. 21.
5. BA-MA, N 656/27, Hindenburg an Hitler, 04.04.1933, Bl. 10–17; Schleunes, p. 95. For an example of the type of letters Hindenburg received, see Friedländer, p. 16.
6. BA-MA, N 656/27, Hitler an Hindenburg, 05.04.1933, Bl. 10–17; Schleunes, p. 96. It is the author's opinion that Hitler was lying to Hindenburg about the law already being prepared to appease Hindenburg.
7. Gordon A. Craig, *Germany, 1866–1945* (New York, 1978), p. 578; Henry Ashby Turner, *Hitler's Thirty Days to Power: January 1933* (London, 1996), p. 164; Bracher, pp. 48–49; Victor, p. 78; Ian Kershaw, *Profiles in Power: Hitler* (London, 1991), pp. 68–69, 71–72; Friedländer, p. 17; Heinz Guderian, *Panzer Leader* (California, 1988), p. 30. For more details about Hitler's relationship with Hindenburg, see Speer, pp. 64–65; Haffner, p. 17.
8. Kershaw, *Hitler, 1889–1936*, p. 500.
9. Friedländer, p. 35.
10. Kershaw, *Hitler, 1889–1936*, pp. 362, 371–75, 391, 437; Redlich, pp. 88–89, 262, 307.
11. Hans Umbreit in *Das Deutsche Reich und der zweite Weltkrieg.* vol. 5/1, p. 283. Umbreit wrote, "Nach den im Reich ab 1933 angewandten Kriterien war jeder ein Jude, der mindestens einen Eltern- oder Großelternteil jüdischen Glaubens besaß."; Friedländer, p. 27. Saul Friedländer wrote, "The first of them [April 1933 laws]—the most fundamental one because of its definition of the Jew—was the April 7 Law for the Restoration of the Professional Civil Service." This study concurs with Kershaw when he writes that in the Aryan Paragraph, "there was no definition of a Jew." Kershaw, *Hitler, 1889–1936*, p. 474.
12. BA-MA, W 01-5/173, Erste und Dritte Verordnung zur Durchführung des Gesetzes zur Wiederherstellung des Berufsbeamtentums, Erste Verordnung v. 11.04.1933; Friedländer, p. 36.
13. Ibid., Erste Verordnung zur Durchführung des Gesetzes zur Wiederherstellung des Berufsbeamtentums, 11.04.1933; Hilde Kammer and Elisabet Bartsch, eds., *Nationalsozialismus: Begriffe aus der Zeit der Gewaltherrschaft, 1933–1945* (Hamburg, 1992), p. 18; *Reichsgesetzblatt* (RGBl.), I, 11 April- 6 Mai 1933, pp. 135, 175, 195.
14. According to Ascher's grandson, Peter Gaupp, Sammy Ascher was an Oberstabsarzt (equivalent to an army major) during World War I.
15. Although the *Arierparagraph* only addressed civil servants in its legal language, several Jews, regardless of their professions, were forced to retire or leave their work. This was especially the case with those doctors who worked in hospitals.

16. BA-MA, BMRS, interview Peter Gaupp, 17.01.1995, T-87. Tragically, Dr. Ascher felt so patriotically committed to Germany that when war fever was high in 1938, he declared to his family that he would have to serve again if his country called on him. His family laughed at him, but he was serious. BA-MA, BMRS, interview Ursula Gaupp, 08.07.1995, T-158. Ascher was not alone in his desire to serve Germany once again. Half-Jew Gert Beschütz's father, Max, reported to the army in 1938, was rejected, and a few weeks later was sent to the Sachsenhausen concentration camp. BA-MA, BMRS, File Beschütz, Bl. 3.

17. Bracher, p. 253; Kaplan, p. 24.

18. Viktor Klemperer, *Ich will Zeugnis ablegen bis zum letzten, 1933–1945* (Aufbau Verlag, 1996), Buch I, p. 25.

19. BA-B, R 41/581, Partisch an Göring, 07.08.1933, Bl. 199–200.

20. Friedländer, p. 70.

21. BA-B, R 43 II/ 418a. As translated in Noakes, p. 298. See also Friedländer, p. 119.

22. Heeres-Verordnungsblatt (HVBl.), Nr. 73, 1933, p. 73; Rudolf Absolon, Die Wehrmacht im Dritten Reich. Band I-II, 30.1.1933 bis 02.08.1934 (Boppard, 1983); Sammlung wehrrechtlicher Gutachten und Vorschriften. Heft I (1963)-Heft 22 (1984). Bearbeitet v. Rudolf Absolon, Bundesarchiv-Zentralnachweisstelle, Aachen-Kornelimünster, 1985, Heft 9, p. 4; Vogel, p. 200.

23. Militärgeschichtliches Forschungsamt, ed., *Handbuch zur deutschen Militärgeschichte, 1648–1939 VII. Wehrmacht und Nationalsozialismus, 1933–1939* (München, 1978), p. 57.

24. Craig, *Prussian Army*, pp. 373–466; Wallach, pp. 236, 303.

25. Corum, *Luftwaffe*, p. 145; Frei, *National Socialist Rule*, pp. 50, 74; Seaton, *German Army*, p. 104. Although Germany was rearming at an alarming rate, it still had a long way to go. Hitler had originally planned to start war in 1943 or thereafter, but starting the war in 1939 as he did, the Kriegsmarine was still weak compared with Britain, the Luftwaffe was still growing and developing long-range bombers, and the army, besides the Panzer divisions, was still largely a "foot-slogging infantry" dependent on horses and *panje* wagons.

26. BA-MA, BMRS, interview Paul Hirschfeld, 15–16.08.1994, T-12.

27. Creveld, p. 18; Kershaw, *Hitler, 1889–1936*, pp. 436, 446; Bracher, p. 72; David Thomson, *Europe Since Napoleon* (Cambridge, 1962), p. 684.

28. BA-MA, BMRS, File Ernst Prager, Bl. 29.

29. BA-MA, N 656/27, Hitler an Hindenburg, 05.04.1933, Bl. 15. Hitler had cynically written in his second book that if an officer's rank could be bought, then such a profession would be "comprehensible" to the Jews. Hitler, *Hitler's Secret Book*, p. 26.

30. Kershaw, *Hitler, 1889–1936*, p. 96; Fritz Stern, *The Politics of Cultural Despair* (London, 1974), pp. 161–62.

31. *Heeresadjutant bei Hitler, 1938–1943. Aufzeichnungen des Majors Gerhard Engel*. Hrsg. u. kommentiert v. Hildegard von Kotze. (=Schriftenreihe der Vierteljahreshefte für Zeitgeschichte Nr. 29) (Stuttgart, 1974), pp. 31–32. Engel

altered his diary after the war. As Jeremy Noakes writes, "[T]his is not in fact a diary but more like a memoir" (Noakes, "Development of Nazi Policy," p. 333, n. 133). However, there is no reason to doubt the events surrounding the *Mischlinge* described in Engel's diary even if he had added them after the war. Documents in the archives and this study support Engel's activities regarding *Mischlinge*.

32. BA-MA, RW 6/73 a, Antwortentwurf v. 12. 10. 1933 an "Fridericus—Die deutsche Wochenschrift" von Friedrich C. Holtz.

33. Ibid., Pressestelle des Reichsbundes der Höheren Beamten an Reichswehrministerium, 17.01.1934.

34. *Handbuch VII*, pp. 57–59; BA-MA, N 656/27; Manfred Messerschmidt, *Die Wehrmacht im NS-Staat* (Hamburg, 1969), p. 47.

35. Messerschmidt, p. 46; BA-MA, N 328/45, Admiral a.D. Ehrhardt an Admiral a.D. Förste, 14.11.1956.

36. Matthew Cooper, *German Army* (New York, 1978), p. 28; Seaton, *German Army*, p. 44.

37. Wilhelm Deist, "The Rearmament of the Wehrmacht," in *Germany and the Second World War*, vol. 1, *The Build-up of German Aggression*, ed. Militärgeschichtliches Forschungsamt (Oxford, 1998), p. 522.

38. *Hoheitsabzeichen*.

39. Robert J. O'Neill, *The German Army and the Nazi Party, 1933–1939* (London, 1966), p. 38; Wheeler-Bennett, *Nemesis of Power*, p. 678; Creveld, p. 84; Kershaw, *Hitler, 1889–1936*, p. 504; Seaton, *German Army*, p. 44; Craig, *Prussian Army*, p. 476.

40. Kershaw, *Hitler, 1889–1936*, p. 504. See also O'Neill, p. 38; Craig, *Politics of the Prussian Army*, p. 476.

41. Norman H. Baynes, ed., *The Speeches of Adolf Hitler*, vol 2 (Oxford, 1942), p. 1,349.

42. *Handbuch VII*, p. 57; Berliner Morgenpost, 22.04.1934; Rudolf Absolon, *Wehrgesetz und Wehrdienst, 1935–1945. Das Personalwesen in der Wehrmacht* (Boppard, 1960), p. 117; Messerschmidt, pp. 45–46; Kershaw, *Hitler, 1889–1936*, p. 504; O'Neill, p. 39; Jürgen Förster, "Wehrmacht, Krieg und Holocaust," in *Die Wehrmacht*, ed. Müller and Volkmann, p. 950.

43. O'Neill, pp. 38–39, 76.

44. BA-MA, BMRS, general impression gained from data collected for this study; Absolon, *Wehrgesetz und Wehrdienst*, p. 117, n. 20.

45. Messerschmidt, pp. 45–46. See also Absolon, *Wehrgesetz und Wehrdienst*, p. 117, n. 20.

46. *Handbuch VII*, p. 57.

47. The commander was Captain von Schrader. He explained to Lebram that the *Arierparagraph* was necessary for the Reichswehr. BA-MA, N 656/2, Bl. 24.

48. BA-MA, N 656/2, Bl. 9.

49. BA-MA, BMRS, interview Friedrich-Christian Stahl, 12.11.1997, T-406.

50. BA-MA, N 656/2, Bl. 12.

51. BA-MA, N 656/2, Raeder an Lebram, 19.04.1934, Bl. 8.

52. BA-MA, N 328/45, Ehrhardt an Förste; Ludovic Kennedy, *Pursuit: Battleship Bismarck* (London, 1993), p. 35; BA-MA, N 379/109a, 12.09.1956; BA-MA, Pers 6/2236, Personalbogen, Frau: Margarete Backenköhler geb. 09.05.1903, Bl. 2; BA-MA, 656/2, Bl. 13; discussion with Dr. G. Granier on 12.11.1997 in the Bundesarchiv-Militärarchiv about Backenköhler's Jewish past. Interestingly, as the *Bismarck* was in its death throes, Lütjens sent a radiogram to Hitler praising the Führer and the war. Perhaps Lütjens did so because he firmly believed in Hitler, or perhaps he was scared for his *Mischling* wife and children and wanted to ensure their protection by displaying his devotion. It was probably a mixture of both. Burkard Frhr. von Müllenheim-Rechberg, *Schlachtschiff Bismarck, 1940–1941* (Berlin, 1980), pp. 168–69; Jörg Duppler, ed., *Germania auf dem Meere* (Hamburg, 1998), p. 127.

53. BA-MA, N 656/2, Bl. 12; BA-MA, BMRS, File Admiral Conrad Patzig, Bl. 62.

54. BA-MA, N 656/2, Bl. 12–13.

55. Ibid., Dok., Kommando der Marinestation der Ostsee an Oberleutnant z. S. Lebram, 08.05.1934.

56. BA-MA, BMRS, interview Dietrich Beelitz 16.11.1997, T-401; BA-MA, N 656. Lebram disputes the fact that his brother committed suicide. Nonetheless, from eyewitnesses' testimonies and reports, it appears that Lebram's brother, Walter, killed himself. Walter Lebram, a pilot in the army air force, flew his plane into the ground.

57. Charles S. Thomas, *The German Navy in the Nazi Era* (London, 1990), pp. 86–87, 238; BA-MA, BMRS, File Hans-Georg von Friedeburg; BA-MA, BMRS, interview Ludwig von Friedeburg, 01.12.1997, T-415. Perhaps Raeder helped General Admiral Hans Georg von Friedeburg or perhaps it was Himmler, with whom Friedeburg was on good terms. Friedeburg remained at his post throughout the entire war without any problems. He and General Jodl signed the formal surrender documents at General Dwight D. Eisenhower's headquarters in May of 1945. Friedeburg's grandmother was Adelheid Kuh, a half-Jew, perhaps a full Jew. Information gained from the *Mitteilung des Instituts für Personengeschichtliche Forschung,* Bensheim, Germany, and from Baron Niklas Schrenck von Notzing at his personal archive dedicated to genealogies of the German aristocracy in Charlottesville, Virginia. The founder of this Institut in Bensheim was Wilfried Euler, who was a "Mischling expert" during the Third Reich. He worked in the Reichinstitut für Geschichte des Neuen Deutschland (Reich Institute for the History of the New Germany). He worked closely with Achim Gercke. His sources need to be used with caution. Thanks to Dr. Patricia von Papen-Bodek for this information.

58. Thomas, p. 94; BA-MA, BMRS, interview von Friedeburg.

59. Many have previously assumed that Friedeburg was a quarter-Jew. Apparently, they have based this solely on his grandmother's last name (rather than her heritage from both sides). Also, the ignorance and sloppiness of certain officials and historians have created much confusion about Friedeburg's ancestry. Although it has been proven that his grandmother was a half-Jew, it has

not been proven or disproven that both her parents were Jews according to the Nazi racial laws.

60. Hans Breithaupt, *Zwischen Front und Widerstand. Ein Beitrag zur Diskussion um den Feldmarschall Erich von Manstein* (München, 1994), p. 123; BA-MA, BMRS, interview Ursula Freifrau von Knigge, 26.07.1997, T-392.

61. BA-MA, BMRS, File Klaus von Schmeling-Diringshofen, Bl. 5–6.

62. Much speculation has surrounded Manstein's possible Jewish ancestry. The fact that he was born von Lewinski and adopted by the von Mansteins has led some to believe that he descended from Jews. They state that Lewinski could be a variant of Levy with a Polish patronymic suffix. However, only one source has surfaced during this study that might lead one to believe that Manstein had Jewish ancestry. In a December 1994 interview, his adjutant, Alexander Stahlberg, who has Jewish ancestry himself, stated that Manstein claimed that the Lewinskis were Jews. Nonetheless, Stahlberg could not provide any documents to prove that this conversation had taken place or that Manstein in fact had Jewish ancestors. Manstein's son, Rüdiger, claimed that his family could possibly have Jews in their past, but that there is no evidence to prove it either way. The SS investigated Manstein's (they actually called him Lewinski) ancestry in April 1944, after his dismissal. However, the file is incomplete, and it remains unknown what the SS discovered. Alexander Stahlberg, *Die verdammte Pflicht* (Berlin, 1987); BA-MA, BMRS, interview Alexander Stahlberg, 3–4.12.1994, T-68; BA-MA, BMRS, interview Rüdiger von Manstein, 17.11.1994, T-54; BA-B, NS 19/2177.

63. Military district.

64. BA-MA, BMRS, interview Knigge.

65. Breithaupt, p. 123.

66. BA-MA, BMRS, File Schmeling-Diringshofen, Bl. 5–6; BA-MA, BMRS, interview Knigge.

67. Retired (1926) Generaloberst Hans von Seeckt (1866–1936) was the chief of the army leadership *(Chef der Heeresleitung)* of the Reichswehr from 1920 to 1926. Later, he was an important military adviser to Chiang Kai-shek from 1934 to 1935, and some believe that he also helped non-Aryan soldiers get appointments to China. Interestingly, Seeckt's wife, Frau Dorothee von Seeckt née Fabian, was adopted by Jews. It is unclear whether she herself was Jewish, although most assume that this was the case. See Martin, p. 60; Snyder, p. 319.

68. O'Neill, p. 76; Cooper, *German Army*, p. 46; Friedländer, pp. 117–18; Wistrich, p. 14; BA-MA, BMRS, interview Knigge.

69. General Hans Oster and Colonel von Mellentin also helped Borchardt to get to China. BA-MA, BMRS, File Robert Borchardt, Bl. 22–31; BA-MA, BMRS, interview Elisabeth Borchardt, 18.02.1995, T-101; Vogel, pp. 305–6. Borchardt was later posted with the Sonderverband (Special Unit) 288 in Africa under Rommel. He commanded the Fifth Panzerjäger Company. He had been one of the few German officers who had been trained with mechanized units during the Weimar Republic. He was later taken prisoner by the British and survived the war in POW camps in England and Canada.

70. Dal McGuirk, *Rommel's Army in Africa* (Osceola, 1993), p. 45; BA-MA, BMRS, File Robert Borchardt, Bl. 22–31; BA-MA, BMRS, interview Elisabeth Borchardt, 18.02.1995.

71. This phrase should not be confused with the way the Nazis used it to depict agrarian romanticism (after Walter Darré, "the *Blut und Boden* guru" [Kershaw, *Hitler, 1936–1945*, p. 374]). His friends nicknamed Schmeling-Diringshofen this before the Nazis were in power because of his love of the land and of hunting.

72. BA-MA, BMRS, interview Beelitz.

73. In 1938, as Germany was strengthening its alliance with Japan, Hitler decided that Germany "dismantle all the links" with China. See Wilhelm Keitel, *The Memoirs of Field-Marshal Keitel,* ed. Walter Görlitz (London, 1961), p. 41. It was probably at that time that most *Mischling* soldiers in China returned to Germany. On their returns, Hitler granted most of them clemency. BA-MA, BMRS, File Robert Borchardt, "Vorlesung von Robert Borchardt."

74. Löwenstein had "perfected the technique of sound measurement which made possible more accurate and effective artillery fire" during World War I. Marcus, p. 82. From 2 February 1942 until 1 April 1943, the Nazis made him perform forced labor. On 1 July 1943, the Nazis deported him and his wife to Theresienstadt. They both would survive the Holocaust. He died in 1956 while vacationing in Israel, where he was also buried. Walle, in *Deutsche Jüdische Soldaten, 1914–1945*, p. 32.

75. Reichsbund jüdischer Frontsoldaten (RjF). This organization had thirty thousand members. Walle, in *Deutsche Jüdische Soldaten, 1914–1945*, p. 32.

76. BA-MA, RW 6/73, Löwenstein (Reichsbund Jüdischer Frontsoldaten) an Hindenburg, 23.03.1934.

77. Ibid., Löwenstein an Abteilungsleiter im Reichswehrministerium, 24.03.1934.

78. Bundeswehr is the armed forces of the Federal Republic of Germany founded in 1955.

79. BA-MA, BMRS, File Bernhard Rogge, Heft I, Generaladmiral a.D. Boehm an Frankfurter Allgemeine Zeitung, 05.04.1961, Bl. 2.

80. Cooper, *German Army,* p. 29; Breithaupt, pp. 123–27.

81. Breithaupt, pp. 123–24, 126; BA-MA, BMRS, interview von Knigge.

82. Breithaupt, p. 124.

83. Ibid., p. 124.

84. Klaus-Jürgen Müller, *Das Heer und Hitler* (Stuttgart, 1969), p. 594; Breithaupt, p. 125.

85. Müller, *Das Heer,* p. 594.

86. Breithaupt, p. 125.

87. Klaus-Jürgen Müller, "Witzleben, Stülpnagel and Speidel," in *Hitler's Generals,* ed. Correlli Barnett (London, 1989), p. 46.

88. O'Neill, p. 39.

89. Wilhelm Deist, in *Die Wehrmacht,* p. 43; Hans-Ulrich Thamer, "Die Erosion einer Säule. Wehrmacht und NSDAP," in *Die Wehrmacht,* p. 426; Jürgen Förster, "Hitler's Decision in Favor of War against the Soviet Union," in *Ger-*

many and the Second World War, vol. 4, pp. 36–37; Messerschmidt, in *Deutsche Jüdische Soldaten*, pp. 124–25.

90. O'Neill, p. 28; William L. Shirer, *The Nightmare Years* (New York, 1984), pp. 189, 214; Craig, *Prussian Army*, p. 491; Geoffrey P. Megargee, *Inside Hitler's High Command* (Kansas, 2000), p. 22; Cooper, *German Army*, p. 24.
91. BA-MA, BMRS, File R. von Manstein, Manstein to Rigg, 21.07.2001; BA-MA, BMRS, interview R. von Manstein. The nephews were children of his niece Frau von Preuschen née Lewinski.
92. Emmy Göring, *An der Seite meines Mannes* (Göttingen, 1967). Emmy Göring should be used with caution. She wrote this book as an apology for her husband, and many events are misrepresented. See Richard Overy, *Goering* (London, 1984), p. 18. Reichsmarschall Göring's attitude may have been influenced by his contact with Jews as a child. Göring's godfather, namesake, and mother's lover, Ritter Hermann von Eppenstein, was a Jew and probably the father of his youngest brother, Albert, who looked just like Eppenstein. Heinrich Fraenkel, *Göring* (New York, 1972), pp. 9–15; Ewan Butler and Gordon Young, *Marshal without Glory* (London, 1951), pp. 20–30; Paul, p. 33; Asher Lee, *Goering: Air Leader* (New York, 1972), pp. 12–13.
93. See Overy, pp. 15–17.
94. Speer, p. 291.
95. Yahil, pp. 59–60; Carl Hans Hermann, *Deutsche Militärgeschichte* (Frankfurt, 1966), pp. 452–53, 456; Kershaw, *ProFiles in Power*, pp. 72–73; Georg Franz-Willing, *Die Reichskanzlei, 1933–1945* (Tübingen, 1984), p. 54. Although the SA continued to exist as an organization, it never exercised any real power during the Third Reich.
96. Kershaw, *Profiles in Power*, pp. 72–74. See also O'Neill, p. 50.
97. O'Neill, p. 54; Craig, *Prussian Army*, p. 479; Megargee, p. 29.
98. Kershaw, *Hitler, 1889–1936*, p. 437. See also Redlich, p. 100.
99. Kershaw writes that Reichenau was "one of the most thoroughly nazified generals." Kershaw, *Hitler, 1936–1945*, p. 70.
100. Nicolaus von Below, *Als Hitlers Adjutant, 1937–1945* (Mainz, 1980), pp. 72–73; Megargee, p. 27.
101. O'Neill, p. 54; Cooper, *German Army*, p. 30; Kershaw, *Hitler, 1889–1936*, pp. 524–25; Wistrich, p. 19; Messerschmidt, p. 51; Megargee, p. 29.
102. Cooper, *German Army*, p. 30; Franz-Willing, p. 61; Messerschmidt, p. 51.
103. Craig, *Prussian Army*, pp. xviii, 363; Messerschmidt, p. 32; Goerlitz, p. 55.
104. Christoph von L'Estocq, *Soldat in drei Epochen* (Berlin, 1993), pp. 112–13.
105. Goerlitz, p. 290; Kershaw, *Hitler, 1889–1936*, p. 525; O'Neill, p. 55; Seaton, *German Army*, p. 53; Messerschmidt, p. 52; Megargee, p. 29.
106. BA-MA, BMRS, File Walter Falk, Bl. 4. Falk would later be promoted to Gefreiter.
107. See BA-MA, BMRS, interview Spitz; BA-MA, BMRS, interview Hans Mühlbacher, 18.09.1994, T-22; BA-MA, BMRS, File Gerhard Bier, Bier an Rigg, 26.03.2001.
108. Fest, *Face*, p. 144.
109. Kershaw, *Hitler, 1889–1936*, p. 436.

110. Hoßbach, pp. 10–12; O'Neill, p. 58; Seaton, *German Army*, p. 52.

111. Hermann, p. 455; Messerschmidt, p. 52. See also Craig, *Germany, 1866–1945*, pp. 585–86; Kitchen, *Military History*, p. 293; Megargee, p. 29.

112. Kershaw, *Profiles in Power*, p. 74.

113. Kershaw, *Hitler, 1889–1936*, pp. 497, 521.

114. Yahil, p. 60; Haffner, pp. 27–31; Guderian, pp. 59–60.

115. RGBl., I, 1935, Nr. 28, p. 375 (Gesetz für den Aufbau der Wehrmacht) bzw. Nr. 52, p. 602 ff. v. 22.05.1935 (Wehrgesetz v. 21.05.1935).

116. Frei, Manfred Funke, "Großmachtpolitik und Weltmachtstreben," in *Das Dritte Reich*, eds. Broszat and Frei, p. 140; Cooper, *German Army*, p. 130; Kershaw, *Hitler, 1889–1936*, p. 551; Kershaw, *Profiles in Power*, p. 121; Friedländer, p. 115; Kitchen, *Military History*, p. 295; Wallach, p. 219; Megargee, p. 32.

117. Friedländer, p.115. By 1939, the army would be fifty-two active divisions strong. Craig, *Prussian Army*, p. 482.

118. BA-MA, BMRS, data collected throughout this study; Absolon, *Wehrgesetz und Wehrdienst*, pp. 117–18.

119. BA-B, R 43 II/1273; Walk, *Sonderrecht für den Juden*, pp. 114–16; RGBl. I, 1935, p. 1,047.

120. BA-MA, BMRS, File Wolfgang Lauinger, Bl. 23; BA-MA, BMRS, interview Lüderitz.

121. For a discussion of the total number of eligible *Mischlinge* for military service, see chapter 3 on assimilation.

122. Friedländer, p. 144.

123. BA-B, R 43 II/1273, Akten betreffend Wehrgesetz, Bl. 112, Löwenstein an Lammers, 23.03.1935.

124. Ibid., Akten betreffend Wehrgesetz, Bl. 116–18, Löwenstein an Hitler, 05.10.1935.

125. BA-B. R 43 II/1273, Verband Nationaldeutscher Juden E. V. Geschäftsstelle Berlin, Verbandsführer Dr. Naumann an Hitler, 20.03.1935, Bl. 110–12.

126. Vital, pp. 814–15. See Schoeps, *Deutschland*, p. 25.

127. Schleunes, p. 117.

128. Oberkommando der Wehrmacht, the armed forces high command.

129. *Sonderrecht für den Juden im NS-Staat*, p. 318, Gesetz von 04.03.1940. Between 1940 and 1942, over thirty Jews tried to obtain special permission to enter the Wehrmacht. All were rejected. BA-B, DZA, Bl. 29. See also Klemperer, Buch II, 05.07.1942, p. 157.

130. BA-MA, Pers 6/ 7363, Bl. 9, Bericht über Major der L[andes] P[olizei] Karl Helwig.

131. O'Neill, p. 76.

132. Kershaw, *Hitler, 1889–1936*, p. 564.

133. O'Neill, p. 77; Kershaw, *Hitler, 1889–1936*, p. 564; Messerschmidt, p. 76; Vogel, p. 239.

134. Vogel, pp. 233–34.

135. BA-MA, BMRS, general impression gained from this study; Vogel, p. 230. One could not become an officer, marry, and so on, without showing his *Abstammungsnachweis* (certificate of descent). Sometimes it was called

Ariernachweis (certificate of Aryanhood). In addition, one had an *Ahnenpaß* (ancestral passport), which was a small booklet with the certificate of descent and a detailed family tree. This document replaced previously required birth, baptismal, and marriage certificates. After the Nuremberg Laws, every German had to show he or she was an Aryan. A document without any gaps was requirement for full citizenship rights. Ironically, since Hitler could not prove who his grandfather was, he could not fulfill this law he had sanctioned for Germany. See chapters 7 and 8 on exemptions.

136. BA-MA, BMRS, File Richard Cohn, Bl. 7, Arische Erklärung, 09.02.1939.

137. BA-MA, BMRS, File Hans-Joachim Körner, Beglaubigte Abschrift, 26.11.1954, Bl. 2–3, 4–6, Körner an Generalstaatsanwalt bei dem Kammergericht. Körner lost fifteen relatives in the concentration camps. Throughout 1942, it looked like the *Gau-* and *Kreisleitungen* found many *Mischling* soldiers and were reporting them to the proper authorities. *Heeresadjutant bei Hitler*, p. 122.

138. BA-MA, W 01–6/359, Kröner an Wehrmeldamt, 13.06.1941.

139. BA-MA, BMRS, File Edgar Jacoby; BA-MA, BMRS, interview Frau Jacoby, 11.01.1994, T-45; BA-MA, BMRS, interview Frau Edgar Jacoby, 19.11.1996, T-243; BA-MA, BMRS, interview Barbara Jacoby, 17.11.1994, T-52; BA-MA, W 01–6/359. Remarkably, Jacoby was later released and survived the war at his home because his brave Aryan wife (Marianne née Günther) refused to divorce him. Käthe Himmelheber was later sent to Theresienstadt. She would survive the war.

140. BA-MA, BMRS, interview Rolf von Sydow; BA-MA, BMRS, File Rolf von Sydow.

141. BA-MA, BMRS, File Rolf von Sydow, Bl. 44, Sydow an seine Eltern, 15.01.1944.

142. Ibid., Sydow an seine Eltern, 22.03.1944, Bl. 35–36.

143. Obergefreiter was an acting corporal.

144. Colonel Seegers, in the Army Personnel Office P2 (Department for Personnel Matters of High-Ranking Officers and Education and Welfare), seemed to help several *Mischlinge* present their cases to the authorities. He probably worked closely with Major Klug (P2 Gruppe I: Deutschblütigkeit, Heirat) and Major Werneyer (P2 Gruppe I-Ic: Deutschblütigkeit) on these cases. Wolf Keilig, *Das Deutsche Heer, 1939–1945: Gliederung, Einsatz, Stellenbesetzung* (Bad Nauheim, 1956), p. 7. See also BA-MA, Pers 6/10046 or BA-A, Pers 14492 to read how Seegers went about helping a *Mischling*. See also *Der Prozess gegen die Hauptkriegsverbrecher vor dem Internationalen Militärgerichtshof*, Nürnberg 14. November 1945–1. Oktober 1946, Nürnberg, 1948, p. 421.

145. BA-MA, Pers 6/11122, Bl. 3, General-Kommando XVII. Armeekorps (Wehrkreis-Kommando XVII) an OKH-H.P.A, 19.08.1939, Bl. 9, 11, Deutschblütigkeitserklärung für Robert Colli, 24.06.1941; *Die Ritterkreuz Träger; Die Träger des Deutschen Kreuzes in Gold*, p. 68; *Die Träger des Eisernen Kreuzes, 1939–1945*, p. 154; Archiv der Republik Österreich, Wien, Pers. Akt. Robert Colli.

146. DDS, Pers Marine-Oberbaurat Franz Mendelssohn; BA-MA, BMRS, File Franz Mendelssohn, Abschrift des Stammbaums von Moses Mendelssohn von

Professor Dr. Peter Witt, *Moses Mendelssohn und Fromet Guggenheim und ihre Nachkommen,* p. 43, A.) II. Franz Viktor Mendelssohn; BA-MA, BMRS, interview Frau Mendelssohn-Eder, 26.02.1995, T-108; BA-MA, BMRS, interview Frau Mendelssohn-Barz, 17.03.1995, T-120.

147. *Nachr. Tr. U. Pion.* Fricke was in charge of this section from 15.11.1942 until 01.10.1944. Keilig, p. 6.

148. Amtsgruppen.

149. Department for Personnel Matters of Officers and Their Offspring (not including General Staff Officers). Keilig, p. 1.

150. BA-MA, BMRS, File Karl-Heinrich Fricke, *Erinnerungen aus 70 Lebensjahren von 1914–1984* (Köln, 1984), p. 182.

151. He registered himself as *gottgläubig* (a believer in God) but without any particular confession *(konfessionslos).*

152. BA-MA, BMRS, interview Hirschfeld, 15–16.08.1994, T-12; BA-MA, BMRS, interview Hirschfeld, 22.11.1996, T-247.

153. BA-MA, BMRS, File Hirschfeld, Hirschfeld an Rigg 18.09.1994, Bl. 17–18: BA-MA, BMRS, interview Hirschfeld, 15–16.08.1994, T-12; BA-MA, BMRS, interview Hirschfeld, 22.11.1996, T-247.

154. BA-MA, BMRS, File Hirschfeld, Hirschfeld an Rigg, 18.09.1994, Bl. 17. Hirschfeld named three other Jews who served in the Wehrmacht.

155. BA-MA, BMRS, interview Hirschfeld, 15–16.08.1994, T-12.

156. BA-MA, BMRS, interview Rabbi Chaskel Besser, 15.01.1995, T-86.

157. Deborah Hertz, "The Genealogy Bureaucracy in the Third Reich," *Jewish History,* Haifa (fall 1997): 28.

158. Hertz, p. 28. Observant Jews do not allow non-Jews to be buried in Jewish cemeteries.

159. A literal translation of *Judenbengel* is "Jewish rascal" or "rogue."

160. Krackow, pp. 309–10.

161. Krackow, p. 98; BA-MA, BMRS, interview J. Krackow, 14.11.1994, T-50; BA-MA, BMRS, interview J. Krackow, 18.11.1994, T-56; BA-MA, BMRS, interview R. Krackow.

162. See Bracher, p. 197.

163. BA-MA, RH 53–7/468, Bl. 8, Wehrmachtamt/Keitel an V.A. (V1), 09.01.1936; BA-MA, RW 6/73.

164. BA-MA, RH 53–7/468, Bl. 9, Generalkommando VII. Armeekorps an Chef des Heerespersonalamts.

165. *Der deutsche Verwaltungsbeamte,* 17.10.1937; See also Friedländer, p. 32; Gellately, *Gestapo and German Society,* pp. 132–58.

166. Kershaw, *Hitler, 1889–1936,* p. 530; Kershaw, *Hitler, 1936–1945,* pp. 233–34; Friedländer, p. 161; Victor, p. 164.

167. Vogel, pp. 234–38; Das Reichsbürgergesetz vom 15.09.1935 (RGBl. 1935, Teil I, Nr. 100, p. 1,146); Gesetz zum Schutze des deutschen Blutes und der deutschen Ehre vom 15.09.1935 (RGBl. 1935, Teil I, p. 1,146); Erste Verordnung zum Reichsbürgergesetz vom 14.11.1935 (RGBl., Teil I, 1935, Nr. 125, pp. 1,333–36).

168. Kershaw, *Hitler, 1889–1936,* p. 567.

169. Lösener, p. 273; Bracher, p. 253.

170. BA-B, *Bestände aus der Zeit von 1867 bis 1945: Zivile Behörden und Einrichtungen des Deutschen Reiches*, p. 56; BA-K, File 8/ RP 39, Kurt Meyer an Gustav Scholten, 03.10.1942; Hertz, p. 44.

171. Yahil, p. 43.

172. Kershaw, *Hitler Myth*, p. 236; Kershaw, *Hitler, 1889–1936*, p. 570; Baynes, *Speeches of Adolf Hitler*, vol 1, p. 732.

173. Kershaw, *Hitler, 1889–1936*, p. 570.

174. Benz, p. 62.

175. Kershaw, *Hitler Myth*, p. 236; Kershaw, *Hitler, 1889–1936*, p. 570; Bauer, p. 110.

176. Hitler, *Mein Kampf*, p. 150.

177. Lösener, p. 281.

178. BA-B, R 18/5514, Bl. 28, Schreiben Reichs- und Preußisches Ministerium des Innern. Abteilung I. Gegenüberstellung der Fassung Dr. Wagner, betrifft: Ausführungsverordnungen zum Reichsbürgergesetz und zum Blutschutzgesetz, 02.11.1935, Bl. 28; Lösener, pp. 274–76; Schleunes, p. 127; Redlich, p. 155; Friedländer, p. 148; Kershaw, *Hitler, 1889–1936*, p. 571; Kershaw, *Hitler, 1936–1945*, p. 256.

179. BA-B, R 18/5514, Bl. 28, Schreiben Reichs- und Preußisches Ministerium des Innern, Abteilung I, I. Gegenüberstellung der Fassung Dr. Wagner, betrifft: Ausführungsverordnungen zum Reichsbürgergesetz und zum Blutschutzgesetz, 02.11.1935, Bl. 29; Noakes, "Development of Nazi Policy," p. 341.

180. BA-B, 15.09/52, Bl. 46–48. The Nazis used Mendel's name as a verb to describe genetic expression between mixed breeds. Johann Gregor Mendel (1822–1884) was an Austrian monk and was the first scientist to formulate the principles of heredity. *Encyclopedia Americana*, vol. 18 (Danbury, 1984), p. 686.

181. Kershaw, *Profiles in Power*, p. 101.

182. IfZ, N-71–73, Diktat Stuckart im Verbindungsstab am 06.11.1935.

183. Lösener, pp. 277–78; Kershaw, *Hitler, 1889–1936*, p. 564; Victor, p. 139; Burleigh, p. 291. The unintelligent Streicher probably took this idea from Arthur Dinter's book *The Sin Against the Blood*, a work of fiction. See also Stoltzfus, *Resistance*, p. xxviii.

184. Lösener, p. 278.

185. IfZ, N 71–73, Reichs- und Preußisches Ministerium des Innern, Abt. I Referent: Lösener, 11.10.1935.

186. IfZ, N 71–73, 11.10.1935; BA-B, R 18/5514, Bl. 30–31.

187. BA-B, R 18/5514, Bl. 29, Schreiben Reichs- und Preußisches Ministerium des Innern Abteilung I, I. Gegenüberstellung der Fassung Dr. Wagner, 02.11.1935; Hilberg, p. 47.

188. Lösener, pp. 278–79; "Authentische Äußerungen zu den Nürnberger Gesetzen," CV Ztg., 05.12.1935, Supplement 2; Yahil, p. 78.

189. Lösener, pp. 268, 273. As translated by Noakes. Noakes, "Development of Nazi Policy," p. 353.

190. Kershaw, *Hitler, 1889–1936*, p. 572; Jeremy Noakes and Geoffrey Pridham, eds., *Nazism 1919–1945*, vol. 4 (Exeter, 1983), p. 1; Hilberg, p. 47.

191. Stoltzfus, *Resistance*, p. 65.

192. Verordnung zum Reichsbürgergesetz 14.11.1935 (RGBl., Teil I, 1935, Nr. 135), pp. 1,333–36; Hilberg, p. 48; *The Holocaust: 1*, p. 31.

193. Hilberg, p. 48; Adler, *Der Verwaltete Mensch*, p. 280; If a Jewish woman had a child out of wedlock and the father's identity was not able to be determined, then the Nazis classified the child as a full Jew. See *Akten-NSDAP*, 107-00404.

194. *Heeresadjutant bei Hitler*, p. 32.

195. If a person was "three-eighths-Jewish," he or she was most often classified as quarter-Jewish. Countless men and women documented in this study were actually 37.5 percent Jewish, and the majority were classified as quarter-Jews by the Nazis. See *Akten-NSDAP*, 107-00389-390. When a person was more than 37.5 percent Jewish but not 50 percent Jewish, he or she was then usually classified as a half-Jew. Likewise, when a person was more than 12.5 percent Jewish, for example, 18.75 percent Jewish, then he or she was usually classified as a quarter-Jew.

196. *Nationalsozialismus. Begriffe aus der Zeit der Gewaltherrschaft, 1933–1945*, pp. 39–40; Kershaw, *Hitler, 1889–1936*, p. 572; Norman Rich, *Hitler's War Aims* (New York, 1974), pp. 1–2.

197. BA-MA, RH 53-7/627, Bl. 12, Auszug aus RGBl. 1935 Teil I, Seite 1334, § 5 (Erste Verordnung zum Reichsbürgergesetz).

198. Stoltzfus, *Resistance*, p. xxv; Kaplan, p. 191.

199. It seems that one reason why the term "non-Aryan" was not used in these new racial laws was to appease Nazi Germany's allies, such as Japan, who took offense at being labeled "non-Aryans." Pommerin, pp. 53–56, 67–69, 102–4; Yahil, p. 71.

200. *Heeresadjutant bei Hitler*, pp. 31–32.

201. BA-MA, BMRS, interview Peter Gaupp, 17.01.1995, T-87.

202. BA-MA, BMRS, interview Peter Gaupp, 27.04.1996, T-198.

203. Redlich, pp. 116, 320; Bauer, pp. 104, 121, 133.

204. Ian Kershaw, "Popular Opinion in the Third Reich," in *Government, Party, and People in Nazi Germany*, ed. Jeremy Noakes (Exeter, 1980), p. 70.

205. Ibid.

206. BA-MA, BMRS, general impressions gained from data collected; Avraham Barkai, "*Volksgemeinschaft*, 'Aryanization' and the Holocaust," in *Final Solution*, p. 37.

207. BA-MA, BMRS, interview Hans Koref, 06.01.1996, T-189.

208. *Kommentare zur Deutschen Rassengesetzgebung*, p. 15. This refers to Ezra, chapter 9 in the Bible, in which the prophet Ezra ordered mixed marriages broken up and all foreign women and children of mixed descent sent away. Some people, like Stuckart, believed that Ezra was racially minded by excluding non-Jews from the nation of Israel. However, Ezra seemed more motivated by a desire to keep the Jewish faith pure. He wanted to maintain the religion. That non-Jews like Ruth and Rahab could become a part of the Jewish community proved the point that Jews were accepting non-Jews when they embraced the Jewish religion (Ezra 8–10, NIV). Nonetheless, Ezra's policy was possibly one of religious discrimination.

209. BA-MA, BMRS, interview Hans Ranke, 09.12.1994, T-75.

210. Yahil, p. 6; *The Holocaust*, vol. 1, *Legalizing the Holocaust—The Early Phase, 1933–1939*, introduction by John Mendelsohn (New York, 1982), pp. 23–25.

211. *Akten der Parteikanzlei der NSDAP: Rekonstruktion eines verlorengegangenen Bestandes: Bundesarchiv, Microfiches*, ed. Institut für Zeitgeschichte, München, 1983, 101–28519, Bl. 90.

212. When historians refer to the Nuremberg Laws, they usually mean both the September laws and the supplementary decree from November 1935. This study follows this convention. See Bauer, p. 102.

213. BA-MA, Pers 6/2304 Admiral Conrad Patzig, Bl. 19. See O'Neill, chapter 5.

214. BA-MA, RW 6/56, Bl. 97.

215. Vogel, pp. 241–42.

216. *Handbuch VIII*, p. 58, "In einer Durchführungsverordnung zum Reichs-bürgergesetz vom 14.11.1935"; Messerschmidt, p. 140.

217. BA-MA, RW 6/73, v. Mackensen an Hitler, 03.12.1935.

218. Ibid., v. Mackensen an Blomberg, 11.01.1936.

219. Wheeler-Bennett, p. 342; Dr. James Corum is of the same opinion as Wheeler-Bennett. Discussion with the author on 28 February 2001.

220. BA-MA, BMRS, general impressions gained from data collected; O'Neill, pp. 75–77.

221. DDS, Pers Franz Mendelssohn.

222. BA-A, Pers 53059 Oberst Peter Sommer, Bl. 22, Generalkommando X. Armee-korps (Wehrkreiskom-man-do X) an OKH, 10.08.1936.

223. BA-MA, RL 14/49.

224. Victor, p. 9.

225. Noakes, "Development of Nazi Policy," pp. 323, 328.

226. BA-B, R 43 II/1275, Blomberg an Frick, 03.04.1936, Bl. 27, Blomberg an den Reichs- und Preußischen Minister des Innern, 03.04.1936; *Akten-NSDAP*, 101–22302, Blomberg an Lammers, 27.03.1936; Noakes, "Development of Nazi Policy," p. 329.

227. BA-B, R 43 II/1275, Blomberg an Lammers, 19.05.1936, Bl. 39, Blomberg an Lammers, 19.05.1936; *Akten-NSDAP* 101–22313, Blomberg an Lammers (countersigned by Keitel); BA-B, R 43 II/1275, Bl. 39; Vogel, p. 254.

228. BA-MA, RH 53–7/ 627, Bl. 25; O'Neill, p. 77. As translated in O'Neill.

229. BA-MA, RH 53–7/ 627, Bl. 25; Messerschmidt, p. 75.

230. Jürgen Förster, "Operation Barbarossa as a War of Conquest and Annihila-tion," in *Germany and the Second World War*, vol. 4, pp. 513–14; Deist in *Germany and the Second World War*, vol. 1 (Oxford, 1998), p. 522; O'Neill, pp. 44–45, 64–66, 70–71; Martin Kitchen, *Military History*, p. 285.

231. *Akten NSDAP*, 101–22299, Bl. 13; *Wehrgesetz* 05.03.1936; *Akten-NSDAP*, 101-22304, Bl. 44, Frick an Lammers 30.03.1936; BA-B, R 43 II/ 1275, Bl. 39, Keitel an Lammers, 18.05.1936, Bl. 37; Walk, pp. 115–16; Vogel, pp. 254–55.

232. BA-MA, BMRS, general impression gained from the data collected; Absolon, *Wehrgesetz und Wehrdienst*, p. 118; Vogel, p. 255.

233. Hertz, pp. 48–49.

234. Hertz, p. 24. At the official exchange rate at the time, eighty million Reichsmarks would equal twenty million dollars. Hilberg, p. 24, n. 22.
235. See chapter 3 on assimilation.
236. Kreisleiter was a district leader of the NSDAP.
237. Gauleiter was a regional leader of the NSDAP. Gauleiter was the second highest rank in the Party. The highest was the Reichsleiter. Benz, p. 90.
238. BA-MA, RH 53–7/514, Gauleitung Baden, Kreisleitung Mannheim an Wagner, 08.01.1936.
239. Ibid., Kommandierender General und Befehlshaber im Wehrkreis VII an Gauleiter der NSDAP, Gauleitung Baden, 20.03.1936.
240. Ibid., Stellv. Gauleiter, Gauleitung Baden an Reichenau, 13.07.1936.
241. BA-A, Pers 48220, Oberst Hans von Schlebrügge, Bl. 2, Dienstlaufbahn, and Bl. 68, Deutscher Verbindungsstab zum Kgl. Ung. AOK 1, Beurteilung über Oberst Hans v. Schlebrügge, 24.06.1944; Walther-Peer Fellgiebel, ed., *Die Träger des Ritterkreuzes des Eisernen Kreuzes, 1939–1945* (Friedberg, 1986).
242. BA-A, Pers 48220, Bl. 14.
243. The German Abwehr was the military intelligence service.
244. BA-MA, RW 6/56, Bl. 122–23.
245. Messerschmidt, pp. 75–76; O'Neill, p. 77.
246. BA-MA, BMRS, File Heinz-Jürgen Kühl, Bl. 1, Hans-Henning Zabel an Rigg, 25.06.1997; *Neue Deutsche Biographie,* ed. Historische Kommission der Bayerischen Akademie der Wissenschaften, Band 18, Familie Morgenstern, p. 110; Karl Friedrich Hildebrand, ed., *Die Generale der deutschen Luftwaffe, 1935–1945,* (Osnabrück, 1992), p. 265.
247. DDS, Pers Kapitän Arnold Techel; BA-MA, BMRS, interview Techel. See also Stoltzfus, *Resistance,* pp. 48–49.
248. BA-MA, RH 53–7/627, Bl. 2, Der Oberbefehlshaber des Heeres, vom 15.01.1936; O'Neill, pp. 76–77.
249. Walk, Gesetz vom 11.10.1936.
250. BA-MA, BMRS, interview Felix Bruck, 18.04.1998, T-422.
251. Oberschütze was a private. In practice, a *Mischlinge* was usually allowed to be promoted to Gefreiter.
252. Vogel, pp. 254–55.
253. Gefreiter was a private first class.
254. Klemperer, Buch I, 08.01.1939, p. 456.
255. BA-MA, RH 53–7/627.
256. BA-MA, RW 19/550; Walk, p. 231.
257. BA-MA, RH 53–7/627, Bl. 16, Generalkommando VII. Armeekorps (Wehrkreiskommando VII) an Kriegschule München, 24.01.1938. See also BA-MA, BMRS, File Hans Sander.
258. BA-MA, BMRS, File Karl Henle, Harald Henle to Rigg, 17.07.2001; BA-MA, BMRS, interview August Sohn, 17.05.1996, T-204; BA-MA, BMRS, File Franz Henle, Bl. 11, Sohn an Rigg, 05.04.1995, Bl. 30, Sohn an Rigg, 05.11.1995, Bl. 20, Sohn an Rigg, 30.06.1996. Henle came from a strong military back-

ground. His father, Franz, was a captain in the Bavarian army and received the EKII for his bravery in World War I. His uncle, Ernst, was also a captain in the Bavarian army and received the EKII and EKI for his bravery in World War I. His grandfather, Carl Henle, was an active officer in the Bavarian army. He served as a first lieutenant in the Königlich Bayrischen Infantrie Leibregiment. Henle's father, Franz, fearing the worst, committed suicide in 1944.

259. Kershaw, *Hitler, 1936–1945*, p. 52. There seems to be some confusion about Blomberg's wife's name. In Cooper's book on the German army, it is spelled Erna Grühn (the umlaut is false). In *Handbuch zur deutschen Militärgeschichte,* cited earlier, she is listed as Eva, which is wrong. In the *Gothaisches Genealogisches Taschenbuch der Adligen Häuser* from 1939, she is cited as Elsbeth Grunow. In the *Genealogisches Handbuch des Adels Bd. XVI* from 1985, she is listed as Margarethe (Elsbeth) Gruhn. In this section, Kershaw's version is used. Hitler's Luftwaffe adjutant, Nicolaus von Below, also mentions this problem about Frau Gruhn's name. Below, p. 62.

260. Hitler also felt embarrassed because he had been a witness at Blomberg's wedding. As Hitler said to his adjutant Fritz Wiedemann, "If a German Field-Marshal marries a whore, anything in the world is possible." Kershaw, *Hitler, 1936–1945*, pp. 52–53. See also Megargee, pp. 39–40.

261. Goerlitz, p. 319; Speer, p. 128; Keegan, *Second World War,* p. 38; Craig, *Germany, 1866–1945,* p. 700; Bracher, p. 308; Guderian, pp. 48–49, 436; O'Neill, p. 136; Kershaw, *Profiles in Power,* pp. 129, 133.

262. Alan Clark, *Barbarossa: The Russian-German Conflict, 1941–1945* (New York, 1965), p. 14; Craig, *Prussian Army, 1640–1945,* p. 495; RGBL,II, 04.02.1938.

263. Wilhelm Deist, in *Germany and the Second World War,* vol. 1 (Oxford, 1998), p. 521.

264. Ibid. See also O'Neill, p. 72.

265. Kershaw, *Hitler, 1936–1945,* p. 57.

266. Ibid., p. 188.

267. BA-MA, RW 6/56, Bl. 397–415, Vortrag von Admiral Canaris bei der Ic-Besprechung im OKW am 03.03.1938, Bl. 400–402. Some have suggested that maybe Canaris said this because he knew Nazi informers would report back on his activities if they felt he did not support Hitler. Those who believe that Canaris really did not believe what he said here cite his later actions against Hitler. No one really knows what Canaris really believed about Hitler and the Third Reich.

268. Kershaw, *Hitler, 1936–1945,* pp. 78–86; Stoltzfus, *Resistance,* pp. 89–93.

269. BA-MA, RH 15/419, Bl. 21, OKW (Keitel) an OKH, OKM, OKL, 03.11.1938; BA-MA, RH 53-7/627, Bl. 14.

270. Vienna, according to the historian Ian Kershaw, was "one of the most virulently anti-Jewish cities in Europe." Kershaw, *Hitler, 1889–1936,* p. 65. See also Friedländer, p. 241; Bauer, pp. 105–6; Evan Burr Bukey, *Hitler's Austria: Popular Sentiment in the Nazi Era* (North Carolina, 2000).

271. BA-MA, BMRS, Dokumente Heft 8, Erwin Mairamhof an Martin Senekowitsch, 14.09.1995, Matzling, Ruhestandsversetzungen am 15.März 1938; Schmidl, p. 149; Deák, p. 210.

272. Ibid., Oberstlt. Georg Bartl: KZ Dachau, KZ Mauthausen, Freitod; Oberstlt. Ferdinand Celar: Haft; Oberstlt. Mathias Gruber: Haft; Oberstlt. Franz Heckenast: KZ Buchenwald, gest. 1939; Hauptmann Franz Kaiser: Haft; Gen. Maj. Karl Kotik: in Haft verstorben; Major Marioncovich: in Haft gestorben; und Gen. der. Inf. Wilhelm Zehner: 1938 angeblich ermordet.

273. Schmidl, p. 149.

274. BA-MA, BMRS, File Dieter fischer, Heft II, Amelis von Mettenheim, *Die Zwölf Langen Jahre 1933–1945*, Bl. 9.

275. Gilbert, *Holocaust*, p. 60; Kaplan, p. 180.

276. BA-MA, BMRS, File Yosef Getreuer, Bl. 1, Yosef Getreuer to Rigg, 18.03.1997.

277. From now on, German means German and Austrian.

278. Navy high command.

279. Luftwaffe high command.

280. BA-MA, RH 15/421, Bl. 21–22, OKW-Keitel an OKH, OKM, OKL, 03.11.1938.

281. BA-MA, BMRS, interview Braun, 10–14.08.1994, T-10; BA-MA, BMRS, interview Braun, 07.01.1996, T-190.

282. BA-MA, RH 15/421, Bl. 22, OKW (Keitel), "Vorstehender Erlaß wird bekanntgegeben" 23.11.1938.

283. BA-MA, Wi VIII/ 45, 18.10.1938.

284. BA-MA, RH 53–7/8, Bl. 88; IfZ, N 71–73; BA-MA, RH 39/222, Beauftragter für den Vierjahresplan—Schnellbrief an Reichsminister des Innern, Reichswirtschaftsminister, die übrigen Reichsminister, 28.12.1938. In practice, this study has found that both types of intermarriages experienced certain privileges during the Third Reich, especially when a son was in the Wehrmacht.

285. Redlich, p. 116; Kaplan, p. 80.

286. BA-MA, RH 53–7/627, Bl. 11–12, Hitler an OKH, OKM, OKL, 20.01.1939; BA-MA, RM 92/5173, Bl. 141.

287. Besondere Marine-Bestimmungen (B.M.B.), 5.Jahrg., Blatt 12 v. 20.09.1939, 138. "Jüdische Mischlinge in der Wehrwirtschaft" Ziff.2.), p. 159 f.

288. Office of the United States Chief Counsel for Prosecution of Axis Criminality, ed., *Nazi Conspiracy and Aggression*, vol. 2 (Washington, D.C., 1946), p. 869; Messerschmidt, p. 78. Although it is true that people's speech in public is often different from how they act in private, Raeder's speech did not have to talk about the Jews as he did. He simply could have spoken about the German fallen and veterans of World War I.

289. Gilbert, *Holocaust*, p. 76.

290. Lucy Dawidowicz, ed., *A Holocaust Reader* (New Jersey, 1976), pp. 57, 72–74.

291. Aschheim, pp. 143–45, 150–51. Jürgen Matthäus, "German *Judenpolitik* in Lithuania during the First World War," in *Leo Baeck Yearbook* 43 (1998): 162–64; Trude Maurer, *Ostjuden in Deutschland, 1918–1933* (Hamburg, 1986), pp. 26–28.

292. BA-MA, BMRS, interview Heinz Günter Angreß, 10.12.1994, T-78.

293. Ahasverus, Wandering Jew *(Ewiger Jude)*, was a medieval invention. Supposedly, this tale describes the Jew Ahasverus's curse for jeering at Jesus on the way to his Crucifixion. Consequently, according to the myth, God cursed him with eternal wandering and an unhappy life until "death should finally redeem him at the Last Judgement." Paul Lawrence Rose, *German Question/Jewish Question: Revolutionary Anti-Semitism from Kant to Wagner* (Princeton, 1990), pp. 23–24; Friedländer, pp. 196–97. The Nazis used *Ewiger Jude* in their anti-Semitic propaganda films and literature to show the racial inferiority of Jewry. Ahasverus should not be confused with the biblical king of Persia and Media. Trepp, pp. 158–60; Miles, pp. 357, 359–62.

294. BA-MA, BMRS, File Hans Mühlbacher, Bl. 52, Tagebuch, Teil V, 14.05.1941.

295. Landser was the ordinary German infantryman of World War II.

296. BA-MA, BMRS, interview Friedrich Schlesinger, 10.12.1994, T-77.

297. See BA-MA, BMRS, interview Braun, 10–14.08.1994, T-10; BA-MA, BMRS, interview Braun, 07.01.1996, T-190; BA-MA, BMRS, interview Michael Günther, 19.02.1997, T-308; BA-MA, BMRS, interview Hans B. (Bernheim), 29.10.1998, T-428. BA-MA, BMRS, interview Hermann Aub, 14.12. 1996, T-275. See also Gilbert, *Holocaust,* p. 90.

298. Not his real name.

299. BA-MA, BMRS, interview Bernheim.

300. Krüger, p. 66; BA-MA, BMRS, interview Krüger.

301. BA-MA, BMRS, general impressions gained from data collected; BA-MA, BMRS, File Joachim Leidloff, Teil II, Bl. 7a, Tagebucheintragung v. 17.09.1940 und 04.10.1940.

302. Ordinary soldier (artillery).

303. BA-MA, BMRS, File Brücher, Tagebuch, Bl. 17–18.

304. BA-MA, BMRS, File Brücher, Tagebuch, Bl. 18. One night while riding his motorcycle as the battery messenger, two Polish soldiers intercepted Florey. Shocked, Florey jumped up. At that moment, one of the soldiers shoved his bayonet into Florey. Fortunately for Florey, he was able to escape and only suffered a flesh wound. Florey received the Wound Badge. BA-MA, BMRS, File Klaus Florey, Florey to Rigg, 15.07.2001.

305. BA-MA, BMRS, File Brücher, Schlike to Brücher, 21.11.1939.

306. Stabsgefreiter (administrative private first class) is the equivalent of an E-4 in the U.S. Army. It was basically a consolation prize.

307. BA-MA, BMRS, File Fritz Steinwasser, *Autobiographie,* p. 71; BA-MA, BMRS, interview Fritz Steinwasser, 13.12.1994, T-79; BA-MA, BMRS, interview Fritz Steinwasser, 07.02.1997, T-302.

308. In the case of the Günther family, Michael's grandmother, Gertrud Hensel née Hahn, was 100 percent Jewish. Her husband, Kurt Hensel, had three Jewish grandparents, but his grandfather, Wilhelm Hensel (a famous painter), was a non-Jew. Because of this Aryan grandparent, some civil servants classified Michael and his siblings as quarter-Jews. From the data collected for this study, they should have been classified as half-Jews. This is especially the case, since they had two grandparents who were racially Jewish.

309. BA-MA, BMRS, File Konrad Schenck, Heft I, Bl. 6.

310. Günther had passed his *Abitur,* or high school diploma, which was a requirement to become an officer.

311. BA-MA, BMRS, File Achim von Bredow, Heft I, Bl. 34, Achim an Ada,
25.08.1942.

312. Ibid., Heft I, Bl. 34.

313. Kershaw, *Hitler, 1936–1945,* p. 131; Bauer, p. 107; Benz, p. 26; Bering,
p. 145.

314. BA-MA, BMRS, general impressions gained from interviewees.

315. From 1903 until 1918, Clara von Mettenheim was married to Lieutenant
Colonel Erwin Fischer. Fischer was the chief of the General Staff of the army
Abteilung (an *Abteilung* was a formation larger than a corps but smaller than
an army) under General Strantz during World War I.

316. The crown prince had many Jewish friends—something that irritated Goebbels.
See *Goebbels Diaries, 1942–1943,* pp. 47–48.

317. BA-MA, BMRS, File Dieter Fischer, Heft I, Bl. 42.

318. She had to go to the *Judenstelle* of the Gestapo to get the large red *J* stamped
in her identification papers and add Sara to her name as prescribed by Nazi
law.

319. BA-MA, BMRS, File Dieter Fischer, Heft I, Bl. 42.

320. BA-MA, BMRS, File Fischer, Heft I, Bl. 41, OKH an Clara v. Mettenheim,
16.12.1939.

321. Ibid., Heft I, Bl. 39–41, Keitel an Prof. v. Mettenheim, 24.12.1939.

322. The General Wehrmacht Office was the Allgemeines Wehrmachtamt (AWA).

323. BA-MA, BMRS, File Fischer, Heft I, Bl. 41, Reinecke an Clara v. Mettenheim,
16.01.1940.

324. HVBl., Nr. 131, 1940, p. 42. This order seemed to be given to most units. See
BA-MA, BMRS, File Heinz Georg Heymann, "Meldung des Flak-Ersatz-
Depots," Ende Februar 1940.

325. BA-B, DZA, Bl. 200, Aktennotiz, 14.02.1940.

326. Rudolf Absolon, *Die Wehrmacht im Dritten Reich. Band V 1. September 1939
bis 18. Dezember 1941, (=Schriften des Bundesarchivs 16/V)* (Boppard, 1988),
p. 148.

327. Absolon, *Die Wehrmacht im Dritten Reich. Band V,* p. 148; Absolon, *Wehrgesetz
und Wehrdienst,* p. 118, n. 26; Messerschmidt, p. 358.

328. Kershaw, *Profiles in Power,* pp. 142–43.

329. BA-MA, BMRS, File Wolfram Günther, Bl. 22–23.

330. For more information on Willy Rohr, see Bruce I. Gudmundsson, *Stormtroop
Tactics: Innovation in the German Army, 1914–1918* (London, 1995); Timothy
T. Lupfer, *The Dynamics of Doctrine: The Changes in German Tactical Doc-
trine during the First World War* (Fort Leavenworth, 1981), pp. 27–28.

331. BA-B, DZA 62 Ka. 1 83, Bl. 200, Aktennotiz, Vorsprache beim OKW,
14.02.1940; Heinz Rohr, *Geschichte einer Lübecker Familie* (Hamburg,
1994), p. 86; IfZ, N 71–73, 27.05.1941, Anträge und positive Entscheidungen
gemäß §7 der Ersten Verordnung zum Reichsbürgergesetz.

332. BA-B, DZA 62 Ka. 1 83, Bl. 200–200b.

CHAPTER 5: THE POLICY TOWARD *MISCHLINGE* TIGHTENS,
1940–1943

1. BA-MA, BMRS, File Fischer, Bl. 37. Grüber helped many converted and unconverted Jews and was eventually sent to a concentration camp for his activities. He survived the war. Bauer, p. 135.

2. Viktor Brack worked in the notorious T-4 office in the KdF that dealt with
the euthanasia program. On 1 September 1939, Hitler signed a document that
authorized Bouhler and Brandt in the KdF to murder those deemed unworthy to live. Brack was Bouhler's deputy.

3. BA-B, DZA 62 Ka. 1 83, Bl. 198, "Aktennotiz für Reichsamtsleiter Brack."

4. Klemperer, Buch I, 11.08.1940, p. 546.

5. BA-B, DZA 62 Ka. 1 83, Bl. 125–26, Blankenburg an Engel, 28.03.1940.

6. Ibid., Bl. 126, Blankenburg an Engel, 28.03.1940.

7. Ibid., Bl. 116, "Aktennotiz" von Brack, 10.07.1942.

8. BA-B, DZA 62 Ka. 1 83, Bl. 192, OKW Az. 12 i 10–20 J (Jc) Nr. 524/40;
BA-MA, RH 7/v. 23; Walk, p. 319; BA-MA, RW 19/853, Bl. 1–2. According
to Rolf Vogel, Jesuit priests and members of former dynastic families of Germany were also discharged. Vogel, p. 256.

9. Vogel, p. 256.

10. BA-B, DZA 62 Ka. 1 83, Bl. 155–56, Blankenburg an Engel, 23.05.1942, and
Bl. 67, "Aktennotiz, IIb/Schr. Jüdische Mischlinge im Wehrdienst", 28.10.1943.

11. BA-B, DZA 62 Ka. 1 83, Bl. 26; BA-B, DZA 62 Ka. 1 83, Bl. 192, OKW Az.
12 i 10–20 J (Jc) Nr. 524/40; BA-MA, RH 7/ v. 23. See also Lösener, p. 310.

12. BA-MA, BMRS, File Du Bois-Reymond, Bl. 5, Lona Du Bois-Reymond to
Rigg, 07.04.1997, and for a similar case, see BA-MA, BMRS, File Helmuth
Baum.

13. BA-B, DZA 62 Ka. 1 83, Bl. 67, "Jüdische Mischlinge im Wehrdienst," Vf.:
Blankenburg; BA-B, DZA 62 Ka. 1 83, Bl. 89, Aktennotiz v. Parteikanzlei II
B 4, 20.10.1942.

14. BA-MA, RH 7/v. 23, OKH, Nr. 2761/40 g PA 2 (Ic), 20.04.1940; Walk,
p. 320; BA-MA, BMRS, general data collected on half-Jews.

15. This in fact would happen to Bamberger. On the night of 6 June 1940,
Bamberger prevented a French attack from taking out his sleeping company.
His officer, Lieutenant Schmidt, praised him and told him that had he not been
a *Mischling*, he would have mentioned his name to the regiment and awarded
him a medal for his bravery. BA-MA, BMRS, File Bamberger, Bl. 30; BA-MA,
BMRS, interview Heinrich Bamberger, 08.11.1994, T-49.

16. BA-MA, BMRS, File Heinrich Bamberger, Bl. 22; BA-MA, BMRS, interview
Bamberger.

17. BA-MA, BMRS, File Horst Geitner, Bl. 3–4, 14–15; BA-MA, BMRS, interview Horst Geitner, 38.03.1997, T-337. Tragically, as Geitner served on the
front lines, his sister, uncle, and aunt were all sent to Auschwitz. They did not
survive the war. After the war, Geitner entered the Bundeswehr. He served as
a first lieutenant and wanted to prove to others and himself that he was worthy
of the rank. Others did the same. See BA-MA, BMRS, File Rolf Vogel; BA-MA,
BMRS, interview Frau Rolf Vogel, 18.03.1995, T-124.

18. BA-MA, BMRS, general impression gained from the interviewees.

19. BA-MA, BMRS, File Fischer, Heft I, Bl. 84, Pfarrer Grüber an Clara von Mettenheim, 29.05.1940; BA-MA, BMRS, interview Dieter Fischer, 12.12.1996, T-270.

20. This fact strongly contradicts the theory put out by the Wehrmachtsaustellung that all German officers were supportive of the Nazi regime and strong supporters of Hitler's. See Heer and Reemtsma, *Vernichtungskrieg.*

21. BA-MA, BMRS, interview Techel.

22. BA-MA, BMRS, interview Lüderitz.

23. BA-MA, BMRS, File Gerd zu Klampen, Bl. 1; BA-MA, BMRS, interview Gerd zu Klampen, 28.10.1998, T-427. See also BA-MA, BMRS, File Meissinger, Bl. 3.

24. BA-MA, BMRS, File Hans Günzel, Bl. 4, Marion Freuh an Rigg, 05.04.1997; BA-MA, BMRS, interview Hans Günzel, 23–24.07.1997, T-387.

25. BA-MA, BMRS, interview Braun, 10–14.08.1994, T-10; BA-MA, BMRS, interview Braun, 07.01.1996, T-190.

26. BA-MA, BMRS, interview Techel.

27. Schütze was an ordinary soldier.

28. BA-MA, BMRS, interview Joachim Le Coutre, 25.01.1997, T-389; BA-MA, BMRS, File Joachim Le Coutre, Joachim Le Coutre an Rigg, 09.04.1997. For a similar case, see BA-MA, BMRS; File Heinz Günther Angreß.

29. BA-MA, BMRS, interview Wolfgang Behrendt, 21.11.1994, T-58; BA-MA, BMRS, interview Goldberg; BA-MA; BMRS, File Meissinger, Bl. 3; BA-MA, BMRS, interview Meissinger.

30. BA-MA, BMRS, interview Krüger; BA-MA, BMRS, File Meissinger, Bl. 3.

31. BA-MA, BMRS, interview Wolfgang Spier, 06.12.1994, T-70.

32. Interestingly, one day while having an argument, a comrade called Gaupp a "*Saujud* (Jewish pig)" in front of many of their fellow soldiers. Gaupp reported this instance to his lieutenant, who then reported it to the captain, the company commander. The captain later met with Gaupp and asked him whether he wanted the man to make his apology privately or publicly. Gaupp asked that it be done privately. The captain then made this man do as he had promised Gaupp. Ironically, this comrade would become one of Gaupp's best friends. As Gaupp said, "[T]he whole time is full of puzzles." BA-MA, BMRS, interview Gaupp, 17.01.1995, T-87; BA-MA, BMRS, interview Gaupp, 27.04.1996, T-198.

33. BA-MA, BMRS, interview Gaupp, 17.01.1995, T-87; BA-MA, BMRS, interview Gaupp, 27.04.1996, T-198. According to Gaupp, the rejection letter was signed by Keitel.

34. BA-MA, BMRS, interview Christoph-Michael Salinger, 08.10.1998, T-424. Salinger takes the phrase at the end from the Bible where Jesus says, "Father, forgive them, for they do not know what they are doing." Jesus said this about those who crucified him. Luke 23:34 NIV.

35. BA-MA, BMRS, interview Braun, 10–14.08.1994, T-10; BA-MA, BMRS, interview Braun, 11.03.1995, T-118; BA-MA, BMRS, interview Braun, 07.01.1996, T-190. See also BA-MA, BMRS, File Meissinger, Bl. 3.

36. BA-MA, BMRS, interview Gerd Grimm, 24.09.1994, C-26; BA-MA, BMRS, interview Gerd Grimm, 09.01.1996, T-194.
37. BA-MA, BMRS, interview Schlesinger.
38. Unlike in the United States, it is quite common in Germany for organizations to write a recommendation when someone has fulfilled a certain task. Germans are obsessed with certificates.
39. BA-B, R 21 (76)/878, Bl. 141, "Bescheinigung von Oberleutnant und Kompaniechef Mertes", 17.07.1941.
40. BA-MA, BMRS, interview Hildegard von Gierke, 29.11.1997, T-413.
41. BA-MA, BMRS, interview Riess. *Mazel tov* means "good luck" in Hebrew. Riess witnessed the execution of French Senegalese soldiers at the Somme River from the fourth through the eighth of June 1940.
42. BA-MA, BMRS, interview Karl-Heinz Scheffler, 09.03.1995, T-113.
43. BA-MA, BMRS, interview Wilhelmina Benasuli, 19.01.1997, T-284.
44. BA-MA, BMRS, File Heinz Bleicher, "Wie ich den 8. Mai 1945 erlebte: Ein persönlicher Bericht eines Betroffenen." See also BA-MA, BMRS, interview Egon Bahr, 13.02.1995, T-95.
45. Funker is an ordinary soldier (signal).
46. BA-MA, BMRS, File Ferdinand Lichtwitz, Heft I, Teil II, Bl. 11. See also Creveld, p. 163, n. 2.
47. BA-MA, BMRS, File Bergmann, Heft II, 06.09.1940.
48. See chapters 7 and 8 on exemptions.
49. Over 60 percent of the half-Jews documented in this study fell after 1941.
50. BA-MA, BMRS, interview Bahr. The rations allotted to German Jews were "considerably fewer" than what was given to Aryans. Benz, p. 41. Also these ration cards were stamped with the word *Jew*, making it difficult for them to shop at certain stores. Kaplan, p. 151.
51. Kaplan, pp. 150–52. Jews usually had only one hour a day in which to shop for food.
52. Regional Party Office.
53. BA-MA, BMRS, File Walter Hamburger, B. Hamburger an Rigg, 15.12.2000; BA-MA, BMRS, File Hamburger, Hamburger an Rigg, 25.11.2000. See also BA-MA, BMRS, File Werner Brück, Bl. 134; BA-MA, BMRS, interview Krüger.
54. Krüger, p. 69.
55. BA-MA, BMRS, File Brücher, Tagebuch, 01.09.1939, Bl. 2.
56. BA-MA, BMRS, File Hans Christian Lankes, Tagebuch, 1939, Bl. 41.
57. BA-MA, BMRS, File Bergmann, Heft III, 09.06.1940.
58. Ibid., Heft II, Bl. 6–7, 02.08.1940.
59. Ibid., Bl. 77, 22.08.1940.
60. Kaplan, p. 160.
61. BA-MA, BMRS, interview Lux.
62. BA-MA, BMRS, interview Bergmann.
63. BA-MA, BMRS, File Karl-Arnd Techel, Tagebuch, 23–30.04.1941; BA-MA, BMRS, interview Techel. See also BA-MA, BMRS, File Hans Sander, Teil II,

Tagebuch, 1939, Bl. 16. See Schmidt, *Politischer Rückblick auf eine unpolitische Jugend, in: Kindheit und Jugend unter Hitler* (Berlin, 1994), p. 221.

64. BA-MA, BMRS, File Christian Rosenthal, Bl. 3; BA-MA, BMRS, interview Partsch.

65. BA-MA, BMRS, interview Gert Ascher, 17.11.1997, T-408; BA-MA, BMRS, interview Ursula Ascher, 17.11.1997, T-409; Kennedy, p. 30; Dudley Pope, *The Battle of the River Plate* (Maryland, 1987), pp. 9, 97, 185.

66. BA-MA, BMRS, File Bergmann, Heft III, Bl. 9, 02.08.1940.

67. BA-MA, BMRS, interview Bergmann.

68. BA-MA, BMRS, interview Hans Meissinger, 17.09.1996, T-216; BA-MA, BMRS, File Meissinger, Meissinger to Rigg, 29.10.2000.

69. BA-B, DZA 62 Ka. 1 83, Bl. 67, 116, "Aktennotiz in Blankenburgs Büro, nach Besprechung mit Engel," 10.07.1942.

70. BA-B, DZA 62 Ka. 1 83, Bl. 123, 190–91, Oberst Schmundt an Reichsleiter Bouhler, 02.10.1940.

71. BA-B, DZA 62 Ka. 1 83, Bl. 184, Blankenburg an Lösener, 18.12.1940; BA-B, R 21/448, Bl. 18.

72. BA-B, R 21/448, Bl. 18. See also Noakes, "Development of Nazi Policy," p. 349.

73. BA-MA, BMRS, interview Beelitz; BA-MA, BMRS, interview Otto Wolters, 18.03.1995, T-123; BA-MA, BMRS, interview Otto Wolters, 06.12.1996, T-252; BA-B, NS 18/482.

74. BA-MA, BMRS, interview Otto Wolters. See also Krüger, pp. 94, 107.

75. Bernhard Kroener, "Die Personellen Ressourcen des Dritten Reiches im Spannungsfeld zwischen Wehrmacht, Bürokratie und Kriegswirtschaft, 1939–1942," in *Das Deutsche Reich und der zweite Weltkrieg. Kriegsverwaltung, Wirtschaft und personelle Ressourcen, 1939–1941*, vol. 5/1 (Stuttgart, 1988), Teil III. p. 834.

76. Bernhard Kroener, in *Das Deutsche Reich und der zweite Weltkrieg. Kriegsverwaltung, Wirtschaft und Personelle Ressourcen, 1939–1941*, vol. 5/1, pp. 833–38; Seaton, *German Army*, pp. 145, 158; Kershaw, *Profiles in Power*, p. 153; Weinberg, *Germany, Hitler*, pp. 158–59; Megargee, p. 130; Keegan, *Mask of Command*, p. 261.

77. Weinberg, *Germany, Hitler*, p. 161.

78. Clark, p. 20. See also O'Neill, p. 135.

79. Jürgen Förster, "Hitler's Decision in Favor of War against the Soviet Union," in *Germany and the Second World War*, vol. 4 (Oxford, 1998), p. 13. See also Redlich, p. 158; Kershaw, *Hitler, 1936–1945*, p. 311.

80. Office of the United States Chief Counsel for Prosecution of Axis Criminality, ed., *U.S.A. Military Tribunals: Case No. 12—German Generals* (Nuremberg, 1949), p. 10,120.

81. Luftgaukommando VI was the VI Luftwaffe regional office.

82. BA-MA, RL 14/49, Luftgaukommando VI, Betr.: Nachweis der deutschblütigen Abstammung und Beförderungen, 08.01.1941.

83. IfZ, N 71–73; Lösener.

84. IfZ, Eichmann Prosecution Document, Police d'Israel Quartier General 6-ème Bureau No. 1355, Bl. 1–2, Betrifft: Verbot der Eheschließung mit Juden— Der Generalkommissar für das Sicherheitswesen an den Reichskommissar v. 18.08.1941, 19.09.1941.

85. *Endlösung* (Final Solution) was the cover name for the systematic extermination of European Jews under Nazi control. See Gideon Hausner, *Justice in Jerusalem* (New York, 1966), p. 95.

86. IfZ, Eichmann Prosecution Document, Police d'Israel Quartier General 6-ème Bureau No. 1355, Bl. 1–2.

87. BA-MA, BMRS, File Fischer, Heft I, Bl. 85–86, "Deutsches Ärzteblatt," Nr. 14/71, 05.04.1941, Generaloberstabsarzt Prof. Dr. Anton Waldmann, "Wege zur Lösung der Judenfrage," pp. 155–57.

88. Walter Groß, *Die rassenpolitischen Voraussetzungen zur Lösung der Judenfrage* (München, 1943), pp. 28–32; Uwe Adam, *Judenpolitik im Dritten Reich* (Düsseldorf, 1972), pp. 319–20; Adler, *Der Verwaltete Mensch*, p. 282.

89. State of Israel Ministry of Justice, ed., *The Trial of Adolf Eichmann: Record of Proceedings in the District Court of Jerusalem*, vol. 5 (Jerusalem, 1992), Session 118–119, p. 2,170. See also Hausner, pp. 102–3.

90. IfZ, N 71–73, Aufzeichnung Dr. Lösener, 04.12.1941.

91. BA-B, DZA 62 Ka. 1 83, Bl. 180 Lammers an Reichsminister des Innern, 04.03.1941; Walk, p. 336.

92. BA-MA, BMRS, interview Maria-Anna van Menxel, 22.04.1995, T-150.

93. BA-MA, BMRS, File Hans Mühlbacher, *1941–1945. Im Zeitalter der Gestapo,* Erinnerungen von Olga Mühlbacher, Teil II, Bl. 6.

94. Büttner, p. 287.

95. A translation of *Arisierung* is "Aryanization." It seems this term for a *Befreiung* (exemption) happened most often between 1935 and 1938. See BA-MA, BMRS, File Ludwig Ganghofer. This term of *Arisierung* should not be confused with the other Aryanization the Nazis conducted, which forced Jewish business owners to sell their property to Aryans or forced Aryan businesses to rid themselves of any Jewish employees. See Hilberg, pp. 60–90.

96. BA-MA, BMRS, File Hans Mühlbacher, *1941–1945. Im Zeitalter der Gestapo,* Erinnerungen von Olga Mühlbacher, Teil II, Bl. 16.

97. Yahil, p. 250; Dallin, p. 30, n. 2.

98. Seaton, *German Army*, pp. 129, 161, 200.

99. Absolon, *Die Wehrmacht im Dritten Reich. Band V*, p. 150.

100. The first sergeant was the Kompaniefeldwebel; among the soldiers he was known as the "Spieß"—a popular slang word for "sarge."

101. BA-MA, BMRS, interview Wolfgang Voigt, 09.04.1995, T-137; BA-MA, BMRS, File Wolfgang Voigt.

102. BA-MA, BMRS, interview Felix Bruck, 18.04.1998, T-422.

103. BA-MA, N 656/27, Bl.2, Hans Dieter Henning an Lebram, 30.06.1977; BA-MA, N 379/87, speech from Vice Admiral Ruge, 11.11.60; BA-MA, File Bernhard Rogge, Heft III, Bl. 69; Raeder, p. 111.

104. BA-MA, BMRS, interview Horst von Oppenfeld, 05.01.1995, T-84; Klemperer, Buch II, p. 212; BA-MA, BMRS, File Heinz Schlieper, Bl. 9; BA-MA, BMRS,

interview Ruth Rilk, 05.02.1997, T-298; BA-MA, BMRS, File Borchardt; BA-MA, BMRS, File Otto Buchinger; BA-MA, BRMS, interview Robert Czempin, 09.02.1995, T-89; Klemperer, Buch II, 18.08.1942.

105. BA-MA, BMRS, interview Horst von Oppenfeld, 05.01.1995, T-84. According to Oppenfeld, the only time he had to concern himself with his ancestry was in 1938 when someone, probably in the Party, denounced him. He was required to go to a Wehrkreis officer in Stettin to examine his ancestry. When the official, a veteran of World War I, saw that his father and three uncles were World War I veterans and that two of them had died in action, the official said something like "*Unsinn* (nonsense)," closed his file, and dismissed him. Oppenfeld never heard about his ancestry again. He probably remained an officer either because he continued to fall under the Hindenburg exemptions of the *Arierparagraph* or because someone was protecting him. According to Manstein's adjutant, Alexander Stahlberg, Stauffenberg was responsible for helping Oppenfeld. Also, Oppenfeld's father, Rittmeister (captain in the cavalry) Moritz von Oppenfeld, was the adviser for agriculture and food security attached to headquarters staff of Hindenburg and Ludendorff during World War I. Oppenfeld feels that his father's service under Hindenburg must have helped him tremendously.

106. Meyer, p. 236.

107. Wallach, p. 282.

108. BA-MA, BMRS, File Oppenfeld, Oppenfeld an Rigg, 16.12.2000. See also Seaton, *German Army*, p. 197.

109. Samuel W. Mitcham Jr., *Rommel's Greatest Victory: The Desert Fox and the Fall of Tobruk, Spring of 1942* (Novato, 1998), pp. 114–15. See also Paul Carell, *The Foxes of the Desert* (New York, 1961), p. 181.

110. BA-MA, BMRS, interview Riess.

111. BA-MA, BMRS, File Hans Mühlbacher; BA-MA, BMRS, File Meissinger; BA-MA, BMRS, interview Mühlbacher; BA-MA, BMRS, interview Meissinger. Meissinger worked for NASA after the war.

112. BA-MA, BMRS, File Mühlbacher; BA-MA, BMRS, interview Mühlbacher.

113. German Research Institute for Aviation.

114. BA-MA, BMRS, File Meissinger, 19.07.2001.

115. BA-MA, BMRS, interview Kurt Hohenemser, 28.11.1994, T-62. This Hohenemser is not to be confused with Kurt Heinrich Hohenemser, a quarter-Jew who during World War II helped design the first German combat helicopters. One of these helicopters, the F1 282 *Kolibri,* was used on reconnaissance and antisubmarine patrols from platforms on convoy escort vessels in the Aegean, Mediterranean, and Baltic Seas. BA-MA, BMRS, File Kurt Heinrich Hohenemser.

116. Krüger, pp. 81–83.

117. BA-MA, BMRS, interview Dietmar Brücher, 17.02.1995, T-99; Dietmar Brücher's personal archive, Photoalbum; BA-MA, BMRS, File Bergmann, Heft I, Tagebuch, 28–29.09.1941.

118. *Ersatzreserve II* or *Landwehr II*. See BA-B, DZA 62 Ka. 1 83, Bl. 155, Blankenburg an Engel, 23.05.1942; BA-MA, RH 7/23.

119. BA-MA, BMRS, from the data collected on half-Jews. See Absolon, *Wehrgesetz und wehrdienst*, pp. 118–19; *Sammlung wehrrechtlicher Gutachten und Vorschriften*, Heft 20/21, p. 174; *Sammlung wehrrechtlicher Gutachten und Vorschriften*, Heft 4, p. 73; Vogel, p. 257.

120. Absent without leave.

121. Lang, "Writing Holocaust," in *Holocaust Remembrance*. See also Vuletic, p. 33.

122. *The Holocaust: 2. Legalizing the Holocaust—The Later Phase, 1939–1943*, introduction by John Mendelsohn (New York, 1982), Bl. 249, Pfundtner an Stellvertreter des Führers, 07.05.1941. Apparently the Nuremberg Laws from 1935, which prohibited sexual relations between half-Jews and Aryans, were not being followed.

123. Hilberg, p. 262; Peterson, p. 30.

124. The SD (Sicherheitsdienst) was the security and intelligence service of the SS.

125. Yahil, p. 249; Seaton, *German Army*, p. 169; Jürgen Förster, "Operation Barbarossa as a War of Conquest and Annihilation," in *Germany and the Second World War*, vol. 4, p. 491; Browning, *Nazi Policy, Jewish Workers, German Killers*, p. 3.

126. Jürgen Förster, "Operation Barbarossa as a War of Conquest and Annihilation," in *Germany and the Second World War*, vol. 4, p. 514. See also Jürgen Förster, "Securing 'Living-space,'" in *Germany and the Second World War*, vol. 4, pp. 1,193, 1,210–11; Dawidowicz, *War against Jews*, p. 124; Omer Bartov, "Operation Barbarossa and the Final Solution," in *The Final Solution*, p. 120.

127. Jürgen Förster, "Securing 'Living-space,'" in *Germany and the Second World War*, vol. 4, pp. 1,227–29, 1,233; Jürgen Förster, "Operation Barbarossa in Historical Perspective," in *Germany and the Second World War*, vol. 4, p. 1,249.

128. Jürgen Förster, "Securing 'Living-space,'" in *Germany and the Second World War*, vol. 4, pp. 1,225; Jürgen Förster, in *Die Wehrmacht*, p. 953; Dallin, pp. 30–34; Omer Bartov, *Hitler's Army* (New York, 1991), pp. 84–88; Dawidowicz, War against Jews, pp. 123–24; Kershaw, *Profiles in Power*, pp. 154–55; Weinberg, *Germany Hitler*, pp. 162–63; Messerschmidt, pp. 398–407; Wilhelm Deist, *Militär, Staat und Gesellschaft. Studien zur preußisch-deutschen Militärgeschichte* (München, 1991), pp. 380–84. Although no one protested this order, there are documented cases of officers simply not enforcing the decree once hostilities between Germany and the Soviet Union started. See Burleigh, p. 520.

129. *Barbarossa* ("Red Beard") was the code name for the German attack on the Soviet Union on 22 June 1941. This battle plan was named after Frederick I *(von Staufen)* or Frederick Barbarossa (1123–1190), holy Roman emperor and German king.

130. Craig, *Germany, 1866–1945*, pp. 729–30.

131. Jürgen Förster, "Operation Barbarossa as a War of Conquest and Annihilation," in *Germany and the Second World War*, vol. 4, p. 483.

132. Wilhelm Deist, in *Die Wehrmacht*, p. 45; Burleigh, p. 520.

133. Wallach, p. 266; Megargee, pp. 73, 80.

134. Percy Ernst Schramm, *Hitler: The Man and the Military Leader* (Chicago, 1971), p. 198.

135. Gerhard L. Weinberg, *A World at Arms* (New York, 1994), p. 170.

136. BA-MA, N 39/62, Bl. 47–49, v. Mackensen, "Wie ich zu Adolf Hitler gekommen bin," v. 16.12.1939, abgeschlossen am 01.02.1942.

137. These SS units were special killing squads used to locate and exterminate Jews and commissars.

138. Paul Gordon Lauren, *Power and Prejudice* (London, 1988), pp. 129–30.

139. Gilbert, *Second World War*, p. 207. In the first five weeks, the Germans murdered over thirty thousand Jews.

140. BA-MA, BMRS, File Franz and Thomas Haller, Bl. 19–22. Schmundt probably believed, as Hitler did, that the Soviet leadership was and had been controlled by Jews (i.e., Trotsky).

141. Gilbert, *Holocaust*, p. 175.

142. Dawidowicz, *War against Jews*, p. 145.

143. *Monologe im Führerhauptquartier, 1941–1944*, p. 90.

144. Messerschmidt, p. 358.

145. BA-B, DZA 62 Ka. 1 83, OKW an Kanzlei des Führers, Bl. 73.

146. Messerschmidt, p. 358; Absolon, *Die Wehrmacht im Dritten Reich. Band V*, p. 150.

147. Lifton, p. 24.

148. Kershaw, *Hitler, 1889–1936*, p. 487; Redlich, p. 111; Friedländer, p. 40; Frei, p. 122; Victor, p. 175; Georg Denzler and Volker Fabricius, *Die Kirchen im Dritten Reich* (Frankfurt, 1984), p. 113.

149. *The Holocaust: 2. Legalizing the Holocaust*, p. 285, 13.10.1941. See also Hilberg, pp. 268–69.

150. A literal translation would be "frontline probation company." This company was probably part of a Bewährungsbataillon (probation battalion). Probation battalions were punishment battalions of the German army that allowed one the possibility of rehabilitation—a grim possibility.

151. BA-MA, BMRS, interview Alfred Posselt, 04.01.1996, T-185; Martin Senekowitsch, *Feldmarschalleutnant Johann Friedländer, 1882–1945: Ein vergessener Offizier des Bundesheeres* (Wien, 1995).

152. Bewährungsbataillon is a probation battalion. To read about how one of these battalions operated, see Fritz Molden, *Fepolinski und Waschlapski* (München, 1991).

153. BA-MA, BMRS, interview Heinz Schindler, 26.10.1997, T-404.

154. Meyer, p. 235.

155. BA-MA, BMRS, File Fischer, Fischer an Rigg, 01.12.2000; BA-MA, BMRS, interview Fischer.

156. BA-B, Sammlung Schumacher, Aktenvermerk für III A, III V, II, 19.12.1943; Keitel, pp. 13, 189.

157. Eichmann Prosecution Document, Police d'Israel Quartier General 6-ème Bureau No. 1355, Bl. 2, Generalkommissar für das Sicherheitswesen an den Reichskommissar, 18.08.1941, 19.09.1941.

158. Dawidowicz, *War against Jews*, p. 124; Gilbert, *Holocaust*, p. 195.

159. Jürgen Förster, "Hitler's Decision in Favor of War against the Soviet Union," in *Germany and the Second World War*, vol. 4, pp. 25–27, 34; Jürgen Förster, "Operation Barbarossa as a War of Conquest and Annihilation," in *Germany and the Second World War*, vol. 4, pp. 481–84, 492; Jürgen Förster, "Operation Barbarossa in Historical Perspective," in *Germany and the Second World War*, vol. 4, pp. 1,245–46.

160. HVBl., Nr. 848, 05.09.1941, pp. 579–80.

161. Christopher R. Browning, *Ordinary Men: Reserve Police Battalion 101 and the Final Solution in Poland* (New York, 1992), p. 177.

162. BA-MA, BMRS, interview Lankes.

163. BA-MA, BMRS, File Johannes Heckert, Bl. 1.

164. Jonathan Steinberg, "Types of Genocide: Croatians, Serbs and Jews, 1941–5," in *The Final Solution* p. 190.

165. BA-MA, BMRS, File Konrad Schenck, Wolfram Günther an Schenck, 22.01.1943, Bl. 20.

166. BA-MA, BMRS, File Friedrich Schlesinger, Berurteilung, 13.07.1943.

167. *The Trial of Adolf Eichmann*, vol. 5, sec. 115–118, p. 2,297.

168. IfZ, N 71–73, Aufzeichnung von Dr. Lösener betr. die Frage der Halbjuden und der privilegierten Mischehen, 04.12.1941; BA-MA, BMRS, interview Stephan Prager.

169. Interviews conducted by Colin Heaton with General Johannes Steinhoff from 26–28 January 1984.

170. BA-MA, BMRS, interview Lux.

171. BA-MA, BMRS, File Bernt von Helmolt, Bl. 2, Bernt von Helmolt an Bryan Rigg, 11.07.1997; BA-MA, BMRS, interview Bernt von Helmolt, 22.07.1997, T-385.

172. Ibid. Helmolt had been decorated with the EKII and the Silver Wound Badge (he had lost a foot). His brother, Eiche, was promoted to lieutenant and died in action in 1944.

173. Krackow, pp. 221–28.

174. Ibid., pp. 333–34.

175. At the request of the family, Lt. Ruge's Christian name has been deleted.

176. BA-MA, BMRS, interview Jürgen Ruge, 15.04.1995, T-143.

177. BA-MA, BMRS, interview Bergmann.

178. Not his real name.

179. J. W. v. Oechelhaeuser, *Adelheit es ist soweit. Soldatisches Erleben* (München, 1981), pp. 67–71.

180. Stoltzfus, *Resistance*, pp. 115–16; BA-MA, BMRS, interview Goldberg.

181. BA-MA, BMRS, File Heinrich Schlepegrell, Bl. 3, Hauptmann Ehrlich, P[an]z[er]. Art[illerie]. Rgt. 33, Kommandeur, Bestätigung für Ogfr. Schlepegrell, 29.12.1943.

182. BA-MA, BMRS, File Schlepegrell, Bl.1, Heinrich Schlepegrell an Rigg, 06.04.1997.

183. BA-MA, BMRS, interview Ludwig Reinhard, 13.01.1996, T-196.

184. IfZ, N 71–73, Aufzeichnung von Dr. Lösener, 04.12.1941.

185. *The Trial of Adolf Eichmann*, vol. 5, sec. 115–118, p. 2,297.

186. Adam, p. 320; Hilberg, pp. 268–69.
187. *The Trial of Adolf Eichmann*, vol. 5, sec. 115–118, p. 2,298; see also Rich, p. 2.
188. Hilberg, pp. 268–69.
189. BA-MA, BMRS, general impression gained through documenting several quarter-Jewish cases; Noakes, "Development of Nazi Policy," p. 318.
190. Friedländer, p. 291.
191. See BA-MA, BMRS, interview Eva Heinrichs, 09.02.1997, T-305; BA-MA, BMRS, interview Kurt Heinrichs, 09.02.1997, T-306.
192. BA-MA, BMRS, File Karl Taraba; BA-MA, BMRS, interview Rosa Taraba, 08.01.1996, T-193. Most couples who married during the Third Reich received a copy of *Mein Kampf.* Kershaw, *Hitler, 1889–1936*, p. 242; Redlich, p. 69.
193. *Hitlers Tischgespräche im Führerhauptquartier*, p. 79; *Monologe im Führerhauptquartier, 1941–1944*, p. 148.
194. *Hitlers Tischgespräche im Führerhauptquartier*, p. 79; *Monologe im Führerhauptquartier, 1941–1944*, p. 148. For Hitler's thoughts on Mendel's theory of genetics, see Hitler, *Hitler's Secret Book*, p. 101.
195. *Hitlers Tischgespräche im Führerhauptquartier*, p. 78.
196. A few quarter-Jews documented in this study had two quarter-Jewish parents.
197. IfZ, N71–73, Aufzeichnung von Dr. Lösener betr. die Frage der Halbjuden und der privilegierten Mischehen, 04.12.1941.
198. Ibid.
199. Office of the United States Chief Counsel for Prosecution of Axis Criminality, ed., *U.S.A. Military Tribunals: Case No. 11* (Nuremberg, 1949,) pp. 28,526–27; Lösener, pp. 311–12; Peterson, p. 147. See also Rebentisch, p. 113, n. 268; Klaus Oldenhage, Hermann Schreyer, and Wolfram Werner, eds., Wilhelm Lenz, "Die Handakten von Bernhard Lösener, 'Rassereferent' im Reichsministerium des Innern," in *Archiv und Geschichte. Festschrift für Friedrich P. Kahlenberg (Schriften des Bundesarchivs; 57)* (Düsseldorf, 2000), pp. 686, 691–93, 696. Lösener was arrested on 11 November 1944 by the Gestapo for having hidden two people involved with the 20 July 1944 bomb plot against Hitler. The Nazis sent him to a prison in Berlin, where he remained for the duration of the war.
200. Lösener, p. 311.
201. Jochen von Lang, *The Secretary: Martin Bormann* (New York, 1979), pp. 235–38.
202. Wheeler-Bennett, p. 525; Cooper, *German Army*, p. 344; Creveld, p. 43; Kershaw, *Hitler, 1936–1945*, pp. 451–52.
203. Fest, *Face*, p. 246; Keegan, *Mask of Command*, p. 272.
204. Hermann, p. 495.
205. Gordon A. Craig, "The Political Leader as Strategist," in *Makers of Modern Strategy from Machiavelli to the Nuclear Age*, ed. Peter Paret (Princeton, 1986), p. 497.
206. Kershaw, *Hitler, 1936–1945*, pp. 459, 472–73; Gilbert, *Holocaust*, p. 285. What Hitler said here was in reference to his famous "prophecy" of 30 January 1939. Benz, p. 61; Kershaw, *Hitler, 1936–1945*, pp. 152–53.

207. BA-MA, BMRS, interview Wolfgang Ebert, 13.07.1997, T-373; Wolfgang Ebert, *Das Porzellan war so nervös. Memoiren eines verwöhnten Kindes* (München, 1975), pp. 231–32.

208. *Die Wehrmacht. Mythos und Realität*, Wilhelm Deist, p. 39; *Die Wehrmacht. Mythos und Realität*, Jürgen Förster, p. 948; *Deutsche Dienststelle (WASt) [=Wehrmacht-Auskunft-Stelle] für die Benachrichtigung der nächsten Angehörigen von Gefallenen der ehemaligen deutschen Wehrmacht: Arbeitsbericht 1994–1996*, Berlin, 1996.

209. BA-B, DZA 62 Ka. 1 83, Bl. 170.

210. SA-Gruppenführer is a General Major in the SA.

211. BA-B, DZA 62 Ka. 1 83, Bl. 171, Blankenburg an Girgensohn, 12.02.1942.

212. BA-MA, BMRS, interview Walter Scheinberger, 02.07.1995, T-157.

213. BA-MA, BMRS, File Werner Seldis, Bl. 14, Dr. Werner Seldis an Rigg, Sept. 1996. See also Klemperer, Buch II, 21.09.1943, pp. 440, 443.

214. BA-B, Sammlung Schumacher, Aktenvermerk, 19.12.1943.

215. BA-MA, BMRS, File Edgar Francken, p. 97, John Francken to Rigg, 08.03.1997.

216. When war broke out, Hermann told a Sippen-Gericht in Berlin what his mother, Julie Francken née Spier, had told him on her death bed; namely, that an Aryan man and not her husband, Max Francken, was the father of her son, Hermann Francken. Hermann's testimony was accepted by the Nazis. Hermann no longer had to wear the yellow star and could drive his car.

217. BA-MA, BMRS, John Francken to Rigg, 08.03.1997, p. 97.

218. *Akten-NSDAP*, 101-15518/13, Lammers an Bormann, 16.01.1942.

219. Benz, pp. 8–9, 12, 81–82; Kershaw, *Hitler, 1936–1945*, p. 482.

220. Browning, *Ordinary Men*, pp. 14, 25, 58–70; Lifton, p. 159. Rudolf Höss, "Commandant of Auschwitz," in *The Norton Book of Modern War*, ed. Paul Fussell (New York, 1991), p. 508.

221. Bauer, pp. 200–201; Weinberg, *Germany, Hitler*, pp. 204, 224.

222. *The Holocaust*, vol. 11, *The Wannsee Protocol and a 1944 Report on Auschwitz by the Office of Strategic Services*, introduction by Robert Wolfe (New York, 1982), p. 87; Bauer, pp. 200–206; BA-MA, N 642/12. The address of the villa was Am Großen Wannsee 57.

223. Yehuda Bauer, "Conclusion: The Significance of the Final Solution," in *The Final Solution*, p. 302.

224. Hilberg, pp. 257–62; *The Final Solution*, introduction by David Cesarani, p. 5; Jürgen Förster, "Securing 'Living-space,'" in *Germany and the Second World War*, vol. 4, p. 1,237; *Nationalsozialismus*, p. 58.

225. Gilbert, *Second World War*, p. 292.

226. *Holocaust*, vol. 11, pp. 10–12; *U.S.A. Military Tribunals: Case No. 11*, p. 28,306; IfZ, N 71–73; Benz, p. 11.

227. *Holocaust*, vol. 11, pp. 10–12; Adam, pp. 320–21; Benz, p. 11.

228. *Trials of German Major War Criminals*, vol. 14, *Nuremberg, 14–24 May 1946*, pp. 234–35; Adam, p. 321; Benz, p. 10.

229. Klemperer, Buch II, 18.08.1942; BA-MA, BMRS, File Henle; BA-MA, BMRS, File Prager; BA-MA, BMRS, File D. Fischer; BA-MA, BMRS, File

Hamburger; BA-MA, BMRS, File Günther Mirauer; BA-MA, BMRS, File Fritz Rosenhaupt.

230. BA-B, DZA 62 Ka. 1 83, Bl. 73, OKW an Kanzlei des Führers, Betr. Deutsch-blütigkeitserklärung jüdischer *Mischlinge*, 16.09.1943. See BA-MA, BMRS, File Georg-Friedrich Müller, Bl. 52; BA-MA, BMRS, File Haller.

231. *U.S.A. Tribunals: Case No. 11*, p. 28,308; Adam, pp. 322–23; IfZ, N 71–73, Eichmanns Büro, Ergebnis der Besprechung im Hauptamt Sicherheitspolizei über die Lösung der europäischen Judenfrage, Notizen von Besprechungen von August und September 1941.

232. Office of the United States Chief Counsel for Prosecution of Axis Criminality, ed., *U.S.A. Military Tribunals: Case No. 11.2* (Nuremberg, 1949), p. 48,473.

233. *Holocaust*, vol. 11, pp. 129–31.

234. *Holocaust*, vol. 11, pp. 88–89, 99–103; *U.S.A. Tribunals: Case No. 11*, pp. 28,307, 28,315.

235. *Goebbels Diaries 1942–1943*, p. 116.

236. *Holocaust*, vol. 11, p. 217; Adam, p. 324; Meyer, p. 99.

237. *Holocaust*, vol. 11, pp. 215–17; Lösener, pp. 299–301; Adler, *Der Verwaltete Mensch*, p. 288.

238. *Holocaust*, vol. 11, p. 219.

239. Yehuda Bauer, "Conclusion: The Significance of the Final Solution," in *The Final Solution*, p. 302.

240. Krüger, p. 11; BA-MA, BMRS, interview Krüger; BA-MA; BMRS, File Krüger, Bl. 29. See also BA-MA, BMRS, File Florey, Bl. 1; BA-MA, BMRS, File Gaehde, Bl. 17; BA-MA, BMRS, File Bergmann, Tagebuch, 06.05.1942.

241. See BA-MA, BMRS, File Johannes Reich, Bl. 6, Dr. J. Reich to Rigg, 11.12.1995; BA-MA, BMRS, interview Johannes Reich, 28.12.1995, T-181; BA-MA, BMRS, interview Kopp; BA-MA, BMRS, interview Scholz; BA-MA, BMRS, interview Bergmann; BA-MA, BMRS, interview Margold.

242. Paul Sauer, ed., *Dokumente über die Verfolgung der jüdischen Bürger in Baden-Württemberg durch das nationalsozialistische Regime, 1933–1945* (Stuttgart, 1966), Bd. II, p. 378; Laze, Teil II, Bl. 12.

243. See, for example, BA-MA, BMRS, interview Sachs; BA-MA, BMRS, interview Lüderitz; BA-MA, BMRS, interview Angreß; BA-MA, BMRS, File Heinz Günther Angreß, Bl. 3.

244. HVBl., Nr. 202, 1942C, p. 165, Behandlung jüdischer Mischlinge in der Wehrmacht.

245. HVBl., Nr. 384, 1942C, pp. 315–16.

246. HVBl., Nr. 202, 1942C, pp. 315–16; BA-A, H 20/490.

247. *Trials of German Major War Criminals*, vol. 14, *Nuremberg, 14–24 May 1946*, p. 235.

248. Adam, p. 327; Broszat and Frei, pp. 156–57; Lösener, pp. 298–301; Noakes, "Development of Nazi Policy," pp. 345–46.

249. For an example of the confusion, see *Akten-NSDAP*, 107-00387, 107-00390.

250. BA-B, DZA 62 Ka. 1 83, Bl. 113, Bouhler an Bormann, 10.07.1942.

251. Lang, pp. 204–7; Rebentisch, pp. 452–53.

252. *The Trial of Adolf Eichmann*, sec. 113, p. 2,039; *U.S.A. Tribunals: Case No. 11*,

p. 28,528; Lang, p. 236; Noakes, "Development of Nazi Policy," p. 344. See also *The Trial of Adolf Eichmann*, sec. 115–118, p. 2,170; Hilberg, p. 606; Gilbert, *Second World War*, p. 340; Adler, *Der Verwaltete Mensch*, p. 288.

253. Adam, p. 329.

254. *U.S.A. Tribunals: Case No. 11*, pp. 28,308, 28,314; Lösener, p. 300; *Trials of German Major War Criminals*, vol. 14, *Nuremberg, 14–24 May 1946*, pp. 235–36.

255. Charles Burdick, ed., *The Halder War Diary 1939–1942* (London, 1950), p. 678.

256. HVBl, Nr. 926, 25.09.1942, pp. 131, 501; Adam, p. 327; *Sammlung wehrrechtlicher Gutachten und Vorschriften*, Heft 20/21, p. 175.

257. BA-MA, BMRS, interview Eduard Hesse, 30.10.1998, T-430; Landgericht München I, Akten Werner Eisner, Protokoll aufgenommen in öffentlicher Sitzung des Einzelrichters des 17. Zivilsenats des Oberlandesgerichts München, Bericht von Zeuge Walter Julius Eisner, 3 Juli 1968, Heft IV, Bl. 648, Eduard Hesses Bericht über Werner Eisner, 20 Januar 1969, Heft IV, Bl. 693, Aktenzeichen 17EU 529/66, Heft I, Aktenzeichen: 7 EK 2316/60, Bl. 2–3, report about Eisner written by Dr. H. March on 16 May 1961, Bl. 2–3, report by Dr. Jose Alvarado, 3 June 1965, La Paz, Bolivia, Bl. 455; BA-MA, BMRS, interview Byk.

258. The next three cases (Schinek, Kohn, and Mayer) are also described in Professor Steven Welch's Leo Baeck essay from 1999. Steven R. Welch, "Mischling Deserters from the Wehrmacht," *Leo Baeck Yearbook* 44 (1999): 273–324.

259. Ordinary sailor.

260. BA-A, RW 55/15043, Bl. 69, Lt.. Berlling, 1. Batterie Marineflakabt. 814 an Kommando M. Flak. A. 814, 14.10.1942, Einsatzort. Special thanks to Professor Steven Welch for finding this document.

261. Ibid., Bl. 66, Thea Liebe an Gericht des Marinebefehlshabers Dänemark, 08.10.1942.

262. Ibid., Bl. 74, Gericht des Marinebefehlshabers Dänemark, Verfügung v. 29.10.1942. During the Third Reich, military courts handed down fifty thousand death sentences. Manfred Messerschmidt and Fritz Wüllner, *Die Wehrmachtjustiz im Dienste des Nationalsozialismus. Zerstörung einer Legende* (Baden-Baden, 1987); Redlich, p. 107.

263. He apparently did not know his Jewish father, Otto Kohn.

264. BA-A, RW 55/1589, Bl. 25, Gericht der Wehrmachtkommandantur Berlin, 09.06.1942.

265. Ibid., Bl. 25, 70–80.

266. BA-A, RM 123/335944, Gericht der Wehrmachtkommandantur Wien, Urteil gegen Anton Mayer, 13.03.1944.

267. Ibid., Anton Mayer an Großadmiral Dönitz, 23.07.1944.

268. Allgemeines Marineamt was a branch of the navy supreme command.

269. BA-A, RM 123/335944, OKM an Gericht der Kriegsmarine Berlin, Betrifft: Strafsache gegen den M.A.Gefr. Anton Mayer, 23.04.1944; DDS, Pers Anton Mayer, Gericht der Kriegsmarine Berlin, 25.08.1944. Over fifty thousand death sentences were issued by the Wehrmacht throughout the Third Reich. Messerschmidt and Wüllner; Weinberg, *Germany, Hitler*, p. 309, n. 6. See also Manfred Messerschmidt, "German Military Law in the Second World War," in *The German Military in the Age of Total War*, ed. Wilhelm Deist (Dover, 1985), pp. 323–35.

270. DDS, Pers Adm. Martin Baltzer, Bl. 3; BA-MA, BMRS, File Conrad Patzig, Dr. Günter Patzig über C. Patzig, p. 14.
271. Messerschmidt, p. 355.
272. *U.S.A. Tribunals: Case No. 11*, pp. 28,315; Hilberg, p. 273.
273. Adam, pp. 328–29.
274. *AWA (I)= Allgemeines Wehrmachtamt (Inland)*.
275. *Akten-NSDAP*, 103–22530, Engel an Frey, 02.11.1942.
276. BA-B, Sammlung Schumacher, Rundschreiben der NSDAP, SS Abschnitt, 01.12.1942, Hamburg; BA-B. Reichskanzlei 4123, Bl. 74, Vermerk Lammers', RM Nr. 2566/43/A. Hitler enacted thirty restrictions on marriage according to how Jewish one was. Victor, p. 18.
277. Hertz, p. 35.

CHAPTER 6: TURNING POINT AND FORCED LABOR, 1943–1944
1. *Akten-NSDAP*, 107-00392-393.
2. The author feels that this was probably the number of half-Jews registered only in Berlin because the number is so low.
3. BA-B, NS 18/482, Gussmann an Hauptverbindungsamt, Pg. Spangenberg, 10.02.1943.
4. Ibid., Der Chef der Sicherheitspolizei und des SD Kaltenbrunner an OKW, Goebbels, Speer und Reichsminister für Bewaffnung und Munition, 03.03.1943.
5. Although the documents used that have Dietz's signature for this study do not contain his first name, it probably was none other than Heinrich Dietz, who had been a member of the Prussian army legal service since 1901. In 1933, he became the editor of the journal for military lawyers called the *Zeitschrift für Wehrrecht* "and subsequently was a high-ranking civil servant in the war ministry." Manfred Messerschmidt, "German Military Law in the Second World War," in *The German Military in the Age of Total War*, pp. 325–26. In 1938, the War Ministry was reorganized into OKW.
6. BA-B, DZA 62 Ka. 1 83, Bl. 84, Aktennotiz, Anruf über Feldwebel Dr. Vogtherr, 03.06.1943.
7. BA-B, NS 18/482, Aktennotiz, Betrifft: Heranziehung der jüdischen Mischlinge und jüdisch Versippten zur Dienstleistung im Kriege, 17.07.1943.
8. *Akten-NSDAP*, 103-22534, Aktennotiz Bormann für Dr. Klopfer [Stellvertreter Bormanns als Leiter der Parteikanzlei], 14.10.1943.
9. Noakes, "Development of Nazi Policy," p. 351.
10. Dieter Maier, *Arbeitseinsatz und Deportation. Die Mitwirkung der Arbeitsverwaltung bei der nationalsozialistischen Judenverfolgung in den Jahren, 1938–1945* (Berlin, 1994), p. 217.
11. BA-MA, RH53–7/ 271, Bl. 51–53, Kommandeurbesprechung, 18.10.1943.
12. BA-MA, BMRS, interview Gerhard Wundermacher, 20.11.1995, T-167.
13. Meyer, p. 239.
14. BA-B, R 3/1583, Bl. 108, Speer an Himmler, 16.10.1944; Walk, p. 405; Adam, p. 381.
15. BA-B, Sammlung Schumacher, Aktenvermerk, 19.12.1943; Keitel, p. 189. Keitel had abandoned not only his friend Bürkner but also his aunt Ottilie (Tilly)

Cahn née Schulze, her Jewish husband, Max Ludwig, and their half-Jewish children, who were deported to OT camps. BA-MA, BMRS, File Peter Cahn,
Bl. 6; BA-MA, BMRS, interview Peter Cahn, 11.12.1996, T-269.

16. The Deutscher Volkssturm (German home guard, or literally "people's
militia") was made up of young boys and old men between the ages of sixteen
and sixty during the last months of the war. With the Führer's decree of 25 September 1944, the Deutscher Volkssturm was founded. Bormann was in charge
of its organization and political education. Himmler was in charge of arming
the units. Most who fought in the Deutscher Volkssturm received poor training
and were sent to the fronts in eastern and western Germany to try and stop the
Allied offensives. Close to 175,000 Germans probably died while fighting in the
Volkssturm. Kershaw, *Hitler, 1936–1945*, p. 715.

17. Kershaw, *Hitler, 1936–1945*, p. 714.

18. *Akten-NSDAP*, 101-12427, Deutscher Volkssturm, Anordnung 443/44,
09.12.1944; BA-B, NS 6/764, Bl. 133–34, Klopfer an Bormann, 30.10.1944;
Speer, pp. 329, 391.

19. BA-MA, BMRS, interview Hermann Nast-Kolb, 22.11.1994, T-59.

20. Bloch, under orders from Canaris, rescued the Lubavitcher Rebbe Schneersohn
in 1939–1940. Schneersohn was later able to make it to the United States via
the Baltic states, Sweden, and the Atlantic.

21. BA-MA, BMRS, File Ernst Bloch.

22. Bruno Blau writes that in April 1944, half-Jews who did not have work or were
not serving in the armed forces were sent to OT. Blau, "Die Mischehe im
Nazireich," p. 54. Interestingly, from the cases documented in this study, most
of the Jewish wives of Aryan men deported to OT survived the war. They simply remained home and waited for the end of the war.

23. In *Aktion Hasse*, half-Jews wore uniforms and performed mostly construction work. Some half-Jews claim that it was not nearly as bad as *Aktion Mitte*.
BA-MA, BMRS, interview Gerhard Schiller, 11.02.1995, T-92.

24. In *Aktion Mitte*, half-Jews performed forced labor and did not wear uniforms.
BA-MA, BMRS, interview Schiller.

25. BA-MA, BMRS, general data collected; *Sammlung wehrrechtlicher Gutachten
und Vorschriften*, Heft 2, p. 27. "B-men" stands for *Bewährungsmänner*. Some
half-Jews may have been deported to OT camps in 1943, but most of them
were deported to such camps only in 1944.

26. *Akten-NSDAP*, 107-00394; Noakes, "Development of Nazi Policy," p. 351.

27. BA-MA, BMRS, File Herbert Beyer, Bl. 3, 6, 50, *Lebensbeschreibung*.

28. Maier, p. 219; Noakes, p. 351.

29. BA-MA, BMRS, interview Angreß.

30. BA-MA, BMRS, interview Friederich Schlesinger, 10.12.1994, T-77.

31. BA-MA, BMRS, interview Salinger.

32. BA-MA, BMRS, general impression gained from interviewees; Noakes, "Development of Nazi Policy," p. 351.

33. Maier, p. 219.

34. Ibid., p. 228.

35. For an example of a Gestapo notification for OT, see BA-MA, BMRS, File Bleicher, Gestapo Stuttgart an Bleicher, 13.10.1944; BA-MA, BMRS, File Carl Neubronner, Arbeitsamt Frankfurt an Neubronner, 01.03.1945. Others were arrested and deported, but they were a minority.

36. BA-MA, BMRS, File Brücher, "Amtliche Anzeigen," des Leiter des Arbeitsamts Stuttgart; BA-MA, BMRS, interview Brücher.

37. BA-MA, BMRS, File Rehfeld. Helmut Rehfeld worked for the railroads between Liegnitz and Breslau as an engineer. During his work, he witnessed the transports with their human cargo on their way to Auschwitz and other extermination camps. One day, disgusted with the whole regime, he took down the Führer's picture from his office wall, muttering that he could not work under his gaze. His boss denounced him to the Gestapo and after spending several weeks in a Breslau prison, the Nazis deported him to Buchenwald.

38. BA-MA, BMRS, File Gerhard Guttstadt, Bl. 1, Elisabeth Guttstadt an Rigg, 11.08.1997. See also Werner Schmidt, *Leben an Grenzen* (Zürich, 1989), pp. 159–60.

39. BA-MA, BMRS, File H. Beyer, Bl. 49, *Lebensbeschreibung.*

40. Schmidt, p. 173.

41. On 1 August 1944, *Sippenhaft[ung]* was imposed as a result of the 20 July bomb plot. See Seaton, *German Army*, pp. 232–33.

42. BA-MA, BMRS, File Hermann Steinthal, Hermann Steinthal an Rigg, Bl. 3, Steinthal an Rigg, 14.11.1996.

43. BA-MA, BMRS, general impression gained from the data collected; BA-MA, BMRS, interview Behrendt; Schmidt, pp. 170–73.

44. Krüger, pp. 100–101; Klaus Budzinski, *Der Riss durchs Ganze. Kolportage einer gestörten Deutschwerdung* (Berlin, 1993), pp. 226.

45. Adam, p. 332.

46. *Akten-NSDAP,* 101-07575-Bl. 3, Bormann an Lammers, Betrifft: "Beamte, die jüdische Mischlinge oder mit Juden oder jüdischen Mischlingen verheiratet sind."; BA-B, R 43 II/599a, Bl. 71.

47. Neue Züricher Zeitung, Montag, 15.01.1945, Bl. 6.

48. BA-MA, BMRS, File H. Beyer, Bl. 51, *Lebensbeschreibung;* BA-MA, BMRS, interview H. Beyer.

49. BA-MA, BMRS, interview Hanna Wollenberg, 19.06.1996, T-213.

50. BA-MA, BMRS, File H. Beyer, Bl. 52, *Lebensbeschreibung;* BA-MA, BMRS, interview Hans-Geert Falkenberg, 02.02.1997, T-289; BA-MA, BMRS, interview Krüger; BA-MA, BMRS, interview Schliesser.

51. BA-MA, BMRS, File H. Beyer, Bl. 49, 52, *Lebensbeschreibung.*

52. BA-MA, BMRS, general impression gained from data collected; Meyer, p. 241.

53. U.S. Holocaust Museum researcher Dr. Geoffrey Megargee, who is working on the numbers of Nazi camps, claims that the Nazis probably constructed over ten thousand camps; *Nationalsozialismus,* p. 17.

54. *Trials of German Major War Criminals, Part 17, Nuremberg 20 June–1 July 1946,* p. 52.

55. Ibid.

56. BA-MA, BMRS, interview Hans Radványi, 07.01.1996, T-192; BA-MA, BMRS, interview Reiner Wiehl, 17.05.1996, T-205.

57. BA-MA, BMRS, File Kurt Einstein, Bl. 2, Kurt Einstein an Rigg, 10.12.1996.

58. BA-MA, BMRS, interview Brücher.

59. BA-MA, BMRS, interview Techel; BA-MA, BMRS, interview Behrendt; BA-MA, BMRS, interview Werner Gramsch, 16.11.1996, T-238; BA-MA, BMRS, interview Kurt Zeunert, 06.02.1997, T-300.

60. BA-MA, BMRS, File Ernst Ludwig, Bl.12, Ernst Ludwig, Anlage zu meiner Erklärung, meine Verfolgung in den Jahren 1941–45 betreffend, 11.06.1949; BA-MA, BMRS, interview Ernst Ludwig, 22.01.1997, T-286. See also BA-MA, BMRS, File Rudolf Löwenfeld, Bl. 2.

61. BA-MA, BMRS, interview Bergmann.

62. BA-MA, BMRS, interview Heinz Neumaier, 21.04.1995, T-145; BA-MA, BMRS, interview Klaus Budzinski, 15.11.1994, T-51.

63. BA-MA, BMRS, interview Rath.

64. BA-MA, BMRS, interview Schliesser.

65. BA-MA, BMRS, interview Wiehl.

66. BA-MA, BMRS, interview Zeunert.

67. BA-MA, BMRS, interview Radványi; BA-MA, BMRS, interview Wiehl. Beate Meyer has drawn the same conclusion. See Meyer, p. 247.

68. BA-MA, BMRS, interview Salinger. See also BA-MA, BMRS, interview Schliesser.

69. BA-MA, BMRS, interview Wiehl; BA-MA, BMRS, interview Peter Cahn, 17.03.1995, T-121; BA-MA, BMRS, interview Peter Cahn, 11.12.1996, T-268; BA-MA, BMRS, interview Hans Cahn 11.12.1996, T-269; BA-MA, BMRS, interview Walter Scheinberger, 18.03.1995, T-121a; BA-MA, BMRS, interview Karl Neubronner, 09.04.1995, T-136; BA-MA, BMRS, interview Hans Homberger, 08.04.1995, T-132.

70. BA-MA, BMRS, interview Lichtwitz.

71. BA-MA, BMRS, interview Falkenberg. Ironically, after the war, the Allies put Falkenberg in prison because they thought he really was an OT officer.

72. BA-MA, BMRS, interview Harald Ettheimer, 02.09.1995, T-164.

73. Vogel, p. 262.

74. Frontführer or Bauführer in the OT was a second lieutenant.

75. BA-MA, BMRS, interview Horst Schmechel, 29.11.1994, T-65. Schmechel was in several OT camps. They were Hazebrouk, Watten, Vizernes, and Boulogne Sur-Mer in France.

76. BA-MA, BMRS, interview Budzinski.

77. Niedersächsischer Verband Deutscher Sinti, ed., *"Es war unmenschenmöglich." Sinti aus Niedersachsen erzählen—Verfolgung und Vernichtung im Nationalsozialismus und Diskriminierung bis heute* (Hannover, 1995), pp. 50, 87. This unit was named after SS Oberführer Oskar Dirlewanger, who was a sadist and necrophiliac. Clark, p. 391, n.3; Keegan, *Second World War,* p. 482; Guderian, p. 356.

78. BA-MA, H 6/172, Schreiben Chef des Heeres-Personalamts Burgdorf, 03.01.1945; BA-MA, Pers 7786.

79. B. H. Liddell Hart, *The German Generals Talk* (New York, 1979), p. 178. General Heinrici's wife was half-Jewish.

80. Adam, pp. 332–33.

81. Kershaw, *Profiles in Power*, p. 165; Redlich, pp. 232–34, 275; Maser, pp. 376, 394, 402; Keegan, *Mask of Command*, p. 309.

82. Schleunes, pp. 3–4; Eberhard Jäckel, *Hitler's Weltanschauung* (Stuttgart, 1981), p. 78; Kershaw, *Profiles in Power*, p. 30.

83. Büttner, "Persecution," p. 288.

84. *Holocaust, vol. 1, Legalizing the Holocaust*, p. 31.

85. Globke and Stuckart, p. 17.

86. A. Rüter-Ehlermann and C. F. Rüter, eds., *Sammlung deutscher Strafurteile wegen nationalsozialistischer Tötungsverbrechen* (Amsterdam 1968–1981), Bd. VI, p. 406.

87. Schleunes, p. 130.

88. *U.S.A. Military Tribunals: Case No. 11.2*, p. 125.

89. SS colonel.

90. BA-B, NS 19/1047, Bl. 2–3, Hildebrandt an Himmler, 17.03.1943. See also Noakes, "Development of Nazi Policy," pp. 339–40.

91. BA-MA, NS 19/1047, Bl. 10; Adam, p. 328.

92. Stoltzfus, *Resistance*, p. 57.

93. *Akten-NSDAP*, 107-00409-410.

94. Eichmann Prosecution Document, Police d'Israel Quartier General 6-ème Bureau No. 1102, Der Reichsminister für die besetzten Ostgebiete (Schmitz), 30.01.1942; IfZ Hefte N-71-73, Dr. Feldscher, betr. "Verschärfung des Judenbegriffs," 13.08.1941; BA-B, NS 19/1772, Bl. 2; *Holocaust, vol. 2, Legalizing the Holocaust*, Bl. 103; Noakes, "Development of Nazi Policy," pp. 344–45.

95. Ibid.

96. Hilberg, p. 309.

97. Ibid., p. 152

98. Noakes, "Development of Nazi Policy," p. 338; Kurt Pätzold, ed., *Verfolgung, Vertreibung, Vernichtung. Dokumente des faschistischen Antisemitismus 1933 bis 1942* (Leipzig, 1984), pp. 249, 264–65.

99. Rüter-Ehlermann and Rüter, p. 15.

100. Klemperer, Buch II, 12.05.1943, p. 377, 23.01.1944, p. 475.

101. Arendt, p. 174. One half-Jew who escaped from Denmark was the famous scientist Niels Bohr, who later found his way to the United States and worked on the atomic bomb project.

102. *Trial of Adolf Eichmann*, vol. 7, session 42, p. 752, Witness Charlotte Salzburger née Wreschner; and Lösener, pp. 299–302; Eichmann Prosecution Document, Police d'Israel Quartier General 6-ème Bureau No. 1102, Reichsminister für die besetzten Ostgebiete (Schmitz), 30.01.1942, Aufzeichnung, pp. 2–3; BA-B, NS 19/1772, Bl. 2, Reichsminister für die besetzten Ostgebiete, 02.05.1942; Bauer, p. 229; IfZ, N 71-73, Der Judenbegriff in den besetzten Gebieten; Hausner, p. 256; Meyer, p. 9; Adler, *Der Verwaltete Mensch*, pp. 283–84.

103. See Stoltzfus, *Resistance;* Kaplan, pp. 149, 193.

104. Maier, p. 203; Rebentisch, p. 439.

105. Lifton, p. 56.
106. Kershaw, *Hitler, 1936–1945*, p. 486; Arendt, p. 96.
107. Hilberg, p. 296, n. 164. Müller became head of the Gestapo in 1939 under Himmler. Gellately, *Gestapo and German Society*, p. 55.
108. David Roskies, ed., *The Literature of Destruction: Jewish Responses to Catastrophe* (New York, 1989); Chaim A. Kaplan, "Scribes of the Warsaw Ghetto: Scroll of Agony," p. 446.
109. This was an SS Captain.
110. Stoltzfus, *Resistance*, pp. 184–86.
111. Ernst Klee, *Euthanasie im NS-Staat: Die Vernichtung lebensunwerten Lebens* (Frankfurt, 1985), p. 419; Noakes, "Development of Nazi Policy," p. 348; Victor, p. 172; Weinberg, *Germany, Hitler*, p. 240; Adler, *Der Verwaltete Mensch*, p. 16.
112. *Der Stürmer*, 09.11.1944.
113. Bauer, pp. 190–91, 206; Büttner, "Persecution," p. 289.
114. *Trial of Adolf Eichmann*, vol. 2, sec. 42, p. 755; BA-MA, BMRS, File Hanns-Heinz Bauer. BA-MA, interview Hanns-Heinz Bauer, 29.03.1998, T-421.
115. BA-MA, BMRS, File Hans Kirchholtes, Bl. 4.
116. Wolf Zuelzer, "Keine Zukunft als 'Nicht-Arier' im Dritten Reich," in *Der Judenpogrom*, p. 154.
117. BA-MA, BMRS, interview Hans Döppes, 19.05.1996, T-207; BA-MA, BMRS, interview Bauer; BA-MA, BMRS, interview Ferdinand Lichtwitz, 18.07.1997; BA-MA, BMRS, interview R. Schenk, 23.05.1997, T-349; BA-MA, BMRS, File Herbert Simon, Bl. 11; BA-MA, BMRS, File Erik Blumenfeld; BA-MA, BMRS, File Helmuth Rosenbaum, Bl. 9; BA-MA, BMRS, File Werner Eisner. See also Meyer, pp. 236, 251, 469; Hans A. Schmitt, *Quakers and Nazis: Inner Light in Outer Darkness* (Missouri, 1997), pp. 174–75; Adler, *Der Verwaltete Mensch*, p. 320; Owings, p. 48.
118. Kershaw, *Hitler, 1889–1936*, p. 487; Redlich, p. 111; Frei, p. 122; Lifton, p. 27; Denzler and Fabricus, pp. 112–13.
119. BA-MA, BMRS, interview Hans-Oskar Löwenstein de Witt, 06.12.1994, T-71. See also Alfred Posselt, *Soldat des Feindes* (Wien, 1993), pp. 18–19.
120. BA-MA, BMRS, File G. Bier, Bier an Rigg, 26.03.2001.
121. Bauer, p. 206.
122. BA-MA, BMRS, interview Steinwasser.
123. Kershaw, *Hitler Myth*, pp. 238–40, 250–51; Gilbert, *Holocaust*, pp. 73–75; William Sheridan Allen, "Die deutsche Öffentlichkeit und die 'Reichskristallnacht'—Konflikte zwischen Werthierarchie und Propaganda im Dritten Reich," in *Die Reihen fest geschlossen. Beiträge zur Geschichte des Alltags unterm Nationalsozialismus* (Wuppertal, 1981), pp. 397–411; Hilberg, p. 29; Kaplan, p. 148.
124. Redlich, p. 156; Bormann Lang, p. 221; Noakes, "Development of Nazi Policy," p. 354; *Nazism 1919–1945*, vol. 3, pp. 1,031–43; Denzler and Fabricius, pp. 98, 116–32; Rebentisch, p. 431; Victor, pp. 93, 172. Over seventy thousand mentally ill and deformed patients were murdered because of this program. Kershaw, *Profiles in Power*, p. 141; Kershaw, *Hitler, 1936–1945*, pp. 261, 427–30; Redlich, p. 154; Stoltzfus, *Resistance*, pp. 15, 145; Gellately, *Consent and*

Coercion, p. 103. Gellately notes that Hitler might have also felt that it was a good time to stop the euthanasia program because the expertise of the person-nel who had been working in the euthanasia centers was needed for the ex-termination now going on in the East.

125. In February 1943, Goebbels ordered around two thousand Jews living with Aryan spouses arrested. The government planned to deport these Jews. How-ever, wives, children, family, and friends in Berlin protested day and night for one week. Sometimes almost six thousand people protested. Amazingly, under such pressure, the Nazi regime relented and freed the Jews in March. *Geschichte und Gesellschaft. Zeitschrift für Historische Sozialwissenschaft 21. Jahrgang/ Heft 2 April–Juni 1995, Protest und Widerstand* (Göttingen, 1995), Nathan Stoltzfus, "Widerstand des Herzens," pp. 218–47; Stoltzfus, pp. xvi–xxii; Noakes, "Development of Nazi Policy," p. 354; Weinberg, *Germany, Hitler,* p. 231; BA-MA, BMRS, interview Goldberg; BA-MA, BMRS, interview Elisabeth Behrend, 03.03.1997, T-321; Meyer, p. 57; Schmitt, p. 175; Richard J. Evans, *Lying About Hitler: History, Holocaust, and the David Irving Trial* (New York, 2001), p. 84; Owings, p. 462; *Goebbels Diaries, 1942–1943,* pp. 276, 288, 294.

126. Arendt, p. 159; see also Schmitt, p. 174.
127. BA-MA, BMRS, interview Wiehl.
128. BA-MA, BMRS, interview Braun, 10–14.08.1994, T-10; BA-MA, BMRS, in-terview Braun, 07.01.1996, T-190.
129. BA-MA, BMRS, File Wilhelm Dröscher.

CHAPTER 7: EXEMPTIONS FROM THE RACIAL LAWS
GRANTED BY HITLER

1. Many interviewees, fellow students, and academics have expressed this view.
2. Ibid.
3. Hamann, pp. 71–77; Kershaw, *Profiles in Power,* p.19; Redlich, pp. 11–13; Vic-tor, pp. 9, 13, 16, 123.
4. Discussion with Dr. Fritz Redlich at his home in Connecticut on 23 Septem-ber 2000. See also *Monologe im Führerhauptquartier, 1941–1944,* p. 357.
5. Kershaw, *Hitler, 1889–1936,* p. xxv.
6. Hamann, pp. 8, 73–76; Redlich, pp. 6–8, 11, 223–224, 255; Robert G. L. Waite, *The Psychopathic God Adolf Hitler* (New York, 1977), p. 131.
7. Victor, p. 8; Redlich, pp. 34, 43, 46, 82, 99; Bormann Lang, p. 119.
8. Hamann, p. 76; Maser, p. 21; Bormann Lang, pp. 129–30. For more about Patrick Hitler, see Kershaw, *Hitler, 1889–1936,* pp. 8–9, 604 n. 28.
9. Redlich, pp. 11, 224, 255.
10. Maser, pp. 15, 36–38; Redlich, p. 6.
11. Redlich, pp. 7–8; Maser, p. 17; Victor, p. 20; Heiden, p. 43.
12. Kershaw, *Hitler, 1889–1936,* pp. 351–53; Redlich, pp. 79–80, 285–86; Victor, p. 154.
13. Redlich, pp. 9, 257; Maser, p. 61; Heiden, p. 43.
14. Maser, pp. 315, 598–622. Maser is convinced that Hitler fathered an illegiti-mate son, Jean Marie Loret, during World War I.

15. Waite, pp. 33, 127–37.
16. Kershaw, *Hitler, 1889–1936*, p. 11; Redlich, pp. 10, 255–56; Victor, p. 22.
17. Maser, pp. 36–37.
18. Kershaw, *Hitler, 1889–1936*, p. 13; Hamann, p. 16; Redlich, p. 258; Maser, p. 329; Victor, pp. 19–20, 23, 29.
19. Victor, pp. 20, 22.
20. Redlich, pp. 7–8, 223, 256, 281; Victor, p. 20.
21. Kershaw, *Profiles in Power*, p. 19; Redlich, pp. 6, 11–13, 256; Ralph Giordano, *Wenn Hitler den Krieg gewonnen hätte* (Hamburg, 1989), p. 103; Victor, pp. 20; Waite, pp. 33, 127–37.
22. Kershaw, *Hitler, 1889–1936*, p. 7; Hamann, p. 268; Maser, p. 14.
23. Kershaw, *Hitler, 1889–1936*, p. 7.
24. Victor, p. 17; Hansjürgen Koehler, *Inside Information* (London, 1940); Hans Frank, *Im Angesicht des Galgens* (Schliersee, 1955).
25. Victor, pp. 17, 155.
26. Koehler, pp. 145–49. Koehler claims that while he worked under Heydrich, he came across a file created by the chancellors of the Austrian Republic, Engelbert Dollfuß and Kurt von Schuschnigg, both political enemies of Hitler, that claimed that Hitler's grandmother had worked in the Rothschilds' mansion in Vienna, where she became pregnant.
27. BA-MA, BMRS, interview Niklas Frank, 16.10.1996, T-227. See also Maser, pp. 46–47, 269. Frank had even claimed after the war that he was part Jewish. Joseph E. Persico, *Nuremberg: Infamy on Trial* (New York, 1994), p. 22. Frank's son, Niklas, states that no documents have been found to prove that his family has Jewish ancestry. BA-MA, BMRS, interview N. Frank.
28. Kershaw, *Hitler, 1889–1936*, p. 9.
29. Waite, p. 127.
30. Supposedly, no records are available to confirm or disprove whether there was a Jewish family by the name of Frankenberger in Graz during this time. According to Kershaw, there were no Jews called Frankenberger in Graz during the 1830s. Moreover, Jews were not allowed in the whole of Styria (Steiermark) because they were not allowed to live in that part of Austria until the 1860s. Kershaw, *Hitler, 1889–1936*, p. 8. See also Redlich, p. 12; Maser, p. 27.
31. Victor, p. 17.
32. Hamann, pp. 72–74; Redlich, pp. 11, 257; Waite, pp. 130–31; Speer, p. 117; Bracher, pp. 58, 64. There has been much speculation that the town was destroyed by the Russians after the war. The sources are unclear on this point. It is possible that both the Russians and Hitler did their fair share of destruction for their own reasons. Most likely, as mentioned earlier, Hitler had documents from Döllersheim removed and destroyed. Hitler may have known that the parish priest of Döllersheim had altered Hitler's father's birth register by marking out the name Schicklgruber, "replacing 'out of wedlock' by 'within wedlock,' and entering 'Georg Hitler' in the hitherto empty box for the father's name." Kershaw, *Hitler, 1889–1936*, p. 5; Redlich, pp. 7–8. See also Maser, pp. 23–24.
33. Redlich, p. 11.

34. Kershaw, *Hitler, 1889–1936*, p. 86. Hitler's evasion of the Austrian draft does not mean he was a coward. His war record as a dispatch runner in the German army during World War I, where he was wounded three times and awarded both the EKII and EKI (unusual for a corporal), was proof that he was indeed a brave soldier. Kershaw, *Hitler, 1889–1936*, pp. 91–97; Redlich, pp. 40, 259; O'Neill, p. 5; Keegan, *Mask of Command*, p. 236.

35. Bormann Lang, p. 119.

36. Victor, pp. 13–14, 17, 147.

37. Redlich, p. 320. See also *Monologe im Führerhauptquartier, 1941–1944*, p. 310.

38. Waite, p. 129. See also *Monologe im Führerhauptquartier, 1941–1944*, p. 293.

39. Secretary of Treasury (Reichsfinanzminister) Matthias Erzberger was the leader of the Catholic Zentrum party and was perhaps one of the most hated members of the Middle by the Right in Germany. He had advocated peace at the end of World War I and had attacked the military leadership in the Reichstag during the war. He was assassinated in August 1921. Bauer, p. 78. Craig, *Prussian Army*, pp. 325, 368.

40. Persico, pp. 327–29; Redlich, pp. 13, 320; Kershaw, *Hitler, 1889–1936*, p. 569; Friedländer, p. 150; Victor, pp. 18, 125.

41. Redlich, pp. 320, 116, n. 72.

42. BA-B, NS 6/ 487, Bl. 4. See also Maser, p. 388.

43. Redlich, pp. 3, 223–24.

44. Ibid., p. 11.

45. Redlich, pp. 11–12, 72; Giordano, p. 103.

46. Maser, p. 323; Redlich, pp. 78, 284.

47. Hamann, pp. 53–57; Redlich, pp. 22, 115, 323; Victor, p. 41.

48. *Heeresadjutant bei Hitler*, pp. 31–32.

49. Kershaw, *Hitler, 1889–1936*, p. 96; Bauer, p. 81; Stern, pp. 161–62; Maser, p. 144; Joachim C. Fest, *Hitler* (Frankfurt, 1987), p. 103.

50. Kershaw, *Hitler, 1889–1936*, p. 348; Cooper, *German Army*, p. 20; Frei, p. 14; Victor, p. 78. Hitler not only knew about the homosexuality of the commander of the SA, Ernst Röhm, but also knew that several of Röhm's lieutenants (e.g., SA leader Edmund Heines) were also "notorious" homosexuals. Kershaw, *Hitler, 1889–1936*, p. 514; Redlich, pp. 98–99, 273; Friedländer, p. 208.

51. Kershaw, *Hitler, 1889–1936*, p. 348; Bormann Lang, p. 65.

52. The name Izzy or Isi, derived from the Jewish name Itzig, may have achieved its popular usage as denoting a "dirty Jew" from books such as Gustav Freytag's *Debit and Credit (Soll und Haben)*, published in 1855. Freytag's widely read book portrayed the Jewish merchant Veital Itzig as everything a Nazi would view a Jew as being: dirty, dishonest, and evil. Course on German literature taken with Professor Liselotte Davis at Yale University, spring 1994.

53. Günther Deschner, *Reinhard Heydrich* (Berlin, 1987), p. 67; Victor, p. 146. Another biography on Heydrich, which thoroughly deals with Heydrich's supposed Jewish ancestry, was written by Shlomo Aronson: *Reinhard Heydrich und die Frühgeschichte von Gestapo und SD* (Stuttgart, 1971). This book is often referred to in order to refute the claim that Heydrich may have been Jewish. See Aronson, pp. 12–17. Historian and professor Hugh Trevor-Roper

of Oxford believed that Heydrich did have Jewish ancestry. See G. S. Graber, *The Life and Times of Reinhard Heydrich* (New York, 1980), p. 81. See also Cornberg and Steiner, p. 161.

54. BA-MA, N 656/9, Bl. 9, p. 3.

55. Callum MacDonald, *The Killing of SS Obergruppenführer Reinhard Heydrich* (New York, 1989), p. 11.

56. BA-MA, BMRS, interview Joachim Schaper, 25.05.1997, T-351. This seemed to be the general belief in Halle. See Edouard Calic, *Reinhard Heydrich: The Chilling Story of the Man Who Masterminded the Nazi Death Camps* (New York), 1985, p. 21.

57. Calic, p. 22. The Gauleiter of Halle, Rudolf Jordan, believed that Heydrich's father was Jewish. He cited *Riemanns Musik Lexikon* from 1916 for proof. He stated that next to Bruno Heydrich's name was the statement that his last name should actually be "Süss." BA-B, NS 22/1051.

58. Felix Kersten, *The Kersten Memoirs, 1940–1945* (New York, 1957), pp. 96–97. Joachim Fest believes that Kersten's memoirs have "so far stood up to all checks." Fest believes that they prove that Himmler definitely believed that Heydrich was of Jewish descent. Fest, *Face,* pp. 335–37, n. 11. Professor Richard Evans of Cambridge University believes Kersten's memoirs are full of errors and need to be used with caution. Calic believes that Kersten only "tried to exonerate the SS by claiming that" Heydrich was responsible for the mass murder of Jews and that his murderous lust to kill Jews resulted from "an inferiority complex produced" by his knowledge that he was partially Jewish (Calic, p. 52). This study believes that the memoirs can be used to show that there were many around Heydrich, among them Hitler and Himmler, who may have believed he was Jewish, which must have had a severe effect on Heydrich.

59. Speer, p. 146.

60. Fest, *Face,* p. 101.

61. Helmut Maurer, *Von Mensch zu Mensch. In Canaris' Abwehr* (Berlin, 1975), p. 125; Snyder, p. 145.

62. Maurer, pp. 124–26; Charles Wighton, *Heydrich: Hitler's Most Evil Henchman* (London, 1962), p. 25; Fest, *Face,* p. 105 n. 26; BA-MA, BMRS, interview Alexander Stahlberg, 3–4.12.1994, T-68; BA-MA, BMRS, interview Theodor Oberländer, 19.09.1994, T-23; Engelmann, pp. 210–11; Walter Schellenberg, *The Schellenberg Memoirs* (London, 1956), p. 207. Schellenberg's memoirs need to be looked at with caution, since he was fighting for his life when he wrote them and was doing everything he could to cover up his past. Another dubious work that mentions Heydrich's possible Jewish past is that of SS officer Wilhelm Hoettl. See Wilhelm Hoettl, *The Secret Front: The Story of Nazi Political Espionage* (New York, 1954), pp. 20–30. See Hilberg, p. 677, about Hoettl.

63. BA-MA, N 179, Milchs Tagebücher, Notiz vom 31.01.1933.

64. Office of the United States Chief Counsel for Prosecution of Axis Criminality, ed., *U.S.A. Military Tribunals: Case No. 1–2, Nuremberg Trials* (Nuremberg, 1949), p. 1776.

65. BA-MA, N 179, Milchs Tagebücher, Notiz vom 01.11.1933, Bl. 46; BA-B, R 15.09/90, Bl. 2, Göring an den Leiter der Reichsstelle für Sippenforschung, 07.08.1935; BA-MA, BMRS, File Erhard Milch, Heft III; BA-MA, Pers 8-385 Horst Boog über Erhard Milch, *Die Militärelite*, p. 351; Wistrich, p. 210; Heiden, p. 500.

66. Williamson Murray, *Luftwaffe* (Baltimore, 1985), pp. 6–7.

67. Corum, *Luftwaffe*, pp. 161–62. See also Murray, p. 9.

68. Corum, *Luftwaffe*, p. 181.

69. Cooper, *German Air-Force*, p. 13.

70. Adam R. A. Claasen, *Hitler's Northern War: The Luftwaffe's Ill-Fated Campaign, 1940–1945* (Kansas, 2001), pp. 99–100.

71. Ibid., pp. 121, 140.

72. Ibid., p. 140.

73. Joel S. A. Hayward, *Stopped at Stalingrad: The Luftwaffe and Hitler's Defeat in the East, 1942–1943* (Kansas, 1998), p. 286.

74. Hayward, pp. 286–310; Murray, p. 148.

75. Heiden, p. 352.

76. Hajo Herrmann, *Eagle's Wings* (England, 1991), pp. 38–43; James S. Corum, *The Roots of Blitzkrieg* (Kansas, 1992), pp. 144–68; Corum, *Luftwaffe*, pp. 30, 34, 52, 59–61, 125–27, 142–46, 180; James S. Corum, "The Old Eagle as Phoenix: The Luftstreitkräfte Creates an Operational Air War Doctrine, 1919–1920," *Air Power History*, (1992): 13–21; Cooper, *German Air-Force*, pp. 39, 379–89; Dr. A. Baeumker, *Ein Beitrag zur Geschichte der Führung der deutschen Luftfahrttechnik im ersten halben Jahrhundert 1900–1945*, Heft XXXXIV der Schriftenreihe "Langfristiges Planen der Forschung und Entwicklung" (Juli 1971); Helmut Wilberg, *Abschließender flieger=Erfahrungsbericht über die Schlacht in flandern* (Gedruckt in der Buch- und Steindruckerei der Artillerie-fliegerschule Ost I); Hildebrand, pp. 513–14.

77. Corum, *Roots of Blitzkrieg*, p. 152.

78. Ibid., p. 153.

79. Ibid., p. 151.

80. Ibid., p. 162. Wilberg was instrumental in making arrangements with the Soviets to allow German pilots to train at the Russian air base of Lipetsk.

81. Ibid., p. 167. The manual was called *Luftwaffe Regulation 16, The Conduct of Air Operations (Luftkriegsführung)*.

82. Ibid., p. 168.

83. The Condor Legion "comprised of four fighter-bomber, four fighter, one reconnaissance, and two seaplane squadrons detached from the *Luftwaffe*." Craig, *Prussian Army*, p. 487.

84. BA-MA, N 761/7, Bl. 2, Bericht General Erwin Jaenecke; Herbert Molly Mason Jr., *The Rise of the Luftwaffe* (New York, 1973), pp. 168–71, 218–21; Corum, *Luftwaffe*, pp. 147, 183–84, 219–21. The office in Berlin that conducted the operations for the Condor Legion was called Sonderstab W (Special Office W; the *W* is for Wilberg).

85. BA-MA, N 761/7, Bl.1–3, Bericht General Erwin Jaenecke.

86. BA-MA, BMRS, File Achim von Bredow, Heft II, Bl.55, Bredow an seine Mutter, 24.10.1941.

87. General Studnitz commanded the Eighty-seventh Infantry Division that invaded Russia in 1941 with Field Marshal Ritter von Leeb's Army Group North.

88. BA-MA, BMRS, interview Wilhelm von Gwinner, 17.11.1994, T-53; BA-MA, BMRS, interview Wilhelm von Gwinner, 16.12.1996, T-280.

89. BA-MA, N 379/ 260, Lebram an Ruge, 10.04.1976.

90. BA-MA, N 379/ 260, Lebram an Ruge, 10.04.1976; BA-MA, N 328/32, Förste an Ehrhardt, 12.12.56.

91. Cajus Bekker, *Hitler's Naval War* (New York, 1977), p. 70; M. J. Whitley, *Destroyer! German Destroyers in World War II* (Maryland, 1983), pp. 118, 130; BA-MA, BMRS, File Georg Langheld. For example, from 10 October 1942 until 9 April 1943, Langheld was fleet commander of the Fourth Destroyer Flotilla. From January 1944 until April 1944, he was fleet commander of the Eighth Destroyer Flotilla, and from 20 April 1944 until 10 May 1945, he was fleet commander of the Fifth Destroyer Flotilla.

92. Kurt Pritzkoleit, *Die Neuen Herren* (München, 1955), pp. 96–97; Meyer, p. 152; Cornberg and Steiner, p. 156.

93. Friedländer, pp. 52–53, 153; Stoltzfus, *Resistance,* p. viii; Cornberg and Steiner, p. 159.

94. BA-B, R 21/874–878, Bl. 103.

95. Lörzer and Göring had served together during World War I as pilots and were good friends.

96. BA-MA, BMRS, File Lt. Fränzel, Bl. 2.

97. Meyer, p. 152; Gerhard Bracke, *Melitta Gräfin Stauffenberg. Das Leben einer Fliegerin* (München, 1990); BA-MA, BMRS, File H. Lange. She flew over twenty-five hundred *Sturzflüge* with the Stuka dive-bombers *Ju 87* and *Ju 88.* Göring also awarded her the Gold Military Flyer Medal with diamonds and rubies. In 1945, she was shot down by an American fighter.

98. *Nazism, 1919–1945,* vol. 4, p. 31.

99. Oberfüsilier is a private.

100. General von Briesen and Keitel were good friends, which must have also played a role in helping Rüdiger von Briesen to get the *Genehmigung.* This especially could have been the case, since Hitler thought highly of General von Briesen. See Keitel, p. 95.

101. BA-A, Sammlung Jüdische Soldaten, Oberst v. Briesen, Kommandant von Prag, an einen ungenannten Regimentskommandeur, 07.11.1940; BA-MA, BMRS, File v. Briesen.

102. Thomas, p. 103, n. 39. Nevertheless, Raeder's son-in-law found it advisable to live abroad during the Third Reich.

103. Erich Raeder, *Mein Leben. Von 1935 bis Spandau 1955* (Tübingen, 1957), p. 112.

104. BA-B, NS 6/78, Bl. 13–14, Der Stellvertreter des Führers an Gauleiter des Gaues Schleswig-Holstein der NSDAP, Pg. Hinrich Lohse, 03.09.1938, Abschrift von Schreiben Hitlers über Konteradmiral a.D. Karl Kühlenthal, 06.07.1938.

105. BA-MA, N 328/20, Kühlenthal an Förste, 28.10.1950.

106. BA-MA, BMRS, interview Gerhart von Gierke, 05.04.1997, T-344; BA-MA, BMRS, interview Rolf von Gierke, 29.11.1997, T-414.
107. Information gained from Dr. Georg Meyer of the Militärgeschichtliches Forschungsamt (Military Research Center), Potsdam/Freiburg, March 1998, "Glückliche Mischung aus preußischem Charme und jüdischer Bescheidenheit."
108. Bernd Gericke, ed., *Die Inhaber des Deutschen Kreuzes in Gold, des Deutschen Kreuzes in Silber der Kriegsmarine* (Osnabrück, 1993), p. 201.
109. BA-MA, N 328/32, Raeder an Katz, 06.01.1940.
110. Ibid., Bestätigung für Katz, 06.01.1940.
111. Lieutenant field marshal (Feldmarschalleutnant) is a general's rank. It is the equivalent to the British rank of lieutenant general (Generalleutnant in the Wehrmacht) and was used in the Habsburg monarchy until 1918. From 1918 until 1920, it was used in the Volkswehr of Austria. Afterward, the rank was not used throughout the 1920s and early 1930s. In 1933, the Austrian military (Österreichisches Bundesheer) reinstated the rank until its incorporation into the Wehrmacht in March of 1938. See *1918–1968 Die Streitkräfte der Republik Österreich. Katalog zur Sonderausstellung im Heeresgeschichtlichen Museum Wien 1968* (hrsg.), Heeresgeschichtlichen Museum/Militärwissenschaftlichen Institut Wien (Wien, 1968), pp. 149–57.
112. Johann Friedländer distinguished himself on the General Staff before and during World War I. After 1928, he "headed the defense ministry's department of training, equipment and education." In 1936, he was transferred to the inspector general's office. He retired in 1937. Schmidl, p. 148.
113. As the Russians invaded Poland, where many of the death camps were located, the Nazis evacuated the camps and forced the inmates to walk long distances to concentration camps in the West. During these forced marches, called "death marches," many of the inmates died of exhaustion and disease. Many also were executed on the side of the road.
114. Senekowitsch, *Feldmarschalleutnant Johann Friedländer,* pp. 20–28; BA-MA, BMRS, interview Posselt.
115. Office of the United States Chief Counsel for Prosecution of Axis Criminality, ed., *Nazi Conspiracy and Aggression, Supplement B* (Washington, D.C.), 1946, p. 1,246. This man was probably Ribbentrop's personal physician, Dr. Oscar Bosch. According to family friends, Bosch's contact with Ribbentrop saved Bosch's mother. BA-MA, BMRS, File Oscar Bosch, Bl. 4–5. If it was not Bosch, then it might have been SS Captain Thorner. He was Ribbentrop's secretary in London and a "12.5 percent Jew." Ribbentrop had helped Thorner by taking his case personally to Hitler. John Weitz, *Hitler's Diplomat: The Life and Times of Joachim von Ribbentrop* (New York, 1992), p. 132.
116. *Nazi Conspiracy and Aggression: Supplement B,* p. 1,246.
117. Kesselring: BA-MA, N 431/1154, Beglaubigte Abschrift von Irmgard Horn, 18.03.1947; Sauckel: BA-MA, BMRS, File Hans Sander; Lammers: BA-MA, BMRS, File Ernst Prager and BA-B, Reichskanzlei 7.01 4112, Bl. 363–65; Canaris: BA-MA, BMRS, File Robert Borchardt, BA-MA, BMRS, File Ernst Bloch; Bormann/Heydrich: BA-MA, WF-01/10230; Dönitz: Messerschmidt, p. 356, BA-MA, BMRS, File di Simoni; Ribbentrop: BA-MA, BMRS, File

Joachim von Ribbentrop, BA-MA, BMRS, File Bosch; v. Manstein, Schmundt v. Gottberg and Raeder: documented throughout this book; v. Schirach: Krackow, p. 98; BA-MA, BMRS, interviews J. Krackow; BA-MA, BMRS, interview R. Krackow; Kaltenbrunner: BA-MA, BMRS, interview Koref.

118. Meyer, p. 152; Cornberg and Steiner, p. 148.

119. Gilbert, *Holocaust*, p. 615; Craig, *Germany, 1866–1945*, p. 750.

120. Clark, pp. 339–40. Pringsheim was a well-known professor for Roman and German civil rights in Freiburg and Göttingen, and then in Oxford from 1939 to 1946.

121. Even Adolf Eichmann helped save a half-Jewish cousin and a Jewish couple in Vienna; in addition, he had a Jewish stepmother. While working in Vienna in the late 1930s, Eichmann had a Jewish mistress, an old flame from his youth. Arendt, pp. 30, 88, 137. Eichmann was not alone in committing *Rassenschande* among the Nazi elite. The famous Stuka pilot and fanatic Nazi, Luftwaffe Colonel Hans-Ulrich Rudel, had a half-Jewish lover, Frau Erika Leykam, during the war. Personal interview conducted with Leykam by Günter Czernetzky, director of the film project *ZeitZeugenVideo* in Munich; BA-MA, BMRS, File Erika Leykam. Alfred Rosenberg, the Nazi racial theorist and Reich minister of eastern regions, also had a Jewish mistress. Wighton, p. 126.

122. Hitler renamed Lodz Litzmannstadt in honor of General Litzmann. Benz, p. 49. General Litzmann had become famous in 1914 during World War I for breaking through the Russian front near Lodz. He conquered the fortress Brest-Litovsk.

123. They actually were "18.75" Jewish and thus, according to Nazi practice with racial policy, regarded as quarter-Jews.

124. BA-MA, BMRS, File Walter Lehweß-Litzmann, Bl. 7, Stammbaum Lehweß-Litzmann, Bl. 11, and Bl. 37, Der Kommandierende General des VIII. Fliegerkorps an Frau Dr. med. Lehweß-Litzmann, 01.11.1941; BA-MA, BMRS, interview Jörn Lehweß-Litzmann, 27.05.1997, T-354.

125. *Die Träger des Ritterkreuzes des Eisernen Kreuzes, 1939–1945. Die Inhaber der höchsten Auszeichnung des Zweiten Weltkrieges aller Wehrmachtteile* (Osnabrück, 1993), p. 166. Walter Lehweß-Litzmann became a General Staff officer and a squadron commander.

126. BA-MA, BMRS, interview Friedrich Rubien, 27.07.1997, T-394.

127. BA-MA, BMRS, interview Rubien. According to Rubien, the family member Senator Fritz Beindorff paid this amount.

128. *Goebbels Diaries, 1942–1943*, p. 285.

129. BA-MA, BMRS, File Werner Bujakowsky, Bl. 16.

130. BA-MA, BMRS, File Ludwig Mayer, Bl. 23, Telegram M. Steinhardt to Mayer 27.09. 1935, Bl. 25, H. Mayer an ihre Mutter, 06.10.1935 and Bl.30, H. Mayer to v. Tschammer, October 1935.

131. BA-MA, BMRS, File Ludwig Mayer, Bl. 31, H. Mayer to Mr. Avery Brundage, president of the American Olympic Committee, 26.10.1935, Bl. 35, H. Mayer to Dr. Aurelia Henry Reinhardt, 10.12.1935.

132. Klemperer, Buch I, 12.08.1936, pp. 292–93.

133. BA-MA, BMRS, File Mayer, Bl. 31; BA-MA, BMRS, interview Erika Mayer; Shirer, *Nighmare Years*, pp. 230–33. See also Friedländer, p. 181.

134. BA-MA, BMRS, File Mayer, Bl. 35; Yahil, p. 71.

135. Apparently, after the women's fencing event was over, Hitler refused to congratulate Mayer; Iona Elek, the gold medalist from Hungary; and Ellen Preis, the bronze medalist from Austria, because they were all of Jewish descent. Engelmann, opp. p. 353.

136. Friedländer, p. 181. Several reports state that Ball was half-Jewish (Cornberg and Steiner, p. 160). Since Friedländer is an authority on German Jews, his data has been taken for Ball's case.

137. *BA-MA, BMRS, File Wolfgang Fürstner; Richard D. Mandell, The Nazi Olympics* (New York, 1971), pp. 88, 93. He committed suicide in 1936 because of the persecution he experienced as a half-Jew.

138. Lutz Graf Schwerin von Krosigk, *Persönliche Erinnerungen: II. Teil, 25 Jahre Berlin, 1930–1945* (Essen, 1973), p. 173; Cornberg and Steiner, pp. 159–60; Vuletić, p. 22, n. 37. Lewald was the man who introduced the tradition of carrying the torch from Olympia in Greece to the host city.

139. Mandell, pp. 71–77. Gretel Bergmann, a German athlete of Jewish descent, was not as lucky as Mayer or Ball. Two weeks before the Games, the Nazis informed her that she could not participate because of her Jewish ancestry. She was predicted to win the gold in the high jump, had she been allowed to compete. See also Friedländer, p. 181.

140. Keegan, *Second World War*, p. 486; Keegan, *Mask of Command*, p. 281.

141. Hitler, *Mein Kampf*, pp. 290–91. See also *Hitlers Tischgespräche im Führerhauptquartier*, p. 310.

142. Speer, p. 145. See also *Goebbels Diaries, 1942–1943*, pp. 51, 60; John W. Dower, *War Without Mercy: Race and Power in the Pacific War* (New York, 1986), p. 207.

143. Hilberg, p. 45; Lauren, p. 124, Stoltzfus, *Resistance*, p. 42; Dower, pp. 207, 269; Yahil, p. 71.

144. Snyder, p. 170; Craig, *Germany, 1866–1945*, p. 696.

145. Snyder, p. 170; see also H. R. Trevor-Roper, *The Last Days of Hitler* (New York, 1947), pp. 21–22; Otto Klineberg, "Racialism in Nazi Germany," in *The Third Reich*, ed. Maurice Baumont, John H. E. Fried and Edmond Vermeil (New York, 1955), p. 859; Dower, p. 269; *Goebbels Diaries, 1942–1943*, pp. 77, 79, 86, 91. Hitler called the Japanese the "Prussians of the East." *Hitlers Tischgespräche im Führerhauptquartier*, p. 398, n. 388.

146. *Goebbels Diaries, 1942–1943*, p. 138; Redlich, p. 149; Kershaw, *Hitler, 1936–1945*, p. 504.

147. Otto Klineberg, "Racialism in Nazi Germany," in *The Third Reich*, p. 859.

148. The mufti left Beirut in 1939, took up residence in Baghdad, and put himself at the pro-Axis political effort there, which culminated in a "pro-Axis coup" in 1941. The mufti proclaimed over the airways a jihad (holy war) against the British, who were occupying Iraq at the time. Although the Germans promised support, it did not arrive in time, and the mufti and his forces were

defeated. After the defeat, the mufti left for Berlin in September 1941. The mufti stayed in Germany until the end of the war. Conor Cruise O'Brien, *The Siege: The Saga of Israel and Zionism* (New York, 1986), pp. 250–52.

149. Lepre, p. 31.

150. Hitler had promised Hajj Amin el-Husseini that he would slaughter the Jewish community in Palestine once German forces had taken over that area. Weinberg, *Germany, Hitler,* p. 220; Browning, *Nazi Policy, Jewish Workers,* pp. 49–50.

151. Bauer, p. 44.

152. O'Brien, pp. 251–52. Hitler felt that Arab men with blond hair and blue eyes were descendants of the Vandals who had occupied northern Africa. *Monologe im Führerhauptquartier 1941–1944,* p. 124.

153. *Hitlers Tischgespräche im Führerhauptquartier,* p. 403. As translated in O'Brien, pp. 251–52. Hitler even claimed that Turkey's leader Atatürk could not have descended from the Turks because he had blue eyes. *Monologe im Führerhauptquartier, 1941–1944,* p. 217.

154. Hilberg, p. 7; BA-B, NS 19/3134, Bl. 1–2; Maser, p. 282; *Hitlers Tischgespräche im Führerhauptquartier,* Einführung von Picker, p. 45; Bormann Lang, p. 156; Dimont, pp. 331–32.

155. Horst von McGraw, *The Evolution of Hitler's Germany* (New York, 1973), p. 56; *Monologe im Führerhauptquartier, 1941–1944,* pp. 96–99, 412–13; Redlich, p. 309; Friedländer, pp. 102, 177; *The Speeches of Adolf Hitler,* vol 1, p. 19.

156. *Institut zur Erforschung und Beseitigung des jüdischen Einflusses auf das deutsche kirchliche Leben.* See Friedländer, pp. 326–27.

157. Bauer, p. 133; Redlich, p. 302; Burleigh, pp. 13–14, 259–60.

158. Omer Bartov, *Hitler's Army* (New York, 1991), pp. 14, 39; see also Megargee, p. 174.

159. Rüdiger Overmans, *Deutsche militärische Verluste im Zweiten Weltkrieg* (München, 1999), pp. 266, 278.

160. BA-MA, BMRS, File Gert Beschütz, Bl. 3.

161. BA-MA, N 328/45, Ehrhardt an Förste, 14.11.1956; *Heeresadjutant bei Hitler,* p. 32; Noakes, "Development of Nazi Policy," pp. 316, 333.

162. BA-MA, N 328/45, Ehrhardt an Förste, 14.11.1956.

163. *Heeresadjutant bei Hitler,* pp. 121–22, n. 375; BA-B, DZA 62 Ka. 1 83, Bl. 140, Engel an Blankenburg, 17.06.1942.

164. BA-MA, BMRS, interview Gert Ascher, 17.11.1997, T-408; BA-MA, BMRS, interview Ursula Ascher, 17.11.1997, T-409.

165. BA-MA, BMRS, File Heinrici, Heft I, Bl. 21, Dr. Heinrici an Rigg, 05.12.1995; BA-MA, BMRS, interview Dr. Heinrici, 16.05.1996, T-203.

166. Ibid.

167. BA-B, DZA 62 Ka. 1 83, Bl. 140, Engel an Blankenburg, 17.06.1942.

168. BA-MA, WF01/10230, Bl. 1–2, Engel an Käpitan z.S. a.D. Vanselow, 19.11.1940.

169. BA-MA, N 118/4.

170. Deutsche Arbeitsfront (DAF) (German Labor Front).

171. BA-B, DZA 62 Ka. 1 83, Bl. 93, Engel an die Kanzlei des Führers der NSDAP, 26.09.1941.
172. *Stufe* means "level." For example, *Stufe* III wounded soldiers had lost either an arm, a leg, or both feet—to name just a few of the wounds that qualified a soldier for this classification. These soldiers also received fifty Reichsmarks a month. BA-MA, RH 12–23/ 834, p. 93.
173. Absolon, *Wehrgesetz und Wehrdienst*, p. 120; See also BA-B, DZA 62 Ka. 1 83, Bl. 91–92, Parteikanzlei, Beförderung von Schwerstbeschädigten, 11.10.1941.
174. This number was probably small because only those who applied were considered for the exemption. In other words, once a *Mischlinge* was injured, he did not get an exemption de facto. He, like any other *Mischlinge* attempting to receive an exemption, had to apply for it.
175. BA-B, R 21/448, Bl. 34, Der Reichsminister des Innern (Schönfeldt) an Rust, 20.02.1942.
176. BA-B, DZA 62 Ka. 1 83, Bl. 72.
177. Ibid., Bl. 73, OKW an Kanzlei des Führers, 16.09.1943.
178. Ibid., Bl. 67b, "Jüdische Mischlinge im Wehrdienst," von Blankenburg.
179. BA-MA, BMRS, File Bamberger, Bl. 2, Lammers und Keitel an Bamberger, 17.08.1943 and Bl. 35–36, *Autobiographie*.
180. See BA-B, R 21-448, Bl. 35, von Schönfeldt an Rust, 20.2.1942.
181. BA-MA, BMRS, File Emil Lux, Heft IV, Bl. 8. Knoll/Hochschule für Welthandel an Regierungsdirektor Dr. Kock, 20.07.1944, and Bl. 12, OKW an Rust, 08.10.1943; BA-MA, BMRS, interview Lux. While Lux served in Russia, his mother, Jenny née Schultz, was persecuted at home and forced to wear the Jewish star. When he returned home from the front and his hospitalization, he found that his mother was gone. The Gestapo had forced her to enter the Jewish Hospital in Berlin at Iranische Straße.
182. BA-B, DZA 62 Ka. 1 83, Bl. 67b–68.
183. BA-B, DZA 62 Ka. 1 83, Bl. 82.
184. BA-B, DZA 62 Ka. 1 83, Bl. 73, OKW an Kanzlei des Führers, 16.09.1943; BA-MA, BMRS, File G. F. Müller, Bl. 52; BA-MA, BMRS, File Haller.
185. Two men in this study received Hitler's declarations this way. However, it is difficult to document men who received this award because of the problems of finding their families or military files.
186. BA-B, DZA 62 Ka. 1 83, Bl. 72.
187. *Kampfzeit* (time of struggle) was between 1920 and 1933 when the Nazis struggled for power.
188. *Heeresadjutant bei Hitler,* pp. 31–32.
189. BA-MA, RH 53-7/ 1120.
190. BA-MA, BMRS, interview Wolter; *Das Deutsche Reich und der zweite Weltkrieg.* vol. 5/1, Kroener, pp. 709–12.
191. IfZ,N 71–73, Anträge und positive Entscheidungen gemäß §7 der Ersten Verordnung zum Reichsbürger-gesetz, 22.05.1941; Lösener, pp. 284–85.
192. Meyer, p. 157.
193. BA-B, DZA 62 Ka. 1 83, Bl. 136–39.
194. Ibid., Bl. 147–48.

195. IfZ, N 71–73, Bl. 106, Zahl der Gnadenentscheidungen nach dem Reichs-bürgergesetz, 10.09.1942; Lösener, p. 310.
196. BA-B, DZA 62 Ka. 1 83, Bl. 29–45.
197. Ibid., Bl. 43.
198. Rebentisch, p. 435, n. 200. H. G. Adler also said that exemptions probably ran into the thousands. Adler, *Der Verwaltete Mensch*, p. 302.
199. BA-B, DZA 62 Ka. 1 83, Bl. 117, "Aktennotiz" von Brack, 10.07.1942.
200. BA-MA, BMRS, interview W. v. Gwinner.
201. BA-MA, BMRS, interview Hamburger; BA-MA, BMRS, File Hamburger, Hamburger an Rigg, 25.11.2000.
202. BA-MA, BMRS, File Prager.
203. BA-MA, WF01–20740, Koken an Engel, 15.10.1942.
204. Ibid., Engel an Koken, 19.10.1942.
205. BA-MA, BMRS, interview Arnim Leidoff, 02.12.1995, T-93.
206. Königsberg is now Kaliningrad, Russia.
207. Actually, Göring said this phrase. Hitler was never recorded as saying anything like the above.
208. BA-A, Pers 36790 Georg Meyer, Beurteilung vom 01.03.1944. Margot Meyer von Rühle maintains that this military report was only written as it was because it was a necessary condition for promotion. In other words, it was a formality. BA-MA, BMRS, File Georg Meyer, Meyer von Rühle an Rigg, 11.01.2001.
209. BA-MA, BMRS, interview Margot Meyer von Rühle 02.09.1995, T-163; BA-MA, BMRS, interview Helmut Meyer-Krahmer, 27.07.1997, T-393; BA-A, Pers 36848 Helmut Meyer-Krahmer. According to Margot Meyer von Rühle, Georg was only "12.5 percent or 18.75 percent" Jewish. However, Georg Meyer's cousin, Helmut Meyer-Krahmer, says that this is incorrect. He and his four cousins were all quarter-Jews. According to Meyer-Krahmer, Georg must have obtained false documents to prove that their grandmother was not a full Jew but a half-Jew. He naturally did so to mitigate his situation. Since Meyer-Krahmer knows his family's personal history better than most, his version has been used.
210. BA-MA, BMRS, File Prager.
211. Vogel, p. 313. Philipp Borchardt was later released, and he and his daughter left for England, where they spent the rest of the war.
212. BA-MA, BMRS, interview E. Borchardt; McGuirk, p. 45.
213. BA-A, Pers 4393, Beurteilung, 13.05.1942.
214. BA-MA, BMRS, File Borchardt, Bl. 46, E.M. Heard to Rigg, 02.12.1996. Borchardt defended himself after the war, claiming that he fought for Germany and that his family had a long history of military service and cultural accomplishments. Two brothers of his great-grandfather fought in the War of Independence of 1813–1815. One died in Leipzig. During the Franco-Prussian War, two brothers of his grandfather served in the Prussian army. One was terribly wounded in the Battle of Sedan. One of his father's brothers, Rudolf, was a poet and translator and was friends with Hugo von Hofmannsthal and Rudolf Alexander Schröder. During World War I, Rudolf Borchardt served four years in the German army. Another uncle, Ernst Borchardt, served as a lieutenant

and died soon after the war because of his battle injuries. Another uncle, Robert Borchardt, served as an Unteroffizier and died in battle in 1916. Borchardt's father would have served in the army, had he not been born with a deformed left leg. Robert Borchardt claimed that serving Germany as he did was no different from what his Jewish ancestors had done before him.

215. BA-MA, BMRS, File Eike Schweitzer, Bl. 24, Eike Schweitzer an Tante Dorle, 11.01.1942.

216. BA-MA, BMRS, File Schweitzer, Bl. 13.

217. Although Wilberg was in charge of the operations of the Condor Legion, was in charge of the officer school, and was responsible for developing Luftwaffe air doctrine, he still did not become chief of staff, probably because of his ancestry.

218. See Kershaw, *Hitler, 1936–1945*, pp. 105–6, 289, 386, 417; *Nazism 1919–1945*, vol. 4, pp. 8–13; Keitel, p. 105; Megargee, p. 65.

219. BA-MA, BMRS, File Gerd Schneider, Bl. 77, Frey an Schiller, 10.02.1943 and Bl. 82, Wehrmachtfürsorge, Bescheid—Rente, 26.03.1943.

220. *Germany and the Second World War*, vol. 4, M. Messerschmidt, p. 8; Seaton, *German Army*, p. 80; Speer, p. 157; Kershaw, *Hitler, 1936–1945*, pp. 576–77. See also Wallach, pp. 306–7; Keegan, *Mask of Command*, pp. 295–98.

CHAPTER 8: THE PROCESS OF OBTAINING AN EXEMPTION

1. BA-MA, BMRS, general impression gained from this study; Lösener, p. 310; Noakes, "Development of Nazi Policy," p. 318; BA-MA, N 328/32, Förste an Ehrhardt, 12.12.56.

2. BA-MA, BMRS, N 328/32, Förste an Ehrhardt, 12.12.1956; Gericke, p. 128.

3. BA-MA, BMRS, File Prager.

4. Kershaw, *Hitler, 1889–1936*, p. 328; Kershaw, *Hitler, 1936–1945*, pp. 93–94.

5. Kershaw, *Hitler, 1889–1936*, p. 344.

6. Bauer, p. 100; Yahil, p. 66.

7. BA-B, R 43 II/1273, Bl. 70–84.

8. Vogel, pp. 233–34.

9. BA-MA, BMRS, File Sander, Bl. 3, Hitler an Sander, 30.07.1935 and Bl. 62–64, Major a.D. Sander an Hans Sander, 27.02.1935; BA-MA, BMRS, interview Stefan Sander, 10.07.1997, T-366.

10. BA-MA, RH 39/154, Schreiben von Frick, 19.08.1937. An exception in the Party did not automatically allow one to become an officer. In January 1938, the Wehrmacht announced that although a *Mischling* may have received Hitler's approval to remain in the Party and enter the Wehrmacht, he could not become an officer without an additional approval. BA-MA, RH 53-7/627, Bl. 8, General-Kommando VII. Armee-Korps an Kriegsschule München, 24.01.1938. For example, Hitler declared Sander *deutschblütig* in 1940, and only then could he become an officer. BA-MA, BMRS, File Sander, Bl. 2, Lammers an Sander, 29.08.1940.

11. It was probably at this time that the clemency forms of *Deutschblütigkeitserklärung* and *Genehmigung* came into being.

12. *Holocaust, vol. 1, Legalizing the Holocaust*, p. 31; Erste Verordnung zum Reichsbürgergesetz vom 14.11.1935 (RGBl., Teil I, 1935, Nr. 125, pp. 1,333–36); Vogel, p. 238.

13. Schleunes, p. 257.
14. Friedländer, p. 188.
15. Absolon, *Die Wehrmacht im Dritten Reich. Band III*, p. 353.
16. BA-MA, BMRS, general impression gained from this study; Lösener, p. 284.
17. Lösener, pp. 270–85.
18. For more about Keitel's and Lammers's roles in implementing policy, see Speer, pp. 300–301.
19. BA-MA, BMRS, general data collected; BA-MA, N 328/45, Eherhardt an Förste, 18.12.1956. Noakes in his essay claims that the certificates were bright blue (Noakes, "Development of Nazi Policy," p. 319; see also Stoltzfus, *Resistance*, p. 117; Cornberg and Steiner, p. 154). The several certificates signed by Meyer and obtained during this study show that they were green, not blue.
20. No one could be a farmer *(Bauer)* who had a Jewish ancestor after 1800. Cohn, "Bearers of a Common Fate."p. 330. According to Büttner, non-Aryans were allowed to work in agriculture, but could not own a farm that their heirs could inherit *(Erbhofstellen)*. Büttner, "Persecution," p. 272. See also *Akten-NSDAP*, 107-00390-391; RGBl. 1933, Teil I, Nr. 108, p. 686.
21. *Akten-NSDAP*, 107—00392, p. 7. See also BA-B, NS 19/1614, Bl. 3, Lammers an Himmler, 31.08.1942.
22. BA-B, NS 19/1614, Bl. 3, Lammers an Himmler, 31.08.1942; BA-MA, BMRS, File Walter Hollaender, see also BA-MA, BMRS, File Karl Helwig; BA-MA, BMRS, File Erich Mußgnug.
23. BA-MA, BMRS, interview Otto Wolters; BA-MA, BMRS, interview Frau Hertha-Barbara Hollaender, 21.11.1995, T-171; BA-MA, BMRS, interview Frau Hertha-Barbara Hollaender, 12.11.1996, T-234; *Die Träger des Deutschen Kreuzes in Gold*, p. 162; BA-MA, BMRS, File Walter Hollaender, Bl. 113, Ritterkreuz-Urkunde, 18.07.1943; BA-A, Pers Walter Hollaender, Beurteilung vom 11.01.1943; BA-MA, BMRS, interview Jochen Hollaender, 14.12.1996, T-276; BA-MA, BMRS, File Wilhelm Hollaender.
24. BA-B, Sammlung Schumacher, Reichskommissar für die Festigung des deutschen Volkstums/ Stabshauptamt: Mitteilung Nr. 3, 29.09.1942.
25. Lösener, p. 310; *Heeresadjutant bei Hitler*, pp. 120–22; *Dictionary of Nazi Terms*, David Bankier *Mischlinge;* BA-MA, N 328/45, Ebhardt an Förste, 14.11.1956.
26. BA-MA, RW 19/550, Lammers an Reichsminister, Preußischen Minister-präsidenten und Finanzminister, Staatssekretär und Chef der Präsidialkanzlei, Chef der Kanzlei, und Adj. des Führers, 25.10.1937; BA-MA, Wi/ VIII 45; Noakes, "Development of Nazi Policy," p. 319: Craig, *Germany, 1866–1945*, p. 592; for more information about Lammers, see Georg Franz-Willing's book, *Die Reichskanzlei, 1933–1945*.
27. Robert Koehl, "Feudal Aspects of National Socialism," *American Political Science Review* 54 (1960). See also Redlich, p. 104.
28. At this time, Lammers had the power to decide whether an application was worthy of Hitler's time. Applications not good enough for an exemption according to Lammers's initial review were rejected without being seen by Hitler. See also Rebentisch, p. 434; *Akten-NSDAP*, 107-00392.

29. *Gleichschaltung* means "coordination."

30. *Nazism, 1919–1945,* vol. 4, p. 1.

31. Lammers had lost an eye during World War I and wore a glass eye, which gave him a cross-eyed appearance. Rebentisch, p. 49.

32. Rebentisch, pp. 425–26.

33. BA-B, R 43 II/1036, 15.12.1936; Kershaw, *Profiles in Power,* p. 113; Kershaw, *Hitler, 1889–1936,* pp. 485, 533; Hilberg, p. 264; Jochen Lang, p. 180.

34. Kershaw, *Hitler, 1936–1945,* p. 313.

35. *U.S.A. Military Tribunals: Case No. 11.2,* Heinrich Lammers, p. 161. *Monologe im Führerhauptquartier, 1941–1944,* p. 141.

36. Friedemann Bedürftig and Christian Zentner, eds., *The Encyclopedia of the Third Reich,* vol. 1 (New York, 1991), p. 524.

37. Stoltzfus, *Resistance,* pp. 73, 120, 246–47. Most *Schutzjuden* escaped deportation. See Stoltzfus, p. 120 n. 14. See also Cornberg and Steiner, pp. 149–51.

38. BA-MA, N 39/62, Lammers an v. Mackensen, 03.02.1939. See also Friedländer, pp. 270–71.

39. The Spanish Blue Division (250th Infantry Division, "División Azúl") was made up of Spanish volunteers commanded by General Esteban Infantes and sent by Franco to the eastern front to fight with the army against Russia. Over forty-seven thousand men fought in this division, forty-five hundred were killed in action, and the Wehrmacht estimated that these Spaniards inflicted over forty-nine thousand casualties on the Soviets. Corum, *Luftwaffe,* p. 219.

40. BA-MA, BMRS, File Erich Rose, Schnez an Rigg, 30.01.2001.

41. BA-MA, Pers 6/ 10046, Alfred Simon, Bl. 49, Generalkommando V. Armeekorps an OKH-P[ersonal] A[mt], 06.09.1937.

42. Ibid., Bl. 45, v. Reichenau an Chef des Heerespersonalamts, 03.08.1937.

43. Ibid., Bl. 50, OKH an Reichs- und Preußischen Minister des Innern, 11.09.1937.

44. Ibid., Bl. 96, Keitel an Generalkommando VII. Armeekorps, 17.06.1938.

45. BA-MA, Pers 6/ 10046, Pionier-Kommandeur 1, Berurteilung über Alfred Simon, 01.03.1944.

46. Kriegsschule is a military academy.

47. Rohr, pp. 42–46, 84–85.

48. BA-MA, BMRS, interview Knigge.

49. *Heeresadjutant bei Hitler,* pp. 10–11, 33, 94, 103

50. Ibid., p. 10.

51. *Heeresadjutant bei Hitler,* pp. 53, 80; BA-MA, BMRS, interview Beelitz. Hitler's Luftwaffe adjutant, Nicolaus von Below, wrote that the military adjutants often took walks with Hitler. Below, p. 29.

52. *Heeresadjutant bei Hitler,* pp. 20, 30–32, 76, 78, 94, 141–42.

53. BA-MA, N 118; BA-MA, BMRS, interview von Knigge; BA-MA, BMRS, interview Beelitz; BA-MA, BMRS, interview v. Helmolt.

54. Schmundt took over Hoßbach's position after the Blomberg-Fritsch crisis in 1938. He was above the other military adjutants ("Chefadjutant der Wehrmacht"). Luftwaffe adjutant Nicolaus von Below dubbed him *Primus inter pares.* Below, p. 90.

55. BA-B, DZA 62 Ka. 1 83, Bl. 67b, "Jüdische Mischlinge im Wehrdienst," von Blankenburg; BA-B, DZA 62 Ka. 1 83, Bl. 167, Engel an Blankenburg, 28.04.1942; *Heeresadjutant bei Hitler*, pp. 32–33, 126–29, 138, 143.

56. *Heeresadjutant bei Hitler*, pp. 70, 75, 79–80, 127; BA-MA, BMRS, interview Beelitz.

57. Below, p. 27.

58. BA-MA, BMRS, general impression gained from the files on Engel and v. Puttkamer; Below, p. 32.

59. Below, p. 35.

60. BA-MA, BMRS, general data gathered on *Mischling* soldiers; BA-MA, N 328/58, Puttkamer an Förste, 15.04.1957; BA-MA, N 328/58, Ehrhardt an Förste, 14.11.56; see also Meyer, p. 231; BA-MA, BMRS, File Bernhard Rogge; BA-MA, BMRS, interview Helmut Schmoeckel, 25.11.1994, T-63; BA-MA, BMRS, File Helmut Schmoeckel.

61. BA-MA, Pers 6/2094, OKH Betr.: Deutschblütigkeitserklärung von Offizieren, 02.09.1939.

62. Absolon, *Die Wehrmacht im Dritten Reich. Band V*, p. 148. Their number is unknown.

63. BA-MA, N 328/45, Ehrhardt an Förste, 14.11.1956; BA-MA, BMRS, File Schmoeckel. It seems that the one navy officer not taken back was Lebram, which made the young man furious. Lebram tried four times to return to the navy (1934, 1935, 1939, and 1941). BA-MA, N 656/27, Lebram an Ruge, 08.04.1976; BA-MA, N 656/2. Eventually, Canaris helped Lebram get a job with Siemens as a Marinebaurat. BA-MA, N 656/2, Bl. 43.

64. BA-MA, N 328/45, Ehrhardt an Förste, 14.11.1956.

65. BA-MA, N 328/32, Förste an Ehrhardt, 12.12.1956.

66. Rogge notes that the Party official that attacked him was the Kreisleiter of Eutin, but it is clear from the document that Rogge was unsure of the spelling of that name.

67. BA-MA, BMRS, File Rogge, Vertraulich, Betr. Absetzung Landrat Bernhard Rogge, Schleswig, Persönliche Ausführungen zur Sache, 06.11.1945, Heft I. Special thanks to Peter Tamm, director of the Institut für Schiffahrts- und Marinegeschichte in Hamburg, for access to Rogge's file. Special thanks for information gained about this incident during a discussion with Dr. Georg Meyer of the Militärgeschichtliches Forschungsamt (Military Research Center), Potsdam/Freiburg, March 1998; Karl-Friedrich Merten, *Nach Kompass* (Cloppenburg, 1994), p. 274.

68. Muggenthaler, p. 136; BA-MA, BMRS, File Friedrich-Karl Rogge, *Lebenserinnerungen* (Amorbach, 1993), p. 36; Gilbert, *Second World War*, pp. 35, 51; Edward P. von der Porten, *The German Navy in World War II* (New York, 1969), p. 134.

69. Charles W. Koburger Jr., *Steel Ships, Iron Crosses, and Refugees: The German Navy in the Baltic, 1939–1945* (New York, 1989), pp. 45, 49. An interesting side note about Rogge's military career. At the war's end, he had several men executed for desertion. After the war, he was brought up on charges but was found innocent. Rogge had received so much help from others because of

his Jewish past, but did not show much mercy on those who no longer wanted to fight for Nazi Germany. The information gathered on Rogge indicates that he simply claimed that he was following orders. As Georg Meyer said of Rogge in respect to this event, "[H]e was hard as steel."

70. Muggenthaler, p. 140. Without Rogge's support of the army in the Baltic, the Kurland pocket would have never continued its resistance, which tied down thousands of Russian soldiers in 1944. He also allowed twenty-nine divisions and much of their equipment to escape Russian encirclement in 1944 by keeping a thirty-mile choke point open at Riga. He also used his ships to cover the millions of refugees leaving Prussia under the savage advance of the Soviet army in 1944 and 1945. Koburger, pp. 47–48.

71. Fähnrich is an officer candidate.

72. BA-MA, BMRS, interview Helmut Schmoeckel, 25.11.1994, T-63; BA-MA, BMRS, File Helmut Schmoeckel. Before Schmoeckel became a U-boat captain, he was the first adjutant on the heavy cruiser *Admiral Hipper*. As a U-boat captain, he sank one ship for a total of 1.621 tons.

73. BA-MA, BMRS, interview Thilo Bode, 24.02.1995, T-104.

74. Rohr, p. 108.

75. Rohr, pp. 91, 103; BA-A, Pers 45573, Joachim Rohr an OKH, 03.12.1939.

76. BA-A, Pers 45570, Heinz Rohr an Panzerabwehrabteilung 30, 07.03.1940; BA-MA, BMRS, interview Rohr.

77. BA-MA, BMRS, File Heinz Rohr, Heft II, Teil III, Bl. 25, Rohr an Rigg, 09.02.1997.

78. BA-MA, BMRS, File Joachim Rohr, Bl. 44, Sterbeurkunde.

79. *Die Träger des Deutschen Kreuzes in Gold*, p. 304; BA-A, Pers 45573, Grenadier Regiment 6: Beurteilung zum 1. April 1943 über Hptm. Joachim Rohr; BA-MA, BMRS, File H. Rohr, Wehrpaß, pp. 22–23, Beförderungen und Ernennungen; BA-A, Pers 45570, Major Heinz Rohr, Panzerregiment 11, Beurteilung über Heinz Rohr, 08.02.1941.

80. BA-A, Pers 45570, Beurteilung vom 11.04.1944; BA-A, Pers 45573, Beurteilung vom 01.03.1943.

81. BA-MA, BMRS, interview Knigge; BA-MA, N 118/4. Captain von Schmeling-Diringhofen took over the First Company in the Seventy-third Infantry Regiment in Celle.

82. BA-MA, BMRS, interview Beelitz.

83. BA-MA, BMRS, interview Beelitz; BA-MA, BMRS, interview Ulrich de Maizière, 24.03.1997, T-323; Ulrich de Maizière, *In der Pflicht* (Bonn, 1989), p. 31; *Gedenkschrift. Der Jahrgang 30. 10. Offizier Ergänzungsjahrgang des Reichsheeres 1930–1. April 1980*, p. 85.

84. Ursula von Knigge, *Meine liebste Mamming. Briefe an Clara Freifrau Knigge, geschrieben von Sohn und Schwiegertochter in den Jahren, 1928–1945* (Grünwald, 1981), [Privatdruck], p. 170.

85. BA-MA, BMRS, interview Beelitz.

86. General Hans-Heinrich Sixt von Armin was the son of the famous World War I Fourth Army Commander Friedrich Sixt von Armin. General Hans-Heinrich Sixt von Armin led the 113th Infantry Division during the battle for

Stalingrad, and when Field Marshal von Paulus surrendered, Armin also surrendered. He went into Russian captivity and would die on 1 April 1952 as a
POW in the Soviet Union.

87. BA-MA, N 431/ 803, Günther Blumentritts Eidesstattliche Erklärung,
10.06.1946; BA-MA, BMRS, File Sixt von Armin; *Die Träger des Ritterkreuzes,*
pp. 399–402; *Die Träger des Deutschen Kreuzes in Gold,* p. 353; BA-MA, Pers
6/1808, Günter Sachs, Luftflottenkommando 6 Gen. Kdo. II. Flakkorps an
OKL, 10.09.1944; ed. Karl Friedrich Hildebrand, ed., *Die Generale der deutschen
Luftwaffe, 1935–1945: Band 3* (Osnabrück 1992), pp. 158–59; BA-MA, Pers
6/871, Hans-Heinrich Sixt von Armin, Personal-Nachweis; Goerlitz, p. 454.

88. BA-B, DZA 62 Ka. 1 83, Bl. 200, "Aktennotiz, Vorsprache beim OKW",
14.02.1940; Rohr, p. 86; IfZ, N 71–73, 27.05.1941; *U.S.A. Military Tribunals:
Case No. 11.2,* Heinrich Lammers, p. 161.

89. BA-MA, BMRS, interview W. Günther; BA-MA, BMRS, interview Bergmann;
see also BA-A, RW 55/3843, Bl. 58.

90. Oberkanonier was a private (artillery).

91. BA-MA, BMRS, File W. Günther, Bl. 24–31, Gnadengensuch durch Rechtsan-
wälte Dr. Alfred Holl and Dr. Fritz Hamann für Wolfram Günther an Hitler,
17.05.1939.

92. BA-MA, BMRS, interview Wolfram Günther.

93. BA-MA, BMRS, interview W. Günther.

94. Reichsstelle für Sippenforschung.

95. BA-MA, BMRS, File Martin Bier, Bl. 56; BA-MA, BMRS, interview Martin
Bier, 25.09.1994, T-28.

96. Bier had courageously defended a defensive position while being heavily attacked by Polish forces. Although his comrade was shot through the head and
died, Bier did not give up the position and held it against the enemy. Bier served
with the Thirteenth Company of One Hundredth Mountain Regiment.

97. BA-MA, BMRS, File Martin Bier, Bl. 56; BA-MA, BMRS, interview Martin
Bier, 25.09.1994, T-28.

98. Ibid.

99. BA-MA, File M. Bier, Bl. 4.

100. Ibid., Bl. 57.

101. Ibid., Bl. 56.

102. BA-MA, WF01/20740, Schoch an Engel, 10.11.1942.

103. Ibid., Beurteilung des Uffz. Cadek durch Oberst Schoch, 10.11.1942.

104. BA-MA, BMRS, File Georg Struzyna, Bl. 1–2. Many thanks to Dr. Georg
Meyer for this File.

105. IfZ, N71–73, "Herrn Minister auf dem Dienstwege," Zu I e Ei 1 IV/40-5017a,
22.05.1940; Lösener, p. 285.

106. Ibid.

107. His name has been kept anonymous.

108. BA-MA, BMRS, File Hermann Lange, Teil II, Bl. 7.

109. Offiziersanwärter was an officer candidate.

110. BA-MA, BMRS, File Walther Hofmann, Bl. 22–24, Maier an Hitler, 19.06.1940.

111. Ibid., Bl. 20–21, Hofmann an OKW, 07.06.1940.

112. Oberfähnrich was a rank between Stabsoberfeldwebel and Oberfeldwebel. It was a senior officer candidate.
113. BA-MA, BMRS, File Wilhelm von Gottberg, Heft I, Teil I, Bl. 41.
114. SS General von Gottberg led anti-partisan units in White Russia. While there, he reported throughout 1942 and 1943 that his men had executed thousands of Jews. Hilberg, pp. 251–52; Burleigh, p. 562.
115. BA-MA, BMRS, File Wilhelm von Gottberg, Heft I, Teil II, Band C: "Geschichte der Familie von Gottberg im Zwanzigsten Jahrhundert" (1984), Bl. 25–27; BA-MA, BMRS, interview Helmut von Gottberg, 09–10.11.1996, T-229–230.
116. BA-A, Pers 45573, Bl. 14–15, Elisabeth Rohr an Brauchitsch, 14.01.1940.
117. Ibid., Bl. 19, Chef P[ersonal] A[mt] an Elisabeth Rohr, 29.01.1940.
118. BA-MA, N 118/3, Engel an Elisabeth Rohr, 26.11.1940. Apparently, her brother Joachim had a contact with a high-ranking officer in the General Staff, who got his sister's case seen by Hitler. As a result of her *Deutschblütig-keitserklärung,* she was able to marry in 1943. BA-MA, BMRS, File Heinz Rohr, Rohr an Rigg, 22.11.2000.
119. BA-B, DZA 62 Ka. 1 83, Bl. 167, Engel an Blankenburg, 28.04.1942. See also BA-B. DZA 62 Ka. 1 83, Bl. 110–11, Bouhler an Bormann, 10.06.1942.
120. See BA-MA, BMRS, File Fischer; BA-MA, BMRS, interview Fischer; BA-MA, BMRS, interview A. von Mettenheim; BA-MA, BMRS, File Krackow; BA-MA, BMRS, interview R. Krackow; BA-MA, BMRS, interview J. Krackow; BA-MA, BMRS, interview Gwinner.
121. BA-MA, BMRS, File Haller, Bl. 4.
122. BA-MA, BMRS, File Haller, Schmundt an Haller, 13.05.1942, Bl. 2.
123. BA-MA, BMRS, File Haller, Frey an Schmundt, 25.05.1942, Bl. 2–3.
124. More precisely, the report stated that OKH wanted proof that the *Mischlinge* in question had played an important role during an engagement with the enemy.
125. Absolon, *Die Wehrmacht im Dritten Reich.* Band V, p. 149; *Sammlung wehr-rechtlicher Gutachten und Vorschriften,* Heft 4, p. 73; *Sammlung wehrrecht-licher Gutachten und Vorschriften,* Heft 20/21, p. 175.
126. This study was unable to document whether some of the 967 half-Jews documented received an EKII and EKI. The numbers presented here are lower than in reality.
127. BA-B, DZA 62 Ka. 1 83, Bl. 122.
128. BA-MA, BMRS, File Heinrich Levin, Bl. 11.
129. Kanonier was an ordinary soldier in the artillery.
130. BA-MA, BMRS, File Viktor Mendel.
131. Absolon, *Die Wehrmacht im Dritten Reich.* Band V, pp. 149–50.
132. BA-MA, Pers 6/2094, Berurteilung über K. Zukertort, 21.04.1939.
133. Ibid., Schell to Heeres-personal-Amt, 10.07.1939.
134. Ibid., Berurteilung v. 03.07.1941.
135. Ibid., Der Chef des Heereswaffenamtes to Zukertort, 30.07.1941.
136. BA-MA, Pers 6/2094, Brauchitsch to PA 2, 14.08.1941; BA-MA, BMRS, File Karl Zukertort.
137. BA-MA, File Karl Zukertort, Bl. 1.

138. Information gathered during a personal discussion with Kurt-Dagobert Zukertort, 24.07.2001.

139. BA-MA, BMRS, File Johann Zukertort.

140. BA-MA, BMRS, interview Walter Hamburger, 5–6.11.1994, T-47; BA-MA, BMRS, File Walter Hamburger, B. Hamburger an Rigg, 15.12.2000; BA-MA, BMRS, File Hamburger, Hamburger an Rigg, 25.11.2000.

141. BA-MA, BMRS, File Hamburger, Perfall zum Abschied an Fräulein Hamburger, 31.05.1941.

142. Zossen is located south of Berlin and was where the OKH was located.

143. General Bodewin Keitel was head of the Army Personnel Office (Heerespersonalamt) from 26 August 1939 until 2 October 1942. Keilig, p. 4.

144. BA-MA, RH 20–18/71, Kriegstagebuch [Nr.] 3 b der Abt. Ia des AOK 18, Bl. 97. See also Steven R. Welch, "Mischling *Deserters from the Wehrmacht*," *Leo Baeck Yearbook* 44 (1999): 281.

145. BA-MA, RH 21–3/v. 46 (=Panzergruppe 3/I a; Anlagen zum Kriegstagebuch, Bd. IV, 25.5.–22.7.41, Bl. 34.

146. BA-MA, RH 20-18/71, Kriegstagebuch [Nr.] 3 b der Abt. Ia des AOK 18, Bl. 97.

147. Such as the Iron Cross or the Wound Badge.

148. BA-MA, RH 7/23, OKH Nr. 6840/41 g. P[ersonal] A[mt] 2 (Ic), 16.07.1941; BA-MA, RH 7/11, Bl. 7; Vogel, p. 256.

149. *Hitlers Tischgespräche im Führerhauptquartier*, p. 277. This is a play on words, based on the name of scientist Gregor Mendel. He was a nineteenth-century geneticist, known to many as the father of genetics.

150. One of the criteria Hitler used to measure a person's worth was whether or not he or she looked Jewish. For instance, Hitler only "reluctantly" presented the fighter-ace Adolf Galland with his Ritterkreuz because he looked Jewish (Keegan, *Second World War*, p. 96). One can be sure that Hitler had his bureaucrats look into Galland's ancestry, just as he had them do with Liebig.

151. *Hitlers Tischgespräche im Führerhauptquartier*, pp. 277, 398–99; Noakes, "Development of Nazi Policy," pp. 333–34.

152. BA-B, DZA 62 Ka. 1 83, Bl. 155–59, Blankenburg an Engel, 23.05.1942; Wistrich, p. 26; Fred Mielke and Alexander Mitscherlich, *Doctors of Infamy* (New York, 1949), pp. 94, 135.

153. *Heeresadjutant bei Hitler*, pp. 121–22.

154. Ibid., pp. 31–32, 42, 70, 79, 103, 105, 108, 120–22.

155. Ibid., pp. 52, 79, 109.

156. *Heeresadjutant bei Hitler*, pp. 31–32. Many documents and a few books have claimed that "hiding" soldiers of Jewish descent happened often. See O'Neill, pp. 77–78; BA-MA, BMRS, File Karl-Heinrich Fricke, *Erinnerungen aus 70 Lebensjahren von 1914–1984* (Köln, 1984).

157. Regional Party offices.

158. District Party offices.

159. Lösener in the RMI supposedly also helped people falsify their ancestry. See Lösener, p. 309.

160. *Heeresadjutant bei Hitler*, pp. 31–32.

161. Ibid., p. 122.

162. See Speer, p. 328; *Heeresadjutant bei Hitler,* pp. 121–22.

163. *Heeresadjutant bei Hitler,* pp. 121–22.

164. Guderian, p. 449. Guderian's postwar account must be looked at critically. Although it contains valuable information, Guderian wrote it primarily to glorify his role in the development of the Wehrmacht and gives the impression that Guderian could have won the war for Germany had Hitler only allowed him to conduct operations during the 1940s. Guderian also wrote this to present himself as an anti-Nazi. Guderian was anything but anti-Nazi, as Megargee proves in his book *Inside Hitler's High Command.* See Megargee, p. 213; Kershaw, *Hitler, 1936–1945,* p. 414.

165. *Mogeleiversuchen* literally means "attempts to cheat."

166. *Heeresadjutant bei Hitler,* p. 122. See also *Hitlers Tischgespräche im Führerhauptquartier,* Notiz von Picker, p. 399.

167. Kershaw, *Profiles in Power,* p. 114–15.

168. BA-B, DZA 62 Ka. 1 83, Bl. 117, "Aktennotiz" von Brack, 10.07.1942.

169. Kershaw, *Profiles in Power,* p. 137; Speer, p. 302; Jochen Lang, pp. 187, 267–69.

170. Jochen Lang, p. 7.

171. Ibid., p. 208.

172. Kershaw, *Profiles in Power,* p. 137. See also Speer, pp. 300–301; Engelmann, p. 212; Bracher, p. 346.

173. Kershaw, *Profiles in Power,* p. 136.

174. Ibid., p. 138.

175. *The Encyclopedia of the Third Reich,* vol. 1, p. 102. This is a play on what Jesus told his disciples, quoted in John 14:6, NIV.

176. *Nazi Conspiracy and Aggression: Supplement B,* p. 1093; see also Speer, pp. 104–5, for more insight into the relationship Bormann had with Hitler.

177. Rebentisch, p. 400. See also Below, p. 31.

178. *Hitlers Tischgespräche im Führerhauptquartier,* p. 425; Messerschmidt, p. 358.

179. BA-B, DZA 62 Ka. 1 83, Bl. 136, Bormann an Bouhler, 02.06.1942; Rebentisch, p. 435.

180. Kershaw, *Profiles in Power,* p. 138; Rebentisch, p. 411; Kershaw, *Hitler, 1936–1945,* pp. 378, 421.

181. *Hitlers Tischgespräche im Führerhauptquartier,* pp. 399–400.

182. BA-B, DZA 62 Ka. 1 83, Bl. 26, Reichsverfügungsblatt Anordnung A 34/42, 23.06.1942; BA-B, DZA 62 Ka. 1 83, Bl. 131–32.

183. Sir Stafford Cripps (1899–1952) became the executive head of the Labor Party from 1937 to 1940, and then was the British ambassador to the USSR from 1940 to 1942.

184. When Hitler met with the German military attaché to Washington in February 1939, he only wanted to discuss with him Roosevelt's alleged Jewish ancestry. This belief that Roosevelt had Jewish ancestry was shared by many high-ranking Nazi officials. Weinberg, *A World at Arms,* p. 87; Keegan, *Second World War,* p. 537; Jochen Lang, p. 235; *Hitlers Tischgespräche im Führerhauptquartier,* p. 399; Victor, p. 18. It was common for Hitler to believe that

the leaders of countries who opposed him were Jews. For example, he believed
the majority of the Soviet and American leaders were Jews. Kershaw, *Hitler
Myth,* pp. 237–38; Friedländer, pp. 103, 185; Below, p. 39; Victor,
p. 18. See also Hitler, *Hitler's Secret Book,* p. xxii.
185. BA-B, DZA 62 Ka. 1 83, Bl. 131–32, Bormann an Bouhler, 02.07.1942.
186. BA-B, DZA 62 Ka. 1 83, Bl. 115, Bouhler an Bormann, 10.07.1942, BA-B,
DZA 62 Ka. 1 83, Bl. 128, Reichsverfügungsblatt, Ausgabe A Folge 27/42,
04.07.1942.
187. The Reich's ordinance bulletin (the official gazette of the Parteikanzlei).
188. BA-B, DZA 62 Ka. 1 83, Bl. 128, Reichsverfügungsblatt, Ausgabe A Folge 27/
42, 04.07.1942; BA-B, R 58/276; BA-B, R 21/488, Bl. 41; Adams, p. 326;
BA-B, Sammlung Schumacher.
189. BA-B, DZA 62 Ka. 1 83, Bl. 111.
190. Ibid., Bl. 112, Bouhler an Bormann, 10.07.1942.
191. Reichsamtsleiter Dr. Kurt Blome in the Parteikanzlei.
192. BA-B, DZA 62 Ka. 1 83, Bl. 112–13, Bouhler an Bormann, 10.07.1942.
193. Ibid., Bl. 113, Bouhler an Bormann, 10.07.1942.
194. BA-B, DZA 62 Ka. 1 83, Bl. 114, Bouhler an Bormann, 10.07.1942; BA-B, DZA
62 Ka. 1 83, Bl. 147, "Aktennotiz" von Blankenburg, 09.07.1942.
195. BA-B, DZA 62 Ka. 1 83, Bl. 114, Bouhler an Bormann, 10.07.1942.
196. *Judenfrage* was a Nazi catchword used to justify the expulsion of the Jews.
197. BA-B, DZA 62 Ka. 1 83, Bl. 115, Bouhler an Bormann, 10.07.1942. Although
Bouhler said to Bormann, "*Lösung der Judenfrage,*" it was clear that he
meant the extermination of the Jews that was taking place at that time. See
Hilberg, p. 562; Peter Padfield, *Himmler: Reichsführer-SS* (New York, 1990),
p. 303.
198. The Führer's private chancellery dealt mainly with the flood of mail addressed
to Hitler. Interestingly enough, although Albert and Martin Bormann worked
near to each other and were brothers, they grew to detest each other. Jochen
Lang, pp. 60, 140; Kershaw, *Hitler, 1936–1945,* p. 32. According to Hitler's
Luftwaffe adjutant, Nicolaus von Below, these brothers hardly ever spoke to
one another although they often were in the same room together during meetings and other functions. According to Below, this hatred started with a dis-
pute over whom Albert had married. Below, p. 30.
199. BA-B, DZA 62 Ka. 1 83, Bl. 103, Bouhler an A. Bormann, 13.07.1942.
200. Ibid., Bl. 117, "Aktennotiz" von Brack, 10.07.1942.
201. Ibid., Bl. 116a, "Aktennotiz" von Brack, 10.07.1942.
202. Ibid., Bl. 100.
203. Ibid., Bl. 116, "Aktennotiz" aus der Kanzlei des Führers, 10.07.1942.
204. Adam, p. 319.
205. Hilberg, pp. 272–73.
206. BA-B, DZA 62 Ka. 1 83, Bl. 28, Rundschreiben 164/42, 24.10.1942; BA-B,
Sammlung Schumacher, SS-Abschnitt XV Abt. I Ao AZ. 1 qu W/Wo.
207. BA-MA, BMRS, File Rolf Schenk, Frey an R. Schenk, 09.09.1942.
208. Below, p. 348. Below puts the date for Engel's dismissal at the end of
September 1943. However, according to Hildegard von Kotze's commen-

tary on Engel's diary, Engel left his position as Hitler's adjutant in
March 1943. See *Heeresadjutant bei Hitler*, p. 145, Notiz von Hildegard von
Kotze.

209. BA-B, DZA 62 Ka. 1 83, Bl. 46–48, A. Bormann an Blankenburg, 13.03.1943.
210. Ibid., Bl. 48, Blankenburg an A. Bormann, 17.02.1942.
211. Ibid., Bl. 129–129b.
212. *Rundschreiben* is a circular.
213. BA-B, DZA 62 Ka. 1 83, Bl. 28, 46–48.
214. Lifton, p. 452; Hilberg, p. 601.
215. Wachtmeister is a staff sergeant.
216. BA-B, DZA 62 Ka. 1 83, Bl. 87–88.
217. BA-B, DZA 62 Ka. 1 83, Bl. 77, OKW an Blankenburg, 03.08.1943.
218. BA-B, DZA 62 Ka. 1 83, Bl. 48b.
219. Rudolf Absolon, *Die Wehrmacht im Dritten Reich. Band VI*, p. 315.
220. BA-B, DZA 62 Ka. 1 83, Bl. 25–25a, Bormann an Bouhler, 27.09.1943.
221. Ibid.
222. Noakes, "Development of Nazi Policy," p. 335.
223. Guderian, p. 362.
224. BA-B, DZA 62 Ka. 1 83, Bl. 70, Aktennotiz, IIbDi/Schr., Betrifft: Politische Beurteilung von jüdischen Mischlingen, 12.10.1943.
225. Ibid., Bl. 71, "Aktennotiz für Herrn Blankenburg," Betrifft: Bearbeitung der Mischlingssachen, 19.10.1943.
226. BA-MA, BMRS, File Haller, Bl. 37–38, Schmundt an Irmgard Böhrne, 03.11.1943.
227. BA-B, DZA 62 Ka. 1 83, Bl. 67–68, IIa/Schr., Jüdische Mischlinge im Wehrdienst, 28.10.1943. See also BA-B, DZA 62 Ka. 1 83, Bl. 84b.
228. Ibid., Bl. 68.
229. In addition to Schmundt's responsibility as Hitler's Wehrmacht adjutant, he was head of the Army Personnel Office from 2 October 1942 until 20 July 1944. Keilig, p. 4.
230. D. Bradley and R. Schulze-Kossens, eds., *Tätigkeitsbericht des Chefs des Heerespersonalamtes General der Infanterie Rudolf Schmundt: 1.10.1942–29.10.1944. Fortgef. v. Wilhelm Burgdorf* (Osnabrück, 1984), p. 128 (cited from now on as: *Schmundt, Tätigkeitsbericht*).
231. Department for Personnel Matters of Officers and Their Offspring (not including General Staff officers). Keilig, p. 5.
232. Department for Personnel Matters of High-Ranking Officers and Education and Welfare. Keilig, p. 7.
233. *Schmundt, Tätigkeitsbericht*, p. 128.
234. Group IV *(Gruppe IV)* in P2 was responsible for officers, officer cadets, and Sonderführer. Keilig, p. 8.
235. Department for Awards. Keilig, p. 12.
236. BA-B, NS 19/87, Bl. 2, Brandt an Klopfer, betr. Liste der Berufsoffiziere, die teils vor Kriegsbeginn, teils auch erst im Kriege Deutschblütigen gleichgestellt wurden, 05.09.1944; BA-A, Sammlung Jüdische Mischlinge.
237. Joachim von Schmeling-Diringshofen was recalled to active duty in 1939 from China. He died in battle during the summer of 1942.

238. BA-A, Mischlinge in der Wehrmacht, Schreiben Amtsgruppe P2/ 3 Abt. an P5, 11.01.1944.
239. BA-MA, BMRS, interview Otto Wolters, 18.03.1995, T-123; BA-MA, BMRS, interview Otto Wolters, 06.12.1996, T-252.
240. *Akten-NSDAP,* 101-07569-07588; BA-B, R 43 II/599.
241. BA-B, DZA 62 Ka. 1 83, Bl. 53, OKW an Kanzlei des Führers der NSDAP, 18.02.1944.
242. BA-B, DZA 62 Ka. 1 83, Bl. 52, Blankenburg an OKW, 11.03.1944.
243. *Akten-NSDAP,* 107-00401/402, 4. Die Führerverfügung 48/44; BA-B, Sammlung Schumacher; BA-B, NS 6/347, Bl. 162; Martin Moll, ed., *Führererlasse, 1939–1945* (Stuttgart, 1997), pp. 395–96.
244. Jochen Lang, pp. 236–37.
245. Ibid., p. 262.
246. Ibid., p. 266.
247. BA-B, DZA 62 Ka. 1 83, Bl. 54, OKW an Kanzlei des Führers, betr. Ausnahmebehandlung jüdischer Mischlinge, 03.03.1944.
248. Adam, p. 331.
249. Unterarzt Erich Rauchfüß. BA-MA, BMRS, interview Erich Rauchfüß, 02.04.1995, T-127.
250. Adam, pp. 331–32; Meyer, pp. 100, 108, 153.
251. BA-MA, N 179, Telegramm Milchs an Hitler, 21.07.1944.
252. *Akten-NSDAP,* 107-00386, I. Derzeitiger Stand des Mischlingsproblems.
253. Ibid., 107-00399, 2. Ausnahmen vom Gesetz der Blutreinheit, a) Jüdische-Mischlinge.
254. Ibid., 107-00392.
255. Ibid., 107-00405, 4. Die Rangfolge bei der Ausnahmebehandlung von Mischlingen.
256. Ibid., 107-00406-407, 6. Die Tarnung der jüdischen Mischlinge durch die Gleichstellung mit Deutschblütigen.
257. Ibid., 107-00406-414.
258. Ibid., 107-00415, III. Richtlinien für die künftige Sachbearbeitung.
259. Ibid., 107-00417-00418, 3. Die Stellungnahme der NSDAP zu Ausnahmeanträgen im Bereich des Staates und der Wehrmacht.
260. Ibid.
261. *Stufe* IV wounded soldiers lost, for example, either both hands, both legs, or their eyesight, to name just a few of the wounds that qualified one for this classification. Such soldiers also received eighty Reichsmarks a month. BA-MA, RH 12-23/ 834, p. 93.
262. *Akten-NSDAP,* 107-00417-00418, 3. Die Stellungnahme der NSDAP zu Ausnahmeanträgen im Bereich des Staates und der Wehrmacht.
263. *Schmundt, Tätigkeitsbericht,* p. 186. For reports on Sachs's 257th Infantry Division in Russia, see BA-MA, RH 26/257. For example, from June 1941 until April 1942, Sachs's division had killed 12,500 Russians, destroyed thirty tanks, shot down six planes, and taken 2,626 prisoners.
264. *Schmundt, Tätigkeitsbericht,* p. 186.

265. BA-MA, RH 26/257, Schreiben Sachs an 257. Div., 19.08.1941.

266. BA-B, NS 19/87, Bl. 1,Vermerk für Dr. Brandt, 30.08.1944, and Bl. 2, Dr. Brandt an Klopfer, 05.09.1944.

267. *Schmundt, Tätigkeitsbericht,* p. 247.

268. BA-B, R 43 II/599, Bormann an Lammers, 02.11.1944; BA-B, 43II/603b.

269. Absolon, *Wehrgesetz und Wehrdienst,* p. 119.

270. Kershaw, *Profiles in Power,* pp. 163–64.

271. This study has documented two soldiers not on the list who were possibly discharged because of this order—Obergefreiter Dieter Fischer and Unterarzt Erich Rauchfüß. BA-MA, BMRS, File Dieter Fischer, Heft II, Amelis von Mettenheim, *Die Zwölf Langen Jahre, 1933–1945,* Bl. 38; BA-MA, BMRS, interview Erich Rauchfüß, 02.04.1995, T-127.

272. BA-MA, BMRS, File Werner Maltzahn.

273. BA-MA, Pers 6/7363, Major Friedrich Gebhard, Gebhard an General-kommando XI. A.K., Hannover, 21.10.1944.

274. Waffen-SS/SS lieutenant colonel.

275. BA-MA, Pers 6/9887, Bl. 41, Suchanek an Burgdorf, 15.09.1944.

276. Ibid., Bl. 41, Burgdorf an Suchanek, 26.09.1944.

277. Ibid., Bl. 25, Beurteilung vom 27.11.1943.

278. Ibid., Burgdorf an Bloch, 15.02.1945.

279. BA-MA, BMRS, File Bloch, Walther Brockhoff an Sabine Bloch, 31.10.1945; BA-MA, BMRS, interview M. Bloch.

280. BA-MA, BMRS, File Bloch, Brockhoff an Sabine Bloch, 31.10.1945.

281. BA-MA, 6/7363, Friedrich Gebhard, Ag 1/1. (Zentral-) Abt. (IIc) an Stellv. Generalkommando XI. A.K. Hannover, 30.09.1944; BA-MA, Pers. Karl Helwig, Ag 1/1. (Zentral-) Abt. (IIc) an Stellv. Generalkommando VII.A.K. München, 30.09.1944.

282. BA-MA, BMRS, File Binder, Bl. 68, 81; BA-MA, BMRS, interview Binder. Binder was told in February 1945 that Hitler had declared him an *Ehrenarier* (honorable Aryan) and promoted him to first lieutenant.

283. BA-A, Pers 14492, Hans-Günther von Gersdorff, Dienstlaufbahn, Bl. 4.

284. Ibid., Bl. 5–6, 4. Artillerieregiment Aktz. 22a/34II vom 08.05.1934 ("Ein-schreiben"). This description of Aryan ancestry most probably comes from Minister Frick's description of it. See BA-B, R 43 II/ 418a.

285. Supposedly this woman was a rather famous horseback rider in her youth.

286. BA-A, Pers 14492, Bl. 5–6.

287. Ibid., Bl. 23, v. Schwedler an Frau Marie Fritsch (frühere v. Gersdorff), 30.08.1935.

288. Ibid., Bl. 25, Fritsch an v. Schwedler, 02.09.1935.

289. Ibid., Bl. 28–31, Fritsch an v. Blomberg, 05.09.1935.

290. Ibid., v. Blomberg an Fritsch, 18.09.1935.

291. Ibid., Bl. 34–37, Fritsch an v. Blomberg, 02.10.1935.

292. Ibid., Bl. 46–50, Fritsch an v. Schwedler, 28. 10.1935, Bl. 58–61, Fritsch an Adolf Hitler 17.12.1935, Bl. 66–67, Fritsch an v. Schwedler, 07.01.1936, and Bl. 68, v. Schwedler an Fritsch, 17.01.1936.

293. BA-A, Pers 14492, Bl. 82, Engel an OKW, 05.04.1940; MA-A, Pers 15499, Wilhelm von Gottberg, Bl. 2, Dienstlaufbahn, 27.08.1939; BA-MA, BMRS, interview H. von Gottberg.

294. BA-MA, BMRS, File Wilhelm von Gottberg, Bl. 41, Brauchitsch an Brockhusen, 29.02.1940.

295. Ibid., Bl. 42, Meissner an Irmgard von Brockhusen, 29.02.1940.

296. BA-A, Pers 14492, Bl. 100–105, 109, Gericht der Division Nr. 154, Dresden, Feldurteil unterzeichnet von Dr. Schirmer, 16.02.1942.

297. BA-A, Pers 14492, Bl. 75–82.

298. BA-MA, BMRS, File Ernst Prager, Heft III, Bl. 1, Polizeipräsident in Berlin, Abt. II, Justrowski an Prager, 01.04.1937; Ibid., Bl. 60–61, Prager an Stephan Prager, 07.04.1937.

299. Ibid., Bl. 8, Prager an Stephan Prager, 19.07.1937.

300. Ibid., Bl. 9, Prager an Stephan Prager, 27.08.1937.

301. Haehnelt was the commander of the Second Army's Air Group during World War I and had been a strong proponent of air defense. Corum, *Luftwaffe*, p. 78.

302. BA-MA, BMRS, File Ernst Prager, Heft III, Bl. 9, Prager an Stephan Prager, 27.08.1937, & Bl. 132, Bestätigung von Heinrich Prager, Vater Ernst Pragers, 20.11.1945.

303. Ibid., Bl. 11, Prager an Stephan Prager, 22.12.1937.

304. Ibid., Bl. 14, Prager an Stephan Prager, 14.02.1938.

305. BA-MA, BMRS, File Ernst Prager, Heft II, Bl. 27–30, Prager an OKW, Betrifft: Anlage 1 zum Gesuch um Wiederverwendung, 24.05.1941.

306. BA-MA, BMRS, interview Stephan Prager, 11.10.1997, T-402.

307. BA-MA, BMRS, File Prager, Heft III, Bl. 50, Prager an Stephan Prager, 15.06.1941.

308. BA-MA, BMRS, interview S. Prager.

309. BA-MA, BMRS, File Prager, Heft III, Bl. 50, Prager an Stephan Prager, 15.06.1941.

310. BA-MA, BMRS, File Prager, Heft III, Bl. 57–58, Prager an Stephan Prager, 06.07.1941. Lösener reported that after the war, no more than a dozen mixed marriages were approved, which was a very small number compared with the large number of applications they received. Lösener, pp. 284–85.

311. BA-MA, BMRS, File Prager, Heft III, Bl. 57–58, Prager an Stephan Prager, 06.07.1941.

312. Ibid., Bl. 57–58, Prager an Stephan Prager, 06.07.1941.

313. Ibid., Bl. 54–55, Prager an Stephan Prager, 26.06.1941.

314. Ibid., Bl. 133, Heinrich Prager an Gericht in Kulmbach, 20.11.1941.

315. Ibid., Bl. 17, Prager an Stephan Prager, 17.11.1941.

316. Ibid., S. Prager to Rigg, 05.07.2001.

317. Ibid., Bl. 16.

318. Jews could not travel as of 10 October 1941 without special permission. Maser, p. 266.

319. BA-MA, BMRS, File Prager, Heft III, Bl. 17.

320. Ibid., Bl. 16. Prager an Stephan Prager, 17.11.1941.

321. Ibid.
322. Prager had described half-Jew Robert Borchardt.
323. BA-MA, BMRS, File Prager, Heft III, Bl. 21, Prager an Stephan Prager, 26.11.1941.
324. *Amt für Rassenforschung.*
325. BA-MA, BMRS, File Prager, Heft III, Bl. 17, Prager an Stephan Prager, 17.11.1941.
326. BA-MA, BMRS, File Prager, Heft II, Bl. 53, Prager an Fräulein Kürschner, 21.12.1941.
327. Ibid., Bl. 65–73, 168, Abschiedsansprache für Hella Prager von Stephan Prager, 10.06.1996.
328. BA-B, R 7.01 Reichskanzlei 4112, Bl. 292, Haehnelt an Lammers, 02.04.1943.
329. Ibid., Bl. 294, Lammers an Haehnelt, 08.04.1943.
330. Messerschmidt, p. 355.
331. Prager's aunt and uncle, Mathilde and Stefan Blanck, both died in Theresienstadt. Another aunt, Elisabeth Schmitt née Prager, died in Bergen-Belsen sometime in 1942. See also BA-MA, BMRS, File Ernst Prager, Heft II, Bl. 167.
332. An interesting side note to Prager's case happened a few days before the U.S. Army captured Beyreuth when he had four Luftwaffe deserters executed. He claimed after the war that had he not executed these men, who had tried to escape before and had planned to murder their guard, he might have been shot himself and discipline among the 1,000 men he commanded might have broken down. Regardless of Prager's reasons, this act caused him some problems after 1945. Although it was known that he and his family were victims of the Nazis, he was denounced as a Nazi sympathizer. As a result, he had to go through a denazification process. Despite humiliating deliberations, Prager was eventually found innocent of all charges of being a Nazi. BA-MA, BMRS, File Prager, Heft II, Bl. 133–140; BA-MA, BMRS, interview Prager. Another interesting note to the Prager story happened several years after the war when the German government awarded him the rank of colonel. This happened after Prager had taken his case to court arguing that without the racial laws, he would have attained this rank. He was proud to receive what he termed "his rightful place in the army." BA-MA, BMRS, interview Prager.
333. BA-MA, BMRS, File Rainer Gärtner, Heft IV, Bl. 8–9; Ibid., Bl. 11–14, Gärtner an seine Eltern, 02.02.1942.
334. Ibid., Bl. 9, Gärtner an seine Eltern, 05.01.1942, Gärtner an seine Mutter, 02.02.1942.
335. BA-MA, BMRS, File Gärtner, Heft III, Bl. 63–65, Dr. Robert Gärtner an Emil Gärtner, 20.03.1942.
336. Ibid., Bl. 65.
337. Ibid.
338. Ibid., Bl. 64, Dr. Biermann an Dr. Robert Gärtner, (o.D.).
339. Ibid., Bl. 42–44, Gärtner an seinen Vater, 12.02.1942.
340. Ibid, Heft IV, Bl. 9, Gärtner an seine Eltern, 05.01.1942; Ibid., Heft IV, Bl. 9, Gärtner an seinen Vater, 05.01.1942.
341. Ibid., Heft IV, Bl. 1, Gärtner an seinen Vater, 07.03.1942.
342. Ibid., Heft III, Bl. 40, Dr. Robert Gärtner an Rainer Gärtner, 15.03.1942.

343. Ibid., Bl. 38, Notiz auf Schreiben Dr. Biermann-Ratjen an Dr. Robert Gärtner, 17.03.1942.
344. Ibid., Bl. 63, Dr. Robert Gärtner an Emil Gärtner, 26.03.1942.
345. Ibid., Bl. 45–55.
346. Ibid., Heft III, Bl. 55, Dr. Robert Gärtner an Rainer Gärtner, 27.03.1942.
347. Ibid., Bl. 42, Bestätigung von Schwenn Lindemann, 30.03.1942.
348. Ibid., Heft II, Bl. 7–8, Hannerle an Rainer Gärtner, 20.08.1942.
349. Ibid., Bl. 42, Hauptmann Giese an Eltern Gärtner, 14.01.1945.
350. Ibid., Heft IV, Bl. 115, Gärtner an Giese, 10.02.1945.
351. BA-MA, BMRS, File Dieter Fischer, Heft I, Bl. 80–81, Mettenheim an OKW, 09.09.1941.
352. Ibid., Frey an Mettenheim, 13.09.1941.
353. Ibid., Bl. 77, Frey an Mettenheim, 21.10.1941.
354. BA-MA, BMRS, File Dieter Fischer, Heft I, Bl. 64, Mettenheim an OKW, 04.11.1943.
355. BA-MA, BMRS, File Dieter Fischer, Heft II, *Die Zwölf Langen Jahre 1933–1945,* von Amelis von Mettenheim, Bl. 18–23.
356. Ibid., Bl. 19.
357. BA-MA, BMRS, File Dieter Fischer, Heft I, Bl. 63, OKW an v. Mettenheim, 22.11.1943.

CHAPTER 9: WHAT DID *MISCHLINGE* KNOW ABOUT THE HOLOCAUST?

1. Stephen G. Fritz, *Frontsoldaten: The German Soldier in World War II* (Lexington, 1995), p. 3.
2. A literal translation of *Judenlümmel* is "Jewish lout" or "jerk."
3. Krackow, pp. 69–79; BA-MA, BMRS, interview J. Krackow.
4. BA-MA, BMRS, interview Reinhard.
5. BA-MA, BMRS, interview Scholz.
6. Noakes, "Development of Nazi Policy," p. 305.
7. BA-MA, BMRS, interview Hans Pollak, 07.12.1995, T-72. Pollak was wounded five times during the war.
8. BA-MA, BMRS, File Hans Günzel, Bl. 43; BA-MA, BMRS, interview Rosemarie Mirauer, 24.02.1997, T-315; BA-MA, BMRS, File Günther Mirauer, Bl. 56; BA-MA, BMRS, interview Czempin; BA-MA, BMRS, File Hans-Geert Falkenberg, Heft I, Bl. 34–42; BA-MA, BMRS, interview Hans-Geert Falkenberg, 02.02.1997, T-289; BA-MA, BMRS, Hans Günzel, Bl. 43.
9. BMRS, File Hans-Geert Falkenberg, Heft I, Bl. 34–42, 56; BA-MA, BMRS, interview Hans-Geert Falkenberg, 02.02.1997, T-289. Richard Albert Falkenberg (Mountfalcon) served as a private from January 1940 to 1943. In 1943, he was promoted to sergeant and remained at this rank until his honorable discharge in 1945.
10. BA-MA, BMRS, interview Heinz-Georg Heymann, 09.04.1995, T-138.
11. BA-MA, BMRS, interview Dietrich Moll, 04.03.1995, T-111.
12. BA-MA, BMRS, interview Hamburger.
13. BM-MA, BMRS, interview Bergmann; Bergmann, pp. 6–7.
14. BA-MA, BMRS, File Hans-Geert Falkenberg, Bl. 56–57.

15. Ibid., File Hans-Geert Falkenberg, Bl. 60–61, Klein an Falkenberg, 08.07.1940.
16. Ibid., Bl. 60–61.
17. Ibid., Bl. 57, Klein an Falkenberg, 05.04.1942.
18. Ibid., Bl. 58, Klein an Falkenberg, 10.05.1942.
19. Owings, p. 460.
20. BA-MA, BMRS, File Werner Maltzahn, Bl. 2–4.
21. BA-MA, Msg 1/1364, Bl. 59–60.
22. BA-MA, BMRS, File Wolfgang Lennert, Bl. 18, Lennert an seine Mutter, 17.01.1941; BA-MA, BMRS, File Wolfgang Lennert, Bl. 17, Lennert an seine Mutter, 13.01.1941.
23. Ibid., Bl. 1.
24. BA-MA, BMRS, Bl. 20, Lennert an seine Mutter, 28.07.1942; Freie Universität Berlin: Zentralinstitut für Sozialwissenschaftliche Forschung, ed., *Gedenkbuch Berlins der jüdischer Opfer des Nationalsozialismus* (Berlin, 1995).
25. BA-MA, BMRS, File Wolfgang Lennert, Lennert an seine Mutter, 12.10.1942.
26. *Gedenkbuch jüdischen Opfer.*
27. Feldwebel is a staff sergeant.
28. BA-MA, BMRS, File Georg-Friedrich Müller, Bl. 48; BA-MA, BMRS, interview Georg-Friedrich Müller, 04.02.1997, T-293.
29. BA-MA, BMRS, interview Bergmann; BA-MA, BMRS, interview Peter Cahn, 17.03.1995, T-121 and 11.12.1996, T-268. See also Bergmann, pp. 136, 147.
30. Bergmann, pp. 208–9; BA-MA, BMRS, interview Bergmann.
31. Posselt, p. 42.
32. BA-MA, BMRS, interview Posselt; Posselt, pp. 42–44.
33. BA-MA, BMRS, interview Posselt.
34. BA-MA, BMRS, File Angreß, Bl. 3, 16; BA-MA, BMRS, interview Angreß.
35. BA-MA, BMRS, interview H. Pollak.
36. BA-MA, BMRS, interview H. S., 16.11.1995, C-52.
37. BA-MA, BMRS, File Hermann Schucht, Bl. 3, Abschiedsbrief seiner Mutter an Hermann Schucht, 15.10.1942.
38. BA-MA, BMRS, File Richard Czempin, Bl. 62.
39. BA-MA, BMRS, interview Czempin. Czempin's Jewish father had also committed suicide to prevent his deportation.
40. BA-MA, BMRS, File Joachim Gaehde, Bl. 38.
41. Kershaw, *Hitler, 1936–1945,* pp. 134–35, 320, 321–24, 349–52, 383, 470, 521; Hilberg, pp. 3, 128, 138, 141, 258, 260–61; Lösener, p. 296; Burleigh, p. 592; Gordon, p. 97; BA-MA, BMRS, File H. Rehfeld.
42. BA-MA, BMRS, interview Horst Schmechel; BA-MA, BMRS, interview Hans Schmechel.
43. Not his real name.
44. BA-MA, BMRS, interview Horst G. (Reinhard), 20.11.1994, T-57.
45. BA-MA, BMRS, interview Steinwasser.
46. BA-MA, BMRS, interview Steinwasser; BA-MA, BMRS, File Fritz Steinwasser, Bl. 102.
47. BA-MA, BMRS, interview Steinwasser; BA-MA, BMRS, File Steinwasser, Bl. 102.

48. BA-MA, BMRS, interview Frau Hertha-Barbara Hollaender, 21.11.1995, T-171; BA-MA, BMRS, interview Frau Hertha-Barbara Hollaender, 12.11.1996, T-234.

49. BA-MA, BMRS, interview Braun, 10–14.08.1994, T-10; BA-MA, BMRS, interview Braun, 07.01.1996, T-190.

50. BA-MA, BMRS, interview Braun, 10–14.08.1994, T-10; BA-MA, BMRS, interview Braun, 07.01.1996, T-190; BA-MA, BMRS, File Braun, Braun an Rigg, 22.12.2000.

51. Bergmann, p. 238.

52. BA-MA, BMRS, interview Bergmann.

53. BA-MA, BMRS, File Klaus Florey.

54. Ibid., Florey to Rigg, 05.07.2001.

55. BA-MA, BMRS, File Bleicher, "Wie ich den 8. Mai 1945 erlebte: Ein persönlicher Bericht eines Betroffenen": BA-MA, interview Heinz Bleicher, 10.02.1995, T-90.

56. See also Kaplan, p. 195.

57. BA-MA, BMRS, File Hanns Rehfeld.

58. BA-MA, BMRS, interview Löwy.

59. Although some Waffen-SS personnel did serve in the concentration camps, Dr. Josef Mengele being one of the most famous examples, most Waffen-SS did not serve in the concentration camps. Lifton, p. 340.

60. BA-MA, BMRS, File Heinz-Günther Löwy, Bl. 2, Löwy an Rigg, 16.03.1996; BA-MA, BMRS, interview Löwy.

61. BA-MA, BMRS, File Florey.

62. BA-MA, BMRS, interview Catharin; BA-MA, BMRS, File Catharin, Bl. 7, Catharin an Rigg.

63. BA-MA, BMRS, interview Hans Döppes, 19.05.1996, T-207; BA-MA, BMRS, interview Hanns Bauer, 29.03.1998, T-421; BA-MA, interview Ferdinand Lichtwitz, 18.07.1997; BA-MA, BMRS, File Ferdinand Lichtwitz; BA-MA, BMRS, interview Rolf Schenk, 23.05.1997, T-349; BA-MA, BMRS, File Rolf Schenk; BA-MA, BMRS, File Herbert Simon., Bl. 11; BA-MA, BMRS, File Erik Blumenfeld; BA-MA, BMRS, File Eisner; BA-MA, BMRS, File Helmuth Rosenbaum, Bl. 9.

64. BA-MA, BMRS, interview Lichtwitz.

65. BA-MA, BMRS, File R. Schenk; BA-MA, BMRS, interview Schenk.

66. *U.S.A. Military Tribunals: Case No. 1–2, Nuremberg Trials*, p. 2,524.

67. Lifton, p. 286; Persico, p. 370.

68. Office of the United States Chief Counsel for Prosecution of Axis Criminality, ed., *Nazi Conspiracy and Aggression*, vol. 2 (Washington, D.C., 1946), p. 445.

69. Ibid., p. 446.

70. Hilberg, p. 599.

71. *U.S.A. Military Tribunals: Case No. 12*, p. 10,261.

72. Discussion with the author on 28 October 1998.

73. Senior civil servant. Killy was responsible for finance, budget, labor, audit and civil service matters in the Reichskanzlei. Hilberg, p. 44.

74. Rebentisch, pp. 59–60; Hilberg, p. 53; Meyer, p. 153; Cornberg and Steiner, pp. 155–56.
75. Hilberg, p. 53. Rebentisch disputes Hilberg's claim about Killy. See Rebentisch, p. 437, n. 207. Since Killy was a high-ranking official in the Reichskanzlei, he could not have avoided taking part in the Holocaust, actively or passively. However, Lösener writes that Killy was a good friend of his and helped him with *Mischlinge*. Lösener, p. 272.
76. BA-MA, BMRS, File Hans Eppinger. He is credited with formulating many significant concepts in hepatology. He identified what is now called viral hepatitis as a hepatocellular disorder and even developed the classification of jaundice.
77. Ibid.
78. Ibid., Bl. 1. Eppinger was not only distraught about his upcoming trial, but also apparently grieving his son's death, which had happened on the Russian front.
79. For a complete biography on Stella Goldschlag see Peter Wyden, *Stella: One Woman's True Tale of Evil, Betrayal, and Survival in Hitler's Germany;* see also Stoltzfus, *Resistance,* p. 222; Beate Meyer and Hermann Simon, *Juden in Berlin, 1938–1945* (Berlin, 2000), pp. 237–52.
80. Wyden, pp. 300–301.
81. Ibid., p. 17.
82. Ibid., p. 231.
83. Stoltzfus, *Resistance,* pp. 166, 184, 279–81. There were other "catchers" who worked with Stella and Abrahamsohn—Bruno Goldstein, Ruth Danziger, Ralf Isaaksohn, and a man named Frieldaender, to name just a few. See Wyden, pp. 139–42, 240, 274–76.
84. Kaplan, p. 210.
85. SS first lieutenant.
86. This camp operated from 18 August 1943 until 29 July 1944. The inmates worked at the Factory Lenta (S.D. Werkstätten). *Internationaler Suchdienst,* Verzeichnis der Haftstätten unter dem Reichsführer-SS, Comité International Genève (Red Cross), 1979, p. 251.
87. BA-MA, BMRS, File Fritz Scherwitz, Bl. 13.
88. BA-MA, BMRS, File Fritz Scherwitz, Bl. 22. Others have claimed that he helped people in the camp (see BA-MA, BMRS, File Scherwitz, Bl. 25–31). Anita Kugler, however, disputes the accuracy of these sources, which originally came from the Simon Wiesenthal Center in Israel, in her forthcoming biography of Scherwitz, *Der jüdische SS-Offizier* (personal communication from Kugler, 21 March 2002).
89. The rabbi who said this wishes to remain unknown.
90. BA-MA, BMRS, interview H. Pollak.
91. BA-MA, BMRS, interview Gaupp, 27.04.1996, T-198.
92. BA-MA, BMRS, File Schliesser.
93. They had just been pulled out of the combat zone west of Moscow, where they had been in constant combat for eleven months. BA-MA, BMRS, File Horst von Oppenfeld, Oppenfeld to Rigg, 12.02.2001.

94. BA-MA, BMRS, interview Oppenfeld.
95. BA-MA, BMRS, interview Rudolf Sachs, 20.11.1995, T-168.
96. BA-MA, BMRS, interview Fritz Kassowitz, 04.01.1996, T-183; BA-MA, BMRS, File Fritz Kassowitz.
97. BA-MA, BMRS, File Ernst Prager, Heft I, Bl. 144; BA-MA, BMRS, File Ernst Prager, S. Prager to Rigg, 05.07.2001.
98. Ibid.; BA-MA, BMRS, interview S. Prager.
99. BA-MA, BMRS, File Ernst Prager, Heft III, Bl. 121.
100. BA-MA, N 379/v. 226, Bl. 39, Langheld an Ruge, 12.05.1956.
101. BA-MA, N 328/45, Ehrhardt an Förste, 14.11.1956. This intervention must have happened sometime between 1940 and 1941 because it was stated that Heß secured her protection. After Bormann took over Heß's duties in May 1941, it is not known what happened to Frau Langheld née Gerson. However, in the letters Langheld wrote after the war, he mentioned that only his aunts and not his mother died, so one might conclude that she made it safely through the war.
102. Klemperer, Buch II, p. 477, 32.01.1944.
103. SS major.
104. BA-MA, BMRS, interview Krüger; Krüger, pp. 92–94.
105. Krüger, p. 94.
106. Rose had fought on the side of Franco's forces during the Spanish Civil War.
107. Rose's father, Siegbert Emil Rose, had been a medical officer (Oberstabsarzt) in the army during World War I.
108. The literal translation for *Schwein* is "pig," but here it means "jerk."
109. BA-MA, BMRS, File Rose, Schnez an Rigg, 30.01.2001. Rose's parents were killed in Auschwitz soon after their arrival.
110. de Maizière, p. 31; BA-MA, BMRS, interview Albert Schnez, 24.03.1997, T-323.
111. BA-MA, BMRS, File Schliesser; BA-MA, BMRS, Effenberg, Bl. 9 pp. 1–6.
112. BA-MA, BMRS, interview Techel.
113. Bergmann, p. 257.
114. BA-MA, BMRS, interview Bergmann.
115. BA-MA, BMRS, File Schliesser.
116. BA-MA, BMRS, File Hans Schmitt, Schmitt to Rigg, 30.03.2001.
117. Captain Sternberg would later go down with his U-boat.
118. BA-MA, BMRS, File Martin Bier, Bl. 33.
119. BA-MA, BMRS, File M. Bier, Bl. 17; BA-MA, BMRS, File Gerhard Bier, Bl. 13; BA-MA, BMRS, interview M. Bier; BA-MA, BMRS, interview Gerhard Bier, 25.09.1995, T-27; BA-MA, BMRS, interview Schlesinger.
120. BA-MA, BMRS, File Meissinger, Meissinger to Rigg, 21.07.2001.
121. Ibid.
122. Ibid., Meissinger to Rigg, 27.01.2001.
123. BA-MA, BMRS, interview Günzel; BA-MA, BMRS, File Günzel, Bl. 3. Hans Günzel received the Wound Badge and the EKII. Peter Günzel received the EKII and the EKI.
124. BA-MA, BMRS, interview Herder.

125. BA-MA, BMRS, interview Dieckmann.
126. BA-MA, BMRS, interview Sydow, 17.12.1994.
127. BA-MA, BMRS, interview Max Mannheimer, 18.11.1994, T-55.
128. Johannes Steinhoff, Peter Pechel, and Dennis Showalter, eds., *Deutsche im Zweiten Weltkrieg: Zeitzeugen Sprechen* (München, 1989), pp. 218, 452.
129. Schmidt, "Politischer Rückblick auf eine unpolitische Jugend," in *Kindheit unter Hitler,* p. 236.
130. BA-MA, BMRS, interview Fuchs.
131. BA-MA, BMRS, interview Harald Etheimer, 02.09.1995, T-164. See also BA-MA, BMRS, interview Bleicher.
132. Dawidowicz, *War against Jews,* pp. 349–50. See also Bauer, p. 247.
133. Steinberg, *All or Nothing,* pp. 50–51. See also Kaplan, pp. 184, 227.
134. Yahil, p. 99. See also Langer, *Holocaust Testimonies,* p. 138; Kaplan, p. 172.
135. Kaplan, p. 194.
136. Ian Kershaw, "Popular Opinion in the Third Reich," in *Government, Party, and People in Nazi Germany,* p. 71.
137. Dawidowicz, *War against Jews,* p. 306.

CONCLUSION

1. Charles Kelly Barrow, R. B. Rosenburg, and J. H. Segars, eds., *Forgotten Confederates: An Anthology about Black Southerners* (Atlanta, 1995); Richard Rollins, *Black Southerners in Gray: Essays on Afro-Americans in Confederate Armies* (California, 1994); Patricia W. Romero and Charles H. Wesley, *International Library of Negro Life and History* (New York, 1969), pp. 27, 56–58, 112–14, 143–44; James I. Robertson, *Soldiers Blue and Gray* (South Carolina, 1998), pp. 30–35; Richard Beringer, Herman Hattaway, Archer Jones, and William Stil, *The Elements of Confederate Defeat: Nationalism, War Aims, and Religion* (London, 1988), p. 177.
2. Ervin L. Jordan Jr., "Different Drummers," in *Black Southerners in Gray,* p. 67.
3. Romero and Wesley, p. 39. See also Richard Rollins, "Black Southerners in Gray," in *Black Southerners in Gray,* pp. 7–8, 17; Arthur W. Bergeron Jr., "Louisiana's Free Men of Color," in *Black Southerners in Gray,* pp. 37–38.
4. Rudolph Young, "Black Confederates in Lincoln County, North Carolina," in *Black Southerners in Gray;* p. 121; James H. Brewer, *The Confederate Negro* (Durham, 1969), p. 3. Brewer puts the number of African-Americans who served in the Confederate military between fifty thousand and sixty thousand.
5. Samuel Eliot Morison and Henry Steele Commager, *The Growth of the American Republic,* vol. 2, (Oxford, 1958), pp. 785–87; Charles B. MacDonald, *The Mighty Endeavor: American Armed Forces in the European Theater in World War II* (Oxford, 1969), pp. 248, 263, 498–500; Lauren, pp. 72–75, 188; Allen Millett and Peter Maslowski, *For the Common Defense* (New York, 1984), p. 349; Omar N. Bradley and Clay Blair, *A General's Life: An Autobiography by General of the Army Omar N. Bradley* (New York, 1981), pp. 484–86, 543.

6. Robert B. Edgerton, *Warriors of the Rising Sun* (New York, 1997), p. 226; William Manchester, *Goodbye Darkness* (New York, 1979), pp. 166, 183; Robert T. Oliver, *A History of the Korean People in Modern Times: 1800 to the Present* (Newark, 1993), pp. 110–24. Many Koreans were conscripted by the Japanese armed forces and sent to battle in Manchuria and the Pacific Islands. Several kamikaze pilots were in fact brainwashed Korean high school students. Although Koreans were severely discriminated against in the army, several reached high ranks. For example, Lieutenant General Sa-ick Hong, the commandant of the infamous Manila POW camp, was a Korean and was later executed by the Americans as a war criminal (Japan deliberately transferred him to the prison post near the end of the war). Former Korean president Chung-hee Park was a graduate of the Japanese Military Academy and fought for Japan in Manchuria as an officer. Many thanks to Dr. Kwan-sa You for translating this information from Kap-jae Cho: "Spit on my Grave—The Life of Park Chung-hee," Chosun Ilbo, Seoul, Korea, article no. 104-116, 1998.

7. It seems that only Japanese living in the coastal areas of California, Oregon, and Washington had to leave for the internment camps. Those Japanese who lived in Hawaii, for example, were not put into camps.

8. Morison and Commager, p. 788; Lauren, pp. 132–33. Not until 21 June 2000 were twenty-two Japanese Americans awarded the Medal of Honor for actions performed during World War II. They had been denied these honors because of their ancestry. These Japanese Americans served in the 442nd Army Regiment, the most decorated regiment of the war. Some people claim that this was a political move on President Clinton's part during election year to secure the American Asian vote for Gore. For example, every World War II army regiment averaged around one Medal of Honor, but the fact that twenty-two men received this medal from one regiment is quite remarkable if not impossible. As historian and army colonel James Corum says, "It smells of politics."

9. See Stoltzfus, *Resistance*, pp. 85, 248.

10. Turner, p. 36.

11. Walter Görlitz, "Reichenau," in *Hitler's Generals*, p. 215.

12. *Heeresadjutant bei Hitler*, p. 70. See also Guderian, p. 86.

13. Bartov, pp. 129–30; Jürgen Förster, in *The Final Solution*, p. 97; Jürgen Förster, "Securing 'Living-Space,'" in *Germany and the Second World War*, vol. 4, pp. 1,209–14.

14. Jürgen Förster, "Securing 'Living-Space,'" in *Germany and the Second World War*, vol. 4, p. 1,213.

15. Bartov, p. 130; Breithaupt, pp. 135–37; Jürgen Förster, *The Final Solution*, p. 97; Jürgen Förster, *Germany and the Second World War*, vol. 4, pp. 1213–16.

16. Jürgen Förster, "Hitler's Decision in Favor of War against the Soviet Union," in *Germany and the Second World War*, vol. 4, pp. 36–37.

17. See Yahil, pp. 257–58, 272–74; Gilbert, *Holocaust*, p. 210.

18. Kershaw, *Hitler, 1936–1945*, pp. 406, 709.

19. Hitler quite often let his ideological beliefs get in the way of military necessity. For example, during the war with Russia, Hitler could have mobilized five mil-

lion women to work in the factories, thereby freeing up to three million men for military service. However, he did not use these women because of "both the physical and moral harm upon German women and damage to their psychic and emotional life and possibly their potential as mothers" if they worked. Craig, *Germany, 1866–1945*, pp. 735–36, 745–46. See also Rebentisch, p. 403 n. 93; Stephan Salter, "Class Harmony or Class Conflict? The Industrial Working Class and the National Socialist Regime," in *Government, Party, and People in Nazi Germany*, pp. 89–91; Kershaw, *Hitler, 1936–1945*, pp. 563, 567–68.

20. BA-MA, BMRS, general impression gained from this study; Rebentisch, p. 435, n. 200; Adler, *Der Verwaltete Mensch*, p. 302.

21. Victor, p. 197.

22. Bracher, p. 404.

23. Lösener, pp. 281, 311. *Judenfreund* was described by Robert Gellately as a "term of abuse and a catch-all accusation that could be levelled at persons who had uttered a mild disagreement with some aspect of the racial policies, or had otherwise given reason for suspicion that they did not accept the letter or spirit of Nazi anti-Semitism." Gellately, *Gestapo and German Society*, p. 160.

24. Lösener, p. 311; see also Noakes, "Development of Nazi Policy," pp. 313, 353–54.

25. For evidence of Hitler's direct handling of the Holocaust, see Kershaw, *Profiles in Power*, pp. 82, 115, 157, 178; Kershaw, *Nazi Dictatorship*, pp. 80–107; Kershaw, *Hitler, 1936–1945*, pp. 147, 152, 461–64, 468–69, 487, 520–21, 583–84, 636; Richard Breitman "Himmler, The Architect of Genocide," in *Final Solution*, p. 73; Christopher R. Browning, "Hitler and the Euphoria of Victory: The Path to the Final Solution," in *Final Solution*, pp. 137, 143–45; *Goebbels Diaries, 1942–1943*, pp. 86, 92, 148, 244, 300; Redlich, pp. 54–55, 104–5, 170–76, 264, 316; *Monologe im Führerhauptquartier, 1941–1944*, pp. 90, 99, 130, 195, 229; Weinberg, *Germany, Hitler*, p. 223; Friedländer, p. 3; Maser, pp. 256, 384; Browning, *Nazi Policy, Jewish Workers*, pp. 1–3; Browning, *Ordinary Men*, p. 49; Evans, pp. 85, 213–15, 220.

26. Helmut Krausnick and Hildegard von Kotze, eds., *Es spricht der Führer: Sieben exemplarische Hitler-Reden* (Gütersloh, 1966), p. 147. As translated by Friedländer, p. 187.

27. Kershaw, *Profiles in Power*, p. 110. See also Kershaw, *Hitler, 1889–1936*, p. 532; Kershaw, *Hitler, 1936–1945*, pp. 93, 421.

28. Kershaw, *Profiles in Power*, p. 157; Redlich, pp. 170, 321; Evans, pp. 11, 78, 82, 89–90.

29. Kershaw, *Profiles in Power*, pp. 157, 178; Kershaw, *Hitler, 1889–1936*, p. 345; Kershaw, *Hitler, 1936–1945*, pp. 244, 248, 349, 352–58, 461–69, 479, 488, 492, 520–22, 589; Kershaw, *Nazi Dictatorship*, p. 105; *Die Wehrmacht*, Jürgen Förster, pp. 953, 960; Bauer, pp. 155, 194–95; Martin Broszat, *German National Socialism, 1919–1945* (California, 1966), p. 52; Weinberg, *Germany, Hitler*, p. 226; Rebentisch, p. 429; Benz, p. 1; Redlich, pp. 154, 173–75, 177, 321–22, 327–28; Browning, *Nazi Policy, Jewish Workers*, pp. 3, 14–15, 33, 39; Browning, *Ordinary Men*, p. 10; Evans, pp. 57, 81.

30. Redlich, p. 170.

BIBLIOGRAPHY

PRIMARY WRITTEN SOURCES (ARCHIVES)

Bundesarchiv Aachen (BA-A), Germany
BA-A

H 20/490	Pers 36848	RM 123/15043
Sammlung Jüdische	Pers 45570	RM 123/335944
Soldaten	Pers 45573	RW 55/1589
Pers 4393	Pers 48220	RW 55/2163
Pers 14492	Pers 49110	RW 55/3843
Pers 15380	Pers 53022	RW 55/7211
Pers 15499	Pers 53059	RW 55/7224
Pers 19147	Pers 63210	RW 55/15043
Pers 36790	RM 45/3375	RW 160/55

Archiv der Republik Österreich–Vienna, Austria
Archiv der Republik Österreich (ARÖ) Wien, Pers. Akt. Robert Colli

Bundesarchiv-Berlin (BA-B), Germany
BA-B

15.09/36N	NS 6/764	R 18/520
15.09/39	NS 15/39	R 18/5514
15.09/43	NS 15/40	R 21/448
15.09/52	NS 15/41	R 21 (76)/874
15.09/58	NS 15/42	R 21 (76)/875
15.09/90	NS 18/482	R 21 (76)/876
NS 6/78	NS 19/87	R 21 (76)/877
NS 6/98	NS 19/199	R 21 (76)/878
NS 6/200	NS 19/415	R 41/581
NS 6/221	NS 19/453	R 43 II/418a
NS 6/285	NS 19/1194	R 43 II/599
NS 6/338	NS 19/1614	R 43 II/ 1036
NS 6/339	NS 19/1772	R 43 II/1273
NS 6/341	NS 19/2177	R 58/276
NS 6/342	NS 19/3134	
NS 6/346	NS 19/3857	Sammlung Schumacher
NS 6/347	NS 22/1051	II 240
NS 6/349	R 3/1583	DZA (Potsdam) 62 Ka.
NS 6/ 487	R 7.01 Reichskanzlei 4112	I 83

Bundesarchiv-Militararchiv-Freiburg (BA-MA), Germany
BA-MA

H 6/172	Msg 1/1364	Msg 1/3417
Msg 1/531	Msg 1/1365	Msg 2/5078
Msg 1/793	Msg 1/1570	Msg 44/101
Msg 1/1363	Msg 1/3414	N 39/62

N 59/4
N 107/1
N 113/2
N 113/3
N 113/4
N 118
N 179
N 328/20
N 328/32
N 328/45
N 328/58
N 379/109a
N 379/223
N 379/224
N 379/225
N 379/226
N 379/260
N 431/803
N 431/1154
N 607/4
N 642
N 656/2
N 656/3
N 656/4

N 656/5
N 656/6
N 656/9
N 656/27
N 761/7

Pers 6/11
Pers 6/541
Pers 6/871
Pers 6/1808
Pers 6/2094
Pers 6/2236
Pers 6/2304
Pers 6/7363
Pers 6/9887
Pers 6/10046
Pers 6/10595
Pers 6/11122
Pers 6/11545
Pers 8–385

RH 7/11
RH 7/23
RH 12-23/834
RH 15/419

RH 15/421
RH 20-18/71
RH 21-3/v. 46
RH 26/257
RH 39/154
RH 39/222
RH 53-7/8
RH53-7/271
RH 53-7/468
RH 53-7/514
RH 53-7/627

RL 14/49

RM 92/5173

RW 6/56
RW 6/73
RW 19/550
RW 19/853

W 01-5/173
W 01-6/359
WF-01/10230
WF01/20740
Wi VIII/45

Deutsche Dienststelle–Berlin (DDS), Germany

DDS

Pers Paul Ascher
Pers Erich Astheimer
Pers Martin Baltzer

Pers Franz Mendelssohn
Pers Anton Mayer
Pers Conrad Patzig

Pers Arnold Techel
Deutsche Dienststelle-
Berlin Library

Allgemeine Heeresmitteilungen (AHM), Ziff. Nr. 1041, 18.08.1941
Heeres-Verordnungsblatt (HVBL.), Nr. 73, 1933

HVBl., Nr. 131, 1940
HVBl., Nr. 848, 05.09.1941

HVBl., Nr. 202, 1942

HVBl., Nr. 926, 25.09.1942

Deutsche Dienststelle (WAST) für die Benachrichtigung der nächsten Angehörigen von Gefallenen der Ehemaligen deutschen Wehrmacht, Arbeitsbericht 1994–1996. Berlin, 1996.

Institut für Zeitgeschichte–Munich (IFZ), Germany

Akten der Parteikanzlei der NSDAP: Rekonstruktion eines verlorengegangenen Bestandes: Bundesarchiv, Microfiches, hrsg. v. Institut für Zeitgeschichte. München, 1983.
IfZ, N 71-73

Eichmann Prosecution Document, Police d'Israel Quartier General 6-ème Bureau No.
878, 994, 1102, 1205, 1355

MA 103/1

MA 125/8 380458

Munich's Legal Records—Munich, Germany

Landgericht München I, Akten Werner Eisner, Protokoll aufgenommen in öffentlicher
Sitzung des Einzelrichters des 17. Zivilsenats des Oberlandesgerichts München
Stadtarchiv Bonn, Germany
D 2797, P 18/130

Bryan Mark Rigg-Sammlung (Collection), Bundesarchiv–Militärarchiv–Freiburg (BA-MA, BMRS), Germany

BA-MA, BMRS,

File Heinz Günther
  Angreß
File Heinrich Bamberger
File Fritz Baruch
File Hanns-Heinz Bauer
File Helmuth Baum
File Dieter Bergmann
File Gert Beschütz
File Herbert Beyer
File Gerhard Bier
File Martin Bier
File Heinz Bleicher
File Ernst Bloch
File Erik Blumenfeld
File Robert Borchardt
File Oscar Bosch
File Achim von Bredow
File Dietmar Brücher
File Otto Buchinger
File Werner Bujakowsky
File Walter Bürck
File Peter Cahn
File Alfred Catharin
File Richard Cohn
File Robert Czempin
File di Simoni
File Wilhelm Dröscher
File Du Bois-Reymond
File Heinz Eder
File Dieter Effenberg
File Kurt Einstein
File Werner Eisner
File Hans Eppinger
File Walter Falk
File Hans-Geert
  Falkenberg
File Bettina Fehr
File Dieter Fischer
File Klaus Florey
File Eugen Frank

File Lt. Fränzel
File Karl-Heinrich Fricke
File Hans-Georg von
  Friedeburg
File Ludwig Ganghofer
File Rainer Gärtner
File Horst Geiger
File Horst Geitner
File Yosef Getreuer
File Gerhart von Gierke
File Helmut von Gottberg
File Wilhelm von
  Gottberg
File Wolfram Günther
File Hans Günzel
File Gerhard Guttstadt
File Franz and Thomas
  Haller
File Walter Hamburger
File Johannes Heckert
File Gotthard Heinrici
File Hartmut Heinrici
File Bernt von Helmolt
File Franz Henle
File Karl Henle
File Heinz Georg
  Heymann
File Hans Hiefner
File Paul-Ludwig
  Hirschfeld
File Walther Hofmann
File Kurt Heinrich
  Hohenemser
File Walter Hollaender
File Wilhelm Hollaender
File Helmuth Jacobsen
File Edgar Jacoby
File Georg-Wilhelm Jäger
File Hans Kirchholtes
File Gerd zu Klampen

File Otto Kohn
File Hans-Joachim
  Körner
File Heinz-Jürgen Kühl
File Hermann Lange
File Georg Langheld
File Hans Christian
  Lankes
File Wolfgang Lauinger
File Joachim Le Coutre
File Herbert Lefévre
File Walter Lehweß-
  Litzmann
File Joachim Leidloff
File Wolfgang Lennert
File Heinrich Levin
File Erika Leykam
File Ferdinand Lichtwitz
File Rudolf Löwenfeld
File Heinz-Günther Löwy
File Ernst Ludwig
File Emil Lux
File Werner Maltzahn
File Alfred Marian
File Ludwig Mayer
File Hans Meissinger
File Viktor Mendel
File Franz Mendelssohn
File Georg Meyer
File Günther Mirauer
File Georg-Friedrich
  Müller
File Hans Mühlbacher
File Heino Nave
File Carl Neubronner
File Helmut Niemann
File Peter Noah
File Horst von Oppenfeld
File August Oestreicher
File Conrad Patzig

File Ernst Prager
File Hanns Rehfeld
File Johannes Reich
File Anton Paul Rengers
File Joachim von
  Ribbentrop
File Heinz Rohr
File Joachim Rohr
File Bernhard Rogge
File Friedrich-Karl Rogge
File Helmuth Rosenbaum
File Fritz Rosenhaupt
File Christian Rosenthal
File Hans Sander
File Günther Scheffler
File Karl Heinz Scheffler
File Konrad Schenck

File Rolf Schenk
File Fritz Scherwitz
File Heinrich
  Schlepegrell.
File Friedrich Schlesinger
File Heinz Schlieper
File Peter Schliesser
File Klaus von Schmeling-
  Diringshofen
File Hans Schmitt
File Helmut Schmoeckel
File Gerd Schneider
File Hermann Schucht
File Eike Schweitzer
File Werner Seldis
File Herbert Simon
File Wolfgang Spier

File Hermann Steinthal
File Fritz Steinwasser
File Georg Struzyna
File Rolf von Sydow
File Karl Taraba
File Karl-Arnd Techel
File Rolf Vogel
File Wolfgang Voigt
File Helmut Wilberg
File Johann Zukertort
File Karl Zukertort

Lecture given at Yale
  by Shlomo Perel,
  22 April 1994

Liste von aktiven
  Offizieren

INTERVIEWS

BA-MA, BMRS, interview
  H. A., 18.11.1997
  Heinz Günter Angreß, 10.12.1994
  Gert Ascher, 17.11.1997
  Ursula Ascher, 17.11.1997
  Hermann Aub, 14.12.1996
  Egon Bahr, 13.02.1995
  Heinrich Bamberger, 08.11.1994
  Fritz Baruch, 31.07.1997
  Hanns-Heinz Bauer, 29.03.1998
  Dietrich Beelitz 16.11.1997
  Elisabeth Behrend, 03.03.1997
  Wolfgang Behrendt, 21.11.1994
  Wilhelmina Benasuli, 19.01.1997
  Hans B. (Bernheim), 29.10.1998
  Rabbi Chaskel Besser, 15.01.1995
  Gerhard Bier, 25.09.1994
  Martin Bier, 25.09.1994
  Heinz Bleicher, 10.02.1995
  Martin Bloch, 13.10.1996
  Martin Bloch, 04.12.1996
  Adolf Blum, 22.04.1995
  Lenni Blum, 22.04.1995
  Thilo Bode, 24.02.1995
  Elisabeth Borchardt, 18.02.1995
  Margot Braun, 07.01.1996
  Robert Braun, 10–14.08.1994
  Robert Braun, 11.03.1995
  Robert Braun, 07.01.1996
  Felix Bruck, 18.04.1997
  Walter Brück, 12.07.1997

  Dietmar Brücher, 17.02.1995
  Klaus Budzinski, 15.11.1994
  Susi Byk, 23.11.1995
  Hans Cahn, 11.12.1996
  Peter Cahn, 17.03.1995
  Peter Cahn, 11.12.1996
  Alfred Catharin, 04.01.1996
  Richard Czempin, 09.02.1995
  Ulrich de Maizière, 24.03.1997
  Hans-Oskar Löwenstein de Witt,
    06.12.1994
  Yoav Delarea, 05.07.1998
  Hans Döppes, 19.05.1996
  Wolfgang Ebert, 13.07.1997
  Harald Etheimer, 02.09.1995
  Hans-Geert Falkenberg, 02.02.1997
  Gerhard Fecht, 18.11.1997
  Dieter Fischer, 12.12.1996
  Herbert Frank, 27.06.1995
  Niklas Frank, 16.10.1996
  Hugo Freund., 30.11.1994
  Ludwig von Friedeburg, 01.12.1997
  Hugo Fuchs, 08.07.1995
  Peter Gaupp, 17.01.1995
  Peter Gaupp, 27.04.1996
  Ursula Gaupp, 08.07.1995
  Ursula Gaupp, 27.04.1996
  Horst Geitner, 38.03.1997
  Gerhart von Gierke, 05.04.1997
  Hildegard von Gierke, 29.11.1997

Rolf von Gierke, 29.11.1997
Hansotto Goebel, 07.12.1996
Werner Goldberg, 17.10.1994
Horst G. (Reinhard), 20.11.1994
J. G., 05.01.1995
Harald von Gottberg, 09.07.1997
Helmut von Gottberg, 09–10.11.1996
Rolf Gottschalk, 01.12.1994
Werner Gramsch, 16.11.1996
Michael Günther, 19.02.1997
Wolfram Günther, 12.08.1996
Hans Günzel, 23–24.07.1997
Wilhelm von Gwinner, 17.11.1994
Wilhelm von Gwinner, 16.12.1996
Walter Hamburger, 5–6.11.1994
Michael Hauck, 24.11.1994
Bernt von Helmolt, 22.07.1997
Eva Heinrichs, 09.02.1997
Kurt Heinrichs, 09.02.1997
Dr. Heinrici, 16.05.1996
Eduard Hesse, 30.10.1998
Hans von Herwarth, 12.09.1994
Heinz-Georg Heymann, 09.04.1995
Paul Hirschfeld, 15–16.08.1994
Paul Hirschfeld, 22.11.1996
Kurt Hohenmser, 28.11.1994
Jochen Hollaender, 14.12.1996
Hertha-Barbara Hollaender, 21.11.1995
Hertha- Barbara Hollaender, 12.11.1996
Hans Homberger, 08.04.1995
Frhr. von Hornstein, 16.06.1996
Barbara Jacoby, 17.11.1994
Frau Edgar Jacoby, 01.11.1994
Frau Edgar Jacoby, 19.11.1996
Fritz Kassowitz, 04.01.1996
Gerd zu Klampen, 28.10.1998
Ursula Freifrau von Knigge, 26.07.1997
Hans Koref, 06.01.1996
Jürgen Krackow, 14.11.1994
Jürgen Krackow, 18.11.1994
Reinhard Krackow, 20.05.1996
Helmut Krüger, 27, 31.08.1994
J. L., 09.11.1994
Joachim Le Coutre, 25.01.1997
Arnim Leidoff, 02.12.1995
Hannah Leopold, 11.11.1996
Ferdinand Lichtwitz, 18.07.1997
Jörn Lehweß-Litzmann, 27.05.1997
Heinz-Günther Löwy, 12.01.1996
Otto Lüderitz, 28.03.1997

Ernst Ludwig, 22.01.1997
Emil Lux, 30.05.1997
Max Mannheimer, 18.11.1994
Rüdiger von Manstein, 17.11.1994
Franz Margold, 18.05.1996
Hans Meissinger, 17.09.1996
Frau Mendelssohn-Barz, 17.03.1995
Frau Mendelssohn-Eder, 26.02.1995
Margot Meyer von Rühle 02.09.1995
Helmut Meyer-Krahmer, 27.07.1997
Rosemarie Mirauer, 24.02.1997
Dietrich Moll, 04.03.1995
Hans Mühlbacher, 18.09.1994
Hermann Nast-Kolb, 22.11.1994
Karl Neubronner, 09.04.1995
Heinz Neumaier, 21.04.1995
Theodor Oberländer, 19.09.1994
Richard Ohm, 11.02.1995
Horst von Oppenfeld, 05.01.1995
Karl Partsch, 14.12.1994
Shlomo Perel, 10.09.1994
Ingrid Pflettner, 15.04.1995
Hans Pollak, 07.12.1995
Alfred Posselt, 04.01.1996
Stephan Prager, 11.10.1997
Hans Radványi, 07.01.1996
Hans Ranke, 09.12.1994
Hermann Rath, 08.04.1995
Erich Rauchfüß, 02.04.1995
Hanns Rehfeld, 16.11.1996
Johannes Reich, 28.12.1995
Ludwig Reinhard, 13.01.1996
Richard Riess, 15.10.1994
Ruth Rilk, 05.02.1997
Friedrich Rubien, 27.07.1997
Jürgen Ruge, 15.04.1995
H. S., 16.11.1995
Rudolf Sachs, 20.11.1995
Christoph-Michael Salinger, 08.10.1998
Stefan Sander, 10.07.1997
Joachim Schaper, 25.05.1997
Günther Scheffler, 10.03.1995
Günther Scheffler, 14.12.1996
Karl-Heinz Scheffler, 09.03.1995
Karl-Heinz Scheffler, 19.05.1996
Walter Scheinberger, 18.03.1995
Rolf Schenk, 23.05.1997.
Gerhard Schiller, 11.02.1995
Heinz Schindler, 26.10.1997
Friedrich Schlesinger, 10.12.1994

Peter Schliesser, 28.04.1996
Horst Schmechel, 29.11.1994
Helmut Schmidt, 22.11.1995
Helmut Schmidt, 15.10.1996
Egbert von Schmidt-Pauli, 13.09.1994
Hans Schmoeckel , 08.12.1994
Helmut Schmoeckel, 25.11.1994
Walter Schneinberger, 02.07.1995
Albert Schnez, 24.03.1997
Walter Schönewald, 06.01.1996
August Sohn, 17.05.1996
Wolfgang Spier, 06.12.1994
Arno Spitz, 17.06.1996
Friedrich-Christian Stahl, 12.11.1997
Alexander Stahlberg, 3–4.12.1994
Fritz Steinwasser, 13.12.1994

Fritz Steinwasser, 07.02.1997
Rolf von Sydow, 17.12.1994
Rosa Taraba, 08.01.1996
Karl-Arnd Techel, 29.05.1997
Maria-Anna van Menxel, 22.04.1995
Frau Rolf Vogel, 18.03.1995
Wolfgang Voigt, 09.04.1995
Reiner Wiehl, 17.05.1996
Joachim Wilberg, 05.04.1995
Frau Joachim Wilberg, 05.04.1995
Otto Wolters, 18.03.1995
Otto Wolters, 16.12.1996
Gerhard Wundermacher, 20.11.1995
Joachim Zelter, 27.10.1997
Rolf Zelter, 14.05.1996
Kurt Zeunert, 06.02.1997

SECONDARY SOURCES

1918–1968 Die Streitkräfte der Republik Österreich. Katalog zur Sonderausstellung im Heeresgeschichtlichen Museum Wien 1968 (hrsg.). Heeresgeschichtlichen Museum/Militärwissenschaftlichen Institut Wien. Wien, 1968.

Abrams, Alan, *Special Treatment.* New Jersey, 1985.

Abshagen, Karl Heinz. *Canaris.* London, 1956.

Absolon, Rudolf. *Die Wehrmacht im Dritten Reich. Band III, 3. August 1934 bis 4. Februar 1938* (=Schriften des Bundesarchivs 16/III). Boppard, 1975.

———. *Die Wehrmacht im Dritten Reich. Band V, 1. September 1939 bis 18. Dezember 1941* (=Schriften des Bundesarchivs 16/V). Boppard, 1988.

———. *Die Wehrmacht im Dritten Reich. Band VI, 19. Dezember 1941 bis 9. Mai 1945* (=Schriften des Bundesarchivs 16/VI). Boppard, 1995.

———. *Wehrgesetz und Wehrdienst 1935–1945. Das Personalwesen in der Wehrmacht.* Boppard, 1960.

Adam, Peter. *Art of the Third Reich.* New York, 1992.

Adam, Uwe. *Judenpolitik im Dritten Reich.* Düsseldorf, 1972.

Adler, H. G., *Der Verwaltete Mensch. Studien zur Deportation der Juden aus Deutschland.* Tübingen, 1974.

———. *The Jews in Germany.* London, 1969.

Adolf Hitler Monologe im Führerhauptquartier, 1941–1944. Hrsg. u. kommentiert v. Werner Jochmann. Hamburg, 1980.

Alexander, Philip S. *Textual Sources for the Study of Judaism.* Manchester, 1984.

Allen, William Sheridan. "Die deutsche Öffentlichkeit und die 'Reichskristallnacht'— Konflikte zwischen Werthierarchie und Propaganda im Dritten Reich." In *Die Reihen fest geschlossen. Beiträge zur Geschichte des Alltags unterm Nationalsozialismus.* Wuppertal, 1981, S. 397–411.

———. *The Nazi Seizure of Power.* New York, 1984.

Angolia, John R. *For Führer and Fatherland: Military Awards of the Third Reich.* New York, 1976.

Angress, Werner T. "Prussia's Army and the Jewish Reserve Officer Controversy before World War I." *Leo Baeck Yearbook* 17 (1972): 17–54.

Arendt, Hannah. *Eichmann in Jerusalem.* New York, 1984.

Armstrong, Karen, *A History of God: A 4,000-Year Quest of Judaism, Christianity and Islam.* New York, 1993.

Aronson, Shlomo. *Reinhard Heydrich und die Frühgeschichte von Gestapo und SD.* Stuttgart, 1971.

Aschheim, Steven E. *Brothers and Strangers: The East European Jew in German and German Jewish Consciousness, 1800–1923.* Wisconsin, 1982.

Auerbach, Leopold. *Das Judentum und seine Bekenner in Preußen.* Berlin, 1890.

Auman, Hans J. *Mein Leben als Mischmosch.* München, 1977.

Baeumker, A. "Ein Beitrag zur Geschichte der Führung der deutschen Luftfahrt-technik im ersten halben Jahrhundert 1900–1945." Heft 44 der Schriftenreihe "Langfristiges Planen der Forschung und Entwicklung" (Juli 1971).

Balfour, Michael. *The Kaiser and His Times.* Cambridge, 1964.

Bamberger, Bernhard J. *The Story of Judaism.* New York, 1957.

Barnett, Correlli, ed. *Hitler's Generals.* London, 1989.

Barrow, Charles Kelly, J. H. Segars, and R.B. Rosenburg. *Forgotten Confederates: An Anthology about Black Southerners.* Atlanta, 1995.

Bartov, Omer. *Hitler's Army.* New York, 1991.

Bar-Zohar, Michel. *Hitler's Jewish Spy.* London, 1985.

Bauer, Yehuda. *A History of the Holocaust.* New York, 1982.

Bauer, Yehuda and Nathan Rotenstreich, eds. *The Holocaust as Historical Experience.* New York, 1981.

Baumont, Maurice, John H. E. Fried, and Edmond Vermeil, eds. *The Third Reich.* New York, 1955.

Baynes, Norman H., ed. *The Speeches of Adolf Hitler. Vols. 1 and 2, April 1922–August 1939.* Oxford, 1942.

Bedürftig, Friedemann, and Christian Zentner, eds. *The Encyclopedia of the Third Reich.* Vol. 1. New York, 1991.

Beer, Edith Hahn, and Susan Dworkin. *The Nazi Officer's Wife.* New York, 1999.

Behr, Stephan. *Der Bevölkerungsrückgang der deutschen Juden.* Frankfurt, 1932.

Bein, Alex. "Arthur Ruppin: The Man and his Work." *Leo Baeck Yearbook* 17, (1972): 117–41.

Bekker, Cajus. *Hitler's Naval War.* New York, 1977.

Below, Nicolaus von. *Als Hitlers Adjutant, 1937–1945.* Mainz, 1980.

Benz, Wolfgang. *The Holocaust: A German Historian Examines the Genocide.* New York, 1999.

Berghahn, Volker Rolf. *Germany and the Approach of War in 1914.* New York, 1993.

Bergmann, Dieter. *Between Two Benches.* California, 1995.

Bering, Dietz, *Stigma of Names.* Michigan, 1992.

Beringer, Richard, Herman Hattaway, Archer Jones, and William Still. *The Elements of Confederate Defeat: Nationalism, War Aims, and Religion.* London, 1988.

Berkley, George E. *Vienna and Its Jews.* Maryland, 1988.

Berman, Louis A. *Jews and Intermarriage: A Study in Personality and Culture.* New York, 1968.

Best, Geoffrey. *Humanity in Warfare.* New York, 1980.

Beyerchen, Alan D. *Scientists under Hitler.* New Haven, 1977.

Bienenfeld, F. R. *The Germans and the Jews.* London, 1939.
———. *The Religion of the Non-Religious Jews.* London, 1944.
Black, Matthew and H. H. Rowley, eds. *Peake's Commentary on the Bible.* New York, 1963.
Blau, Bruno. *Das Ausnahmerecht für die Juden in Deutschland, 1933–1945.* Düsseldorf, 1954.
———. "Die Christen jüdischer und gemischter Abkunft in Deutschland und Österreich im Jahr 1939." *Judaica: Beiträge zum Verständnis des jüdischen Schicksals in Vergangenheit und Gegenwart.* Bd. 5 (1949): S. 272–88.
———. "Die Juden in Deutschland von 1935–1945." *Judaica: Beiträge zum Verständnis des jüdischen Schicksals in Vergangenheit und Gegenwart.* Bd. 7 (1951): S. 270–84.
———. "Die Mischehe im Nazireich." *Judaica: Beiträge zum Verständnis des jüdischen Schicksals in Vergangenheit und Gegenwart.* Bd. 4 (1948): S. 46–57.
Bloch, Chajim, and Löbel Taubes, eds. *Jüdisches Jahrbuch für Österreich.* Wien, 1932.
Botz, Gerhard, Ivar Oxaal, and Michael Pollak, eds. *Jews, Antisemitism, and Culture in Vienna.* New York, 1987.
Bracher, Karl Dietrich. *The German Dictatorship.* New York, 1970.
Bracke, Gerhard. *Melitta Gräfin Stauffenberg. Das Leben einer Fliegerin.* München, 1990.
Bradley, D., and R. Schulze-Kossens, eds. *Tätigkeitsbericht des Chefs des Heerespersonalamtes General der Infanterie Rudolf Schmundt: 1.10.1942–29.10.1944. Fortgef. v. Wilhelm Burgdorf.* Osnabrück, 1984.
Bradley, Omar N., and Clay Blair. *A General's Life: An Autobiography by General of the Army Omar N. Bradley.* New York, 1981.
Breithaupt, Hans. *Zwischen Front und Widerstand. Ein Beitrag zur Diskussion um den Feldmarschall Erich von Manstein.* München, 1994.
Brewer, James H. *The Confederate Negro.* Durham, 1969.
Brissaud, Andre. *Canaris.* London, 1986.
Broszat, Martin. *Das Dritte Reich.* München, 1989.
———. *German National Socialism, 1919–1945.* California, 1966.
Broszat, Martin and Norbert Frei, eds. *Das Dritte Reich im Überblick. Chronik, Ereignisse, Zusammenhänge.* München, 1989.
Browning, Christopher R. *The Final Solution and the German Foreign Office.* London, 1978.
———. *Nazi Policy, Jewish Workers, German Killers.* Cambridge, 2000.
———. *Ordinary Men: Reserve Police Battalion 101 and the Final Solution in Poland.* New York, 1992.
Budzinski, Klaus. *Der Riss durchs Ganze. Kolportage einer gestörten Deutschwerdung.* Berlin, 1993.
Bukey, Evan Burr. *Hitler's Austria: Popular Sentiment in the Nazi Era.* North Carolina, 2000.
Bullock, Alan. *Hitler: A Study in Tyranny.* New York, 1962.
Burdick, Charles, ed. *The Halder War Diary, 1939–1942.* London, 1950.
Burleigh, Michael. *The Third Reich: A New History.* New York, 2000.

Burrin, Philippe. *Hitler and the Jews: The Genesis of the Holocaust.* London, 1989.
Buschbeck, E. H. *Austria.* London, 1949.
Butler, Ewan and Gordon Young. *Marshal without Glory.* London, 1951.
Büttner, Ursula. *Die Not der Juden teilen.* Hamburg, 1988.
———. "The Persecution of Christian-Jewish Families in the Third Reich." *Leo Baeck Yearbook* 34 (1989): 267–90.
Calic, Edouard. *Reinhard Heydrich: The Chilling Story of the Man Who Masterminded the Nazi Death Camps.* New York, 1985.
Carell, Paul. *The Foxes of the Desert.* New York, 1961.
———. *Unternehmen Barbarossa.* Stuttgart, 1963.
Carr, William. *A History of Germany, 1815–1945.* London, 1969.
Cecil, Lamar. *Albert Ballin: Business and Politics in Imperial Germany, 1888–1918.* Princeton, 1967.
———. *Wilhelm II: Prince and Emperor, 1859–1900.* Chapel Hill, 1989.
Cesarani, David, ed. *The Final Solution: Origins and Implementation.* New York, 1994.
Cho, Kap-jae. "Spit on my Grave—The Life of Park Chung-hee." Chosun Ilbo, Seoul, Korea. Article no. 104-116 1998.
Claasen, Adam R. A. *Hitler's Northern War: The Luftwaffe's Ill-Fated Campaign, 1940–1945.* Kansas, 2001.
Clark, Alan. *Barbarossa: The Russian-German Conflict, 1941–1945.* New York, 1965.
Cohen, Asher and Bernard Susser. *Israel and the Politics of Jewish Identity: The Secular-Religious Impasse.* London, 2000.
Cohen, Israel. *Jewish Life in Modern Times.* New York, 1914.
Cohn, Werner. "Bearers of a Common Fate? The 'Non-Aryan' Christian 'Fate-Comrades' of the Paulus-Bund, 1933–1939." *Leo Baeck Yearbook* 33 (1988): 327–68.
Cooper, Matthew. *German Army.* New York, 1978.
———. *The German Air-Force, 1933–1945.* New York, 1981.
Cornberg, Jobst Frhr. von, and John M. Steiner. "Willkür in der Willkür. Hitler und die Befreiungen von den antisemitischen Nürnberger Gesetzen." *Vierteljahreshefte für Zeitgeschichte,* Heft 2 (1998): S. 143–87.
Corum, James S. *The Luftwaffe: Creating the Operational Air War, 1918–1940.* Kansas, 1997.
———. "The Old Eagle as Phoenix: The Luftstreitkräfte Creates an Operational Air War Doctrine, 1919–1920." *Air Power History* (1992).
———. *The Roots of Blitzkrieg.* Kansas, 1992.
Craig, Gordon A. *Germany, 1866–1945.* New York, 1978.
———. *The Politics of the Prussian Army, 1640–1945.* New York, 1964.
Crankshaw, Edward. *Bismarck.* New York, 1981.
Creveld, Martin van. *Fighting Power.* New York, 1982.
Dallin, Alexander. *German Rule in Russia, 1941–1945.* New York, 1957.
Dawidowicz, Lucy, ed. *A Holocaust Reader.* New Jersey, 1976.
Dawidowicz, Lucy. *The War against the Jews, 1933–1945.* New York, 1975.
De Lange, Nicholas. *Judaism.* New York, 1986.

Deák, István. *Beyond Nationalism: A Social and Political History of the Habsburg Officer Corps, 1848–1918.* New York, 1990.

Deist, Wilhelm, ed. *The German Military in the Age of Total War.* Dover, 1985.

Deist, Wilhelm, Militär, Staat und Gesellschaft. Studien zur preußisch-deutschen Militärgeschichte. München, 1991.

———. *The Wehrmacht and German Rearmament.* London, 1981.

Demeter, Karl. *The German Officer Corps, 1650–1945.* New York, 1965.

Denzler, Georg and Volker Fabricius. *Die Kirchen im Dritten Reich.* Frankfurt, 1984.

Der Prozess gegen die Hauptkriegsverbrecher von dem Internationalen Militägerichtshof, Nürnberg 14. November 1945–1. Oktober 1946. Nürnberg, 1948.

Deschner, Günther. *Reinhard Heydrich.* Berlin, 1987.

Dickinson, Robert E. *Germany.* New York, 1953.

Die Träger des Ritterkreuzes des Eisernen Kreuzes 1939–1945. Die Inhaber der höchsten Auszeichnung des Zweiten Weltkrieges aller Wehrmachtteile. Osnabrück, 1993.

Dieckmann, Heinz. *Narren-Schaukel.* München, 1984.

Dimont, Max I. *Jews, God, and History.* New York, 1994.

Donin, Hayim Halevy. *To Be a Jew.* New York, 1991.

Dönitz, Karl. *Memoirs.* London, 1961.

Dower, John W. *War without Mercy: Race and Power in the Pacific War.* New York, 1986.

Duppler, Jörg, ed. *Germania auf dem Meere.* Hamburg, 1998.

Dwork, Deborah. *Children with a Star.* London, 1991.

Ebert, Wolfgang. *Das Porzellan war so nervös. Memoiren eines verwöhnten Kindes.* München, 1975.

Eckart, Wolfgang. "Biopolitical Seizure of Power and Medical Science in Germany, 1933–1945. Law for the Prevention of Genetically Diseased Offspring of July 14, 1933." University of Heidelberg, 2000.

Edgerton, Robert B. *Warriors of the Rising Sun.* New York, 1997.

Engelman, Uriah Zevi. "Intermarriage." *Jewish Social Studies* 2 (1940).

Engelmann, Bernt. *Deutschland ohne Juden.* Köln, 1988.

Epstein, Isidore. *Judaism: A Historical Presentation.* London, 1959.

Evans, Richard J. *Lying about Hitler: History, Holocaust, and the David Irving Trial.* New York, 2001.

Federal Research Division, ed. *Austria: A Country Study.* Washington, D.C., 1994.

———. *Israel: A Country Study.* Washington, D.C., 1990.

Fellgiebel, Walther-Peer, ed. *Die Träger des Ritterkreuzes des Eisernen Kreuzes, 1939–1945.* Friedberg/H., 1986.

Fest, Joachim C. *The Face of Third Reich.* Vermont, 1970.

———. *Hitler. Eine Biographie.* Frankfurt am Main, 1987.

Fischer, Christoph, and Renate Schein, eds. *O ewich is so lanck. Die Historischen Friedhöfe in Berlin-Kreuzberg. Ein Werkstattbericht.* Berlin, 1987.

Fischer, Horst. *Judentum, Staat und Heer in Preußen im frühen 19. Jahrhundert.* Tübingen, 1968.

Flachowsky, Karin. "Neue Quellen zur Abstammung Reinhard Heydrichs," *Vierteljahreshefte für Zeitgeschichte,* Heft 48 (2000): S. 319–27.

Fraenkel, Heinrich. *Göring.* New York, 1972.

Frank, Hans. *Im Angesicht des Galgens.* Schliersee, 1955.

Frank, Wolfgang, and Bernhard Rogge. *The German Raider Atlantis.* New York, 1956.

Frankel, Jonathan, and Steven J. Zipperstein, eds. *Assimilation and Community: The Jews in Nineteenth-Century Europe.* Cambridge, 1992.

Frankl, Viktor. *Man's Search for Meaning.* New York, 1990.

Franz-Willing, Georg. *Die Reichskanzlei, 1933–1945.* Tübingen, 1984.

Fraser, David. *Knight's Cross.* New York, 1993.

Frei, Norbert. *National Socialist Rule in Germany.* Cambridge, 1993.

Freie Universität Berlin: Zentralinstitut für Sozialwissenschaftliche Forschung, ed. *Gedenkbuch Berlins der jüdischer Opfer des Nationalsozialismus.* Berlin, 1995.

Frick, Wilhelm. "Die Rassenfrage in der deutschen Gesetzgebung." In *Deutsche Juristen-Zeitung, Heft 1.* Jahrgang 39, 1 January 1934.

Fricke, Karl-Heinrich. *Erinnerungen aus 70 Lebensjahren von 1914–1984.* Köln, 1984.

Friedländer, Saul. *Nazi Germany and the Jews. Vol. 1: The Years of Persecution, 1933–1939.* New York, 1997.

Friedman, Chaim Shlomo. *Dare to Survive.* New York, 1991.

Frischauer, Willi. *The Rise and Fall of Hermann Goering.* Boston, 1951.

Fritz, Stephen G. *Frontsoldaten: The German Soldier in World War II.* Lexington, 1995.

Frydman-Kohl, Baruch. "Covenant, Conversion and Chosenness: Maimonides and Halvei on 'Who Is a Jew?" *Judaism* 41, no. 1 (winter 1992): 64–79.

Fussell, Paul, ed. *The Norton Book of Modern War.* New York, 1991.

Gay, Ruth. *The Jews of Germany.* New Haven, 1992.

Gedenkschrift. Der Jahrgang 30-10. Offizier-Ergänzungsjahrgang des Reichsheeres 1930-1. April-1980.

Gellately, Robert. *Backing Hitler: Consent and Coercion in Nazi Germany.* Oxford, 2001.

———. *The Gestapo and German Society: Enforcing Racial Policy.* Oxford, 1990.

Genoud, Francois, ed. *The Testament of Adolf Hitler.* London, 1959.

Gericke, Bernd, ed. *Die Inhaber des Deutschen Kreuzes in Gold, des Deutschen Kreuzes in Silber der Kriegsmarine.* Osnabrück, 1993.

Geschichte und Gesellschaft. Zeitschrift für Historische Sozialwissenschaft 21. Jahrgang/Heft 2 April-Juni 1995, Protest und Widerstand. Göttingen, 1995.

Gidal, Nachum T. *Die Juden in Deutschland von der Römerzeit bis zur Weimarer Republik.* Könemann, 1997.

Gilbert, Martin. *The Holocaust: A History of the Jews of Europe during the Second World War.* New York, 1985.

———. *The Second World War.* New York, 1989.

Gilman, Sander L. *Jewish Self-Hatred.* London, 1986.

Giordano, Ralph. *Wenn Hitler den Krieg gewonnen hätte.* Hamburg, 1989.

Glaser, Ephraim. *The Necessity of Returning.* Kibbutz Dallia, Israel, 1997.

Globke, Hans, and Wilhelm Stuckart. *Kommentare zur Deutschen Rassengesetzgebung.* München, 1936.

Godsey, William. "The Nobility, Jewish Assimilation, and the Austro-Hungarian Foreign Service on the Eve of the First World War." *Austrian History Yearbook* 27 (1996): 155–80.

Goebbels, Joseph. *The Goebbels Diaries, 1942–1943.* Ed. and trans. Louis P. Lochner. New York, 1948.

Goerlitz, Walter. *The German General Staff, 1657–1945.* New York, 1971.

Goldhagen, Daniel Jonah. *Hitler's Willing Executioners: Ordinary Germans and the Holocaust.* New York, 1996.

Gorden, Albert. *Intermarriage: Interfaith, Interracial, Interethnic.* Boston, 1964.

Gordon, Sarah. *Hitler, Germans, and the "Jewish Question."* Princeton, 1984.

Göring, Emmy. *An der Seite meines Mannes.* Göttingen, 1967.

Graber, G. S. *The Life and Times of Reinhard Heydrich.* New York, 1980.

Groß, Walter. *Die rassenpolitischen Voraussetzungen zur Lösung der Judenfrage.* München, 1943.

Grossman, David. *On Killing.* New York, 1997.

Grunwald, Max. *History of Jews in Vienna.* Philadelphia, 1936.

Guderian, Heinz. *Panzer Leader.* California, 1988.

Gudmundsson, Bruce I. *Stormtroop Tactics: Innovation in the German Army, 1914–1918.* London, 1995.

Haffner, Sebastian. *The Meaning of Hitler.* Cambridge, 1997.

Halder, Franz. *Kriegstagebuch. Tägliche Aufzeichnungen des Chefs des Generalstabes des Heeres, 1939–1942.* Ed. Hans-Adolf Jacobsen. Stuttgart, 1962.

Hamann, Brigitte. *Hitlers Wien. Lehrjahre eines Diktators.* München, 1997.

Hamilton, Charles. *Leaders and Personalities of the Third Reich.* San Jose, 1985.

Hart, B. H. Liddell. *The German Generals Talk.* New York, 1979.

Hartman, Geoffrey, ed. *Holocaust Remembrance: The Shapes of Memory.* New York, 1994.

Hauck, Michael. *Kompost. Veröffentlichungen und Vorträge aus vier Jahrzehnten.* Frankfurt, 1997.

Hausner, Gideon. *Justice in Jerusalem.* New York, 1966.

Hayward, Joel S. A. *Stopped at Stalingrad: The Luftwaffe and Hitler's Defeat in the East, 1942–1943.* Kansas, 1998.

Heaton, Colin D. *German Anti-Partisan Warfare in Europe: 1939–1945.* New York, 2001.

Hecht, Ben. *Perfidy.* New York, 1961.

Hecht, Ingeborg. *Als unsichtbare Mauern wuchsen. Eine deutsche Familie unter den Nürnberger Rassengesetzen.* Hamburg, 1987.

Heer, Hannes, and J. P. Reemtsma, eds. *Vernichtungskrieg. Verbrechen der Wehrmacht.* Hamburg, 1995.

Heeresadjutant bei Hitler 1938–1943. Aufzeichnungen des Majors Gerhard Engel. Hrsg. u. kommentiert v. Hildegard von Kotze. (=Schriftenreihe der Vierteljahreshefte für Zeitgeschichte Nr. 29). Stuttgart, 1974.

Heid, Ludger, and Julius H. Schoeps, eds. *Juden in Deutschland.* München, 1994.

Heiden, Konrad. *Der Fuehrer: Hitler's Rise to Power.* London, 1967.

Herczeg, Yisrael Isser Zvi, ed. *The Torah: With Rashi's Commentary.* Brooklyn, 1994.

Hermann, Carl Hans. *Deutsche Militärgeschichte.* Frankfurt, 1966.

Herrmann, Hajo. *Eagle's Wings.* England, 1991.

Hertz, Deborah. "The Genealogy Bureaucracy in the Third Reich." *Jewish History,* Haifa (fall 1997).

Herwarth, Hans von. *Zwischen Hitler und Stalin. Erlebte Zeitgeschichte, 1931–1945.* Frankfurt, 1982.

Herwig, Holgar H. *The German Naval Officer Corps: A Social and Political History, 1890–1918.* Oxford, 1973.

Hilberg, Raul. *Destruction of the European Jews.* New York, 1961.

Hildebrand, Karl Friedrich, ed. *Die Generale der deutschen Luftwaffe, 1935–1945.* Bd. I–III. Osnabrück, 1992. (=*Deutschlands Generale und Admirale, Teil 2,* hrsg. v. D. Bradley in Verbindung m. M. Rövekamp).

Hitler, Adolf. *Hitler's Secret Book.* Introduction by Telford Taylor. New York, 1961.

———. *Hitler's Secret Conversations, 1941–1944.* Introductory essay by H. R. Trevor-Roper. New York, 1953.

———. *Mein Kampf.* New York, 1971.

Hoettl, Wilhelm. *The Secret Front: The Story of Nazi Political Espionage.* New York, 1954.

Hoffmann, Joachim. *Kaukasien 1942/43. Das deutsche Heer und die Orientvölker der Sowjetunion* (=Einzelschriften zur Militärgeschichte, 35; hersg. V. Militärgeschichtlichen Forschungsamt). Freiburg, 1991.

Höhne, Heinz. *Canaris und die Abwehr zwischen Anpassung und Opposition.* München, 1985.

The Holocaust. Vol. 1, Legalizing the Holocaust—The Early Phase, 1933–1939. Introduction by John Mendelsohn. New York, 1982.

The Holocaust. Vol. 2, Legalizing the Holocaust—The Later Phase, 1939–1943. Introduction by John Mendelsohn. New York, 1982.

The Holocaust. Vol. 11, The Wannsee Protocol and a 1944 Report on Auschwitz by the Office of Strategic Services. Introduction by Robert Wolfe. New York, 1982.

Horne, John, ed. *State, Society, and Mobilization in Europe during the First World War.* Cambridge, 1997.

Hoßbach, Friedrich. *Zwischen Wehrmacht und Hitler, 1934–1938.* Göttingen, 1965.

Hoss, Rudolf. "Commandant of Auschwitz." In *The Norton Book of Modern War,* ed. Paul Fussell.

Hupka, Herbert. *Unruhiges Gewissen. Ein deutscher Lebenslauf.* München, 1994.

In't Veld N.K.C.A., De SS in Nederland. Documenten vit SS archieven, 1935–1944. Den Haag, 1976.

Internationaler Suchdienst. Verzeichnis der Haftstätten unter dem Reichsführer-SS. Comité International Genève (Red Cross), 1979.

Irving, David. *Die Tragödie der Deutschen Luftwaffe. Aus den Akten und Erinnerungen von Feldmarschall Erhard Milch.* Berlin, 1990.

Israel Religious Action Center, "Assaults against Reform Continue." (*www.irac.org*) 10 September 1997.

Jäckel, Eberhard. *Hitlers Weltanschauung.* Stuttgart, 1981.

James, C. L. R. *The Black Jacobins.* New York, 1989.

Janßen, Karl-Heinz. *30 Januar. Der Tag, der die Welt veränderte.* Hamburg, 1983.

Johnson, Paul. *History of the Jews.* New York, 1987.

Jonas, Hans. *Der Gottesbegriff nach Auschwitz.* Baden-Baden, 1984.

Kahn, David. *Hitler's Spies: German Military Intelligence in World War II.* New York, 1978.

Kahn, Ernst. "Die Mischehen bei den deutschen Juden." Der Jude, Eine Monatsschrift, Erster Jahrgang. Berlin (1916–1917): S. 855–56.

Kaiserliches Statistisches Amt, ed. *Statistisches Jahrbuch für das Deutsche Reich.* Berlin, 1903

Kammer, Hilde, and Elisabet Bartsch, eds. *Nationalsozialismus. Begriffe aus der Zeit der Gewaltherrschaft, 1933–1945.* Hamburg, 1992.

Kaplan, Marion A. *Between Dignity and Despair: Jewish Life in Nazi Germany.* New York, 1998.

Kaploun, Uri, ed. *Likkutei Dibburim: An Anthology of Talks by Rabbi Yosef Yitzchak Schneersohn of Lubavitch.* Vol. 3. New York, 1990.

Katzburg, Nathaniel. *Hungary and the Jews: Policy and Legislation, 1920–1943.* Bar-Ilan Univ., 1981.

Kee, Robert. *A Crowd Is Not Company.* London, 2000.

Keegan, John. *The Mask of Command.* New York, 1987.

——. *The Second World War.* New York, 1989.

——. *Waffen-SS, the Asphalt Soldiers.* New York, 1970.

Keilig, Wolf. *Das Deutsche Heer, 1939–1945: Gliederung, Einsatz, Stellenbesetzung.* Bad Nauheim, 1956.

Keitel, Wilhelm. *The Memoirs of Field-Marshal Keitel.* Ed. Walter Görlitz. London, 1961.

Kennan, George F. *From Prague after Munich: Diplomatic Papers, 1938–1940.* Princeton, 1968.

Kennedy, Ludovic. *Pursuit: Battleship Bismarck.* London, 1993.

Kershaw, Ian. *Hitler, 1889–1936: Hubris.* New York, 1999.

——. *Hitler, 1936–1945: Nemesis.* New York, 2000.

——. *The Hitler Myth.* Oxford, 1987.

——. *The Nazi Dictatorship.* New York, 1985.

——. *Profiles in Power: Hitler.* London, 1991.

Kersten, Felix. *The Kersten Memoirs, 1940–1945.* New York, 1957.

Kessler, David. *The Falashas: A Short History of the Ethiopian Jews.* London, 1996.

Kindheit und Jugend unter Hitler. Mit Beiträgen von Helmut Schmidt u.a. von Wolf Jobst Siedler. Berlin, 1992.

Kitchen, Martin. *German Officer Corps, 1890–1914.* Oxford, 1968.

——. *A Military History of Germany.* London, 1975.

Klee, Ernst. *Euthanasie im NS-Staat: Die Vernichtung lebensunwerten Lebens.* Frankfurt, 1985.

Klein, Fritz. *Verlorene Größe.* München, 1996.

Klemperer, Viktor. *Ich will Zeugnis ablegen bis zum letzten. Tagebücher, 1933–1945.* Darmstadt, 1996.

Klepper, Jochen. *Unter dem Schatten Deiner Flügel.* Stuttgart, 1962.

Knigge, Ursula von. *Meine liebste Mamming. Briefe an Clara Freifrau Knigge, geschrieben von Sohn und Schwiegertochter in den Jahren, 1928–1945.* Grünwald, 1981 [Privatdruck].

Koburger, Charles W. *Steel Ships, Iron Crosses, and Refugees: The German Navy in the Baltic, 1939–1945.* New York, 1989.

Koehl, Robert. "Feudal Aspects of National Socialism," *American Political Science Review* 54 (1960).

Koehler, Hansjürgen. *Inside Information.* London, 1940.

Kolatch, Alfred. *The Jewish Book of Why.* New York, 1981.

Krackow, Jürgen. *Die Genehmigung.* München, 1991.

Krausnick, Helmut, and Hildegard von Kotze, eds. *Es spricht der Führer. Sieben exemplarische Hitler-Reden.* Gütersloh, 1966.

Krüger, Helmut. *Der Halbe Stern. Leben als deutsch-jüdischer Mischlinge im Dritten Reich.* Berlin, 1992.

Kubizek, August. *Young Hitler: The Story of Our Friendship.* London, 1954.

Kuehn, Heinz. *Mixed Blessings: An Almost Ordinary Life in Hitler's Germany.* London, 1988.

Ladenburg, Maria. *Auf dem Weg zu Euch.* München, 1996.

Lang, Berel, ed. *Writing and the Holocaust.* New York, 1988.

Lang, Jochen von. *The Secretary: Martin Bormann.* New York, 1979.

Langer, Lawrence. *Holocaust Testimonies.* New Haven, 1991.

Langer, Walter C. *The Mind of Adolf Hitler.* London, 1978.

Laqueur, Walter, ed. *The Holocaust Encyclopedia.* New Haven, 2001.

Lauer, Kartine. "Schicksale: Leben des Nathan Mendelssohn"; Studien: Beiträge zur neueren deutschen Kultur—und Wirtschaftsgeschichte, Band 8, Berlin, 1993.

Lauren, Paul Gordon. *Power and Prejudice.* London, 1988.

League of Nations Economic Intelligence Service, ed. *Statistical Year-Book of the League of Nations, 1936/37.* Geneva, 1937.

Lee, Asher. *Goering: Air Leader.* New York, 1972.

Lehrer, Steven. *Wannsee House and the Holocaust.* London, 2000.

Lekebusch, Sigrid. *Not und Verfolgung der Christen jüdischer Herkunft im Rheinland.* Köln, 1995.

Lenz, Fritz. *Menschliche Auslese und Rassenhygiene (Eugenik).* München, 1932.

Lenz, Wilhelm. "Die Handakten von Bernhard Lösener, 'Rassereferent' im Reichsministerium des Inner." In Archiv und Geschichte. Festschrift für Friedrich P. Kahlenberg (=Schriften des bundesarchives;57). Hrsg. von K. Oldenhage et al. Düsseldorf, 2000.

Lepre, George. *Himmler's Bosnian Division: The Waffen-SS Handschar Division, 1943–1945.* New York, 2000.

L'Estocq, Christoph von. *Soldat in drei Epochen.* Berlin, 1993.

Levi, Primo. *Moments of Reprieve: A Memoir of Auschwitz.* New York, 1986.

———. *Survival in Auschwitz.* New York, 1960.

Lifton, Robert Jay. *The Nazi Doctors.* New York, 1986.

Loewenthal, Max J. *Das jüdische Bekenntnis als Hinderungsgrund bei der Beförderung zum preussischen Reserveoffizier.* Berlin, 1911.

Lösener, Bernhard. "Als Rassereferent im Reichsministerium des Innern." In Das Reichsministerium des Innern und die Judengesetzgebung, *Vierteljahreshefte für Zeitgeschichte,* Heft 6 (1961): S. 261–313.

Lowenstein, Steven M. *The Berlin Jewish Community: Enlightenment, Family, and Crisis, 1770–1830.* New York, 1994.

Lowenthal, Marvin. *The Jews of Germany: A History of Sixteen Centuries.* Philadelphia, 1936.

Ludwig, Emil. *Bismarck.* Boston, 1927.

Lupfer, Timothy T. *The Dynamics of Doctrine: The Changes in German Tactical Doctrine during the First World War.* Fort Leavenworth, 1981.

MacDonald, Callum. *The Killing of SS-Obergruppenführer Reinhard Heydrich.* New York, 1989.

MacDonald, Charles B. *The Mighty Endeavor: American Armed Forces in the European Theater in World War II.* Oxford, 1969.

Maier, Dieter. *Arbeitseinsatz und Deportation. Die Mitwirkung der Arbeitsverwaltung bei der nationalsozialistischen Judenverfolgung in den Jahren, 1938–1945.* Berlin, 1994.

Maier, Joseph B., and Chaim I. Waxman. *Ethnicity, Identity, and History.* London, 1983.

Maier, Karl-Heinz. *Und höret niemals auf zu kämpfen.* Berlin, 1994.

Maizière, Ulrich de. *In der Pflicht.* Bonn, 1989.

Manchester, William. *Goodbye Darkness.* New York, 1979.

Mandell, Richard D. *The Nazi Olympics.* New York, 1971.

Manoschek, Walter, ed. *"Es gibt nur eines für das Judentum: Vernichtung." Das Judenbild in deutschen Soldatenbriefen, 1939–1944.* Hamburg, 1995.

Manstein, Erich von. *Lose Victories.* New York, 1982.

Maoz, Asher. "Who Is a Convert?" *International Association of Jewish Lawyers and Jurists* 15 (December 1997): 11–19.

———. "Who Is a Jew?" *Midstream* 35 no. 5 (1989): 11–15.

Marcus, Jacob R. *The Rise and Destiny of the German Jew.* Cincinnati, 1934.

Marrus, Michael R., and Robert O. Paxton. *Vichy France and the Jews.* New York, 1981.

Martin, Günther. *Die bürgerlichen Excellenzen. Zur Sozialgeschichte der preußischen Generalität, 1812–1918.* Düsseldorf, 1976.

Maser, Werner. *Adolf Hitler. Legende Mythos Wirklichkeit.* München, 1971.

Mason, David. *U-Boat: The Secret Menace.* London, 1968.

Mason, Herbert Molly, Jr. *The Rise of the Luftwaffe.* New York, 1973.

Matthäus, Jürgen. "German *Judenpolitik* in Lithuania during the First World War." *Leo Baeck Yearbook* 43 (1998): 155–74.

Maurer, Helmut. *Von Mensch zu Mensch. In Canaris' Abwehr.* Berlin, 1975.

Maurer, Trude. *Ostjuden in Deutschland, 1918–1933.* Hamburg, 1986.

McGraw, Horst von. *The Evolution of Hitler's Germany.* New York, 1973.

McGuirk, Dal. *Rommel's Army in Africa.* Osceola, 1993.

Megargee, Geoffrey P. *Inside Hitler's High Command.* Kansas, 2000.

Meiring, Kerstin. *Die Christlich-Jüdische Mischehe in Deutschland, 1840–1933.* Hamburg, 1998.

Mendelssohn, Moses. *Jerusalem: Or on Religious Power and Judaism.* London, 1983.

Merten, Karl-Friedrich. *Nach Kompass.* Cloppenburg, 1994.

Messerschmidt, Manfred. *Die Wehrmacht im NS-Staat.* Hamburg, 1969.

Messerschmidt, Manfred, and Fritz Wüllner. *Die Wehrmachtjustiz im Dienste des Nationalsozialismus. Zerstörung einer Legende.* Baden-Baden, 1987.

Meyer, Beate. *Jüdische Mischlinge. Rassenpolitik und Verfolgungserfahrung, 1933–1945.* Hamburg, 1999.

Meyer, Beate, and Hermann Simon. *Juden in Berlin, 1938–1945.* Berlin, 2000.

Meyer, Michael A., ed. *Deutsch-Jüdische Geschichte in der Neuzeit. 1871–1918.* Band III. München, 1997.

———. *Deutsch-Jüdische Geschichte in der Neuzeit: 1918–1945.* Band IV. München, 1997.

———. *German-Jewish History in Modern Times.* Vol. 4. New York, 1998.

Meyer, Winfried. *Unternehmen Sieben. Eine Rettungsaktion für vom Holocaust Bedrohte im Amt Ausland/Abwehr im Oberkommando der Wehrmacht.* Frankfurt, 1993.

Mielke, Fred, and Alexander Mitscherlich. *Doctors of Infamy.* New York, 1949.

Miles, Jack. *God: A Biography.* New York, 1995.

Militärgeschichtliches Forschungsamt, ed. *Das Deutsche Reich und der zweite Weltkrieg. Kriegsverwaltung, Wirtschaft und personelle Ressourcen, 1939–1941.* Vol. 5/1. Stuttgart, 1988.

———. *Deutsche Jüdische Soldaten, 1914–1945.* Bonn, 1984.

———. *Germany and the Second World War.* Vol. 1, *The Build-up of German Aggression.* Oxford, 1998.

———. *Germany and the Second World War.* Vol. 2, *Germany's Initial Conquests in Europe.* Oxford, 1999.

———. *Germany and the Second World War.* Vol. 4, *The Attack on the Soviet Union.* Oxford, 1998.

———. *Handbuch zur deutschen Militärgeschichte, 1648–1939 Bd. IV, 2: Militärgeschichte im 19 Jahrhundert, 1814–1890.* München, 1976.

———. *Handbuch zur deutschen Militärgeschichte, 1648–1939 Bd. VII. Wehrmacht und Nationalsozialismus, 1933–1939.* München, 1978.

Millett, Allen, and Peter Maslowski. *For the Common Defense.* New York, 1984.

Mitcham, Samuel W. *Rommel's Greatest Victory: The Desert Fox and the Fall of Tobruk, Spring of 1942.* Novato, 1998.

Mitscherlich, Alexander, and Fred Mielke. *Doctors of Infamy: The Story of the Nazi Medical Crime.* New York, 1949.

Mohr, Ulrich, and A. V. Sellwood. *Ship 16: The Story of the Secret German Raider Atlantis.* New York, 1956.

Molden, Fritz. *Fepolinski und Waschlapski.* München, 1991.

Moll, Martin, ed. *Führererlasse, 1939–1945.* Stuttgart, 1997.

Morison, Samuel Eliot, and Henry Steele Commager. *The Growth of the American Republic.* Vol. 2, Oxford, 1958.

Mosberg, Helmuth. *Schlemihls Schatten. Geschichte einer ostpreußischen Familie.* München, 1993.

Mosley, Leonard. *The Reich Marshal.* London, 1974.

Mosse, George L. *The Crisis of German Ideology: Intellectual Origins of the Third Reich.* New York, 1964.

Muggenthaler, Karl August. *German Raiders of World War II.* London, 1977.

Müllenheim-Rechberg, Burkard Frhr. Von. *Schlachtschiff Bismarck, 1940–1941.* Berlin, 1980.

Müller, Klaus-Jürgen. *Das Heer und Hitler.* Stuttgart, 1969.

Müller, Rolf-Dieter, and Hans-Erich Volkmann, eds. *Die Wehrmacht. Mythos und Realität.* Stuttgart, 1999.

Murray, Williamson. *Luftwaffe.* Baltimore, 1985.

Naval Intelligence Division, ed. *Germany.* Vol. 3, *Economic Geography.* Washington, D.C., 1944.

Niedersächsischer Verband Deutscher Sinti, ed. *"Es war unmenschenmöglich." Sinti aus Niedersachsen erzählen—Verfolgung und Vernichtung im Nationalsozialismus und Diskriminierung bis heute.* Hannover, 1995.

Nipperdey, Thomas. *Deutsche Geschichte. Bd. 1: Arbeitswelt und Bürgergeist.* München, 1993.

Noakes, Jeremy. "The Development of Nazi Policy towards the German-Jewish 'Mischlinge' 1933–1945." *Leo Baeck Yearbook* 34, (1989): 291–354.

Noakes, Jeremy, ed. *Government, Party, and People in Nazi Germany.* Exeter, 1980.

Noakes, Jeremy and Geoffrey Pridham, eds. *Nazism, 1919–1945.* Vols. 1–4. Exeter, 1983.

Nolting-Hauff, Wilhelm. *"Imis." Chronik einer Verbannung.* Bremen, 1946.

Oberländer, Erwin. *Hitler-Stalin Pakt 1939.* Frankfurt, 1990.

Oberlander, Franklin A. *Wir aber sind nicht Fisch und nicht Fleisch.* Opladen, 1996.

O'Brien, Conor Cruise. *The Siege: The Saga of Israel and Zionism.* New York, 1986.

Oechelhaeuser, J. W. v., *Adelheit es ist soweit. Soldatisches Erleben.* München, 1981.

Office of the United States Chief Counsel for Prosecution of Axis Criminality, ed. *Nazi Conspiracy and Aggression: Supplement B.* Washington, D.C., 1948.

———. *Nazi Conspiracy and Aggression.* Vol. 2. Washington, D.C., 1946.

———. *Trials of German Major War Criminals. Vol. 14, Nuremberg, 14–24 May 1946.* Washington, D.C., 1946.

———. *U.S.A. Military Tribunals: Case No. 1–2, 11, 11.2, 12.* Nuremberg, 1949.

Oldenhage, Klaus, Hermann Schreyer, and Wolfram Werner, eds. *Archiv und Geschichte. Festschrift für Friedrich P. Kahlenberg (Schriften des Bundesarchivs; 57).* Düsseldorf, 2000.

Oliver, Robert T. *A History of the Korean People in Modern Times: 1800 to the Present.* Newark, 1993.

O'Neill, Robert J. *The German Army and the Nazi Party, 1933–1939.* London, 1966.

Osborne, Sidney. *Germany and Her Jews.* London, 1939.

Overmans, Rüdiger. *Deutsche militärische Verluste im Zweiten Weltkrieg.* München, 1999.

Overy, Richard. *Goering.* London, 1984.

Owings, Alison. *Frauen: German Women Recall the Third Reich.* New Brunswick, 1995.

Padfield, Peter. *Himmler: Reichsführer-SS.* New York, 1990.

Paret, Peter, ed. *Makers of Modern Strategy from Machiavelli to the Nuclear Age.* Princeton, 1986.

Pätzold, Kurt, ed. *Verfolgung, Vertreibung, Vernichtung. Dokumente des faschistischen Antisemitismus 1933 bis 1942.* Leipzig, 1984.

Paul, Wolfgang. *Wer war Hermann Göring?* Esslingen, 1983.

Payer, Andreas G. *Armati Hungarorum.* München, 1985.

Payne, Robert. *The Life and Death of Adolf Hitler.* New York, 1973.

Pehle, Walter H., ed. *Der Judenpogrom 1938: Von der 'Reichskristallnacht' zum Völkermord.* Frankfurt am Main, 1988.

Perel, Sally. *Ich war Hitlerjunge Salomon.* Berlin, 1992.

Persico, Joseph E. *Nuremberg: Infamy on Trial.* New York, 1994.

Peterson, Edward. *The Limits of Hitler's Power.* New Jersey, 1969.

Picker, Henry. *Hitlers Tischgespräche im Führerhauptquartier, 1941–1942.* Ed. Percy Ernst Schramm. Stuttgart, 1976.

Pierson, Ruth. *German Jewish Identity in the Weimar Republic.* New Haven, 1970.

Pommerin, Reiner. *Sterilisierung der Rheinlandbastarde. Das Schicksal einer farbigen deutschen Minderheit, 1918–1937.* Düsseldorf, 1979.

Pope, Dudley. *The Battle of the River Plate.* Maryland, 1987.

Porten, Edward P. von der. *The German Navy in World War II.* New York, 1969.

Posselt, Alfred. *Soldat des Feindes.* Wien, 1993.

Prager, Dennis, and Joseph Telushkin. *The Nine Questions People Ask about Judaism.* New York, 1975.

Pritzkoleit, Kurt. *Die Neuen Herren.* München, 1955.

Raeder, Erich. *Mein Leben. Von 1935 bis Spandau 1955.* Tübingen, 1957.

Rebentisch, Dieter. *Führerstaat und Verwaltung im Zweiten Weltkrieg. Verfassungsentwicklung und Verwaltungspolitik, 1939–1945.* Stuttgart, 1989.

Redlich, Fritz. *Hitler: Diagnosis of a Destructive Prophet.* Oxford, 1998.

Reich, Reinhard. *Chronik des Maschinengewehr-Bataillons 9 (mot) in seinen Garnisonen Königsberg (Pr.) und Heiligenbeil.* Burgdorf/Hannover, 1978 [Masch. Vervielfältigung].

Remarque, Erich Maria. *A Time to Love and a Time to Die.* New York, 1954.

Renner, Karl. *Österreich von der Ersten zur Zweiten Republik II. Band.* Wien, 1953.

Rich, Norman. *Hitler's War Aims.* New York, 1974.

Richter, Hans Peter. *Die Zeit der jungen Soldaten.* Stuttgart, 1980.

Ringelblum, Emanuel. *Notes from the Warsaw Ghetto.* New York, 1958.

Robertson, James I. *Soldiers Blue and Gray.* South Carolina, 1998.

Robertson, Ritchie. *The "Jewish Question" in German Literature, 1749–1939: Emancipation and Its Discontents.* Oxford, 1999.

Röhl, John C. G. *The Kaiser and His Court: Wilhelm II and the Government of Germany.* New York, 1994.

Rohr, Heinz. *Geschichte einer Lübecker Familie.* Hamburg, 1994.

Rollins, Richard, ed. *Black Southerners in Grey: Essays on Afro-Americans in Confederate Armies.* California, 1994.

Romero, Patricia W., and Charles H. Wesley. *International Library of Negro Life and History.* New York, 1969.

Rose, Paul Lawrence. *German Question/Jewish Question: Revolutionary Anti-Semitism from Kant to Wagner.* Princeton, 1990.

Roskies, David, ed. *The Literature of Destruction: Jewish Responses to Catastrophe.* New York, 1989.

Roth, Cecil. *A Short History of the Jewish People.* London, 1936.

Rozenblit, Marsha L. *Reconstructing a National Identity: The Jews of Habsburg Austria during World War I.* Oxford, 2001.

———. *The Jews of Vienna, 1867–1914.* New York, 1983.

Ruppin, Arthur. *The Jews in the Modern World.* London, 1934.

———. *The Jews of Today.* New York, 1913.

Rüter-Ehlermann, A., and C. F. Rüter, eds. *Sammlung deutscher Strafurteile wegen nationalsozialistischer Tötungsverbrechen.* Amsterdam, 1968–1981.

Sachar, Howard M. *A History of Israel. Vol. 2, From the Aftermath of the Yom Kippur War.* Oxford, 1987.

Sagarra, Eda. *A Social History of Germany, 1648–1914.* New York, 1977.

Sammlung wehrrechtlicher Gutachten und Vorschriften. Heft I (1963)–Heft 22 (1984). Bearbeitet v. Rudolf Absolon, Bundesarchiv-Zentralnachweisstelle, Aachen-Kornelimünster.

Sauer, Paul, ed. *Dokumente über die Verfolgung der jüdischen Bürger in Baden-Württemberg durch das nationalsozialistische Regime, 1933–1945.* Stuttgart, 1966.

Scheibert, Horst, ed. *Die Träger des Deutschen Kreuzes in Gold.* Friedberg/H., 1981.

Schellenberg, Walter. *The Schellenberg Memoirs.* London, 1956.

Scherman, Nosson, and Meir Zlotowitz, eds. *The Complete Artscroll Siddur.* Brooklyn, 1984.

Schiffman, Lawrence H. *Who Was a Jew? Rabbinic and Halakhic Perspectives on the Jewish-Christian Schism.* New Jersey, 1985.

Schleunes, Karl A. *The Twisted Road to Auschwitz: Nazi Policy toward German-Jews, 1933–1939.* Illinois, 1970.

Schmidl, Erwin A. *Juden in der K.(u.) K. Armee, 1788–1918. Studia Judaica Austriaca, Band XI.* Eisenstadt, 1989.

Schmidt, Werner. *Leben an Grenzen.* Zürich, 1989.

Schmitt, Hans A. *Quakers and Nazis: Inner Light in Outer Darkness.* Missouri, 1997.

Schochet, Jacob Immanuel. *Who Is a Jew? 30 Questions and Answers about This Controversial and Divisive Issue.* Brooklyn, 1987.

Schoeps, Joachim. *Bereit für Deutschland.* Berlin, 1970.

Schramm, Percy Ernst. *Hitler: The Man and the Military Leader.* Chicago, 1971.

Schwerin von Krosigk, Lutz Graf. *Persönliche Erinnerungen: II. Teil, 25 Jahre Berlin, 1930–1945.* Essen, 1973.

Seaton, Albert. *The German Army, 1933–45.* New York, 1982.

———. *The Russo-German War, 1941–1945.* London, 1971.

Segre, V. D. *Israel: A Society in Transition.* New York, 1971.

Seidler, Franz M. *Die Organization Todt, Bauen für Staat und Wehrmacht.* Koblenz, 1987.

Semigothaisches Genealogisches Taschenbuch aristocratisch-jüdischer Heiraten. München, 1914.

Senekowitsch, Martin. *Feldmarschalleutnant Johann Friedländer, 1882–1945: Ein vergessener Offizier des Bundesheeres.* Wien, 1995.

———. *Gleichberechtigte in einer grossen Armee: Zur Geschichte des Bundes Jüdischer Frontsoldaten Österreichs, 1932–1938.* Wien, 1994.

————. "Ich hatt' einen Kameraden." *Der Soldat,* 12 July 1995.

Senger, Valentin. *Kaiserhofstraße 12.* München, 1995.

Sheehan, James J. *German History, 1770–1866.* Oxford, 1989.

Shirer, William L. *The Nightmare Years.* New York, 1984.

————. *The Rise and Fall of the Third Reich.* New York, 1960.

Smelser, Ronald, and Enrico Syring, eds. *Die Militärelite des Dritten Reiches.* Berlin, 1995.

Snyder, Louis L. *Encyclopedia of The Third Reich.* New York, 1989.

Sokolsky, George E. *We Jews.* London, 1935.

Speer, Albert. *Inside the Third Reich.* New York, 1970.

Staehelin, W. R., ed. Wappenbuch der Stadt Basel. 1 Teil. 1 Folge. Basel, 1934.

Stahlberg, Alexander. *Die verdammte Pflicht.* Berlin, 1987.

State of Israel Ministry of Justice, ed. *The Trial of Adolf Eichmann: Record of Proceedings in the District Court of Jerusalem.* Vols. 1–4, Jerusalem, 1992.

Stegemann, Hermann. *The Struggle for the Rhine.* London, 1927.

Steinberg, Jonathan. *All or Nothing.* New York, 1991.

————. "The Kaiser's Navy." *Past and Present* 28 (24 July 1964).

Steinhoff, Johannes, Peter Pechel, and Dennis Showalter, eds. *Deutsche im Zweiten Weltkreig: Zeitzeugen Sprechen.* München, 1989.

Stern, Fritz. *The Politics of Cultural Despair.* London, 1974.

Stoltzfus, Nathan. *Resistance of the Heart: Intermarriage and the Rosenstrasse Protest in Nazi Germany.* New York, 1996.

————. "Widerstand des Herzens." *Geschichte und Gesellschaft. Zeitschrift für Historische Sozialwissenschaft 21. Jahrgang/Heft 2 April-Juni 1995, Protest und Widerstand.* Göttingen, 1995.

Sydow, Rolf von. *Angst zu atmen.* Berlin, 1986.

Telushkin, Joseph. *Jewish Literacy: The Most Important Things to Know about the Jewish Religion, Its People, and Its History.* New York, 1991.

Theilhaber, Felix A. *Der Untergang der deutschen Juden.* München, 1911.

————. *Jüdische Flieger im Weltkrieg.* Berlin, 1924.

Thomas, Charles S. *The German Navy in the Nazi Era.* London, 1990.

Thomson, David. *Europe Since Napoleon.* Cambridge, 1962.

Toland, John. *Adolf Hitler.* New York, 1976.

————. *In Mortal Combat.* New York, 1991.

Traverso, Enzo. *The Jews and Germany.* Nebraska, 1995.

Trepp, Leo. *The Complete Book of Jewish Observance.* New York, 1980.

Trevor-Roper, H. R. *The Last Days of Hitler.* New York, 1947.

Turner, Henry Ashby. *Hitler's Thirty Days to Power: January 1933.* London, 1996.

Unger, Merrill F., ed. *Unger's Bible Dictionary.* Chicago, 1978.

United States War Department Technical Manual, ed. *Handbook on German Military Forces.* Washington, D.C., 1945.

Valentin, Veit. *Geschichte der Deutschen.* Berlin, 1947.

Victor, George. *Hitler: The Pathology of Evil.* Dulles, 1998.

Vital, David. *A People Apart: The Jews in Europe, 1789–1939.* Oxford, 1999.

Vogel, Rolf. *Ein Stück von uns. Deutsche Juden in deutschen Armeen, 1813–1976. Eine Dokumentation.* Bonn, 1973.

Vuletić, Aleksandar-Saša. *Christen Jüdischer Herkunft im Dritten Reich. Verfolgung und Organisierte Selbsthilfe, 1933–1939.* Mainz, 1999.

Waite, Robert G. L. *The Psychopathic God Adolf Hitler.* New York, 1977.

Walk, Joseph, ed. *Sonderrecht für den Juden im NS-Staat. Eine Sammlung der gesetzlichen Maßnahmen und Richtlinien. Inhalt und Bedeutung.* Heidelberg, 1981.

Wallach, Jehuda L. *The Dogma of the Battle of Annihilation: The Theories of Clausewitz and Schlieffen and Their Impact on the German Conduct of Two World Wars.* London, 1986.

Warburg, G. *Six Years of Hitler: The Jews under the Nazi Regime.* London, 1939.

Watt, Richard M. *The Kinds Depart. The Tragedy of Germany: Versailles and the German Revolution.* New York, 1968.

Weimarer historisch-genealogisches Taschenbuch des gesamten Adels jehudäischen Ursprunges. München, 1912.

Weinberg, Gerhard L. *Germany, Hitler, and World War II.* New York, 1996.

———. *A World at Arms.* New York, 1994.

Weitz, John. *Hitler's Diplomat: The Life and Times of Joachim von Ribbentrop.* New York, 1992.

Welch, David. *Germany, Propaganda and Total War, 1914–1918: The Sins of Omission.* New Brunswick, 2000.

Welch, Steven R. "*Mischling* Deserters from the Wehrmacht." *Leo Baeck Yearbook* 44 (1999): 273–324.

———. "The Case of Anton Meyer." *Journal of the University of Melbourne Library* 2, no. 1 (spring/summer 1996): 8–15.

Werth, Alexander. *Russia at War, 1941–1945.* London, 1964.

Wheeler-Bennett, John. *The Nemesis of Power.* New York, 1980.

White, Charles Edward. *The Enlightened Soldier: Scharnhorst and the Militärische Gesellschaft in Berlin, 1801–1805.* New York, 1989.

Whitley, M. J. *Destroyer! German Destroyers in World War II.* Maryland, 1983.

Wighton, Charles. *Heydrich: Hitler's Most Evil Henchman.* London, 1962.

Wilberg, Helmut. *Abschließender Flieger=Erfahrungsbericht über die Schlacht in Flandern,* Gedruckt in der Buch- und Steindruckerei der Artillerie-Fliegerschule Ost I, 1923.

Wistrich, Robert. *Who's Who in Nazi Germany.* New York, 1982.

Wouk, Herman. *This Is My God: The Jewish Way of Life.* New York, 1959.

Wyden, Peter. *Stella: One Woman's True Tale of Evil, Betrayal, and Survival in Hitler's Germany.* New York, 1993.

Wyman, David. *The Abandonment of the Jews.* New York, 1989.

Yahil, Leni. *The Holocaust.* Tel Aviv, 1987.

INDEX